Netter's Atlas of Human Anatomy for *cpt*® Coding

Netter's Atlas of Human Anatomy for *cpt*® Coding

Celeste G. Kirschner, MHSA

Illustrations by

Frank H. Netter, MD

Contributing Illustrator

Carlos A. G. Machado, MD

Vice President, Business Products, AMA Press: Anthony J. Frankos
Publisher, AMA Press: Michael Desposito
Senior Acquisitions Editor, AMA Press: Elise Schumacher
Art Editor, AMA Press: Mary Ann Albanese
Developmental Editor, AMA Press: Carol Brockman
Director, Marketing, AMA Press: J. D. Kinney
Marketing Manager, AMA Press: Erin Kalitowski

Netter's Atlas of Human Anatomy for CPT® Coding

Internet address: www.ama-assn.org

Netter's Atlas of Human Anatomy for CPT® Coding is intended to serve as an anatomy reference to aid in the understanding of CPT coding. Please refer to the most current edition of the American Medical Association's *Current Procedural Terminology* containing the complete listing and most current CPT codes and descriptions. This publication does not replace the CPT codebook or other appropriate coding authorities.

AMA disclaims all responsibility for any liability, loss or risk, personal or otherwise, which is incurred as a consequence, directly or indirectly, of the use and application of any of the contents of this product.

This book is for informational purposes only. It is not intended to constitute legal or financial advice. If legal, financial, or other professional advice is required, the services of a competent professional should be sought.

Additional copies of this book may be ordered by calling 800 621-8335.
Secure online orders can be taken at www.amapress.com.
Mention product number OP490605.

ISBN 1-57947-669-4
AC33:12/04

Library of Congress Cataloging-in-Publication Data

Kirschner, Celeste G.
    Netter's atlas of human anatomy for CPT coding / Celeste G. Kirschner.
        p. ; cm.
    Summary: "This 4-color resource incorporates more than 400 medical illustrations, drawn by Frank H. Netter, to help explain the application of Current Procedural Terminology (CPT) as it relates to human anatomy. Two indexes are provided: index of CPT codes and index of Anatomical Structures"—Provided by publisher.
    Includes index.
    ISBN 1-57947-669-4
    1. Human anatomy—Atlases. 2. Medicine—Code numbers.
    [DNLM: 1. Anatomy—Atlases. 2. Anatomy—Terminology—English. QS 17 K605n 2005] I. Title: Atlas of human anatomy for CPT coding. II. American Medical Association. III. Current procedural terminology (Standard ed.: 1998) IV. Title.
QM25.K535 2005
611—dc22   2004025328

Contents

About Celeste G. Kirschner, MHSA

Celeste G. Kirschner, MHSA, is one of the nation's leading authorities in coding, reimbursement, and documentation in the medical field. With more than 20 years of experience in health care coding, revenue cycle/reimbursement, compliance, process improvement, and related issues, she is uniquely qualified.

Currently, Ms Kirschner serves as the executive director of a state health care association while continuing to remain involved in coding and nomenclature. Prior to her current role, she served for 16 years as the secretary of the American Medical Association's (AMA's) CPT Editorial Panel and was most recently employed as division director with the AMA. In her role at the AMA, Ms Kirschner was responsible for the CPT Editorial Panel and involved in the development and publication of the AMA's coding product line, including the CPT codebook, *CPT®Assistant, Principles of CPT®, CPT® Companion,* the *CPT® Coding Symposia,* and other related coding products. Ms Kirschner coordinated the efforts of volunteer physician leaders from more than 100 national medical specialty societies and served as liaison with governmental agencies on issues pertaining to coding and reimbursement.

After leaving the AMA, Ms Kirschner served as manager/director with several consulting firms, where she served clients by consulting with major medical device manufacturers concerning reimbursement strategy; consulting in litigation and arbitration concerning compliance issues; working with medical associations in developing physician education and new products for their memberships; and managing a variety of coding, revenue cycle, and compliance projects. Early in her career, Ms Kirschner was employed by the Blue Cross and Blue Shield Association as a consultant in its technology evaluation and coverage group.

About Frank H. Netter, MD

Frank H. Netter, MD, was born in 1906 in New York City. He studied art at the Art Student's League and the National Academy of Design before entering medical school at New York University, where he received his MD degree in 1931. During his student years, Dr Netter's notebook sketches attracted the attention of the medical faculty and other physicians, allowing him to augment his income by illustrating articles and textbooks. He continued illustrating as a sideline after establishing a surgical practice in 1933, but he ultimately opted to give up his practice in favor of a full-time commitment to art. After service in the United States Army during World War II, Dr Netter began his long collaboration with the CIBA Pharmaceutical Company (now Novartis Pharmaceuticals). This 45-year partnership resulted in the production of the extraordinary collection of medical art so familiar to physicians and other medical professionals worldwide.

Icon Learning Systems acquired the Netter Collection in July 2000 and continues to update Dr Netter's original paintings and to add newly commissioned paintings by artists trained in the style of Dr Netter.

Dr Netter's works are among the finest examples of the use of illustration in the teaching of medical concepts. The 13-book *Netter Collection of Medical Illustrations,* which includes the greater part of the more than 20,000 paintings created by Dr Netter, became and remains one of the most famous medical works ever published. *The Atlas of Human Anatomy,* first published in 1989, presents the anatomical paintings from the *Netter Collection* and has been translated into 11 languages.

The Netter illustrations are appreciated not only for their aesthetic qualities but, more importantly, for their intellectual content. As Dr Netter wrote in 1949, ". . . clarification of a subject is the aim and goal of illustration. No matter how beautifully painted, how delicately and subtly rendered a subject may be, it is of little value as a medical illustration if it does not serve to make clear some medical point." Dr Netter's planning, conception, point of view, and approach are what inform his paintings and what makes them so intellectually valuable.

Frank H. Netter, MD, physician and artist, died in 1991.

Introduction

Current Procedural Terminology is, by nature, a synthesis of anatomy, procedures, and pathology. The Current Procedural Terminology (CPT®) code set describes specific medical and surgical procedures, and it is essential that a user of the CPT codes be familiar with the human anatomy underlying the performance of those procedures and services. Appropriate coding cannot be effectively accomplished without a basic grasp of anatomy. *Netter's Atlas of Human Anatomy for CPT® Coding* will serve as an aid in that understanding and as an ongoing reference.

This book in organized in the manner of many anatomic texts. The illustrations are organized by body region, moving from the head to the lower limbs. In contrast, the CPT codebook is predominantly organized based on the practice of medicine. The main sections of Evaluation and Management (E/M); Anesthesia; Surgery; Radiology; Pathology and Laboratory; and Medicine are oriented toward identifying procedures and services in a practical application of clinical practice. However, within each of these sections, there are similarities in the arrangement of codes and descriptors corresponding with anatomic regions. For example, the Anesthesia section has a strong anatomic foundation, categorizing the codes and descriptors under anatomic headings such as head, neck, pelvis, and lower leg.

HOW TO USE THIS BOOK

Netter's Atlas of Human Anatomy for CPT® Coding will serve as a useful reference for those who want to understand the anatomic structures cited within particular CPT codes descriptions or to learn more about underlying anatomic concepts. The illustrations featured within this book represent normal human anatomy and serve as a starting point for the understanding of anatomy as it relates to procedures and services that are performed to treat illness, injury, and pathologic conditions.

Netter's Atlas of Human Anatomy for CPT® Coding does not serve as a primary coding reference, and no attempts should be made to code directly from this book. All of the necessary coding notes, rules, modifiers, and guidelines for proper assignment of procedure and service codes can be found in the most current edition of *Current Procedural Terminology.*

Certain sections of the CPT codebook are deliberately excluded from this text because they are not anatomically specific enough to be included. These sections include E/M; Laboratory and Pathology; some portions of Medicine; and the majority of the Radiology section. Additionally, some subsections (eg, General Musculoskeletal System) contain codes that apply across many different anatomic locations; therefore, due to their nonspecific nature, these subsections are not addressed. Much of the Integumentary System subsection, while containing anatomically specific locations, is likewise not included because the terminology and anatomic locations are general enough for the lay person to understand without the aid of detailed illustrations. Codes may be included in more than one illustration, depending on the structures illustrated. Exclusion of any particular code is not intended to mean that a procedure is not applicable to that anatomic structure.

While the illustrations in this book depict a specific anatomic region, such as head and neck, the coding associated with each anatomic region will cut across many sections of the CPT code system. Throughout this book, four of the major CPT sections are referenced:

> Anesthesia
> Surgery
> Radiology
> Medicine

Under each section heading, the appropriate headings and subheadings are listed as they appear in the CPT codebook along with a list of applicable CPT codes.

To aid in better understanding procedures and services, a special symbol (ᴾ) has been added to the right of any code number in this book that has a corresponding procedure or service illustration in the *CPT® Professional Edition.* In some cases, if a series of codes are illustrated with a single illustration, this special symbol may be noted only on the first code in the series. Readers may make use of this annotation by simply looking up the applicable code or codes in the *CPT® Professional Edition.* The reader will find a side-by-side use of both

Netter's Atlas of Human Anatomy for CPT® Coding and *CPT® Professional Edition* most helpful. Additionally, simplified anatomic drawings can be found in the introduction to *CPT® Professional Edition* (pp. xvi–xxxvii).

At times, the CPT system uses more generic terminology than what is found in this book. The CPT code system often employs broad, encompassing terms to describe particular anatomical areas so as to avoid repeating codes for each area. To alleviate any confusion in terminology between this book and the CPT codebook, a section titled Nomenclature Notes accompanies the illustrations, when needed. Nomenclature Notes also highlight specific clinical and anatomic information that may assist in the coding process.

HOW TO READ CPT CODES AND DESCRIPTIONS

The Current Procedural Terminology (CPT) code set has been developed as stand-alone descriptions of medical procedures. However, some of the procedures in the CPT codebook and in *Netter's Atlas of Human Anatomy for CPT® Coding* are not printed in their entirety but refer back to a common portion of the procedure listed in a preceding entry. This is evident when the CPT code of an entry is followed by an indented description. This practice of deleting common portions of procedure descriptions is done solely to conserve space within the CPT codebook and this book.

Example

25100   Arthrotomy, wrist joint; with biopsy
25105   with synovectomy

The common portion of the procedural description always precedes a semicolon; and, therefore, the full procedure represented by code 25105 should read:

25105   Arthrotomy, wrist joint; with synovectomy

HOW TO USE THIS BOOK WHEN CODING FROM AN OPERATIVE REPORT

When coding from an operative report, it is important to identify key anatomic terms and refer to the illustrations that depict these anatomic areas. Although many codes are reproduced within this anatomy book, it is critical that the index and full text of the CPT codebook be used in tandem with this book because the code listings associated with each illustration are not exhaustive.

The following operative report, with its highlighted anatomic terms, demonstrates the manner in which this book is most useful. Reference to more than one illustration may be necessary, depending on the surgical procedure(s) performed. Regularly using this book as a reference when coding will enable the reader to further understand the relationship of human anatomy to medical and surgical procedures.

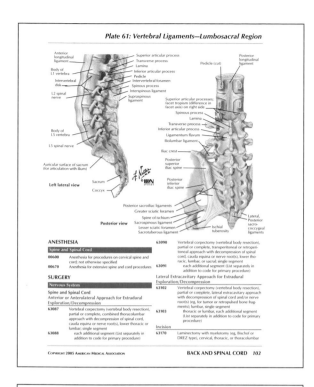

Plate 61: Vertebral Ligaments—Lumbosacral Region

ANESTHESIA

Spine and Spinal Cord

00600	Anesthesia for procedures on cervical spine and cord; not otherwise specified
00670	Anesthesia for extensive spine and cord procedures

SURGERY

Nervous System

Spine and Spinal Cord
Anterior or Anterolateral Approach for Extradural Exploration/Decompression

63087	Vertebral corpectomy (vertebral body resection), partial or complete, combined thoracolumbar approach with decompression of spinal cord, cauda equina or nerve root(s); lumbar; single segment
63088	each additional segment (List separately in addition to code for primary procedure)
63090	Vertebral corpectomy (vertebral body resection), partial or complete, transperitoneal or retroperitoneal approach with decompression of spinal cord, cauda equina or nerve root(s); lower thoracic, lumbar, or sacral; single segment
63091	each additional segment (List separately in addition to code for primary procedure)

Lateral Extracavitary Approach for Extradural Exploration/Decompression

63102	Vertebral corpectomy (vertebral body resection), partial or complete, lateral extracavitary approach with decompression of spinal cord and/or nerve root(s) (eg, for tumor or retropulsed bone fragments); lumbar, single segment
63103	thoracic or lumbar, each additional segment (List separately in addition to code for primary procedure)

Incision

63170	Laminotomy with myelotomy (eg, Bischof or DREZ type), cervical, thoracic, or thoracolumbar

COPYRIGHT 2005 AMERICAN MEDICAL ASSOCIATION BACK AND SPINAL CORD 103

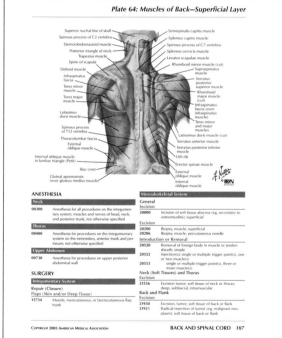

Plate 64: Muscles of Back—Superficial Layer

ANESTHESIA

Neck

00300	Anesthesia for all procedures on the integumentary system, muscles and nerves of head, neck, and posterior trunk, not otherwise specified

Thorax

00400	Anesthesia for procedures on the integumentary system on the extremities, anterior trunk and perineum; not otherwise specified

Upper Abdomen

00730	Anesthesia for procedures on upper posterior abdominal wall

SURGERY

Integumentary System

Repair (Closure)
Flaps (Skin and/or Deep Tissue)

15734	Muscle, myocutaneous, or fasciocutaneous flap; trunk

Musculoskeletal System

General
Incision

20000	Incision of soft tissue abscess (eg, secondary to osteomyelitis); superficial

Excision

20200	Biopsy, muscle; superficial
20206	Biopsy, muscle, percutaneous needle

Introduction or Removal

20520	Removal of foreign body in muscle or tendon sheath; simple
20552	Injection(s); single or multiple trigger point(s), one or two muscle(s)
20553	single or multiple trigger point(s), three or more muscle(s)

Neck (Soft Tissues) and Thorax
Excision

21556	Excision tumor, soft tissue of neck or thorax; deep, subfascial, intramuscular

Back and Flank
Excision

21930	Excision, tumor, soft tissue of back or flank
21935	Radical resection of tumor (eg, malignant neoplasm), soft tissue of back or flank

COPYRIGHT 2005 AMERICAN MEDICAL ASSOCIATION BACK AND SPINAL CORD 107

SPINAL SURGERY

PREOPERATIVE DIAGNOSIS
Spinal stenosis, L3-L4 and L4-L5 with L3-L4 spondylolisthesis
Neurogenic claudication radiculopathy, left greater than right

POSTOPERATIVE DIAGNOSIS
Same

PROCEDURE
1. Decompressive lumbar laminectomy L3-L4 with redecompression of previous laminotomy site. Lateral recess decompression and medial facetectomy bilaterally.
2. L4-L5 and L5-S1 decompressive laminectomy with total removal of L5 lamina, L4 lamina, lateral recess decompression, medial facetectomy, foraminotomy bilaterally at L4-L5 and L3-L4.
3. Posterior spinal fusion, L3-L4.
4. Right iliac crest bone graft.
5. Somatosensory evoked potential monitoring.

ANESTHESIA
General

TECHNIQUE
The patient was brought to the operating room and placed under general anesthesia. She was carefully turned prone onto an Andrew's spinal frame and her back was prepped and draped in the usual sterile fashion. The previous laminotomy site was identified and a midline skin incision was made and carried down through skin and subcutaneous tissue to expose the erector spinae fascia. The erector spinae fascia was incised along the right and left sides of the wound, exposing the lamina of L3, L4, L5, and L5-S1 interlaminar space. Intraoperative X rays were obtained confirming satisfactory localization and alignment.

At this point, under magnified visualization, the lamina of L5 and L4 was removed in total; the inferior lamina of L3 was also removed in total using high-speed bur, Kerrison rongeur of 2, 3, and 4 mm size and 3-0 curette. Lateral recesses were decompressed. Medial facetectomy was performed. Hypertrophic ligamentum flavum was carried down and nerve roots decompressed with foraminotomy performed at L3-L4 and L4-L5 bilaterally.

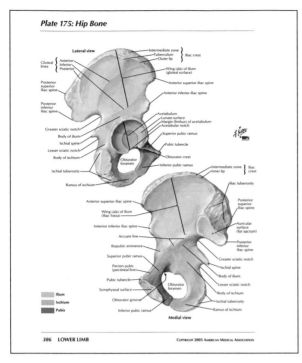

Plate 175: Hip Bone

Lateral view

Medial view

■ Ilium
■ Ischium
■ Pubis

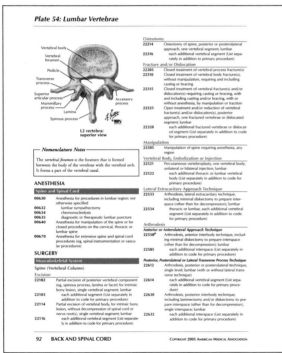

Plate 54: Lumbar Vertebrae

L2 vertebra: superior view

— Nomenclature Notes —

The *vertebral foramen* is the foramen that is formed between the body of the vertebra with the vertebral arch. It forms a part of the vertebral canal.

ANESTHESIA

Spine and Spinal Cord

00630	Anesthesia for procedures in lumbar region; not otherwise specified
00632	lumbar sympathectomy
00634	chemonucleolysis
00635	diagnostic or therapeutic lumbar puncture
00640	Anesthesia for manipulation of the spine or for closed procedures on the cervical, thoracic or lumbar spine
00670	Anesthesia for extensive spine and spinal cord procedures (eg, spinal instrumentation or vascular procedures)

SURGERY

Musculoskeletal System

Spine (Vertebral Column)

Excision

22102	Partial excision of posterior vertebral component (eg, spinous process, lamina or facet) for intrinsic bony lesion, single vertebral segment; lumbar
22103	each additional segment (List separately in addition to code for primary procedure)
22114	Partial excision of vertebral body, for intrinsic bony lesion, without decompression of spinal cord or nerve root(s), single vertebral segment; lumbar
22116	each additional vertebral segment (List separately in addition to code for primary procedure)

Osteotomy

22214	Osteotomy of spine, posterior or posterolateral approach, one vertebral segment; lumbar
22216	each additional vertebral segment (List separately in addition to primary procedure)

Fracture and/or Dislocation

22305	Closed treatment of vertebral process fracture(s)
22310	Closed treatment of vertebral body fracture(s), without manipulation, requiring and including casting or bracing
22315	Closed treatment of vertebral fracture(s) and/or dislocation(s) requiring casting or bracing, with and including casting and/or bracing, with or without anesthesia, by manipulation or traction
22325	Open treatment and/or reduction of vertebral fracture(s) and/or dislocation(s), posterior approach, one fractured vertebra or dislocated segment; lumbar
22328	each additional fractured vertebrae or dislocated (List separately in addition to code for primary procedure)

Manipulation

22505	Manipulation of spine requiring anesthesia, any region

Vertebral Body, Embolization or Injection

22521	Percutaneous vertebroplasty, one vertebral body, unilateral or bilateral injection; lumbar
22522	each additional thoracic or lumbar vertebral body (List separately in addition to code for primary procedure)

Lateral Extracavitary Approach Technique

22533	Arthrodesis, lateral extracavitary technique, including minimal diskectomy to prepare interspace (other than for decompression); lumbar
22534	thoracic or lumbar, each additional vertebral segment (List separately in addition to code for primary procedure)

Arthrodesis

Anterior or Anterolateral Approach Technique

22558	Arthrodesis, anterior interbody technique, including minimal diskectomy to prepare interspace (other than for decompression); lumbar
22585	each additional interspace (List separately in addition to code for primary procedure)

Posterior, Posterolateral or Lateral Transverse Process Technique

22612	Arthrodesis, posterior or posterolateral technique, single level; lumbar (with or without lateral transverse technique)
22614	each additional vertebral segment (List separately in addition to code for primary procedure)
22630	Arthrodesis, posterior interbody technique, including laminectomy and/or diskectomy to prepare interspace (other than for decompression), single interspace; lumbar
22632	each additional interspace (List separately in addition to code for primary procedure)

The disk spaces were inspected. Although bulging, there was no evidence of acute disk herniation. A probe could be easily passed through the L3-L4 and L4-L5 neural foramina at the end of decompression and a probe along the L5 nerve root out through the L5-S1 neural foramina.

The wound was irrigated with copious amounts of saline solution. Attention was then turned to the right iliac crest where, through a separate fascial incision, using the same skin incision, the right iliac crest was exposed. Cancellous and corticocancellous bone graft was harvested, brought to the back table and cleaned of soft tissue for later use in fusion.

This wound was irrigated with copious amounts of saline solution. Thrombin soaked Gelfoam was placed over the exposed bleeding bone. A Jackson-Pratt drain was used to drain the deep spaces and the fascia was closed with interrupted figure-of-eight #1 Vicryl sutures for watertight fascial closure.

Attention was then turned to the midline and the transverse processes of L3 and L4 were exposed laterally and cleaned of soft tissue for later fusion. This was the outer face of the facet joint and pars interarticularis.

Decortication was performed of the transverse process of L4 and L3, outer face of the facet joint and pars interarticularis, cancellous and corticocancellous bone graft was packed laterally and bilaterally. Attention was turned to the midline. There was no evidence of epidural bleeding, dural leak, further neural compression, or aberrant bone graft. The wound was again irrigated with copious amounts of saline solution as well as throughout the operative procedure. Thrombin soaked Gelfoam was placed over the exposed dura in the lateral recesses to prevent migrating bone graft from compressing neural foramina or nerve roots. A Hemovac drain was used to drain the deep spaces and the fascia was now closed with interrupted figure-of-eight #1 Vicryl sutures for watertight fascial closure. A 2-0 Vicryl suture was used in the subcutaneous tissue and staples were used on the skin. Sterile dressing was applied and the patient returned to the recovery room in satisfactory condition.

Throughout the operative procedure, the patient was monitored with somatosensory evoked potentials. The signals remained strong. There was no evidence of complications.

Chapter 1
Head and Neck

The anatomy of the head and neck is among the most complex in the human body. From the bony structure making up the framework of the face and protecting the brain to the specialized sense organs of the eye, ear, nose, and tongue, the complex relationship of soft and hard tissues, blood vessels, and nerves converge to provide vision, hearing, taste, and smell.

The skull consists of 28 bones. Of these bones, 22 consist of 11 pairs of bones, such as the parietal bones, the malar bones, and maxillae. The remaining six bones are single bones, such as the frontal and occipital bones. The skull has two principal divisions: the cranium and the face. The cranium consists of eight bones that enclose and protect the brain; the face consists of 14 bones. The hyoid bone is a single bone in the neck and is considered to be part of the axial skeleton.

The seven cervical vertebrae make up the bony framework of the neck. These vertebrae are smaller than those in the thoracic or lumbar regions of the spine and contain the unique feature of a foramen in the transverse process. The first two cervical vertebrae have specialized names. The first cervical vertebrae is named the *atlas* because it supports the "globe" of the head. The second cervical vertebrae is named the *axis* because it forms the pivot on which the atlas rotates.

Portions of the respiratory system—the nose, pharynx, larynx, and trachea—are included in this chapter. The gastrointestinal tract is also represented in this chapter through the inclusion of the mouth, salivary glands, and teeth. These structures serve an important purpose in preparing food for absorption so that it can be used for energy by the cells of the body.

Portions of the endocrine system also make up the head and neck anatomy; they include the pituitary and pineal glands in the brain and the thyroid and parathyroid glands in the neck. The glands of the endocrine system release secretions (hormones) into the blood stream and are crucial in how the body maintains and integrates its functions.

The central nervous system and peripheral nervous systems, clearly play a central role in head and neck anatomy. The central nervous system consists of the brain and the cervical portion of the spinal cord. A portion of the peripheral nervous system is part of the anatomy of the head and neck, consisting of the 12 cranial nerves arising from the undersurface of the brain (see Table 1-1) and the eight pairs of cervical spinal nerves. Each spinal nerve attaches indirectly to the spinal cord by two short roots: anterior and posterior.

The eye and ocular adenxa are highly complex, specialized sense organs. The principal anatomic divisions of the eye include the orbit—the bony structure of the skull that encases the eyeball—and the eyeball itself that consists of three tissue layers: the sclera, uvea, and retina. The interior area of the eye is divided by the lens into two segments: anterior and posterior. Muscles of the eye include the intraocular muscles, such as the ciliary muscle and iris, and the extraocular muscles that are part of the ocular adnexa.

The auditory system is another complex sensory system.

Table 1-1
Cranial Nerve Chart

I	Olfactory	VII	Facial
II	Optic	VIII	Acoustic
III	Oculomotor	IX	Glossopharyngeal
IV	Trochlear	X	Vagus
V	Trigeminal	XI	Spinal accessory
VI	Abducens	XII	Hypoglossal

Although the ear is divisible into three main parts—the external ear, the middle ear (tympanum), and the internal ear (labyrinth)—the ear communicates with other structures in the head and neck, including the nasopharynx through the Eustachian tubes, and with the mastoid air cells. The middle ear is close to other key structures in the head because the only structure separating the roof of the tympanum from the temporal lobe of the brain is the dura mater and a thin plate of bone. Auditory structures lie in close proximity to the jugular fossa and the carotid canal.

Common procedures performed in this anatomic region include, but are not limited to, the following:

- Skull and brain
  — Craniotomy
  — Craniectomy
  — Fracture treatment
  — Ventricular punctures
  — Repair of dural/cerebrospinal fluid leak
- Cervical spine
  — Diskectomy (an excision of an intervertebral disk during which the disk can be surgically removed or a percutatneous diskectomy can be performed)
  — Laminotomy or laminectomy (a surgical procedure to relieve pressure on the spinal cord or nerve root that is caused by a slipped or herniated disk, or a treatment for spinal stenosis)
  — Exploration or decompression of nerves
  — Nerve destruction
  — Treatment of fractures and dislocations
  — Arthrodesis (joint fusion or surgical immobilization of a joint)
- Eye
  — Lesion removal
  — Cataract removal
  — Retinal repair
  — Strabismus surgery
  — Closure of lacrimal punctum
- Ear
  — Myringotomy
  — Tympanoplasty
  — Excision of tumor or polyps

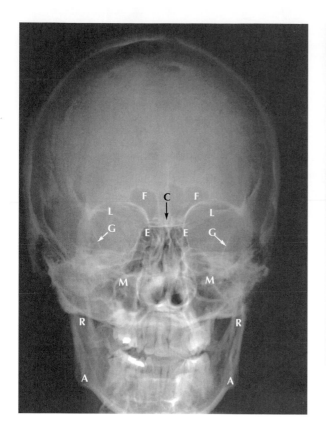

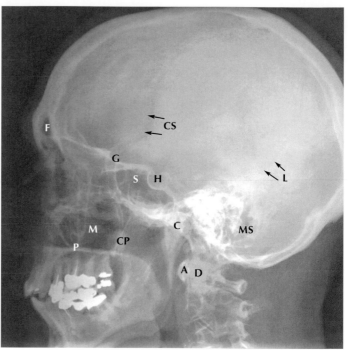

A	Angle of mandible
C	Crista galli
E	Ethmoid sinus
F	Frontal sinus
G	Greater wing of sphenoid
L	Lesser wing of sphenoid
M	Maxillary sinus
R	Ramus of mandible

A	Anterior arch of atlas (CI vertebra)	G	Greater wing of sphenoid
C	Condyle of mandible	H	Hypophyseal fossa
CP	Coronoid process of mandible	L	Lambdoid suture
CS	Coronal suture	M	Maxillary sinus
D	Dens of axis (C2 vertebra)	MS	Mastoid air cells
F	Frontal sinus	P	Palatine process of maxilla
		S	Sphenoid sinus

Nomenclature Notes

Paranasal sinuses include the maxillary sinus, sphenoidal sinus, frontal sinus, and ethmoidal sinus.

RADIOLOGY

Diagnostic Radiology (Diagnostic Imaging)

Head and Neck

70210	Radiologic examination, sinuses, paranasal, less than three views
70250	Radiologic examination, skull; less than four views

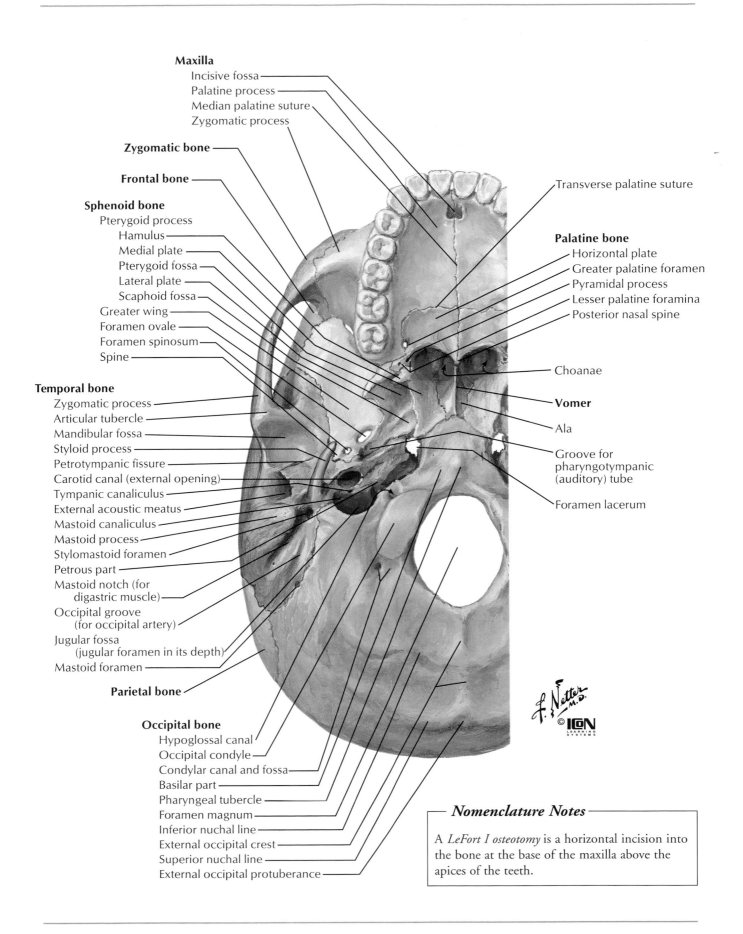

Maxilla
Incisive fossa
Palatine process
Median palatine suture
Zygomatic process

Zygomatic bone

Frontal bone

Sphenoid bone
Pterygoid process
Hamulus
Medial plate
Pterygoid fossa
Lateral plate
Scaphoid fossa
Greater wing
Foramen ovale
Foramen spinosum
Spine

Temporal bone
Zygomatic process
Articular tubercle
Mandibular fossa
Styloid process
Petrotympanic fissure
Carotid canal (external opening)
Tympanic canaliculus
External acoustic meatus
Mastoid canaliculus
Mastoid process
Stylomastoid foramen
Petrous part
Mastoid notch (for digastric muscle)
Occipital groove (for occipital artery)
Jugular fossa (jugular foramen in its depth)
Mastoid foramen

Parietal bone

Occipital bone
Hypoglossal canal
Occipital condyle
Condylar canal and fossa
Basilar part
Pharyngeal tubercle
Foramen magnum
Inferior nuchal line
External occipital crest
Superior nuchal line
External occipital protuberance

Transverse palatine suture

Palatine bone
Horizontal plate
Greater palatine foramen
Pyramidal process
Lesser palatine foramina
Posterior nasal spine

Choanae

Vomer

Ala

Groove for pharyngotympanic (auditory) tube

Foramen lacerum

Nomenclature Notes

A *LeFort I osteotomy* is a horizontal incision into the bone at the base of the maxilla above the apices of the teeth.

Plate 2: Cranial Base—Inferior View

ANESTHESIA

Head

00210 Anesthesia for intracranial procedures; not otherwise specified

SURGERY

Nervous System

Skull, Meninges, and Brain
Approach Procedures

Anterior Cranial Fossa

61580 Craniofacial approach to anterior cranial fossa; extradural, including lateral rhinotomy, ethmoidectomy, sphenoidectomy, without maxillectomy or orbital exenteration

61581 extradural, including lateral rhinotomy, orbital exenteration, ethmoidectomy, sphenoidectomy and/or maxillectomy

61582 extradural, including unilateral or bifrontal craniotomy, elevation of frontal lobe(s), osteotomy of base of anterior cranial fossa

61583 intradural, including unilateral or bifrontal craniotomy, elevation or resection of frontal lobe, osteotomy of base of anterior cranial fossa

61584 Orbitocranial approach to anterior cranial fossa, extradural, including supraorbital ridge osteotomy and elevation of frontal and/or temporal lobe(s); without orbital exenteration

61585 with orbital exenteration

61586 Bicoronal, transzygomatic and/or LeFort I osteotomy approach to anterior cranial fossa with or without internal fixation, without bone graft

Middle Cranial Fossa

61590 Infratemporal pre-auricular approach to middle cranial fossa (parapharyngeal space, infratemporal and midline skull base, nasopharynx), with or without disarticulation of the mandible, including parotidectomy, craniotomy, decompression and/or mobilization of the facial nerve and/or petrous carotid artery

61591 Infratemporal post-auricular approach to middle cranial fossa (internal auditory meatus, petrous apex, tentorium, cavernous sinus, parasellar area, infratemporal fossa) including mastoidectomy, resection of sigmoid sinus, with or without decompression and/or mobilization of contents of auditory canal or petrous carotid artery

61592 Orbitocranial zygomatic approach to middle cranial fossa (cavernous sinus and carotid artery, clivus, basilar artery or petrous apex) including osteotomy of zygoma, craniotomy, extra- or intradural elevation of temporal lobe

Posterior Cranial Fossa

61595 Transtemporal approach to posterior cranial fossa, jugular foramen or midline skull base, including mastoidectomy, decompression of sigmoid sinus and/or facial nerve, with or without mobilization

61596 Transcochlear approach to posterior cranial fossa, jugular foramen or midline skull base, including labyrinthectomy, decompression, with or without mobilization of facial nerve and/or petrous carotid artery

61597 Transcondylar (far lateral) approach to posterior cranial fossa, jugular foramen or midline skull base, including occipital condylectomy, mastoidectomy, resection of C1-C3 vertebral body(s), decompression of vertebral artery, with or without mobilization

61598 Transpetrosal approach to posterior cranial fossa, clivus or foramen magnum, including ligation of superior petrosal sinus and/or sigmoid sinus

Definitive Procedures

Base of Anterior Cranial Fossa

61600 Resection or excision of neoplastic, vascular or infectious lesion of base of anterior cranial fossa; extradural

61601 intradural, including dural repair, with or without graft

Base of Middle Cranial Fossa

61605 Resection or excision of neoplastic, vascular or infectious lesion of infratemporal fossa, parapharyngeal space, petrous apex; extradural

61606 intradural, including dural repair, with or without graft

61607 Resection or excision of neoplastic, vascular or infectious lesion of parasellar area, cavernous sinus, clivus or midline skull base; extradural

61608 intradural, including dural repair, with or without graft

61609 Transection or ligation, carotid artery in cavernous sinus; without repair (List separately in addition to code for primary procedure)

61610 with repair by anastomosis or graft (List separately in addition to code for primary procedure)

61611 Transection or ligation, carotid artery in petrous canal; without repair (List separately in addition to code for primary procedure)

61612 with repair by anastomosis or graft (List separately in addition to code for primary procedure)

61613 Obliteration of carotid aneurysm, arteriovenous malformation, or carotid-cavernous fistula by dissection within cavernous sinus

Base of Posterior Cranial Fossa

61615 Resection or excision of neoplastic, vascular or infectious lesion of base of posterior cranial fossa, jugular foramen, foramen magnum, or C1-C3 vertebral bodies; extradural

61616 intradural, including dural repair, with or without graft

Repair and/or Reconstruction of Surgical Defects of Skull Base

61618 Secondary repair of dura for cerebrospinal fluid leak, anterior, middle or posterior cranial fossa following surgery of the skull base; by free tissue graft (eg, pericranium, fascia, tensor fascia lata, adipose tissue, homologous or synthetic grafts)

61619 by local or regionalized vascularized pedicle flap or myocutaneous flap (including galea, temporalis, frontalis or occipitalis muscle)

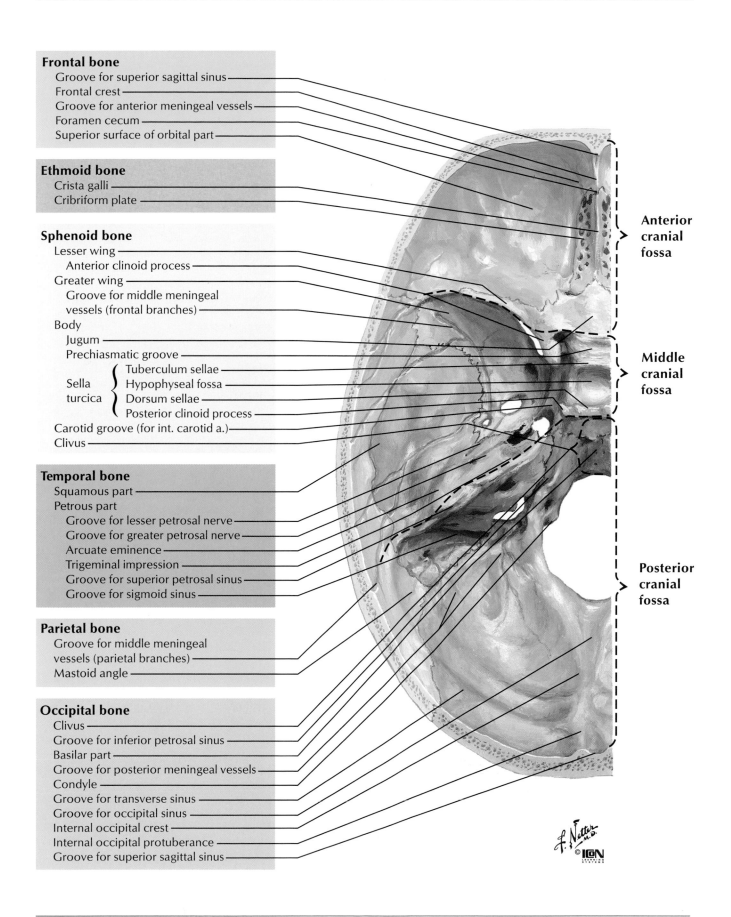

Frontal bone
Groove for superior sagittal sinus
Frontal crest
Groove for anterior meningeal vessels
Foramen cecum
Superior surface of orbital part

Ethmoid bone
Crista galli
Cribriform plate

Sphenoid bone
Lesser wing
Anterior clinoid process
Greater wing
Groove for middle meningeal
vessels (frontal branches)
Body
Jugum
Prechiasmatic groove
Sella turcica {
Tuberculum sellae
Hypophyseal fossa
Dorsum sellae
Posterior clinoid process
}
Carotid groove (for int. carotid a.)
Clivus

Temporal bone
Squamous part
Petrous part
Groove for lesser petrosal nerve
Groove for greater petrosal nerve
Arcuate eminence
Trigeminal impression
Groove for superior petrosal sinus
Groove for sigmoid sinus

Parietal bone
Groove for middle meningeal
vessels (parietal branches)
Mastoid angle

Occipital bone
Clivus
Groove for inferior petrosal sinus
Basilar part
Groove for posterior meningeal vessels
Condyle
Groove for transverse sinus
Groove for occipital sinus
Internal occipital crest
Internal occipital protuberance
Groove for superior sagittal sinus

Anterior cranial fossa

Middle cranial fossa

Posterior cranial fossa

ANESTHESIA

Head

00210 Anesthesia for intracranial procedures; not otherwise specified

SURGERY

Nervous System

Skull, Meninges, and Brain
Approach Procedures

Anterior Cranial Fossa

61580 Craniofacial approach to anterior cranial fossa; extradural, including lateral rhinotomy, ethmoidectomy, sphenoidectomy, without maxillectomy or orbital exenteration

61581 extradural, including lateral rhinotomy, orbital exenteration, ethmoidectomy, sphenoidectomy and/or maxillectomy

61582 extradural, including unilateral or bifrontal craniotomy, elevation of frontal lobe(s), osteotomy of base of anterior cranial fossa

61583 intradural, including unilateral or bifrontal craniotomy, elevation or resection of frontal lobe, osteotomy of base of anterior cranial fossa

61584 Orbitocranial approach to anterior cranial fossa, extradural, including supraorbital ridge osteotomy and elevation of frontal and/or temporal lobe(s); without orbital exenteration

61585 with orbital exenteration

61586 Bicoronal, transzygomatic and/or LeFort I osteotomy approach to anterior cranial fossa with or without internal fixation, without bone graft

Middle Cranial Fossa

61590 Infratemporal pre-auricular approach to middle cranial fossa (parapharyngeal space, infratemporal and midline skull base, nasopharynx), with or without disarticulation of the mandible, including parotidectomy, craniotomy, decompression and/or mobilization of the facial nerve and/or petrous carotid artery

61591 Infratemporal post-auricular approach to middle cranial fossa (internal auditory meatus, petrous apex, tentorium, cavernous sinus, parasellar area, infratemporal fossa) including mastoidectomy, resection of sigmoid sinus, with or without decompression and/or mobilization of contents of auditory canal or petrous carotid artery

61592 Orbitocranial zygomatic approach to middle cranial fossa (cavernous sinus and carotid artery, clivus, basilar artery or petrous apex) including osteotomy of zygoma, craniotomy, extra- or intradural elevation of temporal lobe

Posterior Cranial Fossa

61595 Transtemporal approach to posterior cranial fossa, jugular foramen or midline skull base, including mastoidectomy, decompression of sigmoid sinus and/or facial nerve, with or without mobilization

61596 Transcochlear approach to posterior cranial fossa, jugular foramen or midline skull base, including labyrinthectomy, decompression, with or without mobilization of facial nerve and/or petrous carotid artery

61597 Transcondylar (far lateral) approach to posterior cranial fossa, jugular foramen or midline skull base, including occipital condylectomy, mastoidectomy, resection of C1-C3 vertebral body(s), decompression of vertebral artery, with or without mobilization

61598 Transpetrosal approach to posterior cranial fossa, clivus or foramen magnum, including ligation of superior petrosal sinus and/or sigmoid sinus

Definitive Procedures

Base of Anterior Cranial Fossa

61600 Resection or excision of neoplastic, vascular or infectious lesion of base of anterior cranial fossa; extradural

61601 intradural, including dural repair, with or without graft

Base of Middle Cranial Fossa

61605 Resection or excision of neoplastic, vascular or infectious lesion of infratemporal fossa, parapharyngeal space, petrous apex; extradural

61606 intradural, including dural repair, with or without graft

61607 Resection or excision of neoplastic, vascular or infectious lesion of parasellar area, cavernous sinus, clivus or midline skull base; extradural

61608 intradural, including dural repair, with or without graft

61609 Transection or ligation, carotid artery in cavernous sinus; without repair (List separately in addition to code for primary procedure)

61610 with repair by anastomosis or graft (List separately in addition to code for primary procedure)

61611 Transection or ligation, carotid artery in petrous canal; without repair (List separately in addition to code for primary procedure)

61612 with repair by anastomosis or graft (List separately in addition to code for primary procedure)

61613 Obliteration of carotid aneurysm, arteriovenous malformation, or carotid-cavernous fistula by dissection within cavernous sinus

Base of Posterior Cranial Fossa

61615 Resection or excision of neoplastic, vascular or infectious lesion of base of posterior cranial fossa, jugular foramen, foramen magnum, or C1-C3 vertebral bodies; extradural

61616 intradural, including dural repair, with or without graft

Repair and/or Reconstruction of Surgical Defects of Skull Base

61618 Secondary repair of dura for cerebrospinal fluid leak, anterior, middle or posterior cranial fossa following surgery of the skull base; by free tissue graft (eg, pericranium, fascia, tensor fascia lata, adipose tissue, homologous or synthetic grafts)

61619 by local or regionalized vascularized pedicle flap or myocutaneous flap (including galea, temporalis, frontalis or occipitalis muscle)

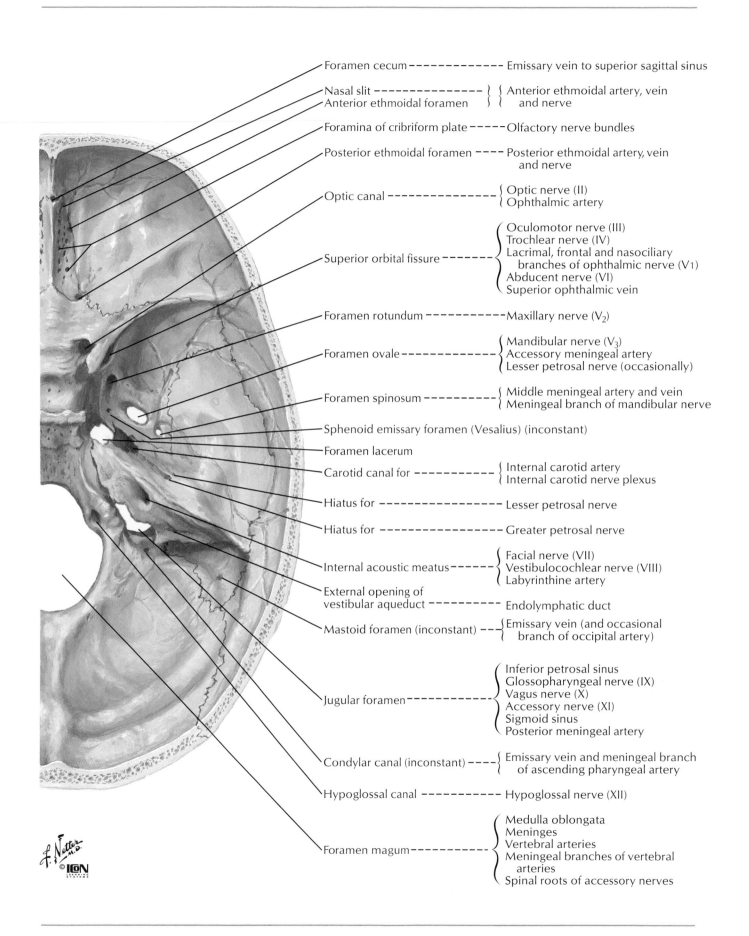

Foramen cecum ------------ Emissary vein to superior sagittal sinus

Nasal slit --------------- } { Anterior ethmoidal artery, vein
Anterior ethmoidal foramen } {   and nerve

Foramina of cribriform plate ----- Olfactory nerve bundles

Posterior ethmoidal foramen ---- Posterior ethmoidal artery, vein
                                    and nerve

Optic canal -------------- { Optic nerve (II)
                           { Ophthalmic artery

Superior orbital fissure ------- { Oculomotor nerve (III)
                                 { Trochlear nerve (IV)
                                 { Lacrimal, frontal and nasociliary
                                 {   branches of ophthalmic nerve (V1)
                                 { Abducent nerve (VI)
                                 { Superior ophthalmic vein

Foramen rotundum ---------- Maxillary nerve (V$_2$)

Foramen ovale ------------ { Mandibular nerve (V$_3$)
                           { Accessory meningeal artery
                           { Lesser petrosal nerve (occasionally)

Foramen spinosum --------- { Middle meningeal artery and vein
                           { Meningeal branch of mandibular nerve

Sphenoid emissary foramen (Vesalius) (inconstant)

Foramen lacerum

Carotid canal for ---------- { Internal carotid artery
                            { Internal carotid nerve plexus

Hiatus for --------------- Lesser petrosal nerve

Hiatus for --------------- Greater petrosal nerve

Internal acoustic meatus ------ { Facial nerve (VII)
                               { Vestibulocochlear nerve (VIII)
                               { Labyrinthine artery

External opening of
vestibular aqueduct --------- Endolymphatic duct

Mastoid foramen (inconstant) --- { Emissary vein (and occasional
                                 {   branch of occipital artery)

Jugular foramen ----------- { Inferior petrosal sinus
                            { Glossopharyngeal nerve (IX)
                            { Vagus nerve (X)
                            { Accessory nerve (XI)
                            { Sigmoid sinus
                            { Posterior meningeal artery

Condylar canal (inconstant) ---- { Emissary vein and meningeal branch
                                 {   of ascending pharyngeal artery

Hypoglossal canal --------- Hypoglossal nerve (XII)

Foramen magum ---------- { Medulla oblongata
                         { Meninges
                         { Vertebral arteries
                         { Meningeal branches of vertebral
                         {   arteries
                         { Spinal roots of accessory nerves

ANESTHESIA

Head

00210   Anesthesia for intracranial procedures; not otherwise specified

SURGERY

Nervous System

Skull, Meninges, and Brain
Approach Procedures

Anterior Cranial Fossa

61580   Craniofacial approach to anterior cranial fossa; extradural, including lateral rhinotomy, ethmoidectomy, sphenoidectomy, without maxillectomy or orbital exenteration

61581   extradural, including lateral rhinotomy, orbital exenteration, ethmoidectomy, sphenoidectomy and/or maxillectomy

61582   extradural, including unilateral or bifrontal craniotomy, elevation of frontal lobe(s), osteotomy of base of anterior cranial fossa

61583   intradural, including unilateral or bifrontal craniotomy, elevation or resection of frontal lobe, osteotomy of base of anterior cranial fossa

61584   Orbitocranial approach to anterior cranial fossa, extradural, including supraorbital ridge osteotomy and elevation of frontal and/or temporal lobe(s); without orbital exenteration

61585   with orbital exenteration

61586   Bicoronal, transzygomatic and/or LeFort I osteotomy approach to anterior cranial fossa with or without internal fixation, without bone graft

Middle Cranial Fossa

61590   Infratemporal pre-auricular approach to middle cranial fossa (parapharyngeal space, infratemporal and midline skull base, nasopharynx), with or without disarticulation of the mandible, including parotidectomy, craniotomy, decompression and/or mobilization of the facial nerve and/or petrous carotid artery

61591   Infratemporal post-auricular approach to middle cranial fossa (internal auditory meatus, petrous apex, tentorium, cavernous sinus, parasellar area, infratemporal fossa) including mastoidectomy, resection of sigmoid sinus, with or without decompression and/or mobilization of contents of auditory canal or petrous carotid artery

61592   Orbitocranial zygomatic approach to middle cranial fossa (cavernous sinus and carotid artery, clivus, basilar artery or petrous apex) including osteotomy of zygoma, craniotomy, extra- or intradural elevation of temporal lobe

Posterior Cranial Fossa

61595   Transtemporal approach to posterior cranial fossa, jugular foramen or midline skull base, including mastoidectomy, decompression of sigmoid sinus and/or facial nerve, with or without mobilization

61596   Transcochlear approach to posterior cranial fossa, jugular foramen or midline skull base, including labyrinthectomy, decompression, with or without mobilization of facial nerve and/or petrous carotid artery

61597   Transcondylar (far lateral) approach to posterior cranial fossa, jugular foramen or midline skull base, including occipital condylectomy, mastoidectomy, resection of C1-C3 vertebral body(s), decompression of vertebral artery, with or without mobilization

61598   Transpetrosal approach to posterior cranial fossa, clivus or foramen magnum, including ligation of superior petrosal sinus and/or sigmoid sinus

Definitive Procedures

Base of Anterior Cranial Fossa

61600   Resection or excision of neoplastic, vascular or infectious lesion of base of anterior cranial fossa; extradural

61601   intradural, including dural repair, with or without graft

Base of Middle Cranial Fossa

61605   Resection or excision of neoplastic, vascular or infectious lesion of infratemporal fossa, parapharyngeal space, petrous apex; extradural

61606   intradural, including dural repair, with or without graft

61607   Resection or excision of neoplastic, vascular or infectious lesion of parasellar area, cavernous sinus, clivus or midline skull base; extradural

61608   intradural, including dural repair, with or without graft

61609   Transection or ligation, carotid artery in cavernous sinus; without repair (List separately in addition to code for primary procedure)

61610   with repair by anastomosis or graft (List separately in addition to code for primary procedure)

61611   Transection or ligation, carotid artery in petrous canal; without repair (List separately in addition to code for primary procedure)

61612   with repair by anastomosis or graft (List separately in addition to code for primary procedure)

61613   Obliteration of carotid aneurysm, arteriovenous malformation, or carotid-cavernous fistula by dissection within cavernous sinus

Base of Posterior Cranial Fossa

61615   Resection or excision of neoplastic, vascular or infectious lesion of base of posterior cranial fossa, jugular foramen, foramen magnum, or C1-C3 vertebral bodies; extradural

61616   intradural, including dural repair, with or without graft

Repair and/or Reconstruction of Surgical Defects of Skull Base

61618   Secondary repair of dura for cerebrospinal fluid leak, anterior, middle or posterior cranial fossa following surgery of the skull base; by free tissue graft (eg, pericranium, fascia, tensor fascia lata, adipose tissue, homologous or synthetic grafts)

61619   by local or regionalized vascularized pedicle flap or myocutaneous flap (including galea, temporalis, frontalis or occipitalis muscle)

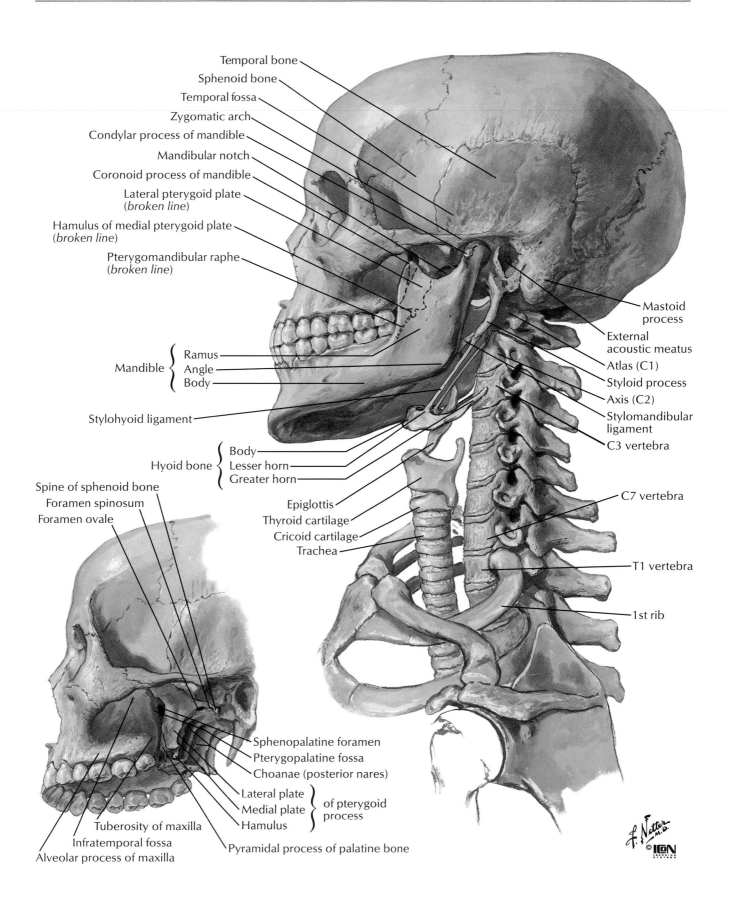

Temporal bone
Sphenoid bone
Temporal fossa
Zygomatic arch
Condylar process of mandible
Mandibular notch
Coronoid process of mandible
Lateral pterygoid plate (*broken line*)
Hamulus of medial pterygoid plate (*broken line*)
Pterygomandibular raphe (*broken line*)

Mandible
Ramus
Angle
Body

Stylohyoid ligament

Hyoid bone
Body
Lesser horn
Greater horn

Spine of sphenoid bone
Foramen spinosum
Foramen ovale

Epiglottis
Thyroid cartilage
Cricoid cartilage
Trachea

Mastoid process
External acoustic meatus
Atlas (C1)
Styloid process
Axis (C2)
Stylomandibular ligament
C3 vertebra

C7 vertebra

T1 vertebra

1st rib

Sphenopalatine foramen
Pterygopalatine fossa
Choanae (posterior nares)
Lateral plate
Medial plate
Hamulus
of pterygoid process
Tuberosity of maxilla
Infratemporal fossa
Alveolar process of maxilla
Pyramidal process of palatine bone

Plate 5: Bony Framework of Head and Neck

ANESTHESIA

Head

00190	Anesthesia for procedures on facial bones or skull; not otherwise specified
00192	radical surgery (including prognathism)

SURGERY

Musculoskeletal System

Head
Excision

21025	Excision of bone (eg, for osteomyelitis or bone abscess); mandible
21026	facial bone(s)
21029	Removal by contouring of benign tumor of facial bone (eg, fibrous dysplasia)
21030	Excision of benign tumor or cyst of maxilla or zygoma by enucleation and curettage
21034	Excision of malignant tumor of maxilla or zygoma
21040	Excision of benign tumor or cyst of mandible, by enucleation and/or curettage
21044	Excision of malignant tumor of mandible;
21045	radical resection
21046	Excision of benign tumor or cyst of mandible; requiring intra-oral osteotomy (eg, locally aggressive or destructive lesion(s))
21047	requiring extra-oral osteotomy and partial mandibulectomy (eg, locally aggressive or destructive lesion(s))
21048	Excision of benign tumor or cyst of maxilla; requiring intra-oral osteotomy (eg, locally aggressive or destructive lesion(s))
21049	requiring extra-oral osteotomy and partial maxillectomy (eg, locally aggressive or destructive lesion(s))
21050	Condylectomy, temporomandibular joint (separate procedure)
21070	Coronoidectomy (separate procedure)

Repair, Revision, and/or Reconstruction

21120	Genioplasty; augmentation (autograft, allograft, prosthetic material)
21121	sliding osteotomy, single piece
21122	sliding osteotomies, two or more osteotomies (eg, wedge excision or bone wedge reversal for asymmetrical chin)
21123	sliding, augmentation with interpositional bone grafts (includes obtaining autografts)
21125	Augmentation, mandibular body or angle; prosthetic material
21127	with bone graft, onlay or interpositional (includes obtaining autograft)

21137	Reduction forehead; contouring only
21138	contouring and application of prosthetic material or bone graft (includes obtaining autograft)
21139	contouring and setback of anterior frontal sinus wall
21193	Reconstruction of mandibular rami, horizontal, vertical, C, or L osteotomy; without bone graft
21194	with bone graft (includes obtaining graft)
21195	Reconstruction of mandibular rami and/or body, sagittal split; without internal rigid fixation
21196	with internal rigid fixation
21198	Osteotomy, mandible, segmental;
21199	with genioglossus advancement
21206P	Osteotomy, maxilla, segmental (eg, Wassmund or Schuchard)
21208	Osteoplasty, facial bones; augmentation (autograft, allograft, or prosthetic implant)
21209	reduction
21210	Graft, bone; nasal, maxillary or malar areas (includes obtaining graft)
21215	mandible (includes obtaining graft)
21230	Graft; rib cartilage, autogenous, to face, chin, nose or ear (includes obtaining graft)
21235	ear cartilage, autogenous, to nose or ear (includes obtaining graft)
21244	Reconstruction of mandible, extraoral, with transosteal bone plate (eg, mandibular staple bone plate)
21245	Reconstruction of mandible or maxilla, subperiosteal implant; partial
21246	complete
21247	Reconstruction of mandibular condyle with bone and cartilage autografts (includes obtaining grafts) (eg, for hemifacial microsomia)
21248	Reconstruction of mandible or maxilla, endosteal implant (eg, blade, cylinder); partial
21249	complete
21255	Reconstruction of zygomatic arch and glenoid fossa with bone and cartilage (includes obtaining autografts)
21256	Reconstruction of orbit with osteotomies (extracranial) and with bone grafts (includes obtaining autografts) (eg, micro-ophthalmia)
21260	Periorbital osteotomies for orbital hypertelorism, with bone grafts; extracranial approach
21261	combined intra- and extracranial approach
21263	with forehead advancement
21267	Orbital repositioning, periorbital osteotomies, unilateral, with bone grafts; extracranial approach
21268	combined intra- and extracranial approach
21270	Malar augmentation, prosthetic material

Fracture/Dislocation

21300	Closed treatment of skull fracture without operation
21355	Percutaneous treatment of fracture of malar area, including zygomatic arch and malar tripod, with manipulation
21356	Open treatment of depressed zygomatic arch fracture (eg, Gillies approach)

21360   Open treatment of depressed malar fracture, including zygomatic arch and malar tripod

21365   Open treatment of complicated (eg, comminuted or involving cranial nerve foramina) fracture(s) of malar area, including zygomatic arch and malar tripod; with internal fixation and multiple surgical approaches

21366   with bone grafting (includes obtaining graft)

21452   Percutaneous treatment of mandibular fracture, with external fixation

21453   Closed treatment of mandibular fracture with interdental fixation

21454   Open treatment of mandibular fracture with external fixation

21461   Open treatment of mandibular fracture; without interdental fixation

21462   with interdental fixation

21465   Open treatment of mandibular condylar fracture

21470   Open treatment of complicated mandibular fracture by multiple surgical approaches including internal fixation, interdental fixation, and/or wiring of dentures or splints

21493   Closed treatment of hyoid fracture; without manipulation

21494   with manipulation

21495   Open treatment of hyoid fracture

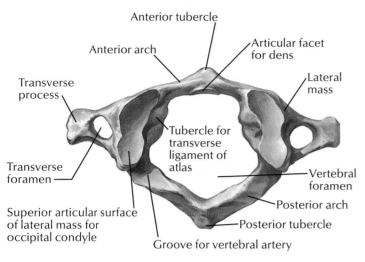

Anterior tubercle

Anterior arch

Articular facet
for dens

Transverse
process

Lateral
mass

Tubercle for
transverse
ligament of
atlas

Transverse
foramen

Vertebral
foramen

Superior articular surface
of lateral mass for
occipital condyle

Posterior arch

Posterior tubercle

Groove for vertebral artery

Atlas (C1): superior view

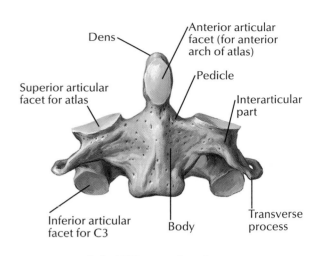

Dens

Anterior articular
facet (for anterior
arch of atlas)

Superior articular
facet for atlas

Pedicle

Interarticular
part

Inferior articular
facet for C3

Body

Transverse
process

Axis (C2): anterior view

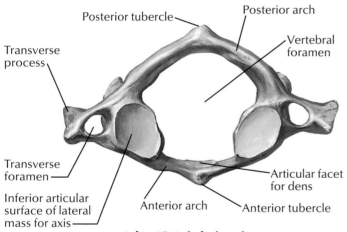

Posterior tubercle

Posterior arch

Transverse
process

Vertebral
foramen

Transverse
foramen

Inferior articular
surface of lateral
mass for axis

Anterior arch

Articular facet
for dens

Anterior tubercle

Atlas (C1): inferior view

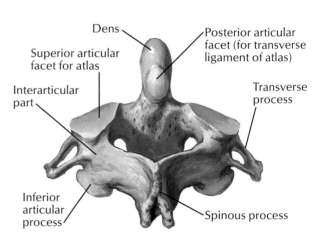

Dens

Posterior articular
facet (for transverse
ligament of atlas)

Superior articular
facet for atlas

Interarticular
part

Transverse
process

Inferior
articular
process

Spinous process

Axis (C2): posterosuperior view

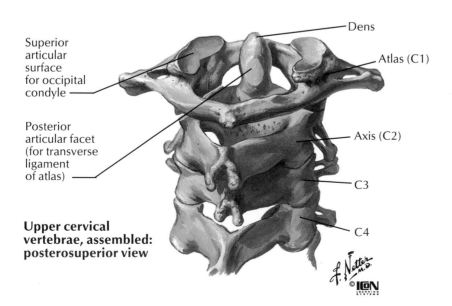

Dens

Atlas (C1)

Superior
articular
surface
for occipital
condyle

Axis (C2)

Posterior
articular facet
(for transverse
ligament
of atlas)

C3

C4

**Upper cervical
vertebrae, assembled:
posterosuperior view**

Nomenclature Notes

Atlas is synonymous with *C1 (cervical vertebrae 1)*.

Axis is synonymous with *C2 (cervical vertebrae 2)*.

The *clivus* is defined as the sloping area from the dorsum sellae to the foramen magnum, made up of part of the sphenoid and part of the occipital bone.

ANESTHESIA

Spine and Spinal Cord

00600	Anesthesia for procedures on cervical spine and cord; not otherwise specified
00604	procedures with patient in the sitting position
00620	Anesthesia for procedures on thoracic spine and cord; not otherwise specified
00640	Anesthesia for manipulation of the spine or for closed procedures on the cervical, thoracic or lumbar spine

SURGERY

Musculoskeletal System

Spine (Vertebral Column)
Excision

22100	Partial excision of posterior vertebral component (eg, spinous process, lamina or facet) for intrinsic bony lesion, single vertebral segment; cervical
22103	each additional segment (List separately in addition to code for primary procedure)
22110	Partial excision of vertebral body, for intrinsic bony lesion, without decompression of spinal cord or nerve root(s), single vertebral segment; cervical
22116	each additional vertebral segment (List separately in addition to code for primary procedure)

Osteotomy

22210	Osteotomy of spine, posterior or posterolateral approach, one vertebral segment; cervical
22216	each additional vertebral segment (List separately in addition to primary procedure)
22220	Osteotomy of spine, including diskectomy, anterior approach, single vertebral segment; cervical
22226	each additional vertebral segment (List separately in addition to code for primary procedure)

Fracture and/or Dislocation

22326	Open treatment and/or reduction of vertebral fracture(s) and/or dislocation(s), posterior approach, one fractured vertebrae or dislocated segment; cervical
22328	each additional fractured vertebrae or dislocated segment (List separately in addition to code for primary procedure)

Arthrodesis

Anterior or Anterolateral Approach Technique

22548[P]	Arthrodesis, anterior transoral or extraoral technique, clivus-C1-C2 (atlas-axis), with or without excision of odontoid process

Posterior, Posterolateral or Lateral Transverse Process Technique

22590	Arthrodesis, posterior technique, craniocervical (occiput-C2)
22595	Arthrodesis, posterior technique, atlas-axis (C1-C2)

Nervous System

Spine and Spinal Cord
Posterior Extradural Laminotomy or Laminectomy for Exploration/Decompression of Neural Elements or Excision of Herniated Intervertebral Disks

63001	Laminectomy with exploration and/or decompression of spinal cord and/or cauda equina, without facetectomy, foraminotomy or diskectomy, (eg, spinal stenosis), one or two vertebral segments; cervical
63015	Laminectomy with exploration and/or decompression of spinal cord and/or cauda equina, without facetectomy, foraminotomy or diskectomy, (eg, spinal stenosis), more than 2 vertebral segments; cervical
63020	Laminotomy (hemilaminectomy), with decompression of nerve root(s), including partial facetectomy, foraminotomy and/or excision of herniated intervertebral disk; one interspace, cervical
63035	each additional interspace, cervical or lumbar (List separately in addition to code for primary procedure)
63040	Laminotomy (hemilaminectomy), with decompression of nerve root(s), including partial facetectomy, foraminotomy and/or excision of herniated intervertebral disk, reexploration, single interspace; cervical
63043	each additional cervical interspace (List separately in addition to code for primary procedure)
63048	Laminectomy, facetectomy and foraminotomy (unilateral or bilateral with decompression of spinal cord, cauda equina and/or nerve root(s), (eg, spinal or lateral recess stenosis)), single vertebral segment; each additional segment, cervical, thoracic, or lumbar (List separately in addition to code for primary procedure)

Anterior or Anterolateral Approach for Extradural Exploration/Decompression

63075	Diskectomy, anterior, with decompression of spinal cord and/or nerve root(s), including osteophytectomy; cervical, single interspace
63076	cervical, each additional interspace (List separately in addition to code for primary procedure)
63081	Vertebral corpectomy (vertebral body resection), partial or complete, anterior approach with decompression of spinal cord and/or nerve root(s); cervical, single segment
63082	cervical, each additional segment (List separately in addition to code for primary procedure)

Plate 6: Cervical Vertebrae

Incision

63170   Laminectomy with myelotomy (eg, Bischof or DREZ type), cervical, thoracic, or thoracolumbar

63180   Laminectomy and section of dentate ligaments, with or without dural graft, cervical; one or two segments

63182   more than two segments

63194   Laminectomy with cordotomy, with section of one spinothalamic tract, one stage; cervical

63196   Laminectomy with cordotomy, with section of both spinothalamic tracts, one stage; cervical

63198   Laminectomy with cordotomy with section of both spinothalamic tracts, two stages within 14 days; cervical

Excision, Anterior or Anterolateral Approach, Intraspinal Lesion

63300   Vertebral corpectomy (vertebral body resection), partial or complete, for excision of intraspinal lesion, single segment; extradural, cervical

63304   intradural, cervical

63308   each additional segment (List separately in addition to codes for single segment)

Plate 7: Cervical Vertebrae—Radiograph of Atlantoaxial Joint

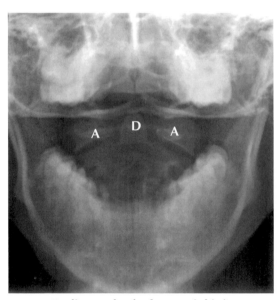

Radiograph of atlantoaxial joint

A Lateral masses of atlas (CI vertebra)
D Dens of axis (C2 vertebra)

RADIOLOGY

Diagnostic Radiology (Diagnostic Imaging)

Spine and Pelvis

72020   Radiologic examination, spine, single view, specify level

72040   Radiologic examination, spine, cervical; two or three views

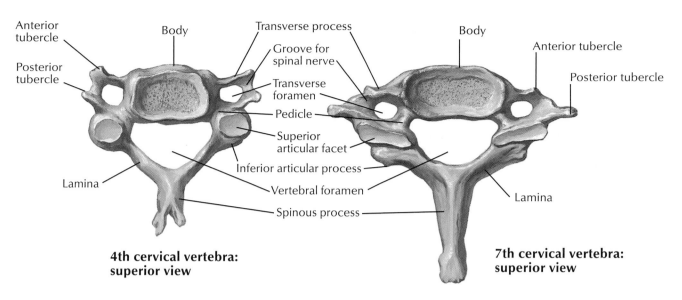

Anterior tubercle

Body

Transverse process

Groove for spinal nerve

Transverse foramen

Pedicle

Superior articular facet

Inferior articular process

Vertebral foramen

Spinous process

Posterior tubercle

Lamina

4th cervical vertebra: superior view

Body

Anterior tubercle

Posterior tubercle

Lamina

7th cervical vertebra: superior view

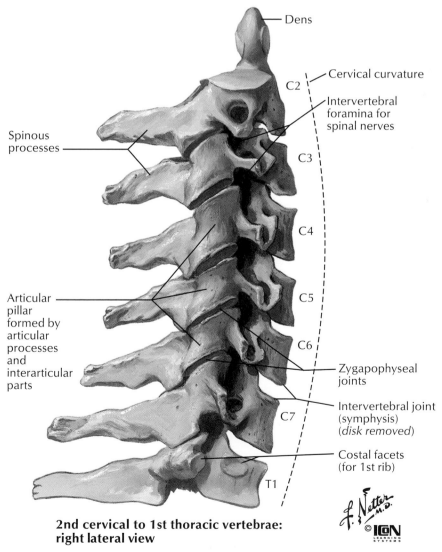

Dens

Cervical curvature

Intervertebral foramina for spinal nerves

Spinous processes

Articular pillar formed by articular processes and interarticular parts

Zygapophyseal joints

Intervertebral joint (symphysis) (*disk removed*)

Costal facets (for 1st rib)

C2
C3
C4
C5
C6
C7
T1

2nd cervical to 1st thoracic vertebrae: right lateral view

Plate 8: Cervical Vertebrae

ANESTHESIA

Spine and Spinal Cord

00600 Anesthesia for procedures on cervical spine and cord; not otherwise specified

00604 Anesthesia for procedures on cervical spine and cord; procedures with patient in the sitting position

SURGERY

Musculoskeletal System

Spine (Vertebral Column)
Excision

22100 Partial excision of posterior vertebral component (eg, spinous process, lamina or facet) for intrinsic bony lesion, single vertebral segment; cervical

22103 each additional segment (List separately in addition to code for primary procedure)

22110 Partial excision of vertebral body, for intrinsic bony lesion, without decompression of spinal cord or nerve root(s), single vertebral segment; cervical

22116 each additional vertebral segment (List separately in addition to code for primary procedure)

Osteotomy

22210 Osteotomy of spine, posterior or posterolateral approach, one vertebral segment; cervical

22216 each additional vertebral segment (List separately in addition to primary procedure)

22220 Osteotomy of spine, including diskectomy, anterior approach, single vertebral segment; cervical

22226 each additional vertebral segment (List separately in addition to code for primary procedure)

Fracture and/or Dislocation

22326 Open treatment and/or reduction of vertebral fracture(s) and/or dislocation(s), posterior approach, one fractured vertebrae or dislocated segment; cervical

22328 each additional fractured vertebrae or dislocated segment (List separately in addition to code for primary procedure)

Arthrodesis

22554[P] Arthrodesis, anterior interbody technique, including minimal diskectomy to prepare interspace (other than for decompression); cervical below C2

22585 each additional interspace (List separately in addition to code for primary procedure)

Posterior, Posterolateral or Lateral Transverse Process Technique

22600 Arthrodesis, posterior or posterolateral technique, single level; cervical below C2 segment

22614 each additional vertebral segment (List separately in addition to code for primary procedure)

Nervous System

Spine and Spinal Cord
Posterior Extradural Laminotomy or Laminectomy for Exploration/Decompression of Neural Elements or Excision of Herniated Intervertebral Disks

63001 Laminectomy with exploration and/or decompression of spinal cord and/or cauda equina, without facetectomy, foraminotomy or diskectomy, (eg, spinal stenosis), one or two vertebral segments; cervical

63015 Laminectomy with exploration and/or decompression of spinal cord and/or cauda equina, without facetectomy, foraminotomy or diskectomy, (eg, spinal stenosis), more than 2 vertebral segments; cervical

63020 Laminotomy (hemilaminectomy), with decompression of nerve root(s), including partial facetectomy, foraminotomy and/or excision of herniated intervertebral disk; one interspace, cervical

63035 Laminotomy (hemilaminectomy), with decompression of nerve root(s), including partial facetectomy, foraminotomy and/or excision of herniated intervertebral disk; each additional interspace, cervical or lumbar (List separately in addition to code for primary procedure)

63040 Laminotomy (hemilaminectomy), with decompression of nerve root(s), including partial facetectomy, foraminotomy and/or excision of herniated intervertebral disk, reexploration, single interspace; cervical

63043 each additional cervical interspace (List separately in addition to code for primary procedure)

63048 Laminectomy, facetectomy and foraminotomy (unilateral or bilateral with decompression of spinal cord, cauda equina and/or nerve root(s), (eg, spinal or lateral recess stenosis)), single vertebral segment; each additional segment, cervical, thoracic, or lumbar (List separately in addition to code for primary procedure)

Anterior or Anterolateral Approach for Extradural Exploration/Decompression

63075 Diskectomy, anterior, with decompression of spinal cord and/or nerve root(s), including osteophytectomy; cervical, single interspace

63076 cervical, each additional interspace (List separately in addition to code for primary procedure)

63081 Vertebral corpectomy (vertebral body resection), partial or complete, anterior approach with decompression of spinal cord and/or nerve root(s); cervical, single segment

63082 cervical, each additional segment (List separately in addition to code for primary procedure)

Incision

63170 Laminectomy with myelotomy (eg, Bischof or DREZ type), cervical, thoracic, or thoracolumbar

63180 Laminectomy and section of dentate ligaments, with or without dural graft, cervical; one or two segments

63182 more than two segments

63194 Laminectomy with cordotomy, with section of one spinothalamic tract, one stage; cervical

63196 Laminectomy with cordotomy, with section of both spinothalamic tracts, one stage; cervical

63198 Laminectomy with cordotomy with section of both spinothalamic tracts, two stages within 14 days; cervical

Excision, Anterior or Anterolateral Approach, Intraspinal Lesion

63300 Vertebral corpectomy (vertebral body resection), partial or complete, for excision of intraspinal lesion, single segment; extradural, cervical

63304 intradural, cervical

63308 each additional segment (List separately in addition to codes for single segment)

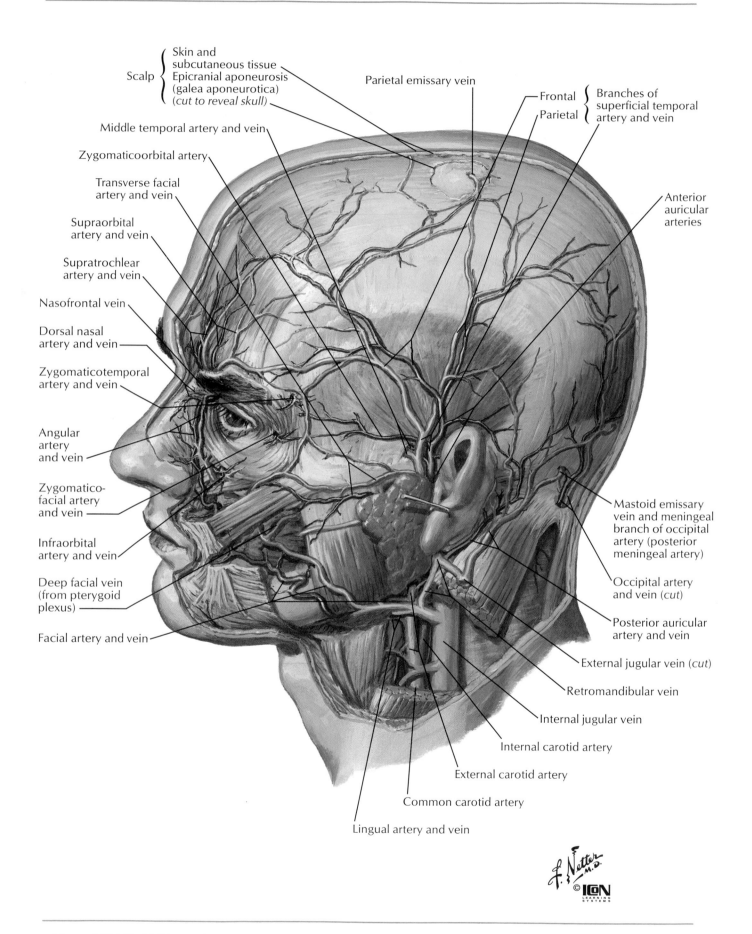

Scalp { Skin and subcutaneous tissue
Epicranial aponeurosis (galea aponeurotica) (cut to reveal skull)

Middle temporal artery and vein

Zygomaticoorbital artery

Transverse facial artery and vein

Supraorbital artery and vein

Supratrochlear artery and vein

Nasofrontal vein

Dorsal nasal artery and vein

Zygomaticotemporal artery and vein

Angular artery and vein

Zygomatico-facial artery and vein

Infraorbital artery and vein

Deep facial vein (from pterygoid plexus)

Facial artery and vein

Parietal emissary vein

Frontal
Parietal } Branches of superficial temporal artery and vein

Anterior auricular arteries

Mastoid emissary vein and meningeal branch of occipital artery (posterior meningeal artery)

Occipital artery and vein (cut)

Posterior auricular artery and vein

External jugular vein (cut)

Retromandibular vein

Internal jugular vein

Internal carotid artery

External carotid artery

Common carotid artery

Lingual artery and vein

Plate 9: Superficial Arteries and Veins of Face and Scalp

ANESTHESIA

Neck

00350   Anesthesia for procedures on major vessels of neck; not otherwise specified

00352   simple ligation

Radiological Procedures

01916   Anesthesia for diagnostic anteriography/venography

SURGERY

Cardiovascular

Arteries and Veins

Embolectomy/Thrombectomy

Arterial, With or Without Catheter

34001   Embolectomy or thrombectomy, with or without catheter; carotid, subclavian or innominate artery, by neck incision

Thromboendarterectomy

35301   Thromboendarterectomy, with or without patch graft; carotid, vertebral, subclavian, by neck incision

Intra-Arterial—Intra-Aortic

36100   Introduction of needle or intracatheter, carotid or vertebral artery

Ligation

37565   Ligation, internal jugular vein

37600   Ligation; external carotid artery

37605   internal or common carotid artery

37606   internal or common carotid artery, with gradual occlusion, as with Selverstone or Crutchfield clamp

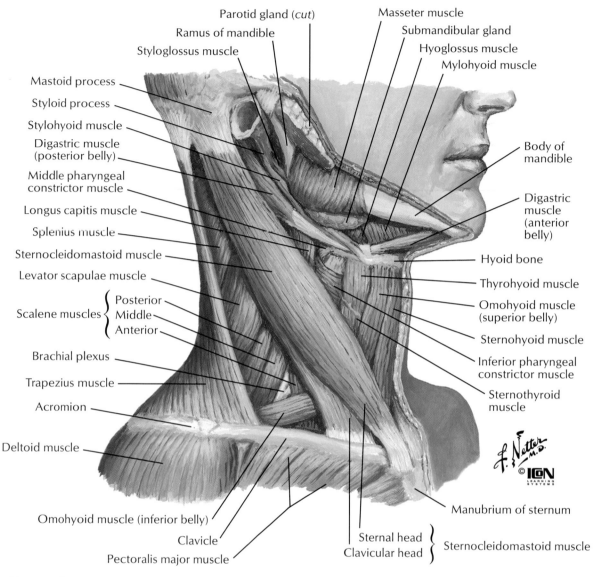

Parotid gland (*cut*)
Ramus of mandible
Styloglossus muscle
Masseter muscle
Submandibular gland
Hyoglossus muscle
Mylohyoid muscle

Mastoid process
Styloid process
Stylohyoid muscle
Digastric muscle (posterior belly)
Middle pharyngeal constrictor muscle
Longus capitis muscle
Splenius muscle
Sternocleidomastoid muscle
Levator scapulae muscle
Scalene muscles { Posterior, Middle, Anterior }
Brachial plexus
Trapezius muscle
Acromion
Deltoid muscle

Body of mandible
Digastric muscle (anterior belly)
Hyoid bone
Thyrohyoid muscle
Omohyoid muscle (superior belly)
Sternohyoid muscle
Inferior pharyngeal constrictor muscle
Sternothyroid muscle

Manubrium of sternum

Omohyoid muscle (inferior belly)
Clavicle
Pectoralis major muscle

Sternal head
Clavicular head } Sternocleidomastoid muscle

Nomenclature Notes

Scalenus anticus is synonomous with *scalenus anterior* or *anteror scalene muscle.*

ANESTHESIA

Neck

00300	Anesthesia for all procedures on the integumentary system, muscles and nerves of head, neck and posterior trunk, not otherwise specified
00350	Anesthesia for procedures on major vessels of neck; not otherwise specified

SURGERY

Musculoskeletal System

Neck (Soft Tissues) and Thorax
Incision

21501	Incision and drainage, deep abscess or hematoma, soft tissues of neck or thorax;

Excision

21550	Biopsy, soft tissue of neck or thorax
21555	Excision tumor, soft tissue of neck or thorax; subcutaneous
21556	deep, subfascial, intramuscular
21557	Radical resection of tumor (eg, malignant neoplasm), soft tissue of neck or thorax
21620	Ostectomy of sternum, partial
21627	Sternal debridement

Repair, Revision, and/or Reconstruction

21685	Hyoid myotomy and suspension
21700	Division of scalenus anticus; without resection of cervical rib

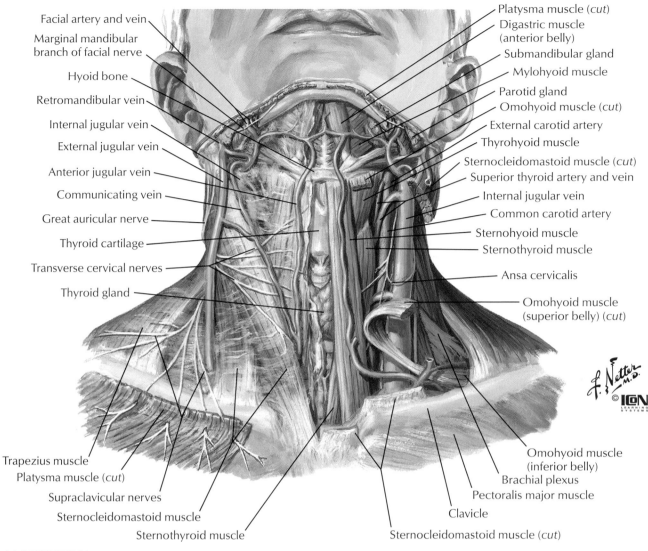

Facial artery and vein
Marginal mandibular branch of facial nerve
Hyoid bone
Retromandibular vein
Internal jugular vein
External jugular vein
Anterior jugular vein
Communicating vein
Great auricular nerve
Thyroid cartilage
Transverse cervical nerves
Thyroid gland

Platysma muscle (*cut*)
Digastric muscle (anterior belly)
Submandibular gland
Mylohyoid muscle
Parotid gland
Omohyoid muscle (*cut*)
External carotid artery
Thyrohyoid muscle
Sternocleidomastoid muscle (*cut*)
Superior thyroid artery and vein
Internal jugular vein
Common carotid artery
Sternohyoid muscle
Sternothyroid muscle
Ansa cervicalis
Omohyoid muscle (superior belly) (*cut*)

Trapezius muscle
Platysma muscle (*cut*)
Supraclavicular nerves
Sternocleidomastoid muscle
Sternothyroid muscle

Omohyoid muscle (inferior belly)
Brachial plexus
Pectoralis major muscle
Clavicle
Sternocleidomastoid muscle (*cut*)

ANESTHESIA

Neck

00300   Anesthesia for all procedures on the integumentary system, muscles and nerves of head, neck and posterior trunk, not otherwise specified

00350   Anesthesia for procedures on major vessels of neck; not otherwise specified

SURGERY

Cardiovascular

Arteries and Veins

Repair Arteriovenous Fistula

35180   Repair, congenital arteriovenous fistula; head and neck

Repair Blood Vessel Other Than for Fistual, With or Without Patch Angioplasty

35201   Repair blood vessel, direct; neck
35231   Repair blood vessel with vein graft; neck
35261   Repair blood vessel with graft other than vein; neck

Thromboendarterectomy

35301   Thromboendarterectomy, with or without patch graft; carotid, vertebral, subclavian, by neck incision

Intra-Arterial—Intra-Aortic

36215   Selective catheter placement, arterial system; each first order thoracic or brachiocephalic branch, within a vascular family
36216   initial second order thoracic or brachiocephalic branch, within a vascular family
36217   initial third order or more selective thoracic or brachiocephalic branch, within a vascular family
36218   additional second order, third order, and beyond, thoracic or brachiocephalic branch, within a vascular family (List in addition to code for initial second or third order vessel as appropriate)

Ligation

37565   Ligation, internal jugular vein
37600   Ligation; external carotid artery
37605   internal or common carotid artery
37606   internal or common carotid artery, with gradual occlusion

Plate 12: Subclavian Artery

Right anterior dissection

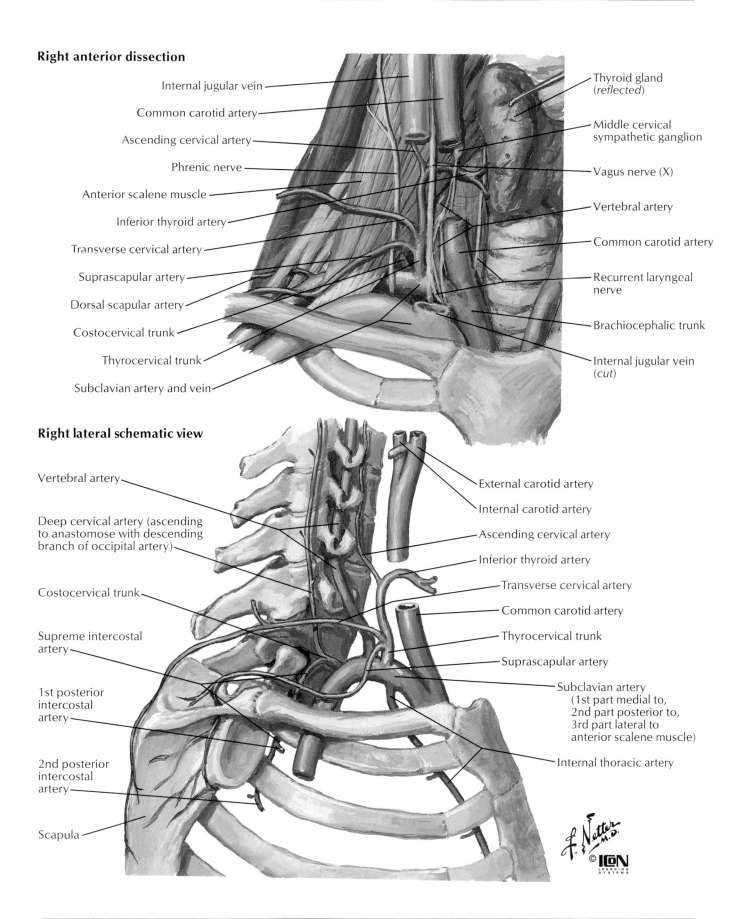

Internal jugular vein

Common carotid artery

Ascending cervical artery

Phrenic nerve

Anterior scalene muscle

Inferior thyroid artery

Transverse cervical artery

Suprascapular artery

Dorsal scapular artery

Costocervical trunk

Thyrocervical trunk

Subclavian artery and vein

Thyroid gland (*reflected*)

Middle cervical sympathetic ganglion

Vagus nerve (X)

Vertebral artery

Common carotid artery

Recurrent laryngeal nerve

Brachiocephalic trunk

Internal jugular vein (*cut*)

Right lateral schematic view

Vertebral artery

Deep cervical artery (ascending to anastomose with descending branch of occipital artery)

Costocervical trunk

Supreme intercostal artery

1st posterior intercostal artery

2nd posterior intercostal artery

Scapula

External carotid artery

Internal carotid artery

Ascending cervical artery

Inferior thyroid artery

Transverse cervical artery

Common carotid artery

Thyrocervical trunk

Suprascapular artery

Subclavian artery (1st part medial to, 2nd part posterior to, 3rd part lateral to anterior scalene muscle)

Internal thoracic artery

ANESTHESIA

Neck

00350 Anesthesia for procedures on major vessels of neck; not otherwise specified

Intrathoracic

00560 Anesthesia for procedures on heart, pericardial sac, and great vessels of chest; without pump oxygenator

Upper Abdomen

00770 Anesthesia for all procedures on major abdominal blood vessels

Shoulder and Axilla

01650 Anesthesia for procedures on arteries of shoulder and axilla; not otherwise specified

01654   bypass graft

SURGERY

Cardiovascular System

Arteries and Veins
Embolectomy/Thrombectomy

Arterial, With or Without Catheter

34001 Embolectomy or thrombectomy, with or without catheter; carotid, subclavian or innominate artery, by neck incision

34051   innominate, subclavian artery, by thoracic incision

34101   axillary, brachial, innominate, subclavian artery, by arm incision

Transluminal Angioplasty

35458 Transluminal balloon angioplasty, open; brachiocephalic trunk or branches, each vessel

Bypass Graft

Vein

35501 Bypass graft, with vein; carotid
35506   carotid-subclavian
35507   subclavian-carotid
35511   subclavian-subclavian
35512   subclavian-brachial
35515   subclavian-vertebral
35516   subclavian-axillary
35526   aortosubclavian or carotid

Other Than Vein

35606 Bypass graft, with other than vein; carotid-subclavian
35612   subclavian-subclavian
35626   aortosubclavian or carotid

Arterial Transposition

35691 Transposition and/or reimplantation; vertebral to carotid artery

35694   subclavian to carotid artery

Exploration/Revision

35701 Exploration (not followed by surgical repair), with or without lysis of artery; carotid artery

Plate 13: Carotid Arteries

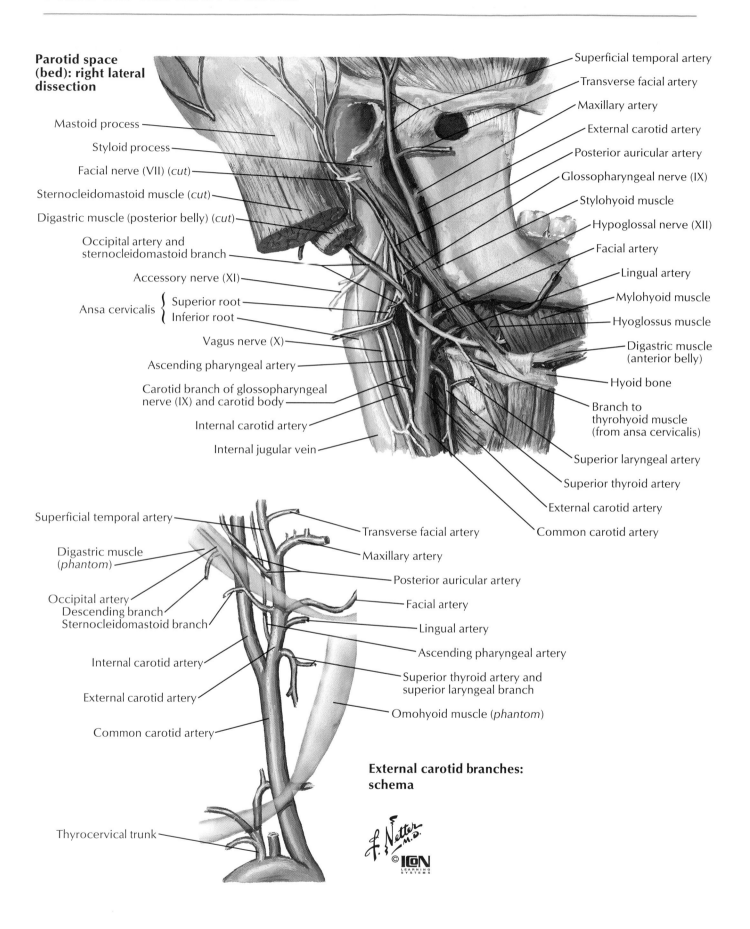

Parotid space (bed): right lateral dissection

Mastoid process

Styloid process

Facial nerve (VII) (*cut*)

Sternocleidomastoid muscle (*cut*)

Digastric muscle (posterior belly) (*cut*)

Occipital artery and sternocleidomastoid branch

Accessory nerve (XI)

Ansa cervicalis { Superior root / Inferior root

Vagus nerve (X)

Ascending pharyngeal artery

Carotid branch of glossopharyngeal nerve (IX) and carotid body

Internal carotid artery

Internal jugular vein

Superficial temporal artery

Transverse facial artery

Maxillary artery

External carotid artery

Posterior auricular artery

Glossopharyngeal nerve (IX)

Stylohyoid muscle

Hypoglossal nerve (XII)

Facial artery

Lingual artery

Mylohyoid muscle

Hyoglossus muscle

Digastric muscle (anterior belly)

Hyoid bone

Branch to thyrohyoid muscle (from ansa cervicalis)

Superior laryngeal artery

Superior thyroid artery

External carotid artery

Common carotid artery

Superficial temporal artery

Digastric muscle (*phantom*)

Occipital artery

Descending branch

Sternocleidomastoid branch

Internal carotid artery

External carotid artery

Common carotid artery

Thyrocervical trunk

Transverse facial artery

Maxillary artery

Posterior auricular artery

Facial artery

Lingual artery

Ascending pharyngeal artery

Superior thyroid artery and superior laryngeal branch

Omohyoid muscle (*phantom*)

External carotid branches: schema

ANESTHESIA

Neck

00350   Anesthesia for procedures on major vessels of neck; not otherwise specified

Radiological Procedures

01916   Anesthesia for diagnostic arteriography/ venography

SURGERY

Cardiovascular

Arteries and Veins
Embolectomy/Thrombectomy

Arterial, With or Without Catheter
34001   Embolectomy or thrombectomy, with or without catheter; carotid, subclavian or innominate artery, by neck incision

Direct Repair of Aneurysm or Excision (Partial or Total) and Graft Insertion for Aneurysm, Pseudoaneurysm, Ruptured Aneurysm, and Associated Occlusive Disease

35001   Direct repair of aneurysm, pseudoaneurysm, or excision (partial or total) and graft insertion, with or without patch graft; for aneurysm and associated occlusive disease, carotid, subclavian artery, by neck incision

35002   for ruptured aneurysm, carotid, subclavian artery, by neck incision
35005   for aneurysm, pseudoaneurysm, and associated occlusive disease, vertebral artery
35011   for aneurysm and associated occlusive disease, axillary-brachial artery, by arm incision

Thromboendarterectomy

35301   Thromboendarterectomy, with or without patch graft; carotid, vertebral, subclavian, by neck incision

Bypass Graft

Vein
35526   Bypass graft, with vein; aortosubclavian or carotid
Other Than Vein
35601   Bypass graft, with other than vein; carotid
35606   carotid-subclavian
35626   aortosubclavian or carotid
35642   carotid-vertebral

Exploration/Revision

35701   Exploration (not followed by surgical repair), with or without lysis of artery; carotid artery

Intra-Arterial—Intra-Aortic

36100   Introduction of needle or intracatheter, carotid or vertebral artery

Plate 14: Nose (Skeleton)—Anterolateral and Inferior Views

Anterolateral view

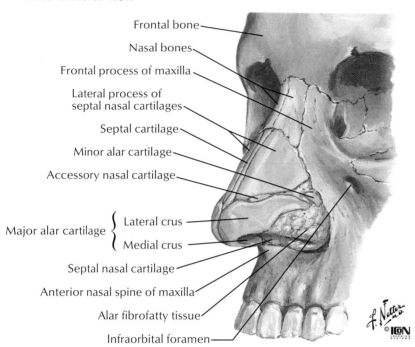

Frontal bone

Nasal bones

Frontal process of maxilla

Lateral process of septal nasal cartilages

Septal cartilage

Minor alar cartilage

Accessory nasal cartilage

Major alar cartilage { Lateral crus

Medial crus

Septal nasal cartilage

Anterior nasal spine of maxilla

Alar fibrofatty tissue

Infraorbital foramen

Inferior view

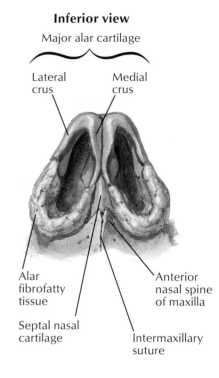

Major alar cartilage

Lateral crus

Medial crus

Alar fibrofatty tissue

Septal nasal cartilage

Anterior nasal spine of maxilla

Intermaxillary suture

ANESTHESIA

Head

00160	Anesthesia for procedures on nose and accessory sinuses; not otherwise specified
00162	radical surgery

SURGERY

Respiratory System

Nose
Incision

30000	Drainage abscess or hematoma, nasal, internal approach
30020	Drainage abscess or hematoma, nasal septum

Repair

30400	Rhinoplasty, primary; lateral and alar cartilages and/or elevation of nasal tip
30410	complete, external parts including bony pyramid, lateral and alar cartilages, and/or elevation of nasal tip
30420	including major septal repair
30430	Rhinoplasty, secondary; minor revision (small amount of nasal tip work)
30435	intermediate revision (bony work with osteotomies)
30450	major revision (nasal tip work and osteotomies)
30460	Rhinoplasty for nasal deformity secondary to congenital cleft lip and/or palate, including columellar lengthening; tip only
30462	tip, septum, osteotomies
30465[P]	Repair of nasal vestibular stenosis (eg, spreader grafting, lateral nasal wall reconstruction)
30520	Septoplasty or submucous resection, with or without cartilage scoring, contouring or replacement with graft

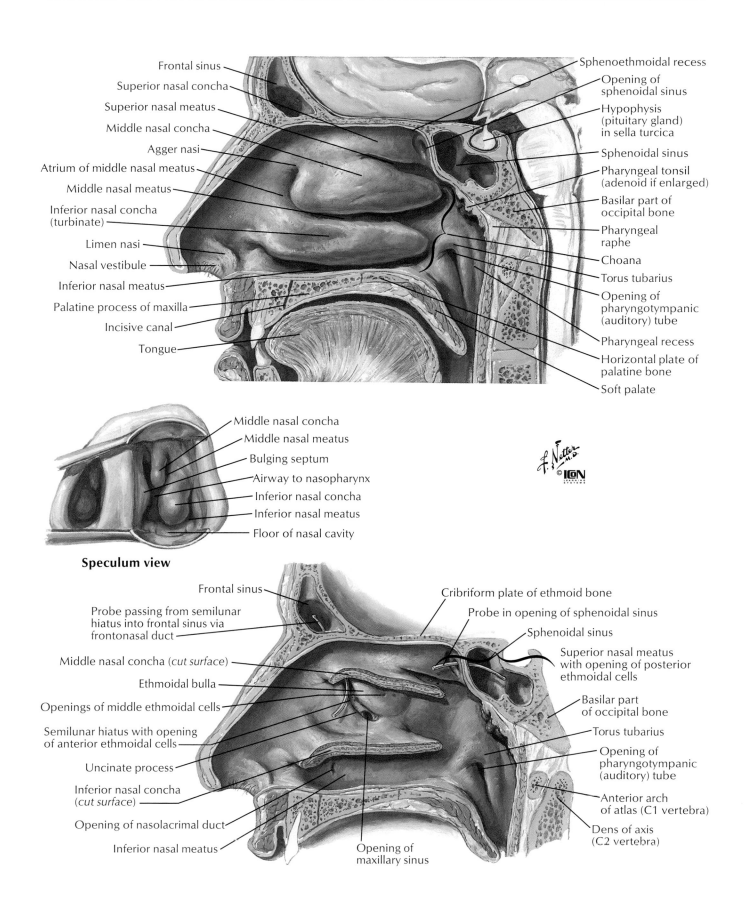

Frontal sinus
Superior nasal concha
Superior nasal meatus
Middle nasal concha
Agger nasi
Atrium of middle nasal meatus
Middle nasal meatus
Inferior nasal concha (turbinate)
Limen nasi
Nasal vestibule
Inferior nasal meatus
Palatine process of maxilla
Incisive canal
Tongue

Sphenoethmoidal recess
Opening of sphenoidal sinus
Hypophysis (pituitary gland) in sella turcica
Sphenoidal sinus
Pharyngeal tonsil (adenoid if enlarged)
Basilar part of occipital bone
Pharyngeal raphe
Choana
Torus tubarius
Opening of pharyngotympanic (auditory) tube
Pharyngeal recess
Horizontal plate of palatine bone
Soft palate

Middle nasal concha
Middle nasal meatus
Bulging septum
Airway to nasopharynx
Inferior nasal concha
Inferior nasal meatus
Floor of nasal cavity

Speculum view

Frontal sinus
Probe passing from semilunar hiatus into frontal sinus via frontonasal duct
Middle nasal concha (*cut surface*)
Ethmoidal bulla
Openings of middle ethmoidal cells
Semilunar hiatus with opening of anterior ethmoidal cells
Uncinate process
Inferior nasal concha (*cut surface*)
Opening of nasolacrimal duct
Inferior nasal meatus

Cribriform plate of ethmoid bone
Probe in opening of sphenoidal sinus
Sphenoidal sinus
Superior nasal meatus with opening of posterior ethmoidal cells
Basilar part of occipital bone
Torus tubarius
Opening of pharyngotympanic (auditory) tube
Anterior arch of atlas (C1 vertebra)
Dens of axis (C2 vertebra)
Opening of maxillary sinus

ANESTHESIA

Head

00160	Anesthesia for procedures on nose and accessory sinuses; not otherwise specified
00162	radical surgery
00164	biopsy, soft tissue

SURGERY

Respiratory System

Nose
Incision

30000	Drainage abscess or hematoma, nasal, internal approach
30020	Drainage abscess or hematoma, nasal septum

Excision

30100	Biopsy, intranasal
30110	Excision, nasal polyp(s), simple
30115	Excision, nasal polyp(s), extensive
30117	Excision or destruction (eg, laser), intranasal lesion; internal approach
30118	external approach (lateral rhinotomy)
30120	Excision or surgical planing of skin of nose for rhinophyma
30124	Excision dermoid cyst, nose; simple, skin, subcutaneous
30125	complex, under bone or cartilage
30130	Excision turbinate, partial or complete, any method
30140	Submucous resection turbinate, partial or complete, any method
30150	Rhinectomy; partial
30160	total

Other Procedures

30901	Control nasal hemorrhage, anterior, simple (limited cautery and/or packing) any method
30903	Control nasal hemorrhage, anterior, complex (extensive cautery and/or packing) any method
30905	Control nasal hemorrhage, posterior, with posterior nasal packs and/or cautery, any method; initial
30906	subsequent

Accessory Sinuses
Endoscopy

31231[P]	Nasal endoscopy, diagnostic, unilateral or bilateral (separate procedure)
31233	Nasal/sinus endoscopy, diagnostic with maxillary sinusoscopy (via inferior meatus or canine fossa puncture)
31235	Nasal/sinus endoscopy, diagnostic with sphenoid sinusoscopy (via puncture of sphenoidal face or cannulation of ostium)
31237	Nasal/sinus endoscopy, surgical; with biopsy, polypectomy or debridement (separate procedure)
31238	with control of nasal hemorrhage
31239	with dacryocystorhinostomy
31240	with concha bullosa resection
31254	with ethmoidectomy, partial (anterior)
31255	with ethmoidectomy, total (anterior and posterior)
31256	Nasal/sinus endoscopy, surgical, with maxillary antrostomy;
31267	with removal of tissue from maxillary sinus
31276	Nasal/sinus endoscopy, surgical with frontal sinus exploration, with or without removal of tissue from frontal sinus
31287	Nasal/sinus endoscopy, surgical, with sphenoidotomy;
31288	with removal of tissue from the sphenoid sinus
31290	Nasal/sinus endoscopy, surgical, with repair of cerebrospinal fluid leak; ethmoid region
31291	sphenoid region
31292	Nasal/sinus endoscopy, surgical; with medial or inferior orbital wall decompression
31293	with medial orbital wall and inferior orbital wall decompression
31294	with optic nerve decompression

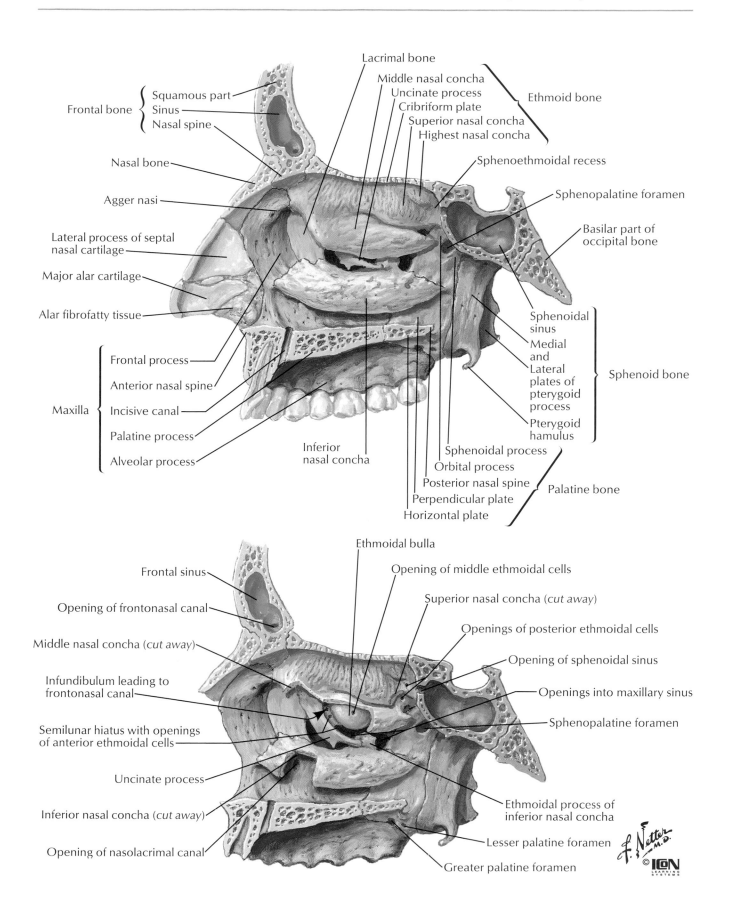

Lacrimal bone
Middle nasal concha
Uncinate process
Cribriform plate
Superior nasal concha
Highest nasal concha

Ethmoid bone

Frontal bone {
Squamous part
Sinus
Nasal spine

Nasal bone

Agger nasi

Lateral process of septal nasal cartilage

Major alar cartilage

Alar fibrofatty tissue

Sphenoethmoidal recess

Sphenopalatine foramen

Basilar part of occipital bone

Sphenoidal sinus
Medial and Lateral plates of pterygoid process

Sphenoid bone

Pterygoid hamulus

Maxilla {
Frontal process
Anterior nasal spine
Incisive canal
Palatine process
Alveolar process

Inferior nasal concha

Sphenoidal process
Orbital process
Posterior nasal spine
Perpendicular plate
Horizontal plate

Palatine bone

Ethmoidal bulla
Opening of middle ethmoidal cells

Frontal sinus

Opening of frontonasal canal

Middle nasal concha (cut away)

Infundibulum leading to frontonasal canal

Semilunar hiatus with openings of anterior ethmoidal cells

Uncinate process

Inferior nasal concha (cut away)

Opening of nasolacrimal canal

Superior nasal concha (cut away)

Openings of posterior ethmoidal cells

Opening of sphenoidal sinus

Openings into maxillary sinus

Sphenopalatine foramen

Ethmoidal process of inferior nasal concha

Lesser palatine foramen

Greater palatine foramen

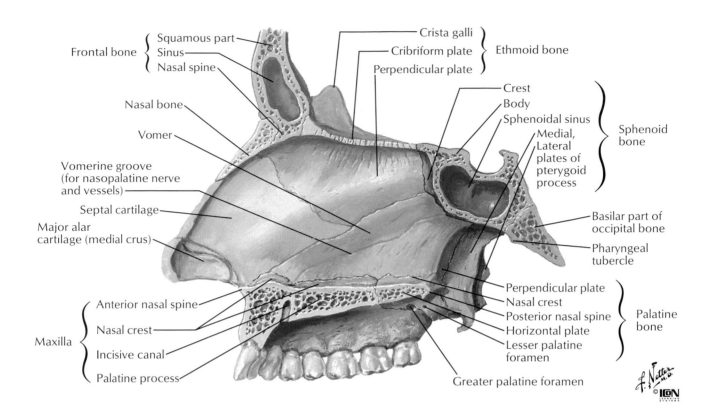

Frontal bone { Squamous part, Sinus, Nasal spine

Crista galli, Cribriform plate, Perpendicular plate } Ethmoid bone

Nasal bone

Vomer

Vomerine groove (for nasopalatine nerve and vessels)

Septal cartilage

Major alar cartilage (medial crus)

Crest, Body, Sphenoidal sinus, Medial, Lateral plates of pterygoid process } Sphenoid bone

Basilar part of occipital bone

Pharyngeal tubercle

Maxilla { Anterior nasal spine, Nasal crest, Incisive canal, Palatine process

Perpendicular plate, Nasal crest, Posterior nasal spine, Horizontal plate, Lesser palatine foramen } Palatine bone

Greater palatine foramen

ANESTHESIA

Head

00160 Anesthesia for procedures on nose and accessory sinuses; not otherwise specified

SURGERY

Musculoskeletal System

Head

Fracture and/or Dislocation

21310	Closed treatment of nasal bone fracture without manipulation
21315	Closed treatment of nasal bone fracture; without stabilization
21320	with stabilization
21325	Open treatment of nasal fracture; uncomplicated
21330	complicated, with internal and/or external skeletal fixation
21335	with concomitant open treatment of fractured septum
21336	Open treatment of nasal septal fracture, with or without stabilization

21337	Closed treatment of nasal septal fracture, with or without stabilization
21338	Open treatment of nasoethmoid fracture; without external fixation
21339	with external fixation
21340	Percutaneous treatment of nasoethmoid complex fracture, with splint, wire or headcap fixation, including repair of canthal ligaments and/or the nasolacrimal apparatus
21343	Open treatment of depressed frontal sinus fracture
21344	Open treatment of complicated (eg, comminuted or involving posterior wall) frontal sinus fracture, via coronal or multiple approaches
21345	Closed treatment of nasomaxillary complex fracture (LeFort II type), with interdental wire fixation or fixation of denture or splint
21346	Open treatment of nasomaxillary complex fracture (LeFort II type); with wiring and/or local fixation
21347	requiring multiple open approaches
21348	with bone grafting (includes obtaining graft)

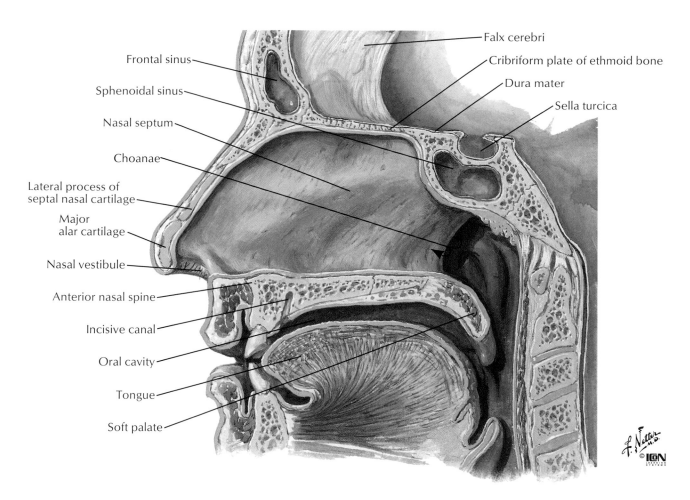

Frontal sinus

Sphenoidal sinus

Nasal septum

Choanae

Lateral process of septal nasal cartilage

Major alar cartilage

Nasal vestibule

Anterior nasal spine

Incisive canal

Oral cavity

Tongue

Soft palate

Falx cerebri

Cribriform plate of ethmoid bone

Dura mater

Sella turcica

ANESTHESIA

Head	
00160	Anesthesia for procedures on nose and accessory sinuses; not otherwise specified
00162	radical surgery
00164	biopsy, soft tissue

SURGERY

Respiratory System	

Nose
Incision

30000	Drainage abscess or hematoma, nasal, internal approach
30020	Drainage abscess or hematoma, nasal septum

Excision

30100	Biopsy, intranasal
30110	Excision, nasal polyp(s), simple
30115	Excision, nasal polyp(s), extensive
30117	Excision or destruction (eg, laser), intranasal lesion; internal approach
30118	external approach (lateral rhinotomy)
30120	Excision or surgical planing of skin of nose for rhinophyma

30124	Excision dermoid cyst, nose; simple, skin, subcutaneous
30125	complex, under bone or cartilage
30130	Excision turbinate, partial or complete, any method
30140	Submucous resection turbinate, partial or complete, any method

Other Procedures

30901	Control nasal hemorrhage, anterior, simple (limited cautery and/or packing) any method
30903	Control nasal hemorrhage, anterior, complex (extensive cautery and/or packing) any method
30905	Control nasal hemorrhage, posterior, with posterior nasal packs and/or cautery, any method; initial
30906	subsequent

Accessory Sinuses
Endoscopy

31231[P]	Nasal endoscopy, diagnostic, unilateral or bilateral (separate procedure)
31233[P]	Nasal/sinus endoscopy, diagnostic with maxillary sinusoscopy (via inferior meatus or canine fossa puncture)

(Endoscopy continued on next page)

Plate 17: Medial Wall of Nasal Cavity

(Endoscopy continued from previous page)

31235   Nasal/sinus endoscopy, diagnostic with sphenoid sinusoscopy (via puncture of sphenoidal face or cannulation of ostium)

31237   Nasal/sinus endoscopy, surgical; with biopsy, polypectomy or debridement (separate procedure)

31238   with control of nasal hemorrhage

31239   with dacryocystorhinostomy

31240   with concha bullosa resection

31254   Nasal/sinus endoscopy, surgical; with ethmoidectomy, partial (anterior)

31255   with ethmoidectomy, total (anterior and posterior)

31256   Nasal/sinus endoscopy, surgical, with maxillary antrostomy;

31267   with removal of tissue from maxillary sinus

31276   Nasal/sinus endoscopy, surgical with frontal sinus exploration, with or without removal of tissue from frontal sinus

31287   Nasal/sinus endoscopy, surgical, with sphenoidotomy;

31288   with removal of tissue from the sphenoid sinus

31290   Nasal/sinus endoscopy, surgical, with repair of cerebrospinal fluid leak; ethmoid region

31291   sphenoid region

31292   Nasal/sinus endoscopy, surgical; with medial or inferior orbital wall decompression

31293   with medial orbital wall and inferior orbital wall decompression

31294   with optic nerve decompression

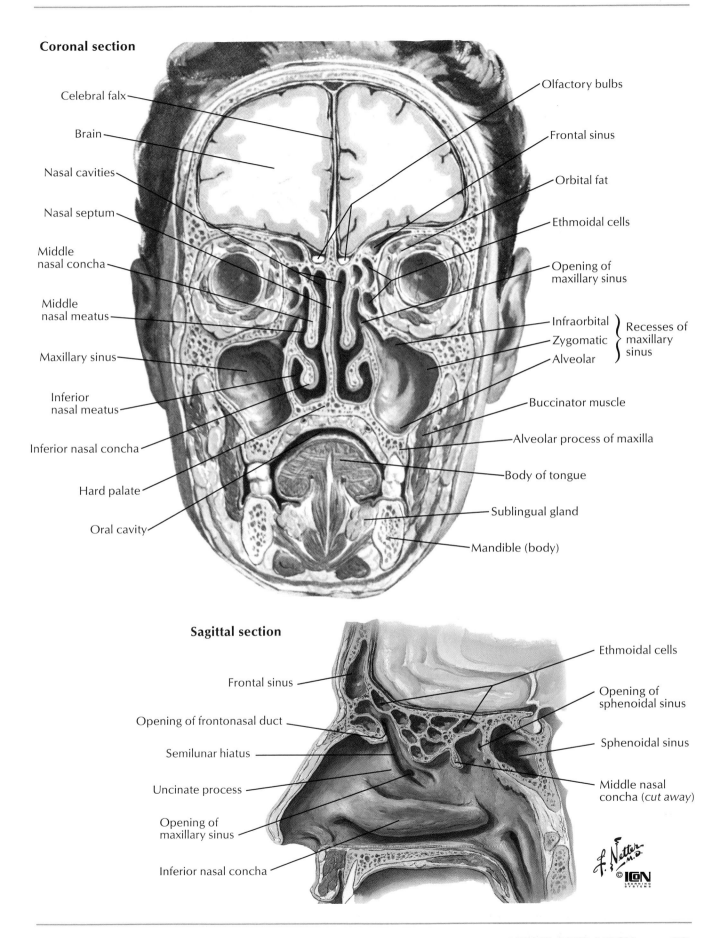

Coronal section

Celebral falx

Brain

Nasal cavities

Nasal septum

Middle nasal concha

Middle nasal meatus

Maxillary sinus

Inferior nasal meatus

Inferior nasal concha

Hard palate

Oral cavity

Olfactory bulbs

Frontal sinus

Orbital fat

Ethmoidal cells

Opening of maxillary sinus

Infraorbital } Recesses of
Zygomatic   } maxillary
Alveolar   } sinus

Buccinator muscle

Alveolar process of maxilla

Body of tongue

Sublingual gland

Mandible (body)

Sagittal section

Frontal sinus

Opening of frontonasal duct

Semilunar hiatus

Uncinate process

Opening of maxillary sinus

Inferior nasal concha

Ethmoidal cells

Opening of sphenoidal sinus

Sphenoidal sinus

Middle nasal concha (*cut away*)

Plate 18: Paranasal Sinuses—Coronal and Sagittal Sections

ANESTHESIA

Head

00160	Anesthesia for procedures on nose and accessory sinuses; not otherwise specified
00162	radical surgery

SURGERY

Respiratory System

Accessory Sinuses
Incision

31000	Lavage by cannulation; maxillary sinus (antrum puncture or natural ostium)
31002	sphenoid sinus
31020	Sinusotomy, maxillary (antrotomy); intranasal
31030	radical (Caldwell-Luc) without removal of antrochoanal polyps
31032	radical (Caldwell-Luc) with removal of antrochoanal polyps
31040	Pterygomaxillary fossa surgery, any approach
31050	Sinusotomy, sphenoid, with or without biopsy;
31051	with mucosal stripping or removal of polyp(s)
31070ᴾ	Sinusotomy frontal; external, simple (trephine operation)
31075	transorbital, unilateral (for mucocele or osteoma, Lynch type)
31080	obliterative without osteoplastic flap, brow incision (includes ablation)
31081	obliterative, without osteoplastic flap, coronal incision (includes ablation)
31084	obliterative, with osteoplastic flap, brow incision
31085	obliterative, with osteoplastic flap, coronal incision
31086	nonobliterative, with osteoplastic flap, brow incision
31087	nonobliterative, with osteoplastic flap, coronal incision
31090	Sinusotomy, unilateral, three or more paranasal sinuses (frontal, maxillary, ethmoid, sphenoid)

Excision

31200	Ethmoidectomy; intranasal, anterior
31201	intranasal, total
31205	extranasal, total
31225	Maxillectomy; without orbital exenteration
31230	with orbital exenteration (en bloc)

Endoscopy

31231ᴾ	Nasal endoscopy, diagnostic, unilateral or bilateral (separate procedure)
31233	Nasal/sinus endoscopy, diagnostic with maxillary sinusoscopy (via inferior meatus or canine fossa puncture)
31235	Nasal/sinus endoscopy, diagnostic with sphenoid sinusoscopy (via puncture of sphenoidal face or cannulation of ostium)
31237	Nasal/sinus endoscopy, surgical; with biopsy, polypectomy or debridement (separate procedure)
31238	with control of nasal hemorrhage
31239	with dacryocystorhinostomy
31240	with concha bullosa resection
31254	Nasal/sinus endoscopy, surgical; with ethmoidectomy, partial (anterior)
31255	with ethmoidectomy, total (anterior and posterior)
31256	Nasal/sinus endoscopy, surgical, with maxillary antrostomy;
31267	with removal of tissue from maxillary sinus
31276	Nasal/sinus endoscopy, surgical with frontal sinus exploration, with or without removal of tissue from frontal sinus
31287	Nasal/sinus endoscopy, surgical, with sphenoidotomy;
31288	with removal of tissue from the sphenoid sinus
31290	Nasal/sinus endoscopy, surgical, with repair of cerebrospinal fluid leak; ethmoid region
31291	sphenoid region
31292	Nasal/sinus endoscopy, surgical; with medial or inferior orbital wall decompression
31293	with medial orbital wall and inferior orbital wall decompression
31294	with optic nerve decompression

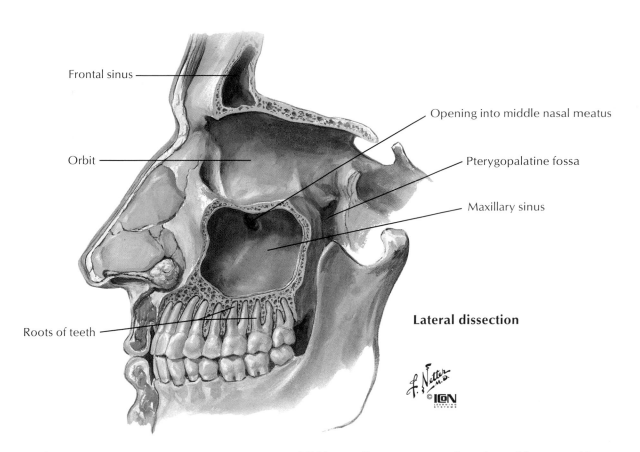

Frontal sinus

Opening into middle nasal meatus

Orbit

Pterygopalatine fossa

Maxillary sinus

Roots of teeth

Lateral dissection

Nomenclature Notes

The *LeFort II fracture* is also called a *pyramidal fracture*. It extends from the nasal bridge through the frontal processes of the maxilla inferolaterally through the lacrimal bones and orbital floor, traveling under the zygoma and through the pterygoid plates.

ANESTHESIA

Head

00160	Anesthesia for procedures on nose and accessory sinuses; not otherwise specified
00162	radical surgery

SURGERY

Musculoskeletal System

Head
Fracture and/or Dislocation

21310	Closed treatment of nasal bone fracture without manipulation
21315	Closed treatment of nasal bone fracture; without stabilization
21320	with stabilization
21325	Open treatment of nasal fracture; uncomplicated
21330	complicated, with internal and/or external skeletal fixation
21335	with concomitant open treatment of fractured septum

21336	Open treatment of nasal septal fracture, with or without stabilization
21337	Closed treatment of nasal septal fracture, with or without stabilization
21343	Open treatment of depressed frontal sinus fracture
21344	Open treatment of complicated (eg, comminuted or involving posterior wall) frontal sinus fracture, via coronal or multiple approaches
21345	Closed treatment of nasomaxillary complex fracture (LeFort II type), with interdental wire fixation or fixation of denture or splint
21346	Open treatment of nasomaxillary complex fracture (LeFort II type); with wiring and/or local fixation
21347	requiring multiple open approaches
21348	with bone grafting (includes obtaining graft)
21385	Open treatment of orbital floor blowout fracture; transantral approach (Caldwell-luc operation)
21386	periorbital approach
21387	combined approach
21390	periorbital approach, with alloplastic or other implant
21395	periorbital approach with bone graft (includes obtaining graft)
21400	Closed treatment of fracture of orbit, except blowout; without manipulation
21401	with manipulation
21406	Open treatment of fracture of orbit, except blowout; without implant
21407	with implant
21408	with bone grafting (includes obtaining graft)

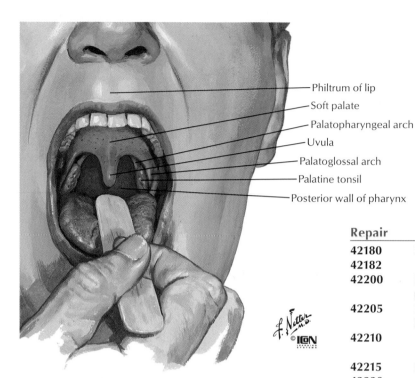

Philtrum of lip
Soft palate
Palatopharyngeal arch
Uvula
Palatoglossal arch
Palatine tonsil
Posterior wall of pharynx

Nomenclature Notes

The *oropharynx* is the part of the throat at the back of the mouth.

The *nasopharynx* is the part of the pharynx extending from the posterior nares to the soft palate.

ANESTHESIA

Head

00170	Anesthesia for intraoral procedures, including biopsy; not otherwise specified

SURGERY

Digestive System

Palate and Uvula
Incision

42000	Drainage of abscess of palate, uvula

Excision, Destruction

42100	Biopsy of palate, uvula
42104	Excision, lesion of palate, uvula; without closure
42106	with simple primary closure
42107	with local flap closure
42120	Resection of palate or extensive resection of lesion
42140	Uvulectomy, excision of uvula
42145	Palatopharyngoplasty (eg, uvulopalatopharyngoplasty, uvulopharyngoplasty)
42160	Destruction of lesion, palate or uvula (thermal, cryo or chemical)

Repair

42180	Repair, laceration of palate; up to 2 cm
42182	over 2 cm or complex
42200	Palatoplasty for cleft palate, soft and/or hard palate only
42205	Palatoplasty for cleft palate, with closure of alveolar ridge; soft tissue only
42210	with bone graft to alveolar ridge (includes obtaining graft)
42215	Palatoplasty for cleft palate; major revision
42220	secondary lengthening procedure
42225	attachment pharyngeal flap
42226	Lengthening of palate, and pharyngeal flap
42227	Lengthening of palate, with island flap
42235	Repair of anterior palate, including vomer flap

Pharynx, Adenoids, and Tonsils
Incision

42700	Incision and drainage abscess; peritonsillar
42720	retropharyngeal or parapharyngeal, intraoral approach
42725	retropharyngeal or parapharyngeal, external approach

Excision, Destruction

42800	Biopsy; oropharynx
42802	hypopharynx
42804	nasopharynx, visible lesion, simple
42806	nasopharynx, survey for unknown primary lesion
42808	Excision or destruction of lesion of pharynx, any method
42820	Tonsillectomy and adenoidectomy; under age 12
42821	age 12 or over
42825	Tonsillectomy, primary or secondary; under age 12
42826	age 12 or over
42830	Adenoidectomy, primary; under age 12
42831	age 12 or over
42835	Adenoidectomy, secondary; under age 12
42836	age 12 or over
42842	Radical resection of tonsil, tonsillar pillars, and/or retromolar trigone; without closure
42844	closure with local flap (eg, tongue, buccal)
42845	closure with other flap
42860	Excision of tonsil tags
42870	Excision or destruction lingual tonsil, any method (separate procedure)

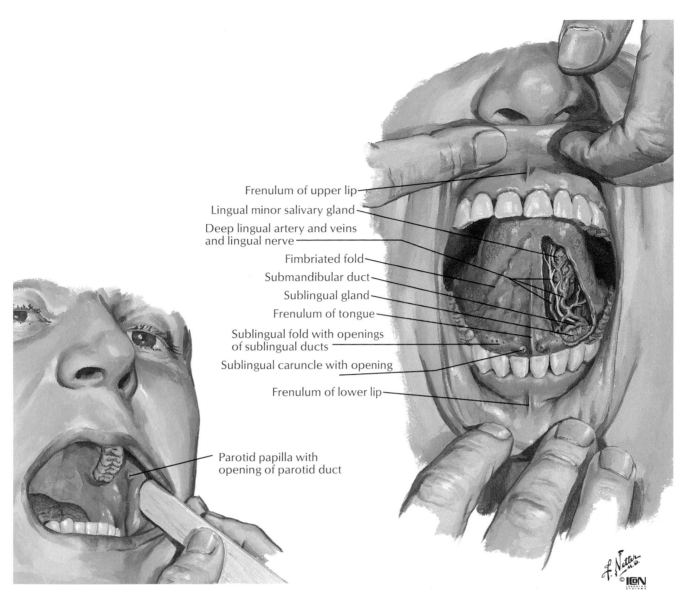

Frenulum of upper lip

Lingual minor salivary gland

Deep lingual artery and veins and lingual nerve

Fimbriated fold

Submandibular duct

Sublingual gland

Frenulum of tongue

Sublingual fold with openings of sublingual ducts

Sublingual caruncle with opening

Frenulum of lower lip

Parotid papilla with opening of parotid duct

Nomenclature Notes

The *vestibule of the mouth* is the part of the oral cavity outside the teeth and gums. It includes the muscosa and submucosa of the lips and cheeks.

Frenum is synonymous with *frenulum*.

Submaxillary gland is synonymous with *submandibular gland*.

ANESTHESIA

Head

00100	Anesthesia for procedures on salivary glands, including biopsy
00170	Anesthesia for intraoral procedures, including biopsy; not otherwise specified

SURGERY

Digestive System

Vestibule of Mouth

Incision

40800	Drainage of abscess, cyst, hematoma, vestibule of mouth; simple
40801	complicated
40804	Removal of embedded foreign body, vestibule of mouth; simple
40805	complicated
40806	Incision of labial frenum (frenotomy)

Excision, Destruction

40808	Biopsy, vestibule of mouth
40810	Excision of lesion of mucosa and submucosa, vestibule of mouth; without repair

(Excision continued on next page)

(Excision continued from previous page)

40812	with simple repair
40814	with complex repair
40816	complex, with excision of underlying muscle
40818	Excision of mucosa of vestibule of mouth as donor graft
40819	Excision of frenum, labial or buccal (frenumectomy, frenulectomy, frenectomy)
40820	Destruction of lesion or scar of vestibule of mouth by physical methods (eg, laser, thermal, cryo, chemical)

Repair

40830	Closure of laceration, vestibule of mouth; 2.5 cm or less
40831	over 2.5 cm or complex
40840	Vestibuloplasty; anterior
40842	posterior, unilateral
40843	posterior, bilateral
40844	entire arch
40845	complex (including ridge extension, muscle repositioning)

Tongue and Floor of Mouth
Excision

41100	Biopsy of tongue; anterior two-thirds
41105	posterior one-third
41108	Biopsy of floor of mouth
41110	Excision of lesion of tongue without closure
41112	Excision of lesion of tongue without closure; anterior two-thirds
41113	posterior one-third
41114	with local tongue flap
41115	Excision of lingual frenum (frenectomy)
41116	Excision, lesion of floor of mouth
41120	Glossectomy; less than one-half tongue
41130	hemiglossectomy

Repair

41250	Repair of laceration 2.5 cm or less; floor of mouth and/or anterior two-thirds of tongue
41251	Repair of laceration 2.5 cm or less; posterior one-third of tongue
41252	Repair of laceration of tongue, floor of mouth, over 2.6 cm or complex

Other Procedures

41500	Fixation of tongue, mechanical, other than suture (eg, K-wire)
41510	Suture of tongue to lip for micrognathia (Douglas type procedure)
41520	Frenoplasty (surgical revision of frenum, eg, with Z-plasty)

Salivary Gland and Ducts
Incision

42310	Drainage of abscess; submaxillary or sublingual, intraoral
42320	submaxillary, external
42325	Fistulization of sublingual salivary cyst (ranula);
42326	with prosthesis
42330	Sialolithotomy; submandibular (submaxillary), sublingual or parotid, uncomplicated, intraoral
42335	submandibular (submaxillary), complicated, intraoral

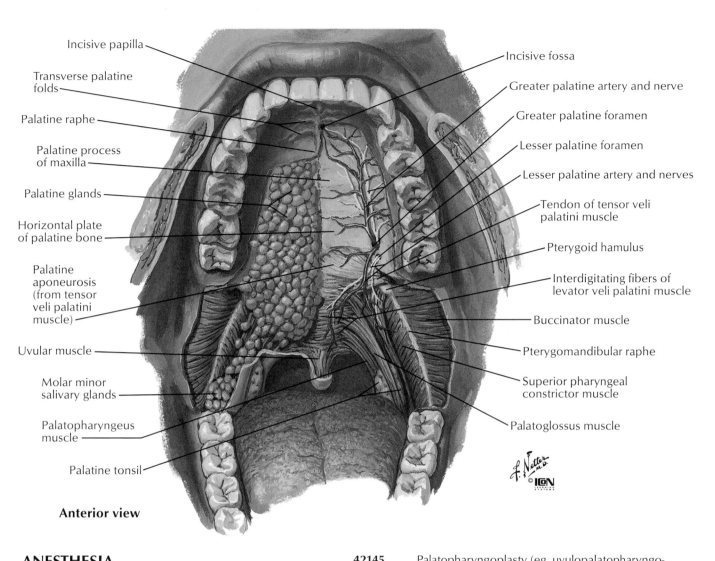

Incisive papilla

Transverse palatine folds

Palatine raphe

Palatine process of maxilla

Palatine glands

Horizontal plate of palatine bone

Palatine aponeurosis (from tensor veli palatini muscle)

Uvular muscle

Molar minor salivary glands

Palatopharyngeus muscle

Palatine tonsil

Incisive fossa

Greater palatine artery and nerve

Greater palatine foramen

Lesser palatine foramen

Lesser palatine artery and nerves

Tendon of tensor veli palatini muscle

Pterygoid hamulus

Interdigitating fibers of levator veli palatini muscle

Buccinator muscle

Pterygomandibular raphe

Superior pharyngeal constrictor muscle

Palatoglossus muscle

Anterior view

ANESTHESIA

Head

00170	Anesthesia for intraoral procedures, including biopsy; not otherwise specified
00172	repair of cleft palate
00176	radical surgery

SURGERY

Digestive System

Palate and Uvula
Incision

42000	Drainage of abscess of palate, uvula

Excision/Destruction

42100	Biopsy of palate, uvula
42104	Excision, lesion of palate, uvula; without closure
42106	with simple primary closure
42107	with local flap closure
42120	Resection of palate or extensive resection of lesion

42145	Palatopharyngoplasty (eg, uvulopalatopharyngo-plasty, uvulopharyngoplasty)
42160	Destruction of lesion, palate or uvula (thermal, cryo or chemical)

Repair

42180	Repair, laceration of palate; up to 2 cm
42182	over 2 cm or complex
42200	Palatoplasty for cleft palate, soft and/or hard palate only
42205	Palatoplasty for cleft palate, with closure of alveolar ridge; soft tissue only
42210	with bone graft to alveolar ridge (includes obtaining graft)
42215	Palatoplasty for cleft palate; major revision
42220	secondary lengthening procedure
42225	attachment pharyngeal flap
42226	Lengthening of palate, and pharyngeal flap
42227	Lengthening of palate, with island flap
42235	Repair of anterior palate, including vomer flap

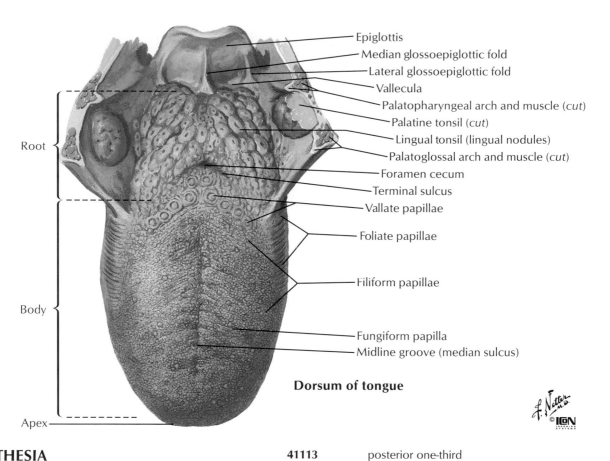

Epiglottis
Median glossoepiglottic fold
Lateral glossoepiglottic fold
Vallecula
Palatopharyngeal arch and muscle (*cut*)
Palatine tonsil (*cut*)
Lingual tonsil (lingual nodules)
Palatoglossal arch and muscle (*cut*)
Foramen cecum
Terminal sulcus
Vallate papillae
Foliate papillae
Filiform papillae
Fungiform papilla
Midline groove (median sulcus)

Root

Body

Apex

Dorsum of tongue

ANESTHESIA

Head

00170 Anesthesia for intraoral procedures, including biopsy; not otherwise specified

SURGERY

Digestive System

Tongue and Floor of Mouth

Incision

41000 Intraoral incision and drainage of abscess, cyst, or hematoma of tongue or floor of mouth; lingual

Excision

41100 Biopsy of tongue; anterior two-thirds
41105 Biopsy of tongue; posterior one-third
41112 Excision of lesion of tongue with closure; anterior two-thirds

41113 posterior one-third
41114 with local tongue flap
41120 Glossectomy; less than one-half tongue
41130 hemiglossectomy
41140 complete or total, with or without tracheostomy, without radical neck dissection

Repair

41250 Repair of laceration 2.5 cm or less; floor of mouth and/or anterior two-thirds of tongue
41251 posterior one-third of tongue
41252 Repair of laceration of tongue, floor of mouth, over 2.6 cm or complex

Other Procedures

41500 Fixation of tongue, mechanical, other than suture (eg, K-wire)

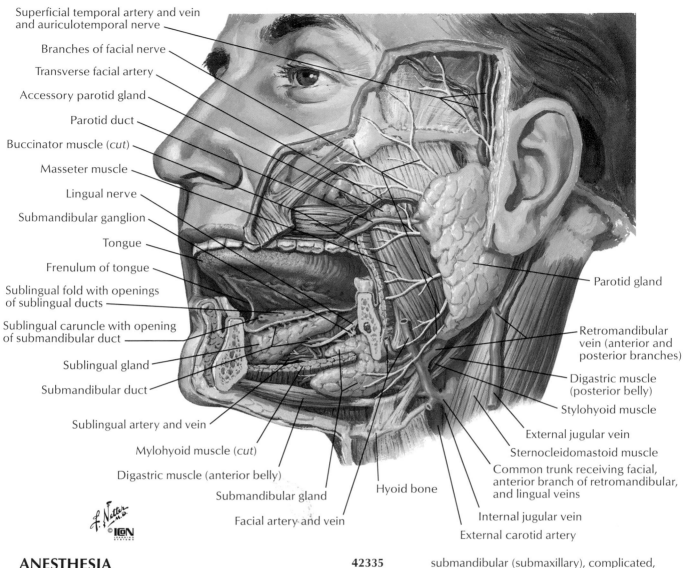

Superficial temporal artery and vein and auriculotemporal nerve

Branches of facial nerve

Transverse facial artery

Accessory parotid gland

Parotid duct

Buccinator muscle (*cut*)

Masseter muscle

Lingual nerve

Submandibular ganglion

Tongue

Frenulum of tongue

Sublingual fold with openings of sublingual ducts

Sublingual caruncle with opening of submandibular duct

Sublingual gland

Submandibular duct

Sublingual artery and vein

Mylohyoid muscle (*cut*)

Digastric muscle (anterior belly)

Submandibular gland

Facial artery and vein

Parotid gland

Retromandibular vein (anterior and posterior branches)

Digastric muscle (posterior belly)

Stylohyoid muscle

External jugular vein

Sternocleidomastoid muscle

Common trunk receiving facial, anterior branch of retromandibular, and lingual veins

Internal jugular vein

External carotid artery

Hyoid bone

ANESTHESIA

Head

00100	Anesthesia for procedures on salivary glands, including biopsy

SURGERY

Digestive System

Salivary Glands and Ducts
Incision

42300	Drainage of abscess; parotid, simple
42305	parotid, complicated
42310	Drainage of abscess; submaxillary or sublingual, intraoral
42320	submaxillary, external
42325	Fistulization of sublingual salivary cyst (ranula);
42326	with prosthesis
42330	Sialolithotomy; submandibular (submaxillary), sublingual or parotid, uncomplicated, intraoral

42335	submandibular (submaxillary), complicated, intraoral
42340	parotid, extraoral or complicated intraoral

Excision

42400	Biopsy of salivary gland; needle
42405	incisional
42408	Excision of sublingual salivary cyst (ranula)
42409	Marsupialization of sublingual salivary cyst (ranula)
42410	Excision of parotid tumor or parotid gland; lateral lobe, without nerve dissection
42415	lateral lobe, with dissection and preservation of facial nerve
42420	total, with dissection and preservation of facial nerve
42425	total, en bloc removal with sacrifice of facial nerve
42426	Excision of parotid tumor or parotid gland; total, with unilateral radical neck dissection

(Excision continued on next page)

Plate 24: Salivary Glands

(Excision continued from previous page)

42440	Excision of submandibular (submaxillary) gland
42450	Excision of sublingual gland

Repair

42500	Plastic repair of salivary duct, sialodochoplasty; primary or simple
42505	secondary or complicated
42507	Parotid duct diversion, bilateral (Wilke type procedure);
42508	with excision of one submandibular gland
42509	with excision of both submandibular glands
42510	with ligation of both submandibular (Wharton's) ducts

Other Procedures

42550	Injection procedure for sialography
42600	Closure salivary fistula
42650	Dilation salivary duct
42660	Dilation and catheterization of salivary duct, with or without injection
42665	Ligation salivary duct, intraoral

RADIOLOGY

Diagnostic Radiology (Diagnostic Imaging)

Head and Neck

70380	Radiologic examination, salivary gland for calculus
70390	Sialography, radiological supervision and interpretation

Plate 25: Pharynx—Median Section

ANESTHESIA

Head

00170	Anesthesia for intraoral procedures, including biopsy; not otherwise specified
00174	excision of retropharyngeal tumor

Neck

00320	Anesthesia for all procedures on esophagus, thyroid, larynx, trachea and lymphatic system of neck; not otherwise specified, age 1 year or older
00326	Anesthesia for all procedures on the larynx and trachea in children less than 1 year of age

SURGERY

Digestive System

Pharynx, Adenoids, and Tonsils
Excision, Destruction

42800	Biopsy; oropharynx
42802	hypopharynx
42804	nasopharynx, visible lesion, simple
42806	nasopharynx, survey for unknown primary lesion
42808	Excision or destruction of lesion of pharynx, any method
42809	Removal of foreign body from pharynx
42810	Excision branchial cleft cyst or vestige, confined to skin and subcutaneous tissues
42815	Excision branchial cleft cyst, vestige, or fistula, extending beneath subcutaneous tissues and/or into pharynx
42870	Excision or destruction lingual tonsil, any method (separate procedure)
42890	Limited pharyngectomy
42892	Resection of lateral pharyngeal wall or pyriform sinus, direct closure by advancement of lateral and posterior pharyngeal walls
42894	Resection of pharyngeal wall requiring closure with myocutaneous flap

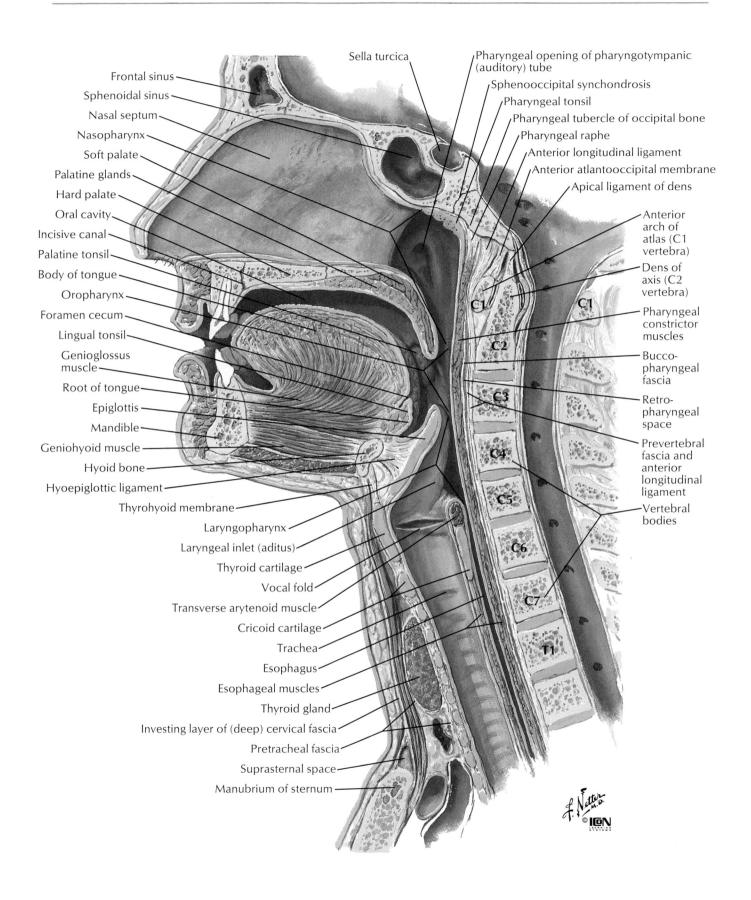

Frontal sinus

Sphenoidal sinus

Nasal septum

Nasopharynx

Soft palate

Palatine glands

Hard palate

Oral cavity

Incisive canal

Palatine tonsil

Body of tongue

Oropharynx

Foramen cecum

Lingual tonsil

Genioglossus muscle

Root of tongue

Epiglottis

Mandible

Geniohyoid muscle

Hyoid bone

Hyoepiglottic ligament

Thyrohyoid membrane

Laryngopharynx

Laryngeal inlet (aditus)

Thyroid cartilage

Vocal fold

Transverse arytenoid muscle

Cricoid cartilage

Trachea

Esophagus

Esophageal muscles

Thyroid gland

Investing layer of (deep) cervical fascia

Pretracheal fascia

Suprasternal space

Manubrium of sternum

Sella turcica

Pharyngeal opening of pharyngotympanic (auditory) tube

Sphenooccipital synchondrosis

Pharyngeal tonsil

Pharyngeal tubercle of occipital bone

Pharyngeal raphe

Anterior longitudinal ligament

Anterior atlantooccipital membrane

Apical ligament of dens

Anterior arch of atlas (C1 vertebra)

Dens of axis (C2 vertebra)

Pharyngeal constrictor muscles

Bucco-pharyngeal fascia

Retro-pharyngeal space

Prevertebral fascia and anterior longitudinal ligament

Vertebral bodies

C1

C2

C3

C4

C5

C6

C7

T1

C1

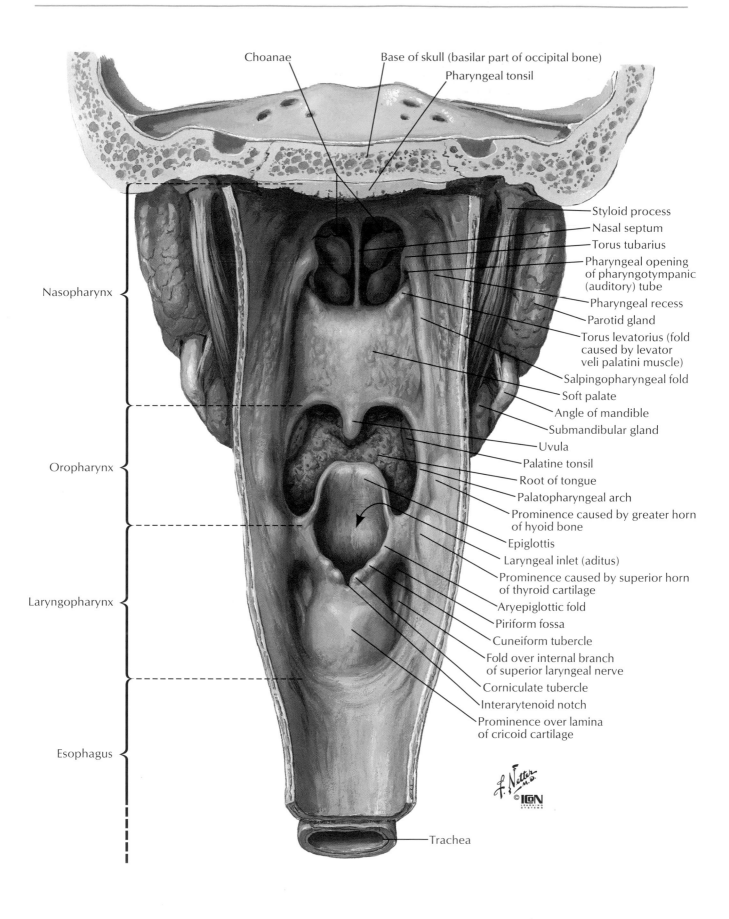

Choanae

Base of skull (basilar part of occipital bone)

Pharyngeal tonsil

Styloid process

Nasal septum

Torus tubarius

Pharyngeal opening of pharyngotympanic (auditory) tube

Pharyngeal recess

Parotid gland

Torus levatorius (fold caused by levator veli palatini muscle)

Salpingopharyngeal fold

Soft palate

Angle of mandible

Submandibular gland

Uvula

Palatine tonsil

Root of tongue

Palatopharyngeal arch

Prominence caused by greater horn of hyoid bone

Epiglottis

Laryngeal inlet (aditus)

Prominence caused by superior horn of thyroid cartilage

Aryepiglottic fold

Piriform fossa

Cuneiform tubercle

Fold over internal branch of superior laryngeal nerve

Corniculate tubercle

Interarytenoid notch

Prominence over lamina of cricoid cartilage

Nasopharynx

Oropharynx

Laryngopharynx

Esophagus

Trachea

ANESTHESIA

Neck

00320	Anesthesia for all procedures on esophagus, thyroid, larynx, trachea and lymphatic system of neck; not otherwise specified, age 1 year or older
00322	needle biopsy of thyroid
00326	Anesthesia for all procedures on the larynx and trachea in children less than 1 year of age

SURGERY

Respiratory System

Larynx
Excision

31300	Laryngotomy (thyrotomy, laryngofissure); with removal of tumor or laryngocele, cordectomy
31320	diagnostic
31360	Laryngectomy; total, without radical neck dissection
31365	total, with radical neck dissection
31367	subtotal supraglottic, without radical neck dissection
31368	subtotal supraglottic, with radical neck dissection
31370	Partial laryngectomy (hemilaryngectomy); horizontal
31375	laterovertical
31380	anterovertical
31382	antero-latero-vertical
31390	Pharyngolaryngectomy, with radical neck dissection; without reconstruction
31395	with reconstruction
31400	Arytenoidectomy or arytenoidopexy, external approach
31420	Epiglottidectomy

Endoscopy

31505	Laryngoscopy, indirect; diagnostic (separate procedure)
31510	with biopsy
31511	with removal of foreign body
31512	with removal of lesion
31513	with vocal cord injection
31515	Laryngoscopy direct, with or without tracheoscopy; for aspiration
31520	diagnostic, newborn
31525	diagnostic, except newborn
31526	diagnostic, with operating microscope
31527	with insertion of obturator
31528	with dilatation, initial
31529	with dilatation, subsequent
31530	Laryngoscopy, direct, operative, with foreign body removal
31531	with operating microscope
31535	Laryngoscopy, direct, operative, with biopsy
31536	with operating microscope
31540	Laryngoscopy, direct, operative, with excision of tumor and/or stripping of vocal cords or epiglottis
31541	with operating microscope
31545	Laryngoscopy, direct, operative, with operating microscope or telescope, with submucosal removal of non-neoplastic lesion(s) of vocal cord; reconstruction with local tissue flap(s)

31546	reconstruction with graft(s), includes obtaining autograft
31560	Laryngoscopy, direct, operative, with arytenoidectomy
31561	with operating microscope
31570	Laryngoscopy, direct, with injection into vocal cord(s), therapeutic
31571	with operating microscope
31575	Laryngoscopy, flexible fiberoptic; diagnostic
31576	with biopsy
31577	with removal of foreign body
31578	with removal of lesion
31579	Laryngoscopy, flexible or rigid fiberoptic, with stroboscopy

Repair

31580	Laryngoplasty; for laryngeal web, two stage, with keel insertion and removal
31582	for laryngeal stenosis, with graft or core mold, including tracheotomy
31584	with open reduction of fracture
31585	Treatment of closed laryngeal fracture; without manipulation
31586	with closed manipulative reduction
31587	Laryngoplasty, cricoid split
31588	Laryngoplasty, not otherwise specified
31590	Laryngeal reinnervation by neuromuscular pedicle

Digestive System

Pharynx, Adenoids, and Tonsils
Incision

42720	Incision and drainage abscess; retropharyngeal or parapharyngeal, intraoral approach
42725	retropharyngeal or parapharyngeal, external approach

Excision, Destruction

42800	Biopsy; oropharynx
42802	hypopharynx
42804	nasopharynx, visible lesion, simple
42806	nasopharynx, survey for unknown primary lesion
42808	Excision or destruction of lesion of pharynx, any method
42809	Removal of foreign body from pharynx
42890	Limited pharyngectomy
42892	Resection of lateral pharyngeal wall or pyriform sinus, direct closure by advancement of lateral and posterior pharyngeal walls
42894	Resection of pharyngeal wall requiring closure with myocutaneous flap

Repair

42900	Suture pharynx for wound or injury
42950	Pharyngoplasty (plastic or reconstructive operation on pharynx)
42953	Pharyngoesophageal repair

Other Procedures

42955	Pharyngostomy (fistulization of pharynx, external for feeding)

Plate 27: Muscles of Pharynx—Lateral View

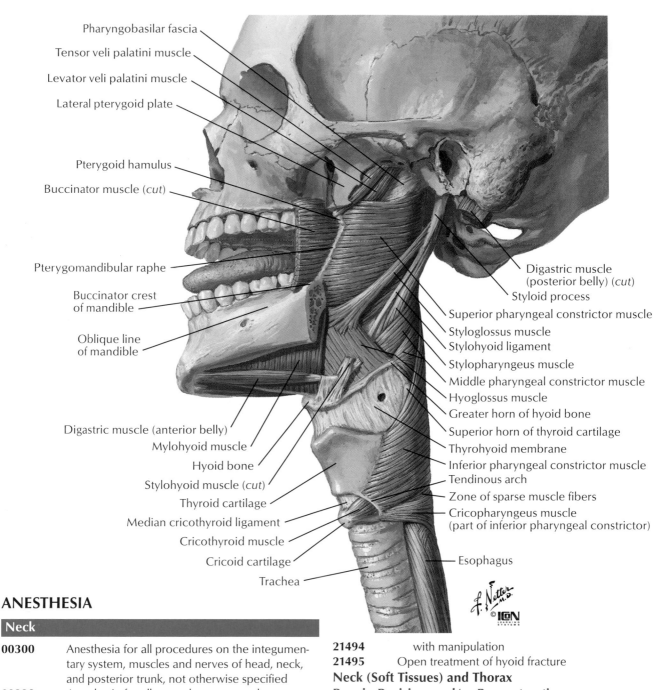

Pharyngobasilar fascia
Tensor veli palatini muscle
Levator veli palatini muscle
Lateral pterygoid plate

Pterygoid hamulus
Buccinator muscle (cut)

Pterygomandibular raphe

Buccinator crest of mandible

Oblique line of mandible

Digastric muscle (anterior belly)
Mylohyoid muscle
Hyoid bone
Stylohyoid muscle (cut)
Thyroid cartilage
Median cricothyroid ligament
Cricothyroid muscle
Cricoid cartilage
Trachea

Digastric muscle (posterior belly) (cut)
Styloid process
Superior pharyngeal constrictor muscle
Styloglossus muscle
Stylohyoid ligament
Stylopharyngeus muscle
Middle pharyngeal constrictor muscle
Hyoglossus muscle
Greater horn of hyoid bone
Superior horn of thyroid cartilage
Thyrohyoid membrane
Inferior pharyngeal constrictor muscle
Tendinous arch
Zone of sparse muscle fibers
Cricopharyngeus muscle (part of inferior pharyngeal constrictor)
Esophagus

ANESTHESIA

Neck

00300 Anesthesia for all procedures on the integumentary system, muscles and nerves of head, neck, and posterior trunk, not otherwise specified

00320 Anesthesia for all procedures on esophagus, thyroid, larynx, trachea and lymphatic system of neck; not otherwise specified, age 1 year or older

00326 Anesthesia for all procedures on the larynx and trachea in children less than 1 year of age

SURGERY

Musculoskeletal System

Head
Fracture and/or Dislocation

21493 Closed treatment of hyoid fracture; without manipulation

21494 with manipulation
21495 Open treatment of hyoid fracture
Neck (Soft Tissues) and Thorax
Repair, Revision, and/or Reconstruction

21685 Hyoid myotomy and suspension

Respiratory System

Larynx
Repair

31587 Laryngoplasty, cricoid split

Trachea and Bronchi
Incision

31603 Tracheostomy, emergency procedure; transtracheal
31605 cricothyroid membrane

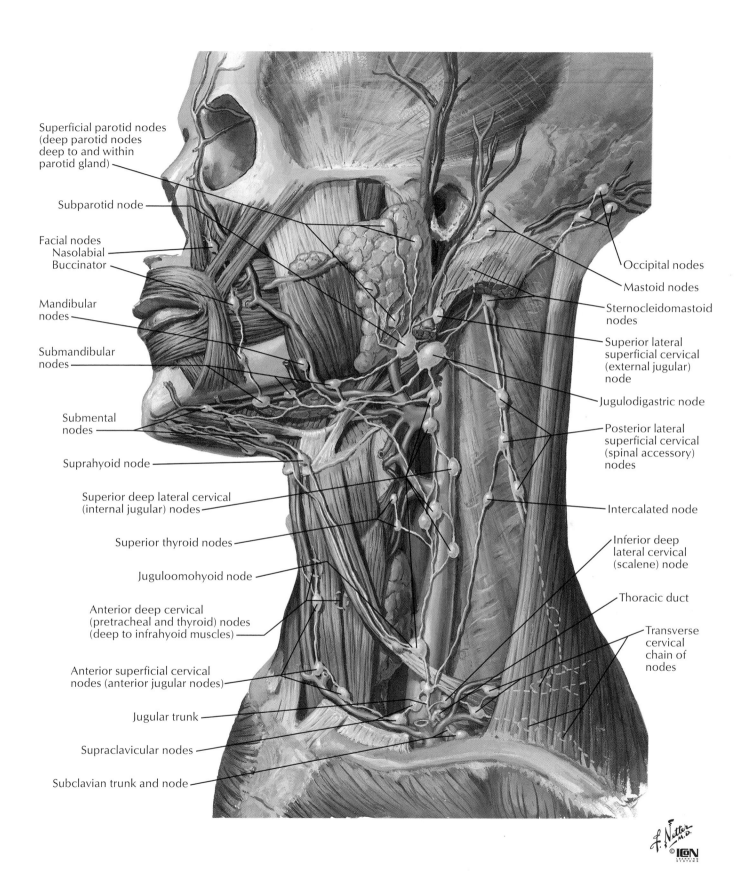

Superficial parotid nodes (deep parotid nodes deep to and within parotid gland)

Subparotid node

Facial nodes
Nasolabial
Buccinator

Mandibular nodes

Submandibular nodes

Submental nodes

Suprahyoid node

Superior deep lateral cervical (internal jugular) nodes

Superior thyroid nodes

Juguloomohyoid node

Anterior deep cervical (pretracheal and thyroid) nodes (deep to infrahyoid muscles)

Anterior superficial cervical nodes (anterior jugular nodes)

Jugular trunk

Supraclavicular nodes

Subclavian trunk and node

Occipital nodes

Mastoid nodes

Sternocleidomastoid nodes

Superior lateral superficial cervical (external jugular) node

Jugulodigastric node

Posterior lateral superficial cervical (spinal accessory) nodes

Intercalated node

Inferior deep lateral cervical (scalene) node

Thoracic duct

Transverse cervical chain of nodes

Plate 28: Lymph Vessels and Nodes of Head and Neck

ANESTHESIA

Head

00320	Anesthesia for all procedures on esophagus, thyroid, larynx, trachea and lymphatic system of neck; not otherwise specified, age 1 year or older

SURGERY

Hemic and Lymphatic Systems

Lymph Nodes and Lymphatic Channels
Incision

38300	Drainage of lymph node abscess or lymphadenitis; simple
38305	Drainage of lymph node abscess or lymphadenitis; extensive
38308	Lymphangiotomy or other operations on lymphatic channels

Excision

38500	Biopsy or excision of lymph node(s); open, superficial
38505	by needle, superficial (eg, cervical, inguinal, axillary)
38510	open, deep cervical node(s)
38520	open, deep cervical node(s) with excision scalene fat pad
38550	Excision of cystic hygroma, axillary or cervical; without deep neurovascular dissection
38555	with deep neurovascular dissection

Radical Lymphadenectomy (Radical Resection of Lymph Nodes)

38700	Suprahyoid lymphadenectomy
38720	Cervical lymphadenectomy (complete)
38724	Cervical lymphadenectomy (modified radical neck dissection)

Introduction

38790	Injection procedure; lymphangiography
38792	for identification of sentinel node

RADIOLOGY

Nuclear Medicine

Diagnostic

Hematopoietic, Reticuloendothelial and Lymphatic System

78195	Lymphatics and lymph nodes imaging

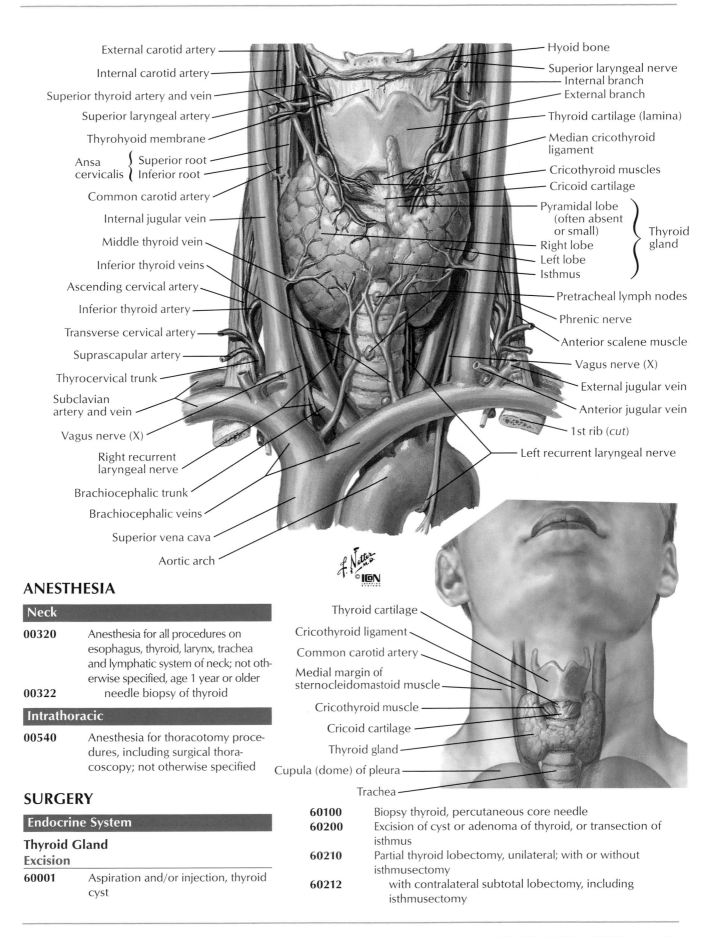

External carotid artery
Internal carotid artery
Superior thyroid artery and vein
Superior laryngeal artery
Thyrohyoid membrane
Ansa cervicalis { Superior root
               { Inferior root
Common carotid artery
Internal jugular vein
Middle thyroid vein
Inferior thyroid veins
Ascending cervical artery
Inferior thyroid artery
Transverse cervical artery
Suprascapular artery
Thyrocervical trunk
Subclavian artery and vein
Vagus nerve (X)
Right recurrent laryngeal nerve
Brachiocephalic trunk
Brachiocephalic veins
Superior vena cava
Aortic arch

Hyoid bone
Superior laryngeal nerve
Internal branch
External branch
Thyroid cartilage (lamina)
Median cricothyroid ligament
Cricothyroid muscles
Cricoid cartilage
Pyramidal lobe (often absent or small)
Right lobe
Left lobe
Isthmus
} Thyroid gland
Pretracheal lymph nodes
Phrenic nerve
Anterior scalene muscle
Vagus nerve (X)
External jugular vein
Anterior jugular vein
1st rib (cut)
Left recurrent laryngeal nerve

Thyroid cartilage
Cricothyroid ligament
Common carotid artery
Medial margin of sternocleidomastoid muscle
Cricothyroid muscle
Cricoid cartilage
Thyroid gland
Cupula (dome) of pleura
Trachea

ANESTHESIA

Neck

00320   Anesthesia for all procedures on esophagus, thyroid, larynx, trachea and lymphatic system of neck; not otherwise specified, age 1 year or older

00322   needle biopsy of thyroid

Intrathoracic

00540   Anesthesia for thoracotomy procedures, including surgical thoracoscopy; not otherwise specified

SURGERY

Endocrine System

Thyroid Gland
Excision

60001   Aspiration and/or injection, thyroid cyst

60100   Biopsy thyroid, percutaneous core needle
60200   Excision of cyst or adenoma of thyroid, or transection of isthmus
60210   Partial thyroid lobectomy, unilateral; with or without isthmusectomy
60212   with contralateral subtotal lobectomy, including isthmusectomy

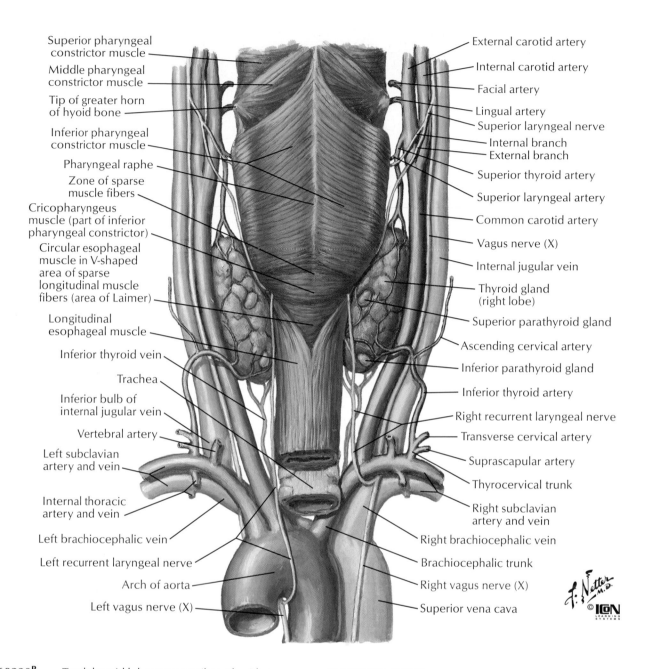

Superior pharyngeal constrictor muscle
Middle pharyngeal constrictor muscle
Tip of greater horn of hyoid bone
Inferior pharyngeal constrictor muscle
Pharyngeal raphe
Zone of sparse muscle fibers
Cricopharyngeus muscle (part of inferior pharyngeal constrictor)
Circular esophageal muscle in V-shaped area of sparse longitudinal muscle fibers (area of Laimer)
Longitudinal esophageal muscle
Inferior thyroid vein
Trachea
Inferior bulb of internal jugular vein
Vertebral artery
Left subclavian artery and vein
Internal thoracic artery and vein
Left brachiocephalic vein
Left recurrent laryngeal nerve
Arch of aorta
Left vagus nerve (X)

External carotid artery
Internal carotid artery
Facial artery
Lingual artery
Superior laryngeal nerve
Internal branch
External branch
Superior thyroid artery
Superior laryngeal artery
Common carotid artery
Vagus nerve (X)
Internal jugular vein
Thyroid gland (right lobe)
Superior parathyroid gland
Ascending cervical artery
Inferior parathyroid gland
Inferior thyroid artery
Right recurrent laryngeal nerve
Transverse cervical artery
Suprascapular artery
Thyrocervical trunk
Right subclavian artery and vein
Right brachiocephalic vein
Brachiocephalic trunk
Right vagus nerve (X)
Superior vena cava

60220[P]	Total thyroid lobectomy, unilateral; with or without isthmusectomy
60225	with contralateral subtotal lobectomy, including isthmusectomy
60240	Thyroidectomy, total or complete
60252	Thyroidectomy, total or subtotal for malignancy; with limited neck dissection
60254	with radical neck dissection
60260	Thyroidectomy, removal of all remaining thyroid tissue following previous removal of a portion of thyroid
60270	Thyroidectomy, including substernal thyroid; sternal split or transthoracic approach
60271	cervical approach
60280	Excision of thyroglossal duct cyst or sinus;
60281	recurrent

RADIOLOGY

Nuclear Medicine

Diagnostic
Endocrine System

78000	Thyroid uptake; single determination
78001	multiple determinations
78003	stimulation, suppression or discharge (not including initial uptake studies)
78006	Thyroid imaging, with uptake; single determination
78007	multiple determinations
78010	Thyroid imaging; only
78011	with vascular flow

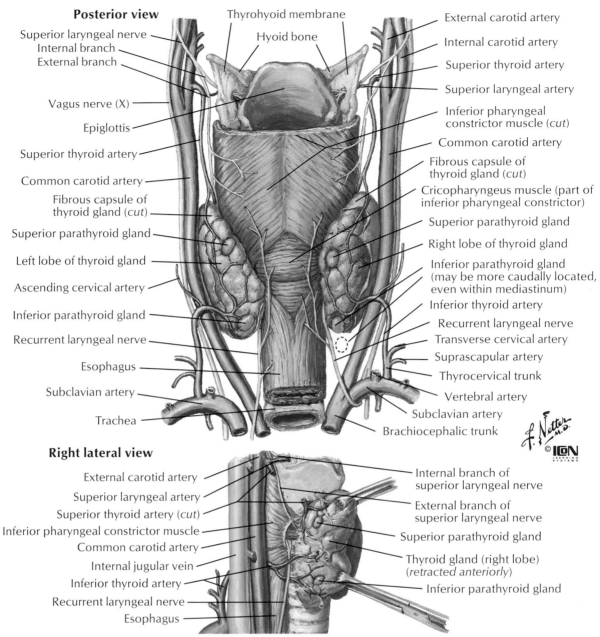

Posterior view

Superior laryngeal nerve
Internal branch
External branch

Vagus nerve (X)

Epiglottis

Superior thyroid artery

Common carotid artery

Fibrous capsule of thyroid gland (*cut*)

Superior parathyroid gland

Left lobe of thyroid gland

Ascending cervical artery

Inferior parathyroid gland

Recurrent laryngeal nerve

Esophagus

Subclavian artery

Trachea

Thyrohyoid membrane
Hyoid bone

External carotid artery
Internal carotid artery
Superior thyroid artery
Superior laryngeal artery
Inferior pharyngeal constrictor muscle (*cut*)
Common carotid artery
Fibrous capsule of thyroid gland (*cut*)
Cricopharyngeus muscle (part of inferior pharyngeal constrictor)
Superior parathyroid gland
Right lobe of thyroid gland
Inferior parathyroid gland (may be more caudally located, even within mediastinum)
Inferior thyroid artery
Recurrent laryngeal nerve
Transverse cervical artery
Suprascapular artery
Thyrocervical trunk
Vertebral artery
Subclavian artery
Brachiocephalic trunk

Right lateral view

External carotid artery
Superior laryngeal artery
Superior thyroid artery (*cut*)
Inferior pharyngeal constrictor muscle
Common carotid artery
Internal jugular vein
Inferior thyroid artery
Recurrent laryngeal nerve
Esophagus

Internal branch of superior laryngeal nerve
External branch of superior laryngeal nerve
Superior parathyroid gland
Thyroid gland (right lobe) (*retracted anteriorly*)
Inferior parathyroid gland

ANESTHESIA

Head

00320   Anesthesia for all procedures on esophagus, thyroid, larynx, trachea and lymphatic system of neck; not otherwise specified, age 1 year or older

SURGERY

Endocrine System

Parathyroid, Thymus, Adrenal Glands, Pancreas, and Carotid Body
Excision

60500   Parathyroidectomy or exploration of parathyroid(s);

60502   re-exploration
60505   with mediastinal exploration, sternal split or transthoracic approach
60512   Parathyroid autotransplantation (List separately in addition to code for primary procedure)

RADIOLOGY

Nuclear Medicine

Diagnostic
Endocrine System

78070   Parathyroid imaging

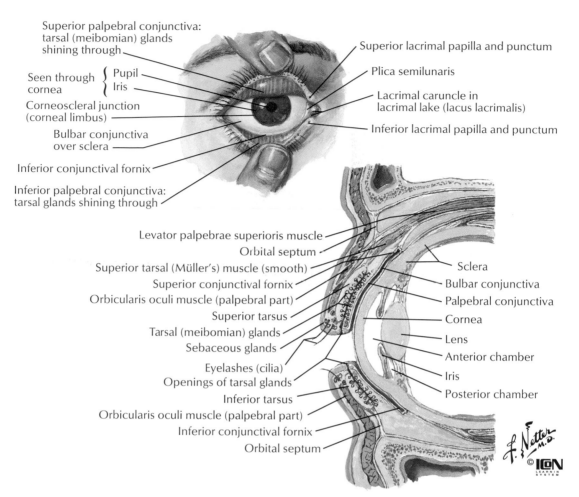

Superior palpebral conjunctiva: tarsal (meibomian) glands shining through

Seen through cornea { Pupil / Iris

Corneoscleral junction (corneal limbus)

Bulbar conjunctiva over sclera

Inferior conjunctival fornix

Inferior palpebral conjunctiva: tarsal glands shining through

Superior lacrimal papilla and punctum

Plica semilunaris

Lacrimal caruncle in lacrimal lake (lacus lacrimalis)

Inferior lacrimal papilla and punctum

Levator palpebrae superioris muscle

Orbital septum

Superior tarsal (Müller's) muscle (smooth)

Superior conjunctival fornix

Orbicularis oculi muscle (palpebral part)

Superior tarsus

Tarsal (meibomian) glands

Sebaceous glands

Eyelashes (cilia)

Openings of tarsal glands

Inferior tarsus

Orbicularis oculi muscle (palpebral part)

Inferior conjunctival fornix

Orbital septum

Sclera

Bulbar conjunctiva

Palpebral conjunctiva

Cornea

Lens

Anterior chamber

Iris

Posterior chamber

ANESTHESIA

Head

00103	Anesthesia for reconstructive procedures of eyelid (eg, blepharoplasty, ptosis surgery)

Neck

00300	Anesthesia for all procedures on the integumentary system, muscles and nerves of head, neck and posterior trunk, not otherwise specified

SURGERY

Eye and Ocular Adnexa

Ocular Adnexa
Eyelids

Incision

67700	Blepharotomy, drainage of abscess, eyelid
67710	Severing of tarsorrhaphy
67715	Canthotomy (separate procedure)

Excision

67800	Excision of chalazion; single
67801	multiple, same lid
67805	multiple, different lids
67808	under general anesthesia and/or requiring hospitalization, single or multiple

67810	Biopsy of eyelid
67820^P	Correction of trichiasis; epilation, by forceps only
67825	epilation by other than forceps (eg, by electro-surgery, cryotherapy, laser surgery)
67830	incision of lid margin
67835	incision of lid margin, with free mucous membrane graft
67840	Excision of lesion of eyelid (except chalazion) without closure or with simple direct closure
67850	Destruction of lesion of lid margin (up to 1 cm)

Repair (Brow Ptosis, Blepharoptosis, Lid Retraction, Ectropion, Entropion)

67914	Repair of ectropion; suture
67915	thermocauterization
67916	excision tarsal wedge
67917	extensive (eg, tarsal strip operations)
67921	Repair of entropion; suture
67922	thermocauterization
67923	excision tarsal wedge
67924	extensive (eg, tarsal strip or capsulopalpebral fascia repairs operation)

Reconstruction

67930	Suture of recent wound, eyelid, involving lid margin, tarsus, and/or palpebral conjunctiva direct closure; partial thickness
67935	full thickness
67938	Removal of embedded foreign body, eyelid

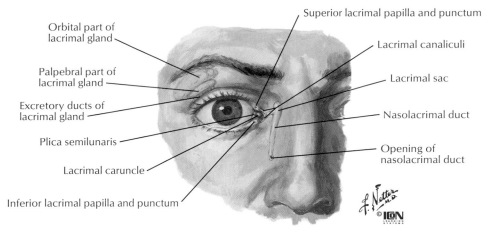

Orbital part of lacrimal gland

Palpebral part of lacrimal gland

Excretory ducts of lacrimal gland

Plica semilunaris

Lacrimal caruncle

Inferior lacrimal papilla and punctum

Superior lacrimal papilla and punctum

Lacrimal canaliculi

Lacrimal sac

Nasolacrimal duct

Opening of nasolacrimal duct

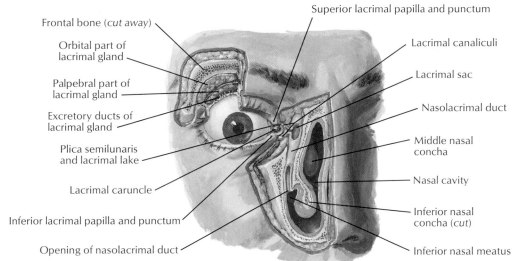

Frontal bone (*cut away*)

Orbital part of lacrimal gland

Palpebral part of lacrimal gland

Excretory ducts of lacrimal gland

Plica semilunaris and lacrimal lake

Lacrimal caruncle

Inferior lacrimal papilla and punctum

Opening of nasolacrimal duct

Superior lacrimal papilla and punctum

Lacrimal canaliculi

Lacrimal sac

Nasolacrimal duct

Middle nasal concha

Nasal cavity

Inferior nasal concha (*cut*)

Inferior nasal meatus

ANESTHESIA

Head

00140   Anesthesia for procedures on eye; not otherwise specified

SURGERY

Eye and Ocular Adnexa

Conjunctiva
Lacrimal System

Incision
68400   Incision, drainage of lacrimal gland
68420   Incision, drainage of lacrimal sac (dacryocyst-otomy or dacryocystostomy)
68440   Snip incision of lacrimal punctum

Excision
68500   Excision of lacrimal gland (dacryoadenectomy), except for tumor; total
68505   partial
68510   Biopsy of lacrimal gland
68520   Excision of lacrimal sac (dacryocystectomy)
68525   Biopsy of lacrimal sac
68530   Removal of foreign body or dacryolith, lacrimal passages

68540   Excision of lacrimal gland tumor; frontal approach
68550   involving osteotomy

Repair
68700   Plastic repair of canaliculi
68705   Correction of everted punctum, cautery
68720   Dacryocystorhinostomy (fistulization of lacrimal sac to nasal cavity)
68745   Conjunctivorhinostomy (fistulization of conjunctiva to nasal cavity); without tube
68750   with insertion of tube or stent
68760   Closure of the lacrimal punctum; by thermocau-terization, ligation, or laser surgery
68761[P]   by plug, each
68770   Closure of lacrimal fistula (separate procedure)

Probing and/or Related Procedures
68801   Dilation of lacrimal punctum, with or without irrigation
68810   Probing of nasolacrimal duct, with or without irrigation;
68811   requiring general anesthesia
68815[P]   with insertion of tube or stent
68840   Probing of lacrimal canaliculi, with or without irrigation
68850   Injection of contrast medium for dacryocyst-ography

Plate 33: Extrinsic Eye Muscles

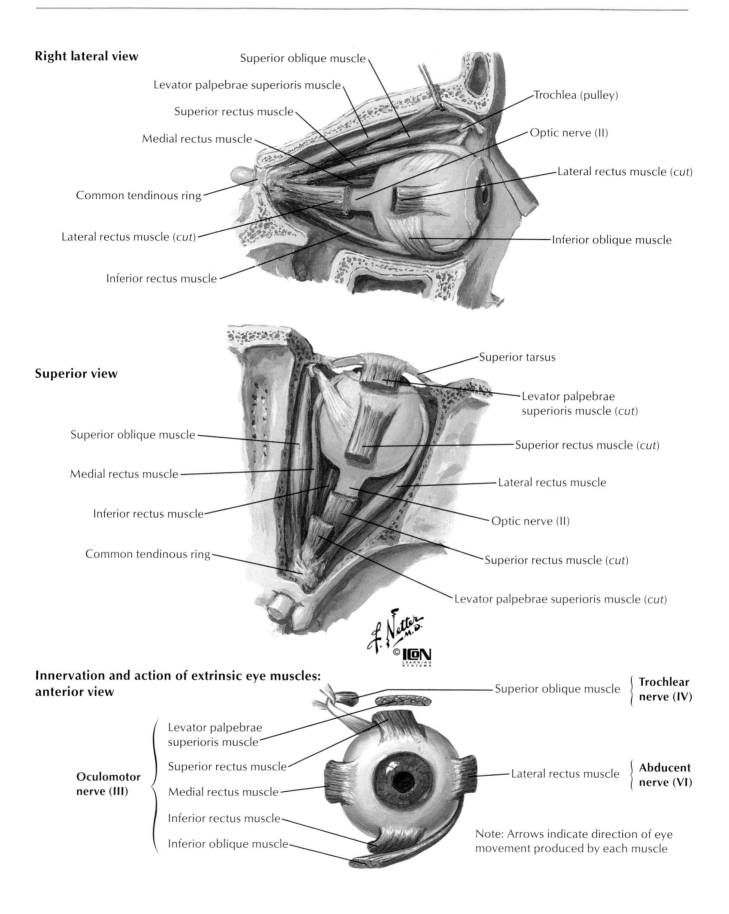

Right lateral view

Superior oblique muscle

Levator palpebrae superioris muscle

Superior rectus muscle

Medial rectus muscle

Common tendinous ring

Lateral rectus muscle (*cut*)

Inferior rectus muscle

Trochlea (pulley)

Optic nerve (II)

Lateral rectus muscle (*cut*)

Inferior oblique muscle

Superior view

Superior oblique muscle

Medial rectus muscle

Inferior rectus muscle

Common tendinous ring

Superior tarsus

Levator palpebrae superioris muscle (*cut*)

Superior rectus muscle (*cut*)

Lateral rectus muscle

Optic nerve (II)

Superior rectus muscle (*cut*)

Levator palpebrae superioris muscle (*cut*)

Innervation and action of extrinsic eye muscles: anterior view

Oculomotor nerve (III)

Levator palpebrae superioris muscle

Superior rectus muscle

Medial rectus muscle

Inferior rectus muscle

Inferior oblique muscle

Superior oblique muscle — Trochlear nerve (IV)

Lateral rectus muscle — Abducent nerve (VI)

Note: Arrows indicate direction of eye movement produced by each muscle

---

┌───┐
│ ─ *Nomenclature Notes* ─   │
│   │
│ *Horizontal muscles* are the lateral rectus muscle and the │
│ medial rectus muscle.   │
│   │
│ *Vertical muscles* are the superior rectus muscle, the inferior │
│ rectus muscle, superior oblique muscle, and the inferior │
│ oblique muscle.   │
└───┘

ANESTHESIA

Head

00140   Anesthesia for procedures on eye; not otherwise
               specified

SURGERY

Eye and Ocular Adenexa

Ocular Adenxa

Extraocular Muscles

67311^P   Strabismus surgery, recession or resection
               procedure; one horizontal muscle
67312   two horizontal muscles
67314^P   one vertical muscle (excluding superior
                  oblique)
67316   two or more vertical muscles (excluding
                  superior oblique)
67318   Strabismus surgery, any procedure, superior
               oblique muscle

67320^P   Transposition procedure (eg, for paretic extra-
               ocular muscle), any extraocular muscle (specify)
               (List separately in addition to code for primary
               procedure)
67331   Strabismus surgery on patient with previous eye
               surgery or injury that did not involve the extra-
               ocular muscles (List separately in addition to code
               for primary procedure)
67332   Strabismus surgery on patient with scarring of
               extraocular muscles (eg, prior ocular injury,
               strabismus or retinal detachment surgery) or
               restrictive myopathy (eg, dysthyroid ophthal-
               mopathy) (List separately in addition to code for
               primary procedure)
67334   Strabismus surgery by posterior fixation suture
               technique, with or without muscle recession (List
               separately in addition to code for primary
               procedure)
67335^P   Placement of adjustable suture(s) during strabis-
               mus surgery, including postoperative adjust-
               ment(s) of suture(s) (List separately in addition to
               code for specific strabismus surgery)
67340   Strabismus surgery involving exploration and/or
               repair of detached extraocular muscle(s) (List sep-
               arately in addition to code for primary procedure)
67343   Release of extensive scar tissue without detaching
               extraocular muscle (separate procedure)
67345   Chemodenervation of extraocular muscle

Other Procedures
67350   Biopsy of extraocular muscle

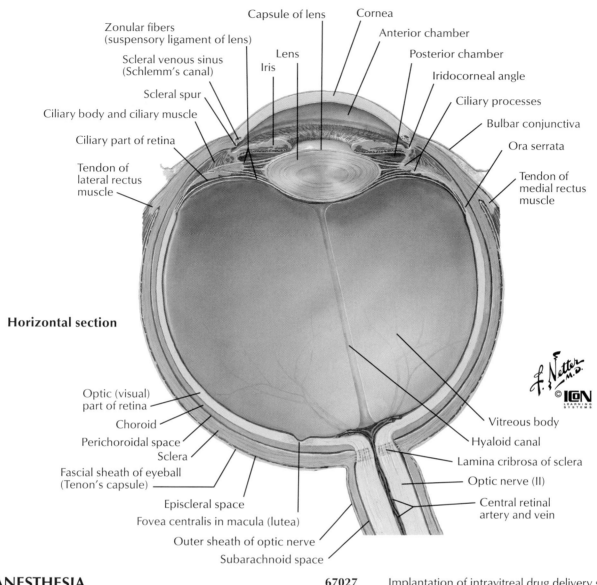

Horizontal section

Labels (clockwise from top): Zonular fibers (suspensory ligament of lens), Capsule of lens, Cornea, Anterior chamber, Posterior chamber, Iridocorneal angle, Ciliary processes, Bulbar conjunctiva, Ora serrata, Tendon of medial rectus muscle, Lens, Iris, Scleral venous sinus (Schlemm's canal), Scleral spur, Ciliary body and ciliary muscle, Ciliary part of retina, Tendon of lateral rectus muscle, Optic (visual) part of retina, Choroid, Perichoroidal space, Sclera, Fascial sheath of eyeball (Tenon's capsule), Episcleral space, Fovea centralis in macula (lutea), Outer sheath of optic nerve, Subarachnoid space, Vitreous body, Hyaloid canal, Lamina cribrosa of sclera, Optic nerve (II), Central retinal artery and vein

ANESTHESIA

Head

00142	Anesthesia for procedures on eye; lens surgery
00145	vitreoretinal surgery
00147	iridectomy

SURGERY

Eye and Ocular Adnexa

Posterior Segment
Vitreous

67005	Removal of vitreous, anterior approach (open sky technique or limbal incision); partial removal
67010	subtotal removal with mechanical vitrectomy
67015	Aspiration or release of vitreous, subretinal or choroidal fluid, pars plana approach (posterior sclerotomy)
67025	Injection of vitreous substitute, pars plana or limbal approach, (fluid-gas exchange), with or without aspiration (separate procedure)

67027	Implantation of intravitreal drug delivery system (eg, ganciclovir implant), includes concomitant removal of vitreous
67028	Intravitreal injection of a pharmacologic agent (separate procedure)
67030	Discission of vitreous strands (without removal), pars plana approach
67031	Severing of vitreous strands, vitreous face adhesions, sheets, membranes or opacities, laser surgery (one or more stages)
67036	Vitrectomy, mechanical, pars plana approach;
67038	with epiretinal membrane stripping
67039	with focal endolaser photocoagulation
67040	with endolaser panretinal photocoagulation

Ocular Adnexa
Orbit

Other Procedures

67570	Optic nerve decompression (eg, incision or fenestration of optic nerve sheath)

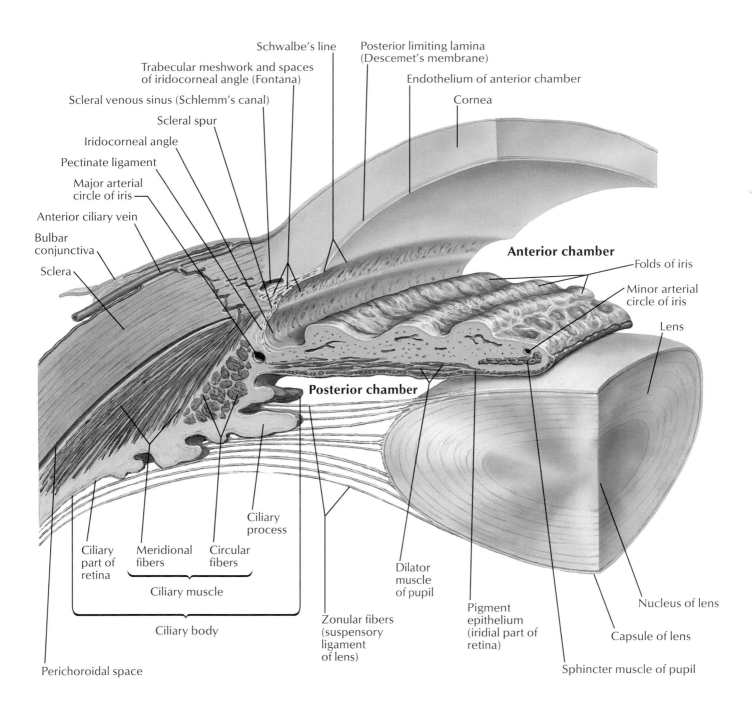

Schwalbe's line

Trabecular meshwork and spaces
of iridocorneal angle (Fontana)

Scleral venous sinus (Schlemm's canal)

Scleral spur

Iridocorneal angle

Pectinate ligament

Major arterial
circle of iris

Anterior ciliary vein

Bulbar
conjunctiva

Sclera

Posterior limiting lamina
(Descemet's membrane)

Endothelium of anterior chamber

Cornea

Anterior chamber

Folds of iris

Minor arterial
circle of iris

Lens

Posterior chamber

Ciliary
part of
retina

Meridional
fibers

Circular
fibers

Ciliary muscle

Ciliary body

Ciliary
process

Dilator
muscle
of pupil

Zonular fibers
(suspensory
ligament
of lens)

Pigment
epithelium
(iridial part of
retina)

Sphincter muscle of pupil

Nucleus of lens

Capsule of lens

Perichoroidal space

Note: For clarity, only single plane of zonular fibers shown;
actually, fibers surround the entire circumference of lens.

ANESTHESIA

Head

00140	Anesthesia for procedures on eye; not otherwise specified
00145	vitreoretinal surgery
00147	iridectomy

SURGERY

Eye and Ocular Adnexa

Anterior Segment

Anterior Chamber

Incision

65800	Paracentesis of anterior chamber of eye (separate procedure); with diagnostic aspiration of aqueous
65805	with therapeutic release of aqueous
65810	with removal of vitreous and/or discission of anterior hyaloid membrane, with or without air injection
65815	with removal of blood, with or without irrigation and/or air injection
65820	Goniotomy
65850	Trabeculotomy ab externo
65855	Trabeculoplasty by laser surgery, one or more sessions (defined treatment series)
65860	Severing adhesions of anterior segment, laser technique (separate procedure)

Other Procedures

65865	Severing adhesions of anterior segment of eye, incisional technique (with or without injection of air or liquid) (separate procedure); goniosynechiae
65870	anterior synechiae, except goniosynechiae
65875	posterior synechiae
65880	corneovitreal adhesions
65900	Removal of epithelial downgrowth, anterior chamber of eye
65920	Removal of implanted material, anterior segment of eye
65930	Removal of blood clot, anterior segment of eye
66020	Injection, anterior chamber of eye (separate procedure); air or liquid
66030	Injection, anterior chamber of eye (separate procedure); medication

Iris, Ciliary Body

Repair

66680	Repair of iris, ciliary body (as for iridodialysis)
66682	Suture of iris, ciliary body (separate procedure) with retrieval of suture through small incision (eg, McCannel suture)

Destruction

66700	Ciliary body destruction; diathermy
66710	cyclophotocoagulation, transscleral
66711	cyclophotocoagulation, endoscopic
66720	cryotherapy
66740	cyclodialysis

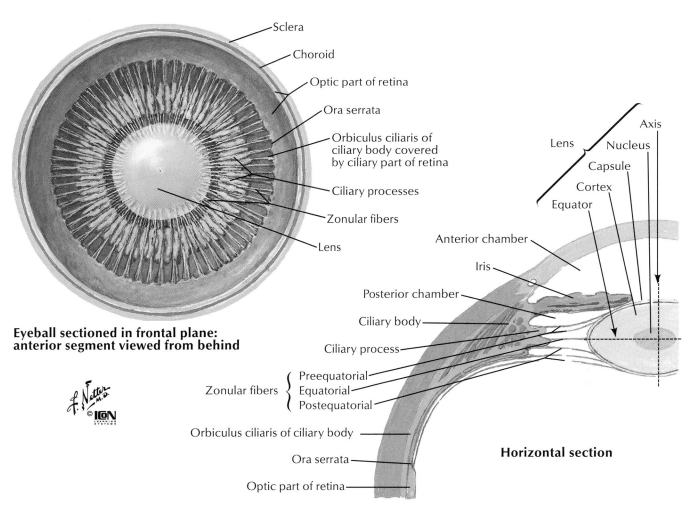

Eyeball sectioned in frontal plane: anterior segment viewed from behind

Labels (upper left diagram): Sclera, Choroid, Optic part of retina, Ora serrata, Orbiculus ciliaris of ciliary body covered by ciliary part of retina, Ciliary processes, Zonular fibers, Lens

Horizontal section

Labels (right diagram): Axis, Lens, Nucleus, Capsule, Cortex, Equator, Anterior chamber, Iris, Posterior chamber, Ciliary body, Ciliary process, Zonular fibers { Preequatorial, Equatorial, Postequatorial }, Orbiculus ciliaris of ciliary body, Ora serrata, Optic part of retina

ANESTHESIA

Head

00140	Anesthesia for procedures on eye; not otherwise specified
00142	lens surgery
00144	corneal transplant
00145	vitreoretinal surgery
00147	iridectomy

SURGERY

Eye and Ocular Adnexa

Anterior Segment

Cornea

Excision

65400	Excision of lesion, cornea (keratectomy, lamellar, partial), except pterygium
65410	Biopsy of cornea
65420	Excision or transposition of pterygium; without graft
65426	with graft

Removal or Destruction

65430	Scraping of cornea, diagnostic, for smear and/or culture
65435	Removal of corneal epithelium; with or without chemocauterization (abrasion, curettage)
65436	with application of chelating agent (eg, EDTA)
65450[P]	Destruction of lesion of cornea by cryotherapy, photocoagulation or thermocauterization
65600	Multiple punctures of anterior cornea (eg, for corneal erosion, tattoo)

Keratoplasty

65710	Keratoplasty (corneal transplant); lamellar
65730	penetrating (except in aphakia)
65750[P]	penetrating (in aphakia)
65755	penetrating (in pseudophakia)

Other Procedures

65760	Keratomileusis
65765	Keratophakia
65767	Epikeratoplasty
65770	Keratoprosthesis
65771	Radial keratotomy
65772	Corneal relaxing incision for correction of surgically induced astigmatism
65775	Corneal wedge resection for correction of surgically induced astigmatism
65780	Ocular surface reconstruction; amniotic membrane transplantation

65781	limbal stem cell allograft (eg, cadaveric or living donor)
65782	limbal conjunctival autograft (includes obtaining graft)

Anterior Chamber

Incision

65800	Paracentesis of anterior chamber of eye (separate procedure); with diagnostic aspiration of aqueous
65805	with therapeutic release of aqueous
65810	with removal of vitreous and/or discission of anterior hyaloid membrane, with or without air injection
65815	with removal of blood, with or without irrigation and/or air injection
65820	Goniotomy
65850	Trabeculotomy ab externo
65855	Trabeculoplasty by laser surgery, one or more sessions (defined treatment series)
65860	Severing adhesions of anterior segment, laser technique (separate procedure)

Other Procedure

65865	Severing adhesions of anterior segment of eye, incisional technique (with or without injection of air or liquid) (separate procedure); goniosynechiae
65870	anterior synechiae, except goniosynechiae
65875	posterior synechiae
65880	corneovitreal adhesions
65900	Removal of epithelial downgrowth, anterior chamber of eye
65920	Removal of implanted material, anterior segment of eye
65930	Removal of blood clot, anterior segment of eye
66020	Injection, anterior chamber of eye (separate procedure); air or liquid
66030	Injection, anterior chamber of eye (separate procedure); medication

Iris, Ciliary Body

Incision

66500	Iridotomy by stab incision (separate procedure); except transfixion
66505	with transfixion as for iris bombe

Excision

66600	Iridectomy, with corneoscleral or corneal section; for removal of lesion
66605	with cyclectomy
66625	peripheral for glaucoma (separate procedure)
66630	sector for glaucoma (separate procedure)
66635	optical (separate procedure)

Repair

66680	Repair of iris, ciliary body (as for iridodialysis)
66682	Suture of iris, ciliary body (separate procedure) with retrieval of suture through small incision (eg, McCannel suture)

Destruction

66700	Ciliary body destruction; diathermy
66710	cyclophotocoagulation, transscleral
66711	cyclophotocoagulation, endoscopic
66720	cryotherapy
66740	cyclodialysis
66761	Iridotomy/iridectomy by laser surgery (eg, for glaucoma) (one or more sessions)
66762	Iridoplasty by photocoagulation (one or more sessions) (eg, for improvement of vision, for widening of anterior chamber angle)
66770	Destruction of cyst or lesion iris or ciliary body (nonexcisional procedure)

Lens

Incision

66820	Discission of secondary membranous cataract (opacified posterior lens capsule and/or anterior hyaloid); stab incision technique (Ziegler or Wheeler knife)
66821	laser surgery (eg, YAG laser) (one or more stages)
66825	Repositioning of intraocular lens prosthesis, requiring an incision (separate procedure)

Removal Cataract

66830	Removal of secondary membranous cataract (opacified posterior lens capsule and/or anterior hyaloid) with corneo-scleral section, with or without iridectomy (iridocapsulotomy, iridocapsulectomy)
66840	Removal of lens material; aspiration technique, one or more stages
66850	phacofragmentation technique (mechanical or ultrasonic) (eg, phacoemulsification), with aspiration
66852	pars plana approach, with or without vitrectomy
66920	intracapsular
66930	intracapsular, for dislocated lens
66940	extracapsular (other than 66840, 66850, 66852)
66982	Extracapsular cataract removal with insertion of intraocular lens prosthesis (one stage procedure), manual or mechanical technique (eg, irrigation and aspiration or phacoemulsification), complex, requiring devices or techniques not generally used in routine cataract surgery (eg, iris expansion device, suture support for intraocular lens, or primary posterior capsulorrhexis) or performed on patients in the amblyogenic developmental stage
66983	Intracapsular cataract extraction with insertion of intraocular lens prosthesis (one stage procedure)
66984	Extracapsular cataract removal with insertion of intraocular lens prosthesis (one stage procedure), manual or mechanical technique (eg, irrigation and aspiration or phacoemulsification)
66985	Insertion of intraocular lens prosthesis (secondary implant), not associated with concurrent cataract removal
66986	Exchange of intraocular lens

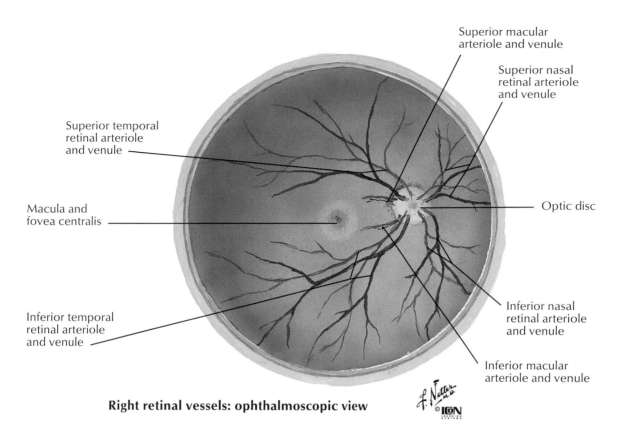

Superior macular arteriole and venule

Superior nasal retinal arteriole and venule

Superior temporal retinal arteriole and venule

Macula and fovea centralis

Optic disc

Inferior temporal retinal arteriole and venule

Inferior nasal retinal arteriole and venule

Inferior macular arteriole and venule

Right retinal vessels: ophthalmoscopic view

MEDICINE

Opthalmology

Special Ophthalmological Services

Ophthalmoscopy

92225	Ophthalmoscopy, extended, with retinal drawing (eg, for retinal detachment, melanoma), with interpretation and report; initial

92226	subsequent
92230	Fluorescein angioscopy with interpretation and report
92235ᴾ	Fluorescein angiography (includes multiframe imaging) with interpretation and report
92240	Indocyanine-green angiography (includes multiframe imaging) with interpretation and report
92250	Fundus photography with interpretation and report

Plate 38: Pathway of Sound Reception

Frontal section

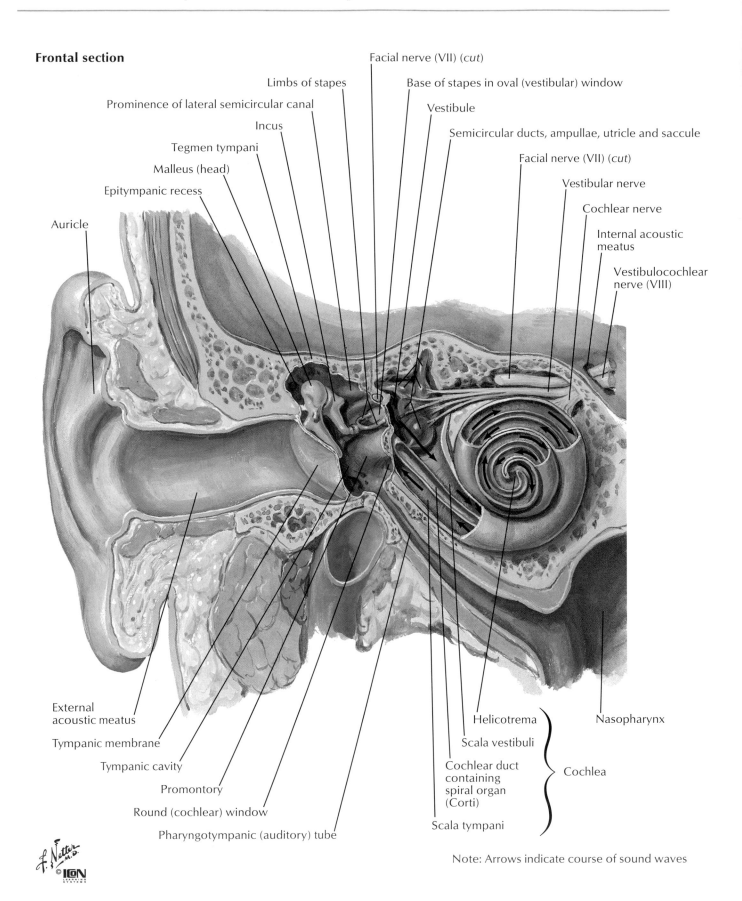

Facial nerve (VII) (*cut*)

Limbs of stapes

Base of stapes in oval (vestibular) window

Prominence of lateral semicircular canal

Vestibule

Incus

Semicircular ducts, ampullae, utricle and saccule

Tegmen tympani

Facial nerve (VII) (*cut*)

Malleus (head)

Vestibular nerve

Epitympanic recess

Cochlear nerve

Auricle

Internal acoustic meatus

Vestibulocochlear nerve (VIII)

External acoustic meatus

Tympanic membrane

Tympanic cavity

Promontory

Round (cochlear) window

Pharyngotympanic (auditory) tube

Helicotrema

Scala vestibuli

Nasopharynx

Cochlear duct containing spiral organ (Corti)

Cochlea

Scala tympani

Note: Arrows indicate course of sound waves

ANESTHESIA

Head

00120 Anesthesia for all procedures on external, middle, and inner ear including biopsy; not otherwise specified
00124 otoscopy
00126 tympanotomy
00190 Anesthesia for all procedures on facial bone or skull; not otherwise specified

Neck

00320 Anesthesia for all procedures on esophagus, thyroid, larynx, trachea and lymphatic system of neck; not otherwise specified, age 1 year or older

SURGERY

Auditory System

External Ear
Incision

69000 Drainage external ear, abscess or hematoma; simple
69005 complicated
69020 Drainage external auditory canal, abscess
69090 Ear piercing

Excision

69100 Biopsy external ear
69105 Biopsy external auditory canal
69110 Excision external ear; partial, simple repair
69120 complete amputation
69140 Excision exostosis(es), external auditory canal
69145 Excision soft tissue lesion, external auditory canal
69150 Radical excision external auditory canal lesion; without neck dissection
69155 with neck dissection

Removal of Foreign Body

69200 Removal foreign body from external auditory canal; without general anesthesia
69205 with general anesthesia
69210 Removal impacted cerumen (separate procedure), one or both ears
69220 Debridement, mastoidectomy cavity, simple (eg, routine cleaning)
69222 Debridement, mastoidectomy cavity, complex (eg, with anesthesia or more than routine cleaning)

Repair

69300 Otoplasty, protruding ear, with or without size reduction
69310 Reconstruction of external auditory canal (meatoplasty) (eg, for stenosis due to injury, infection) (separate procedure)
69320 Reconstruction external auditory canal for congenital atresia, single stage

Other Procedures

69399 Unlisted procedure, external ear

Middle Ear
Introduction

69400 Eustachian tube inflation, transnasal; with catheterization
69401 without catheterization
69405 Eustachian tube catheterization, transtympanic
69410 Focal application of phase control substance, middle ear (baffle technique)

Incision

69420 Myringotomy including aspiration and/or eustachian tube inflation
69421 Myringotomy including aspiration and/or eustachian tube inflation requiring general anesthesia
69424 Ventilating tube removal requiring general anesthesia
69433[P] Tympanostomy (requiring insertion of ventilating tube), local or topical anesthesia
69436 Tympanostomy (requiring insertion of ventilating tube), general anesthesia
69440 Middle ear exploration through postauricular or ear canal incision
69450 Tympanolysis, transcanal

Excision

69501 Transmastoid antrotomy (simple mastoidectomy)
69502 Mastoidectomy; complete
69505 modified radical
69511 radical
69530 Petrous apicectomy including radical mastoidectomy
69535 Resection temporal bone, external approach
69540 Excision aural polyp
69550 Excision aural glomus tumor; transcanal
69552 transmastoid
69554 extended (extratemporal)

Repair

69601 Revision mastoidectomy; resulting in complete mastoidectomy
69602 resulting in modified radical mastoidectomy
69603 resulting in radical mastoidectomy
69604 resulting in tympanoplasty
69605 with apicectomy
69610 Tympanic membrane repair, with or without site preparation of perforation for closure, with or without patch
69620 Myringoplasty (surgery confined to drumhead and donor area)
69631 Tympanoplasty without mastoidectomy (including canalplasty, atticotomy and/or middle ear surgery), initial or revision; without ossicular chain reconstruction
69632 with ossicular chain reconstruction (eg, postfenestration)

(Repair continued on next page)

(Repair continued from previous page)

69633   with ossicular chain reconstruction and synthetic prosthesis (eg, partial ossicular replacement prosthesis (PORP), total ossicular replacement prosthesis (TORP))

69635ᴾ Tympanoplasty with antrotomy or mastoidotomy (including canalplasty, atticotomy, middle ear surgery, and/or tympanic membrane repair); without ossicular chain reconstruction

69636   with ossicular chain reconstruction

69637   with ossicular chain reconstruction and synthetic prosthesis (eg, partial ossicular replacement prosthesis (PORP), total ossicular replacement prosthesis (TORP))

69641 Tympanoplasty with mastoidectomy (including canalplasty, middle ear surgery, tympanic membrane repair); without ossicular chain reconstruction

69642   with ossicular chain reconstruction

69643   with intact or reconstructed wall, without ossicular chain reconstruction

69644   with intact or reconstructed canal wall, with ossicular chain reconstruction

69645   radical or complete, without ossicular chain reconstruction

69646   radical or complete, with ossicular chain reconstruction

69650 Stapes mobilization

69660 Stapedectomy or stapedotomy with reestablishment of ossicular continuity, with or without use of foreign material;

69661   with footplate drill out

69662 Revision of stapedectomy or stapedotomy

69666 Repair oval window fistula

69667 Repair round window fistula

69670 Mastoid obliteration (separate procedure)

69676 Tympanic neurectomy

Other Procedures

69700 Closure postauricular fistula, mastoid (separate procedure)

69710 Implantation or replacement of electromagnetic bone conduction hearing device in temporal bone

69711 Removal or repair of electromagnetic bone conduction hearing device in temporal bone

69714 Implantation, osseointegrated implant, temporal bone, with percutaneous attachment to external speech processor/cochlear stimulator; without mastoidectomy

69715   with mastoidectomy

69717 Replacement (including removal of existing device), osseointegrated implant, temporal bone, with percutaneous attachment to external speech processor/cochlear stimulator; without mastoidectomy

69718   with mastoidectomy

69720 Decompression facial nerve, intratemporal; lateral to geniculate ganglion

69725   including medial to geniculate ganglion

69740 Suture facial nerve, intratemporal, with or without graft or decompression; lateral to geniculate ganglion

69745   including medial to geniculate ganglion

69799 Unlisted procedure, middle ear

Inner Ear
Incision and/or Destruction

69801 Labyrinthotomy, with or without cryosurgery including other nonexcisional destructive procedures or perfusion of vestibuloactive drugs (single or multiple perfusions); transcanal

69802   with mastoidectomy

69805 Endolymphatic sac operation; without shunt

69806   with shunt

69820 Fenestration semicircular canal

69840 Revision fenestration operation

Excision

69905 Labyrinthectomy; transcanal

69910   with mastoidectomy

69915 Vestibular nerve section, translabyrinthine approach

Introduction

69930ᴾ Cochlear device implantation, with or without mastoidectomy

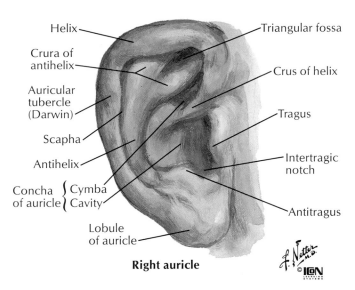

Helix
Crura of antihelix
Auricular tubercle (Darwin)
Scapha
Antihelix
Concha { Cymba
of auricle { Cavity
Lobule of auricle

Triangular fossa
Crus of helix
Tragus
Intertragic notch
Antitragus

Right auricle

Nomenclature Notes

The *external ear* includes the auricle and the external auditory canal.

ANESTHESIA

Head

00120 Anesthesia for procedures on external, middle, and inner ear including biopsy; not otherwise specified

00124 otoscopy

SURGERY

Integumentary System

Repair (Closure)
Repair—Simple

12011 Simple repair of superficial wounds of face, ears, eyelids, nose, lips and/or mucous membranes; 2.5 cm or less

12013 2.6 cm to 5.0 cm
12014 5.1 cm to 7.5 cm
12015 7.6 cm to 12.5 cm
12016 12.6 cm to 20.0 cm
12017 20.1 cm to 30.0 cm
12018 over 30.0 cm

Repair—Intermediate

12051 Layer closure of wounds of face, ears, eyelids, nose, lips and/or mucous membranes; 2.5 cm or less

---

12052 2.6 cm to 5.0 cm
12053 5.1 cm to 7.5 cm
12054 7.6 cm to 12.5 cm
12055 12.6 cm to 20.0 cm
12056 20.1 cm to 30.0 cm
12057 over 30.0 cm

Repair—Complex

13150 Repair, complex, eyelids, nose, ears and/or lips; 1.0 cm or less
13151 1.1 cm to 2.5 cm
13152 2.6 cm to 7.5 cm
13153 each additional 5 cm or less (List separately in addition to code for primary procedure)

Adjacent Tissue Transfer or Rearrangement

14060 Adjacent tissue transfer or rearrangement, eyelids, nose, ears and/or lips; defect 10 sq cm or less
14061 defect 10.1 sq cm to 30.0 sq cm

Auditory System

External Ear
Incision

69000 Drainage external ear, abscess or hematoma; simple
69005 complicated
69020 Drainage external auditory canal, abscess
69090 Ear piercing

Excision

69100 Biopsy external ear
69105 Biopsy external auditory canal
69110 Excision external ear; partial, simple repair
69120 complete amputation
69140 Excision exostosis(es), external auditory canal
69145 Excision soft tissue lesion, external auditory canal
69150 Radical excision external auditory canal lesion; without neck dissection

Removal of Foreign Body

69200 Removal foreign body from external auditory canal; without general anesthesia
69205 with general anesthesia
69210 Removal impacted cerumen (separate procedure), one or both ears

Repair

69300 Otoplasty, protruding ear, with or without size reduction
69310 Reconstruction of external auditory canal (meatoplasty) (eg, for stenosis due to injury, infection) (separate procedure)
69320 Reconstruction external auditory canal for congenital atresia, single stage

---

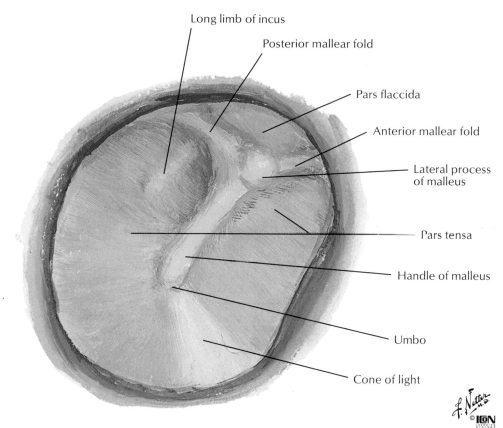

Long limb of incus

Posterior mallear fold

Pars flaccida

Anterior mallear fold

Lateral process of malleus

Pars tensa

Handle of malleus

Umbo

Cone of light

**Right tympanic membrane (eardrum)
viewed through speculum**

Nomenclature Notes

Tympanic membrane is synonymous with *ear drum*.

The tympanic membrane divides the external ear from the middle ear.

ANESTHESIA

Head

00120   Anesthesia for all procedures on external, middle, and inner ear including biopsy; not otherwise specified

SURGERY

Auditory System

Middle Ear
Introduction

69405   Eustachian tube catheterization, transtympanic

Incision

69433[P]   Tympanostomy (requiring insertion of ventilating tube), local or topical anesthesia

69436   Tympanostomy (requiring insertion of ventilating tube), general anesthesia

69440   Middle ear exploration through postauricular or ear canal incision

69450   Tympanolysis, transcanal

Repair

69610   Tympanic membrane repair, with or without site preparation of perforation for closure, with or without patch

69620   Myringoplasty (surgery confined to drumhead and donor area)

69631   Tympanoplasty without mastoidectomy (including canalplasty, atticotomy and/or middle ear surgery), initial or revision; without ossicular chain reconstruction

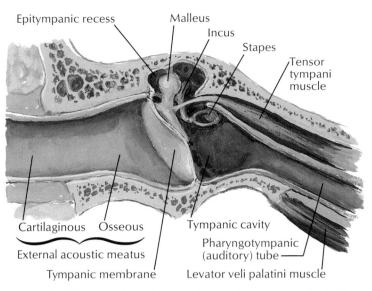

Coronal oblique section of external acoustic meatus and middle ear

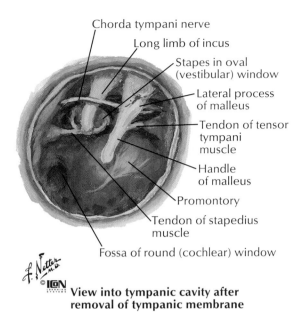

View into tympanic cavity after removal of tympanic membrane

ANESTHESIA

Head

00120	Anesthesia for procedures on external, middle, and inner ear including biopsy; not otherwise specified
00126	tympanotomy

SURGERY

Auditory System

Middle Ear

Introduction

69405	Eustachian tube catheterization, transtympanic
69410	Focal application of phase control substance, middle ear (baffle technique)

Incision

69420	Myringotomy including aspiration and/or eustachian tube inflation
69421	Myringotomy including aspiration and/or eustachian tube inflation requiring general anesthesia
69424	Ventilating tube removal requiring general anesthesia
69433[P]	Tympanostomy (requiring insertion of ventilating tube), local or topical anesthesia
69436[P]	Tympanostomy (requiring insertion of ventilating tube), general anesthesia
69440	Middle ear exploration through postauricular or ear canal incision
69450	Tympanolysis, transcanal

Excision

69501	Transmastoid antrotomy (simple mastoidectomy)
69502	Mastoidectomy; complete
69530	Petrous apicectomy including radical mastoidectomy

Repair

69631	Tympanoplasty without mastoidectomy (including canalplasty, atticotomy and/or middle ear surgery), initial or revision; without ossicular chain reconstruction
69632	with ossicular chain reconstruction (eg, postfenestration)
69633	with ossicular chain reconstruction and synthetic prosthesis (eg, partial ossicular replacement prosthesis (PORP), total ossicular replacement prosthesis (TORP))
69635[P]	Tympanoplasty with antrotomy or mastoidotomy (including canalplasty, atticotomy, middle ear surgery, and/or tympanic membrane repair); without ossicular chain reconstruction
69636[P]	with ossicular chain reconstruction
69637[P]	with ossicular chain reconstruction and synthetic prosthesis (eg, partial ossicular replacement prosthesis (PORP), total ossicular replacement prosthesis (TORP))
69650	Stapes mobilization
69660	Stapedectomy or stapedotomy with reestablishment of ossicular continuity, with or without use of foreign material;
69661	with footplate drill out
69662	Revision of stapedectomy or stapedotomy
69666	Repair oval window fistula
69667	Repair round window fistula
69676	Tympanic neurectomy

Lateral wall of tympanic cavity: medial (internal) view

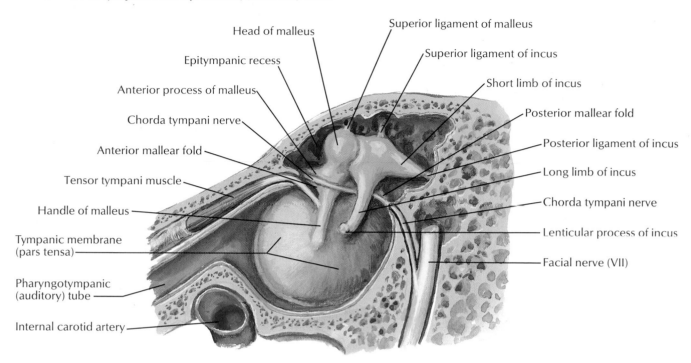

Head of malleus

Superior ligament of malleus

Epitympanic recess

Superior ligament of incus

Anterior process of malleus

Short limb of incus

Chorda tympani nerve

Posterior mallear fold

Anterior mallear fold

Posterior ligament of incus

Tensor tympani muscle

Long limb of incus

Handle of malleus

Chorda tympani nerve

Tympanic membrane (pars tensa)

Lenticular process of incus

Pharyngotympanic (auditory) tube

Facial nerve (VII)

Internal carotid artery

Medial wall of tympanic cavity: lateral view

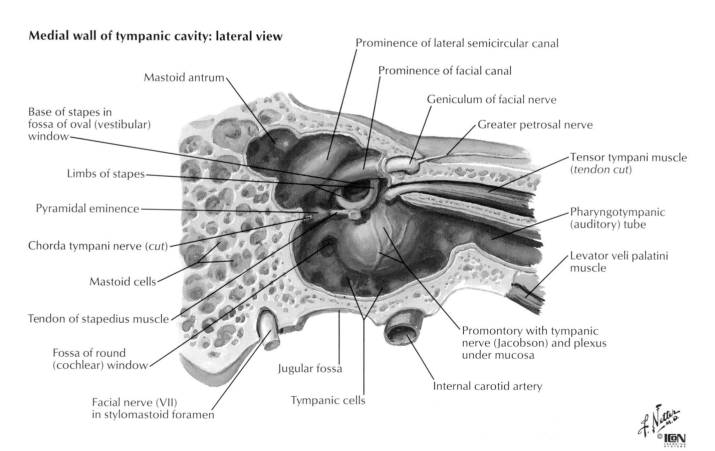

Prominence of lateral semicircular canal

Mastoid antrum

Prominence of facial canal

Geniculum of facial nerve

Base of stapes in fossa of oval (vestibular) window

Greater petrosal nerve

Limbs of stapes

Tensor tympani muscle (tendon cut)

Pyramidal eminence

Pharyngotympanic (auditory) tube

Chorda tympani nerve (cut)

Levator veli palatini muscle

Mastoid cells

Tendon of stapedius muscle

Fossa of round (cochlear) window

Promontory with tympanic nerve (Jacobson) and plexus under mucosa

Jugular fossa

Internal carotid artery

Facial nerve (VII) in stylomastoid foramen

Tympanic cells

ANESTHESIA

Head

00120 Anesthesia for procedures on external, middle, and inner ear including biopsy; not otherwise specified

00126   tympanotomy

SURGERY

Auditory System

Middle Ear
Introduction

69405 Eustachian tube catheterization, transtympanic

69410 Focal application of phase control substance, middle ear (baffle technique)

Incision

69420 Myringotomy including aspiration and/or eustachian tube inflation

69421 Myringotomy including aspiration and/or eustachian tube inflation requiring general anesthesia

69424 Ventilating tube removal requiring general anesthesia

69433^P Tympanostomy (requiring insertion of ventilating tube), local or topical anesthesia

69436^P Tympanostomy (requiring insertion of ventilating tube), general anesthesia

69440 Middle ear exploration through postauricular or ear canal incision

69450 Tympanolysis, transcanal

Excision

69501 Transmastoid antrotomy (simple mastoidectomy)

69502 Mastoidectomy; complete

69505   modified radical

69511   radical

69530 Petrous apicectomy including radical mastoidectomy

69535 Resection temporal bone, external approach

69540 Excision aural polyp

69550 Excision aural glomus tumor; transcanal

69552   transmastoid

69554   extended (extratemporal)

Repair

69601 Revision mastoidectomy; resulting in complete mastoidectomy

69602   resulting in modified radical mastoidectomy

69603   resulting in radical mastoidectomy

69604   resulting in tympanoplasty

69605   with apicectomy

69635^P Tympanoplasty with antrotomy or mastoidotomy (including canalplasty, atticotomy, middle ear surgery, and/or tympanic membrane repair); without ossicular chain reconstruction

69636^P with ossicular chain reconstruction

69637^P with ossicular chain reconstruction and synthetic prosthesis (eg, partial ossicular replacement prosthesis (PORP), total ossicular replacement prosthesis (TORP))

69650 Stapes mobilization

69660 Stapedectomy or stapedotomy with reestablishment of ossicular continuity, with or without use of foreign material;

69661   with footplate drill out

69662 Revision of stapedectomy or stapedotomy

69666 Repair oval window fistula

69667 Repair round window fistula

69676 Tympanic neurectomy

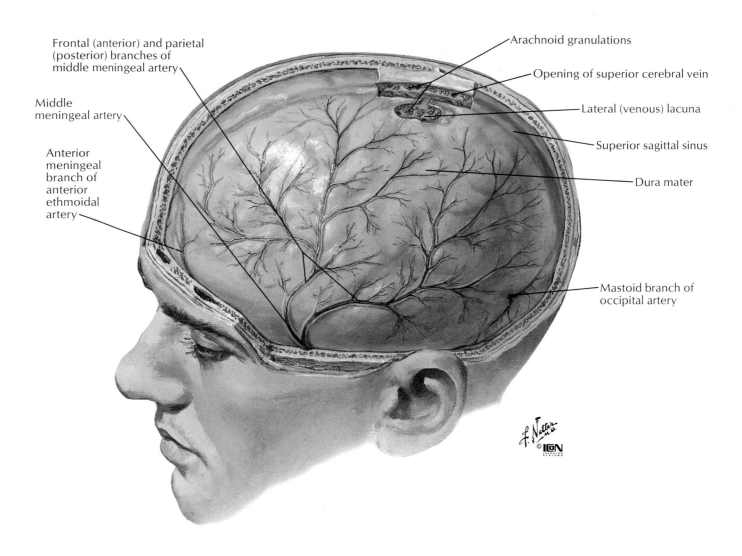

Frontal (anterior) and parietal (posterior) branches of middle meningeal artery

Middle meningeal artery

Anterior meningeal branch of anterior ethmoidal artery

Arachnoid granulations

Opening of superior cerebral vein

Lateral (venous) lacuna

Superior sagittal sinus

Dura mater

Mastoid branch of occipital artery

Nomenclature Notes

The term *supratentorial* refers to the part of the brain above the tentorium, which is a process of dura mater between the cerebrum and cerebellum, that supports the occipital lobes.

The term *infratentorial* refers to the part of the brain below the tentorium, which is a process of dura mater between the cerebrum and cerebellum, that supports the occipital lobes.

ANESTHESIA

Head	
00210	Anesthesia for intracranial procedures; not otherwise specified
00216	vascular procedures

SURGERY

Nervous System	

Skull, Meninges, and Brain
Craniectomy or Craniotomy

61312	Craniectomy or craniotomy for evacuation of hematoma, supratentorial; extradural or subdural
61314	Craniectomy or craniotomy for evacuation of hematoma, infratentorial; extradural or subdural
61512	Craniectomy, trephination, bone flap craniotomy; for excision of meningioma, supratentorial
61519	Craniectomy for excision of brain tumor, infratentorial or posterior fossa; meningioma

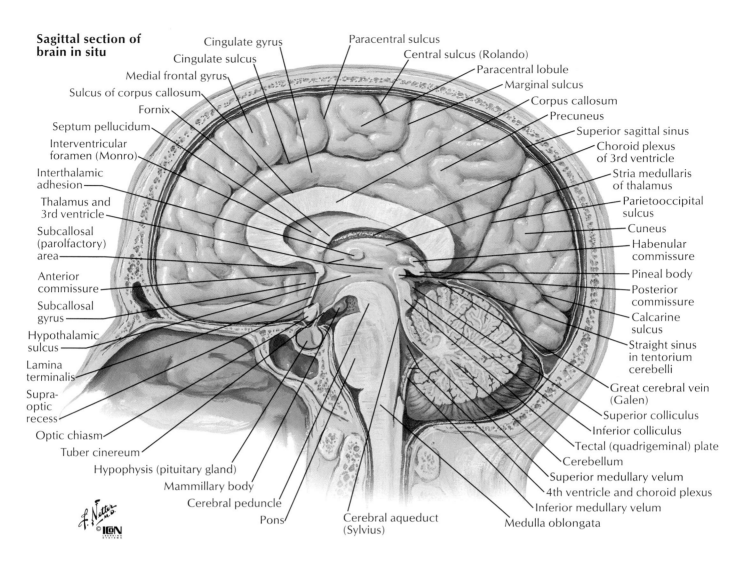

Sagittal section of brain in situ

Cingulate gyrus
Cingulate sulcus
Medial frontal gyrus
Sulcus of corpus callosum
Fornix
Septum pellucidum
Interventricular foramen (Monro)
Interthalamic adhesion
Thalamus and 3rd ventricle
Subcallosal (parolfactory) area
Anterior commissure
Subcallosal gyrus
Hypothalamic sulcus
Lamina terminalis
Supra-optic recess
Optic chiasm
Tuber cinereum
Hypophysis (pituitary gland)
Mammillary body
Cerebral peduncle
Pons

Paracentral sulcus
Central sulcus (Rolando)
Paracentral lobule
Marginal sulcus
Corpus callosum
Precuneus
Superior sagittal sinus
Choroid plexus of 3rd ventricle
Stria medullaris of thalamus
Parietooccipital sulcus
Cuneus
Habenular commissure
Pineal body
Posterior commissure
Calcarine sulcus
Straight sinus in tentorium cerebelli
Great cerebral vein (Galen)
Superior colliculus
Inferior colliculus
Tectal (quadrigeminal) plate
Cerebellum
Superior medullary velum
4th ventricle and choroid plexus
Inferior medullary velum
Medulla oblongata

Cerebral aqueduct (Sylvius)

ANESTHESIA

Head

00210	Anesthesia for intracranial procedures; not otherwise specified
00212	subdural taps
00214	burr holes, including ventriculography
00215	cranioplasty or elevation of depressed skull fracture, extradural (simple or compound)
00216	vascular procedures
00218	procedures in sitting position
00220	cerebrospinal fluid shunting procedures
00222	electrocoagulation of intracranial nerve

SURGERY

Nervous System

Skull, Meninges, and Brain
Twist Drill, Burr Hole(s), or Trephine

61105	Twist drill hole for subdural or ventricular puncture;

61107	for implanting ventricular catheter or pressure recording device
61108	for evacuation and/or drainage of subdural hematoma
61120	Burr hole(s) for ventricular puncture (including injection of gas, contrast media, dye, or radioactive material)
61140	Burr hole(s) or trephine; with biopsy of brain or intracranial lesion
61150	with drainage of brain abscess or cyst
61151	with subsequent tapping (aspiration) of intracranial abscess or cyst
61154	Burr hole(s) with evacuation and/or drainage of hematoma, extradural or subdural
61156	Burr hole(s); with aspiration of hematoma or cyst, intracerebral
61210	for implanting ventricular catheter, reservoir, EEG electrode(s) or pressure recording device (separate procedure)

(Twist Drill continued on next page)

Plate 44: Cerebrum—Medial View

(Twist Drill continued from previous page)

61215 Insertion of subcutaneous reservoir, pump or continuous infusion system for connection to ventricular catheter

61250 Burr hole(s) or trephine, supratentorial, exploratory, not followed by other surgery

61253 Burr hole(s) or trephine, infratentorial, unilateral or bilateral

Craniectomy or Craniotomy

61304 Craniectomy or craniotomy, exploratory; supratentorial

61305 infratentorial (posterior fossa)

61312 Craniectomy or craniotomy for evacuation of hematoma, supratentorial; extradural or subdural

61313 intracerebral

61314 Craniectomy or craniotomy for evacuation of hematoma, infratentorial; extradural or subdural

61315 intracerebellar

61316 Incision and subcutaneous placement of cranial bone graft (List separately in addition to code for primary procedure)

61320 Craniectomy or craniotomy, drainage of intracranial abscess; supratentorial

61321 infratentorial

61322 Craniectomy or craniotomy, decompressive, with or without duraplasty, for treatment of intracranial hypertension, without evacuation of associated intraparenchymal hematoma; without lobectomy

61323 with lobectomy

61330 Decompression of orbit only, transcranial approach

61332 Exploration of orbit (transcranial approach); with biopsy

61333 with removal of lesion

61334 with removal of foreign body

61340 Subtemporal cranial decompression (pseudotumor cerebri, slit ventricle syndrome)

61343 Craniectomy, suboccipital with cervical laminectomy for decompression of medulla and spinal cord, with or without dural graft (eg, Arnold-Chiari malformation)

61345 Other cranial decompression, posterior fossa

61440 Craniotomy for section of tentorium cerebelli (separate procedure)

61450 Craniectomy, subtemporal, for section, compression, or decompression of sensory root of gasserian ganglion

61458 Craniectomy, suboccipital; for exploration or decompression of cranial nerves

61460 for section of one or more cranial nerves

61470 for medullary tractotomy

61480 for mesencephalic tractotomy or pedunculotomy

61490 Craniotomy for lobotomy, including cingulotomy

61500 Craniectomy; with excision of tumor or other bone lesion of skull

61501 for osteomyelitis

61510 Craniectomy, trephination, bone flap craniotomy; for excision of brain tumor, supratentorial, except meningioma

61512 for excision of meningioma, supratentorial

61514 for excision of brain abscess, supratentorial

61516 for excision or fenestration of cyst, supratentorial

61517 Implantation of brain intracavitary chemotherapy agent (List separately in addition to code for primary procedure)

61518 Craniectomy for excision of brain tumor, infratentorial or posterior fossa; except meningioma, cerebellopontine angle tumor, or midline tumor at base of skull

61519 meningioma

61520 cerebellopontine angle tumor

61521 midline tumor at base of skull

61522 Craniectomy, infratentorial or posterior fossa; for excision of brain abscess

61524 for excision or fenestration of cyst

61526 Craniectomy, bone flap craniotomy, transtemporal (mastoid) for excision of cerebellopontine angle tumor;

61530 combined with middle/posterior fossa craniotomy/craniectomy

61531 Subdural implantation of strip electrodes through one or more burr or trephine hole(s) for long term seizure monitoring

61533 Craniotomy with elevation of bone flap; for subdural implantation of an electrode array, for long term seizure monitoring

61534 for excision of epileptogenic focus without electrocorticography during surgery

61535 for removal of epidural or subdural electrode array, without excision of cerebral tissue (separate procedure)

61536 for excision of cerebral epileptogenic focus, with electrocorticography during surgery (includes removal of electrode array)

61537 for lobectomy, temporal lobe, without electrocorticography during surgery

61538 for lobectomy, temporal lobe, with electrocorticography during surgery

61539 for lobectomy, other than temporal lobe, partial or total, with electrocorticography during surgery

61540 for lobectomy, other than temporal lobe, partial or total, without electrocorticography during surgery

61541 for transection of corpus callosum

61542 for total hemispherectomy

61543 for partial or subtotal (functional) hemispherectomy

61544 for excision or coagulation of choroid plexus

61545 for excision of craniopharyngioma

61546 Craniotomy for hypophysectomy or excision of pituitary tumor, intracranial approach

61548 Hypophysectomy or excision of pituitary tumor, transnasal or transseptal approach, nonstereotactic

61550 Craniectomy for craniosynostosis; single cranial suture

61552 multiple cranial sutures

61556	Craniotomy for craniosynostosis; frontal or parietal bone flap
61557	bifrontal bone flap
61558	Extensive craniectomy for multiple cranial suture craniosynostosis (eg, cloverleaf skull); not requiring bone grafts
61559	recontouring with multiple osteotomies and bone autografts (eg, barrel-stave procedure) (includes obtaining grafts)
61563	Excision, intra and extracranial, benign tumor of cranial bone (eg, fibrous dysplasia); without optic nerve decompression
61564	with optic nerve decompression
61566	Craniotomy with elevation of bone flap; for selective amygdalohippocampectomy
61567	for multiple subpial transections, with electrocorticography during surgery
61570	Craniectomy or craniotomy; with excision of foreign body from brain
61571	with treatment of penetrating wound of brain

Repair

62000	Elevation of depressed skull fracture; simple, extradural
62005	compound or comminuted, extradural
62010	with repair of dura and/or debridement of brain
62100	Craniotomy for repair of dural/cerebrospinal fluid leak, including surgery for rhinorrhea/otorrhea
62115	Reduction of craniomegalic skull (eg, treated hydrocephalus); not requiring bone grafts or cranioplasty
62116	with simple cranioplasty
62117	requiring craniotomy and reconstruction with or without bone graft (includes obtaining grafts)
62120	Repair of encephalocele, skull vault, including cranioplasty
62121	Craniotomy for repair of encephalocele, skull base
62140	Cranioplasty for skull defect; up to 5 cm diameter
62141	larger than 5 cm diameter

Neuroendoscopy

62160	Neuroendoscopy, intracranial, for placement or replacement of ventricular catheter and attachment to shunt system or external drainage (List separately in addition to code for primary procedure)
62161	Neuroendoscopy, intracranial; with dissection of adhesions, fenestration of septum pellucidum or intraventricular cysts (including placement, replacement, or removal of ventricular catheter)
62162	with fenestration or excision of colloid cyst, including placement of external ventricular catheter for drainage
62163	with retrieval of foreign body
62164	with excision of brain tumor, including placement of external ventricular catheter for drainage
62165	with excision of pituitary tumor, transnasal or trans-sphenoidal approach

Cerebrospinal Fluid (CSF) Shunt

62180	Ventriculocisternostomy (Torkildsen type operation)
62190	Creation of shunt; subarachnoid/subdural-atrial, -jugular, -auricular
62192	subarachnoid/subdural-peritoneal, -pleural, other terminus
62194	Replacement or irrigation, subarachnoid/subdural catheter
62200	Ventriculocisternostomy, third ventricle;
62201	stereotactic, neuroendoscopic method
62220	Creation of shunt; ventriculo-atrial, -jugular, -auricular
62223[P]	ventriculo-peritoneal, -pleural, other terminus
62225	Replacement or irrigation, ventricular catheter
62230	Replacement or revision of cerebrospinal fluid shunt, obstructed valve, or distal catheter in shunt system
62252	Reprogramming of programmable cerebrospinal shunt
62256	Removal of complete cerebrospinal fluid shunt system; without replacement
62258	with replacement by similar or other shunt at same operation

Plate 45: Brainstem—Posteriolateral and Anterior Views

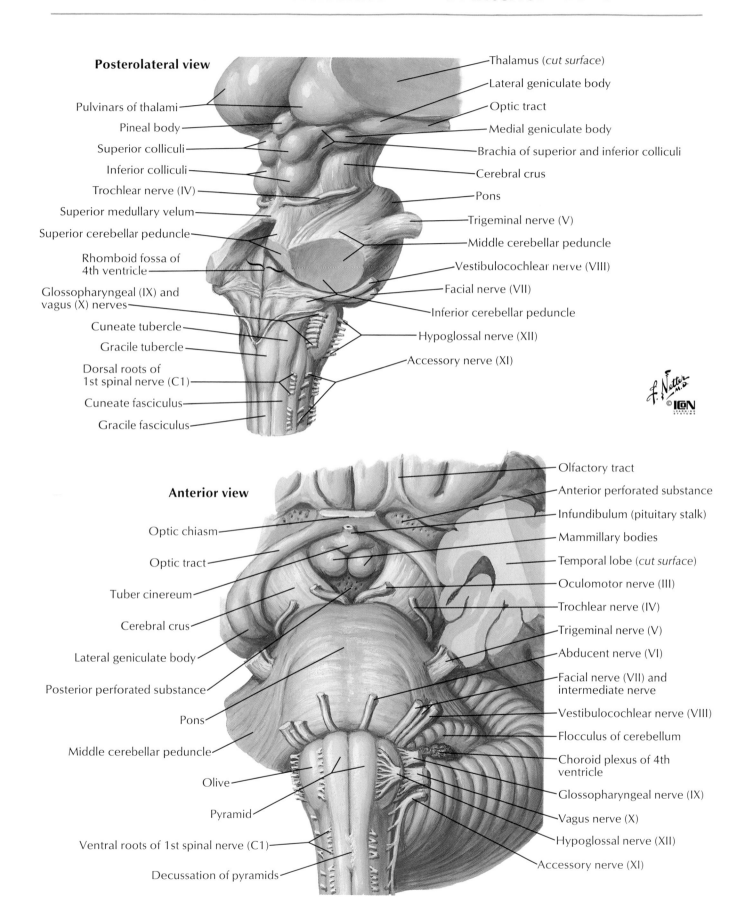

Posterolateral view

Pulvinars of thalami
Pineal body
Superior colliculi
Inferior colliculi
Trochlear nerve (IV)
Superior medullary velum
Superior cerebellar peduncle
Rhomboid fossa of 4th ventricle
Glossopharyngeal (IX) and vagus (X) nerves
Cuneate tubercle
Gracile tubercle
Dorsal roots of 1st spinal nerve (C1)
Cuneate fasciculus
Gracile fasciculus

Thalamus (*cut surface*)
Lateral geniculate body
Optic tract
Medial geniculate body
Brachia of superior and inferior colliculi
Cerebral crus
Pons
Trigeminal nerve (V)
Middle cerebellar peduncle
Vestibulocochlear nerve (VIII)
Facial nerve (VII)
Inferior cerebellar peduncle
Hypoglossal nerve (XII)
Accessory nerve (XI)

Anterior view

Optic chiasm
Optic tract
Tuber cinereum
Cerebral crus
Lateral geniculate body
Posterior perforated substance
Pons
Middle cerebellar peduncle
Olive
Pyramid
Ventral roots of 1st spinal nerve (C1)
Decussation of pyramids

Olfactory tract
Anterior perforated substance
Infundibulum (pituitary stalk)
Mammillary bodies
Temporal lobe (*cut surface*)
Oculomotor nerve (III)
Trochlear nerve (IV)
Trigeminal nerve (V)
Abducent nerve (VI)
Facial nerve (VII) and intermediate nerve
Vestibulocochlear nerve (VIII)
Flocculus of cerebellum
Choroid plexus of 4th ventricle
Glossopharyngeal nerve (IX)
Vagus nerve (X)
Hypoglossal nerve (XII)
Accessory nerve (XI)

ANESTHESIA

Head

00210   Anesthesia for intracranial procedures; not otherwise specified

SURGERY

Nervous System

Skull, Meninges, and Brain
Craniectomy or Craniotomy

61575   Transoral approach to skull base, brain stem or
upper spinal cord for biopsy, decompression or
excision of lesion;

61576   requiring splitting of tongue and/or mandible
(including tracheostomy)

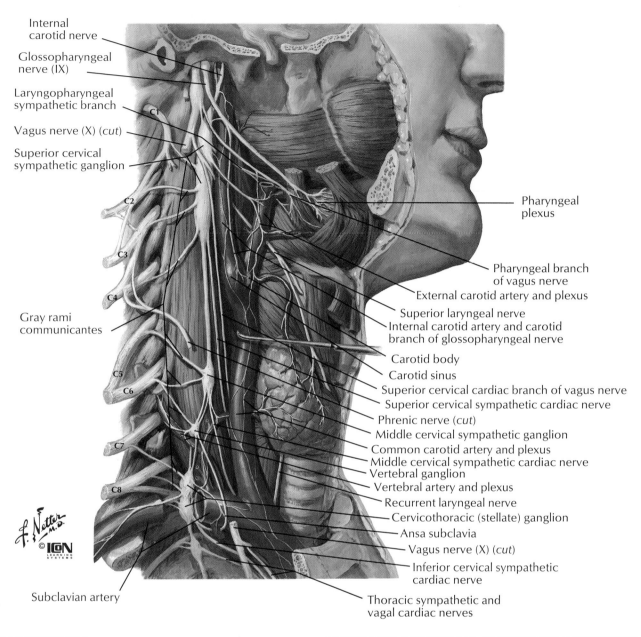

Internal carotid nerve
Glossopharyngeal nerve (IX)
Laryngopharyngeal sympathetic branch
Vagus nerve (X) (cut)
Superior cervical sympathetic ganglion
Gray rami communicantes
Subclavian artery

C1
C2
C3
C4
C5
C6
C7
C8

Pharyngeal plexus
Pharyngeal branch of vagus nerve
External carotid artery and plexus
Superior laryngeal nerve
Internal carotid artery and carotid branch of glossopharyngeal nerve
Carotid body
Carotid sinus
Superior cervical cardiac branch of vagus nerve
Superior cervical sympathetic cardiac nerve
Phrenic nerve (cut)
Middle cervical sympathetic ganglion
Common carotid artery and plexus
Middle cervical sympathetic cardiac nerve
Vertebral ganglion
Vertebral artery and plexus
Recurrent laryngeal nerve
Cervicothoracic (stellate) ganglion
Ansa subclavia
Vagus nerve (X) (cut)
Inferior cervical sympathetic cardiac nerve
Thoracic sympathetic and vagal cardiac nerves

ANESTHESIA

Neck

00300   Anesthesia for all procedures on the integumentary system, muscles and nerves of head, neck, and posterior trunk, not otherwise specified

SURGERY

Endocrine System

Parathyroid, Thymus, Adrenal Glands, Panceas, and Carotid Body
Excision

60600   Excision of carotid body tumor; without excision of carotid artery
60605   with excision of carotid artery

Nervous System

Extracranial Nerves, Peripheral Nerves, and Autonomic Nervous System
Introduction/Injection of Anesthetic Agent (Nerve Block), Diagnostic or Therapeutic
Somatic Nerves
64408   Injection, anesthetic agent; vagus nerve
64470   Injection, anesthetic agent and/or steroid, paravertebral facet joint or facet joint nerve; cervical or thoracic, single level
64472   cervical or thoracic, each additional level (List separately in addition to code for primary procedure)

Excision

Sympathetic Nerves
64802   Sympathectomy, cervical

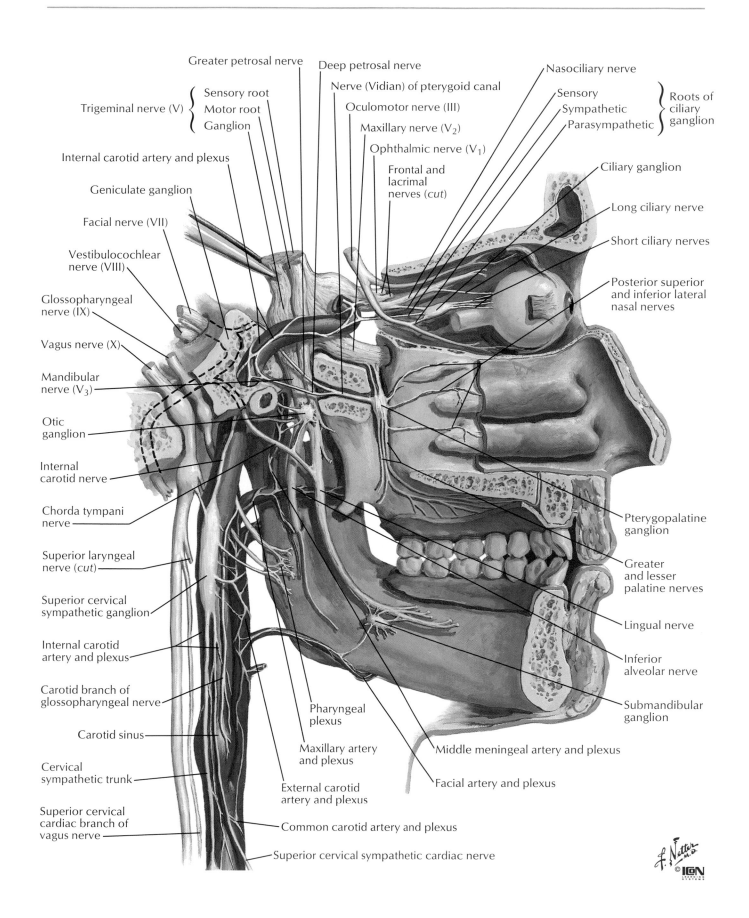

Greater petrosal nerve

Deep petrosal nerve

Nerve (Vidian) of pterygoid canal

Nasociliary nerve

Trigeminal nerve (V) { Sensory root / Motor root / Ganglion }

Oculomotor nerve (III)

Maxillary nerve (V₂)

Ophthalmic nerve (V₁)

Sensory
Sympathetic
Parasympathetic } Roots of ciliary ganglion

Internal carotid artery and plexus

Frontal and lacrimal nerves (cut)

Ciliary ganglion

Geniculate ganglion

Long ciliary nerve

Facial nerve (VII)

Short ciliary nerves

Vestibulocochlear nerve (VIII)

Posterior superior and inferior lateral nasal nerves

Glossopharyngeal nerve (IX)

Vagus nerve (X)

Mandibular nerve (V₃)

Otic ganglion

Pterygopalatine ganglion

Internal carotid nerve

Chorda tympani nerve

Greater and lesser palatine nerves

Superior laryngeal nerve (cut)

Lingual nerve

Superior cervical sympathetic ganglion

Inferior alveolar nerve

Internal carotid artery and plexus

Submandibular ganglion

Carotid branch of glossopharyngeal nerve

Pharyngeal plexus

Carotid sinus

Maxillary artery and plexus

Middle meningeal artery and plexus

Cervical sympathetic trunk

Facial artery and plexus

External carotid artery and plexus

Superior cervical cardiac branch of vagus nerve

Common carotid artery and plexus

Superior cervical sympathetic cardiac nerve

ANESTHESIA

Neck

00300   Anesthesia for all procedures on the integumentary system, muscles and nerves of head, neck, and posterior trunk, not otherwise specified

SURGERY

Nervous System

Extracranial Nerves, Peripheral Nerves, and Autonomic Nervous System

Introduction/Injection of Anesthetic Agent (Nerve Block), Diagnostic or Therapeutic

Somatic Nerves

64400   Injection, anesthetic agent; trigeminal nerve, any division or branch

64402   facial nerve

Sympathetic Nerves

64505   Injection, anesthetic agent; sphenopalatine ganglion

64508   carotid sinus (separate procedure)

Neurostimulators (Peripheral Nerve)

64553   Percutaneous implantation of neurostimulator electrodes; cranial nerve

64555   peripheral nerve (excludes sacral nerve)

64560   autonomic nerve

64565   neuromuscular

64573^P   Incision for implantation of neurostimulator electrodes; cranial nerve

64575   peripheral nerve (excludes sacral nerve)

64577   autonomic nerve

64580   neuromuscular

64585   Revision or removal of peripheral neurostimulator electrodes

64590   Insertion or replacement of peripheral neurostimulator pulse generator or receiver, direct or inductive coupling

64595   Revision or removal of peripheral neurostimulator pulse generator or receiver

Destruction by Neurolytic Agent (eg, Chemical, Thermal, Electrical or Radiofrequency)

Somatic Nerves

64600   Destruction by neurolytic agent, trigeminal nerve; supraorbital, infraorbital, mental, or inferior alveolar branch

64605   second and third division branches at foramen ovale

64610   second and third division branches at foramen ovale under radiologic monitoring

64612   Chemodenervation of muscle(s); muscle(s) innervated by facial nerve (eg, for blepharospasm, hemifacial spasm)

Transection or Avulsion

64732   Transection or avulsion of; supraorbital nerve

64734   infraorbital nerve

64736   mental nerve

64738   inferior alveolar nerve by osteotomy

64740   lingual nerve

64742   facial nerve, differential or complete

64744   greater occipital nerve

Neurorrhaphy

64864   Suture of facial nerve; extracranial

64865   infratemporal, with or without grafting

64866   Anastomosis; facial-spinal accessory

64868   facial-hypoglossal

Neurorrhaphy With Nerve Graft

64885   Nerve graft (includes obtaining graft), head or neck; up to 4 cm in length

64886   more than 4 cm length

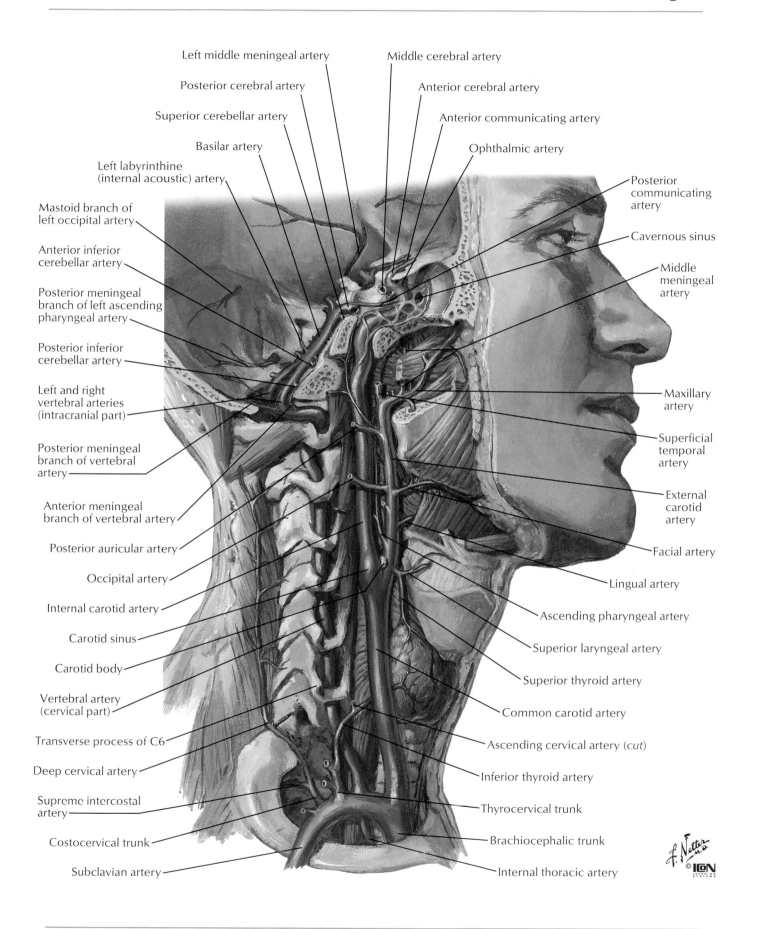

Left middle meningeal artery

Posterior cerebral artery

Superior cerebellar artery

Basilar artery

Left labyrinthine (internal acoustic) artery

Mastoid branch of left occipital artery

Anterior inferior cerebellar artery

Posterior meningeal branch of left ascending pharyngeal artery

Posterior inferior cerebellar artery

Left and right vertebral arteries (intracranial part)

Posterior meningeal branch of vertebral artery

Anterior meningeal branch of vertebral artery

Posterior auricular artery

Occipital artery

Internal carotid artery

Carotid sinus

Carotid body

Vertebral artery (cervical part)

Transverse process of C6

Deep cervical artery

Supreme intercostal artery

Costocervical trunk

Subclavian artery

Middle cerebral artery

Anterior cerebral artery

Anterior communicating artery

Ophthalmic artery

Posterior communicating artery

Cavernous sinus

Middle meningeal artery

Maxillary artery

Superficial temporal artery

External carotid artery

Facial artery

Lingual artery

Ascending pharyngeal artery

Superior laryngeal artery

Superior thyroid artery

Common carotid artery

Ascending cervical artery (cut)

Inferior thyroid artery

Thyrocervical trunk

Brachiocephalic trunk

Internal thoracic artery

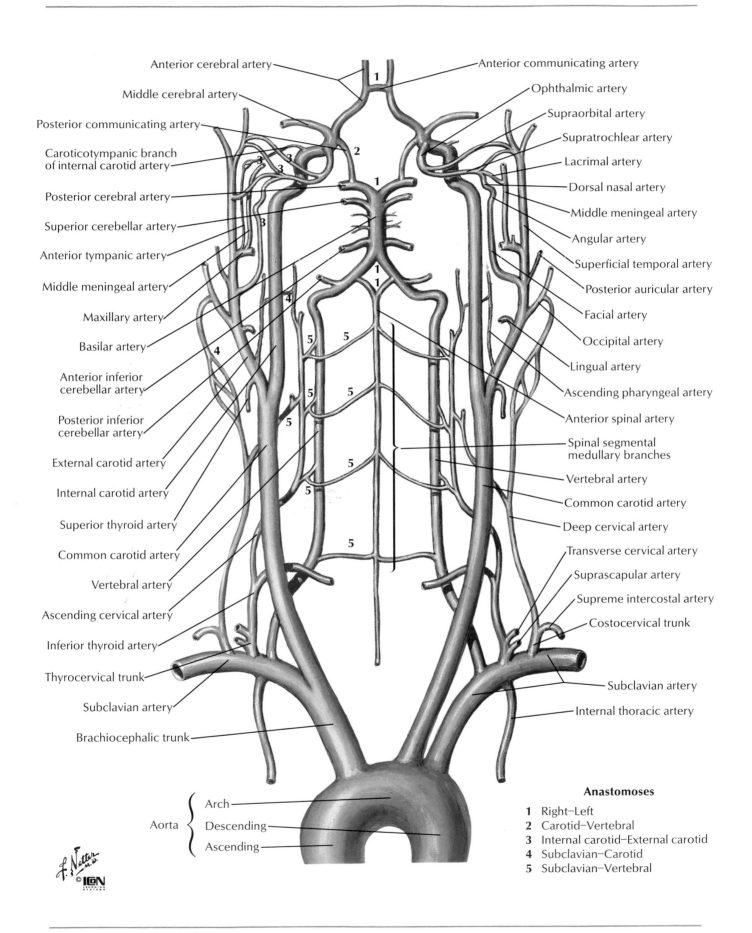

Anterior cerebral artery

Middle cerebral artery

Posterior communicating artery

Caroticotympanic branch of internal carotid artery

Posterior cerebral artery

Superior cerebellar artery

Anterior tympanic artery

Middle meningeal artery

Maxillary artery

Basilar artery

Anterior inferior cerebellar artery

Posterior inferior cerebellar artery

External carotid artery

Internal carotid artery

Superior thyroid artery

Common carotid artery

Vertebral artery

Ascending cervical artery

Inferior thyroid artery

Thyrocervical trunk

Subclavian artery

Brachiocephalic trunk

Anterior communicating artery

Ophthalmic artery

Supraorbital artery

Supratrochlear artery

Lacrimal artery

Dorsal nasal artery

Middle meningeal artery

Angular artery

Superficial temporal artery

Posterior auricular artery

Facial artery

Occipital artery

Lingual artery

Ascending pharyngeal artery

Anterior spinal artery

Spinal segmental medullary branches

Vertebral artery

Common carotid artery

Deep cervical artery

Transverse cervical artery

Suprascapular artery

Supreme intercostal artery

Costocervical trunk

Subclavian artery

Internal thoracic artery

Aorta {
Arch

Descending

Ascending

Anastomoses

1 Right−Left
2 Carotid−Vertebral
3 Internal carotid−External carotid
4 Subclavian−Carotid
5 Subclavian−Vertebral

ANESTHESIA

Head

00216   Anesthesia for intracranial procedures; vascular procedures

SURGERY

Cardiovascular System

Arteries and Veins

Transluminal Angioplasty

Open

35458   Transluminal balloon angioplasty, open; brachio-cephalic trunk or branches, each vessel

Percutaneous

35475   Transluminal balloon angioplasty, percutaneous; brachiocephalic trunk or branches, each vessel

Transluminal Atherectomy

Open

35484   Transluminal peripheral atherectomy, open; bra-chiocephalic trunk or branches, each vessel

Percutaneous

35494   Transluminal peripheral atherectomy, percutaneous; brachiocephalic trunk or branches, each vessel

Bypass Graft

Vein

35501   Bypass graft, with vein; carotid
35506   carotid-subclavian
35507   subclavian-carotid
35508   carotid-vertebral
35509   carotid-carotid
35511   subclavian-subclavian
35515   subclavian-vertebral

Other Than Vein

35601   Bypass graft, with other than vein; carotid
35606   carotid-subclavian
35612   subclavian-subclavian
35642   carotid-vertebral
35645   subclavian-vertebral

Arterial Transposition

35691   Transposition and/or reimplantation; vertebral to carotid artery
35693   vertebral to subclavian artery
35694   subclavian to carotid artery
35695   carotid to subclavian artery

Plate 49: Head Scans—Sagittal MR Images

Median (A) and paramedian (B,C) sagittal MR images

A

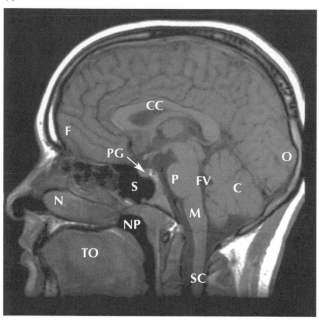

C	Cerebellum	**N**	Inferior nasal concha
CC	Corpus callosum	**NP**	Nasopharynx
E	Extraocular muscles	**O**	Occipital pole
		ON	Optic nerve
F	Frontal pole	**P**	Pons
FV	Fourth ventricle	**PG**	Pituitary gland
L	Lateral ventricle	**S**	Sphenoid sinus
		SC	Spinal cord
M	Medulla oblongata	**T**	Thalamus
		TC	Tentorium cerebelli
MB	Midbrain	**TO**	Tongue
MS	Maxillary sinus		

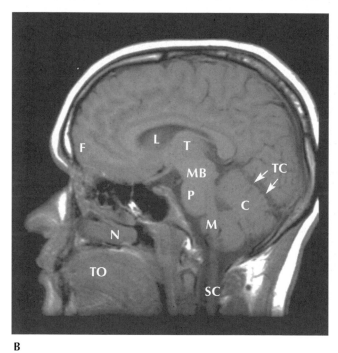

B

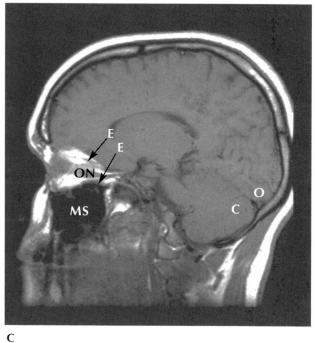

C

RADIOLOGY

Diagnostic Radiology (Diagnostic Imaging)

Head and Neck

70551   Magnetic resonance (eg, proton) imaging, brain (including brain stem); without contrast material

70552   with contrast material(s)

70553   without contrast material, followed by contrast material(s) and further sequences

Axial MR images of the head from inferior (A) to superior (C)

A

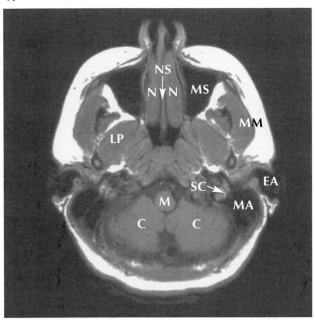

B	Basilar artery		**M**	Medulla oblongata
C	Cerebellum		**MA**	Mastoid air cells
CH	Cerebral hemisphere		**MB**	Midbrain
CS	Confluence of sinuses		**MM**	Masseter muscle
E	Eye		**MR**	Medial rectus muscle
EA	External acoustic meatus		**MS**	Maxillary sinus
ES	Ethmoid sinus		**N**	Nasal concha
F	Fat in orbit		**NS**	Nasal septum
FV	Fourth ventricle		**P**	Pons
L	Lens		**S**	Sphenoid sinus
LP	Lateral pterygoid muscle		**SC**	Semicircular canals
LR	Lateral rectus muscle		**SS**	Superior sagittal sinus
			T	Temporalis muscle
			TL	Temporal lobe

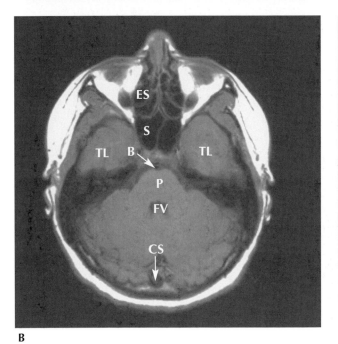

B

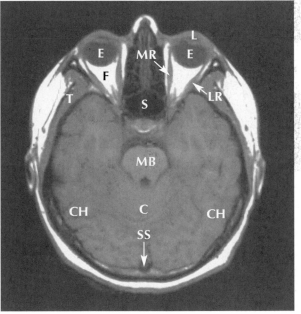

C

RADIOLOGY

Diagnostic Radiology (Diagnostic Imaging)

Head and Neck

70450   Computed tomography, head or brain; without contrast material

70460   with contrast material(s)

70470   without contrast material, followed by contrast material(s) and further sections

Plate 51: Head Scans—Coronal CT Images

Coronal CT images of the head from anterior (A) to posterior (C)

A

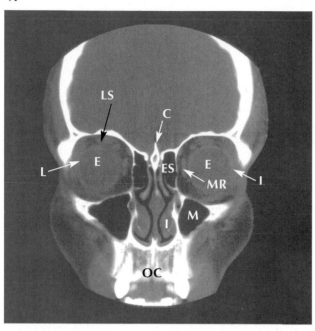

A	Anterior clinoid process	**LS**	Levator palpebrae superioris and superior rectus muscles
C	Crista galli		
E	Eye (vitreous chamber)	**M**	Maxillary sinus
ES	Ethmoid sinus	**MR**	Medial rectus muscle
I	Inferior nasal concha	**N**	Nasal septum
IR	Inferior rectus muscle	**O**	Optic nerve
		OC	Oral cavity
L	Lateral rectus muscle	**S**	Sphenoid sinus

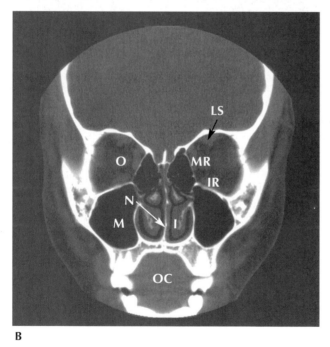

B

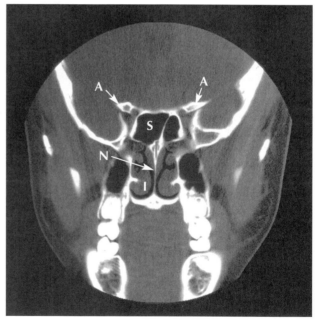

C

RADIOLOGY

Diagnostic Radiology (Diagnostic Imaging)

Head and Neck

70450	Computed tomography, head or brain; without contrast material
70460	with contrast material(s)
70470	without contrast material, followed by contrast material(s) and further sections

Chapter 2
Back and Spinal Cord

This chapter contains illustrations of the bones and ligaments of the spinal column (also called the *vertebral column*), the spinal cord, the muscles of the dorsum of the trunk (the back), the nerves arising from the spinal cord, and parts of the peripheral nervous system. This chapter does not include detailed illustrations of the bones, ligaments, muscles, and nerves of the neck (the cervical area); these are illustrated in Chapter 1, Head and Neck. The illustrations of the ribs are also excluded from this chapter but do appear in Chapter 3, Thorax.

The spinal column consists of a series of bones called vertebrae. The vertebrae are named by their location (eg, cervical, thoracic) and by number within their location. The 33 paired vertebrae found in the human adult can be divided as follows:

- Seven cervical: C1-C7
- Twelve thoracic: T1-T12
- Five lumbar: L1-L5
- Five sacral (typically fused into a single bone called the sacrum): S1-S5
- Four coccygeal (sometimes fused into a single bone called the coccyx)

Disks of cartilage, known as intervertebral disks, separate the spinal vertebrae. The vertebral interspace is the nonbony compartment between two adjacent vertebral bodies that contains the intervertebral disk. The term *vertebral segment* describes the basic constituent parts into which the spine may be divided. A vertebral segment consists of one complete vertebral bone and its articular processes and laminae.

The spinal cavity (or vertebral canal) houses the spinal cord, which extends from the foramen magnum to the lower edge of the first lumbar vertebrae. The subarachnoid space ends at the level of the second sacral vertebrae. The spinal cavity contains not only the cord but also the meninges, spinal fluid, fat tissue, and blood vessels. Thirty-one pairs of spinal nerves arise from the spinal cord. Each spinal nerve is attached indirectly to the cord via the spinal nerve roots. The nerve root itself is only 1 to 2 mm in length. The nerve roots exit the bony spinal cavity through an interveterbral foramen.

In the lumbosacral region, the nerve roots of the lumbar sacral and coccygeal nerves, located in the lower spinal cord, combine to form the cauda equina (literally translated as *horse's tail*, which describes the appearance of this area). The cauda equina is composed of the nerve roots and not the spinal nerves themselves.

The brachial plexus consists of nerve fibers from C5-8 and T1 and is located in the shoulder region from the neck to the axilla. The lumbar plexus consists of nerve fibers from L1-5 and is located in the lumbar spine region of the back in the psoas muscle. The sacral plexus consists of nerve fibers from L4-5 S 1-3 and is located in the pelvic cavity on the anterior surface of the piriformis muscle.

The term *peripheral nerve* often refers to the part of a spinal nerve that is distal to the root and plexus.

Common procedures performed in this anatomic region include, but are not limited to, the following:

- Diagnostic fluid aspirations (spinal tap or lumbar puncture)
- Spinal and nerve injections
- Catheter implantation
- Diskectomy (an excision of an intervertebral disk during which the disk can be surgically removed or a percutatneous diskectomy can be performed)
- Laminotomy or laminectomy (a surgical procedure to relieve pressure on the spinal cord or nerve root that is cause by a slipped or herniated disk, or a treatment for spinal stenosis)
- Exploration or decompression of nerves
- Nerve destruction
- Treatment of fractures and dislocations
- Arthrodesis (joint fusion or surgical immobilization of a joint)
- Vertebroplasty
- Exploration or re-exploration
- Spinal instrumentation (fixation)
- Soft tissue and/or muscle biopsies (soft tissue is considered nonskeletal tissue, ie, it excludes bone, ligament, cartilage, and connective tissue but includes skin, subcutaneous tissue, and muscle tissue)
- Tumor excision
- Myelography (a diagnostic procedure that requires the injection of contrast dye into the spinal canal so that an X ray can be performed to reveal the anatomy of the spinal canal)
- Radiographs
- Magnetic resonance imaging
- Computed axial tomography

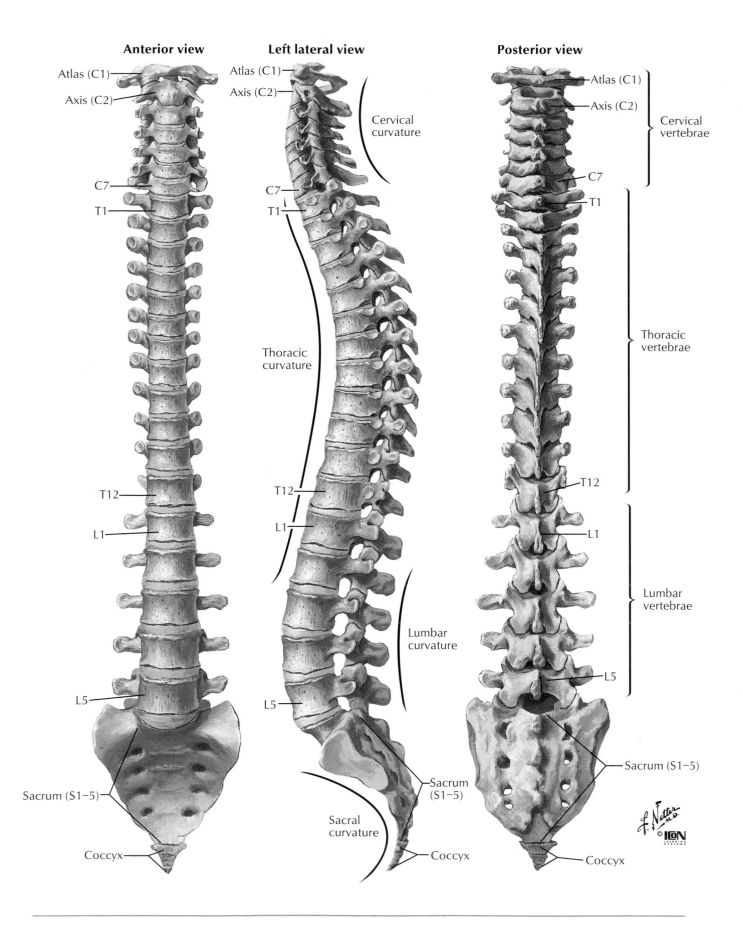

Anterior view

Atlas (C1)
Axis (C2)
C7
T1
T12
L1
L5
Sacrum (S1–5)
Coccyx

Left lateral view

Atlas (C1)
Axis (C2)
Cervical curvature
C7
T1
Thoracic curvature
T12
L1
Lumbar curvature
L5
Sacrum (S1–5)
Sacral curvature
Coccyx

Posterior view

Atlas (C1)
Axis (C2)
Cervical vertebrae
C7
T1
Thoracic vertebrae
T12
L1
Lumbar vertebrae
L5
Sacrum (S1–5)
Coccyx

ANESTHESIA

Spine and Spinal Cord

00600   Anesthesia for procedures on cervical spine and cord; not otherwise specified
00604   procedures with patient in the sitting position
00620   Anesthesia for procedures on thoracic spine and cord; not otherwise specified
00622   thoracolumbar sympathectomy
00630   Anesthesia for procedures in lumbar region; not otherwise specified
00632   lumbar sympathectomy
00634   chemonucleolysis
00635   diagnostic or therapeutic lumbar puncture
00640   Anesthesia for manipulation of the spine or for closed procedures on the cervical, thoracic or lumbar spine
00670   Anesthesia for extensive spine and spinal cord procedures (eg, spinal instrumentation or vascular procedures)

SURGERY

Musculoskeletal System

Spine (Vertebral Column)
Excision

22100   Partial excision of posterior vertebral component (eg, spinous process, lamina or facet) for intrinsic bony lesion, single vertebral segment; cervical
22101   thoracic
22102   lumbar
22103   each additional segment (List separately in addition to code for primary procedure)
22110   Partial excision of vertebral body, for intrinsic bony lesion, without decompression of spinal cord or nerve root(s), single vertebral segment; cervical
22112   thoracic
22114   lumbar
22116   each additional vertebral segment (List separately in addition to code for primary procedure)

Osteotomy

22210   Osteotomy of spine, posterior or posterolateral approach, one vertebral segment; cervical
22212   thoracic
22214   lumbar
22216   each additional vertebral segment (List separately in addition to primary procedure)
22220   Osteotomy of spine, including diskectomy, anterior approach, single vertebral segment; cervical
22222   thoracic
22224   lumbar
22226   each additional vertebral segment (List separately in addition to code for primary procedure)

Fracture and/or Dislocation

22305   Closed treatment of vertebral process fracture(s)
22310   Closed treatment of vertebral body fracture(s), without manipulation, requiring and including casting or bracing

22315   Closed treatment of vertebral fracture(s) and/or dislocation(s) requiring casting or bracing, with and including casting and/or bracing, with or without anesthesia, by manipulation or traction
22318   Open treatment and/or reduction of odontoid fracture(s) and or dislocation(s) (including os odontoideum), anterior approach, including placement of internal fixation; without grafting
22319   with grafting
22325   Open treatment and/or reduction of vertebral fracture(s) and/or dislocation(s), posterior approach, one fractured vertebrae or dislocated segment; lumbar
22326   cervical
22327   thoracic
22328   each additional fractured vertebrae or dislocated segment (List separately in addition to code for primary procedure)

Manipulation

22505   Manipulation of spine requiring anesthesia, any region

Spinal Instrumentation

22840[P]   Posterior non-segmental instrumentation (eg, Harrington rod technique, pedicle fixation across one interspace, atlantoaxial transarticular screw fixation, sublaminar wiring at C1, facet screw fixation)
22841   Internal spinal fixation by wiring of spinous processes
22842[P]   Posterior segmental instrumentation (eg, pedicle fixation, dual rods with multiple hooks and sublaminar wires); 3 to 6 vertebral segments
22843[P]   7 to 12 vertebral segments
22844[P]   13 or more vertebral segments
22845   Anterior instrumentation; 2 to 3 vertebral segments
22846   4 to 7 vertebral segments
22847   8 or more vertebral segments
22848   Pelvic fixation (attachment of caudal end of instrumentation to pelvic bony structures) other than sacrum
22849   Reinsertion of spinal fixation device
22850   Removal of posterior nonsegmental instrumentation (eg, Harrington rod)
22851[P]   Application of intervertebral biomechanical device(s) (eg, synthetic cage(s), threaded bone dowel(s), methylmethacrylate) to vertebral defect or interspace
22852   Removal of posterior segmental instrumentation
22855   Removal of anterior instrumentation

RADIOLOGY

Diagnostic Radiology (Diagnostic Imaging)

Spine and Pelvis

72010   Radiologic examination, spine, entire, survey study, anteroposterior and lateral

(Spine and Pelvis continued on next page)

(Spine and Pelvis continued from previous page)

72020 Radiologic examination, spine, single view, specify level

72040 Radiologic examination, spine, cervical; two or three views

72050 minimum of four views

72052 complete, including oblique and flexion and/or extension studies

72069 Radiologic examination, spine, thoracolumbar, standing (scoliosis)

72070 Radiologic examination, spine; thoracic, two views

72072 thoracic, three views

72074 thoracic, minimum of four views

72080 thoracolumbar, two views

72090 scoliosis study, including supine and erect studies

72100 Radiologic examination, spine, lumbosacral; two or three views

72110 minimum of four views

72114 complete, including bending views

72120 Radiologic examination, spine, lumbosacral, bending views only, minimum of four views

72125 Computed tomography, cervical spine; without contrast material

72126 with contrast material

72127 without contrast material, followed by contrast material(s) and further sections

72128 Computed tomography, thoracic spine; without contrast material

72129 with contrast material

72130 without contrast material, followed by contrast material(s) and further sections

72131 Computed tomography, lumbar spine; without contrast material

72132 with contrast material

72133 without contrast material, followed by contrast material(s) and further sections

Plate 53: Thoracic Vertebrae

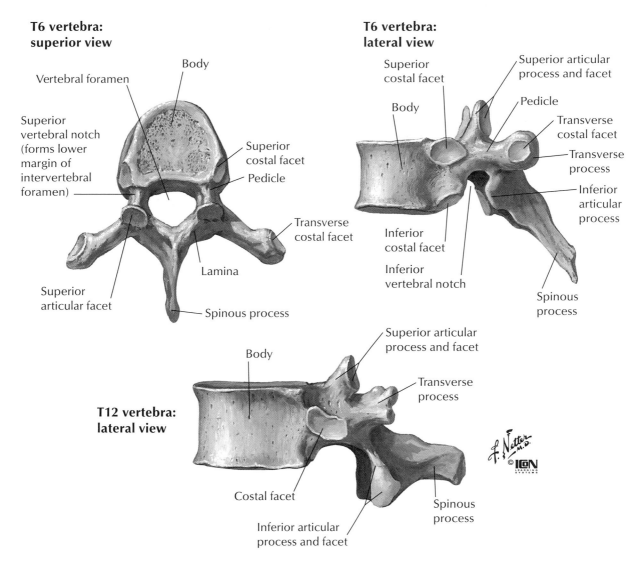

T6 vertebra: superior view

Vertebral foramen

Body

Superior vertebral notch (forms lower margin of intervertebral foramen)

Superior costal facet

Pedicle

Transverse costal facet

Lamina

Superior articular facet

Spinous process

T6 vertebra: lateral view

Superior costal facet

Body

Superior articular process and facet

Pedicle

Transverse costal facet

Transverse process

Inferior articular process

Inferior costal facet

Inferior vertebral notch

Spinous process

T12 vertebra: lateral view

Body

Superior articular process and facet

Transverse process

Costal facet

Inferior articular process and facet

Spinous process

Nomenclature Notes

Spinal canal is synonymous with *vertebral canal*.

ANESTHESIA

Spine and Spinal Cord

00620 Anesthesia for procedures on thoracic spine and cord; not otherwise specified

00640 Anesthesia for manipulation of the spine or for closed procedures on the cervical, thoracic or lumbar spine

SURGERY

Musculoskeletal System

Spine (Vertebral Column)
Excision

22101 Partial excision of posterior vertebral component (eg, spinous process, lamina or facet) for intrinsic bony lesion, single vertebral segment; thoracic

22103 each additional segment (List separately in addition to code for primary procedure)

22112 Partial excision of vertebral body, for intrinsic bony lesion, without decompression of spinal cord or nerve root(s), single vertebral segment; thoracic

22116 each additional vertebral segment (List separately in addition to code for primary procedure)

Osteotomy

22212 Osteotomy of spine, posterior or posterolateral approach, one vertebral segment; thoracic

22216 each additional vertebral segment (List separately in addition to primary procedure)

22222 Osteotomy of spine, including diskectomy, anterior approach, single vertebral segment; thoracic

22226 each additional vertebral segment (List separately in addition to code for primary procedure)

Fracture and/or Dislocation

22305 Closed treatment of vertebral process fracture(s)

(Fracture and/or Dislocation continued on next page)

COPYRIGHT 2005 AMERICAN MEDICAL ASSOCIATION   **BACK AND SPINAL CORD   89**

Plate 53: Thoracic Vertebrae

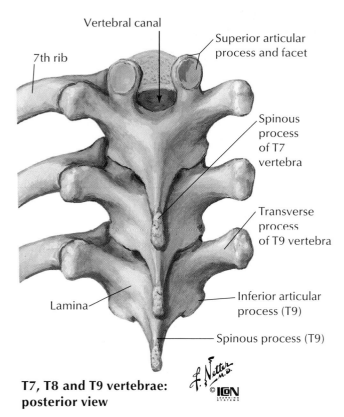

Vertebral canal

7th rib

Superior articular process and facet

Spinous process of T7 vertebra

Transverse process of T9 vertebra

Inferior articular process (T9)

Lamina

Spinous process (T9)

T7, T8 and T9 vertebrae: posterior view

(Fracture and/or Dislocation continued from previous page)

22310 Closed treatment of vertebral body fracture(s), without manipulation, requiring and including casting or bracing

22315 Closed treatment of vertebral fracture(s) and/or dislocation(s) requiring casting or bracing, with and including casting and/or bracing, with or without anesthesia, by manipulation or traction

22327 Open treatment and/or reduction of vertebral fracture(s) and/or dislocation(s), posterior approach, one fractured vertebrae or dislocated segment; thoracic

22328 each additional fractured vertebrae or dislocated segment (List separately in addition to code for primary procedure)

Manipulation

22505 Manipulation of spine requiring anesthesia, any region

Vertebral Body, Embolization or Injection

22520 Percutaneous vertebroplasty, one vertebral body, unilateral or bilateral injection; thoracic

Arthrodesis

Anterior or Anterolateral Approach Technique

22556 Arthrodesis, anterior interbody technique, including minimal diskectomy to prepare interspace (other than for decompression); thoracic

22585 each additional interspace (List separately in addition to code for primary procedure

Posterior, Posterolateral or Lateral Transverse Process Technique

22610 Arthrodesis, posterior or posterolateral technique, single level; thoracic (with or without lateral transverse technique)

Nervous System

Spine and Spinal Cord
Posterior Extradural Laminotomy or Laminectomy for Exploration/Decompression of Neural Elements or Excision of Herniated Intervertebral Disks

63003[P] Laminectomy with exploration and/or decompression of spinal cord and/or cauda equina, without facetectomy, foraminotomy or diskectomy, (eg, spinal stenosis), one or two vertebral segments; thoracic

63016 Laminectomy with exploration and/or decompression of spinal cord and/or cauda equina, without facetectomy, foraminotomy or diskectomy, (eg, spinal stenosis), more than 2 vertebral segments; thoracic

63046 Laminectomy, facetectomy and foraminotomy (unilateral or bilateral with decompression of spinal cord, cauda equina and/or nerve root(s), (eg, spinal or lateral recess stenosis)), single vertebral segment; thoracic

63048 each additional segment, cervical, thoracic, or lumbar (List separately in addition to code for primary procedure)

Transpedicular or Costovertebral Approach for Posterolateral Extradural Exploration/Decompression

63055 Transpedicular approach with decompression of spinal cord, equina and/or nerve root(s) (eg, herniated intervertebral disk), single segment; thoracic

63057 each additional segment, thoracic or lumbar (List separately in addition to code for primary procedure)

63064 Costovertebral approach with decompression of spinal cord or nerve root(s), (eg, herniated intervertebral disk), thoracic; single segment

63066 each additional segment (List separately in addition to code for primary procedure)

Anterior or Anterolateral Approach for Extradural Exploration/Decompression

63085 Vertebral corpectomy (vertebral body resection), partial or complete, transthoracic approach with decompression of spinal cord and/or nerve root(s); thoracic, single segment

63086 thoracic, each additional segment (List separately in addition to code for primary procedure)

63087 Vertebral corpectomy (vertebral body resection), partial or complete, combined thoracolumbar approach with decompression of spinal cord, cauda equina or nerve root(s), lower thoracic or lumbar; single segment

63088 each additional segment (List separately in addition to code for primary procedure)

63090 Vertebral corpectomy (vertebral body resection), partial or complete, transperitoneal or retroperitoneal approach with decompression of spinal cord, cauda equina or nerve root(s), lower thoracic, lumbar, or sacral; single segment

63091 each additional segment (List separately in addition to code for primary procedure)

Lateral Extracavitary Approach for Extradural Exploration/Decompression

63101 Vertebral corpectomy (vertebral body resection), partial or complete, lateral extracavitary approach with decompression of spinal cord and/or nerve root(s) (eg, for tumor or retropulsed bone fragments); thoracic, single segment

63103 thoracic or lumbar, each additional segment (List separately in addition to code for primary procedure)

Incision

63195 Laminectomy with cordotomy, with section of one spinothalamic tract, one stage; thoracic

63197 Laminectomy with cordotomy, with section of both spinothalamic tracts, one stage; thoracic

63199 Laminectomy with cordotomy with section of both spinothalamic tracts, two stages within 14 days; thoracic

Excision by Laminectomy of Lesion Other Than Herniated Disk

63251 Laminectomy for excision or occlusion of arteriovenous malformation of spinal cord; thoracic

63266 Laminectomy for excision or evacuation of intraspinal lesion other than neoplasm, extradural; thoracic

63271 Laminectomy for excision of intraspinal lesion other than neoplasm, intradural; thoracic

63276 Laminectomy for biopsy/excision of intraspinal neoplasm; extradural, thoracic

63281 intradural, extramedullary, thoracic

63286 intradural, intramedullary, thoracic

Excision, Anterior or Anterolateral Approach, Intraspinal Lesion

63301 Vertebral corpectomy (vertebral body resection), partial or complete, for excision of intraspinal lesion, single segment; extradural, thoracic by transthoracic approach

63302 extradural, thoracic by thoracolumbar approach

63305 intradural, thoracic by transthoracic approach

63306 intradural, thoracic by thoracolumbar approach

63308 each additional segment (List separately in addition to codes for single segment)

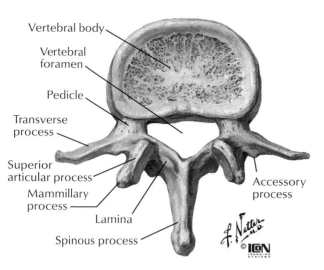

Vertebral body
Vertebral foramen
Pedicle
Transverse process
Superior articular process
Mammillary process
Lamina
Spinous process
Accessory process

L2 vertebra: superior view

Nomenclature Notes

The *vertebral foramen* is the foramen that is formed between the body of the vertebrae with the vertebral arch. It forms a part of the vertebral canal.

ANESTHESIA

Spine and Spinal Cord

00630	Anesthesia for procedures in lumbar region; not otherwise specified
00632	lumbar sympathectomy
00634	chemonucleolysis
00635	diagnostic or therapeutic lumbar puncture
00640	Anesthesia for manipulation of the spine or for closed procedures on the cervical, thoracic or lumbar spine
00670	Anesthesia for extensive spine and spinal cord procedures (eg, spinal instrumentation or vascular procedures)

SURGERY

Musculoskeletal System

Spine (Vertebral Column)

Excision

22102	Partial excision of posterior vertebral component (eg, spinous process, lamina or facet) for intrinsic bony lesion, single vertebral segment; lumbar
22103	each additional segment (List separately in addition to code for primary procedure)
22114	Partial excision of vertebral body, for intrinsic bony lesion, without decompression of spinal cord or nerve root(s), single vertebral segment; lumbar
22116	each additional vertebral segment (List separately in addition to code for primary procedure)

Osteotomy

22214	Osteotomy of spine, posterior or posterolateral approach, one vertebral segment; lumbar
22216	each additional vertebral segment (List separately in addition to primary procedure)

Fracture and/or Dislocation

22305	Closed treatment of vertebral process fracture(s)
22310	Closed treatment of vertebral body fracture(s), without manipulation, requiring and including casting or bracing
22315	Closed treatment of vertebral fracture(s) and/or dislocation(s) requiring casting or bracing, with and including casting and/or bracing, with or without anesthesia, by manipulation or traction
22325	Open treatment and/or reduction of vertebral fracture(s) and/or dislocation(s), posterior approach, one fractured vertebrae or dislocated segment; lumbar
22328	each additional fractured vertebrae or dislocated segment (List separately in addition to code for primary procedure)

Manipulation

22505	Manipulation of spine requiring anesthesia, any region

Vertebral Body, Embolization or Injection

22521[P]	Percutaneous vertebroplasty, one vertebral body, unilateral or bilateral injection; lumbar
22522	each additional thoracic or lumbar vertebral body (List separately in addition to code for primary procedure)

Lateral Extracavitary Approach Technique

22533	Arthrodesis, lateral extracavitary technique, including minimal diskectomy to prepare interspace (other than for decompression); lumbar
22534	thoracic or lumbar, each additional vertebral segment (List separately in addition to code for primary procedure)

Arthrodesis

Anterior or Anterolateral Approach Technique

22558[P]	Arthrodesis, anterior interbody technique, including minimal diskectomy to prepare interspace (other than for decompression); lumbar
22585	each additional interspace (List separately in addition to code for primary procedure)

Posterior, Posterolateral or Lateral Transverse Process Technique

22612	Arthrodesis, posterior or posterolateral technique, single level; lumbar (with or without lateral transverse technique)
22614	each additional vertebral segment (List separately in addition to code for primary procedure)
22630	Arthrodesis, posterior interbody technique, including laminectomy and/or diskectomy to prepare interspace (other than for decompression), single interspace; lumbar
22632	each additional interspace (List separately in addition to code for primary procedure)

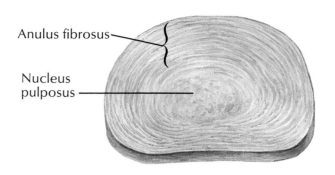

Anulus fibrosus

Nucleus pulposus

Intervertebral disk

ANESTHESIA

Spine and Spinal Cord

00630   Anesthesia for procedures in lumbar region; not otherwise specified

Radiological Procedures

01905   Anesthesia for myelography, diskography, vertebroplasty

SURGERY

Nervous System

Spine and Spinal Cord
Injection, Drainage, or Aspiration

62287   Aspiration or decompression procedure, percutaneous, of nucleus pulposus of intervertebral disk, any method, single or multiple levels, lumbar (eg, manual or automated percutaneous diskectomy, percutaneous laser diskectomy)

62290   Injection procedure for diskography, each level; lumbar

62292   Injection procedure for chemonucleolysis, including diskography, intervertebral disk, single or multiple levels, lumbar

RADIOLOGY

Diagnostic Radiology (Diagnostic Imaging)

Spine and Pelvis

72295   Diskography, lumbar, radiological supervision and interpretation

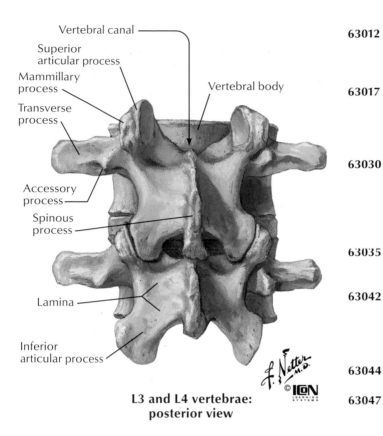

Vertebral canal

Superior
articular process

Mammillary
process

Transverse
process

Vertebral body

Accessory
process

Spinous
process

Lamina

Inferior
articular process

**L3 and L4 vertebrae:
posterior view**

Nomenclature Notes

Vertebral canal is synonymous with *spinal canal*.

ANESTHESIA

Spine and Spinal Cord

00630	Anesthesia for procedures in lumbar region; not otherwise specified
00632	lumbar sympathectomy
00634	chemonucleolysis
00635	diagnostic or therapeutic lumbar puncture
00640	Anesthesia for manipulation of the spine or for closed procedures on the cervical, thoracic or lumbar spine
00670	Anesthesia for extensive spine and spinal cord procedures (eg, spinal instrumentation or vascular procedures)

SURGERY

Nervous System

Spine and Spinal Cord
Posterior Extradural Laminotomy or Laminectomy for Exploration/Decompression of Neural Elements or Excision of Herniated Intervertebral Disks

63005^P	Laminectomy with exploration and/or decompression of spinal cord and/or cauda equina, without facetectomy, foraminotomy or diskectomy, (eg, spinal stenosis), one or two vertebral segments; lumbar, except for spondylolisthesis

63012	Laminectomy with removal of abnormal facets and/or pars inter-articularis with decompression of cauda equina and nerve roots for spondylolisthesis, lumbar (Gill type procedure)
63017	Laminectomy with exploration and/or decompression of spinal cord and/or cauda equina, without facetectomy, foraminotomy or diskectomy, (eg, spinal stenosis), more than 2 vertebral segments; lumbar
63030	Laminotomy (hemilaminectomy), with decompression of nerve root(s), including partial facetectomy, foraminotomy and/or excision of herniated intervertebral disk; one interspace, lumbar (including open or endoscopically-assisted approach)
63035	each additional interspace, cervical or lumbar (List separately in addition to code for primary procedure)
63042	Laminotomy (hemilaminectomy), with decompression of nerve root(s), including partial facetectomy, foraminotomy and/or excision of herniated intervertebral disk, reexploration, single interspace; lumbar
63044	each additional lumbar interspace (List separately in addition to code for primary procedure)
63047	Laminectomy, facetectomy and foraminotomy (unilateral or bilateral with decompression of spinal cord, cauda equina and/or nerve root(s), (eg, spinal or lateral recess stenosis)), single vertebral segment; lumbar
63048	each additional segment, cervical, thoracic, or lumbar (List separately in addition to code for primary procedure)

Transpedicular or Costovertebral Approach for Posterolateral Extradural Exploration/Decompression

63056	Transpedicular approach with decompression of spinal cord, equina and/or nerve root(s) (eg, herniated intervertebral disk), single segment; lumbar (including transfacet, or lateral extraforaminal approach) (eg, far lateral herniated intervertebral disk)
63057	each additional segment, thoracic or lumbar (List separately in addition to code for primary procedure)

Anterior or Anterolateral Approach for Extradural Exploration/Decompression

63087	Vertebral corpectomy (vertebral body resection), partial or complete, combined thoracolumbar approach with decompression of spinal cord, cauda equina or nerve root(s), lower thoracic or lumbar; single segment
63088	each additional segment (List separately in addition to code for primary procedure)
63090	Vertebral corpectomy (vertebral body resection), partial or complete, transperitoneal or retroperitoneal approach with decompression of spinal cord, cauda equina or nerve root(s), lower thoracic, lumbar, or sacral; single segment

63091   each additional segment (List separately in addition to code for primary procedure)

Lateral Extracavitary Approach for Extradural Exploration/Decompression

63102   Vertebral corpectomy (vertebral body resection), partial or complete, lateral extracavitary approach with decompression of spinal cord and/or nerve root(s) (eg, for tumor or retropulsed bone fragments); lumbar, single segment

63103   thoracic or lumbar, each additional segment (List separately in addition to code for primary procedure)

Incision

63170   Laminectomy with myelotomy (eg, Bischof or DREZ type), cervical, thoracic, or thoracolumbar

63200   Laminectomy, with release of tethered spinal cord, lumbar

Excision by Laminectomy of Lesion Other Than Herniated Disk

63251   Laminectomy for excision or occlusion of arteriovenous malformation of spinal cord; thoracic

63267   Laminectomy for excision or evacuation of intraspinal lesion other than neoplasm, extradural; lumbar

63272   Laminectomy for excision of intraspinal lesion other than neoplasm, intradural; lumbar

63282   Laminectomy for biopsy/excision of intraspinal neoplasm; intradural, extramedullary, lumbar

Excision, Anterior or Anterolateral Approach, Intraspinal Lesion

63303   Vertebral corpectomy (vertebral body resection), partial or complete, for excision of intraspinal lesion, single segment; extradural, lumbar or sacral by transperitoneal or retroperitoneal approach

63307   intradural, lumbar or sacral by transperitoneal or retroperitoneal approach

63308   each additional segment (List separately in addition to codes for single segment)

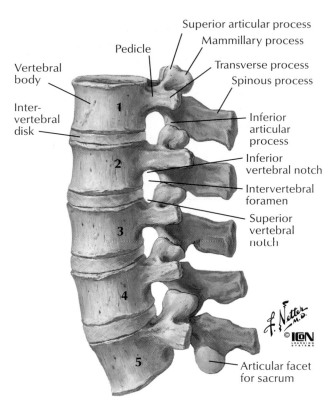

Vertebral body
Inter-vertebral disk
Pedicle
Superior articular process
Mammillary process
Transverse process
Spinous process
Inferior articular process
Inferior vertebral notch
Intervertebral foramen
Superior vertebral notch
Articular facet for sacrum

**Lumbar vertebrae, assembled:
left lateral view**

Nomenclature Notes

The term *transforaminal* means through the intervertebral foramen.

Spinal puncture is synonymous with the terms *lumbar puncture* and *spinal tap*. A spinal puncture is performed at the midline of the back in the space between the L4-L5 vertebrae.

ANESTHESIA

Spine and Spinal Cord

00630   Anesthesia for procedures in lumbar region; not otherwise specified
00635   diagnostic or therapeutic lumbar puncture
00640   Anesthesia for manipulation of the spine or for closed procedures on the cervical, thoracic or lumbar spine
00670   Anesthesia for extensive spine and spinal cord procedures (eg, spinal instrumentation or vascular procedures)

Other Procedures

01992   Anesthesia for diagnostic or therapeutic nerve blocks and injections; prone position

---

SURGERY

Musculoskeletal System

Spine (Vertebral Column)
Excision

22102   Partial excision of posterior vertebral component (eg, spinous process, lamina or facet) for intrinsic bony lesion, single vertebral segment; lumbar
22103   each additional segment (List separately in addition to code for primary procedure)
22114   Partial excision of vertebral body, for intrinsic bony lesion, without decompression of spinal cord or nerve root(s), single vertebral segment; lumbar
22116   each additional vertebral segment (List separately in addition to code for primary procedure)

Osteotomy

22214   Osteotomy of spine, posterior or posterolateral approach, one vertebral segment; lumbar
22216   each additional vertebral segment (List separately in addition to primary procedure)
22224   Osteotomy of spine, including diskectomy, anterior approach, single vertebral segment; lumbar
22226   each additional vertebral segment (List separately in addition to code for primary procedure)

Fracture and/or Dislocation

22305   Closed treatment of vertebral process fracture(s)
22310   Closed treatment of vertebral body fracture(s), without manipulation, requiring and including casting or bracing
22315   Closed treatment of vertebral fracture(s) and/or dislocation(s) requiring casting or bracing, with and including casting and/or bracing, with or without anesthesia, by manipulation or traction
22325   Open treatment and/or reduction of vertebral fracture(s) and/or dislocation(s), posterior approach, one fractured vertebrae or dislocated segment; lumbar
22328   each additional fractured vertebrae or dislocated segment (List separately in addition to code for primary procedure)

Manipulation

22505   Manipulation of spine requiring anesthesia, any region

Vertebral Body, Embolization or Injection

22521   Percutaneous vertebroplasty, one vertebral body, unilateral or bilateral injection; lumbar
22522   each additional thoracic or lumbar vertebral body (List separately in addition to code for primary procedure)

Lateral Extracavitary Approach Technique

22533   Arthrodesis, lateral extracavitary technique, including minimal diskectomy to prepare interspace (other than for decompression); lumbar

---

22534   thoracic or lumbar, each additional vertebral segment (List separately in addition to code for primary procedure)

Arthrodesis

Anterior or Anterolateral Approach Technique

22558[P]   Arthrodesis, anterior interbody technique, including minimal diskectomy to prepare interspace (other than for decompression); lumbar

22585   each additional interspace (List separately in addition to code for primary procedure)

Posterior, Posterolateral or Lateral Transverse Process Technique

22612   Arthrodesis, posterior or posterolateral technique, single level; lumbar (with or without lateral transverse technique)

22614   each additional vertebral segment (List separately in addition to code for primary procedure)

22630   Arthrodesis, posterior interbody technique, including laminectomy and/or diskectomy to prepare interspace (other than for decompression), single interspace; lumbar

22632   each additional interspace (List separately in addition to code for primary procedure)

Spine Deformity (eg, Scoliosis, Kyphosis)

22818   Kyphectomy, circumferential exposure of spine and resection of vertebral segment(s) (including body and posterior elements); single or 2 segments

22819   3 or more segments

Exploration

22830   Exploration of spinal fusion

Nervous System

Spine and Spinal Cord

Injection, Drainage, or Aspiration

62270   Spinal puncture, lumbar, diagnostic

62287   Aspiration or decompression procedure, percutaneous, of nucleus pulposus of intervertebral disk, any method, single or multiple levels, lumbar (eg, manual or automated percutaneous diskectomy, percutaneous laser diskectomy)

62290   Injection procedure for diskography, each level; lumbar

62292   Injection procedure for chemonucleolysis, including diskography, intervertebral disk, single or multiple levels, lumbar

62311   Injection, single (not via indwelling catheter), not including neurolytic substances, with or without contrast (for either localization or epidurography), of diagnostic or therapeutic substance(s) (including anesthetic, antispasmodic, opioid, steroid, other solution), epidural or subarachnoid; cervical or lumbar, sacral (caudal)

62319   Injection, including catheter placement, continuous infusion or intermittent bolus, not including neurolytic substances, with or without contrast (for either localization or epidurography), of diagnostic or therapeutic substance(s) (including anesthetic, antispasmodic, opioid, steroid, other solution), epidural or subarachnoid; lumbar, sacral (caudal)

Posterior Extradural Laminotomy or Laminectomy for Exploration/Decompression Neural Elements or Excision of Herniated Intervertebral Disks

63005[P]   Laminectomy with exploration and/or decompression of spinal cord and/or cauda equina, without facetectomy, foraminotomy or diskectomy, (eg, spinal stenosis), one or two vertebral segments; lumbar, except for spondylolisthesis

63014   Laminectomy with exploration and/or decompression of spinal cord and/or cauda equina, without facetectomy, foraminotomy or diskectomy, (eg, spinal stenosis), more than 2 vertebral segments; lumbar

63047   Laminectomy, facetectomy and foraminotomy (unilateral or bilateral with decompression of spinal cord, cauda equina and/or nerve root(s), (eg, spinal or lateral recess stenosis)), single vertebral segment; lumbar

63048   each additional segment, cervical, thoracic, or lumbar (List separately in addition to code for primary procedure)

Transpedicular or Costovertebral Approach for Posterolateral Extradural Exploration/Decompression

63056   Transpedicular approach with decompression of spinal cord, equina and/or nerve root(s) (eg, herniated intervertebral disk), single segment; lumbar

63057   each additional segment, thoracic or lumbar (List separately in addition to code for primary procedure)

Anterior or Anterolateral Approach for Extradural Exploration/Decompression

63087   Vertebral corpectomy (vertebral body resection), partial or complete, combined thoracolumbar approach with decompression of spinal cord, cauda equina or nerve root(s), lower thoracic or lumbar; single segment

63088   each additional segment (List separately in addition to code for primary procedure)

63090   Vertebral corpectomy (vertebral body resection), partial or complete, transperitoneal or retroperitoneal approach with decompression of spinal cord, cauda equina or nerve root(s), lower thoracic, lumbar, or sacral; single segment

63091   each additional segment (List separately in addition to code for primary procedure)

Lateral Extracavitary Approach for Extradural Exploration/Decompression

63102   Vertebral corpectomy (vertebral body resection), partial or complete, lateral extracavitary approach with decompression of spinal cord and/or nerve root(s) (eg, for tumor or retropulsed bone fragments); lumbar, single segment

63103   thoracic or lumbar, each additional segment (List separately in addition to code for primary procedure)

Incision

63200	Laminectomy with release of tethered spinal cord, lumbar

Excision by Laminectomy of Lesion Other Than Herniated Disk

63252	Laminectomy for excision or occlusion of arteriovenous malformation of spinal cord; thoracolumbar
63267	Laminectomy for excision or evacuation of intraspinal lesion other than neoplasm, extradural; lumbar
63272	Laminectomy for excision of intraspinal lesion other than neoplasm, intradural; lumbar
63277	Laminectomy for biopsy/excision of intraspinal neoplasm; extradural, lumbar
63282	intradural, extramedullary, lumbar
63287	intradural, intramedullary, thoracolumbar

Excision, Anterior or Anterolateral Approach, Intraspinal Lesion

63303	Vertebral corpectomy (vertebral body resection), partial or complete, for excision of intraspinal lesion, single segment; extradural, lumbar or sacral by transperitoneal or retroperitoneal approach
63307	intradural, lumbar or sacral by transperitoneal or retroperitoneal approach
63308	each additional segment (List separately in addition to codes for single segment)

Extracranial Nerves, Peripheral Nerves, and Autonomic Nervous System

Introduction/Injection of Anesthetic Agent (Nerve Block), Diagnostic or Therapeutic

Somatic Nerves

64483	Injection, anesthetic agent and/or steroid, transforaminal epidural; lumbar or sacral, single level
64484	lumbar or sacral, each additional level (List separately in addition to code for primary procedure)

Anteroposterior radiograph

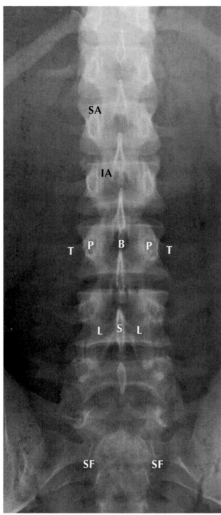

Lateral radiograph

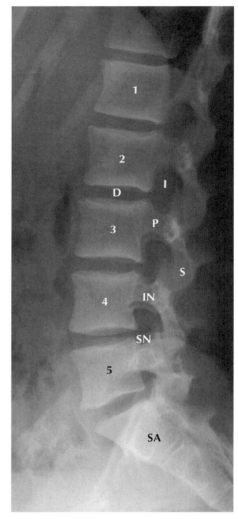

B	Body of L3 vertebra	**SA**	Superior articular process of L1 vertebra
IA	Inferior articular process of L1 vertebra	**SF**	Sacral foramen
L	Lamina of L4 vertebra	**T**	Transverse process of L3 vertebra
P	Pedicle of L3 vertebra		
S	Spinous process of L4 vertebra		

D	Intervertebral disk space	**S**	Spinous process of L3 vertebra
I	Intervertebral foramen	**SA**	Sacrum
IN	Inferior vertebral notch of L4 vertebra	**SN**	Superior vertebral notch of L5 vertebra
P	Pedicle of L3 vertebra	**Note:** The lumbar vertebral bodies are numbered	

Nomenclature Notes

The term *anterorposterior* (A/P) is used with X-ray images to describe the direction of the X-ray beam through the patient, from front to back. An A/P radiograph is a single view.

The term *lateral* is used with X-ray images to describe the direction of the X-ray beam through the patient, from either the right or left side. A lateral radiograph is a single view.

When A/P and lateral radiographs are taken, this constitutes two views.

RADIOLOGY

Diagnostic Radiology (Diagnostic Imaging)

Spine and Pelvis

72020	Radiologic examination, spine, single view, specify level
72100	Radiologic examination, spine, lumbosacral; two or three views

Plate 59: Sacrum and Coccyx

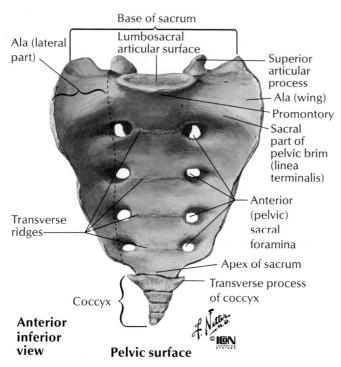

Base of sacrum

Ala (lateral part)

Lumbosacral articular surface

Superior articular process

Ala (wing)

Promontory

Sacral part of pelvic brim (linea terminalis)

Transverse ridges

Anterior (pelvic) sacral foramina

Apex of sacrum

Transverse process of coccyx

Coccyx

Anterior inferior view

Pelvic surface

Nomenclature Notes

The *sacrum* joins on each side at the auricular surface with the bones of the pelvis, forming the sacroiliac joints.

Caudal is synonymous with *sacral*.

ANESTHESIA

Spine and Spinal Cord

00630	Anesthesia for procedures in lumbar region; not otherwise specified
00640	Anesthesia for manipulation of the spine or for closed procedures on the cervical, thoracic or lumbar spine

SURGERY

Integumentary System

Repair (Closure)
Pressure Ulcers (Decubitus Ulcers)

15920	Excision, coccygeal pressure ulcer, with coccygectomy; with primary suture
15922	with flap closure

Musculoskeletal System

Pelvis and Hip Joint
Excision

27050	Arthrotomy, with biopsy; sacroiliac joint
27080	Coccygectomy, primary

Introduction or Removal

27096	Injection procedure for sacroiliac joint, arthrography and/or anesthetic/steroid

Fracture and/or Dislocation

27200	Closed treatment of coccygeal fracture
27202	Open treatment of coccygeal fracture
27218	Open treatment of posterior ring fracture and/or dislocation with internal fixation (includes ilium, sacroiliac joint and/or sacrum)

Digestive System

Abdomen, Peritoneum, and Omentum
Excision, Destruction

49215	Excision of presacral or sacrococcygeal tumor

Nervous System

Spine and Spinal Cord
Injection, Drainage, or Aspiration

62282	Injection/infusion of neurolytic substance (eg, alcohol, phenol, iced saline solutions), with or without other therapeutic substance; epidural, lumbar, sacral (caudal)
62311	Injection, single (not via indwelling catheter), not including neurolytic substances, with or without contrast (for either localization or epidurography), of diagnostic or therapeutic substance(s) (including anesthetic, antispasmodic, opioid, steroid, other solution), epidural or subarachnoid; lumbar, sacral (caudal)

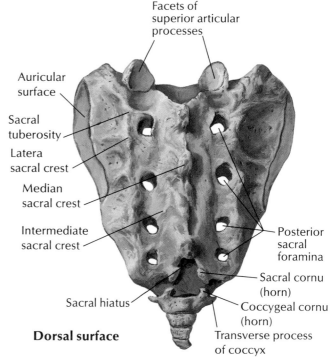

Facets of superior articular processes

Auricular surface

Sacral tuberosity

Latera sacral crest

Median sacral crest

Intermediate sacral crest

Posterior sacral foramina

Sacral cornu (horn)

Coccygeal cornu (horn)

Transverse process of coccyx

Sacral hiatus

Dorsal surface

Posterior superior view

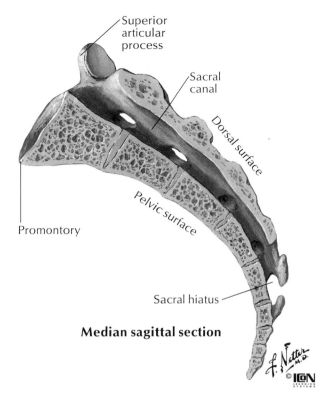

Superior articular process

Sacral canal

Dorsal surface

Pelvic surface

Promontory

Sacral hiatus

Median sagittal section

62319   Injection, including catheter placement, continuous infusion or intermittent bolus, not including neurolytic substances, with or without contrast (for either localization or epidurography), of diagnostic or therapeutic substance(s) (including anesthetic, antispasmodic, opioid, steroid, other solution), epidural or subarachnoid; lumbar, sacral (caudal)

Posterior Extradural Laminotomy or Laminectomy for Exploraion/Decompression of Neural Elements or Excision of Herniated Intervertebral Disks

63011   Laminectomy with exploration and/or decompression of spinal cord and/or cauda equina, without facetectomy, foraminotomy or diskectomy, (eg, spinal stenosis), one or two vertebral segments; sacral

Anterior or Anterolateral Approach for Extradural Exploration/Decompression

63090   Vertebral corpectomy (vertebral body resection), partial or complete, transperitoneal or retroperitoneal approach with decompression of spinal cord, cauda equina or nerve root(s), lower thoracic, lumbar, or sacral; single segment

63091   each additional segment (List separately in addition to code for primary procedure)

Excision by Laminectomy of Lesion Other Than Herniated Disk

63268   Laminectomy for excision or evacuation of intraspinal lesion other than neoplasm, extradural; sacral

63273   Laminectomy for excision of intraspinal lesion other than neoplasm, intradural; sacral

63278   Laminectomy for biopsy/excision of intraspinal neoplasm; extradural, sacral

63283   intradural, sacral

Excision, Anterior or Anterolateral Approach, Intraspinal Lesion

63303   Vertebral corpectomy (vertebral body resection), partial or complete, for excision of intraspinal lesion, single segment; extradural, lumbar or sacral by transperitoneal or retroperitoneal approach

63307   intradural, lumbar or sacral by transperitoneal or retroperitoneal approach

63308   each additional segment (List separately in addition to codes for single segment)

Extracranial Nerves, Peripheral Nerves, and Autonomic Nervous System

Introduction/Injection of Anesthetic Agent (Nerve Block), Diagnostic or Therapeutic

64475   Injection, anesthetic agent and/or steroid, paravertebral facet joint or facet joint nerve; lumbar or sacral, single level

64476   lumbar or sacral, each additional level (List separately in addition to code for primary procedure)

64483   Injection, anesthetic agent and/or steroid, transforaminal epidural; lumbar or sacral, single level

64484   lumbar or sacral, each additional level (List separately in addition to code for primary procedure)

Neurostimulators (Peripheral Nerve)

64561   Percutaneous implantation of neurostimulator electrodes; sacral nerve (transforaminal placement)

64581^P Incision for implantation of neurostimulator electrodes; sacral nerve (transforaminal placement)

Destruction by Neurolytic Agent (eg, Chemical, Thermal, Electrical or Radiofrequency)

Somatic Nerves

64623   Destruction by neurolytic agent, paravertebral facet joint nerve; lumbar or sacral, each additional level (List separately in addition to code for primary procedure)

RADIOLOGY

Diagnostic Radiology (Diagnostic Imaging)

Spine and Pelvis

72100   Radiologic examination, spine, lumbosacral; two or three views

72110   minimum of four views

72114   complete, including bending views

72120   Radiologic examination, spine, lumbosacral, bending views only, minimum of four views

72200   Radiologic examination, sacroiliac joints; less than three views

72202   three or more views

72220   Radiologic examination, sacrum and coccyx, minimum of two views

72265   Myelography, lumbosacral, radiological supervision and interpretation

Lower Extremities

73542   Radiological examination, sacroiliac joint arthrography, radiological supervision and interpretation

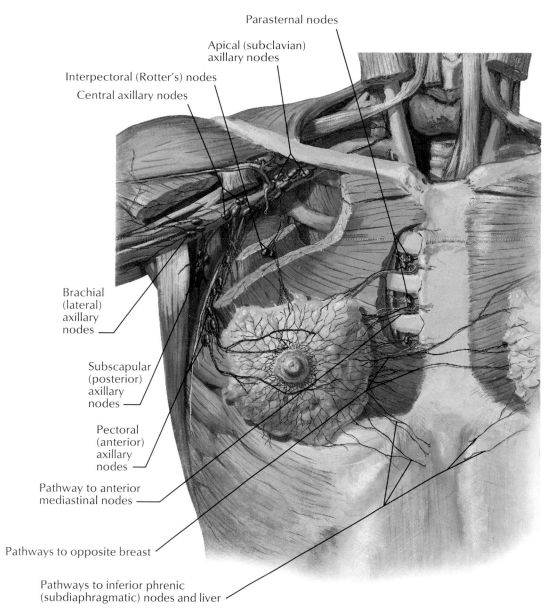

Parasternal nodes

Apical (subclavian) axillary nodes

Interpectoral (Rotter's) nodes

Central axillary nodes

Brachial (lateral) axillary nodes

Subscapular (posterior) axillary nodes

Pectoral (anterior) axillary nodes

Pathway to anterior mediastinal nodes

Pathways to opposite breast

Pathways to inferior phrenic (subdiaphragmatic) nodes and liver

ANESTHESIA

Thorax (Chest Wall and Shoulder Girdle)

00404	Anesthesia for procedures on the integumentary system on the extremities, anterior trunk and perineum; radical or modified radical procedures on breast
00406	radical or modified radical procedures on breast with internal mammary node dissection

SURGERY

Integumentary System

Breast
Excision

19180	Mastectomy, simple, complete
19182	Mastectomy, subcutaneous

19200	Mastectomy, radical, including pectoral muscles, axillary lymph nodes
19220	Mastectomy, radical, including pectoral muscles, axillary and internal mammary lymph nodes (Urban type operation)
19240	Mastectomy, modified radical, including axillary lymph nodes, with or without pectoralis minor muscle, but excluding pectoralis major muscle
19260	Excision of chest wall tumor including ribs
19271	Excision of chest wall tumor involving ribs, with plastic reconstruction; without mediastinal lymphadenectomy
19272	with mediastinal lymphadenectomy

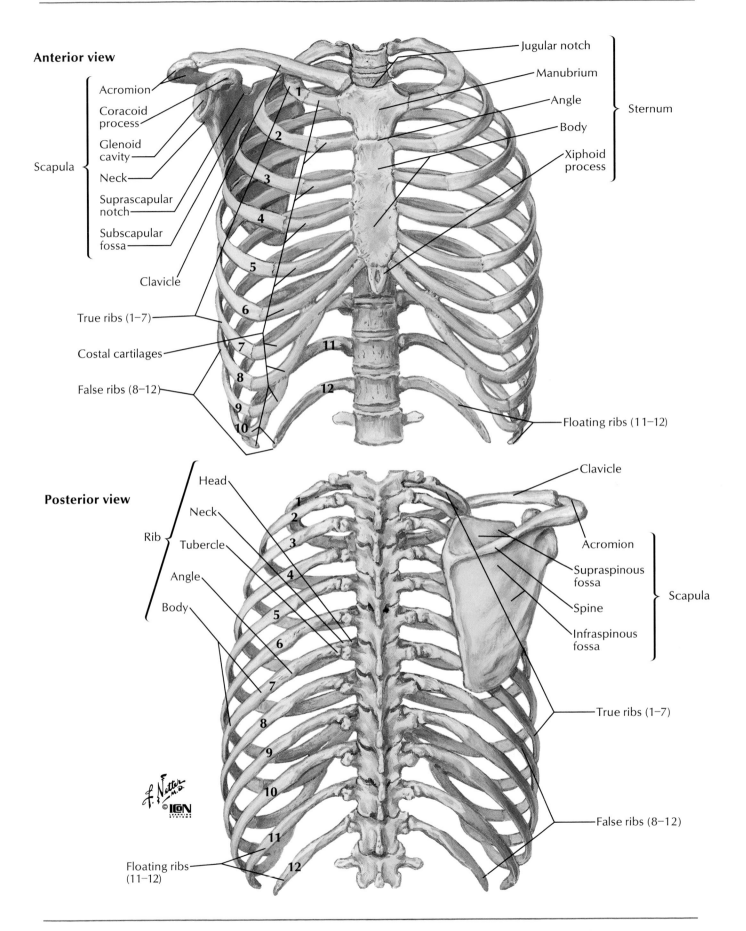

Anterior view

Acromion

Coracoid process

Glenoid cavity

Neck

Suprascapular notch

Subscapular fossa

Scapula

Clavicle

True ribs (1–7)

Costal cartilages

False ribs (8–12)

Jugular notch

Manubrium

Angle

Body

Xiphoid process

Sternum

1
2
3
4
5
6
7
8
9
10
11
12

Floating ribs (11–12)

Posterior view

Head

Neck

Tubercle

Angle

Body

Rib

1
2
3
4
5
6
7
8
9
10
11
12

Clavicle

Acromion

Supraspinous fossa

Spine

Infraspinous fossa

Scapula

True ribs (1–7)

False ribs (8–12)

Floating ribs (11–12)

Nomenclature Notes

Pectus excavatum is a congenital abnormality of the sternum, in which the sternum is depressed.

Pectus carinatum is an abnormal prominence of the chest.

Scalenus anticus is a syndrome characterized by brachial neuritis, with or without vascular and/or vasomotor disturbance of the upper extremity. The scalenus muscles, located on each side of the neck and extending from the third through sixth cervical vertebrae to the first or second rib, are involved in the syndrome.

ANESTHESIA

Thorax (Chest Wall and Shoulder Girdle)

00450	Anesthesia for procedures on clavicle and scapula; not otherwise specified
00452	radical surgery
00454	biopsy of clavicle
00470	Anesthesia for partial rib resection; not otherwise specified
00472	thoracoplasty (any type)
00474	radical procedures (eg, pectus excavatum)

SURGERY

Musculoskeletal System

Neck (Soft Tissues) and Thorax
Incision

21510	Incision, deep, with opening of bone cortex (eg, for osteomyelitis or bone abscess), thorax

Excision

21600	Excision of rib, partial
21610	Costotransversectomy (separate procedure)
21615	Excision first and/or cervical rib;
21616	with sympathectomy
21620	Ostectomy of sternum, partial
21627	Sternal debridement
21630	Radical resection of sternum;

Repair, Revision, and/or Reconstruction

21700	Division of scalenus anticus; without resection of cervical rib
21705	with resection of cervical rib

21720	Division of sternocleidomastoid for torticollis, open operation; without cast application
21725	with cast application
21740	Reconstructive repair of pectus excavatum or carinatum; open
21742	minimally invasive approach (Nuss procedure), without thoracoscopy
21743	minimally invasive approach (Nuss procedure), with thoracoscopy
21750	Closure of median sternotomy separation with or without debridement (separate procedure)

Fracture and/or Dislocation

21800	Closed treatment of rib fracture, uncomplicated, each
21805	Open treatment of rib fracture without fixation, each
21810	Treatment of rib fracture requiring external fixation (flail chest)
21820	Closed treatment of sternum fracture
21825	Open treatment of sternum fracture with or without skeletal fixation

Shoulder
Excision

23200	Radical resection for tumor; clavicle
23210	scapula

Fracture and/or Dislocation

23500	Closed treatment of clavicular fracture; without manipulation
23505	with manipulation
23515	Open treatment of clavicular fracture, with or without internal or external fixation
23520	Closed treatment of sternoclavicular dislocation; without manipulation
23525	with manipulation
23530	Open treatment of sternoclavicular dislocation, acute or chronic;
23532	with fascial graft (includes obtaining graft)
23570	Closed treatment of scapular fracture; without manipulation
23575	with manipulation, with or without skeletal traction (with or without shoulder joint involvement)
23585	Open treatment of scapular fracture (body, glenoid or acromion) with or without internal fixation

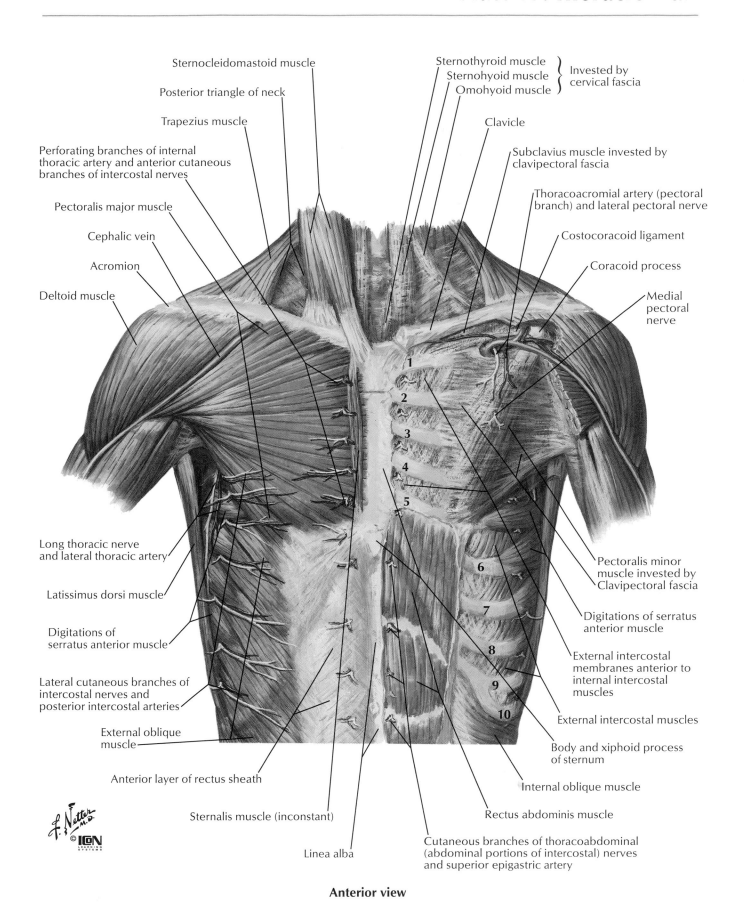

Sternocleidomastoid muscle

Posterior triangle of neck

Trapezius muscle

Perforating branches of internal thoracic artery and anterior cutaneous branches of intercostal nerves

Pectoralis major muscle

Cephalic vein

Acromion

Deltoid muscle

Sternothyroid muscle
Sternohyoid muscle
Omohyoid muscle
} Invested by cervical fascia

Clavicle

Subclavius muscle invested by clavipectoral fascia

Thoracoacromial artery (pectoral branch) and lateral pectoral nerve

Costocoracoid ligament

Coracoid process

Medial pectoral nerve

Long thoracic nerve and lateral thoracic artery

Latissimus dorsi muscle

Digitations of serratus anterior muscle

Lateral cutaneous branches of intercostal nerves and posterior intercostal arteries

External oblique muscle

Pectoralis minor muscle invested by Clavipectoral fascia

Digitations of serratus anterior muscle

External intercostal membranes anterior to internal intercostal muscles

External intercostal muscles

Body and xiphoid process of sternum

Internal oblique muscle

Rectus abdominis muscle

Sternalis muscle (inconstant)

Anterior layer of rectus sheath

Linea alba

Cutaneous branches of thoracoabdominal (abdominal portions of intercostal) nerves and superior epigastric artery

Anterior view

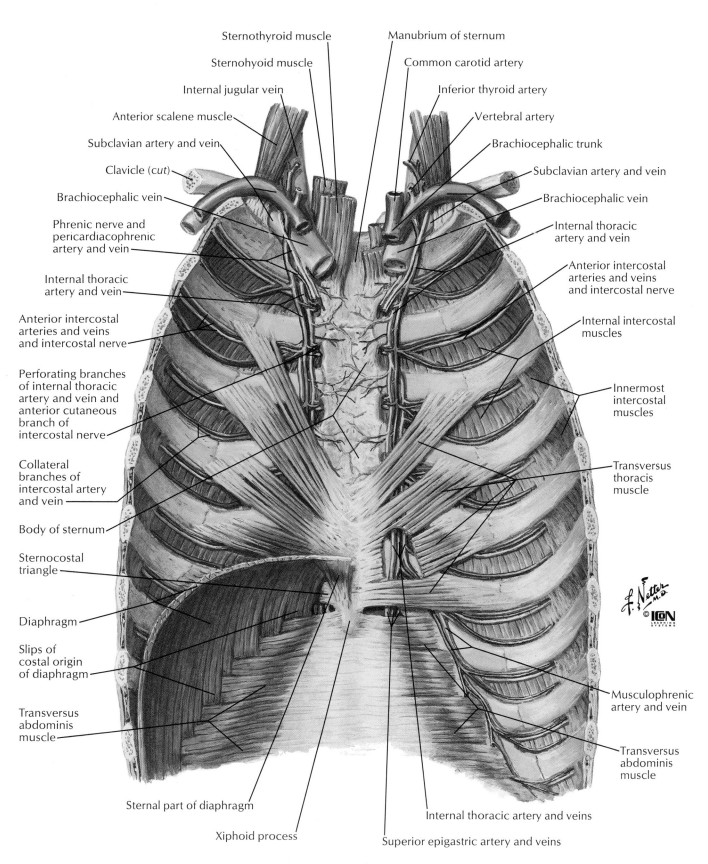

Sternothyroid muscle

Sternohyoid muscle

Internal jugular vein

Anterior scalene muscle

Subclavian artery and vein

Clavicle (*cut*)

Brachiocephalic vein

Phrenic nerve and pericardiacophrenic artery and vein

Internal thoracic artery and vein

Anterior intercostal arteries and veins and intercostal nerve

Perforating branches of internal thoracic artery and vein and anterior cutaneous branch of intercostal nerve

Collateral branches of intercostal artery and vein

Body of sternum

Sternocostal triangle

Diaphragm

Slips of costal origin of diaphragm

Transversus abdominis muscle

Sternal part of diaphragm

Xiphoid process

Manubrium of sternum

Common carotid artery

Inferior thyroid artery

Vertebral artery

Brachiocephalic trunk

Subclavian artery and vein

Brachiocephalic vein

Internal thoracic artery and vein

Anterior intercostal arteries and veins and intercostal nerve

Internal intercostal muscles

Innermost intercostal muscles

Transversus thoracis muscle

Musculophrenic artery and vein

Transversus abdominis muscle

Internal thoracic artery and veins

Superior epigastric artery and veins

Internal view

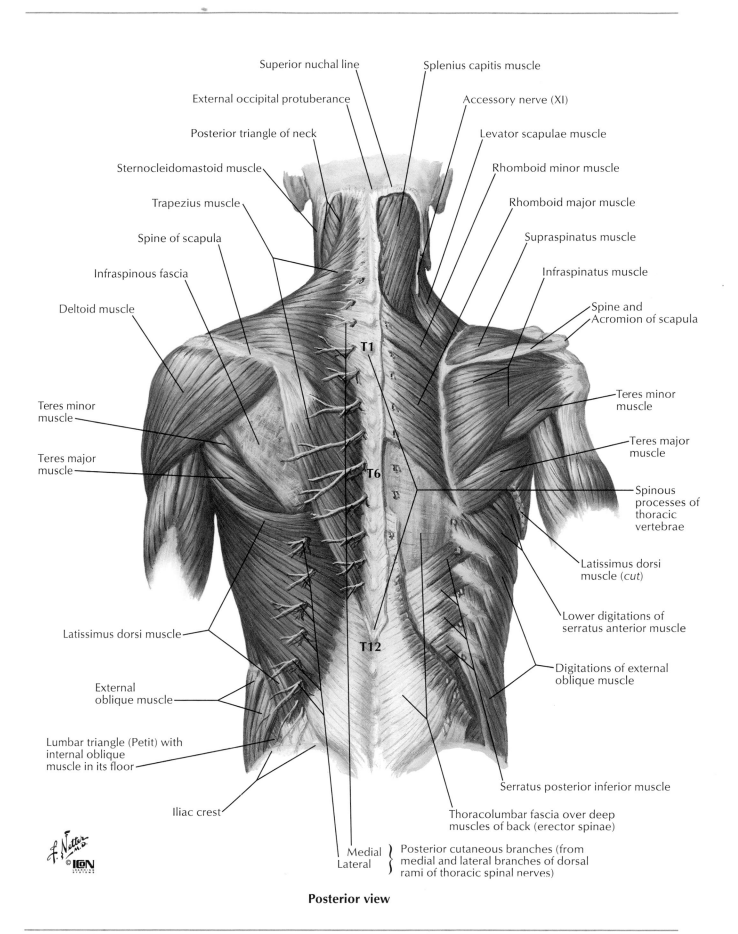

Superior nuchal line

External occipital protuberance

Posterior triangle of neck

Sternocleidomastoid muscle

Trapezius muscle

Spine of scapula

Infraspinous fascia

Deltoid muscle

Teres minor muscle

Teres major muscle

Latissimus dorsi muscle

External oblique muscle

Lumbar triangle (Petit) with internal oblique muscle in its floor

Iliac crest

Splenius capitis muscle

Accessory nerve (XI)

Levator scapulae muscle

Rhomboid minor muscle

Rhomboid major muscle

Supraspinatus muscle

Infraspinatus muscle

Spine and Acromion of scapula

Teres minor muscle

Teres major muscle

Spinous processes of thoracic vertebrae

Latissimus dorsi muscle (*cut*)

Lower digitations of serratus anterior muscle

Digitations of external oblique muscle

Serratus posterior inferior muscle

Thoracolumbar fascia over deep muscles of back (erector spinae)

T1

T6

T12

Medial
Lateral } Posterior cutaneous branches (from medial and lateral branches of dorsal rami of thoracic spinal nerves)

Posterior view

ANESTHESIA

Thorax (Chest Wall and Shoulder Girdle)

00400 Anesthesia for procedures on the integumentary system on the extremities, anterior trunk and perineum; not otherwise specified

00450 Anesthesia for procedures on clavicle and scapula; not otherwise specified

00452 Anesthesia for procedures on clavicle and scapula; radical surgery

00454 Anesthesia for procedures on clavicle and scapula; biopsy of clavicle

00472 Anesthesia for partial rib resection; thoracoplasty (any type)

00474 Anesthesia for partial rib resection; radical procedures (eg, pectus excavatum)

SURGERY

Integumentary System

Skin, Subcutaneous and Accessory Structures
Excision—Debridement

11040 Debridement; skin, partial thickness
11041 Debridement; skin, full thickness
11042 Debridement; skin, and subcutaneous tissue
11043 Debridement; skin, subcutaneous tissue, and muscle
11044 Debridement; skin, subcutaneous tissue, muscle, and bone

Breast
Excision

19260 Excision of chest wall tumor including ribs
19271 Excision of chest wall tumor involving ribs, with plastic reconstruction; without mediastinal lymphadenectomy

Musculoskeletal System

Neck (Soft Tissues) and Thorax
Incision

21501 Incision and drainage, deep abscess or hematoma, soft tissues of neck or thorax;
21502 with partial rib ostectomy
21510 Incision, deep, with opening of bone cortex (eg, for osteomyelitis or bone abscess), thorax

Excision

21550 Biopsy, soft tissue of neck or thorax
21555 Excision tumor, soft tissue of neck or thorax; subcutaneous
21556 deep, subfascial, intramuscular
21557 Radical resection of tumor (eg, malignant neoplasm), soft tissue of neck or thorax

Repair, Revision, and/or Reconstruction

21720 Division of sternocleidomastoid for torticollis, open operation; without cast application
21725 with cast application
21740 Reconstructive repair of pectus excavatum or carinatum; open
21742 minimally invasive approach (Nuss procedure), without thoracoscopy
21743 minimally invasive approach (Nuss procedure), with thoracoscopy

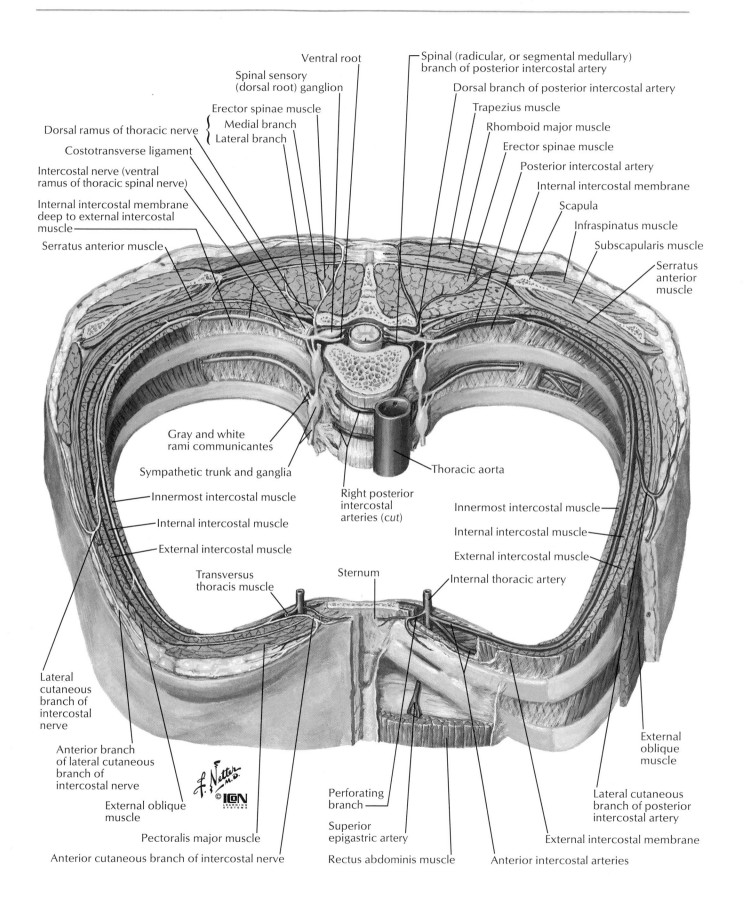

Ventral root

Spinal sensory (dorsal root) ganglion

Erector spinae muscle

Medial branch

Lateral branch

Dorsal ramus of thoracic nerve

Costotransverse ligament

Intercostal nerve (ventral ramus of thoracic spinal nerve)

Internal intercostal membrane deep to external intercostal muscle

Serratus anterior muscle

Spinal (radicular, or segmental medullary) branch of posterior intercostal artery

Dorsal branch of posterior intercostal artery

Trapezius muscle

Rhomboid major muscle

Erector spinae muscle

Posterior intercostal artery

Internal intercostal membrane

Scapula

Infraspinatus muscle

Subscapularis muscle

Serratus anterior muscle

Gray and white rami communicantes

Sympathetic trunk and ganglia

Innermost intercostal muscle

Internal intercostal muscle

External intercostal muscle

Right posterior intercostal arteries (cut)

Thoracic aorta

Innermost intercostal muscle

Internal intercostal muscle

External intercostal muscle

Internal thoracic artery

Transversus thoracis muscle

Sternum

Lateral cutaneous branch of intercostal nerve

Anterior branch of lateral cutaneous branch of intercostal nerve

External oblique muscle

Pectoralis major muscle

Anterior cutaneous branch of intercostal nerve

Perforating branch

Superior epigastric artery

Rectus abdominis muscle

Anterior intercostal arteries

External intercostal membrane

Lateral cutaneous branch of posterior intercostal artery

External oblique muscle

F. Netter M.D.

© ICON LEARNING SYSTEMS

Plate 70: Intercostal Nerves and Arteries

ANESTHESIA

Other Procedures

01991 Anesthesia for diagnostic or therapeutic nerve blocks and injections (when block or injection is performed by a different provider); other than the prone position

01992 prone position

SURGERY

Nervous System

Extracranial Nerves, Peripheral Nerves, and Autonomic Nervous System

Introduction/Injection of Anesthetic Agent (Nerve Block), Diagnostic or Therapeutic

Somatic Nerves

64420 Injection, anesthetic agent; intercostal nerve, single

64421 intercostal nerves, multiple, regional block

Destruction by Neurolytic Agent (eg, Chemical, Thermal, Electrical or Radiofrequency)

Somatic Nerves

64620 Destruction by neurolytic agent, intercostal nerve

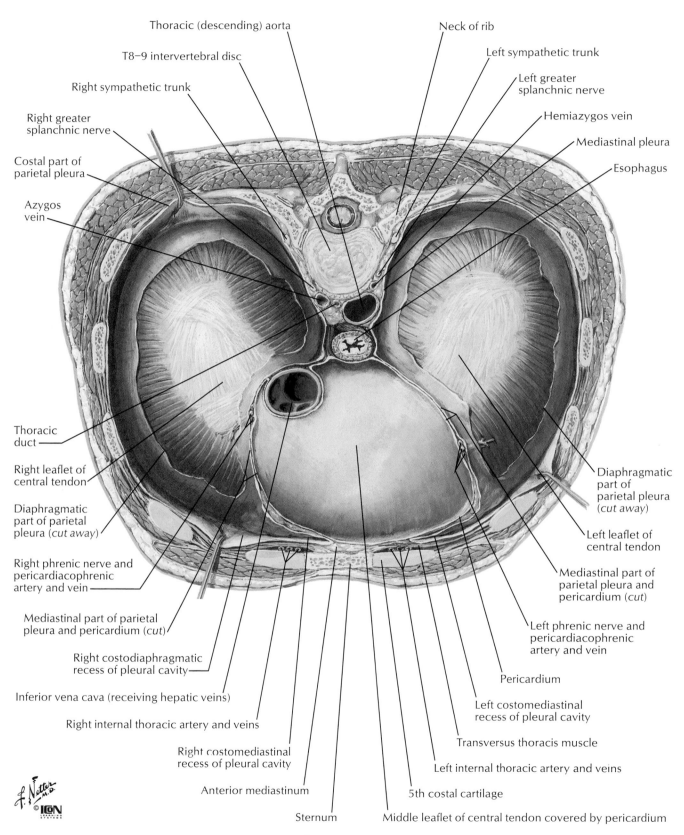

Thoracic (descending) aorta

T8–9 intervertebral disc

Right sympathetic trunk

Right greater splanchnic nerve

Costal part of parietal pleura

Azygos vein

Thoracic duct

Right leaflet of central tendon

Diaphragmatic part of parietal pleura (cut away)

Right phrenic nerve and pericardiacophrenic artery and vein

Mediastinal part of parietal pleura and pericardium (cut)

Right costodiaphragmatic recess of pleural cavity

Inferior vena cava (receiving hepatic veins)

Right internal thoracic artery and veins

Right costomediastinal recess of pleural cavity

Anterior mediastinum

Sternum

Neck of rib

Left sympathetic trunk

Left greater splanchnic nerve

Hemiazygos vein

Mediastinal pleura

Esophagus

Diaphragmatic part of parietal pleura (cut away)

Left leaflet of central tendon

Mediastinal part of parietal pleura and pericardium (cut)

Left phrenic nerve and pericardiacophrenic artery and vein

Pericardium

Left costomediastinal recess of pleural cavity

Transversus thoracis muscle

Left internal thoracic artery and veins

5th costal cartilage

Middle leaflet of central tendon covered by pericardium

Thoracic surface

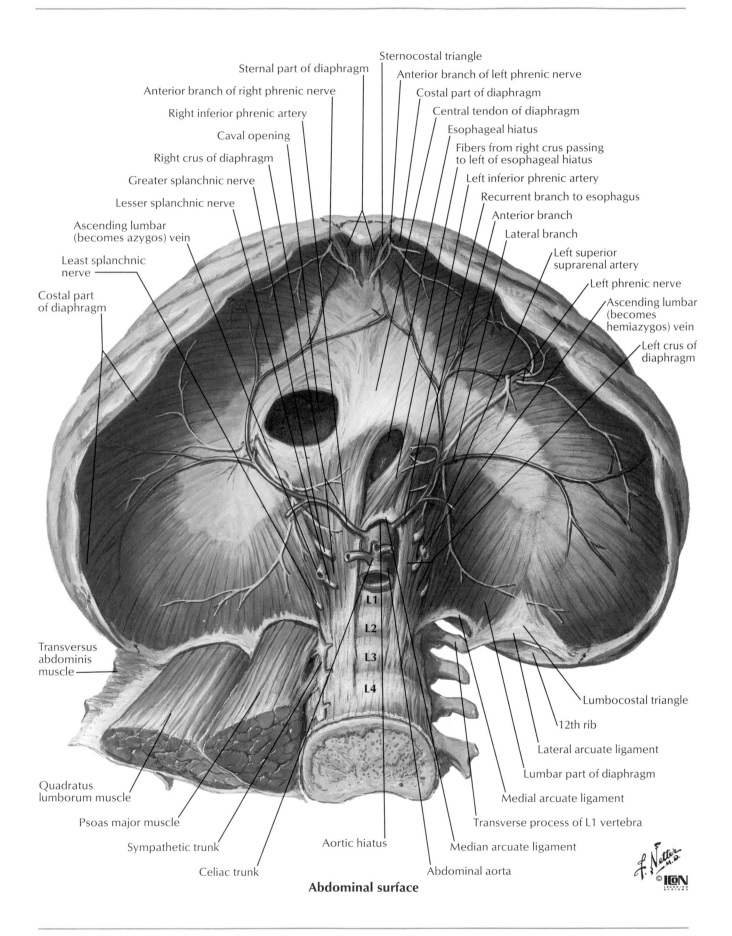

Sternocostal triangle

Sternal part of diaphragm

Anterior branch of left phrenic nerve

Anterior branch of right phrenic nerve

Costal part of diaphragm

Right inferior phrenic artery

Central tendon of diaphragm

Caval opening

Esophageal hiatus

Right crus of diaphragm

Fibers from right crus passing to left of esophageal hiatus

Greater splanchnic nerve

Left inferior phrenic artery

Lesser splanchnic nerve

Recurrent branch to esophagus

Ascending lumbar (becomes azygos) vein

Anterior branch

Lateral branch

Least splanchnic nerve

Left superior suprarenal artery

Costal part of diaphragm

Left phrenic nerve

Ascending lumbar (becomes hemiazygos) vein

Left crus of diaphragm

L1

L2

L3

L4

Transversus abdominis muscle

Lumbocostal triangle

12th rib

Lateral arcuate ligament

Quadratus lumborum muscle

Lumbar part of diaphragm

Psoas major muscle

Medial arcuate ligament

Sympathetic trunk

Transverse process of L1 vertebra

Celiac trunk

Aortic hiatus

Median arcuate ligament

Abdominal aorta

Abdominal surface

ANESTHESIA

Intrathoracic

00540   Anesthesia for thoracotomy procedures involving lungs, pleura, diaphragm, and mediastinum (including surgical thoracoscopy); not otherwise specified

SURGERY

Mediastinum and Diaphragm

Diaphragm
Repair

39501   Repair, laceration of diaphragm, any approach

39502   Repair, paraesophageal hiatus hernia, transabdominal, with or without fundoplasty, vagotomy, and/or pyloroplasty, except neonatal

39503   Repair, neonatal diaphragmatic hernia, with or without chest tube insertion and with or without creation of ventral hernia

39520   Repair, diaphragmatic hernia (esophageal hiatal); transthoracic

39530   combined, thoracoabdominal

39531   combined, thoracoabdominal, with dilation of stricture (with or without gastroplasty)

39540   Repair, diaphragmatic hernia (other than neonatal), traumatic; acute

39541   chronic

39545   Imbrication of diaphragm for eventration, transthoracic or transabdominal, paralytic or nonparalytic

39560   Resection, diaphragm; with simple repair (eg, primary suture)

39561   with complex repair (eg, prosthetic material, local muscle flap)

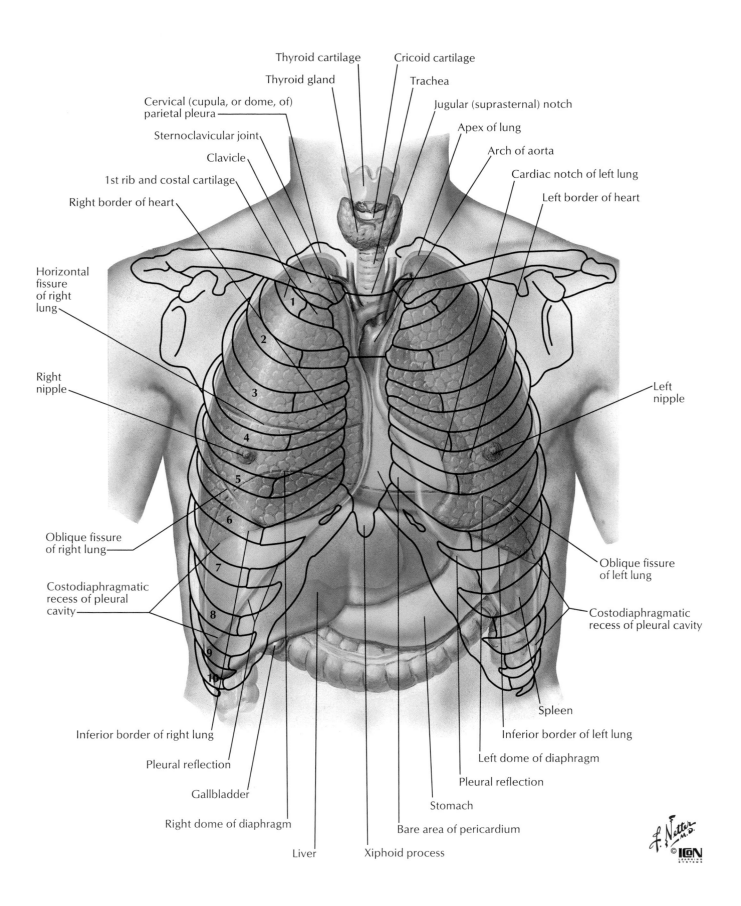

Thyroid cartilage

Cricoid cartilage

Thyroid gland

Trachea

Cervical (cupula, or dome, of) parietal pleura

Jugular (suprasternal) notch

Sternoclavicular joint

Apex of lung

Clavicle

Arch of aorta

1st rib and costal cartilage

Cardiac notch of left lung

Right border of heart

Left border of heart

Horizontal fissure of right lung

Right nipple

Left nipple

Oblique fissure of right lung

Oblique fissure of left lung

Costodiaphragmatic recess of pleural cavity

Costodiaphragmatic recess of pleural cavity

Spleen

Inferior border of right lung

Inferior border of left lung

Pleural reflection

Left dome of diaphragm

Gallbladder

Pleural reflection

Right dome of diaphragm

Stomach

Liver

Xiphoid process

Bare area of pericardium

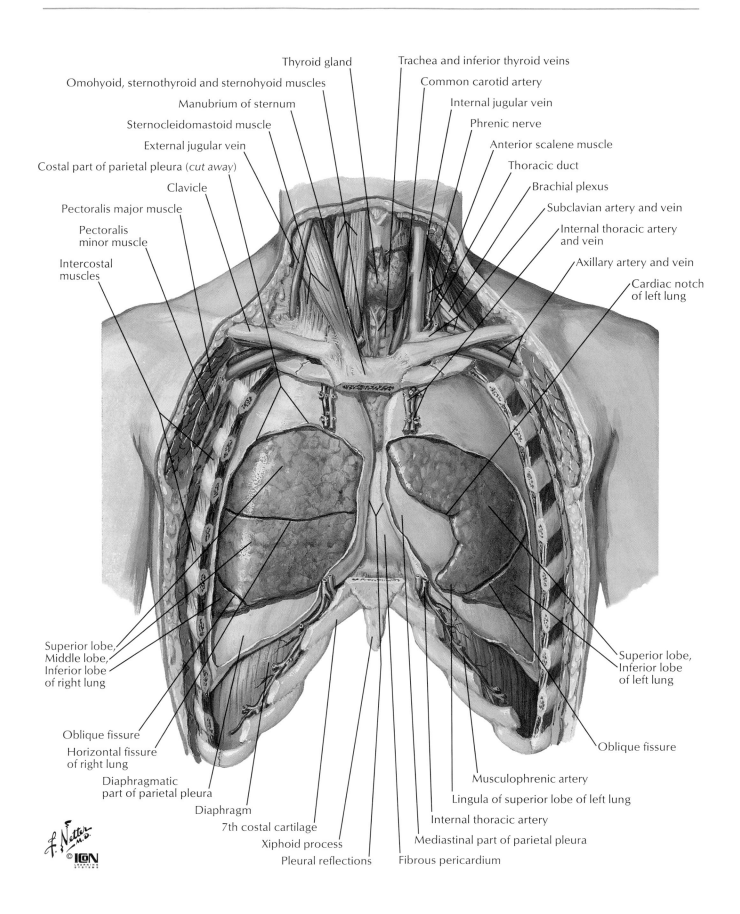

Thyroid gland

Trachea and inferior thyroid veins

Omohyoid, sternothyroid and sternohyoid muscles

Common carotid artery

Manubrium of sternum

Internal jugular vein

Sternocleidomastoid muscle

Phrenic nerve

External jugular vein

Anterior scalene muscle

Costal part of parietal pleura (*cut away*)

Thoracic duct

Clavicle

Brachial plexus

Pectoralis major muscle

Subclavian artery and vein

Pectoralis minor muscle

Internal thoracic artery and vein

Intercostal muscles

Axillary artery and vein

Cardiac notch of left lung

Superior lobe, Middle lobe, Inferior lobe of right lung

Superior lobe, Inferior lobe of left lung

Oblique fissure

Oblique fissure

Horizontal fissure of right lung

Diaphragmatic part of parietal pleura

Musculophrenic artery

Diaphragm

Lingula of superior lobe of left lung

7th costal cartilage

Internal thoracic artery

Xiphoid process

Mediastinal part of parietal pleura

Pleural reflections

Fibrous pericardium

F. Netter M.D.
© ICON
LEARNING SYSTEMS

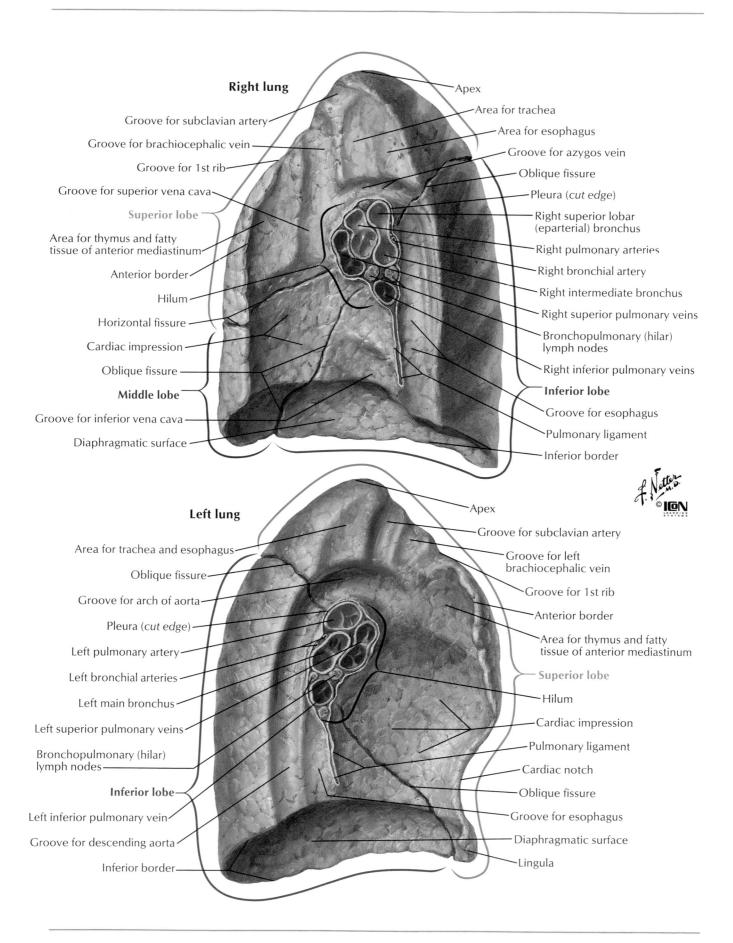

Right lung

Groove for subclavian artery

Groove for brachiocephalic vein

Groove for 1st rib

Groove for superior vena cava

Superior lobe

Area for thymus and fatty tissue of anterior mediastinum

Anterior border

Hilum

Horizontal fissure

Cardiac impression

Oblique fissure

Middle lobe

Groove for inferior vena cava

Diaphragmatic surface

Apex

Area for trachea

Area for esophagus

Groove for azygos vein

Oblique fissure

Pleura (*cut edge*)

Right superior lobar (eparterial) bronchus

Right pulmonary arteries

Right bronchial artery

Right intermediate bronchus

Right superior pulmonary veins

Bronchopulmonary (hilar) lymph nodes

Right inferior pulmonary veins

Inferior lobe

Groove for esophagus

Pulmonary ligament

Inferior border

Left lung

Area for trachea and esophagus

Oblique fissure

Groove for arch of aorta

Pleura (*cut edge*)

Left pulmonary artery

Left bronchial arteries

Left main bronchus

Left superior pulmonary veins

Bronchopulmonary (hilar) lymph nodes

Inferior lobe

Left inferior pulmonary vein

Groove for descending aorta

Inferior border

Apex

Groove for subclavian artery

Groove for left brachiocephalic vein

Groove for 1st rib

Anterior border

Area for thymus and fatty tissue of anterior mediastinum

Superior lobe

Hilum

Cardiac impression

Pulmonary ligament

Cardiac notch

Oblique fissure

Groove for esophagus

Diaphragmatic surface

Lingula

ANESTHESIA

Intrathoracic

00540 Anesthesia for thoracotomy procedures involving lungs, pleura, diaphragm, and mediastinum (including surgical thoracoscopy); not otherwise specified

00541 utilizing one lung ventilation

00542 decortication

00546 pulmonary resection with thoracoplasty

00548 intrathoracic procedures on the trachea and bronchi

SURGERY

Respiratory System

Lungs and Pleura
Incision

32000[P] Thoracentesis, puncture of pleural cavity for aspiration, initial or subsequent

32002 Thoracentesis with insertion of tube with or without water seal (eg, for pneumothorax) (separate procedure)

32005 Chemical pleurodesis (eg, for recurrent or persistent pneumothorax)

32019 Insertion of indwelling tunneled pleural catheter with cuff

32020[P] Tube thoracostomy with or without water seal (eg, for abscess, hemothorax, empyema) (separate procedure)

32035 Thoracostomy; with rib resection for empyema

32036 with open flap drainage for empyema

32095 Thoracotomy, limited, for biopsy of lung or pleura

32100 Thoracotomy, major; with exploration and biopsy

32110 with control of traumatic hemorrhage and/or repair of lung tear

32120 for postoperative complications

32124 with open intrapleural pneumonolysis

32140 with cyst(s) removal, with or without a pleural procedure

32141 with excision-plication of bullae, with or without any pleural procedure

32150 with removal of intrapleural foreign body or fibrin deposit

32151 with removal of intrapulmonary foreign body

32160 with cardiac massage

32200 Pneumonostomy; with open drainage of abscess or cyst

32201 with percutaneous drainage of abscess or cyst

32215 Pleural scarification for repeat pneumothorax

32220 Decortication, pulmonary (separate procedure); total

32225 partial

Excision

32310 Pleurectomy, parietal (separate procedure)

32320 Decortication and parietal pleurectomy

32400 Biopsy, pleura; percutaneous needle

32402 open

32405 Biopsy, lung or mediastinum, percutaneous needle

32420 Pneumocentesis, puncture of lung for aspiration

32440 Removal of lung, total pneumonectomy;

32442 with resection of segment of trachea followed by broncho-tracheal anastomosis (sleeve pneumonectomy)

32445 extrapleural

32480 Removal of lung, other than total pneumonectomy; single lobe (lobectomy)

32482 two lobes (bilobectomy)

32484 single segment (segmentectomy)

32486 with circumferential resection of segment of bronchus followed by broncho-bronchial anastomosis (sleeve lobectomy)

32488 all remaining lung following previous removal of a portion of lung (completion pneumonectomy)

32491 excision-plication of emphysematous lung(s) (bullous or non-bullous) for lung volume reduction, sternal split or transthoracic approach, with or without any pleural procedure

32500 wedge resection, single or multiple

32501 Resection and repair of portion of bronchus (bronchoplasty) when performed at time of lobectomy or segmentectomy (List separately in addition to code for primary procedure)

32520 Resection of lung; with resection of chest wall

32522 with reconstruction of chest wall, without prosthesis

32525 with major reconstruction of chest wall, with prosthesis

32540 Extrapleural enucleation of empyema (empyemectomy)

Endoscopy

32601[P] Thoracoscopy, diagnostic (separate procedure); lungs and pleural space, without biopsy

32602 lungs and pleural space, with biopsy

32603 pericardial sac, without biopsy

32604 pericardial sac, with biopsy

32605 mediastinal space, without biopsy

32606 mediastinal space, with biopsy

32650 Thoracoscopy, surgical; with pleurodesis (eg, mechanical or chemical)

32651 with partial pulmonary decortication

32652 with total pulmonary decortication, including intrapleural pneumonolysis

32653 with removal of intrapleural foreign body or fibrin deposit

32654 with control of traumatic hemorrhage

32655 with excision-plication of bullae, including any pleural procedure

32656 with parietal pleurectomy

32657 with wedge resection of lung, single or multiple

32663 with lobectomy, total or segmental

32664 with thoracic sympathectomy

32665 with esophagomyotomy (Heller type)

Lung Transplantation

32850	Donor pneumonectomy (including cold preservation), from cadaver donor
32851	Lung transplant, single; without cardiopulmonary bypass
32852	with cardiopulmonary bypass
32853	Lung transplant, double (bilateral sequential or en bloc); without cardiopulmonary bypass
32854	with cardiopulmonary bypass
32855	Backbench standard preparation of cadaver donor lung allograft prior to transplantation, including dissection of allograft from surrounding soft tissues to prepare pulmonary venous/atrial cuff, pulmonary artery, and bronchus; unilateral
32856	bilateral

Surgical Collapse Therapy; Thoracoplasty

32900	Resection of ribs, extrapleural, all stages
32905	Thoracoplasty, Schede type or extrapleural (all stages);
32906	with closure of bronchopleural fistula
32940	Pneumonolysis, extraperiosteal, including filling or packing procedures
32960	Pneumothorax, therapeutic, intrapleural injection of air

Other Procedures

32997	Total lung lavage (unilateral)

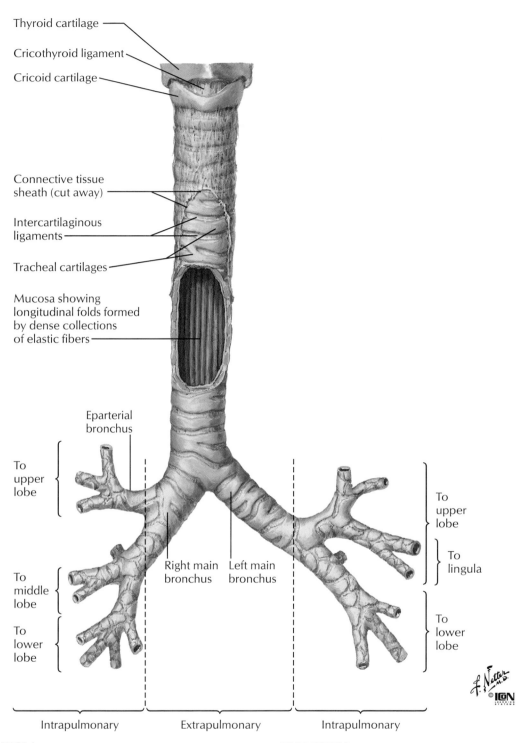

Thyroid cartilage

Cricothyroid ligament

Cricoid cartilage

Connective tissue
sheath (cut away)

Intercartilaginous
ligaments

Tracheal cartilages

Mucosa showing
longitudinal folds formed
by dense collections
of elastic fibers

Eparterial
bronchus

To
upper
lobe

To
middle
lobe

To
lower
lobe

Right main
bronchus

Left main
bronchus

To
upper
lobe

To
lingula

To
lower
lobe

Intrapulmonary

Extrapulmonary

Intrapulmonary

ANESTHESIA

Neck

00320   Anesthesia for all procedures on esophagus, thyroid, larynx, trachea and lymphatic system of neck; not otherwise specified, age 1 year or older

00322   needle biopsy of thyroid

00326   Anesthesia for all procedures on the larynx and trachea in children less than 1 year of age

SURGERY

Respiratory System

Trachea and Bronchi
Incision

31600   Tracheostomy, planned (separate procedure);

(Incision continued on next page)

(Incision continued from previous page)

31601   under two years

31603   Tracheostomy, emergency procedure; transtracheal
31605   cricothyroid membrane

31610   Tracheostomy, fenestration procedure with skin flaps

31611   Construction of tracheoesophageal fistula and subsequent insertion of an alaryngeal speech prosthesis (eg, voice button, Blom-Singer prosthesis)

31612   Tracheal puncture, percutaneous with transtracheal aspiration and/or injection

31613   Tracheostoma revision; simple, without flap rotation

31614   complex, with flap rotation

Endoscopy

31615   Tracheobronchoscopy through established tracheostomy incision

31620   Endobronchial ultrasound (EBUS) during bronchoscopic diagnostic or therapeutic intervention(s) (List separately in addition to code for primary procedure(s))

31622[P]   Bronchoscopy, rigid or flexible, with or without fluoroscopic guidance; diagnostic, with or without cell washing (separate procedure)

31623   with brushing or protected brushings
31624   with bronchial alveolar lavage
31625   with bronchial or endobronchial biopsy(s), single or multiple sites

31628   with transbronchial lung biopsy(s), single lobe
31629   with transbronchial needle aspiration biopsy(s), trachea, main stem and/or lobar bronchus(i)

31630   with tracheal/bronchial dilation or closed reduction of fracture

31631   with placement of tracheal stent(s) (includes tracheal/bronchial dilation as required)

31632   with transbronchial lung biopsy(s), each additional lobe (List separately in addition to code for primary procedure)

31633   with transbronchial needle aspiration biopsy(s), each additional lobe (List separately in addition to code for primary procedure)

31635   with removal of foreign body

31636   with placement of bronchial stent(s) (includes tracheal/bronchial dilation as required), initial bronchus

31637   each additional major bronchus stented (List separately in addition to code for primary procedure)

31638   with revision of tracheal or bronchial stent inserted at previous session (includes tracheal/bronchial dilation as required)

31640   with excision of tumor

31641   Bronchoscopy, (rigid or flexible); with destruction of tumor or relief of stenosis by any method other than excision (eg, laser therapy, cryotherapy)

31643   with placement of catheter(s) for intracavitary radioelement application

31645   with therapeutic aspiration of tracheobronchial tree, initial (eg, drainage of lung abscess)

31646   with therapeutic aspiration of tracheobronchial tree, subsequent

31656   with injection of contrast material for segmental bronchography (fiberscope only)

Introduction

31700   Catheterization, transglottic (separate procedure)
31708   Instillation of contrast material for laryngography or bronchography, without catheterization
31710   Catheterization for bronchography, with or without instillation of contrast material
31715   Transtracheal injection for bronchography
31717   Catheterization with bronchial brush biopsy
31720   Catheter aspiration (separate procedure); nasotracheal
31725   tracheobronchial with fiberscope, bedside
31730   Transtracheal (percutaneous) introduction of needle wire dilator/stent or indwelling tube for oxygen therapy

Repair

31750   Tracheoplasty; cervical
31755   tracheopharyngeal fistulization, each stage
31760   intrathoracic
31766   Carinal reconstruction
31770   Bronchoplasty; graft repair
31775   excision stenosis and anastomosis
31780   Excision tracheal stenosis and anastomosis; cervical
31781   cervicothoracic
31785   Excision of tracheal tumor or carcinoma; cervical
31786   thoracic
31800   Suture of tracheal wound or injury; cervical
31805   intrathoracic
31820   Surgical closure tracheostomy or fistula; without plastic repair
31825   with plastic repair
31830   Revision of tracheostomy scar

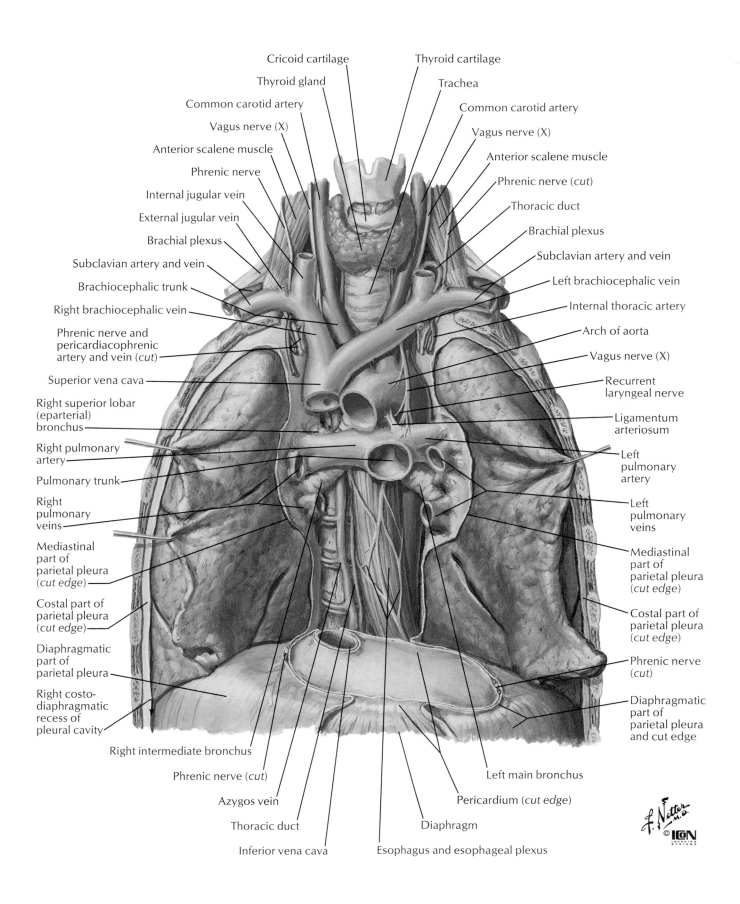

Cricoid cartilage

Thyroid cartilage

Thyroid gland

Trachea

Common carotid artery

Common carotid artery

Vagus nerve (X)

Vagus nerve (X)

Anterior scalene muscle

Anterior scalene muscle

Phrenic nerve

Phrenic nerve (*cut*)

Internal jugular vein

Thoracic duct

External jugular vein

Brachial plexus

Brachial plexus

Subclavian artery and vein

Subclavian artery and vein

Brachiocephalic trunk

Left brachiocephalic vein

Right brachiocephalic vein

Internal thoracic artery

Phrenic nerve and pericardiacophrenic artery and vein (*cut*)

Arch of aorta

Vagus nerve (X)

Superior vena cava

Recurrent laryngeal nerve

Right superior lobar (eparterial) bronchus

Ligamentum arteriosum

Right pulmonary artery

Left pulmonary artery

Pulmonary trunk

Right pulmonary veins

Left pulmonary veins

Mediastinal part of parietal pleura (*cut edge*)

Mediastinal part of parietal pleura (*cut edge*)

Costal part of parietal pleura (*cut edge*)

Costal part of parietal pleura (*cut edge*)

Diaphragmatic part of parietal pleura

Phrenic nerve (*cut*)

Right costo-diaphragmatic recess of pleural cavity

Diaphragmatic part of parietal pleura and cut edge

Right intermediate bronchus

Phrenic nerve (*cut*)

Left main bronchus

Azygos vein

Pericardium (*cut edge*)

Thoracic duct

Diaphragm

Inferior vena cava

Esophagus and esophageal plexus

Nomenclature Notes

The *great vessels* are five blood vessels located above the aortic arch. These include the right and left brachiocephalic veins, the left common carotid artery, the right brachiocephalic artery, and the left subclavian artery.

ANESTHESIA

Intrathoracic

00560	Anesthesia for procedures on heart, pericardial sac, and great vessels of chest; without pump oxygenator
00561	with pump oxygenator, under one year of age
00562	with pump oxygenator
00563	with pump oxygenator with hypothermic circulatory arrest

SURGERY

Cardiovascular System

Heart and Pericardium
Wounds of the Heart and Great Vessels

33320	Suture repair of aorta or great vessels; without shunt or cardiopulmonary bypass
33321	with shunt bypass
33322	with cardiopulmonary bypass
33330	Insertion of graft, aorta or great vessels; without shunt, or cardiopulmonary bypass
33332	with shunt bypass
33335	with cardiopulmonary bypass

Shunting Procedures

33750	Shunt; subclavian to pulmonary artery (Blalock-Taussig type operation)
33755	ascending aorta to pulmonary artery (Waterston type operation)
33762	descending aorta to pulmonary artery (Potts-Smith type operation)
33764	central, with prosthetic graft
33766	superior vena cava to pulmonary artery for flow to one lung (classical Glenn procedure)
33767	superior vena cava to pulmonary artery for flow to both lungs (bidirectional Glenn procedure)

Transposition of the Great Vessels

33770	Repair of transposition of the great arteries with ventricular septal defect and subpulmonary stenosis; without surgical enlargement of ventricular septal defect
33771	with surgical enlargement of ventricular septal defect
33774	Repair of transposition of the great arteries, atrial baffle procedure (eg, Mustard or Senning type) with cardiopulmonary bypass;
33775	with removal of pulmonary band
33776	with closure of ventricular septal defect
33777	with repair of subpulmonic obstruction
33778	Repair of transposition of the great arteries, aortic pulmonary artery reconstruction (eg, Jatene type);
33779	with removal of pulmonary band
33780	with closure of ventricular septal defect
33781	with repair of subpulmonic obstruction

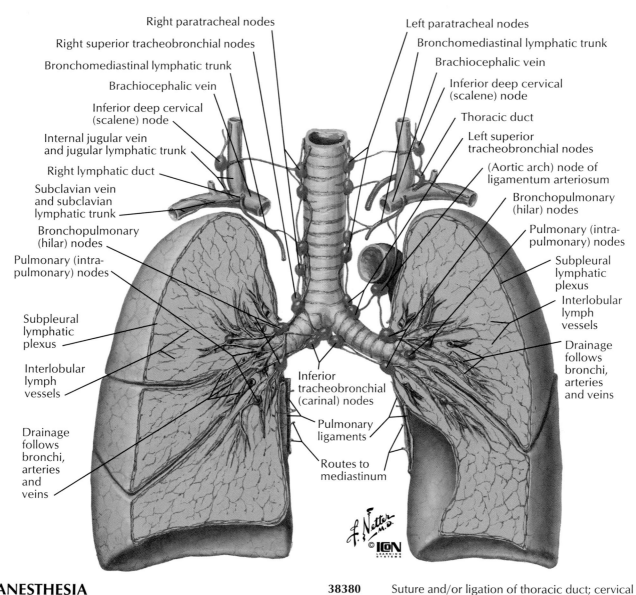

Right paratracheal nodes

Right superior tracheobronchial nodes

Bronchomediastinal lymphatic trunk

Brachiocephalic vein

Inferior deep cervical (scalene) node

Internal jugular vein and jugular lymphatic trunk

Right lymphatic duct

Subclavian vein and subclavian lymphatic trunk

Bronchopulmonary (hilar) nodes

Pulmonary (intra-pulmonary) nodes

Subpleural lymphatic plexus

Interlobular lymph vessels

Drainage follows bronchi, arteries and veins

Left paratracheal nodes

Bronchomediastinal lymphatic trunk

Brachiocephalic vein

Inferior deep cervical (scalene) node

Thoracic duct

Left superior tracheobronchial nodes

(Aortic arch) node of ligamentum arteriosum

Bronchopulmonary (hilar) nodes

Pulmonary (intra-pulmonary) nodes

Subpleural lymphatic plexus

Interlobular lymph vessels

Drainage follows bronchi, arteries and veins

Inferior tracheobronchial (carinal) nodes

Pulmonary ligaments

Routes to mediastinum

ANESTHESIA

Intrathoracic

00540	Anesthesia for thoracotomy procedures involving lungs, pleura, diaphragm, and mediastinum (including surgical thoracoscopy); not otherwise specified
00541	utilizing one lung ventilation
00546	pulmonary resection with thoracoplasty

SURGERY

Hemic and Lymphatic Systems

Lymph Nodes and Lymphatic Channels
Incision

38300	Drainage of lymph node abscess or lymphadenitis; simple
38305	extensive
38308	Lymphangiotomy or other operations on lymphatic channels

38380	Suture and/or ligation of thoracic duct; cervical approach
38381	thoracic approach
38382	abdominal approach

Excision

38510	Biopsy or excision of lymph node(s); open, deep cervical node(s)
38520	open, deep cervical node(s) with excision scalene fat pad

Radical Lymphadenectomy (Radical Resection of Lymph Nodes)

38746	Thoracic lymphadenectomy, regional, including mediastinal and peritracheal nodes (List separately in addition to code for primary procedure)

Introduction

38792	Injection procedure; for identification of sentinel node
38794	Cannulation, thoracic duct

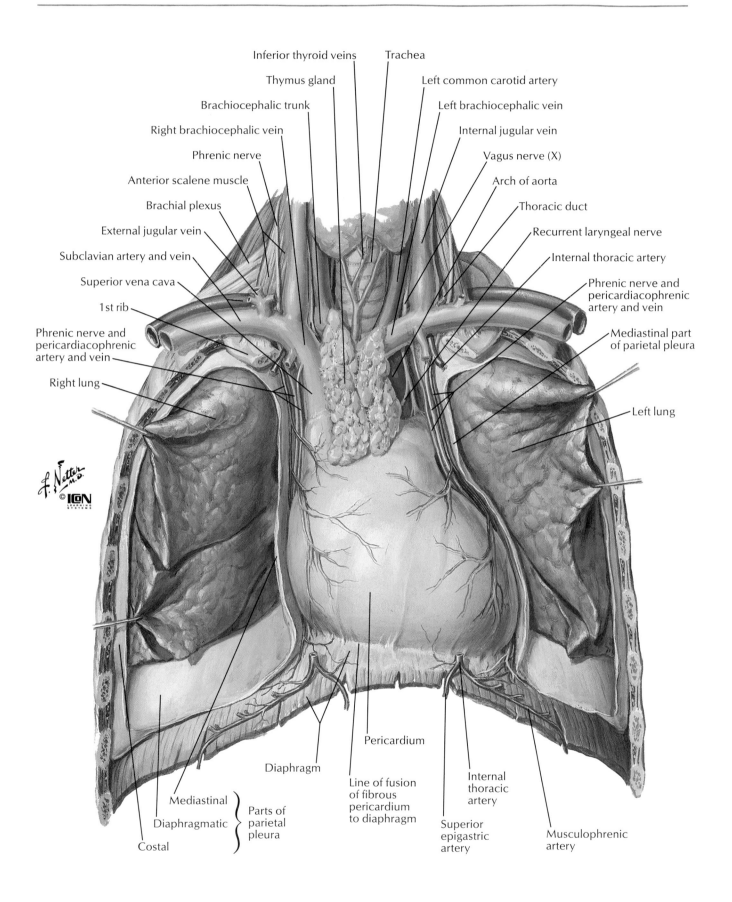

Inferior thyroid veins

Thymus gland

Brachiocephalic trunk

Right brachiocephalic vein

Phrenic nerve

Anterior scalene muscle

Brachial plexus

External jugular vein

Subclavian artery and vein

Superior vena cava

1st rib

Phrenic nerve and pericardiacophrenic artery and vein

Right lung

Trachea

Left common carotid artery

Left brachiocephalic vein

Internal jugular vein

Vagus nerve (X)

Arch of aorta

Thoracic duct

Recurrent laryngeal nerve

Internal thoracic artery

Phrenic nerve and pericardiacophrenic artery and vein

Mediastinal part of parietal pleura

Left lung

Pericardium

Diaphragm

Line of fusion of fibrous pericardium to diaphragm

Internal thoracic artery

Superior epigastric artery

Musculophrenic artery

Mediastinal
Diaphragmatic } Parts of parietal pleura
Costal

ANESTHESIA

Intrathoracic

00560 Anesthesia for procedures on heart, pericardial sac, and great vessels of chest; without pump oxygenator

00561 with pump oxygenator, under one year of age

00562 with pump oxygenator

00563 with pump oxygenator with hypothermic circulatory arrest

00566 Anesthesia for direct coronary artery bypass grafting without pump oxygenator

00580 Anesthesia for heart transplant or heart/lung transplant

SURGERY

Cardiovascular System

Heart and Pericardium
Pericardium

33010 Pericardiocentesis; initial

33011 subsequent

33015 Tube pericardiostomy

33020 Pericardiotomy for removal of clot or foreign body (primary procedure)

33025 Creation of pericardial window or partial resection for drainage

33030 Pericardiectomy, subtotal or complete; without cardiopulmonary bypass

33031 with cardiopulmonary bypass

33050 Excision of pericardial cyst or tumor

Cardiac Tumor

33130 Resection of external cardiac tumor

Heart/Lung Transplantation

33945 Heart transplant, with or without recipient cardiectomy

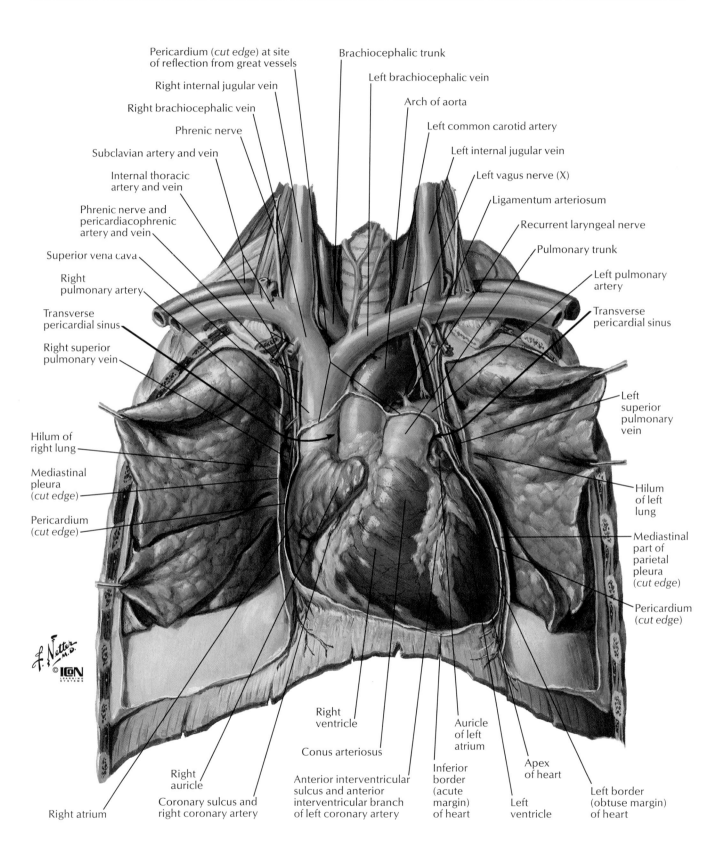

Pericardium (*cut edge*) at site of reflection from great vessels

Right internal jugular vein

Right brachiocephalic vein

Phrenic nerve

Subclavian artery and vein

Internal thoracic artery and vein

Phrenic nerve and pericardiacophrenic artery and vein

Superior vena cava

Right pulmonary artery

Transverse pericardial sinus

Right superior pulmonary vein

Hilum of right lung

Mediastinal pleura (*cut edge*)

Pericardium (*cut edge*)

Brachiocephalic trunk

Left brachiocephalic vein

Arch of aorta

Left common carotid artery

Left internal jugular vein

Left vagus nerve (X)

Ligamentum arteriosum

Recurrent laryngeal nerve

Pulmonary trunk

Left pulmonary artery

Transverse pericardial sinus

Left superior pulmonary vein

Hilum of left lung

Mediastinal part of parietal pleura (*cut edge*)

Pericardium (*cut edge*)

Right ventricle

Conus arteriosus

Right atrium

Right auricle

Coronary sulcus and right coronary artery

Anterior interventricular sulcus and anterior interventricular branch of left coronary artery

Auricle of left atrium

Inferior border (acute margin) of heart

Left ventricle

Apex of heart

Left border (obtuse margin) of heart

ANESTHESIA

Intrathoracic

00560 Anesthesia for procedures on heart, pericardial sac, and great vessels of chest; without pump oxygenator
00561 with pump oxygenator, under one year of age
00562 with pump oxygenator
00563 with pump oxygenator with hypothermic circulatory arrest

SURGERY

Cardiovascular System

Heart and Pericardium
Pacemaker or Pacing Cardioverter-Defibrillator

33200 Insertion of permanent pacemaker with epicardial electrode(s); by thoracotomy
33201 by xiphoid approach
33206 Insertion or replacement of permanent pacemaker with transvenous electrode(s); atrial
33207 ventricular
33208 atrial and ventricular
33210[P] Insertion or replacement of temporary transvenous single chamber cardiac electrode or pacemaker catheter (separate procedure)
33211 Insertion or replacement of temporary transvenous dual chamber pacing electrodes (separate procedure)
33212[P] Insertion or replacement of pacemaker pulse generator only; single chamber, atrial or ventricular
33213 dual chamber
33214 Upgrade of implanted pacemaker system, conversion of single chamber system to dual chamber system (includes removal of previously placed pulse generator, testing of existing lead, insertion of new lead, insertion of new pulse generator)
33215 Repositioning of previously implanted transvenous pacemaker or pacing cardioverter-defibrillator (right atrial or right ventricular) electrode
33216 Insertion of a transvenous electrode; single chamber (one electrode) permanent pacemaker or single chamber pacing cardioverter-defibrillator
33217 dual chamber (two electrodes) permanent pacemaker or dual chamber pacing cardioverter-defibrillator
33218 Repair of single transvenous electrode for a single chamber, permanent pacemaker or single chamber pacing cardioverter-defibrillator
33220 Repair of two transvenous electrodes for a dual chamber permanent pacemaker or dual chamber pacing cardioverter-defibrillator
33222 Revision or relocation of skin pocket for pacemaker
33223 Revision of skin pocket for single or dual chamber pacing cardioverter-defibrillator

33224[P] Insertion of pacing electrode, cardiac venous system, for left ventricular pacing, with attachment to previously placed pacemaker or pacing cardioverter-defibrillator pulse generator (including revision of pocket, removal, insertion and/or replacement of generator)
33225 Insertion of pacing electrode, cardiac venous system, for left ventricular pacing, at time of insertion of pacing cardioverter-defibrillator or pacemaker pulse generator (including upgrade to dual chamber system) (List separately in addition to code for primary procedure)
33226 Repositioning of previously implanted cardiac venous system (left ventricular) electrode (including removal, insertion and/or replacement of generator)
33233 Removal of permanent pacemaker pulse generator
33234 Removal of transvenous pacemaker electrode(s); single lead system, atrial or ventricular
33235 dual lead system
33236 Removal of permanent epicardial pacemaker and electrodes by thoracotomy; single lead system, atrial or ventricular
33237 dual lead system
33238 Removal of permanent transvenous electrode(s) by thoracotomy
33240 Insertion of single or dual chamber pacing cardioverter-defibrillator pulse generator
33241 Subcutaneous removal of single or dual chamber pacing cardioverter-defibrillator pulse generator
33243 Removal of single or dual chamber pacing cardioverter-defibrillator electrode(s); by thoracotomy
33244 by transvenous extraction
33245 Insertion of epicardial single or dual chamber pacing cardioverter-defibrillator electrodes by thoracotomy;
33246 with insertion of pulse generator
33249 Insertion or repositioning of electrode lead(s) for single or dual chamber pacing cardioverter-defibrillator and insertion of pulse generator

Wounds of the Heart and Great Vessels

33300 Repair of cardiac wound; without bypass
33305 with cardiopulmonary bypass
33310 Cardiotomy, exploratory (includes removal of foreign body, atrial or ventricular thrombus); without bypass
33315 with cardiopulmonary bypass
33320 Suture repair of aorta or great vessels; without shunt or cardiopulmonary bypass
33321 with shunt bypass
33322 with cardiopulmonary bypass
33330 Insertion of graft, aorta or great vessels; without shunt, or cardiopulmonary bypass
33332 with shunt bypass
33335 with cardiopulmonary bypass

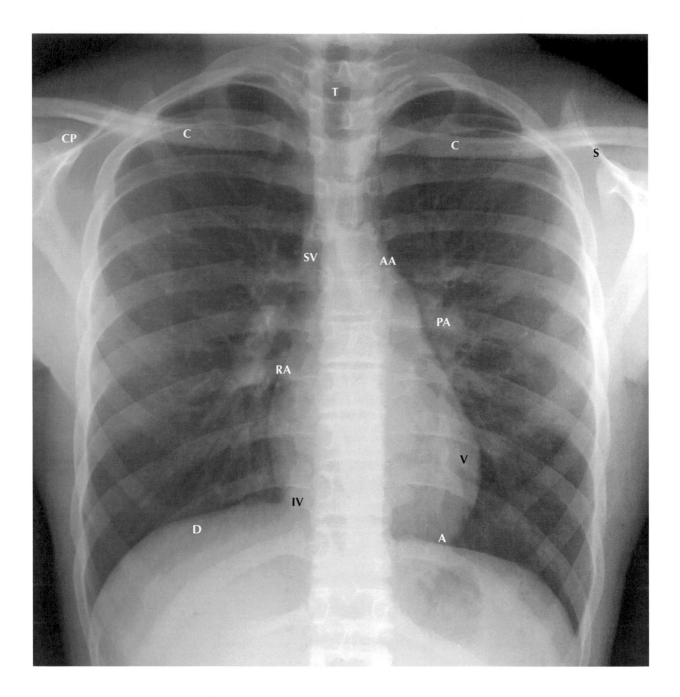

A	Apex of heart	PA	Pulmonary artery (left)
AA	Aortic arch	RA	Right atrium
C	Clavicle	S	Spine of scapula
CP	Coracoid process of scapula	SV	Superior vena cava
D	Dome of diaphragm (right)	T	Trachea (air)
IV	Inferior vena cava	V	Left ventricle

RADIOLOGY

Diagnostic Radiology (Diagnostic Imaging)

Chest
71010   Radiologic examination, chest; single view, frontal

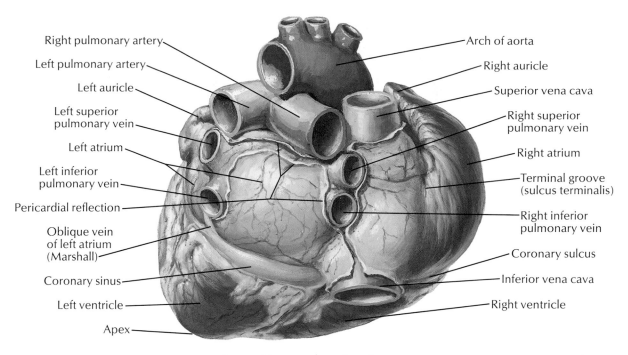

Right pulmonary artery

Left pulmonary artery

Left auricle

Left superior pulmonary vein

Left atrium

Left inferior pulmonary vein

Pericardial reflection

Oblique vein of left atrium (Marshall)

Coronary sinus

Left ventricle

Apex

Arch of aorta

Right auricle

Superior vena cava

Right superior pulmonary vein

Right atrium

Terminal groove (sulcus terminalis)

Right inferior pulmonary vein

Coronary sulcus

Inferior vena cava

Right ventricle

Base of heart: posterior view

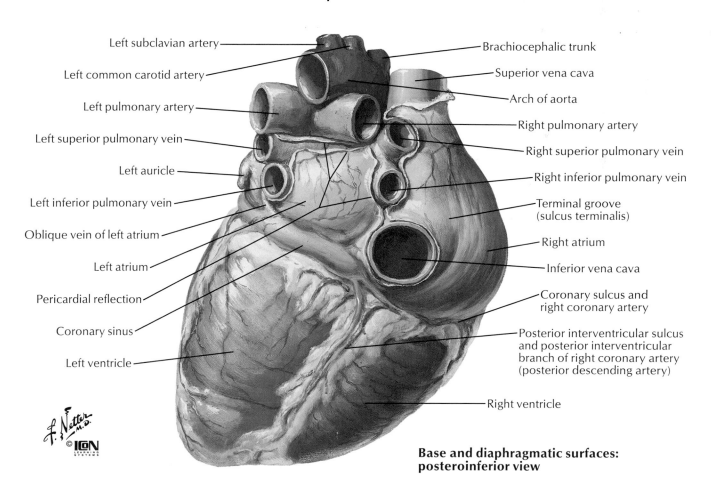

Left subclavian artery

Left common carotid artery

Left pulmonary artery

Left superior pulmonary vein

Left auricle

Left inferior pulmonary vein

Oblique vein of left atrium

Left atrium

Pericardial reflection

Coronary sinus

Left ventricle

Brachiocephalic trunk

Superior vena cava

Arch of aorta

Right pulmonary artery

Right superior pulmonary vein

Right inferior pulmonary vein

Terminal groove (sulcus terminalis)

Right atrium

Inferior vena cava

Coronary sulcus and right coronary artery

Posterior interventricular sulcus and posterior interventricular branch of right coronary artery (posterior descending artery)

Right ventricle

Base and diaphragmatic surfaces: posteroinferior view

ANESTHESIA

Intrathoracic

00560   Anesthesia for procedures on heart, pericardial sac, and great vessels of chest; without pump oxygenator

00561   with pump oxygenator, under one year of age

00562   with pump oxygenator

00563   with pump oxygenator with hypothermic circulatory arrest

SURGERY

Cardiovascular System

Heart and Pericardium
Shunting Procedures

33766   Shunt; superior vena cava to pulmonary artery for flow to one lung (classical Glenn procedure)

33767   superior vena cava to pulmonary artery for flow to both lungs (bidirectional Glenn procedure)

Pulmonary Artery

33910   Pulmonary artery embolectomy; with cardiopulmonary bypass

33915   without cardiopulmonary bypass

33916   Pulmonary endarterectomy, with or without embolectomy, with cardiopulmonary bypass

33917   Repair of pulmonary artery stenosis by reconstruction with patch or graft

33918   Repair of pulmonary atresia with ventricular septal defect, by unifocalization of pulmonary arteries; without cardiopulmonary bypass

33919   with cardiopulmonary bypass

33920   Repair of pulmonary atresia with ventricular septal defect, by construction or replacement of conduit from right or left ventricle to pulmonary artery

33922   Transection of pulmonary artery with cardiopulmonary bypass

33924   Ligation and takedown of a systemic-to-pulmonary artery shunt, performed in conjunction with a congenital heart procedure (List separately in addition to code for primary procedure)

Arteries and Veins
Transluminal Angioplasty

Open

35458   Transluminal balloon angioplasty, open; brachiocephalic trunk or branches, each vessel

Percutaneous

35475   Transluminal balloon angioplasty, percutaneous; brachiocephalic trunk or branches, each vessel

Transluminal Atherectomy

Open

35484   Transluminal peripheral atherectomy, open; brachiocephalic trunk or branches, each vessel

Percutaneous

35494   Transluminal peripheral atherectomy, percutaneous; brachiocephalic trunk or branches, each vessel

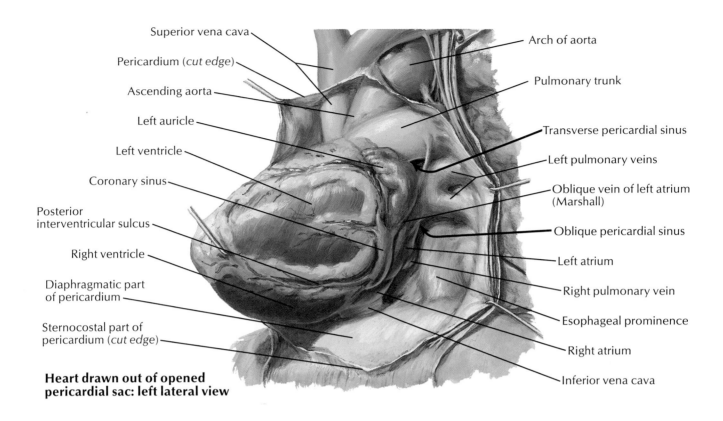

Superior vena cava

Pericardium (*cut edge*)

Ascending aorta

Left auricle

Left ventricle

Coronary sinus

Posterior interventricular sulcus

Right ventricle

Diaphragmatic part of pericardium

Sternocostal part of pericardium (*cut edge*)

Arch of aorta

Pulmonary trunk

Transverse pericardial sinus

Left pulmonary veins

Oblique vein of left atrium (Marshall)

Oblique pericardial sinus

Left atrium

Right pulmonary vein

Esophageal prominence

Right atrium

Inferior vena cava

Heart drawn out of opened pericardial sac: left lateral view

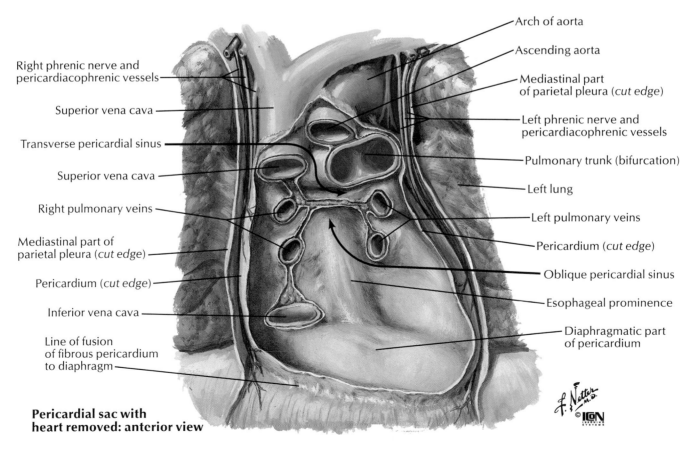

Right phrenic nerve and pericardiacophrenic vessels

Superior vena cava

Transverse pericardial sinus

Superior vena cava

Right pulmonary veins

Mediastinal part of parietal pleura (*cut edge*)

Pericardium (*cut edge*)

Inferior vena cava

Line of fusion of fibrous pericardium to diaphragm

Arch of aorta

Ascending aorta

Mediastinal part of parietal pleura (*cut edge*)

Left phrenic nerve and pericardiacophrenic vessels

Pulmonary trunk (bifurcation)

Left lung

Left pulmonary veins

Pericardium (*cut edge*)

Oblique pericardial sinus

Esophageal prominence

Diaphragmatic part of pericardium

Pericardial sac with heart removed: anterior view

ANESTHESIA

Intrathoracic

00560   Anesthesia for procedures on heart, pericardial sac, and great vessels of chest; without pump oxygenator

00561   with pump oxygenator, under one year of age

00562   with pump oxygenator

00563   with pump oxygenator with hypothermic circulatory arrest

SURGERY

Cardiovascular System

Heart and Pericardium
Pericardium

33010   Pericardiocentesis; initial

33011   subsequent

33015   Tube pericardiostomy

33020   Pericardiotomy for removal of clot or foreign body (primary procedure)

33025   Creation of pericardial window or partial resection for drainage

33030   Pericardiectomy, subtotal or complete; without cardiopulmonary bypass

33031   with cardiopulmonary bypass

33050   Excision of pericardial cyst or tumor

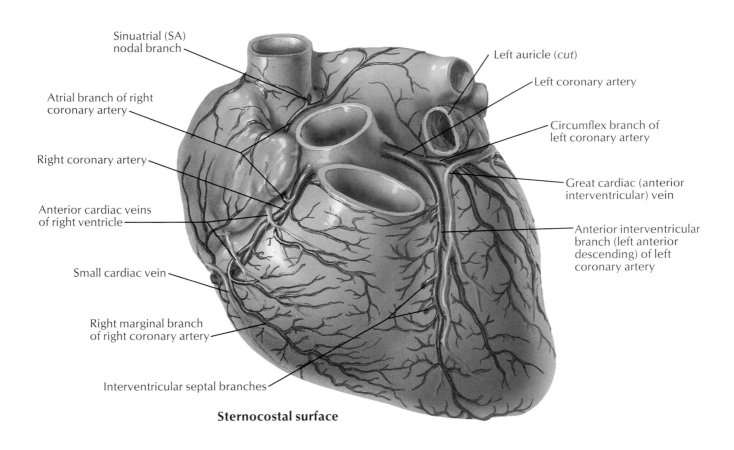

Sinuatrial (SA) nodal branch

Atrial branch of right coronary artery

Right coronary artery

Anterior cardiac veins of right ventricle

Small cardiac vein

Right marginal branch of right coronary artery

Interventricular septal branches

Left auricle (*cut*)

Left coronary artery

Circumflex branch of left coronary artery

Great cardiac (anterior interventricular) vein

Anterior interventricular branch (left anterior descending) of left coronary artery

Sternocostal surface

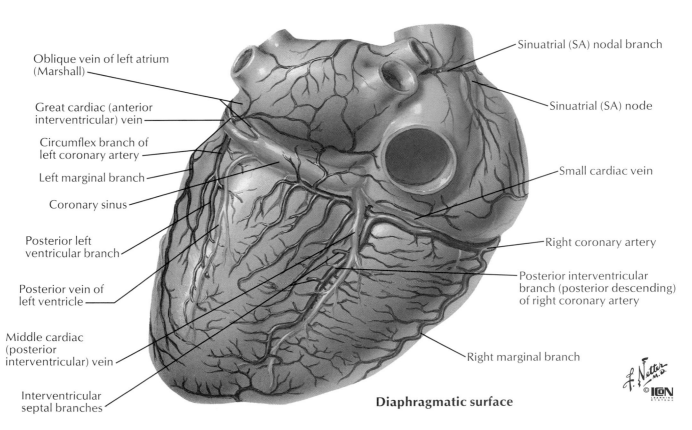

Oblique vein of left atrium (Marshall)

Great cardiac (anterior interventricular) vein

Circumflex branch of left coronary artery

Left marginal branch

Coronary sinus

Posterior left ventricular branch

Posterior vein of left ventricle

Middle cardiac (posterior interventricular) vein

Interventricular septal branches

Sinuatrial (SA) nodal branch

Sinuatrial (SA) node

Small cardiac vein

Right coronary artery

Posterior interventricular branch (posterior descending) of right coronary artery

Right marginal branch

Diaphragmatic surface

ANESTHESIA

Intrathoracic

00560	Anesthesia for procedures on heart, pericardial sac, and great vessels of chest; without pump oxygenator
00561	with pump oxygenator, under one year of age
00562	with pump oxygenator
00563	with pump oxygenator with hypothermic circulatory arrest

SURGERY

Cardiovascular System

Heart and Pericardium
Coronary Artery Anomalies

33500	Repair of coronary arteriovenous or arteriocardiac chamber fistula; with cardiopulmonary bypass
33501	without cardiopulmonary bypass
33502	Repair of anomalous coronary artery; by ligation
33503	by graft, without cardiopulmonary bypass
33504	by graft, with cardiopulmonary bypass
33505	with construction of intrapulmonary artery tunnel (Takeuchi procedure)
33506	by translocation from pulmonary artery to aorta

Endoscopy

33508	Endoscopy, surgical, including video-assisted harvest of vein(s) for coronary artery bypass procedure (List separately in addition to code for primary procedure)

Venous Grafting Only for Coronary Artery Bypass

33510[P]	Coronary artery bypass, vein only; single coronary venous graft
33511	two coronary venous grafts
33512	three coronary venous grafts
33513	four coronary venous grafts
33514	five coronary venous grafts
33516	six or more coronary venous grafts

Combined Arterial-Venous Grafting for Coronary Bypass

33517[P]	Coronary artery bypass, using venous graft(s) and arterial graft(s); single vein graft (List separately in addition to code for arterial graft)
33518	two venous grafts (List separately in addition to code for arterial graft)
33519	three venous grafts (List separately in addition to code for arterial graft)
33521	four venous grafts (List separately in addition to code for arterial graft)
33522	five venous grafts (List separately in addition to code for arterial graft)
33523	six or more venous grafts (List separately in addition to code for arterial graft)
33530	Reoperation, coronary artery bypass procedure or valve procedure, more than one month after original operation (List separately in addition to code for primary procedure)

Arterial Grafting for Coronary Artery Bypass

33533	Coronary artery bypass, using arterial graft(s); single arterial graft
33534	two coronary arterial grafts
33535	three coronary arterial grafts
33536	four or more coronary arterial grafts

Coronary Endarterectomy

33572	Coronary endarterectomy, open, any method, of left anterior descending, circumflex, or right coronary artery performed in conjunction with coronary artery bypass graft procedure, each vessel (List separately in addition to primary procedure)

Right coronary artery: left anterior oblique view

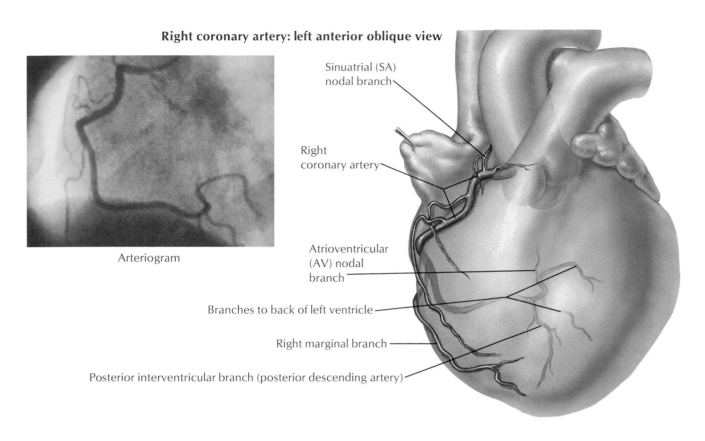

Arteriogram

Sinuatrial (SA) nodal branch

Right coronary artery

Atrioventricular (AV) nodal branch

Branches to back of left ventricle

Right marginal branch

Posterior interventricular branch (posterior descending artery)

Right coronary artery: right anterior oblique view

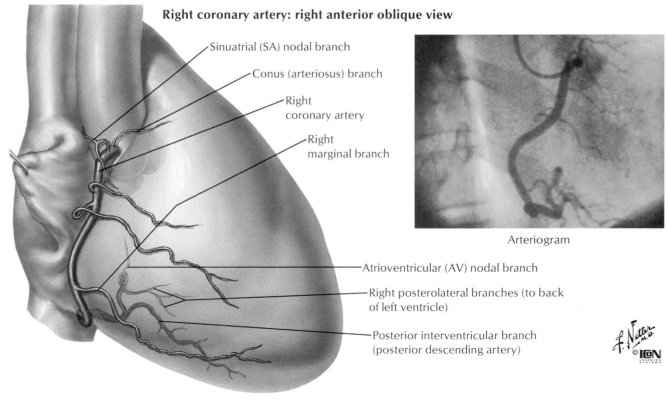

Sinuatrial (SA) nodal branch

Conus (arteriosus) branch

Right coronary artery

Right marginal branch

Arteriogram

Atrioventricular (AV) nodal branch

Right posterolateral branches (to back of left ventricle)

Posterior interventricular branch (posterior descending artery)

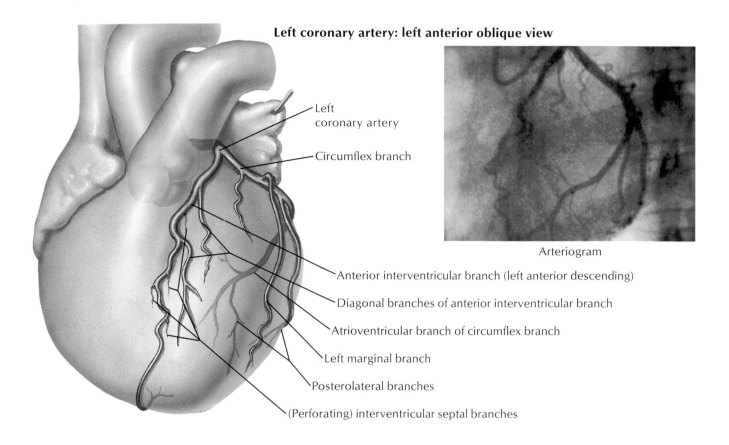

Left coronary artery: left anterior oblique view

Left coronary artery

Circumflex branch

Arteriogram

Anterior interventricular branch (left anterior descending)

Diagonal branches of anterior interventricular branch

Atrioventricular branch of circumflex branch

Left marginal branch

Posterolateral branches

(Perforating) interventricular septal branches

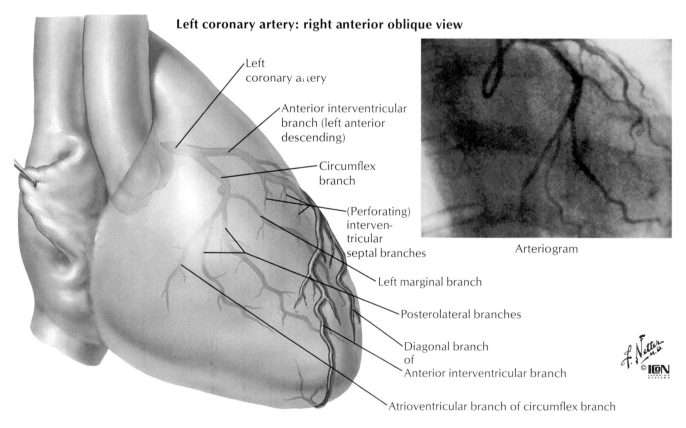

Left coronary artery: right anterior oblique view

Left coronary artery

Anterior interventricular branch (left anterior descending)

Circumflex branch

(Perforating) interventricular septal branches

Arteriogram

Left marginal branch

Posterolateral branches

Diagonal branch of Anterior interventricular branch

Atrioventricular branch of circumflex branch

ANESTHESIA

Radiological Procedures

01916 Anesthesia for diagnostic arteriography/venography

01920 Anesthesia for cardiac catheterization including coronary angiography and ventriculography (not to include Swan-Ganz catheter)

MEDICINE

Cardiovascular

Cardiac Catheterization

93508^P Catheter placement in coronary artery(s), arterial coronary conduit(s), and/or venous coronary bypass graft(s) for coronary angiography without concomitant left heart catheterization

93539 Injection procedure during cardiac catheterization; for selective opacification of arterial conduits (eg, internal mammary), whether native or used for bypass

93540 for selective opacification of aortocoronary venous bypass grafts, one or more coronary arteries

93545 for selective coronary angiography (injection of radiopaque material may be by hand)

93555 Imaging supervision, interpretation and report for injection procedure(s) during cardiac catheterization; ventricular and/or atrial angiography

93556 pulmonary angiography, aortography, and/or selective coronary angiography including venous bypass grafts and arterial conduits (whether native or used in bypass)

93571^P Intravascular Doppler velocity and/or pressure derived coronary flow reserve measurement (coronary vessel or graft) during coronary angiography including pharmacologically induced stress; initial vessel (List separately in addition to code for primary procedure)

93572 each additional vessel (List separately in addition to code for primary procedure)

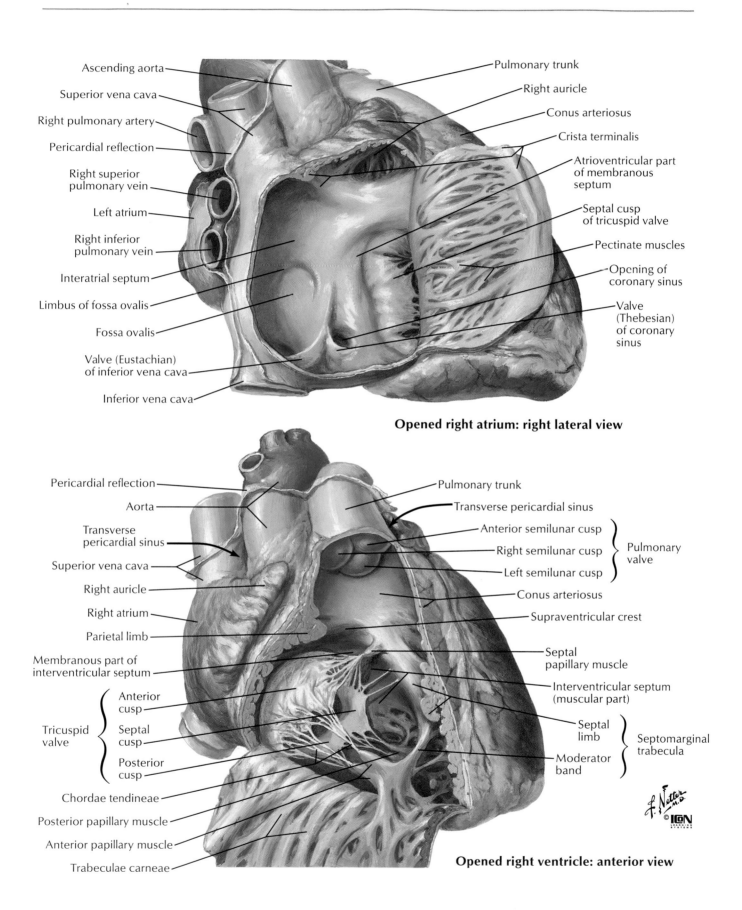

Ascending aorta

Superior vena cava

Right pulmonary artery

Pericardial reflection

Right superior pulmonary vein

Left atrium

Right inferior pulmonary vein

Interatrial septum

Limbus of fossa ovalis

Fossa ovalis

Valve (Eustachian) of inferior vena cava

Inferior vena cava

Pulmonary trunk

Right auricle

Conus arteriosus

Crista terminalis

Atrioventricular part of membranous septum

Septal cusp of tricuspid valve

Pectinate muscles

Opening of coronary sinus

Valve (Thebesian) of coronary sinus

Opened right atrium: right lateral view

Pericardial reflection

Aorta

Transverse pericardial sinus

Superior vena cava

Right auricle

Right atrium

Parietal limb

Membranous part of interventricular septum

Tricuspid valve — Anterior cusp / Septal cusp / Posterior cusp

Chordae tendineae

Posterior papillary muscle

Anterior papillary muscle

Trabeculae carneae

Pulmonary trunk

Transverse pericardial sinus

Anterior semilunar cusp

Right semilunar cusp

Left semilunar cusp

Pulmonary valve

Conus arteriosus

Supraventricular crest

Septal papillary muscle

Interventricular septum (muscular part)

Septal limb

Moderator band

Septomarginal trabecula

Opened right ventricle: anterior view

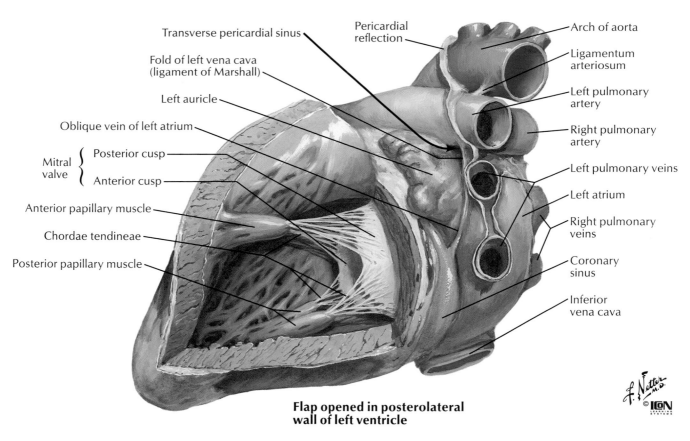

Transverse pericardial sinus

Pericardial reflection

Arch of aorta

Ligamentum arteriosum

Fold of left vena cava (ligament of Marshall)

Left pulmonary artery

Left auricle

Right pulmonary artery

Oblique vein of left atrium

Mitral valve
{ Posterior cusp

Anterior cusp

Left pulmonary veins

Left atrium

Anterior papillary muscle

Right pulmonary veins

Chordae tendineae

Coronary sinus

Posterior papillary muscle

Inferior vena cava

Flap opened in posterolateral wall of left ventricle

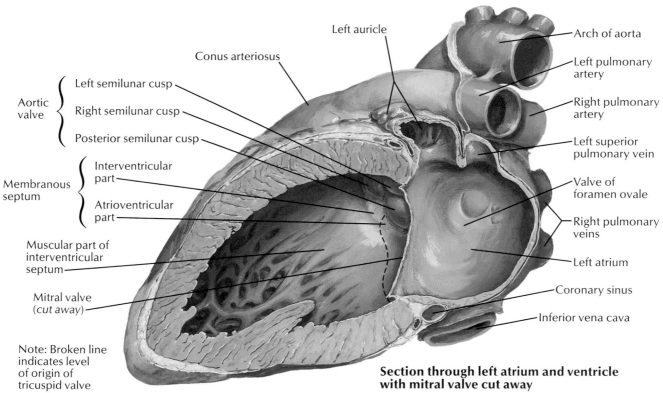

Left auricle

Conus arteriosus

Arch of aorta

Aortic valve
{ Left semilunar cusp

Right semilunar cusp

Posterior semilunar cusp

Left pulmonary artery

Right pulmonary artery

Membranous septum
{ Interventricular part

Atrioventricular part

Left superior pulmonary vein

Valve of foramen ovale

Right pulmonary veins

Muscular part of interventricular septum

Left atrium

Mitral valve (*cut away*)

Coronary sinus

Inferior vena cava

Note: Broken line indicates level of origin of tricuspid valve

Section through left atrium and ventricle with mitral valve cut away

ANESTHESIA

Intrathoracic

00532   Anesthesia for access to central venous circulation

Radiological Procedures

01920   Anesthesia for cardiac catheterization including coronary angiography and ventriculography (not to include Swan-Ganz catheter)

01926   Anesthesia for therapeutic interventional radiologic procedures involving the arterial system; intracranial, intracardiac, or aortic

MEDICINE

Cardiovascular

Cardiac Catheterization

93501[P]   Right heart catheterization

93503   Insertion and placement of flow directed catheter (eg, Swan-Ganz) for monitoring purposes

93505   Endomyocardial biopsy

93508[P]   Catheter placement in coronary artery(s), arterial coronary conduit(s), and/or venous coronary bypass graft(s) for coronary angiography without concomitant left heart catheterization

93510[P]   Left heart catheterization, retrograde, from the brachial artery, axillary artery or femoral artery; percutaneous

93511   by cutdown

93514   Left heart catheterization by left ventricular puncture

93524   Combined transseptal and retrograde left heart catheterization

93526   Combined right heart catheterization and retrograde left heart catheterization

93527   Combined right heart catheterization and transseptal left heart catheterization through intact septum (with or without retrograde left heart catheterization)

93528   Combined right heart catheterization with left ventricular puncture (with or without retrograde left heart catheterization)

93529   Combined right heart catheterization and left heart catheterization through existing septal opening (with or without retrograde left heart catheterization)

93530   Right heart catheterization, for congenital cardiac anomalies

93531   Combined right heart catheterization and retrograde left heart catheterization, for congenital cardiac anomalies

93532   Combined right heart catheterization and transseptal left heart catheterization through intact septum with or without retrograde left heart catheterization, for congenital cardiac anomalies

93533   Combined right heart catheterization and transseptal left heart catheterization through existing septal opening, with or without retrograde left heart catheterization, for congenital cardiac anomalies

93539   Injection procedure during cardiac catheterization; for selective opacification of arterial conduits (eg, internal mammary), whether native or used for bypass

93540   for selective opacification of aortocoronary venous bypass grafts, one or more coronary arteries

93541   for pulmonary angiography

93542   for selective right ventricular or right atrial angiography

93543   for selective left ventricular or left atrial angiography

93544   for aortography

93545   for selective coronary angiography (injection of radiopaque material may be by hand)

93555   Imaging supervision, interpretation and report for injection procedure(s) during cardiac catheterization; ventricular and/or atrial angiography

93556   pulmonary angiography, aortography, and/or selective coronary angiography including venous bypass grafts and arterial conduits (whether native or used in bypass)

93561   Indicator dilution studies such as dye or thermal dilution, including arterial and/or venous catheterization; with cardiac output measurement (separate procedure)

93562   subsequent measurement of cardiac output

Repair of Septal Defect

93580   Percutaneous transcatheter closure of congenital interatrial communication (ie, Fontan fenestration, atrial septal defect) with implant

93581   Percutaneous transcatheter closure of a congenital ventricular septal defect with implant

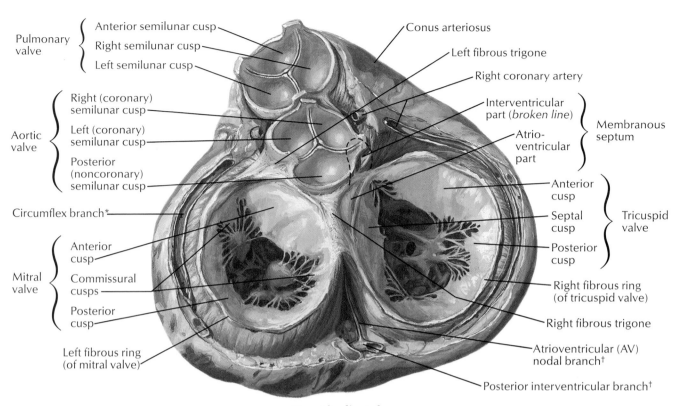

Pulmonary valve
- Anterior semilunar cusp
- Right semilunar cusp
- Left semilunar cusp

Aortic valve
- Right (coronary) semilunar cusp
- Left (coronary) semilunar cusp
- Posterior (noncoronary) semilunar cusp

Circumflex branch*

Mitral valve
- Anterior cusp
- Commissural cusps
- Posterior cusp

Left fibrous ring (of mitral valve)

Conus arteriosus

Left fibrous trigone

Right coronary artery

Membranous septum
- Interventricular part (*broken line*)
- Atrio-ventricular part

Tricuspid valve
- Anterior cusp
- Septal cusp
- Posterior cusp

Right fibrous ring (of tricuspid valve)

Right fibrous trigone

Atrioventricular (AV) nodal branch†

Posterior interventricular branch†

Heart in diastole:
viewed from base with atria removed

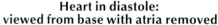

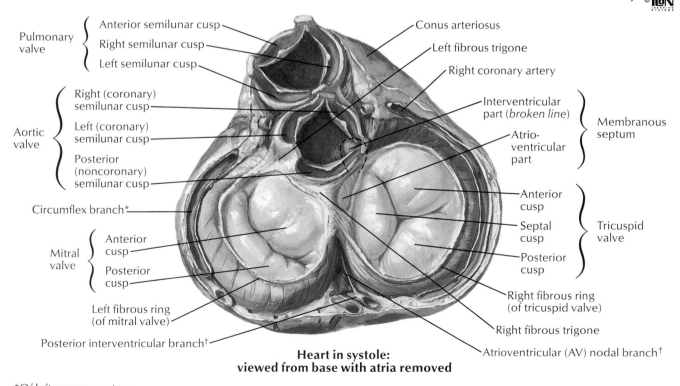

Pulmonary valve
- Anterior semilunar cusp
- Right semilunar cusp
- Left semilunar cusp

Aortic valve
- Right (coronary) semilunar cusp
- Left (coronary) semilunar cusp
- Posterior (noncoronary) semilunar cusp

Circumflex branch*

Mitral valve
- Anterior cusp
- Posterior cusp

Left fibrous ring (of mitral valve)

Posterior interventricular branch†

Conus arteriosus

Left fibrous trigone

Right coronary artery

Membranous septum
- Interventricular part (*broken line*)
- Atrio-ventricular part

Tricuspid valve
- Anterior cusp
- Septal cusp
- Posterior cusp

Right fibrous ring (of tricuspid valve)

Right fibrous trigone

Atrioventricular (AV) nodal branch†

Heart in systole:
viewed from base with atria removed

*Of left coronary artery
†Of right coronary artery

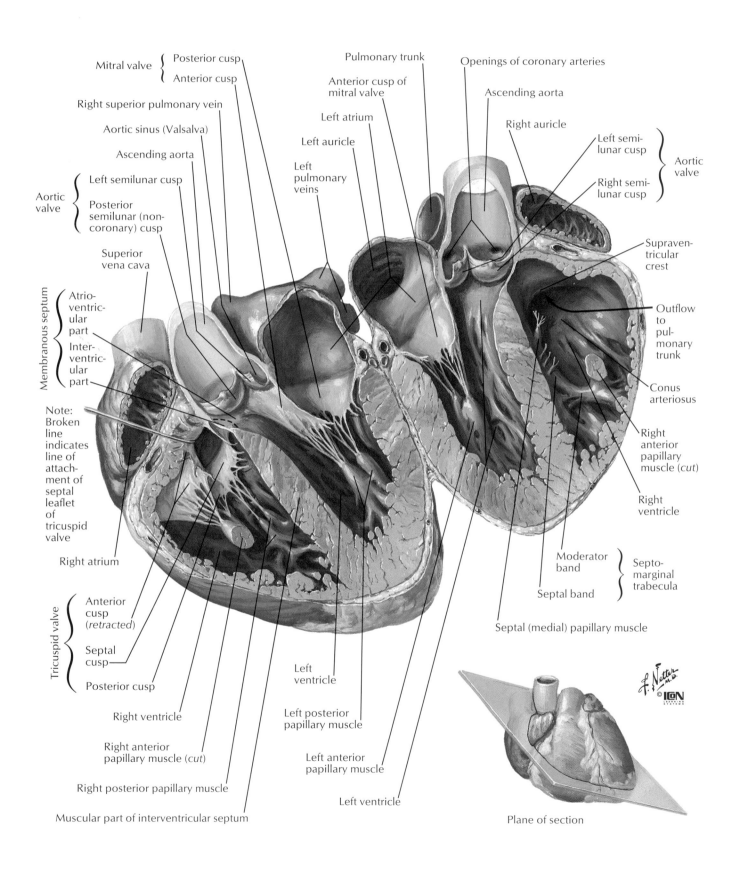

Mitral valve { Posterior cusp / Anterior cusp

Right superior pulmonary vein

Aortic sinus (Valsalva)

Ascending aorta

Aortic valve { Left semilunar cusp / Posterior semilunar (non-coronary) cusp

Superior vena cava

Membranous septum { Atrio-ventricular part / Inter-ventricular part

Note: Broken line indicates line of attachment of septal leaflet of tricuspid valve

Right atrium

Tricuspid valve { Anterior cusp (retracted) / Septal cusp / Posterior cusp

Right ventricle

Right anterior papillary muscle (cut)

Right posterior papillary muscle

Muscular part of interventricular septum

Pulmonary trunk

Anterior cusp of mitral valve

Left atrium

Left auricle

Left pulmonary veins

Left ventricle

Left posterior papillary muscle

Left anterior papillary muscle

Left ventricle

Openings of coronary arteries

Ascending aorta

Right auricle

Left semilunar cusp

Right semilunar cusp

Aortic valve

Supraventricular crest

Outflow to pulmonary trunk

Conus arteriosus

Right anterior papillary muscle (cut)

Right ventricle

Moderator band

Septal band

Septo-marginal trabecula

Septal (medial) papillary muscle

Plane of section

ANESTHESIA

Intrathoracic

00560   Anesthesia for procedures on heart, pericardial sac, and great vessels of chest; without pump oxygenator

00561   with pump oxygenator, under one year of age

00562   with pump oxygenator

00563   with pump oxygenator with hypothermic circulatory arrest

SURGERY

Cardiovascular System

Heart and Pericardium
Cardiac Valves

Aortic Valve

33400   Valvuloplasty, aortic valve; open, with cardiopulmonary bypass

33401   open, with inflow occlusion

33403   using transventricular dilation, with cardiopulmonary bypass

33404   Construction of apical-aortic conduit

33405   Replacement, aortic valve, with cardiopulmonary bypass; with prosthetic valve other than homograft or stentless valve

33406   with allograft valve (freehand)

33410   with stentless tissue valve

33411   Replacement, aortic valve; with aortic annulus enlargement, noncoronary cusp

33412   with transventricular aortic annulus enlargement (Konno procedure)

33413   by translocation of autologous pulmonary valve with allograft replacement of pulmonary valve (Ross procedure)

33414   Repair of left ventricular outflow tract obstruction by patch enlargement of the outflow tract

33415   Resection or incision of subvalvular tissue for discrete subvalvular aortic stenosis

33416   Ventriculomyotomy (-myectomy) for idiopathic hypertrophic subaortic stenosis (eg, asymmetric septal hypertrophy)

33417   Aortoplasty (gusset) for supravalvular stenosis

Mitral Valve

33420   Valvotomy, mitral valve; closed heart

33422   open heart, with cardiopulmonary bypass

33425   Valvuloplasty, mitral valve, with cardiopulmonary bypass;

33426   with prosthetic ring

33427   radical reconstruction, with or without ring

33430   Replacement, mitral valve, with cardiopulmonary bypass

Tricuspid Valve

33460   Valvectomy, tricuspid valve, with cardiopulmonary bypass

33463   Valvuloplasty, tricuspid valve; without ring insertion

33464   with ring insertion

33465   Replacement, tricuspid valve, with cardiopulmonary bypass

33468   Tricuspid valve repositioning and plication for Ebstein anomaly

Pulmonary Valve

33470   Valvotomy, pulmonary valve, closed heart; transventricular

33471   via pulmonary artery

33472   Valvotomy, pulmonary valve, open heart; with inflow occlusion

33474   with cardiopulmonary bypass

33475   Replacement, pulmonary valve

33476   Right ventricular resection for infundibular stenosis, with or without commissurotomy

33478   Outflow tract augmentation (gusset), with or without commissurotomy or infundibular resection

Other Valvular Procedures

33496   Repair of non-structural prosthetic valve dysfunction with cardiopulmonary bypass (separate procedure)

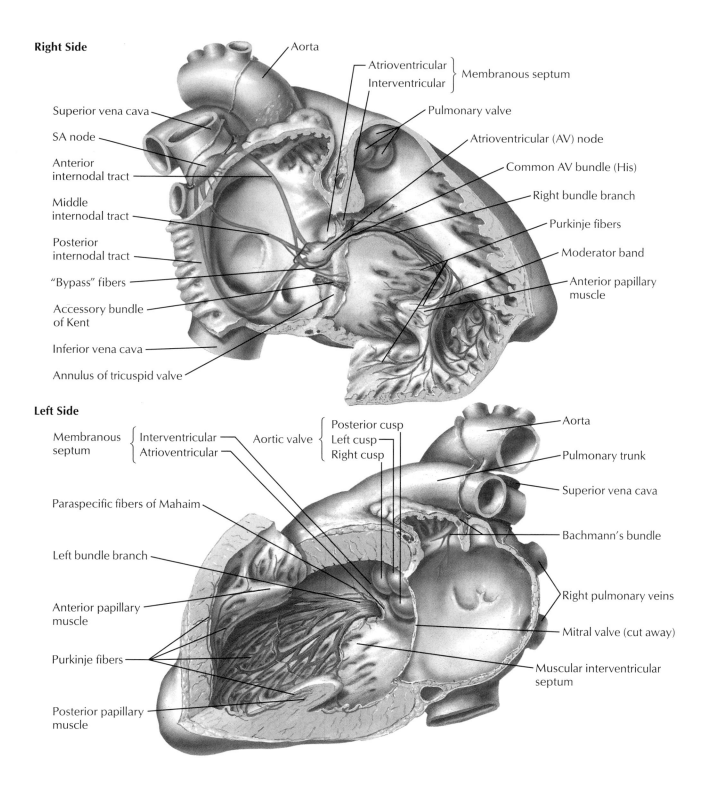

Right Side

Aorta

Atrioventricular
Interventricular
} Membranous septum

Superior vena cava

SA node

Anterior internodal tract

Pulmonary valve

Atrioventricular (AV) node

Common AV bundle (His)

Right bundle branch

Middle internodal tract

Purkinje fibers

Posterior internodal tract

Moderator band

"Bypass" fibers

Anterior papillary muscle

Accessory bundle of Kent

Inferior vena cava

Annulus of tricuspid valve

Left Side

Membranous septum {
Interventricular
Atrioventricular

Aortic valve {
Posterior cusp
Left cusp
Right cusp

Aorta

Pulmonary trunk

Superior vena cava

Paraspecific fibers of Mahaim

Left bundle branch

Bachmann's bundle

Anterior papillary muscle

Right pulmonary veins

Purkinje fibers

Mitral valve (cut away)

Muscular interventricular septum

Posterior papillary muscle

ANESTHESIA

Intrathoracic

00537 Anesthesia for cardiac electrophysiologic procedures including radiofrequency ablation

00560 Anesthesia for procedures on heart, pericardial sac, and great vessels of chest; without pump oxygenator

00562 with pump oxygenator

SURGERY

Cardiovascular System

Heart and Pericardium
Electrophysiologic Operative Procedures

33250 Operative ablation of supraventricular arrhythmogenic focus or pathway (eg, Wolff-Parkinson-White, atrioventricular node re-entry), tract(s) and/or focus (foci); without cardiopulmonary bypass

33251 with cardiopulmonary bypass

33253 Operative incisions and reconstruction of atria for treatment of atrial fibrillation or atrial flutter (eg, maze procedure)

33261 Operative ablation of ventricular arrhythmogenic focus with cardiopulmonary bypass

MEDICINE

Cardiovascular

Intracardiac Electrophysiological Procedures/Studies

93600 Bundle of His recording

93602 Intra-atrial recording

93603 Right ventricular recording

93609 Intraventricular and/or intra-atrial mapping of tachycardia site(s) with catheter manipulation to record from multiple sites to identify origin of tachycardia (List separately in addition to code for primary procedure)

93610 Intra-atrial pacing

93612 Intraventricular pacing

93613 Intracardiac electrophysiologic 3-dimensional mapping (List separately in addition to code for primary procedure)

93615 Esophageal recording of atrial electrogram with or without ventricular electrogram(s);

93616 with pacing

93618 Induction of arrhythmia by electrical pacing

93619 Comprehensive electrophysiologic evaluation with right atrial pacing and recording, right ventricular pacing and recording, His bundle recording, including insertion and repositioning of multiple electrode catheters, without induction or attempted induction of arrhythmia

93620 Comprehensive electrophysiologic evaluation including insertion and repositioning of multiple electrode catheters with induction or attempted induction of arrhythmia; with right atrial pacing and recording, right ventricular pacing and recording, His bundle recording

93621 with left atrial pacing and recording from coronary sinus or left atrium (List separately in addition to code for primary procedure)

93622 with left ventricular pacing and recording (List Programmed stimulation and pacing after intravenous drug infusion (List separately in addition to code for primary procedure)

93624 Electrophysiologic follow-up study with pacing and recording to test effectiveness of therapy, including induction or attempted induction of arrhythmia

93631 Intra-operative epicardial and endocardial pacing and mapping to localize the site of tachycardia or zone of slow conduction for surgical correction

93640 Electrophysiologic evaluation of single or dual chamber pacing cardioverter-defibrillator leads including defibrillation threshold evaluation (induction of arrhythmia, evaluation of sensing and pacing for arrhythmia termination) at time of initial implantation or replacement;

93641 with testing of single or dual chamber pacing cardioverter-defibrillator pulse generator

93642 Electrophysiologic evaluation of single or dual chamber pacing cardioverter-defibrillator (includes defibrillation threshold evaluation, induction of arrhythmia, evaluation of sensing and pacing for arrhythmia termination, and programming or reprogramming of sensing or therapeutic parameters)

93650 Intracardiac catheter ablation of atrioventricular node function, atrioventricular conduction for creation of complete heart block, with or without temporary pacemaker placement

93651 Intracardiac catheter ablation of arrhythmogenic focus; for treatment of supraventricular tachycardia by ablation of fast or slow atrioventricular pathways, accessory atrioventricular connections or other atrial foci, singly or in combination

93652 for treatment of ventricular tachycardia

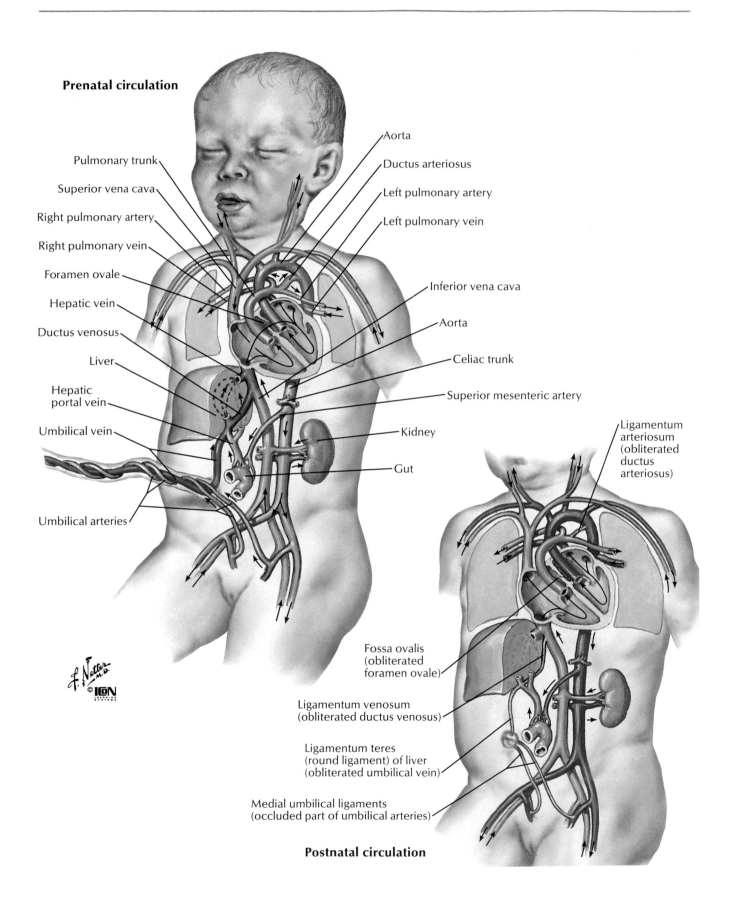

Prenatal circulation

Pulmonary trunk

Superior vena cava

Right pulmonary artery

Right pulmonary vein

Foramen ovale

Hepatic vein

Ductus venosus

Liver

Hepatic portal vein

Umbilical vein

Umbilical arteries

Aorta

Ductus arteriosus

Left pulmonary artery

Left pulmonary vein

Inferior vena cava

Aorta

Celiac trunk

Superior mesenteric artery

Kidney

Gut

Ligamentum arteriosum (obliterated ductus arteriosus)

Fossa ovalis (obliterated foramen ovale)

Ligamentum venosum (obliterated ductus venosus)

Ligamentum teres (round ligament) of liver (obliterated umbilical vein)

Medial umbilical ligaments (occluded part of umbilical arteries)

Postnatal circulation

ANESTHESIA

Intrathoracic

00560   Anesthesia for procedures on heart, pericardial sac, and great vessels of chest; without pump oxygenator
00561   with pump oxygenator, under one year of age
00562   with pump oxygenator
00563   with pump oxygenator with hypothermic circulatory arrest

SURGERY

Cardiovascular System

Heart and Pericardium
Aortic Anomalies

33813   Obliteration of aortopulmonary septal defect; without cardiopulmonary bypass

33814   with cardiopulmonary bypass
33820ᴾ   Repair of patent ductus arteriosus; by ligation
33822   by division, under 18 years
33824   by division, 18 years and older
33840   Excision of coarctation of aorta, with or without associated patent ductus arteriosus; with direct anastomosis
33845   with graft
33851   repair using either left subclavian artery or prosthetic material as gusset for enlargement

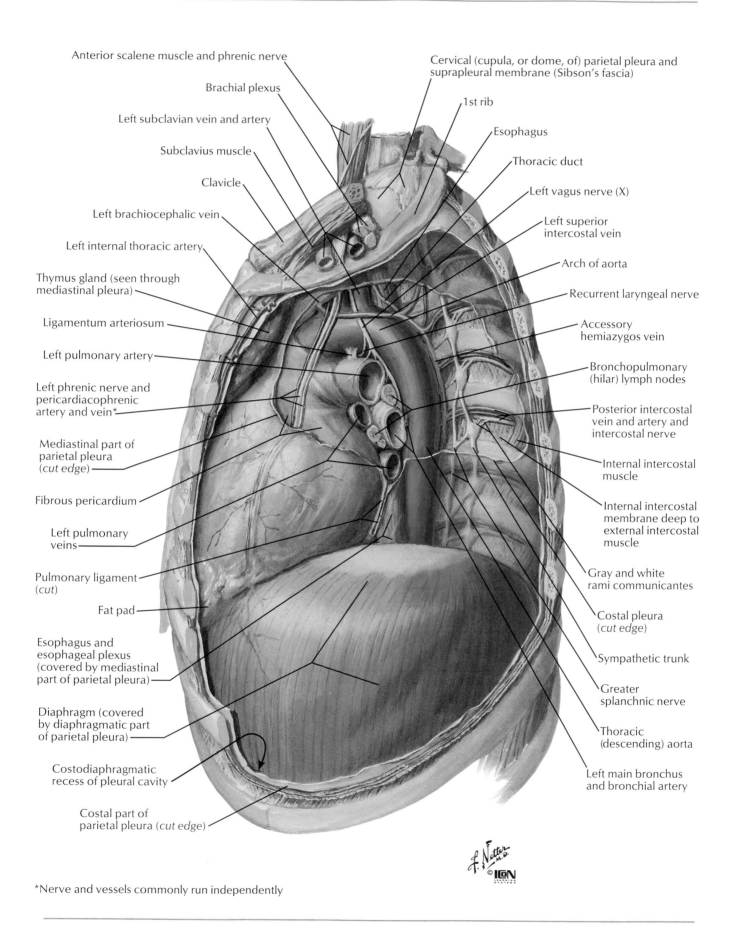

Anterior scalene muscle and phrenic nerve

Brachial plexus

Left subclavian vein and artery

Subclavius muscle

Clavicle

Left brachiocephalic vein

Left internal thoracic artery

Thymus gland (seen through mediastinal pleura)

Ligamentum arteriosum

Left pulmonary artery

Left phrenic nerve and pericardiacophrenic artery and vein*

Mediastinal part of parietal pleura (cut edge)

Fibrous pericardium

Left pulmonary veins

Pulmonary ligament (cut)

Fat pad

Esophagus and esophageal plexus (covered by mediastinal part of parietal pleura)

Diaphragm (covered by diaphragmatic part of parietal pleura)

Costodiaphragmatic recess of pleural cavity

Costal part of parietal pleura (cut edge)

Cervical (cupula, or dome, of) parietal pleura and suprapleural membrane (Sibson's fascia)

1st rib

Esophagus

Thoracic duct

Left vagus nerve (X)

Left superior intercostal vein

Arch of aorta

Recurrent laryngeal nerve

Accessory hemiazygos vein

Bronchopulmonary (hilar) lymph nodes

Posterior intercostal vein and artery and intercostal nerve

Internal intercostal muscle

Internal intercostal membrane deep to external intercostal muscle

Gray and white rami communicantes

Costal pleura (cut edge)

Sympathetic trunk

Greater splanchnic nerve

Thoracic (descending) aorta

Left main bronchus and bronchial artery

*Nerve and vessels commonly run independently

ANESTHESIA

Intrathoracic

00528 Anesthesia for closed chest procedures; mediastinoscopy and diagnostic thoracoscopy not utilizing one lung ventilation

00529 mediastinoscopy and diagnostic thoracoscopy utilizing one lung ventilation

00540 Anesthesia for thoracotomy procedures involving lungs, pleura, diaphragm, and mediastinum (including surgical thoracoscopy); not otherwise specified

SURGERY

Respiratory System

Lungs and Pleura
Excision

32405 Biopsy, lung or mediastinum, percutaneous needle

Mediastinum and Diaphragm

Mediastinum
Incision

39000 Mediastinotomy with exploration, drainage, removal of foreign body, or biopsy; cervical approach

39010 transthoracic approach, including either transthoracic or median sternotomy

Excision

39200 Excision of mediastinal cyst
39220 Excision of mediastinal tumor

Endoscopy

39400 Mediastinoscopy, with or without biopsy

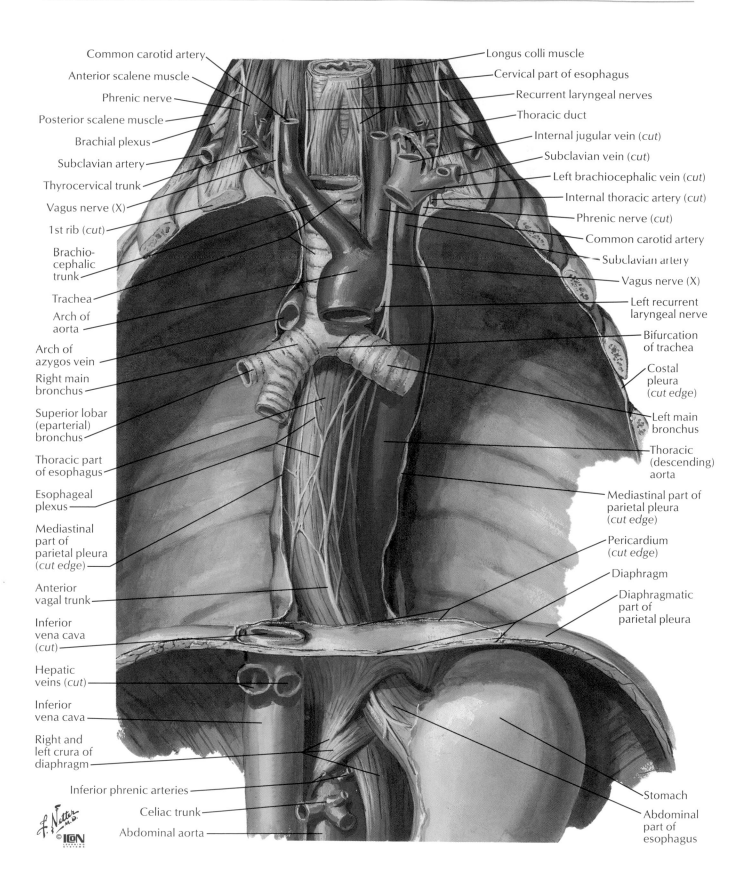

Common carotid artery

Anterior scalene muscle

Phrenic nerve

Posterior scalene muscle

Brachial plexus

Subclavian artery

Thyrocervical trunk

Vagus nerve (X)

1st rib (cut)

Brachio-
cephalic
trunk

Trachea

Arch of
aorta

Arch of
azygos vein

Right main
bronchus

Superior lobar
(eparterial)
bronchus

Thoracic part
of esophagus

Esophageal
plexus

Mediastinal
part of
parietal pleura
(cut edge)

Anterior
vagal trunk

Inferior
vena cava
(cut)

Hepatic
veins (cut)

Inferior
vena cava

Right and
left crura of
diaphragm

Inferior phrenic arteries

Celiac trunk

Abdominal aorta

Longus colli muscle

Cervical part of esophagus

Recurrent laryngeal nerves

Thoracic duct

Internal jugular vein (cut)

Subclavian vein (cut)

Left brachiocephalic vein (cut)

Internal thoracic artery (cut)

Phrenic nerve (cut)

Common carotid artery

Subclavian artery

Vagus nerve (X)

Left recurrent
laryngeal nerve

Bifurcation
of trachea

Costal
pleura
(cut edge)

Left main
bronchus

Thoracic
(descending)
aorta

Mediastinal part of
parietal pleura
(cut edge)

Pericardium
(cut edge)

Diaphragm

Diaphragmatic
part of
parietal pleura

Stomach

Abdominal
part of
esophagus

ANESTHESIA

Neck

00320   Anesthesia for all procedures on esophagus, thyroid, larynx, trachea and lymphatic system of neck; not otherwise specified, age 1 year or older

SURGERY

Digestive System

Esophagus
Incision

43020   Esophagotomy, cervical approach, with removal of foreign body

43030   Cricopharyngeal myotomy

43045   Esophagotomy, thoracic approach, with removal of foreign body

Excision

43100   Excision of lesion, esophagus, with primary repair; cervical approach

43101   thoracic or abdominal approach

43107   Total or near total esophagectomy, without thoracotomy; with pharyngogastrostomy or cervical esophagogastrostomy, with or without pyloroplasty (transhiatal)

43108   with colon interposition or small intestine reconstruction, including intestine mobilization, preparation and anastomosis(es)

43112   Total or near total esophagectomy, with thoracotomy; with pharyngogastrostomy or cervical esophagogastrostomy, with or without pyloroplasty

43113   with colon interposition or small intestine reconstruction, including intestine mobilization, preparation, and anastomosis(es)

43116   Partial esophagectomy, cervical, with free intestinal graft, including microvascular anastomosis, obtaining the graft and intestinal reconstruction

43117   Partial esophagectomy, distal two-thirds, with thoracotomy and separate abdominal incision, with or without proximal gastrectomy; with thoracic esophagogastrostomy, with or without pyloroplasty (Ivor Lewis)

43118   with colon interposition or small intestine reconstruction, including intestine mobilization, preparation, and anastomosis(es)

43121   Partial esophagectomy, distal two-thirds, with thoracotomy only, with or without proximal gastrectomy, with thoracic esophagogastrostomy, with or without pyloroplasty

43122   Partial esophagectomy, thoracoabdominal or abdominal approach, with or without proximal gastrectomy; with esophagogastrostomy, with or without pyloroplasty

43123   with colon interposition or small intestine reconstruction, including intestine mobilization, preparation, and anastomosis(es)

43124   Total or partial esophagectomy, without reconstruction (any approach), with cervical esophagostomy

43130   Diverticulectomy of hypopharynx or esophagus, with or without myotomy; cervical approach

43135   thoracic approach

Endoscopy

43200   Esophagoscopy, rigid or flexible; diagnostic, with or without collection of specimen(s) by brushing or washing (separate procedure)

43201   with directed submucosal injection(s), any substance

43202   with biopsy, single or multiple

43204   with injection sclerosis of esophageal varices

43205   with band ligation of esophageal varices

43215   with removal of foreign body

43216   with removal of tumor(s), polyp(s), or other lesion(s) by hot biopsy forceps or bipolar cautery

43217   with removal of tumor(s), polyp(s), or other lesion(s) by snare technique

43219   with insertion of plastic tube or stent

43220   with balloon dilation (less than 30 mm diameter)

43226   with insertion of guide wire followed by dilation over guide wire

43227   with control of bleeding (eg, injection, bipolar cautery, unipolar cautery, laser, heater probe, stapler, plasma coagulator)

43228   with ablation of tumor(s), polyp(s), or other lesion(s), not amenable to removal by hot biopsy forceps, bipolar cautery or snare technique

43231   with endoscopic ultrasound examination

43232   with transendoscopic ultrasound-guided intramural or transmural fine needle aspiration/biopsy(s)

43234   Upper gastrointestinal endoscopy, simple primary examination (eg, with small diameter flexible endoscope) (separate procedure)

43235   Upper gastrointestinal endoscopy including esophagus, stomach, and either the duodenum and/or jejunum as appropriate; diagnostic, with or without collection of specimen(s) by brushing or washing (separate procedure)

43236   with directed submucosal injection(s), any substance

43237   with endoscopic ultrasound examination limited to the esophagus

43238   with transendoscopic ultrasound-guided intramural or transmural fine needle aspiration/ biopsy(s), esophagus (includes endoscopic ultrasound examination limited to the esophagus)

43239   with biopsy, single or multiple

43240   with transmural drainage of pseudocyst

43241   with transendoscopic intraluminal tube or catheter placement

43242   with transendoscopic ultrasound-guided intramural or transmural fine needle aspiration/ biopsy(s) (includes endoscopic ultrasound examination of the esophagus, stomach, and either the duodenum and/or jejunum as appropriate)

43243 with injection sclerosis of esophageal and/or gastric varices

43244 with band ligation of esophageal and/or gastric varices

43245 with dilation of gastric outlet for obstruction (eg, balloon, guide wire, bougie)

43246 with directed placement of percutaneous gastrostomy tube

43247 with removal of foreign body

43248 with insertion of guide wire followed by dilation of esophagus over guide wire

43249 with balloon dilation of esophagus (less than 30 mm diameter)

43250 with removal of tumor(s), polyp(s), or other lesion(s) by hot biopsy forceps or bipolar cautery

43251 with removal of tumor(s), polyp(s), or other lesion(s) by snare technique

43255 with control of bleeding, any method

43256 with transendoscopic stent placement (includes predilation)

43257 with delivery of thermal energy to the muscle of lower esophageal sphincter and/or gastric cardia, for treatment of gastroesophageal reflux disease

43258 with ablation of tumor(s), polyp(s), or other lesion(s) not amenable to removal by hot biopsy forceps, bipolar cautery or snare technique

43259 with endoscopic ultrasound examination, including the esophagus, stomach, and either the duodenum and/or jejunum as appropriate

43260ᴾ Endoscopic retrograde cholangiopancreatography (ERCP); diagnostic, with or without collection of specimen(s) by brushing or washing (separate procedure)

43261 with biopsy, single or multiple

43262 with sphincterotomy/papillotomy

43263 with pressure measurement of sphincter of Oddi (pancreatic duct or common bile duct)

43264 with endoscopic retrograde removal of calculus/calculi from biliary and/or pancreatic ducts

43265 with endoscopic retrograde destruction, lithotripsy of calculus/calculi, any method

43267 with endoscopic retrograde insertion of nasobiliary or nasopancreatic drainage tube

43268 with endoscopic retrograde insertion of tube or stent into bile or pancreatic duct

43269 with endoscopic retrograde removal of foreign body and/or change of tube or stent

43271 with endoscopic retrograde balloon dilation of ampulla, biliary and/or pancreatic duct(s)

43272 with ablation of tumor(s), polyp(s), or other lesion(s) not amenable to removal by hot biopsy forceps, bipolar cautery or snare technique

Laparoscopy

43280ᴾ Laparoscopy, surgical, esophagogastric fundoplasty (eg, Nissen, Toupet procedures)

Repair

43300 Esophagoplasty (plastic repair or reconstruction), cervical approach; without repair of tracheoesophageal fistula

43305 with repair of tracheoesophageal fistula

43310 Esophagoplasty (plastic repair or reconstruction), thoracic approach; without repair of tracheoesophageal fistula

43312 with repair of tracheoesophageal fistula

43313 Esophagoplasty for congenital defect (plastic repair or reconstruction), thoracic approach; without repair of congenital tracheoesophageal fistula

43314 with repair of congenital tracheoesophageal fistula

43320 Esophagogastrostomy (cardioplasty), with or without vagotomy and pyloroplasty, transabdominal or transthoracic approach

43324ᴾ Esophagogastric fundoplasty (eg, Nissen, Belsey IV, Hill procedures)

43325 Esophagogastric fundoplasty; with fundic patch (Thal-Nissen procedure)

43326 with gastroplasty (eg, Collis)

43330 Esophagomyotomy (Heller type); abdominal approach

43331 Esophagomyotomy (Heller type); thoracic approach

43340 Esophagojejunostomy (without total gastrectomy); abdominal approach

43341 thoracic approach

43350 Esophagostomy, fistulization of esophagus, external; abdominal approach

43351 thoracic approach

43352 cervical approach

43360 Gastrointestinal reconstruction for previous esophagectomy, for obstructing esophageal lesion or fistula, or for previous esophageal exclusion; with stomach, with or without pyloroplasty

43361 with colon interposition or small intestine reconstruction, including intestine mobilization, preparation, and anastomosis(es)

43400 Ligation, direct, esophageal varices

43401 Transection of esophagus with repair, for esophageal varices

43405 Ligation or stapling at gastroesophageal junction for pre-existing esophageal perforation

43410 Suture of esophageal wound or injury; cervical approach

43415 transthoracic or transabdominal approach

43420 Closure of esophagostomy or fistula; cervical approach

43425 transthoracic or transabdominal approach

Manipulation

43450 Dilation of esophagus, by unguided sound or bougie, single or multiple passes

43453 Dilation of esophagus, over guide wire

43456 Dilation of esophagus, by balloon or dilator, retrograde

43458 Dilation of esophagus with balloon (30 mm diameter or larger) for achalasia

43460 Esophagogastric tamponade, with balloon (Sengstaaken type)

Other Procedures

43496 Free jejunum transfer with microvascular anastomosis

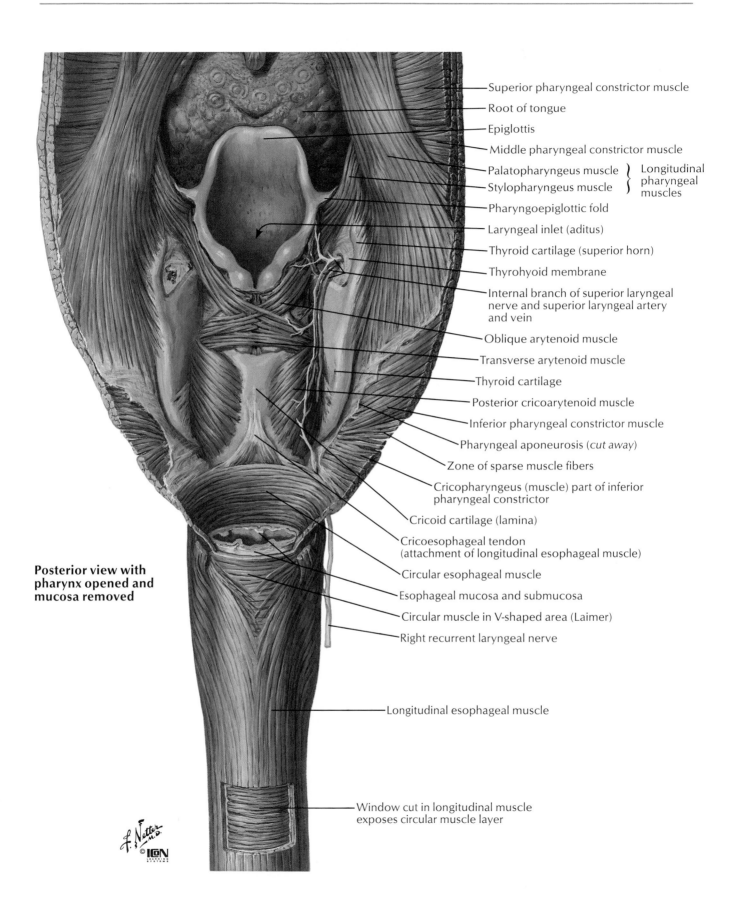

Superior pharyngeal constrictor muscle

Root of tongue

Epiglottis

Middle pharyngeal constrictor muscle

Palatopharyngeus muscle ⎫ Longitudinal
Stylopharyngeus muscle ⎭ pharyngeal muscles

Pharyngoepiglottic fold

Laryngeal inlet (aditus)

Thyroid cartilage (superior horn)

Thyrohyoid membrane

Internal branch of superior laryngeal nerve and superior laryngeal artery and vein

Oblique arytenoid muscle

Transverse arytenoid muscle

Thyroid cartilage

Posterior cricoarytenoid muscle

Inferior pharyngeal constrictor muscle

Pharyngeal aponeurosis (*cut away*)

Zone of sparse muscle fibers

Cricopharyngeus (muscle) part of inferior pharyngeal constrictor

Cricoid cartilage (lamina)

Cricoesophageal tendon (attachment of longitudinal esophageal muscle)

Circular esophageal muscle

Esophageal mucosa and submucosa

Circular muscle in V-shaped area (Laimer)

Right recurrent laryngeal nerve

Longitudinal esophageal muscle

Window cut in longitudinal muscle exposes circular muscle layer

Posterior view with pharynx opened and mucosa removed

Plate 90: Pharyngoesophageal Junction

ANESTHESIA

Neck

00320 Anesthesia for all procedures on esophagus, thyroid, larynx, trachea and lymphatic system of neck; not otherwise specified, age 1 year or older

SURGERY

Digestive System

Esophagus

Excision

43116 Partial esophagectomy, cervical, with free intestinal graft, including microvascular anastomosis, obtaining the graft and intestinal reconstruction

43130 Diverticulectomy of hypopharynx or esophagus, with or without myotomy; cervical approach

43135 thoracic approach

Repair

43300 Esophagoplasty (plastic repair or reconstruction), cervical approach; without repair of tracheoesophageal fistula

43305 with repair of tracheoesophageal fistula

43310 Esophagoplasty (plastic repair or reconstruction), thoracic approach; without repair of tracheoesophageal fistula

43312 with repair of tracheoesophageal fistula

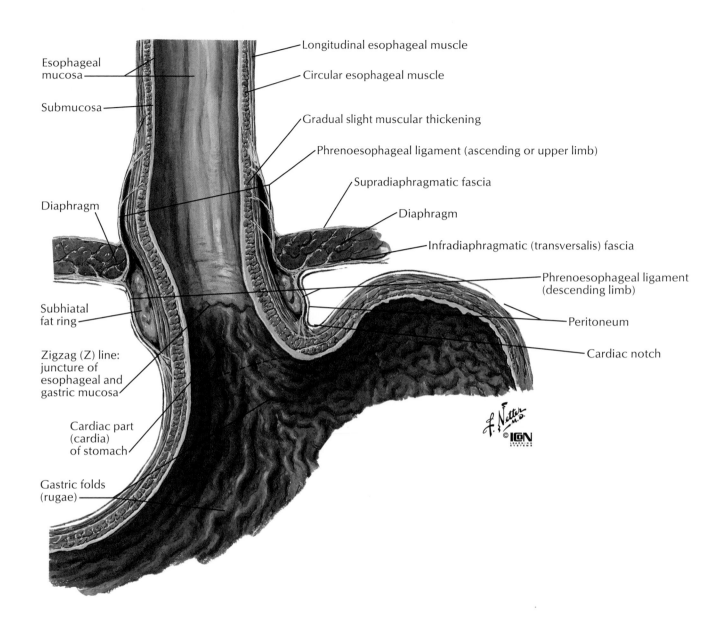

Esophageal mucosa

Longitudinal esophageal muscle

Circular esophageal muscle

Submucosa

Gradual slight muscular thickening

Phrenoesophageal ligament (ascending or upper limb)

Supradiaphragmatic fascia

Diaphragm

Diaphragm

Infradiaphragmatic (transversalis) fascia

Phrenoesophageal ligament (descending limb)

Subhiatal fat ring

Peritoneum

Zigzag (Z) line: juncture of esophageal and gastric mucosa

Cardiac notch

Cardiac part (cardia) of stomach

Gastric folds (rugae)

Nomenclature Notes

Esophagogastric is synonymous with *gastroesophageal*.

ANESTHESIA

Upper Abdomen

00740   Anesthesia for upper gastrointestinal endoscopic procedures, endoscope introduced proximal to duodenum

00790   Anesthesia for intraperitoneal procedures in upper abdomen including laparoscopy; not otherwise specified

SURGERY

Digestive System

Esophagus
Repair

43405   Ligation or stapling at gastroesophageal junction for pre-existing esophageal perforation

Manipulation

43460   Esophagogastric tamponade, with balloon (Sengstaaken type)

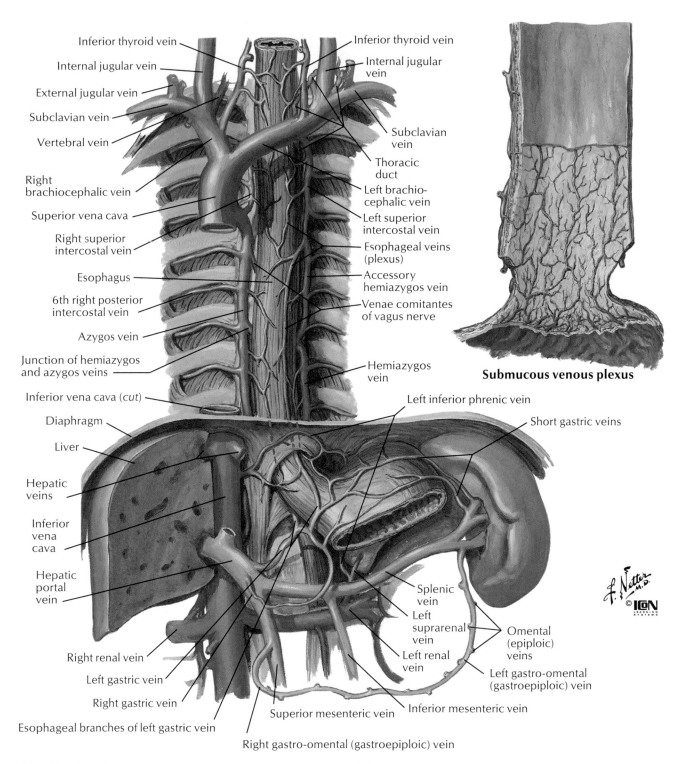

Inferior thyroid vein

Internal jugular vein

External jugular vein

Subclavian vein

Vertebral vein

Right brachiocephalic vein

Superior vena cava

Right superior intercostal vein

Esophagus

6th right posterior intercostal vein

Azygos vein

Junction of hemiazygos and azygos veins

Inferior vena cava (*cut*)

Diaphragm

Liver

Hepatic veins

Inferior vena cava

Hepatic portal vein

Right renal vein

Left gastric vein

Right gastric vein

Esophageal branches of left gastric vein

Superior mesenteric vein

Right gastro-omental (gastroepiploic) vein

Inferior thyroid vein

Internal jugular vein

Subclavian vein

Thoracic duct

Left brachio-cephalic vein

Left superior intercostal vein

Esophageal veins (plexus)

Accessory hemiazygos vein

Venae comitantes of vagus nerve

Hemiazygos vein

Left inferior phrenic vein

Short gastric veins

Splenic vein

Left suprarenal vein

Left renal vein

Omental (epiploic) veins

Left gastro-omental (gastroepiploic) vein

Inferior mesenteric vein

Submucous venous plexus

ANESTHESIA

Neck

| 00320 | Anesthesia for all procedures on esophagus, thyroid, larynx, trachea and lymphatic system of neck; not otherwise specified, age 1 year or older |

SURGERY

Digestive System

Esophagus
Endoscopy

| 43204 | Esophagoscopy, rigid or flexible; with injection sclerosis of esophageal varices |
| 43205 | with band ligation of esophageal varices |

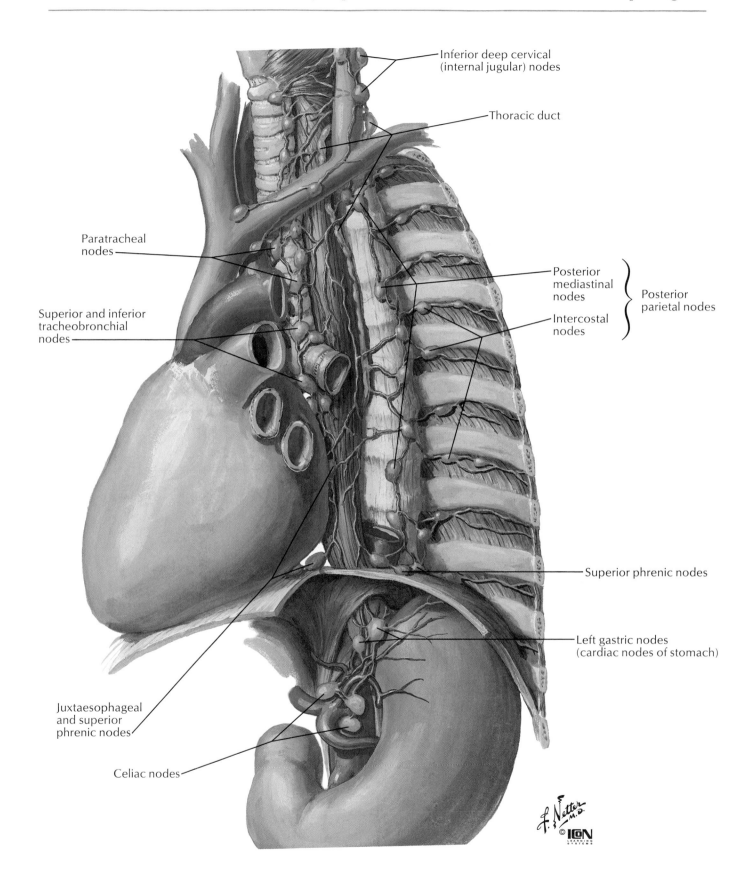

Inferior deep cervical (internal jugular) nodes

Thoracic duct

Paratracheal nodes

Superior and inferior tracheobronchial nodes

Posterior mediastinal nodes

Intercostal nodes

Posterior parietal nodes

Superior phrenic nodes

Left gastric nodes (cardiac nodes of stomach)

Juxtaesophageal and superior phrenic nodes

Celiac nodes

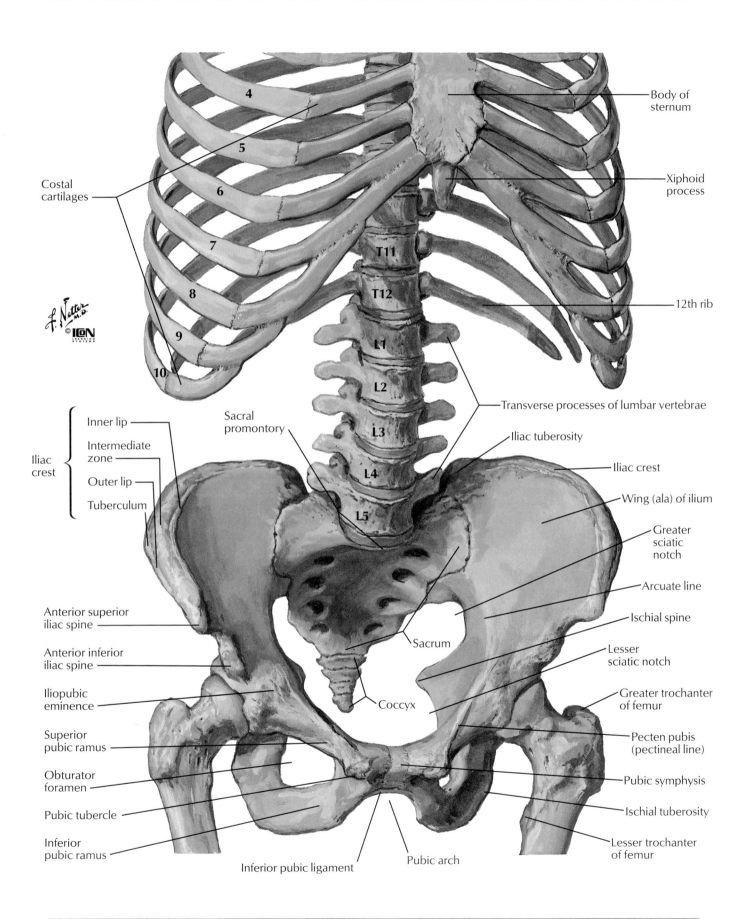

Costal cartilages

4

5

6

7

8

9

10

Body of sternum

Xiphoid process

T11

T12

12th rib

L1

L2

L3

L4

L5

Transverse processes of lumbar vertebrae

Iliac tuberosity

Iliac crest

Wing (ala) of ilium

Greater sciatic notch

Arcuate line

Ischial spine

Lesser sciatic notch

Greater trochanter of femur

Pecten pubis (pectineal line)

Pubic symphysis

Ischial tuberosity

Lesser trochanter of femur

Iliac crest { Inner lip, Intermediate zone, Outer lip, Tuberculum

Sacral promontory

Anterior superior iliac spine

Anterior inferior iliac spine

Iliopubic eminence

Superior pubic ramus

Obturator foramen

Pubic tubercle

Inferior pubic ramus

Inferior pubic ligament

Sacrum

Coccyx

Pubic arch

ANESTHESIA

Thorax (Chest Wall and Shoulder Girdle)

00470 Anesthesia for partial rib resection; not otherwise specified

00472 thoracoplasty (any type)

Intrathoracic

00520 Anesthesia for closed chest procedures; (including bronchoscopy) not otherwise specified

Spine and Spinal Cord

00630 Anesthesia for procedures in lumbar region; not otherwise specified

00670 Anesthesia for extensive spine and spinal cord procedures (eg, spinal instrumentation or vascular procedures)

Pelvis (Except Hip)

01112 Anesthesia for bone marrow aspiration and/or biopsy, anterior or posterior iliac crest

01120 Anesthesia for procedures on bony pelvis

01150 Anesthesia for radical procedures for tumor of pelvis, except hindquarter amputation

01160 Anesthesia for closed procedures involving symphysis pubis or sacroiliac joint

01170 Anesthesia for open procedures involving symphysis pubis or sacroiliac joint

01173 Anesthesia for open repair of fracture disruption of pelvis or column fracture involving acetabulum

Upper Leg (Except Knee)

01210 Anesthesia for open procedures involving hip joint; not otherwise specified

SURGERY

Musculoskeletal System

General
Excision

20220 Biopsy, bone, trocar, or needle; superficial (eg, ilium, sternum, spinous process, ribs)

20225 Biopsy, bone, trocar, or needle; deep (eg, vertebral body, femur)

20240 Biopsy, bone, open; superficial (eg, ilium, sternum, spinous process, ribs, trochanter of femur)

20245 deep (eg, humerus, ischium, femur)

20251 Biopsy, vertebral body, open; lumbar or cervical

Neck (Soft Tissues) and Thorax
Excision

21600 Excision of rib, partial

Fracture and/or Dislocation

21800 Closed treatment of rib fracture, uncomplicated, each

21805 Open treatment of rib fracture without fixation, each

21810 Treatment of rib fracture requiring external fixation (flail chest)

Spine (Vertebral Column)
Spinal Instrumentation

22848 Pelvic fixation (attachment of caudal end of instrumentation to pelvic bony structures) other than sacrum

Pelvis and Hip Joint
Excision

27065 Excision of bone cyst or benign tumor; superficial (wing of ilium, symphysis pubis, or greater trochanter of femur) with or without autograft

27066 deep, with or without autograft

27067 with autograft requiring separate incision

27070 Partial excision (craterization, saucerization) (eg, osteomyelitis or bone abscess); superficial (eg, wing of ilium, symphysis pubis, or greater trochanter of femur)

27071 deep (subfascial or intramuscular)

27075 Radical resection of tumor or infection; wing of ilium, one pubic or ischial ramus or symphysis pubis

27076 ilium, including acetabulum, both pubic rami, or ischium and acetabulum

27077 innominate bone, total

27078 ischial tuberosity and greater trochanter of femur

27079 ischial tuberosity and greater trochanter of femur, with skin flaps

27080 Coccygectomy, primary

Fracture and/or Dislocation

27193 Closed treatment of pelvic ring fracture, dislocation, diastasis or subluxation; without manipulation

27194 with manipulation, requiring more than local anesthesia

27200 Closed treatment of coccygeal fracture

27202 Open treatment of coccygeal fracture

27215 Open treatment of iliac spine(s), tuberosity avulsion, or iliac wing fracture(s) (eg, pelvic fracture(s) which do not disrupt the pelvic ring), with internal fixation

27216 Percutaneous skeletal fixation of posterior pelvic ring fracture and/or dislocation (includes ilium, sacroiliac joint and/or sacrum)

27217 Open treatment of anterior ring fracture and/or dislocation with internal fixation (includes pubic symphysis and/or rami)

27218 Open treatment of posterior ring fracture and/or dislocation with internal fixation (includes ilium, sacroiliac joint and/or sacrum)

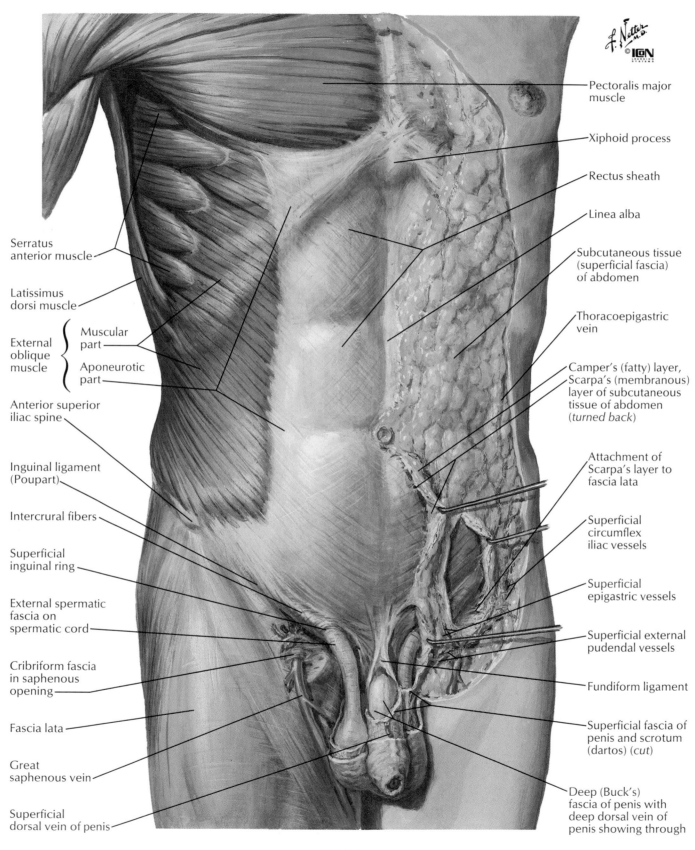

Pectoralis major muscle

Xiphoid process

Rectus sheath

Linea alba

Subcutaneous tissue (superficial fascia) of abdomen

Thoracoepigastric vein

Camper's (fatty) layer, Scarpa's (membranous) layer of subcutaneous tissue of abdomen (*turned back*)

Attachment of Scarpa's layer to fascia lata

Superficial circumflex iliac vessels

Superficial epigastric vessels

Superficial external pudendal vessels

Fundiform ligament

Superficial fascia of penis and scrotum (dartos) (*cut*)

Deep (Buck's) fascia of penis with deep dorsal vein of penis showing through

Serratus anterior muscle

Latissimus dorsi muscle

External oblique muscle — Muscular part / Aponeurotic part

Anterior superior iliac spine

Inguinal ligament (Poupart)

Intercrural fibers

Superficial inguinal ring

External spermatic fascia on spermatic cord

Cribriform fascia in saphenous opening

Fascia lata

Great saphenous vein

Superficial dorsal vein of penis

Superficial dissection

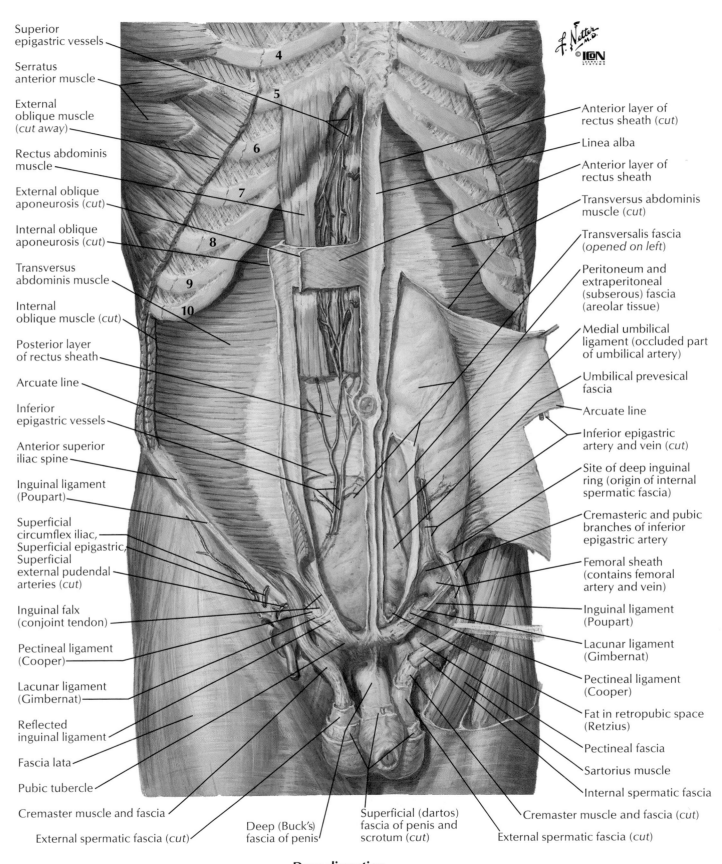

Superior epigastric vessels

Serratus anterior muscle

External oblique muscle (cut away)

Rectus abdominis muscle

External oblique aponeurosis (cut)

Internal oblique aponeurosis (cut)

Transversus abdominis muscle

Internal oblique muscle (cut)

Posterior layer of rectus sheath

Arcuate line

Inferior epigastric vessels

Anterior superior iliac spine

Inguinal ligament (Poupart)

Superficial circumflex iliac, Superficial epigastric, Superficial external pudendal arteries (cut)

Inguinal falx (conjoint tendon)

Pectineal ligament (Cooper)

Lacunar ligament (Gimbernat)

Reflected inguinal ligament

Fascia lata

Pubic tubercle

Cremaster muscle and fascia

External spermatic fascia (cut)

Deep (Buck's) fascia of penis

Superficial (dartos) fascia of penis and scrotum (cut)

Anterior layer of rectus sheath (cut)

Linea alba

Anterior layer of rectus sheath

Transversus abdominis muscle (cut)

Transversalis fascia (opened on left)

Peritoneum and extraperitoneal (subserous) fascia (areolar tissue)

Medial umbilical ligament (occluded part of umbilical artery)

Umbilical prevesical fascia

Arcuate line

Inferior epigastric artery and vein (cut)

Site of deep inguinal ring (origin of internal spermatic fascia)

Cremasteric and pubic branches of inferior epigastric artery

Femoral sheath (contains femoral artery and vein)

Inguinal ligament (Poupart)

Lacunar ligament (Gimbernat)

Pectineal ligament (Cooper)

Fat in retropubic space (Retzius)

Pectineal fascia

Sartorius muscle

Internal spermatic fascia

Cremaster muscle and fascia (cut)

External spermatic fascia (cut)

4

5

6

7

8

9

10

Deep dissection

ANESTHESIA

Upper Abdomen

00700 Anesthesia for procedures on upper anterior abdominal wall; not otherwise specified

00752 Anesthesia for hernia repairs in upper abdomen; lumbar and ventral (incisional) hernias and/or wound dehiscence

Lower Abdomen

00800 Anesthesia for procedures on lower anterior abdominal wall; not otherwise specified

SURGERY

Integumentary System

Skin, Subcutaneous and Accessory Structures
Excision—Debridement

11005 Debridement of skin, subcutaneous tissue, muscle and fascia for necrotizing soft tissue infection; abdominal wall, with or without fascial closure

11006 external genitalia, perineum and abdominal wall, with or without fascial closure

11008 Removal of prosthetic material or mesh, abdominal wall for necrotizing soft tissue infection (List separately in addition to code for primary procedure)

Repair (Closure)
Flaps (Skin and/or Deep Tissues)

15734 Muscle, myocutaneous, or fasciocutaneous flap; trunk

Other Procedures

15877 Suction assisted lipectomy; trunk

Musculoskeletal System

Abdomen
Excision

22900 Excision, abdominal wall tumor, subfascial (eg, desmoid)

Digestive System

Abdomen, Peritoneum, and Omentum
Suture

49900 Suture, secondary, of abdominal wall for evisceration or dehiscence

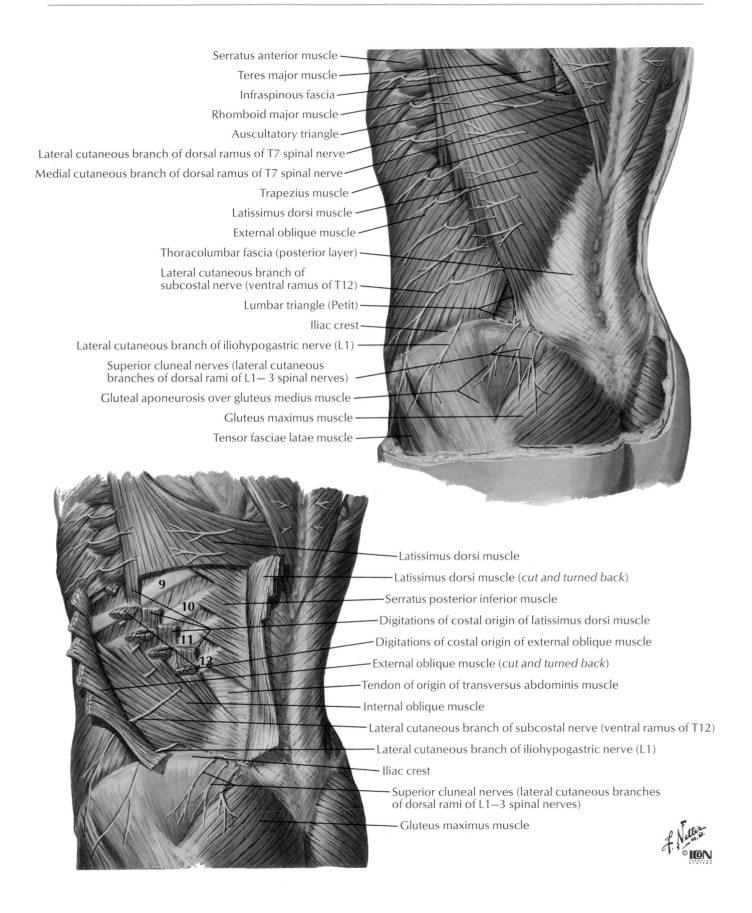

Serratus anterior muscle

Teres major muscle

Infraspinous fascia

Rhomboid major muscle

Auscultatory triangle

Lateral cutaneous branch of dorsal ramus of T7 spinal nerve

Medial cutaneous branch of dorsal ramus of T7 spinal nerve

Trapezius muscle

Latissimus dorsi muscle

External oblique muscle

Thoracolumbar fascia (posterior layer)

Lateral cutaneous branch of subcostal nerve (ventral ramus of T12)

Lumbar triangle (Petit)

Iliac crest

Lateral cutaneous branch of iliohypogastric nerve (L1)

Superior cluneal nerves (lateral cutaneous branches of dorsal rami of L1— 3 spinal nerves)

Gluteal aponeurosis over gluteus medius muscle

Gluteus maximus muscle

Tensor fasciae latae muscle

9

10

11

12

Latissimus dorsi muscle

Latissimus dorsi muscle (*cut and turned back*)

Serratus posterior inferior muscle

Digitations of costal origin of latissimus dorsi muscle

Digitations of costal origin of external oblique muscle

External oblique muscle (*cut and turned back*)

Tendon of origin of transversus abdominis muscle

Internal oblique muscle

Lateral cutaneous branch of subcostal nerve (ventral ramus of T12)

Lateral cutaneous branch of iliohypogastric nerve (L1)

Iliac crest

Superior cluneal nerves (lateral cutaneous branches of dorsal rami of L1—3 spinal nerves)

Gluteus maximus muscle

> **Nomenclature Notes**
>
> The *flank* is the part of the body below the ribs and above the ilium.

ANESTHESIA

Neck

00300 Anesthesia for all procedures on the integumentary system, muscles and nerves of head, neck, and posterior trunk, not otherwise specified

Thorax (Chest Wall and Shoulder Girdle)

00400 Anesthesia for procedures on the integumentary system on the extremities, anterior trunk and perineum; not otherwise specified

Upper Abdomen

00730 Anesthesia for procedures on upper posterior abdominal wall

Lower Abdomen

00820 Anesthesia for procedures on lower posterior abdominal wall

Other Procedures

01991 Anesthesia for diagnostic or therapeutic nerve blocks and injections (when block or injection is performed by a different provider); other than the prone position
01992 prone position

SURGERY

Integumentary System

Skin, Subcutaneous and Accessory Structures
Excision—Debridement

11005 Debridement of skin, subcutaneous tissue, muscle and fascia for necrotizing soft tissue infection; abdominal wall, with or without fascial closure
11006 Debridement of skin, subcutaneous tissue, muscle and fascia for necrotizing soft tissue infection; external genitalia, perineum and abdominal wall, with or without fascial closure

11008 Removal of prosthetic material or mesh, abdominal wall for necrotizing soft tissue infection (List separately in addition to code for primary procedure)

Repair (Closure)
Flaps (Skin and/or Deep Tissues)

15734 Muscle, myocutaneous, or fasciocutaneous flap; trunk

Other Procedures

15877 Suction assisted lipectomy; trunk

Musculoskeletal System

Back and Flank
Excision

21920 Biopsy, soft tissue of back or flank; superficial
21925 deep
21930 Excision, tumor, soft tissue of back or flank
Abdomen
Excision

22900 Excision, abdominal wall tumor, subfascial (eg, desmoid)

Digestive System

Abdomen, Peritoneum, and Omentum
49900 Suture, secondary, of abdominal wall for evisceration or dehiscence

Nervous System

Extracranial Nerves, Peripheral Nerves, and Autonomic Nervous System
Introduction/Injection of Anesthetic Agent (Nerve Block), Diagnostic or Therapeutic

Somatic Nerves
64425 Injection, anesthetic agent; ilioinguinal, iliohypogastric nerves

Excision

Somatic Nerves
64774 Excision of neuroma; cutaneous nerve, surgically identifiable
64788 Excision of neurofibroma or neurolemmoma; cutaneous nerve
64795 Biopsy of nerve

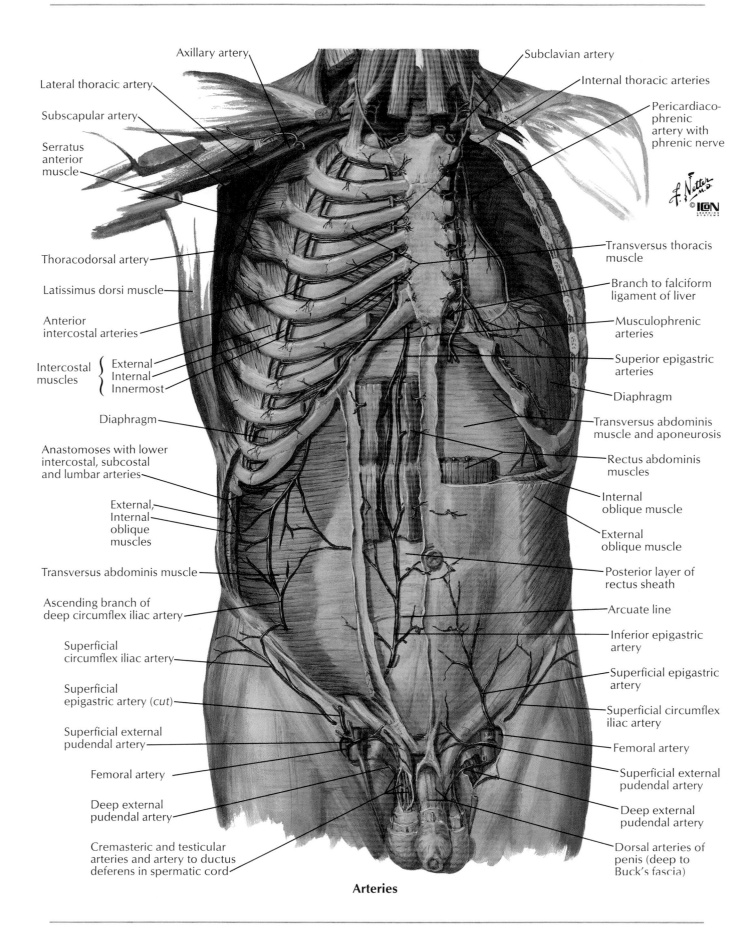

Axillary artery

Lateral thoracic artery

Subscapular artery

Serratus anterior muscle

Thoracodorsal artery

Latissimus dorsi muscle

Anterior intercostal arteries

Intercostal muscles { External Internal Innermost

Diaphragm

Anastomoses with lower intercostal, subcostal and lumbar arteries

External, Internal oblique muscles

Transversus abdominis muscle

Ascending branch of deep circumflex iliac artery

Superficial circumflex iliac artery

Superficial epigastric artery (cut)

Superficial external pudendal artery

Femoral artery

Deep external pudendal artery

Cremasteric and testicular arteries and artery to ductus deferens in spermatic cord

Subclavian artery

Internal thoracic arteries

Pericardiaco-phrenic artery with phrenic nerve

Transversus thoracis muscle

Branch to falciform ligament of liver

Musculophrenic arteries

Superior epigastric arteries

Diaphragm

Transversus abdominis muscle and aponeurosis

Rectus abdominis muscles

Internal oblique muscle

External oblique muscle

Posterior layer of rectus sheath

Arcuate line

Inferior epigastric artery

Superficial epigastric artery

Superficial circumflex iliac artery

Femoral artery

Superficial external pudendal artery

Deep external pudendal artery

Dorsal arteries of penis (deep to Buck's fascia)

Arteries

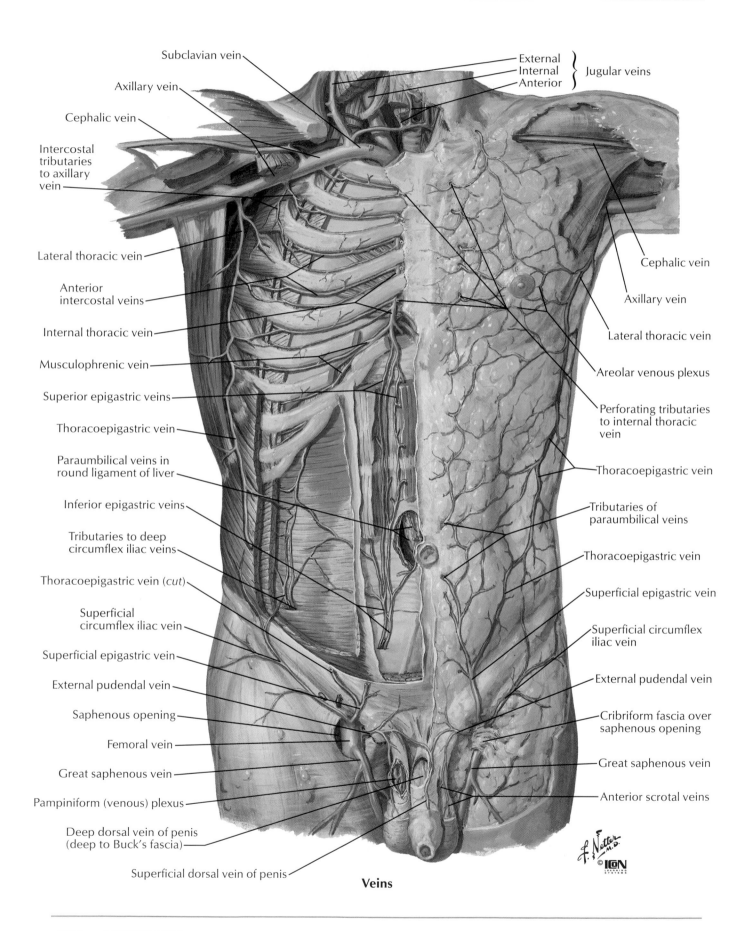

Subclavian vein

External
Internal
Anterior
} Jugular veins

Axillary vein

Cephalic vein

Intercostal tributaries to axillary vein

Cephalic vein

Axillary vein

Lateral thoracic vein

Anterior intercostal veins

Lateral thoracic vein

Internal thoracic vein

Areolar venous plexus

Musculophrenic vein

Perforating tributaries to internal thoracic vein

Superior epigastric veins

Thoracoepigastric vein

Thoracoepigastric vein

Paraumbilical veins in round ligament of liver

Tributaries of paraumbilical veins

Inferior epigastric veins

Thoracoepigastric vein

Tributaries to deep circumflex iliac veins

Superficial epigastric vein

Thoracoepigastric vein (cut)

Superficial circumflex iliac vein

Superficial circumflex iliac vein

External pudendal vein

Superficial epigastric vein

External pudendal vein

Saphenous opening

Cribriform fascia over saphenous opening

Femoral vein

Great saphenous vein

Great saphenous vein

Anterior scrotal veins

Pampiniform (venous) plexus

Deep dorsal vein of penis (deep to Buck's fascia)

Superficial dorsal vein of penis

Veins

ANESTHESIA

Neck

00350   Anesthesia for procedures on major vessels of neck; not otherwise specified

Intrathoracic

00532   Anesthesia for access to central venous circulation

00560   Anesthesia for procedures on heart, pericardial sac, and great vessels of chest; without pump oxygenator

Upper Abdomen

00700   Anesthesia for procedures on upper anterior abdominal wall; not otherwise specified

00770   Anesthesia for all procedures on major abdominal blood vessel

Lower Abdomen

00800   Anesthesia for procedures on lower anterior abdominal wall; not otherwise specified

00880   Anesthesia for procedures on major lower abdominal vessels; not otherwise specified

Upper Leg (Except Knee)

01270   Anesthesia for procedures involving arteries of upper leg, including bypass graft; not otherwise specified

Shoulder and Axilla

01654   Anesthesia for procedures on arteries of shoulder and axilla; bypass graft

Upper Arm and Elbow

01770   Anesthesia for procedures on arteries of upper arm and elbow; not otherwise specified

01772   embolectomy

01780   not otherwise specified

SURGERY

Cardiovascular System

Arteries and Veins

Embolectomy/Thrombectomy

Arterial, With or Without Catheter

34051   Embolectomy or thrombectomy, with or without catheter; innominate, subclavian artery, by thoracic incision

34101   axillary, brachial, innominate, subclavian artery, by arm incision

Venous, Direct or With Catheter

34471   Thrombectomy, direct or with catheter; subclavian vein, by neck incision

34490   axillary and subclavian vein, by arm incision

Direct Repair of Aneurysm or Excision (Partial or Total) and Graft Insertion for Aneurysm, Pseudoaneurysm, Ruptured Aneurysm, and Associated Occlusive Disease

35001   Direct repair of aneurysm, pseudoaneurysm, or excision (partial or total) and graft insertion, with or without patch graft; for aneurysm and associated occlusive disease, carotid, subclavian artery, by neck incision

35002   for ruptured aneurysm, carotid, subclavian artery, by neck incision

35011   for aneurysm and associated occlusive disease, axillary-brachial artery, by arm incision

35013   for ruptured aneurysm, axillary-brachial artery, by arm incision

35021   for aneurysm, pseudoaneurysm, and associated occlusive disease, innominate, subclavian artery, by thoracic incision

35022   for ruptured aneurysm, innominate, subclavian artery, by thoracic incision

35141   for aneurysm, pseudoaneurysm, and associated occlusive disease, common femoral artery (profunda femoris, superficial femoral)

35142   for ruptured aneurysm, common femoral artery (profunda femoris, superficial femoral)

Repair Arteriovenous Fistula

35182   Repair, congenital arteriovenous fistula; thorax and abdomen

35189   Repair, acquired or traumatic arteriovenous fistula; thorax and abdomen

Repair Blood Vessel Other Than for Fistula, With or Without Patch Angioplasty

35221   Repair blood vessel, direct; intra-abdominal

35251   Repair blood vessel with vein graft; intra-abdominal

35281   Repair blood vessel with graft other than vein; intra-abdominal

Thromboendarterectomy

35301   Thromboendarterectomy, with or without patch graft; carotid, vertebral, subclavian, by neck incision

35311   subclavian, innominate, by thoracic incision

35321   axillary-brachial

35371[P]   common femoral

35372[P]   deep (profunda) femoral

Transluminal Angioplasty

Open

35460   Transluminal balloon angioplasty, open; venous

Percutaneous

35476   Transluminal balloon angioplasty, percutaneous; venous

Bypass Graft

Vein

35511   Bypass graft, with vein; subclavian-subclavian

(Bypass Graft continued on next page)

(Bypass Graft continued from previous page)

35516	subclavian-axillary
35558	femoral-femoral
35571[P]	popliteal-tibial, -peroneal artery or other distal vessels

Other Than Vein

35616	Bypass graft, with other than vein; subclavian-axillary

Exploration/Revision

35721	Exploration (not followed by surgical repair), with or without lysis of artery; femoral artery
35761	other vessels
35820	Exploration for postoperative hemorrhage, thrombosis or infection; chest
35840	abdomen
35905	Excision of infected graft; thorax
35907	abdomen

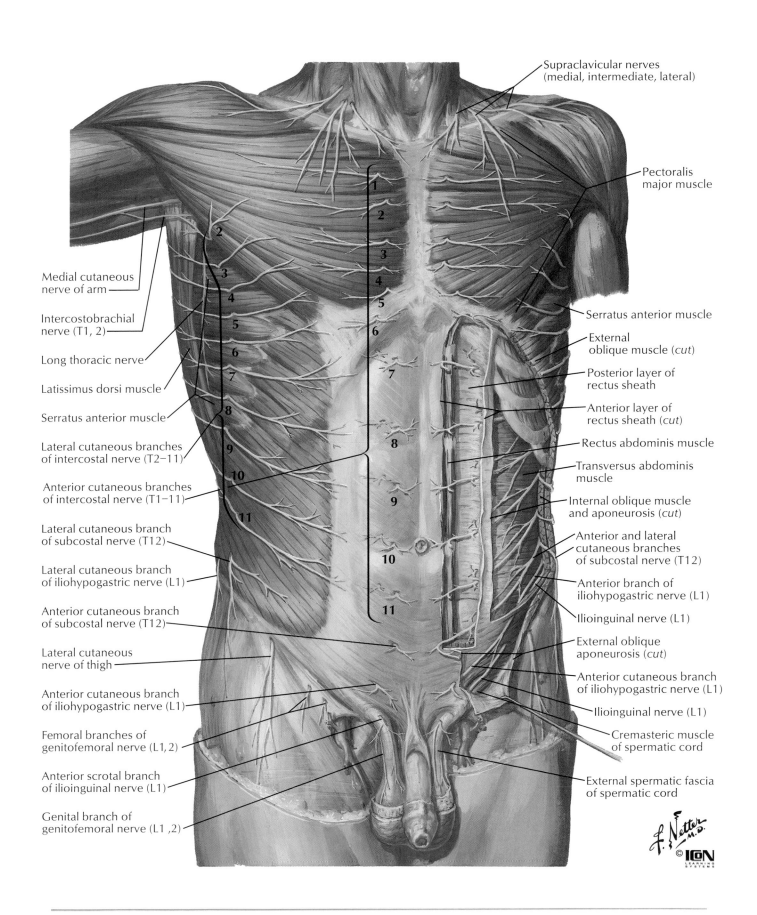

Supraclavicular nerves
(medial, intermediate, lateral)

Pectoralis
major muscle

Serratus anterior muscle

External
oblique muscle (*cut*)

Posterior layer of
rectus sheath

Anterior layer of
rectus sheath (*cut*)

Rectus abdominis muscle

Transversus abdominis
muscle

Internal oblique muscle
and aponeurosis (*cut*)

Anterior and lateral
cutaneous branches
of subcostal nerve (T12)

Anterior branch of
iliohypogastric nerve (L1)

Ilioinguinal nerve (L1)

External oblique
aponeurosis (*cut*)

Anterior cutaneous branch
of iliohypogastric nerve (L1)

Ilioinguinal nerve (L1)

Cremasteric muscle
of spermatic cord

External spermatic fascia
of spermatic cord

Medial cutaneous
nerve of arm

Intercostobrachial
nerve (T1, 2)

Long thoracic nerve

Latissimus dorsi muscle

Serratus anterior muscle

Lateral cutaneous branches
of intercostal nerve (T2–11)

Anterior cutaneous branches
of intercostal nerve (T1–11)

Lateral cutaneous branch
of subcostal nerve (T12)

Lateral cutaneous branch
of iliohypogastric nerve (L1)

Anterior cutaneous branch
of subcostal nerve (T12)

Lateral cutaneous
nerve of thigh

Anterior cutaneous branch
of iliohypogastric nerve (L1)

Femoral branches of
genitofemoral nerve (L1, 2)

Anterior scrotal branch
of ilioinguinal nerve (L1)

Genital branch of
genitofemoral nerve (L1 ,2)

ANESTHESIA

Lower Abdomen

00830   Anesthesia for hernia repairs in lower abdomen; not otherwise specified

00834   Anesthesia for hernia repairs in the lower abdomen not otherwise specified, under 1 year of age

00836   Anesthesia for hernia repairs in the lower abdomen not otherwise specified, infants less than 37 weeks gestational age at birth and less than 50 weeks gestational age at time of surgery

SURGERY

Digestive System

Abdomen, Peritoneum, and Omentum
Repair

Hernioplasty, Herniorrhaphy, Herniotomy

49491   Repair, initial inguinal hernia, preterm infant (less than 37 weeks gestation at birth), performed from birth up to 50 weeks postconception age, with or without hydrocelectomy; reducible

49492   incarcerated or strangulated

49495   Repair, initial inguinal hernia, full term infant under age 6 months, or preterm infant over 50 weeks postconception age and under age 6 months at the time of surgery, with or without hydrocelectomy; reducible

49496   incarcerated or strangulated

49500   Repair initial inguinal hernia, age 6 months to under 5 years, with or without hydrocelectomy; reducible

49501   incarcerated or strangulated

49505   Repair initial inguinal hernia, age 5 years or over; reducible

49507   incarcerated or strangulated

49520   Repair recurrent inguinal hernia, any age; reducible

49521   incarcerated or strangulated

49525   Repair inguinal hernia, sliding, any age

Laparoscopy

49650   Laparoscopy, surgical; repair initial inguinal hernia

49651   repair recurrent inguinal hernia

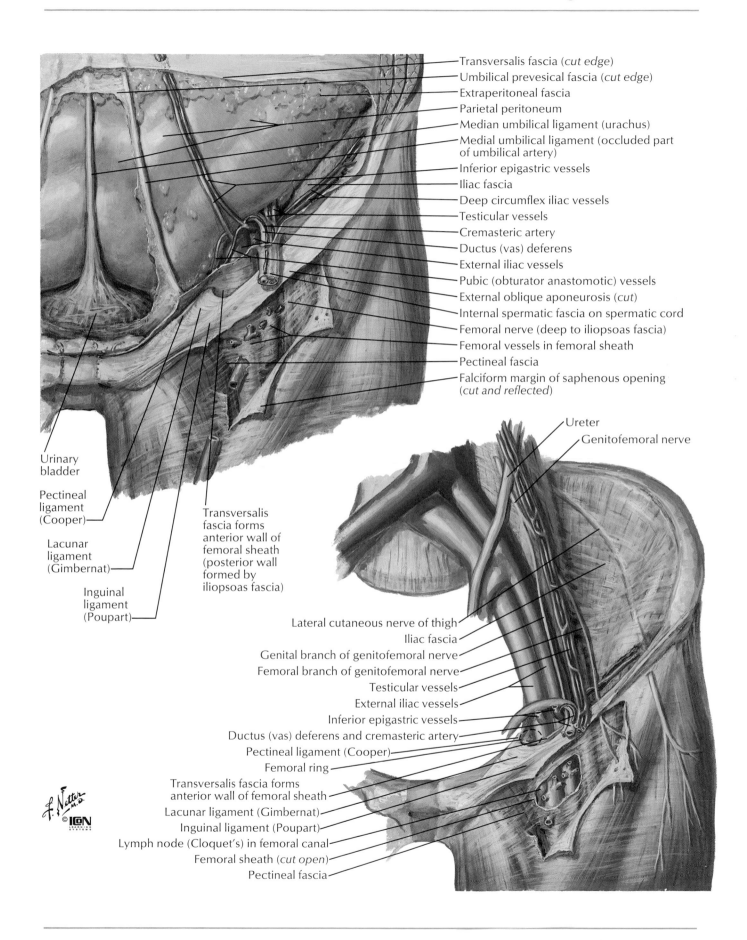

Transversalis fascia (*cut edge*)

Umbilical prevesical fascia (*cut edge*)

Extraperitoneal fascia

Parietal peritoneum

Median umbilical ligament (urachus)

Medial umbilical ligament (occluded part of umbilical artery)

Inferior epigastric vessels

Iliac fascia

Deep circumflex iliac vessels

Testicular vessels

Cremasteric artery

Ductus (vas) deferens

External iliac vessels

Pubic (obturator anastomotic) vessels

External oblique aponeurosis (*cut*)

Internal spermatic fascia on spermatic cord

Femoral nerve (deep to iliopsoas fascia)

Femoral vessels in femoral sheath

Pectineal fascia

Falciform margin of saphenous opening (*cut and reflected*)

Urinary bladder

Pectineal ligament (Cooper)

Lacunar ligament (Gimbernat)

Inguinal ligament (Poupart)

Transversalis fascia forms anterior wall of femoral sheath (posterior wall formed by iliopsoas fascia)

Ureter

Genitofemoral nerve

Lateral cutaneous nerve of thigh

Iliac fascia

Genital branch of genitofemoral nerve

Femoral branch of genitofemoral nerve

Testicular vessels

External iliac vessels

Inferior epigastric vessels

Ductus (vas) deferens and cremasteric artery

Pectineal ligament (Cooper)

Femoral ring

Transversalis fascia forms anterior wall of femoral sheath

Lacunar ligament (Gimbernat)

Inguinal ligament (Poupart)

Lymph node (Cloquet's) in femoral canal

Femoral sheath (*cut open*)

Pectineal fascia

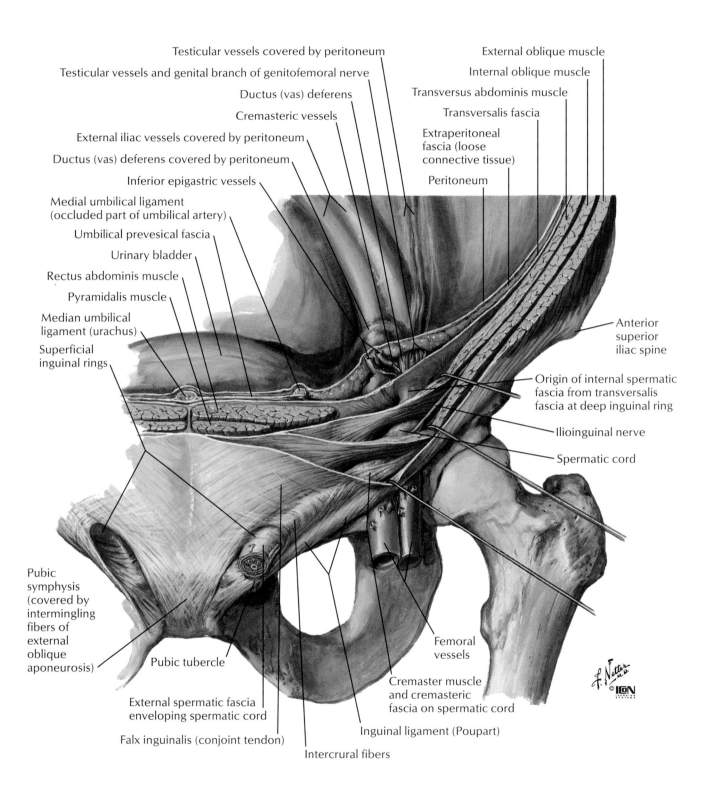

Testicular vessels covered by peritoneum

Testicular vessels and genital branch of genitofemoral nerve

Ductus (vas) deferens

Cremasteric vessels

External iliac vessels covered by peritoneum

Ductus (vas) deferens covered by peritoneum

Inferior epigastric vessels

Medial umbilical ligament (occluded part of umbilical artery)

Umbilical prevesical fascia

Urinary bladder

Rectus abdominis muscle

Pyramidalis muscle

Median umbilical ligament (urachus)

Superficial inguinal rings

Pubic symphysis (covered by intermingling fibers of external oblique aponeurosis)

Pubic tubercle

External spermatic fascia enveloping spermatic cord

Falx inguinalis (conjoint tendon)

Intercrural fibers

External oblique muscle

Internal oblique muscle

Transversus abdominis muscle

Transversalis fascia

Extraperitoneal fascia (loose connective tissue)

Peritoneum

Anterior superior iliac spine

Origin of internal spermatic fascia from transversalis fascia at deep inguinal ring

Ilioinguinal nerve

Spermatic cord

Femoral vessels

Cremaster muscle and cremasteric fascia on spermatic cord

Inguinal ligament (Poupart)

ANESTHESIA

Lower Abdomen

00830 Anesthesia for hernia repairs in lower abdomen; not otherwise specified

00834 Anesthesia for hernia repairs in the lower abdomen not otherwise specified, under 1 year of age

00836 Anesthesia for hernia repairs in the lower abdomen not otherwise specified, infants less than 37 weeks gestational age at birth and less than 50 weeks gestational age at time of surgery

00860 Anesthesia for extraperitoneal procedures in lower abdomen, including urinary tract; not otherwise specified

Perineum

00920 Anesthesia for procedures on male genitalia (including open urethral procedures); not otherwise specified

SURGERY

Digestive System

Abdomen, Peritoneum, and Omentum
Repair

Hernioplasty, Herniorrhaphy, Herniotomy

49491 Repair, initial inguinal hernia, preterm infant (less than 37 weeks gestation at birth), performed from birth up to 50 weeks postconception age, with or without hydrocelectomy; reducible

49492 incarcerated or strangulated

49495 Repair, initial inguinal hernia, full term infant under age 6 months, or preterm infant over 50 weeks postconception age and under age 6 months at the time of surgery, with or without hydrocelectomy; reducible

49496 incarcerated or strangulated

49500 Repair initial inguinal hernia, age 6 months to under 5 years, with or without hydrocelectomy; reducible

49501 incarcerated or strangulated

49505 Repair initial inguinal hernia, age 5 years or over; reducible

49507 incarcerated or strangulated

49520 Repair recurrent inguinal hernia, any age; reducible

49521 incarcerated or strangulated

49525 Repair inguinal hernia, sliding, any age

49550 Repair initial femoral hernia, any age; reducible

49553 incarcerated or strangulated

49555 Repair recurrent femoral hernia; reducible

49557 incarcerated or strangulated

Laparoscopy

49650 Laparoscopy, surgical; repair initial inguinal hernia

49651 repair recurrent inguinal hernia

Male Genital System

Spermatic Cord
Excision

55500 Excision of hydrocele of spermatic cord, unilateral (separate procedure)

55520 Excision of lesion of spermatic cord (separate procedure)

55530 Excision of varicocele or ligation of spermatic veins for varicocele; (separate procedure)

55535 abdominal approach

55540 with hernia repair

Laparoscopy

55550 Laparoscopy, surgical, with ligation of spermatic veins for varicocele

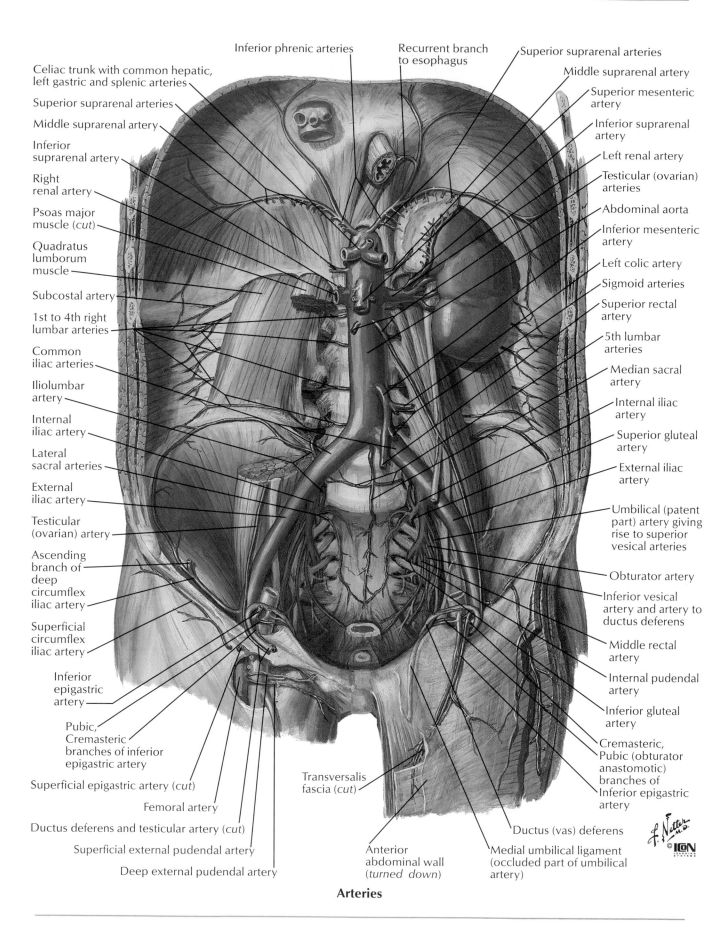

Inferior phrenic arteries

Recurrent branch to esophagus

Superior suprarenal arteries

Middle suprarenal artery

Superior mesenteric artery

Inferior suprarenal artery

Left renal artery

Testicular (ovarian) arteries

Abdominal aorta

Inferior mesenteric artery

Left colic artery

Sigmoid arteries

Superior rectal artery

5th lumbar arteries

Median sacral artery

Internal iliac artery

Superior gluteal artery

External iliac artery

Umbilical (patent part) artery giving rise to superior vesical arteries

Obturator artery

Inferior vesical artery and artery to ductus deferens

Middle rectal artery

Internal pudendal artery

Inferior gluteal artery

Cremasteric, Pubic (obturator anastomotic) branches of Inferior epigastric artery

Ductus (vas) deferens

Medial umbilical ligament (occluded part of umbilical artery)

Anterior abdominal wall (turned down)

Transversalis fascia (cut)

Ductus deferens and testicular artery (cut)

Femoral artery

Superficial epigastric artery (cut)

Pubic, Cremasteric branches of inferior epigastric artery

Inferior epigastric artery

Superficial circumflex iliac artery

Ascending branch of deep circumflex iliac artery

Testicular (ovarian) artery

External iliac artery

Lateral sacral arteries

Internal iliac artery

Iliolumbar artery

Common iliac arteries

1st to 4th right lumbar arteries

Subcostal artery

Quadratus lumborum muscle

Psoas major muscle (cut)

Right renal artery

Inferior suprarenal artery

Middle suprarenal artery

Superior suprarenal arteries

Celiac trunk with common hepatic, left gastric and splenic arteries

Superficial external pudendal artery

Deep external pudendal artery

Arteries

ANESTHESIA

Upper Abdomen

00770   Anesthesia for all procedures on major abdominal blood vessels

SURGERY

Cardiovascular System

Arteries and Veins

Direct Repair of Aneurysm or Excision (Partial or Total) and Graft Insertion for Aneurysm, Pseudoaneurysm, Ruptured Aneurysm, and Associated Occlusive Disease

35081   Direct repair of aneurysm, pseudoaneurysm, or excision (partial or total) and graft insertion, with or without patch graft; for aneurysm, pseudoaneurysm, and associated occlusive disease, abdominal aorta

35082   for ruptured aneurysm, abdominal aorta

35091   for aneurysm, pseudoaneurysm, and associated occlusive disease, abdominal aorta involving visceral vessels (mesenteric, celiac, renal)

35092   for ruptured aneurysm, abdominal aorta involving visceral vessels (mesenteric, celiac, renal)

35102   for aneurysm, pseudoaneurysm, and associated occlusive disease, abdominal aorta involving iliac vessels (common, hypogastric, external)

35103   for ruptured aneurysm, abdominal aorta involving iliac vessels (common, hypogastric, external)

35111   for aneurysm, pseudoaneurysm, and associated occlusive disease, splenic artery

35112   for ruptured aneurysm, splenic artery

35121   for aneurysm, pseudoaneurysm, and associated occlusive disease, hepatic, celiac, renal, or mesenteric artery

35122   for ruptured aneurysm, hepatic, celiac, renal, or mesenteric artery

Repair Arteriovenous Fistula

35182   Repair, congenital arteriovenous fistula; thorax and abdomen

35189   Repair, acquired or traumatic arteriovenous fistula; thorax and abdomen

Repair Blood Vessel Other Than for Fistula, With or Without Patch Angioplasty

35221   Repair blood vessel, direct; intra-abdominal

35251   Repair blood vessel with vein graft; intra-abdominal

35281   Repair blood vessel with graft other than vein; intra-abdominal

Thromboendarterectomy

35331   Thromboendarterectomy, with or without patch graft; abdominal aorta

35341   mesenteric, celiac, or renal

35351   iliac

35355   iliofemoral

35361   combined aortoiliac

35363   combined aortoiliofemoral

35371[P]   common femoral

35372[P]   deep (profunda) femoral

35381   femoral and/or popliteal, and/or tibioperoneal

Transluminal Angioplasty

Open

35450   Transluminal balloon angioplasty, open; renal or other visceral artery

35452   aortic

35454   iliac

35456   femoral-popliteal

35460   venous

Percutaneous

35471   Transluminal balloon angioplasty, percutaneous; renal or visceral artery

35472   aortic

35473   iliac

35476   venous

Transluminal Atherectomy

Open

35480   Transluminal peripheral atherectomy, open; renal or other visceral artery

35481   aortic

35482   iliac

Percutaneous

35490   Transluminal peripheral atherectomy, percutaneous; renal or other visceral artery

35491   aortic

35492   iliac

Bypass Graft

Vein

35531   Bypass graft, with vein; aortoceliac or aortomesenteric

35536   splenorenal

35541   aortoiliac or bi-iliac

35546   aortofemoral or bifemoral

35548   aortoiliofemoral, unilateral

35549   aortoiliofemoral, bilateral

35560   aortorenal

35563   ilioiliac

35565   iliofemoral

Other Than Vein

35631   Bypass graft, with other than vein; aortoceliac, aortomesenteric, aortorenal

35636   splenorenal (splenic to renal arterial anastomosis)

35641   aortoiliac or bi-iliac

35646   aortobifemoral

35647   aortofemoral

(Other Than Vein continued on page 197)

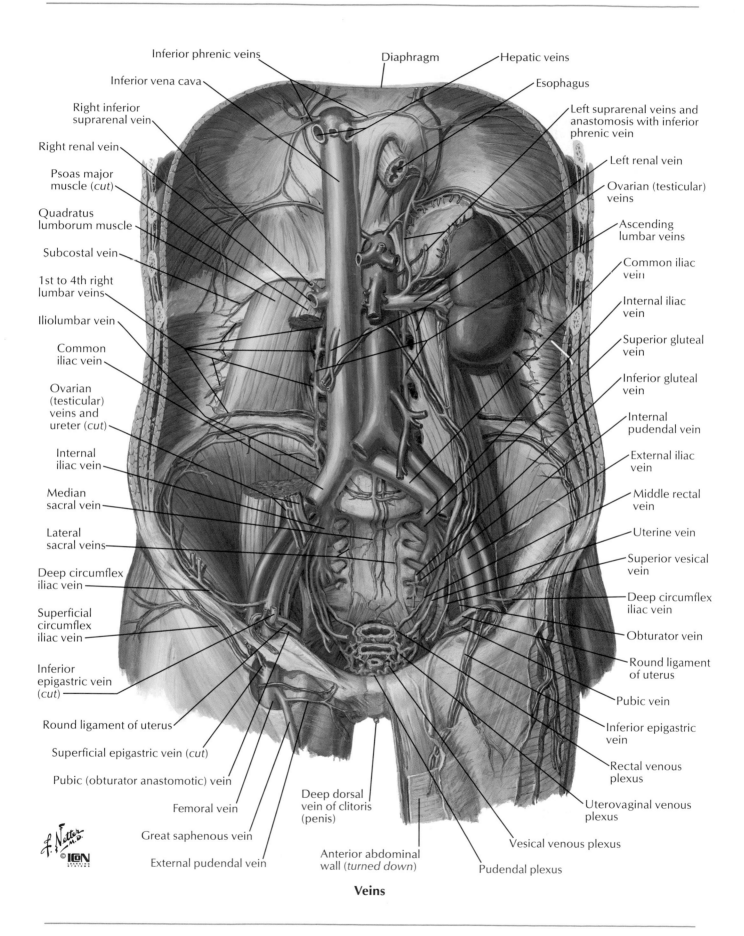

Inferior phrenic veins

Inferior vena cava

Right inferior suprarenal vein

Right renal vein

Psoas major muscle (*cut*)

Quadratus lumborum muscle

Subcostal vein

1st to 4th right lumbar veins

Iliolumbar vein

Common iliac vein

Ovarian (testicular) veins and ureter (*cut*)

Internal iliac vein

Median sacral vein

Lateral sacral veins

Deep circumflex iliac vein

Superficial circumflex iliac vein

Inferior epigastric vein (*cut*)

Round ligament of uterus

Superficial epigastric vein (*cut*)

Pubic (obturator anastomotic) vein

Femoral vein

Great saphenous vein

External pudendal vein

Diaphragm

Hepatic veins

Esophagus

Left suprarenal veins and anastomosis with inferior phrenic vein

Left renal vein

Ovarian (testicular) veins

Ascending lumbar veins

Common iliac vein

Internal iliac vein

Superior gluteal vein

Inferior gluteal vein

Internal pudendal vein

External iliac vein

Middle rectal vein

Uterine vein

Superior vesical vein

Deep circumflex iliac vein

Obturator vein

Round ligament of uterus

Pubic vein

Inferior epigastric vein

Rectal venous plexus

Uterovaginal venous plexus

Vesical venous plexus

Pudendal plexus

Deep dorsal vein of clitoris (penis)

Anterior abdominal wall (*turned down*)

Veins

(Other Than Vein continued from page 195)

35663	ilioiliac
35665	iliofemoral

Exploration/Revision

35721	Exploration (not followed by surgical repair), with or without lysis of artery; femoral artery
35761	other vessels
35840	Exploration for postoperative hemorrhage, thrombosis or infection; abdomen
35870	Repair of graft-enteric fistula
35875	Thrombectomy of arterial or venous graft (other than hemodialysis graft or fistula);
35876	with revision of arterial or venous graft
35907	Excision of infected graft; abdomen

Intravenous

36010	Introduction of catheter, superior or inferior vena cava
36011	Selective catheter placement, venous system; first order branch (eg, renal vein, jugular vein)
36012	second order, or more selective, branch (eg, left adrenal vein, petrosal sinus)

Intra-Arterial—Intra-Aortic

36160	Introduction of needle or intracatheter, aortic, translumbar
36200	Introduction of catheter, aorta
36245	Selective catheter placement, arterial system; each first order abdominal, pelvic, or lower extremity artery branch, within a vascular family
36260	Insertion of implantable intra-arterial infusion pump (eg, for chemotherapy of liver)
36261	Revision of implanted intra-arterial infusion pump
36262	Removal of implanted intra-arterial infusion pump

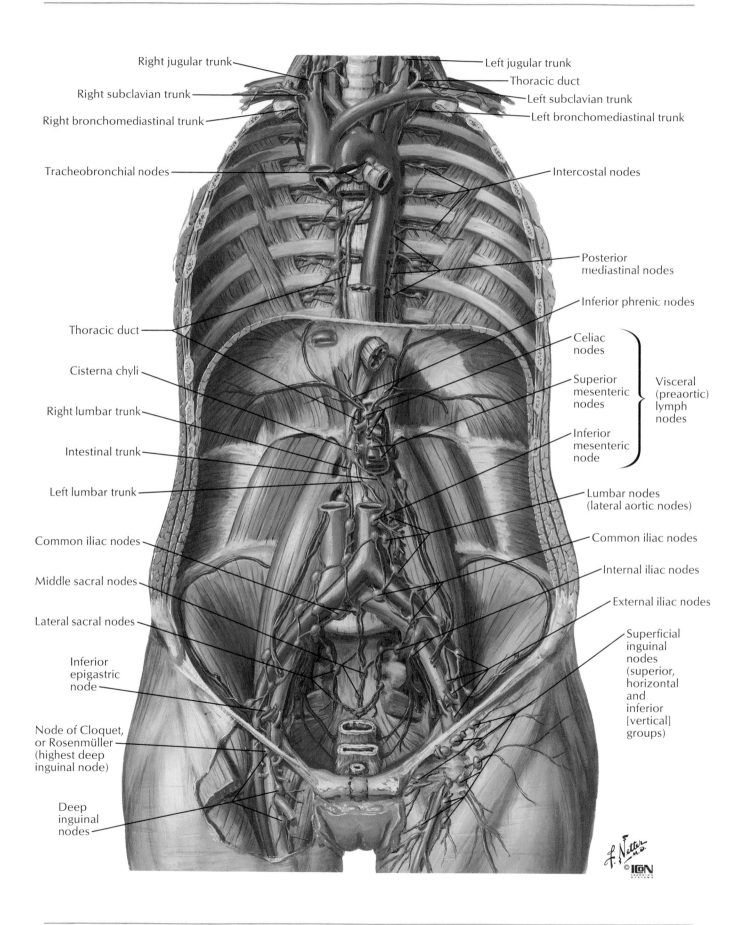

Right jugular trunk

Right subclavian trunk

Right bronchomediastinal trunk

Tracheobronchial nodes

Thoracic duct

Cisterna chyli

Right lumbar trunk

Intestinal trunk

Left lumbar trunk

Common iliac nodes

Middle sacral nodes

Lateral sacral nodes

Inferior epigastric node

Node of Cloquet, or Rosenmüller (highest deep inguinal node)

Deep inguinal nodes

Left jugular trunk

Thoracic duct

Left subclavian trunk

Left bronchomediastinal trunk

Intercostal nodes

Posterior mediastinal nodes

Inferior phrenic nodes

Celiac nodes

Superior mesenteric nodes

Inferior mesenteric node

Visceral (preaortic) lymph nodes

Lumbar nodes (lateral aortic nodes)

Common iliac nodes

Internal iliac nodes

External iliac nodes

Superficial inguinal nodes (superior, horizontal and inferior [vertical] groups)

ANESTHESIA

Neck

00320   Anesthesia for all procedures on esophagus, thyroid, larynx, trachea and lymphatic system of neck; not otherwise specified, age 1 year or older

Lower Abdomen

00800   Anesthesia for procedures on lower anterior abdominal wall; not otherwise specified

00860   Anesthesia for extraperitoneal procedures in lower abdomen, including urinary tract; not otherwise specified

SURGERY

Hemic and Lymphatic Systems

Lymph Nodes and Lymphatic Channels

Incision

38308   Lymphangiotomy or other operations on lymphatic channels

38380   Suture and/or ligation of thoracic duct; cervical approach

38381   thoracic approach

38382   abdominal approach

Excision

38500   Biopsy or excision of lymph node(s); open, superficial

38505   by needle, superficial (eg, cervical, inguinal, axillary)

Limited Lymphadenectomy for Staging

38562   Limited lymphadenectomy for staging (separate procedure); pelvic and para-aortic

38564   retroperitoneal (aortic and/or splenic)

Laparoscopy

38570   Laparoscopy, surgical; with retroperitoneal lymph node sampling (biopsy), single or multiple

38571   with bilateral total pelvic lymphadenectomy

38572   with bilateral total pelvic lymphadenectomy and peri-aortic lymph node sampling (biopsy), single or multiple

Radical Lymphadenectomy (Radical Resection of Lymph Nodes)

38747   Abdominal lymphadenectomy, regional, including celiac, gastric, portal, peripancreatic, with or without para-aortic and vena caval nodes (List separately in addition to code for primary procedure)

38760   Inguinofemoral lymphadenectomy, superficial, including Cloquets node (separate procedure)

38765   Inguinofemoral lymphadenectomy, superficial, in continuity with pelvic lymphadenectomy, including external iliac, hypogastric, and obturator nodes (separate procedure)

Introduction

38790   Injection procedure; lymphangiography

38792   for identification of sentinel node

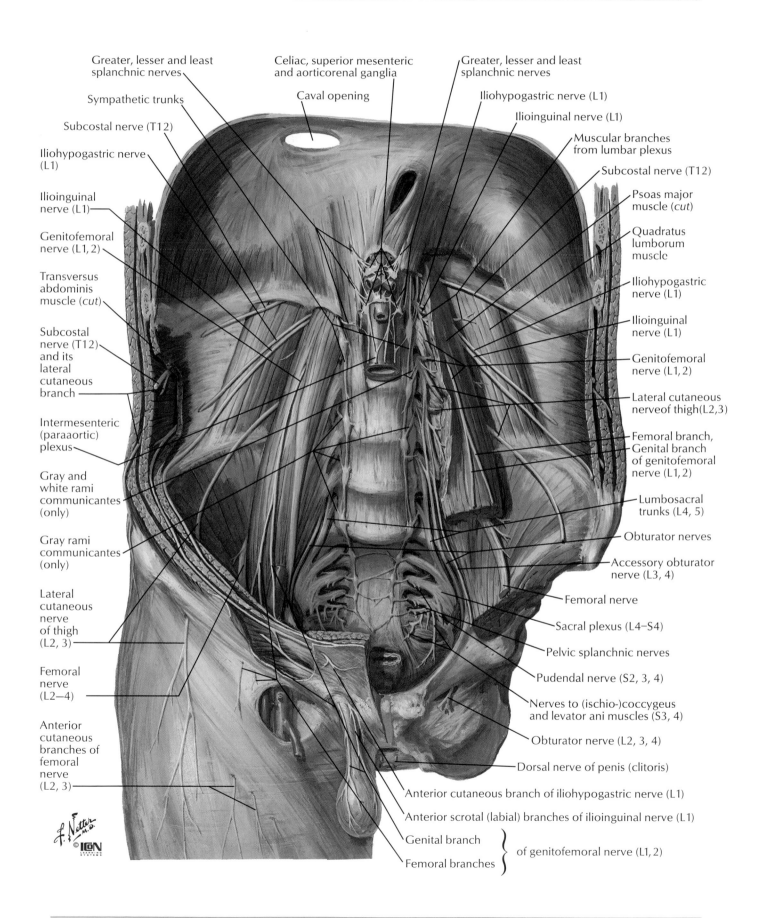

Greater, lesser and least splanchnic nerves

Celiac, superior mesenteric and aorticorenal ganglia

Caval opening

Greater, lesser and least splanchnic nerves

Iliohypogastric nerve (L1)

Ilioinguinal nerve (L1)

Muscular branches from lumbar plexus

Subcostal nerve (T12)

Psoas major muscle (*cut*)

Quadratus lumborum muscle

Iliohypogastric nerve (L1)

Ilioinguinal nerve (L1)

Genitofemoral nerve (L1, 2)

Lateral cutaneous nerve of thigh (L2, 3)

Femoral branch, Genital branch of genitofemoral nerve (L1, 2)

Lumbosacral trunks (L4, 5)

Obturator nerves

Accessory obturator nerve (L3, 4)

Femoral nerve

Sacral plexus (L4–S4)

Pelvic splanchnic nerves

Pudendal nerve (S2, 3, 4)

Nerves to (ischio-)coccygeus and levator ani muscles (S3, 4)

Obturator nerve (L2, 3, 4)

Dorsal nerve of penis (clitoris)

Anterior cutaneous branch of iliohypogastric nerve (L1)

Anterior scrotal (labial) branches of ilioinguinal nerve (L1)

Genital branch }

Femoral branches } of genitofemoral nerve (L1, 2)

Sympathetic trunks

Subcostal nerve (T12)

Iliohypogastric nerve (L1)

Ilioinguinal nerve (L1)

Genitofemoral nerve (L1, 2)

Transversus abdominis muscle (*cut*)

Subcostal nerve (T12) and its lateral cutaneous branch

Intermesenteric (paraaortic) plexus

Gray and white rami communicantes (only)

Gray rami communicantes (only)

Lateral cutaneous nerve of thigh (L2, 3)

Femoral nerve (L2–4)

Anterior cutaneous branches of femoral nerve (L2, 3)

f. Netter
M.D.
©ICON
LEARNING
SYSTEMS

ANESTHESIA

Pelvis (Except Hip)

01180   Anesthesia for obturator neurectomy; extrapelvic
01190   intrapelvic

Other Procedures

01991   Anesthesia for diagnostic or therapeutic nerve blocks and injections (when block or injection is performed by a different provider); other than the prone position
01992   prone position

SURGERY

Nervous System

Extracranial Nerves, Peripheral Nerves, and Autonomic Nervous System
Introduction/Injection of Anesthetic Agent (Nerve Block), Diagnostic or Therapeutic

Somatic Nerves
64425   Injection, anesthetic agent; ilioinguinal, iliohypogastric nerves
64430   pudendal nerve
64447   femoral nerve, single
64448   femoral nerve, continuous infusion by catheter (including catheter placement) including daily management for anesthetic agent administration
64450   other peripheral nerve or branch

Destruction by Neurolytic Agent (eg, Chemical, Thermal, Electrical or Radiofrequency)

Somatic Nerves
64630   Destruction by neurolytic agent; pudendal nerve
64640   other peripheral nerve or branch

Transection or Avulsion

64761   Transection or avulsion of; pudendal nerve
64766   Transection or avulsion of obturator nerve, intrapelvic, with or without adductor tenotomy
64772   Transection or avulsion of other spinal nerve, extradural

Excision

Somatic Nerves
64774   Excision of neuroma; cutaneous nerve, surgically identifiable
64784   major peripheral nerve, except sciatic
64788   Excision of neurofibroma or neurolemmoma; cutaneous nerve
64790   major peripheral nerve
64792   extensive (including malignant type)
64795   Biopsy of nerve

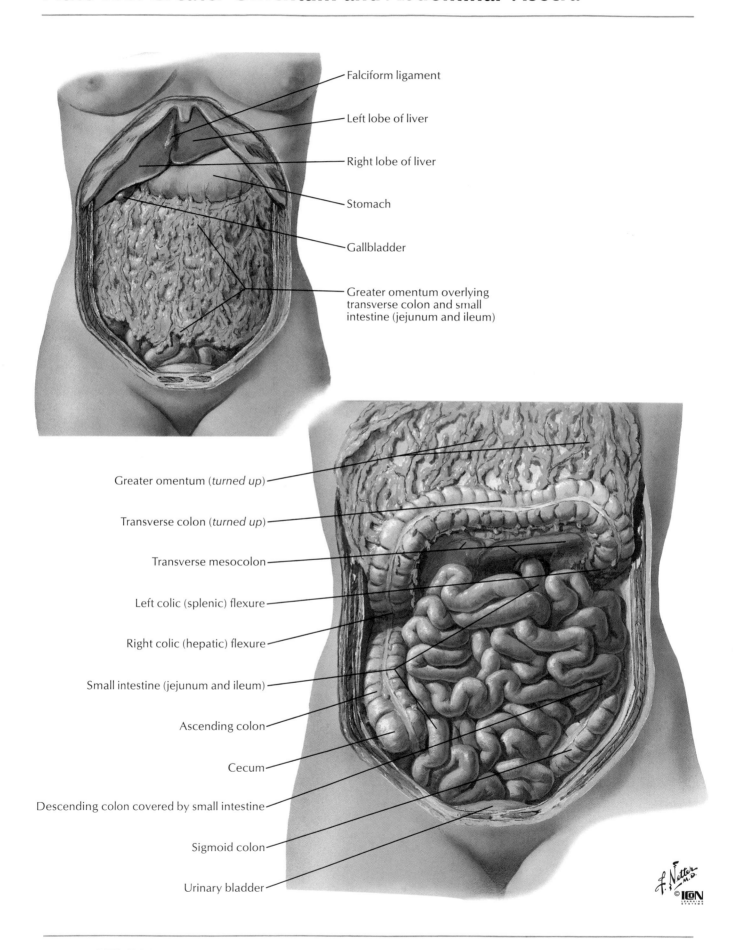

Falciform ligament

Left lobe of liver

Right lobe of liver

Stomach

Gallbladder

Greater omentum overlying transverse colon and small intestine (jejunum and ileum)

Greater omentum (*turned up*)

Transverse colon (*turned up*)

Transverse mesocolon

Left colic (splenic) flexure

Right colic (hepatic) flexure

Small intestine (jejunum and ileum)

Ascending colon

Cecum

Descending colon covered by small intestine

Sigmoid colon

Urinary bladder

ANESTHESIA

Upper Abdomen

00700 Anesthesia for procedures on upper anterior abdominal wall; not otherwise specified

00740 Anesthesia for upper gastrointestinal endoscopic procedures, endoscope introduced proximal to duodenum

00752 Anesthesia for hernia repairs in upper abdomen; lumbar and ventral (incisional) hernias and/or wound dehiscence

00790 Anesthesia for intraperitoneal procedures in upper abdomen including laparoscopy; not otherwise specified

Lower Abdomen

00800 Anesthesia for procedures on lower anterior abdominal wall; not otherwise specified

00810 Anesthesia for lower intestinal endoscopic procedures, endoscope introduced distal to duodenum

00840 Anesthesia for intraperitoneal procedures in lower abdomen including laparoscopy; not otherwise specified

SURGERY

Digestive System

Esophagus
Endoscopy

43234 Upper gastrointestinal endoscopy, simple primary examination (eg, with small diameter flexible endoscope) (separate procedure)

43235 Upper gastrointestinal endoscopy including esophagus, stomach, and either the duodenum and/or jejunum as appropriate; diagnostic, with or without collection of specimen(s) by brushing or washing (separate procedure)

43236 with directed submucosal injection(s), any substance

43237 with endoscopic ultrasound examination limited to the esophagus

43238 with transendoscopic ultrasound-guided intramural or transmural fine needle aspiration/biopsy(s), esophagus (includes endoscopic ultrasound examination limited to the esophagus)

43239 with biopsy, single or multiple

43240 with transmural drainage of pseudocyst

43241 with transendoscopic intraluminal tube or catheter placement

43242 with transendoscopic ultrasound-guided intramural or transmural fine needle aspiration/biopsy(s) (includes endoscopic ultrasound examination of the esophagus, stomach, and either the duodenum and/or jejunum as appropriate)

43243 with injection sclerosis of esophageal and/or gastric varices

43244 with band ligation of esophageal and/or gastric varices

43245 with dilation of gastric outlet for obstruction (eg, balloon, guide wire, bougie)

43246 with directed placement of percutaneous gastrostomy tube

43247 with removal of foreign body

43248 with insertion of guide wire followed by dilation of esophagus over guide wire

43249 with balloon dilation of esophagus (less than 30 mm diameter)

43250 with removal of tumor(s), polyp(s), or other lesion(s) by hot biopsy forceps or bipolar cautery

43251 with removal of tumor(s), polyp(s), or other lesion(s) by snare technique

43255 with control of bleeding, any method

43256 with transendoscopic stent placement (includes predilation)

43257 with delivery of thermal energy to the muscle of lower esophageal sphincter and/or gastric cardia, for treatment of gastroesophageal reflux disease

43258 with ablation of tumor(s), polyp(s), or other lesion(s) not amenable to removal by hot biopsy forceps, bipolar cautery or snare technique

43259 with endoscopic ultrasound examination, including the esophagus, stomach, and either the duodenum and/or jejunum as appropriate

Intestines (Except Rectum)
Incision

44020 Enterotomy, small intestine, other than duodenum; for exploration, biopsy(s), or foreign body removal

44021 for decompression (eg, Baker tube)

Excision

44100 Biopsy of intestine by capsule, tube, peroral (one or more specimens)

44110 Excision of one or more lesions of small or large intestine not requiring anastomosis, exteriorization, or fistulization; single enterotomy

44111 multiple enterotomies

44120 Enterectomy, resection of small intestine; single resection and anastomosis

44121 each additional resection and anastomosis (List separately in addition to code for primary procedure)

44125 with enterostomy

44126 Enterectomy, resection of small intestine for congenital atresia, single resection and anastomosis of proximal segment of intestine; without tapering

44127[P] with tapering

44128 each additional resection and anastomosis (List separately in addition to code for primary procedure)

44130 Enteroenterostomy, anastomosis of intestine, with or without cutaneous enterostomy (separate procedure)

Plate 105: Greater Omentum and Abdominal Viscera

Endoscopy, Small Intestine and Stomal

44360 diagnostic, with or without collection of specimen(s) by brushing or washing (separate procedure)

44361 with biopsy, single or multiple

44363 with removal of foreign body

44364 with removal of tumor(s), polyp(s), or other lesion(s) by snare technique

44365 with removal of tumor(s), polyp(s), or other lesion(s) by hot biopsy forceps or bipolar cautery

44366 with control of bleeding (eg, injection, bipolar cautery, unipolar cautery, laser, heater probe, stapler, plasma coagulator)

44369 with ablation of tumor(s), polyp(s), or other lesion(s) not amenable to removal by hot biopsy forceps, bipolar cautery or snare technique

44370 with transendoscopic stent placement (includes predilation)

44372 with placement of percutaneous jejunostomy tube

44373 with conversion of percutaneous gastrostomy tube to percutaneous jejunostomy tube

44376 Small intestinal endoscopy, enteroscopy beyond second portion of duodenum, including ileum; diagnostic, with or without collection of specimen(s) by brushing or washing (separate procedure)

44377 with biopsy, single or multiple

44378 with control of bleeding (eg, injection, bipolar cautery, unipolar cautery, laser, heater probe, stapler, plasma coagulator)

44379 with transendoscopic stent placement (includes predilation)

Repair

44602 Suture of small intestine (enterorrhaphy) for perforated ulcer, diverticulum, wound, injury or rupture; single perforation

44603 multiple perforations

44604 Suture of large intestine (colorrhaphy) for perforated ulcer, diverticulum, wound, injury or rupture (single or multiple perforations); without colostomy

44605 with colostomy

44615 Intestinal stricturoplasty (enterotomy and enterorrhaphy) with or without dilation, for intestinal obstruction

44620 Closure of enterostomy, large or small intestine;

44625 with resection and anastomosis other than colorectal

44626 with resection and colorectal anastomosis (eg, closure of Hartmann type procedure)

44640 Closure of intestinal cutaneous fistula

44650 Closure of enteroenteric or enterocolic fistula

44660 Closure of enterovesical fistula; without intestinal or bladder resection

44661 with intestine and/or bladder resection

44680 Intestinal plication (separate procedure)

Abdomen, Peritoneum, and Omentum

Suture

49900 Suture, secondary, of abdominal wall for evisceration or dehiscence

Other Procedures

49904 Omental flap, extra-abdominal (eg, for reconstruction of sternal and chest wall defects)

49905 Omental flap, intra-abdominal (List separately in addition to code for primary procedure)

49906 Free omental flap with microvascular anastomosis

Female Genital System

Ovary

Excision

58960 Laparotomy, for staging or restaging of ovarian, tubal or primary peritoneal malignancy (second look), with or without omentectomy, peritoneal washing, biopsy of abdominal and pelvic peritoneum, diaphragmatic assessment with pelvic and limited para-aortic lymphadenectomy

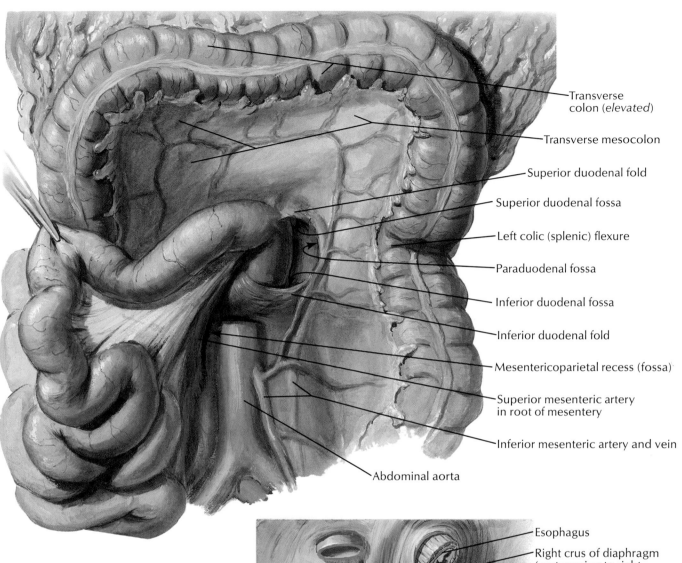

Transverse colon (*elevated*)

Transverse mesocolon

Superior duodenal fold

Superior duodenal fossa

Left colic (splenic) flexure

Paraduodenal fossa

Inferior duodenal fossa

Inferior duodenal fold

Mesentericoparietal recess (fossa)

Superior mesenteric artery in root of mesentery

Inferior mesenteric artery and vein

Abdominal aorta

Esophagus

Right crus of diaphragm (part passing to right of esophageal hiatus)

Right crus of diaphragm (part passing to left of esophageal hiatus)

Left crus of diaphragm

Celiac trunk

Suspensory muscle of duodenum (ligament of Treitz)

Superior mesenteric artery

Duodenojejunal flexure

Ascending (4th) part of duodenum

Jejunum

Inferior (horizontal, or 3rd) part of duodenum

Descending (2nd) part of duodenum

Exposure of suspensory muscle of duodenum (ligament of Treitz)

Plate 106: Mesenteric Relations of Intestines

ANESTHESIA

Upper Abdomen

00740   Anesthesia for upper gastrointestinal endoscopic procedures, endoscope introduced proximal to duodenum

00770   Anesthesia for all procedures on major abdominal blood vessels

00790   Anesthesia for intraperitoneal procedures in upper abdomen including laparoscopy; not otherwise specified

Lower Abdomen

00880   Anesthesia for procedures on major lower abdominal vessels; not otherwise specified

00810   Anesthesia for lower intestinal endoscopic procedures, endoscope introduced distal to duodenum

00840   Anesthesia for intraperitoneal procedures in lower abdomen including laparoscopy; not otherwise specified

00882   Anesthesia for procedures on major lower abdominal vessels; inferior vena cava ligation

Perineum

00902   Anesthesia for; anorectal procedure

Upper Leg (Except Knee)

01270   Anesthesia for procedures involving arteries of upper leg, including bypass graft; not otherwise specified

Radiological Procedures

01924   Anesthesia for therapeutic interventional radiologic procedures involving the arterial system; not otherwise specified

01926   intracranial, intracardiac, or aortic

SURGERY

Cardiovascular System

Arteries and Veins
Embolectomy/Thrombectomy

Venous, Direct or With Catheter

34401   Thrombectomy, direct or with catheter; vena cava, iliac vein, by abdominal incision

Endovascular Repair of Abdominal Aortic Aneurysm

34820   Open iliac artery exposure for delivery of endovascular prosthesis or iliac occlusion during endovascular therapy, by abdominal or retroperitoneal incision, unilateral

34825   Placement of proximal or distal extension prosthesis for endovascular repair of infrarenal abdominal aortic or iliac aneurysm, false aneurysm, or dissection; initial vessel

34826   each additional vessel (List separately in addition to code for primary procedure)

34833   Open iliac artery exposure with creation of conduit for delivery of infrarenal aortic or iliac endovascular prosthesis, by abdominal or retroperitoneal incision, unilateral

Endovascular Repair of Iliac Aneurysm

34900   Endovascular graft placement for repair of iliac artery (eg, aneurysm, pseudoaneurysm, arteriovenous malformation, trauma)

Direct Repair of Aneurysm or Excision (Partial or Total) and Graft Insertion for Aneurysm, Pseudoaneurysm, Ruptured Aneurysm, and Associated Occlusive Disease

35091   Direct repair of aneurysm, pseudoaneurysm, or excision (partial or total) and graft insertion, with or without patch graft; for aneurysm, pseudoaneurysm, and associated occlusive disease, abdominal aorta involving visceral vessels (mesenteric, celiac, renal)

35092   for ruptured aneurysm, abdominal aorta involving visceral vessels (mesenteric, celiac, renal)

35102   for aneurysm, pseudoaneurysm, and associated occlusive disease, abdominal aorta involving iliac vessels (common, hypogastric, external)

35103   for ruptured aneurysm, abdominal aorta involving iliac vessels (common, hypogastric, external)

35121   for aneurysm, pseudoaneurysm, and associated occlusive disease, hepatic, celiac, renal, or mesenteric artery

35122   for ruptured aneurysm, hepatic, celiac, renal, or mesenteric artery

35131   for aneurysm, pseudoaneurysm, and associated occlusive disease, iliac artery (common, hypogastric, external)

35132   for ruptured aneurysm, iliac artery (common, hypogastric, external)

Thromboendarterectomy

35341   Thromboendarterectomy, with or without patch graft; mesenteric, celiac, or renal

35351   iliac

Transluminal Angioplasty

35456   Transluminal balloon angioplasty, open; femoral-popliteal

Transluminal Atherectomy

35482   Transluminal peripheral atherectomy, open; iliac

Bypass Graft

Vein

35531   Bypass graft, with vein; aortoceliac or aortomesenteric

Other Than Vein

35631   Bypass graft, with other than vein; aortoceliac, aortomesenteric, aortorenal

Portal Decompression Procedures

37160   Venous anastomosis, open; caval-mesenteric

Ligation

37660   Ligation of common iliac vein

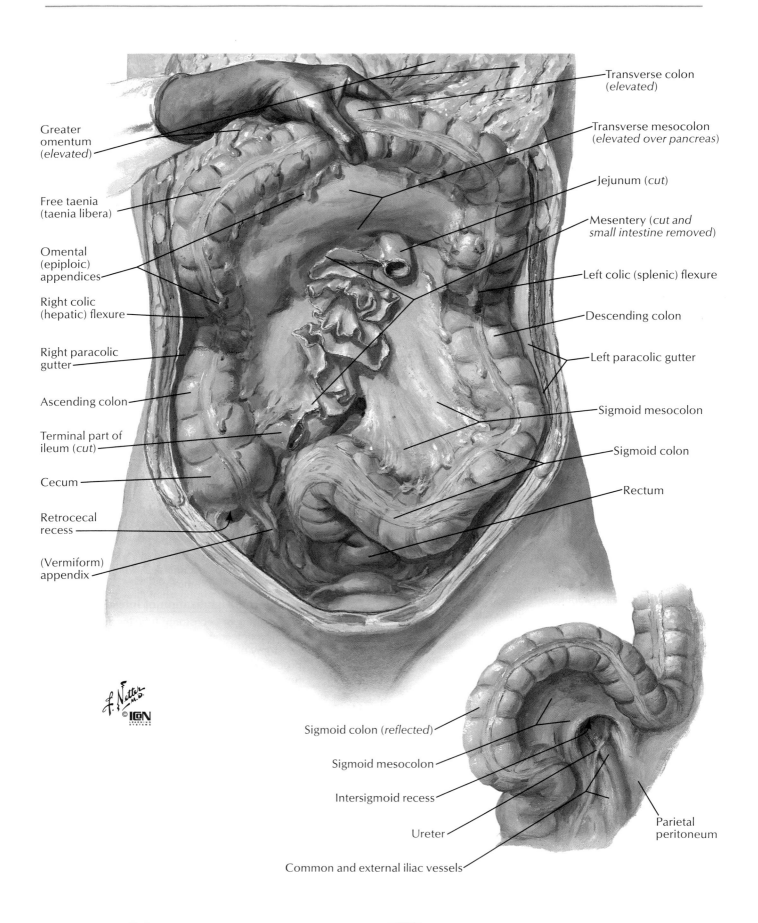

Greater omentum (*elevated*)

Free taenia (taenia libera)

Omental (epiploic) appendices

Right colic (hepatic) flexure

Right paracolic gutter

Ascending colon

Terminal part of ileum (*cut*)

Cecum

Retrocecal recess

(Vermiform) appendix

Transverse colon (*elevated*)

Transverse mesocolon (*elevated over pancreas*)

Jejunum (*cut*)

Mesentery (*cut and small intestine removed*)

Left colic (splenic) flexure

Descending colon

Left paracolic gutter

Sigmoid mesocolon

Sigmoid colon

Rectum

Sigmoid colon (*reflected*)

Sigmoid mesocolon

Intersigmoid recess

Ureter

Common and external iliac vessels

Parietal peritoneum

Plate 106: *Mesenteric Relations of Intestines*

(Endoscopy continued from previous page)

45340	with dilation by balloon, 1 or more strictures
45341	with endoscopic ultrasound examination
45342	with transendoscopic ultrasound guided intramural or transmural fine needle aspiration/biopsy(s)
45345	with transendoscopic stent placement (includes predilation)
45355	Colonoscopy, rigid or flexible, transabdominal via colotomy, single or multiple
45378[P]	Colonoscopy, flexible, proximal to splenic flexure; diagnostic, with or without collection of specimen(s) by brushing or washing, with or without colon decompression (separate procedure)
45379	with removal of foreign body
45380	with biopsy, single or multiple
45381	with directed submucosal injection(s), any substance
45382	with control of bleeding (eg, injection, bipolar cautery, unipolar cautery, laser, heater probe, stapler, plasma coagulator)
45383	with ablation of tumor(s), polyp(s), or other lesion(s) not amenable to removal by hot biopsy forceps, bipolar cautery or snare technique
45384	with removal of tumor(s), polyp(s), or other lesion(s) by hot biopsy forceps or bipolar cautery
45385	with removal of tumor(s), polyp(s), or other lesion(s) by snare technique
45386	with dilation by balloon, 1 or more strictures
45387	with transendoscopic stent placement (includes predilation)
45391	with endoscopic ultrasound examination
45392	with transendoscopic ultrasound guided intramural or transmural fine needle aspiration/biopsy(s)

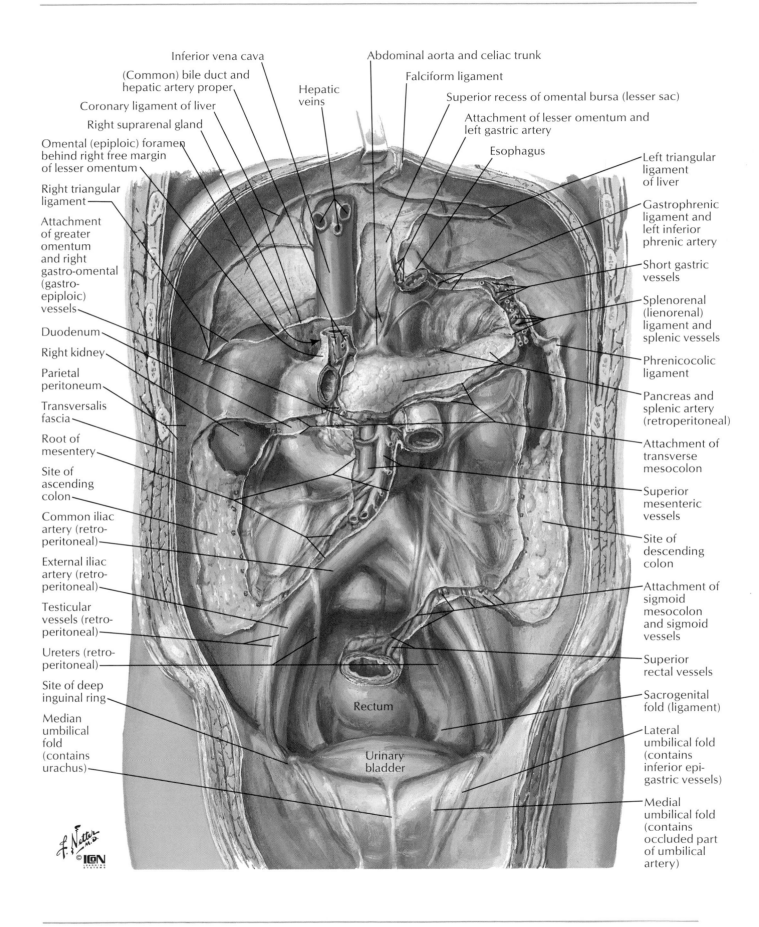

Inferior vena cava

(Common) bile duct and hepatic artery proper

Coronary ligament of liver

Right suprarenal gland

Omental (epiploic) foramen behind right free margin of lesser omentum

Right triangular ligament

Attachment of greater omentum and right gastro-omental (gastro-epiploic) vessels

Duodenum

Right kidney

Parietal peritoneum

Transversalis fascia

Root of mesentery

Site of ascending colon

Common iliac artery (retro-peritoneal)

External iliac artery (retro-peritoneal)

Testicular vessels (retro-peritoneal)

Ureters (retro-peritoneal)

Site of deep inguinal ring

Median umbilical fold (contains urachus)

Hepatic veins

Abdominal aorta and celiac trunk

Falciform ligament

Superior recess of omental bursa (lesser sac)

Attachment of lesser omentum and left gastric artery

Esophagus

Left triangular ligament of liver

Gastrophrenic ligament and left inferior phrenic artery

Short gastric vessels

Splenorenal (lienorenal) ligament and splenic vessels

Phrenicocolic ligament

Pancreas and splenic artery (retroperitoneal)

Attachment of transverse mesocolon

Superior mesenteric vessels

Site of descending colon

Attachment of sigmoid mesocolon and sigmoid vessels

Superior rectal vessels

Sacrogenital fold (ligament)

Lateral umbilical fold (contains inferior epigastric vessels)

Medial umbilical fold (contains occluded part of umbilical artery)

Rectum

Urinary bladder

- Nomenclature Notes -

The term *retroperitoneal* is defined as behind the peritoneum.

ANESTHESIA

Upper Abdominal Wall

00730	Anesthesia for procedures on upper posterior abdominal wall
00790	Anesthesia for intraperitoneal procedures in upper abdomen including laparoscopy; not otherwise specified

Lower Abdominal wall

00820	Anesthesia for procedures on lower posterior abdominal wall
00840	Anesthesia for intraperitoneal procedures in lower abdomen including laparoscopy; not otherwise specified

SURGERY

Digestive System

Abdomen, Peritoneum, and Omentum
Incision

49010	Exploration, retroperitoneal area with or without biopsy(s) (separate procedure)
49020	Drainage of peritoneal abscess or localized peritonitis, exclusive of appendiceal abscess; open
49021	percutaneous
49040	Drainage of subdiaphragmatic or subphrenic abscess; open
49041	percutaneous
49060	Drainage of retroperitoneal abscess; open
49061	percutaneous
49062	Drainage of extraperitoneal lymphocele to peritoneal cavity, open
49080	Peritoneocentesis, abdominal paracentesis, or peritoneal lavage (diagnostic or therapeutic); initial
49081	subsequent
49085	Removal of peritoneal foreign body from peritoneal cavity

Excision, Destruction

49180	Biopsy, abdominal or retroperitoneal mass, percutaneous needle
49200	Excision or destruction, open, intra-abdominal or retroperitoneal tumors or cysts or endometriomas;
49201	extensive

Laparoscopy

49320[P]	Laparoscopy, abdomen, peritoneum, and omentum, diagnostic, with or without collection of specimen(s) by brushing or washing (separate procedure)
49321	Laparoscopy, surgical; with biopsy (single or multiple)
49322	with aspiration of cavity or cyst (eg, ovarian cyst) (single or multiple)
49323	with drainage of lymphocele to peritoneal cavity

Introduction, Revision, and/or Removal

49400	Injection of air or contrast into peritoneal cavity (separate procedure)
49419	Insertion of intraperitoneal cannula or catheter, with subcutaneous reservoir, permanent (ie, totally implantable)
49420	Insertion of intraperitoneal cannula or catheter for drainage or dialysis; temporary
49421	permanent
49422	Removal of permanent intraperitoneal cannula or catheter
49425	Insertion of peritoneal-venous shunt
49426	Revision of peritoneal-venous shunt
49427	Injection procedure (eg, contrast media) for evaluation of previously placed peritoneal-venous shunt
49428	Ligation of peritoneal-venous shunt
49429	Removal of peritoneal-venous shunt

Female Genital System

Ovary
Excision

58960	Laparotomy, for staging or restaging of ovarian, tubal or primary peritoneal malignancy (second look), with or without omentectomy, peritoneal washing, biopsy of abdominal and pelvic peritoneum, diaphragmatic assessment with pelvic and limited para-aortic lymphadenectomy

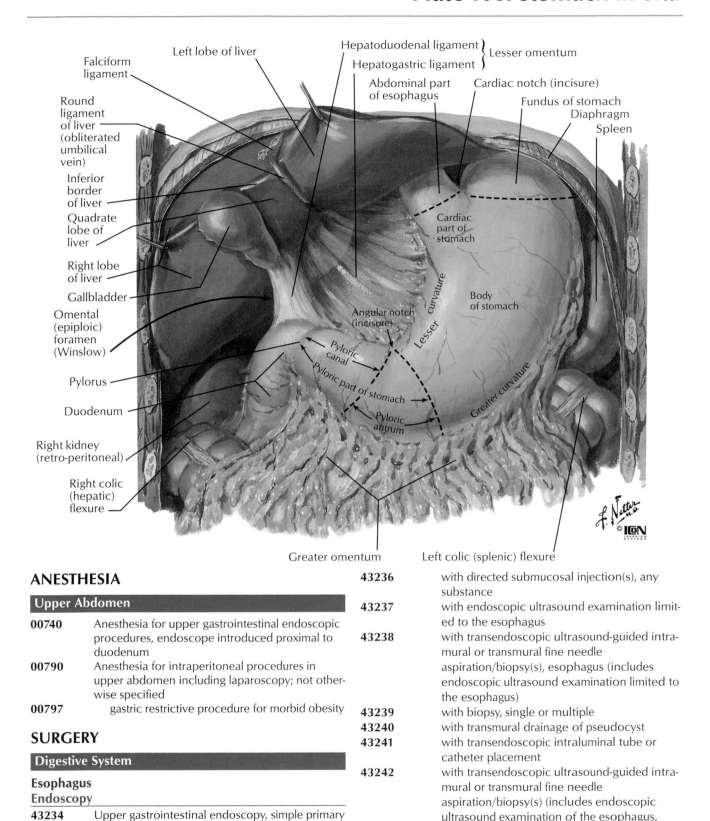

Falciform ligament

Left lobe of liver

Hepatoduodenal ligament ⎱ Lesser omentum
Hepatogastric ligament ⎰

Abdominal part of esophagus

Cardiac notch (incisure)

Fundus of stomach
Diaphragm
Spleen

Round ligament of liver (obliterated umbilical vein)

Inferior border of liver

Quadrate lobe of liver

Right lobe of liver

Gallbladder

Omental (epiploic) foramen (Winslow)

Pylorus

Duodenum

Right kidney (retro-peritoneal)

Right colic (hepatic) flexure

Cardiac part of stomach

Angular notch (incisure)

Pyloric canal

Pyloric part of stomach

Pyloric antrum

Lesser curvature

Body of stomach

Greater curvature

Greater omentum

Left colic (splenic) flexure

ANESTHESIA

Upper Abdomen

00740   Anesthesia for upper gastrointestinal endoscopic procedures, endoscope introduced proximal to duodenum

00790   Anesthesia for intraperitoneal procedures in upper abdomen including laparoscopy; not otherwise specified

00797   gastric restrictive procedure for morbid obesity

SURGERY

Digestive System

Esophagus
Endoscopy

43234   Upper gastrointestinal endoscopy, simple primary examination (eg, with small diameter flexible endoscope) (separate procedure)

43235   Upper gastrointestinal endoscopy including esophagus, stomach, and either the duodenum and/or jejunum as appropriate; diagnostic, with or without collection of specimen(s) by brushing or washing (separate procedure)

43236   with directed submucosal injection(s), any substance

43237   with endoscopic ultrasound examination limited to the esophagus

43238   with transendoscopic ultrasound-guided intramural or transmural fine needle aspiration/biopsy(s), esophagus (includes endoscopic ultrasound examination limited to the esophagus)

43239   with biopsy, single or multiple

43240   with transmural drainage of pseudocyst

43241   with transendoscopic intraluminal tube or catheter placement

43242   with transendoscopic ultrasound-guided intramural or transmural fine needle aspiration/biopsy(s) (includes endoscopic ultrasound examination of the esophagus, stomach, and either the duodenum and/or jejunum as appropriate)

43243   with injection sclerosis of esophageal and/or gastric varices

(Endoscopy continued on next page)

(Endoscopy continued from previous page)

43244   with band ligation of esophageal and/or gastric varices

43245   with dilation of gastric outlet for obstruction (eg, balloon, guide wire, bougie)

43246   with directed placement of percutaneous gastrostomy tube

43247   with removal of foreign body

43248   with insertion of guide wire followed by dilation of esophagus over guide wire

43249   with balloon dilation of esophagus (less than 30 mm diameter)

43250   with removal of tumor(s), polyp(s), or other lesion(s) by hot biopsy forceps or bipolar cautery

43251   with removal of tumor(s), polyp(s), or other lesion(s) by snare technique

43255   with control of bleeding, any method

43256   with transendoscopic stent placement (includes predilation)

43257   with delivery of thermal energy to the muscle of lower esophageal sphincter and/or gastric cardia, for treatment of gastroesophageal reflux disease

43258   with ablation of tumor(s), polyp(s), or other lesion(s) not amenable to removal by hot biopsy forceps, bipolar cautery or snare technique

43259   with endoscopic ultrasound examination, including the esophagus, stomach, and either the duodenum and/or jejunum as appropriate

Stomach
Incision

43500   Gastrotomy; with exploration or foreign body removal

43501   with suture repair of bleeding ulcer

43502   with suture repair of pre-existing esophago-gastric laceration (eg, Mallory-Weiss)

43510   with esophageal dilation and insertion of permanent intraluminal tube (eg, Celestin or Mousseaux-Barbin)

43520   Pyloromyotomy, cutting of pyloric muscle (Fredet-Ramstedt type operation)

Excision

43600   Biopsy of stomach; by capsule, tube, peroral (one or more specimens)

43605   by laparotomy

43610   Excision, local; ulcer or benign tumor of stomach

43611   malignant tumor of stomach

43620   Gastrectomy, total; with esophagoenterostomy

43621   with Roux-en-Y reconstruction

43622   with formation of intestinal pouch, any type

43631   Gastrectomy, partial, distal; with gastro-duodenostomy

43632   with gastrojejunostomy

43633   with Roux-en-Y reconstruction

43634   with formation of intestinal pouch

43635   Vagotomy when performed with partial distal gastrectomy (List separately in addition to code(s) for primary procedure)

43638   Gastrectomy, partial, proximal, thoracic or abdominal approach including esophagogastrostomy, with vagotomy;

43639   with pyloroplasty or pyloromyotomy

43640   Vagotomy including pyloroplasty, with or without gastrostomy; truncal or selective

43641   parietal cell (highly selective)

Laparoscopy

43644   Laparoscopy, surgical, gastric restrictive procedure; with gastric bypass and Roux-en-Y gastroenterostomy (roux limb 150 cm or less)

43645   Laparoscopy, surgical, gastric restrictive procedure; with gastric bypass and small intestine reconstruction to limit absorption

43651   Laparoscopy, surgical; transection of vagus nerves, truncal

43652   transection of vagus nerves, selective or highly selective

43653   gastrostomy, without construction of gastric tube (eg, Stamm procedure) (separate procedure)

Other Procedures

43800   Pyloroplasty

43810   Gastroduodenostomy

43820   Gastrojejunostomy; without vagotomy

43825   with vagotomy, any type

43830   Gastrostomy, open; without construction of gastric tube (eg, Stamm procedure) (separate procedure)

43831   neonatal, for feeding

43832   with construction of gastric tube (eg, Janeway procedure)

43840   Gastrorrhaphy, suture of perforated duodenal or gastric ulcer, wound, or injury

43842   Gastric restrictive procedure, without gastric bypass, for morbid obesity; vertical-banded gastroplasty

43843   other than vertical-banded gastroplasty

43845   Gastric restrictive procedure with partial gastrectomy, pylorus-preserving duodenoileostomy and ileoileostomy (50 to 100 cm common channel) to limit absorption (biliopancreatic diversion with duodenal switch)

43846[P]   Gastric restrictive procedure, with gastric bypass for morbid obesity; with short limb (150 cm or less) Roux-en-Y gastroenterostomy

43847   with small intestine reconstruction to limit absorption

43848   Revision of gastric restrictive procedure for morbid obesity (separate procedure)

43850   Revision of gastroduodenal anastomosis (gastroduodenostomy) with reconstruction; without vagotomy

43855   with vagotomy

43860   Revision of gastrojejunal anastomosis (gastrojejunostomy) with reconstruction, with or without partial gastrectomy or intestine resection; without vagotomy

43865   with vagotomy

43870   Closure of gastrostomy, surgical

43880   Closure of gastrocolic fistula

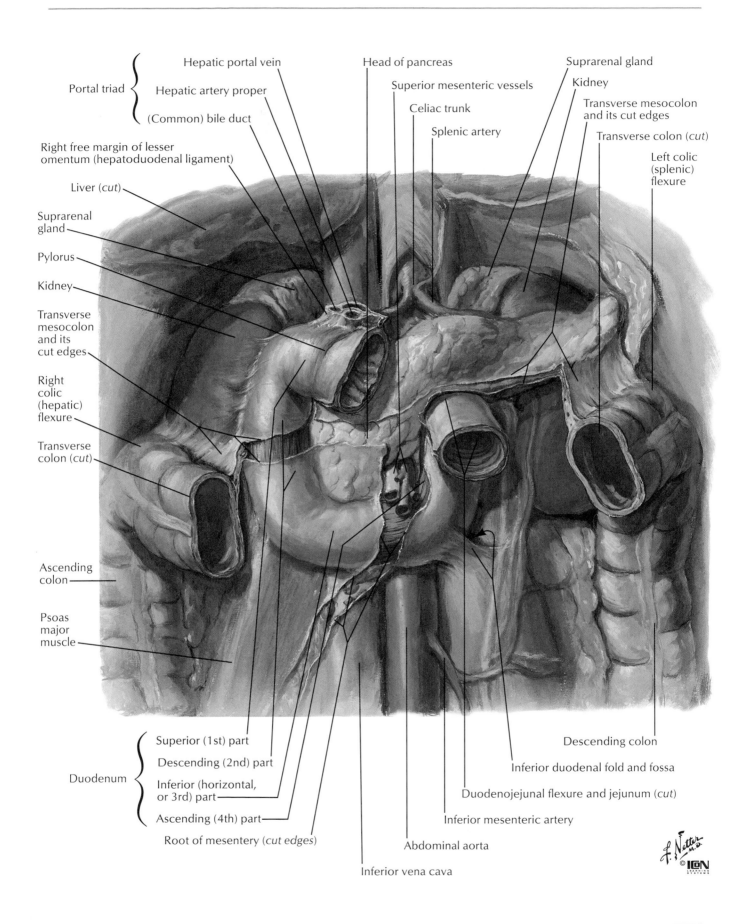

Portal triad
- Hepatic portal vein
- Hepatic artery proper
- (Common) bile duct

Head of pancreas

Superior mesenteric vessels

Celiac trunk

Splenic artery

Suprarenal gland

Kidney

Transverse mesocolon and its cut edges

Transverse colon (*cut*)

Left colic (splenic) flexure

Right free margin of lesser omentum (hepatoduodenal ligament)

Liver (*cut*)

Suprarenal gland

Pylorus

Kidney

Transverse mesocolon and its cut edges

Right colic (hepatic) flexure

Transverse colon (*cut*)

Ascending colon

Psoas major muscle

Duodenum
- Superior (1st) part
- Descending (2nd) part
- Inferior (horizontal, or 3rd) part
- Ascending (4th) part

Root of mesentery (*cut edges*)

Inferior vena cava

Abdominal aorta

Inferior mesenteric artery

Duodenojejunal flexure and jejunum (*cut*)

Inferior duodenal fold and fossa

Descending colon

Plate 109: Duodenum

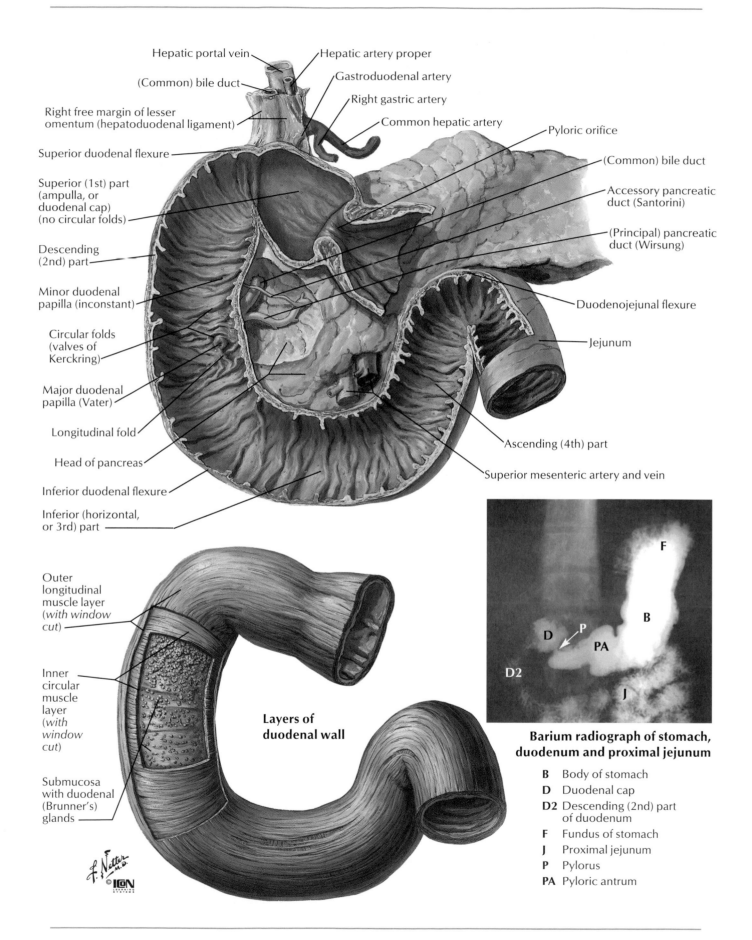

Hepatic portal vein

Hepatic artery proper

(Common) bile duct

Gastroduodenal artery

Right gastric artery

Right free margin of lesser omentum (hepatoduodenal ligament)

Common hepatic artery

Superior duodenal flexure

Pyloric orifice

Superior (1st) part (ampulla, or duodenal cap) (no circular folds)

(Common) bile duct

Accessory pancreatic duct (Santorini)

(Principal) pancreatic duct (Wirsung)

Descending (2nd) part

Minor duodenal papilla (inconstant)

Duodenojejunal flexure

Circular folds (valves of Kerckring)

Jejunum

Major duodenal papilla (Vater)

Longitudinal fold

Head of pancreas

Ascending (4th) part

Inferior duodenal flexure

Superior mesenteric artery and vein

Inferior (horizontal, or 3rd) part

Outer longitudinal muscle layer (*with window cut*)

Inner circular muscle layer (*with window cut*)

Submucosa with duodenal (Brunner's) glands

Layers of duodenal wall

Barium radiograph of stomach, duodenum and proximal jejunum

F

B

D

P

PA

D2

J

B Body of stomach
D Duodenal cap
D2 Descending (2nd) part of duodenum
F Fundus of stomach
J Proximal jejunum
P Pylorus
PA Pyloric antrum

ANESTHESIA

Upper Abdomen

00740   Anesthesia for upper gastrointestinal endoscopic procedures, endoscope introduced proximal to duodenum

00790   Anesthesia for intraperitoneal procedures in upper abdomen including laparoscopy; not otherwise specified

Lower Abdomen

00810   Anesthesia for lower intestinal endoscopic procedures, endoscope introduced distal to duodenum

00840   Anesthesia for intraperitoneal procedures in lower abdomen including laparoscopy; not otherwise specified

SURGERY

Digestive System

Esophagus
Endoscopy

43235   Upper gastrointestinal endoscopy including esophagus, stomach, and either the duodenum and/or jejunum as appropriate; diagnostic, with or without collection of specimen(s) by brushing or washing (separate procedure)

43236   with directed submucosal injection(s), any substance

43237   with endoscopic ultrasound examination limited to the esophagus

43238   with transendoscopic ultrasound-guided intramural or transmural fine needle aspiration/biopsy(s), esophagus (includes endoscopic ultrasound examination limited to the esophagus)

43239   with biopsy, single or multiple

43240   with transmural drainage of pseudocyst

43241   with transendoscopic intraluminal tube or catheter placement

43242   with transendoscopic ultrasound-guided intramural or transmural fine needle aspiration/biopsy(s) (includes endoscopic ultrasound examination of the esophagus, stomach, and either the duodenum and/or jejunum as appropriate)

43243   with injection sclerosis of esophageal and/or gastric varices

43244   with band ligation of esophageal and/or gastric varices

43245   with dilation of gastric outlet for obstruction (eg, balloon, guide wire, bougie)

43246   with directed placement of percutaneous gastrostomy tube

43247   with removal of foreign body

43248   with insertion of guide wire followed by dilation of esophagus over guide wire

43249   with balloon dilation of esophagus (less than 30 mm diameter)

43250   with removal of tumor(s), polyp(s), or other lesion(s) by hot biopsy forceps or bipolar cautery

43251   with removal of tumor(s), polyp(s), or other lesion(s) by snare technique

43255   with control of bleeding, any method

43256   with transendoscopic stent placement (includes predilation)

43257   with delivery of thermal energy to the muscle of lower esophageal sphincter and/or gastric cardia, for treatment of gastroesophageal reflux disease

43258   with ablation of tumor(s), polyp(s), or other lesion(s) not amenable to removal by hot biopsy forceps, bipolar cautery or snare technique

43259   with endoscopic ultrasound examination, including the esophagus, stomach, and either the duodenum and/or jejunum as appropriate

Stomach
Introduction

43761   Repositioning of the gastric feeding tube, any method, through the duodenum for enteric nutrition

Other Procedures

43800   Pyloroplasty

43810   Gastroduodenostomy

Intestines (Except Rectum)
Incision

44010   Duodenotomy, for exploration, biopsy(s), or foreign body removal

Excision

44100   Biopsy of intestine by capsule, tube, peroral (one or more specimens)

44110   Excision of one or more lesions of small or large intestine not requiring anastomosis, exteriorization, or fistulization; single enterotomy

44111   multiple enterotomies

44120   Enterectomy, resection of small intestine; single resection and anastomosis

44121   each additional resection and anastomosis (List separately in addition to code for primary procedure)

44125   with enterostomy

44126   Enterectomy, resection of small intestine for congenital atresia, single resection and anastomosis of proximal segment of intestine; without tapering

44127[P]   with tapering

44128   each additional resection and anastomosis (List separately in addition to code for primary procedure)

Laparoscopy

44202   Laparoscopy, surgical; enterectomy, resection of small intestine, single resection and anastomosis

44203   each additional small intestine resection and anastomosis (List separately in addition to code for primary procedure)

Endoscopy, Small Intestine and Stomal

44360   Small intestinal endoscopy, enteroscopy beyond second portion of duodenum, not including ileum; diagnostic, with or without collection of specimen(s) by brushing or washing (separate procedure)

44361   with biopsy, single or multiple

44363   with removal of foreign body

44364   with removal of tumor(s), polyp(s), or other lesion(s) by snare technique

44365   with removal of tumor(s), polyp(s), or other lesion(s) by hot biopsy forceps or bipolar cautery

44366   with control of bleeding (eg, injection, bipolar cautery, unipolar cautery, laser, heater probe, stapler, plasma coagulator)

44369   with ablation of tumor(s), polyp(s), or other lesion(s) not amenable to removal by hot biopsy forceps, bipolar cautery or snare technique

44370   with transendoscopic stent placement (includes predilation)

44372   with placement of percutaneous jejunostomy tube

44373   with conversion of percutaneous gastrostomy tube to percutaneous jejunostomy tube

44376   Small intestinal endoscopy, enteroscopy beyond second portion of duodenum, including ileum; diagnostic, with or without collection of specimen(s) by brushing or washing (separate procedure)

44377   with biopsy, single or multiple

44378   with control of bleeding (eg, injection, bipolar cautery, unipolar cautery, laser, heater probe, stapler, plasma coagulator)

44379   with transendoscopic stent placement (includes predilation)

Repair

44602   Suture of small intestine (enterorrhaphy) for perforated ulcer, diverticulum, wound, injury or rupture; single perforation

44603   multiple perforations

44620   Closure of enterostomy, large or small intestine;

44625   with resection and anastomosis other than colorectal

44626   with resection and colorectal anastomosis (eg, closure of Hartmann type procedure)

Barium radiograph of jejunum

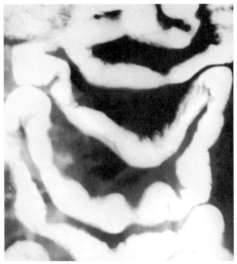

Barium radiograph of ileum

RADIOLOGY

Diagnostic Radiology (Diagnostic Imaging)

Gastrointestinal Tract

74245 Radiologic examination, gastrointestinal tract, upper; with small intestine, includes multiple serial films

74249 Radiological examination, gastrointestinal tract, upper, air contrast, with specific high density barium, effervescent agent, with or without glucagon; with small intestine follow-through

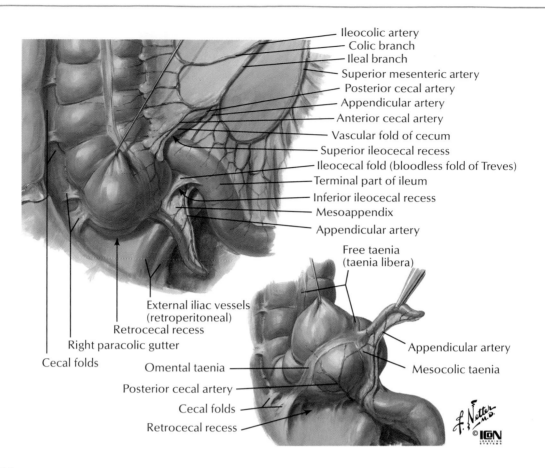

Ileocolic artery
Colic branch
Ileal branch
Superior mesenteric artery
Posterior cecal artery
Appendicular artery
Anterior cecal artery
Vascular fold of cecum
Superior ileocecal recess
Ileocecal fold (bloodless fold of Treves)
Terminal part of ileum
Inferior ileocecal recess
Mesoappendix
Appendicular artery
Free taenia (taenia libera)
Appendicular artery
Mesocolic taenia
External iliac vessels (retroperitoneal)
Retrocecal recess
Right paracolic gutter
Cecal folds
Omental taenia
Posterior cecal artery
Cecal folds
Retrocecal recess

ANESTHESIA

Upper Abdomen

00790   Anesthesia for intraperitoneal procedures in upper abdomen including laparoscopy; not otherwise specified

Lower Abdomen

00810   Anesthesia for lower intestinal endoscopic procedures, endoscope introduced distal to duodenum

00840   Anesthesia for intraperitoneal procedures in lower abdomen including laparoscopy; not otherwise specified

SURGERY

Digestive System

Intestines (Except Rectum)
Excision

44160   Colectomy, partial, with removal of terminal ileum with ileocolostomy

Laparoscopy

44205   Laparoscopy, surgical; colectomy, partial, with removal of terminal ileum with ileocolostomy

Endoscopy, Small Intestine and Stomal

44376   Small intestinal endoscopy, enteroscopy beyond second portion of duodenum, including ileum; diagnostic, with or without collection of specimen(s) by brushing or washing (separate procedure)

44377   with biopsy, single or multiple

44378   with control of bleeding (eg, injection, bipolar cautery, unipolar cautery, laser, heater probe, stapler, plasma coagulator)

44379   with transendoscopic stent placement (includes predilation)

44380   Ileoscopy, through stoma; diagnostic, with or without collection of specimen(s) by brushing or washing (separate procedure)

44382   with biopsy, single or multiple

44383   with transendoscopic stent placement (includes predilation)

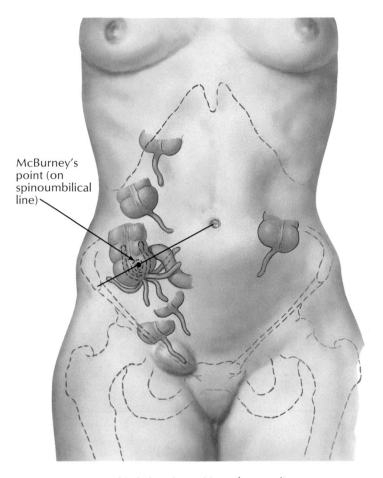

McBurney's point (on spinoumbilical line)

Variations in position of appendix

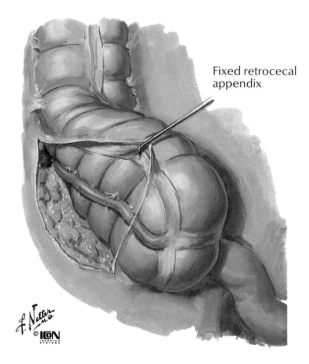

Fixed retrocecal appendix

ANESTHESIA

Lower Abdomen

00800	Anesthesia for procedures on lower anterior abdominal wall; not otherwise specified
00840	Anesthesia for intraperitoneal procedures in lower abdomen including laparoscopy; not otherwise specified

SURGERY

Digestive System

Appendix
Incision

44900	Incision and drainage of appendiceal abscess; open
44901	percutaneous

Excision

44950	Appendectomy;
44955	when done for indicated purpose at time of other major procedure (not as separate procedure) (List separately in addition to code for primary procedure)
44960	for ruptured appendix with abscess or generalized peritonitis

Laparoscopy

44970	Laparoscopy, surgical, appendectomy

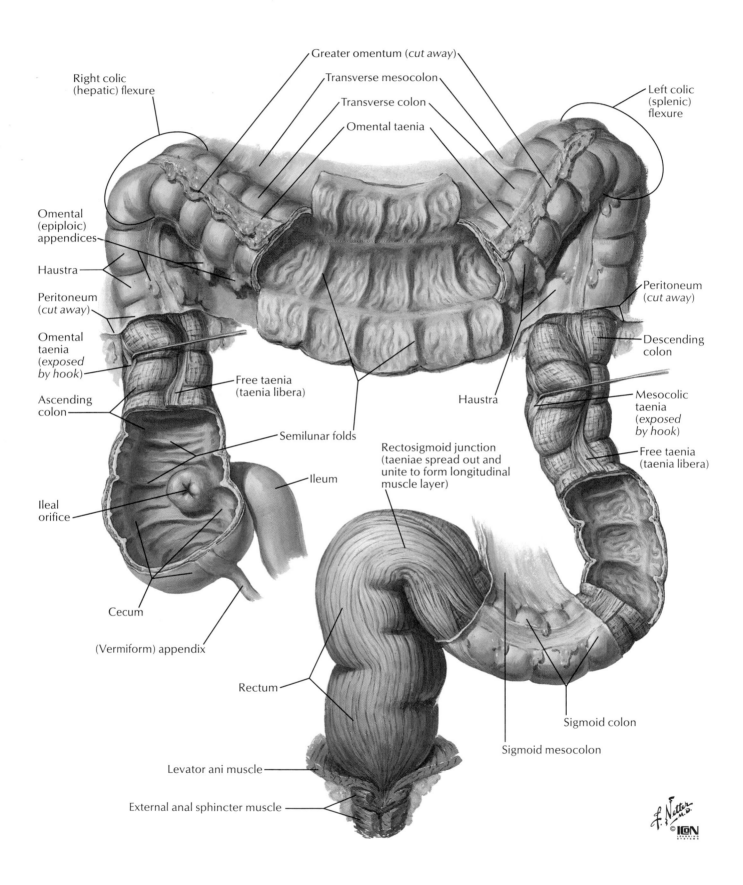

Greater omentum (*cut away*)

Transverse mesocolon

Transverse colon

Omental taenia

Right colic (hepatic) flexure

Left colic (splenic) flexure

Omental (epiploic) appendices

Haustra

Peritoneum (*cut away*)

Omental taenia (*exposed by hook*)

Ascending colon

Ileal orifice

Cecum

(Vermiform) appendix

Rectum

Levator ani muscle

External anal sphincter muscle

Free taenia (taenia libera)

Semilunar folds

Ileum

Rectosigmoid junction (taeniae spread out and unite to form longitudinal muscle layer)

Haustra

Peritoneum (*cut away*)

Descending colon

Mesocolic taenia (*exposed by hook*)

Free taenia (taenia libera)

Sigmoid colon

Sigmoid mesocolon

ANESTHESIA

Thorax (Chest Wall and Shoulder Girdle)

00400   Anesthesia for procedures on the integumentary system on the extremities, anterior trunk and perineum; not otherwise specified

Upper Abdomen

00740   Anesthesia for upper gastrointestinal endoscopic procedures, endoscope introduced proximal to duodenum

00790   Anesthesia for intraperitoneal procedures in upper abdomen including laparoscopy; not otherwise specified

Lower Abdomen

00840   Anesthesia for intraperitoneal procedures in lower abdomen including laparoscopy; not otherwise specified

00810   Anesthesia for lower intestinal endoscopic procedures, endoscope introduced distal to duodenum

00844   Anesthesia for intraperitoneal procedures in lower abdomen including laparoscopy; abdominoperineal resection

Perineum

00902   Anesthesia for; anorectal procedure

00904   radical perineal procedure

SURGERY

Digestive System

Intestines (Except Rectum)

Incision

44005   Enterolysis (freeing of intestinal adhesion) (separate procedure)

44025   Colotomy, for exploration, biopsy(s), or foreign body removal

Excision

44100   Biopsy of intestine by capsule, tube, peroral (one or more specimens)

44110   Excision of one or more lesions of small or large intestine not requiring anastomosis, exteriorization, or fistulization; single enterotomy

44111   multiple enterotomies

44130   Enteroenterostomy, anastomosis of intestine, with or without cutaneous enterostomy (separate procedure)

44139   Mobilization (take-down) of splenic flexure performed in conjunction with partial colectomy (List separately in addition to primary procedure)

44140ᴾ   Colectomy, partial; with anastomosis

44141   with skin level cecostomy or colostomy

44143   with end colostomy and closure of distal segment (Hartmann type procedure)

44144   with resection, with colostomy or ileostomy and creation of mucofistula

44145   with coloproctostomy (low pelvic anastomosis)

44146   with coloproctostomy (low pelvic anastomosis), with colostomy

44147   abdominal and transanal approach

44150   Colectomy, total, abdominal, without proctectomy; with ileostomy or ileoproctostomy

44151   with continent ileostomy

44152   with rectal mucosectomy, ileoanal anastomosis, with or without loop ileostomy

44153   with rectal mucosectomy, ileoanal anastomosis, creation of ileal reservoir (S or J), with or without loop ileostomy

44155   Colectomy, total, abdominal, with proctectomy; with ileostomy

44156   with continent ileostomy

44160ᴾ   Colectomy, partial, with removal of terminal ileum with ileocolostomy

Laparoscopy

44200   Laparoscopy, surgical; enterolysis (freeing of intestinal adhesion) (separate procedure)

44202   enterectomy, resection of small intestine, single resection and anastomosis

44204   colectomy, partial, with anastomosis

44205   colectomy, partial, with removal of terminal ileum with ileocolostomy

44206   colectomy, partial, with end colostomy and closure of distal segment (Hartmann type procedure)

44207   colectomy, partial, with anastomosis, with coloproctostomy (low pelvic anastomosis)

44208   colectomy, partial, with anastomosis, with coloproctostomy (low pelvic anastomosis) with colostomy

44210   colectomy, total, abdominal, without proctectomy, with ileostomy or ileoproctostomy

44211   colectomy, total, abdominal, with proctectomy, with ileoanal anastomosis, creation of ileal reservoir (S or J), with loop ileostomy, with or without rectal mucosectomy

44212   colectomy, total, abdominal, with proctectomy, with ileostomy

Enterostomy—External Fistulization of Intestines

44300   Enterostomy or cecostomy, tube (eg, for decompression or feeding) (separate procedure)

44320   Colostomy or skin level cecostomy; (separate procedure)

44322   with multiple biopsies (eg, for congenital megacolon) (separate procedure)

44340   Revision of colostomy; simple (release of superficial scar) (separate procedure)

44345   complicated (reconstruction in-depth) (separate procedure)

44346   with repair of paracolostomy hernia (separate procedure)

Endoscopy, Small Intestine and Stomal

44388   Colonoscopy through stoma; diagnostic, with or without collection of specimen(s) by brushing or washing (separate procedure)

(Endoscopy continued on next page)

(Endoscopy continued from previous page)

44389	with biopsy, single or multiple
44390	with removal of foreign body
44391	with control of bleeding (eg, injection, bipolar cautery, unipolar cautery, laser, heater probe, stapler, plasma coagulator)
44392	with removal of tumor(s), polyp(s), or other lesion(s) by hot biopsy forceps or bipolar cautery
44393	with ablation of tumor(s), polyp(s), or other lesion(s) not amenable to removal by hot biopsy forceps, bipolar cautery or snare technique
44394	with removal of tumor(s), polyp(s), or other lesion(s) by snare technique
44397	with transendoscopic stent placement (includes predilation)

Repair

44602	Suture of small intestine (enterorrhaphy) for perforated ulcer, diverticulum, wound, injury or rupture; single perforation
44603	multiple perforations
44604	Suture of large intestine (colorrhaphy) for perforated ulcer, diverticulum, wound, injury or rupture (single or multiple perforations); without colostomy
44605	with colostomy
44615	Intestinal stricturoplasty (enterotomy and enterorrhaphy) with or without dilation, for intestinal obstruction
44620	Closure of enterostomy, large or small intestine;
44625	with resection and anastomosis other than colorectal
44626	with resection and colorectal anastomosis (eg, closure of Hartmann type procedure)
44640	Closure of intestinal cutaneous fistula
44680	Intestinal plication (separate procedure)

Other Procedures

44701	Intraoperative colonic lavage (List separately in addition to code for primary procedure)

Rectum
Incision

45005	Incision and drainage of submucosal abscess, rectum
45020	Incision and drainage of deep supralevator, pelvirectal, or retrorectal abscess

Excision

45100	Biopsy of anorectal wall, anal approach (eg, congenital megacolon)
45108	Anorectal myomectomy
45110	Proctectomy; complete, combined abdominoperineal, with colostomy
45111	partial resection of rectum, transabdominal approach
45112	Proctectomy, combined abdominoperineal, pull-through procedure (eg, colo-anal anastomosis)
45113	Proctectomy, partial, with rectal mucosectomy, ileoanal anastomosis, creation of ileal reservoir (S or J), with or without loop ileostomy
45114	Proctectomy, partial, with anastomosis; abdominal and transsacral approach
45116	transsacral approach only (Kraske type)
45119	Proctectomy, combined abdominoperineal pull-through procedure (eg, colo-anal anastomosis), with creation of colonic reservoir (eg, J-pouch), with or without proximal diverting ostomy
45120	Proctectomy, complete (for congenital megacolon), abdominal and perineal approach; with pull-through procedure and anastomosis (eg, Swenson, Duhamel, or Soave type operation)
45121	with subtotal or total colectomy, with multiple biopsies
45123	Proctectomy, partial, without anastomosis, perineal approach
45126	Pelvic exenteration for colorectal malignancy, with proctectomy (with or without colostomy), with removal of bladder and ureteral transplantations, and/or hysterectomy, or cervicectomy, with or without removal of tube(s), with or without removal of ovary(s), or any combination thereof
45130	Excision of rectal procidentia, with anastomosis; perineal approach
45135	abdominal and perineal approach
45136	Excision of ileoanal reservoir with ileostomy
45150	Division of stricture of rectum
45160	Excision of rectal tumor by proctotomy, transsacral or transcoccygeal approach
45170	Excision of rectal tumor, transanal approach

Destruction

45190	Destruction of rectal tumor (eg, electrodessication, electrosurgery, laser ablation, laser resection, cryosurgery) transanal approach

Endoscopy

45300	Proctosigmoidoscopy, rigid; diagnostic, with or without collection of specimen(s) by brushing or washing (separate procedure)
45303	with dilation (eg, balloon, guide wire, bougie)
45305	with biopsy, single or multiple
45307	with removal of foreign body
45308	with removal of single tumor, polyp, or other lesion by hot biopsy forceps or bipolar cautery
45309	with removal of single tumor, polyp, or other lesion by snare technique
45315	with removal of multiple tumors, polyps, or other lesions by hot biopsy forceps, bipolar cautery or snare technique
45317	with control of bleeding (eg, injection, bipolar cautery, unipolar cautery, laser, heater probe, stapler, plasma coagulator)
45320	with ablation of tumor(s), polyp(s), or other lesion(s) not amenable to removal by hot biopsy forceps, bipolar cautery or snare technique (eg, laser)
45321	with decompression of volvulus
45327	with transendoscopic stent placement (includes predilation)

45330	Sigmoidoscopy, flexible; diagnostic, with or without collection of specimen(s) by brushing or washing (separate procedure)
45331	with biopsy, single or multiple
45332	with removal of foreign body
45333	with removal of tumor(s), polyp(s), or other lesion(s) by hot biopsy forceps or bipolar cautery
45334	with control of bleeding (eg, injection, bipolar cautery, unipolar cautery, laser, heater probe, stapler, plasma coagulator)
45335	with directed submucosal injection(s), any substance
45337	with decompression of volvulus, any method
45338	with removal of tumor(s), polyp(s), or other lesion(s) by snare technique
45339	with ablation of tumor(s), polyp(s), or other lesion(s) not amenable to removal by hot biopsy forceps, bipolar cautery or snare technique
45340	with dilation by balloon, 1 or more strictures
45341	with endoscopic ultrasound examination
45342	with transendoscopic ultrasound guided intramural or transmural fine needle aspiration/biopsy(s)
45345	with transendoscopic stent placement (includes predilation)
45355	Colonoscopy, rigid or flexible, transabdominal via colotomy, single or multiple
45378P	Colonoscopy, flexible, proximal to splenic flexure; diagnostic, with or without collection of specimen(s) by brushing or washing, with or without colon decompression (separate procedure)
45379	with removal of foreign body
45380	with biopsy, single or multiple
45381	with directed submucosal injection(s), any substance
45382	with control of bleeding (eg, injection, bipolar cautery, unipolar cautery, laser, heater probe, stapler, plasma coagulator)
45383	with ablation of tumor(s), polyp(s), or other lesion(s) not amenable to removal by hot biopsy forceps, bipolar cautery or snare technique
45384	with removal of tumor(s), polyp(s), or other lesion(s) by hot biopsy forceps or bipolar cautery
45385	with removal of tumor(s), polyp(s), or other lesion(s) by snare technique
45386	with dilation by balloon, 1 or more strictures
45387	with transendoscopic stent placement (includes predilation)
45391	with endoscopic ultrasound examination
45392	with transendoscopic ultrasound guided intramural or transmural fine needle aspiration/biopsy(s)

Repair

45500	Proctoplasty; for stenosis
45505	for prolapse of mucous membrane
45520	Perirectal injection of sclerosing solution for prolapse
45540	Proctopexy for prolapse; abdominal approach
45541	perineal approach
45550	Proctopexy combined with sigmoid resection, abdominal approach
45560	Repair of rectocele (separate procedure)
45562	Exploration, repair, and presacral drainage for rectal injury;
45563	with colostomy

Manipulation

45900	Reduction of procidentia (separate procedure) under anesthesia
45905	Dilation of anal sphincter (separate procedure) under anesthesia other than local
45910	Dilation of rectal stricture (separate procedure) under anesthesia other than local
45915	Removal of fecal impaction or foreign body (separate procedure) under anesthesia

Anus
Incision

46020P	Placement of seton
46030	Removal of anal seton, other marker
46040	Incision and drainage of ischiorectal and/or perirectal abscess (separate procedure)
46045	Incision and drainage of intramural, intramuscular, or submucosal abscess, transanal, under anesthesia
46050	Incision and drainage, perianal abscess, superficial
46060	Incision and drainage of ischiorectal or intramural abscess, with fistulectomy or fistulotomy, submuscular, with or without placement of seton
46070	Incision, anal septum (infant)
46080	Sphincterotomy, anal, division of sphincter (separate procedure)
46083	Incision of thrombosed hemorrhoid, external

Excision

46200	Fissurectomy, with or without sphincterotomy
46210	Cryptectomy; single
46211	multiple (separate procedure)
46220	Papillectomy or excision of single tag, anus (separate procedure)
46221	Hemorrhoidectomy, by simple ligature (eg, rubber band)
46230	Excision of external hemorrhoid tags and/or multiple papillae
46250	Hemorrhoidectomy, external, complete
46255	Hemorrhoidectomy, internal and external, simple;
46257	with fissurectomy
46258	with fistulectomy, with or without fissurectomy
46260	Hemorrhoidectomy, internal and external, complex or extensive;
46261	with fissurectomy
46262	with fistulectomy, with or without fissurectomy
46270	Surgical treatment of anal fistula (fistulectomy/fistulotomy); subcutaneous
46275	submuscular
46280	complex or multiple, with or without placement of seton

(Excision continued on next page)

(Excision continued from previous page)

46285	second stage
46288	Closure of anal fistula with rectal advancement flap
46320	Enucleation or excision of external thrombotic hemorrhoid

Introduction

46500	Injection of sclerosing solution, hemorrhoids

Endoscopy

46600	Anoscopy; diagnostic, with or without collection of specimen(s) by brushing or washing (separate procedure)
46604	with dilation (eg, balloon, guide wire, bougie)
46606	with biopsy, single or multiple
46608	with removal of foreign body
46610	with removal of single tumor, polyp, or other lesion by hot biopsy forceps or bipolar cautery
46611	with removal of single tumor, polyp, or other lesion by snare technique
46612	with removal of multiple tumors, polyps, or other lesions by hot biopsy forceps, bipolar cautery or snare technique
46614	with control of bleeding (eg, injection, bipolar cautery, unipolar cautery, laser, heater probe, stapler, plasma coagulator)
46615	with ablation of tumor(s), polyp(s), or other lesion(s) not amenable to removal by hot biopsy forceps, bipolar cautery or snare technique

Repair

46700	Anoplasty, plastic operation for stricture; adult
46705	infant
46706	Repair of anal fistula with fibrin glue
46715	Repair of low imperforate anus; with anoperineal fistula (cut-back procedure)
46716	with transposition of anoperineal or anovestibular fistula
46730	Repair of high imperforate anus without fistula; perineal or sacroperineal approach
46735	combined transabdominal and sacroperineal approaches
46740	Repair of high imperforate anus with rectourethral or rectovaginal fistula; perineal or sacroperineal approach
46742	combined transabdominal and sacroperineal approaches

46744	Repair of cloacal anomaly by anorectovaginoplasty and urethroplasty, sacroperineal approach
46746	Repair of cloacal anomaly by anorectovaginoplasty and urethroplasty, combined abdominal and sacroperineal approach;
46748	with vaginal lengthening by intestinal graft or pedicle flaps
46750	Sphincteroplasty, anal, for incontinence or prolapse; adult
46751	child
46753	Graft (Thiersch operation) for rectal incontinence and/or prolapse
46754	Removal of Thiersch wire or suture, anal canal
46760	Sphincteroplasty, anal, for incontinence, adult; muscle transplant
46761	levator muscle imbrication (Park posterior anal repair)
46762	implantation artificial sphincter

Destruction

46900	Destruction of lesion(s), anus (eg, condyloma, papilloma, molluscum contagiosum, herpetic vesicle), simple; chemical
46910	electrodesiccation
46916	cryosurgery
46917	laser surgery
46922	surgical excision
46924	Destruction of lesion(s), anus (eg, condyloma, papilloma, molluscum contagiosum, herpetic vesicle), extensive (eg, laser surgery, electrosurgery, cryosurgery, chemosurgery)
46934	Destruction of hemorrhoids, any method; internal
46935	external
46936	internal and external
46937	Cryosurgery of rectal tumor; benign
46938	malignant
46940	Curettage or cautery of anal fissure, including dilation of anal sphincter (separate procedure); initial
46942	subsequent

Suture

46945	Ligation of internal hemorrhoids; single procedure
46946	multiple procedures
46947	Hemorrhoidopexy (eg, for prolapsing internal hemorrhoids) by stapling

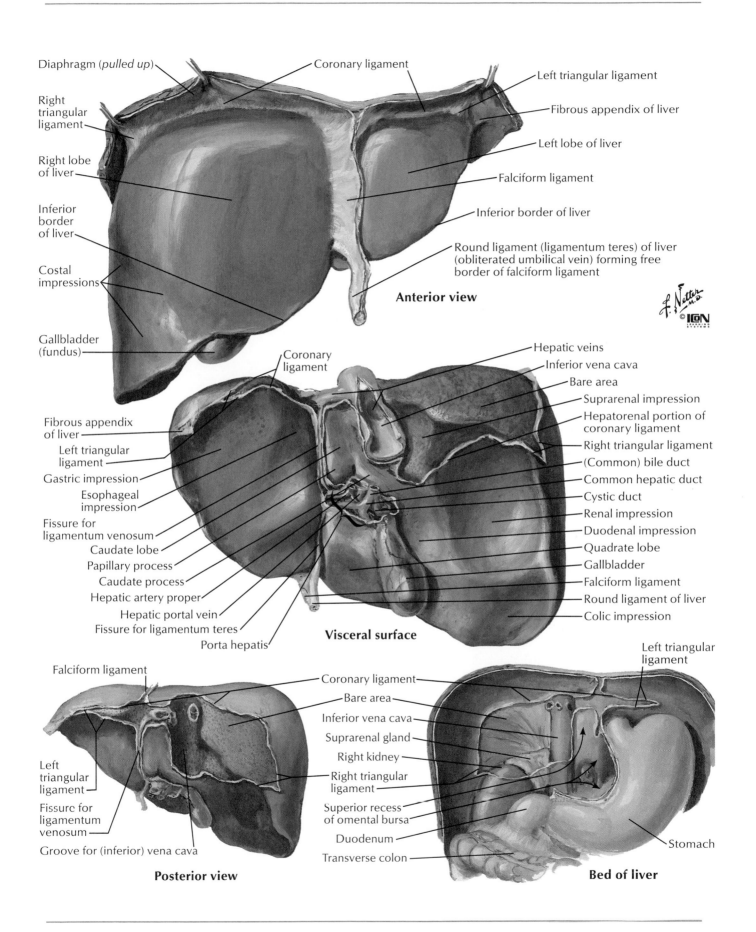

Diaphragm (*pulled up*)

Coronary ligament

Left triangular ligament

Fibrous appendix of liver

Right triangular ligament

Left lobe of liver

Right lobe of liver

Falciform ligament

Inferior border of liver

Inferior border of liver

Costal impressions

Round ligament (ligamentum teres) of liver (obliterated umbilical vein) forming free border of falciform ligament

Gallbladder (fundus)

Anterior view

Coronary ligament

Hepatic veins

Inferior vena cava

Bare area

Suprarenal impression

Fibrous appendix of liver

Hepatorenal portion of coronary ligament

Left triangular ligament

Right triangular ligament

Gastric impression

(Common) bile duct

Esophageal impression

Common hepatic duct

Fissure for ligamentum venosum

Cystic duct

Renal impression

Caudate lobe

Duodenal impression

Papillary process

Quadrate lobe

Caudate process

Gallbladder

Hepatic artery proper

Falciform ligament

Hepatic portal vein

Round ligament of liver

Fissure for ligamentum teres

Colic impression

Porta hepatis

Visceral surface

Falciform ligament

Coronary ligament

Left triangular ligament

Bare area

Inferior vena cava

Suprarenal gland

Right kidney

Left triangular ligament

Right triangular ligament

Fissure for ligamentum venosum

Superior recess of omental bursa

Groove for (inferior) vena cava

Duodenum

Transverse colon

Stomach

Posterior view

Bed of liver

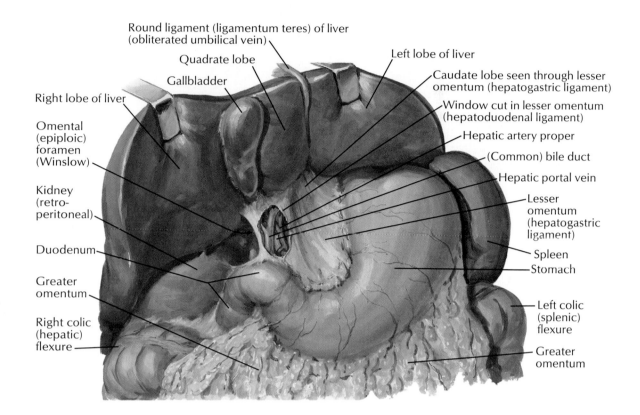

Round ligament (ligamentum teres) of liver (obliterated umbilical vein)

Quadrate lobe

Gallbladder

Right lobe of liver

Omental (epiploic) foramen (Winslow)

Kidney (retro-peritoneal)

Duodenum

Greater omentum

Right colic (hepatic) flexure

Left lobe of liver

Caudate lobe seen through lesser omentum (hepatogastric ligament)

Window cut in lesser omentum (hepatoduodenal ligament)

Hepatic artery proper

(Common) bile duct

Hepatic portal vein

Lesser omentum (hepatogastric ligament)

Spleen

Stomach

Left colic (splenic) flexure

Greater omentum

ANESTHESIA

Intrathoracic

00532   Anesthesia for access to central venous circulation

Upper Abdomen

00702   Anesthesia for procedures on upper anterior abdominal wall; percutaneous liver biopsy

00740   Anesthesia for upper gastrointestinal endoscopic procedures, endoscope introduced proximal to duodenum

00790   Anesthesia for intraperitoneal procedures in upper abdomen including laparoscopy; not otherwise specified

00792   partial hepatectomy or management of liver hemorrhage (excluding liver biopsy)

00796   liver transplant (recipient)

Radiological Procedures

01931   Anesthesia for therapeutic interventional radiologic procedures involving the venous/lymphatic system (not to include access to the central circulation); intrahepatic or portal circulation (eg, transcutaneous porto-caval shunt (TIPS))

SURGERY

Cardiovascular System

Arteries and Veins
Venous

36481   Percutaneous portal vein catheterization by any method

Portal Decompression Procedures

37182   Insertion of transvenous intrahepatic portosystemic shunt(s) (TIPS) (includes venous access, hepatic and portal vein catheterization, portography with hemodynamic evaluation, intrahepatic tract formation/dilatation, stent placement and all associated imaging guidance and documentation)

37183   Revision of transvenous intrahepatic portosystemic shunt(s) (TIPS) (includes venous access, hepatic and portal vein catheterization, portography with hemodynamic evaluation, intrahepatic tract recanulization/dilatation, stent placement and all associated imaging guidance and documentation)

Digestive System

Liver
Incision

47000   Biopsy of liver, needle; percutaneous

47001	when done for indicated purpose at time of other major procedure (List separately in addition to code for primary procedure)
47010	Hepatotomy; for open drainage of abscess or cyst, one or two stages
47011	for percutaneous drainage of abscess or cyst, one or two stages
47015	Laparotomy, with aspiration and/or injection of hepatic parasitic (eg, amoebic or echinococcal) cyst(s) or abscess(es)

Excision

47100	Biopsy of liver, wedge
47120	Hepatectomy, resection of liver; partial lobectomy
47122	trisegmentectomy
47125	total left lobectomy
47130	total right lobectomy

Liver Transplantation

47140	Donor hepatectomy (including cold preservation), from living donor; left lateral segment only (segments II and III)
47141	Donor hepatectomy (including cold preservation), from living donor; total left lobectomy (segments II, III and IV)
47142	total right lobectomy (segments V, VI, VII and VIII)

Repair

47300	Marsupialization of cyst or abscess of liver
47350	Management of liver hemorrhage; simple suture of liver wound or injury

(Repair continued on next page)

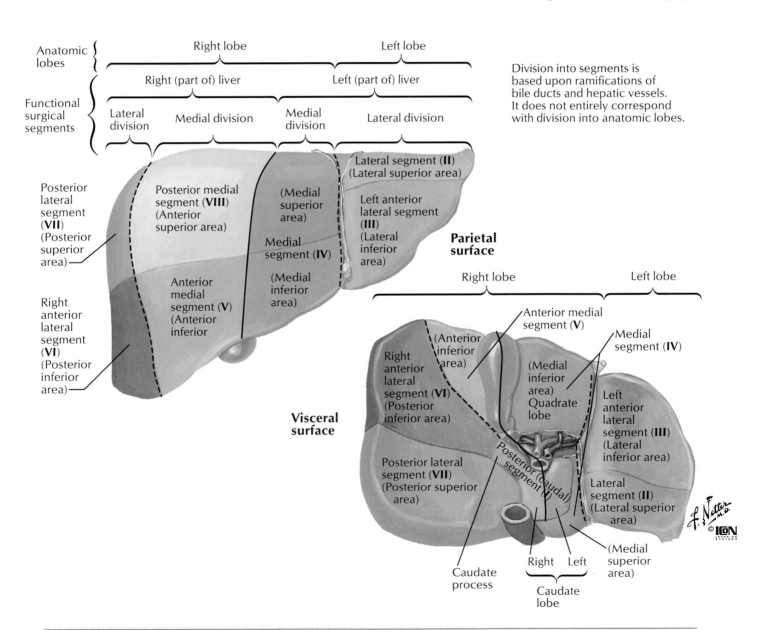

Plate 114: Liver

(Repair continued from previous page)

47360 complex suture of liver wound or injury, with or without hepatic artery ligation

47361 exploration of hepatic wound, extensive debridement, coagulation and/or suture, with or without packing of liver

47362 re-exploration of hepatic wound for removal of packing

Laparoscopy

47370 Laparoscopy, surgical, ablation of one or more liver tumor(s); radiofrequency

47371 cryosurgical

47379 Unlisted laparoscopic procedure, liver

Other Procedures

47380 Ablation, open, of one or more liver tumor(s); radiofrequency

47381 cryosurgical

47382 Ablation, one or more liver tumor(s), percutaneous, radiofrequency

Biliary Tract
Incision

47400 Hepaticotomy or hepaticostomy with exploration, drainage, or removal of calculus

47420 Choledochotomy or choledochostomy with exploration, drainage, or removal of calculus, with or without cholecystotomy; without transduodenal sphincterotomy or sphincteroplasty

47425 with transduodenal sphincterotomy or sphincteroplasty

47460 Transduodenal sphincterotomy or sphincteroplasty, with or without transduodenal extraction of calculus (separate procedure)

47480 Cholecystotomy or cholecystostomy with exploration, drainage, or removal of calculus (separate procedure)

47490 Percutaneous cholecystostomy

Introduction

47500 Injection procedure for percutaneous transhepatic cholangiography

47505 Injection procedure for cholangiography through an existing catheter (eg, percutaneous transhepatic or T-tube)

47510 Introduction of percutaneous transhepatic catheter for biliary drainage

47511 Introduction of percutaneous transhepatic stent for internal and external biliary drainage

47525 Change of percutaneous biliary drainage catheter

47530 Revision and/or reinsertion of transhepatic tube

Endoscopy

47550 Biliary endoscopy, intraoperative (choledochoscopy) (List separately in addition to code for primary procedure)

47552 Biliary endoscopy, percutaneous via T-tube or other tract; diagnostic, with or without collection of specimen(s) by brushing and/or washing (separate procedure)

47553 with biopsy, single or multiple

47554 with removal of calculus/calculi

47555 with dilation of biliary duct stricture(s) without stent

47556 with dilation of biliary duct stricture(s) with stent

Laparoscopy

47560 Laparoscopy, surgical; with guided transhepatic cholangiography, without biopsy

47561 with guided transhepatic cholangiography with biopsy

47562ᴾ cholecystectomy

47563 cholecystectomy with cholangiography

47564 cholecystectomy with exploration of common duct

47570 cholecystoenterostomy

Excision

47605 Cholecystectomy; with cholangiography

47610 Cholecystectomy with exploration of common duct;

47612 with choledochoenterostomy

47620 with transduodenal sphincterotomy or sphincteroplasty, with or without cholangiography

47630 Biliary duct stone extraction, percutaneous via T-tube tract, basket, or snare (eg, Burhenne technique)

47700 Exploration for congenital atresia of bile ducts, without repair, with or without liver biopsy, with or without cholangiography

47701 Portoenterostomy (eg, Kasai procedure)

47711 Excision of bile duct tumor, with or without primary repair of bile duct; extrahepatic

47712 intrahepatic

47715 Excision of choledochal cyst

47716 Anastomosis, choledochal cyst, without excision

Repair

47720 Cholecystoenterostomy; direct

47721 with gastroenterostomy

47740 Roux-en-Y

47741 Roux-en-Y with gastroenterostomy

47760 Anastomosis, of extrahepatic biliary ducts and gastrointestinal tract

47765 Anastomosis, of intrahepatic ducts and gastrointestinal tract

47780 Anastomosis, Roux-en-Y, of extrahepatic biliary ducts and gastrointestinal tract

47785 Anastomosis, Roux-en-Y, of intrahepatic biliary ducts and gastrointestinal tract

47800 Reconstruction, plastic, of extrahepatic biliary ducts with end-to-end anastomosis

47801 Placement of choledochal stent

47802 U-tube hepaticoenterostomy

47900 Suture of extrahepatic biliary duct for pre-existing injury (separate procedure)

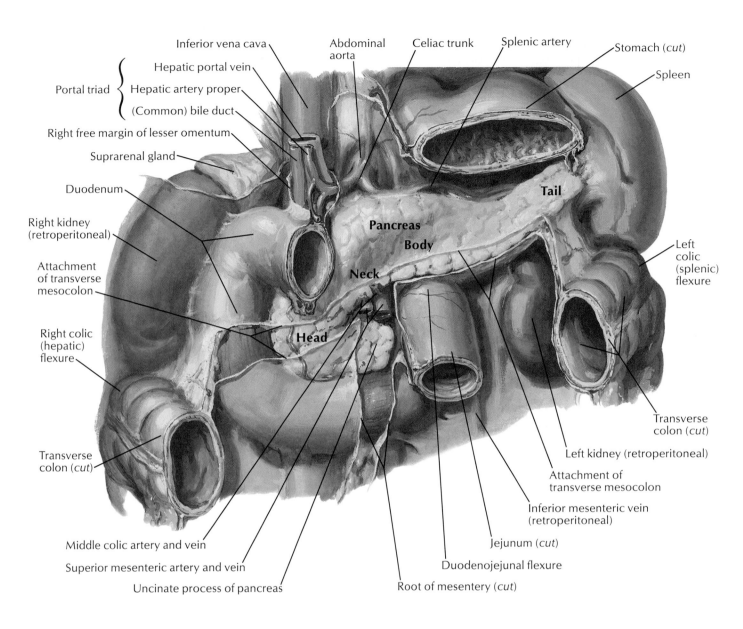

Inferior vena cava

Hepatic portal vein

Portal triad
- Hepatic artery proper
- (Common) bile duct

Right free margin of lesser omentum

Suprarenal gland

Duodenum

Right kidney (retroperitoneal)

Attachment of transverse mesocolon

Right colic (hepatic) flexure

Transverse colon (*cut*)

Middle colic artery and vein

Superior mesenteric artery and vein

Uncinate process of pancreas

Abdominal aorta

Celiac trunk

Splenic artery

Stomach (*cut*)

Spleen

Tail

Pancreas

Body

Neck

Head

Left colic (splenic) flexure

Transverse colon (*cut*)

Left kidney (retroperitoneal)

Attachment of transverse mesocolon

Inferior mesenteric vein (retroperitoneal)

Jejunum (*cut*)

Duodenojejunal flexure

Root of mesentery (*cut*)

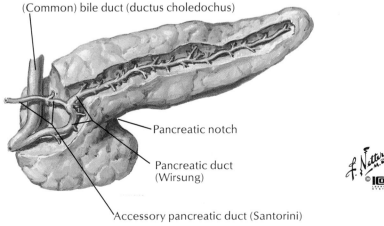

(Common) bile duct (ductus choledochus)

Pancreatic notch

Pancreatic duct (Wirsung)

Accessory pancreatic duct (Santorini)

ANESTHESIA

Upper Abdomen

00740   Anesthesia for upper gastrointestinal endoscopic procedures, endoscope introduced proximal to duodenum

00790   Anesthesia for intraperitoneal procedures in upper abdomen including laparoscopy; not otherwise specified

00794   Anesthesia for intraperitoneal procedures in upper abdomen including laparoscopy; pancreatectomy, partial or total (eg, Whipple procedure)

SURGERY

Digestive System

Esophagus
Endoscopy

43260^P   Endoscopic retrograde cholangiopancreatography (ERCP); diagnostic, with or without collection of specimen(s) by brushing or washing (separate procedure)

43261   with biopsy, single or multiple

43262   with sphincterotomy/papillotomy

43263   with pressure measurement of sphincter of Oddi (pancreatic duct or common bile duct)

43264   with endoscopic retrograde removal of calculus/calculi from biliary and/or pancreatic ducts

43265   with endoscopic retrograde destruction, lithotripsy of calculus/calculi, any method

43267   with endoscopic retrograde insertion of nasobiliary or nasopancreatic drainage tube

43268   with endoscopic retrograde insertion of tube or stent into bile or pancreatic duct

43269   with endoscopic retrograde removal of foreign body and/or change of tube or stent

43271   with endoscopic retrograde balloon dilation of ampulla, biliary and/or pancreatic duct(s)

43272   with ablation of tumor(s), polyp(s), or other lesion(s) not amenable to removal by hot biopsy forceps, bipolar cautery or snare technique

Pancreas
Incision

48000   Placement of drains, peripancreatic, for acute pancreatitis;

48001   with cholecystostomy, gastrostomy, and jejunostomy

48005   Resection or debridement of pancreas and peripancreatic tissue for acute necrotizing pancreatitis

48020   Removal of pancreatic calculus

Excision

48100   Biopsy of pancreas, open (eg, fine needle aspiration, needle core biopsy, wedge biopsy)

48102   Biopsy of pancreas, percutaneous needle

48120   Excision of lesion of pancreas (eg, cyst, adenoma)

48140   Pancreatectomy, distal subtotal, with or without splenectomy; without pancreaticojejunostomy

48145   with pancreaticojejunostomy

48146   Pancreatectomy, distal, near-total with preservation of duodenum (Child-type procedure)

48148   Excision of ampulla of Vater

48150   Pancreatectomy, proximal subtotal with total duodenectomy, partial gastrectomy, choledochoenterostomy and gastrojejunostomy (Whipple-type procedure); with pancreatojejunostomy

48152   without pancreatojejunostomy

48153   Pancreatectomy, proximal subtotal with near-total duodenectomy, choledochoenterostomy and duodenojejunostomy (pylorus-sparing, Whipple-type procedure); with pancreatojejunostomy

48154   without pancreatojejunostomy

48155   Pancreatectomy, total

48160   Pancreatectomy, total or subtotal, with autologous transplantation of pancreas or pancreatic islet cells

48180   Pancreaticojejunostomy, side-to-side anastomosis (Puestow-type operation)

Introduction

48400   Injection procedure for intraoperative pancreatography (List separately in addition to code for primary procedure)

Repair

48500   Marsupialization of pancreatic cyst

48510   External drainage, pseudocyst of pancreas; open

48511   percutaneous

48520   Internal anastomosis of pancreatic cyst to gastrointestinal tract; direct

48540   Roux-en-Y

48545   Pancreatorrhaphy for injury

48547   Duodenal exclusion with gastrojejunostomy for pancreatic injury

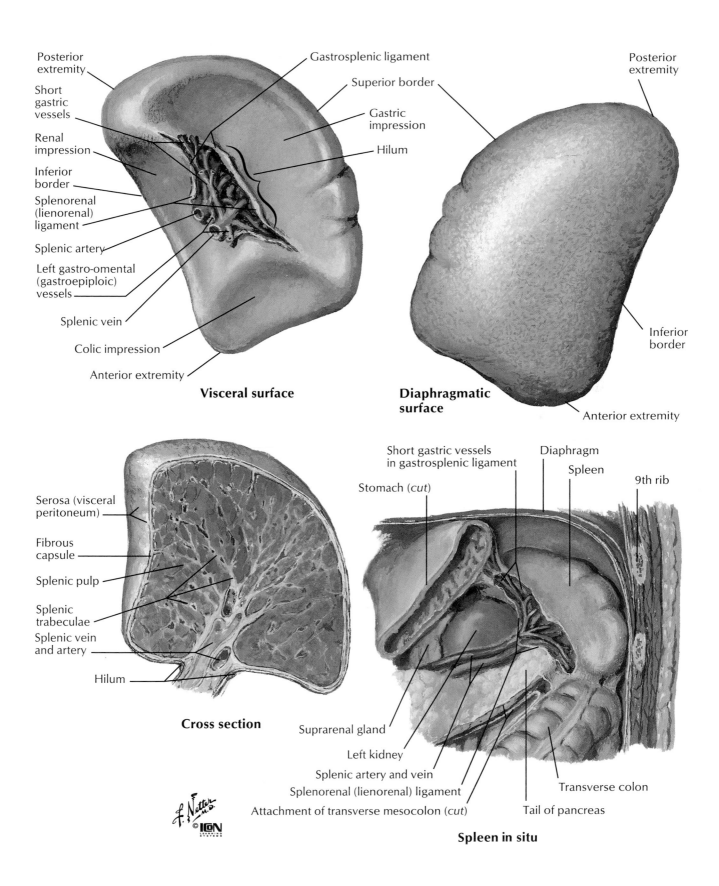

Posterior extremity

Short gastric vessels

Renal impression

Inferior border

Splenorenal (lienorenal) ligament

Splenic artery

Left gastro-omental (gastroepiploic) vessels

Splenic vein

Colic impression

Anterior extremity

Gastrosplenic ligament

Superior border

Gastric impression

Hilum

Visceral surface

Posterior extremity

Inferior border

Anterior extremity

Diaphragmatic surface

Serosa (visceral peritoneum)

Fibrous capsule

Splenic pulp

Splenic trabeculae

Splenic vein and artery

Hilum

Cross section

Short gastric vessels in gastrosplenic ligament

Stomach (*cut*)

Diaphragm

Spleen

9th rib

Suprarenal gland

Left kidney

Splenic artery and vein

Splenorenal (lienorenal) ligament

Attachment of transverse mesocolon (*cut*)

Transverse colon

Tail of pancreas

Spleen in situ

ANESTHESIA

Upper Abdomen

00790 Anesthesia for intraperitoneal procedures in upper abdomen including laparoscopy; not otherwise specified

Radiological Procedures

01916 Anesthesia for diagnostic arteriography/ venography

SURGERY

Hemic and Lymphatic Systems

Spleen
Excision

38100 Splenectomy; total (separate procedure)
38101   partial (separate procedure)

38102   total, en bloc for extensive disease, in conjunction with other procedure (List in addition to code for primary procedure)

Repair

38115 Repair of ruptured spleen (splenorrhaphy) with or without partial splenectomy

Laparoscopy

38120 Laparoscopy, surgical, splenectomy

Introduction

38200 Injection procedure for splenoportography

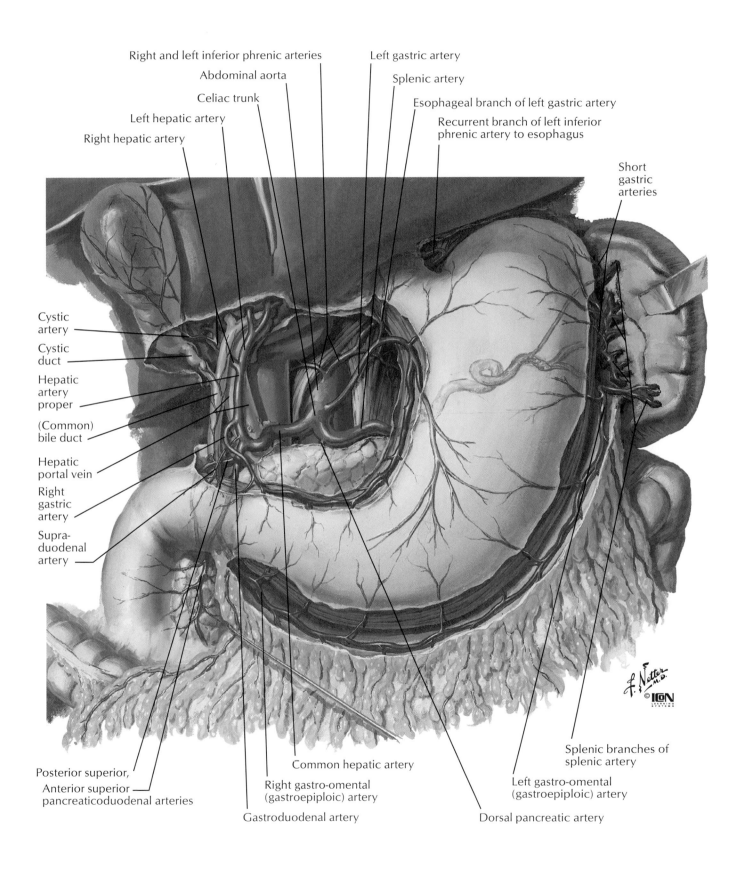

Right and left inferior phrenic arteries

Abdominal aorta

Celiac trunk

Left hepatic artery

Right hepatic artery

Left gastric artery

Splenic artery

Esophageal branch of left gastric artery

Recurrent branch of left inferior phrenic artery to esophagus

Short gastric arteries

Cystic artery

Cystic duct

Hepatic artery proper

(Common) bile duct

Hepatic portal vein

Right gastric artery

Supra-duodenal artery

Posterior superior, Anterior superior pancreaticoduodenal arteries

Right gastro-omental (gastroepiploic) artery

Gastroduodenal artery

Common hepatic artery

Left gastro-omental (gastroepiploic) artery

Dorsal pancreatic artery

Splenic branches of splenic artery

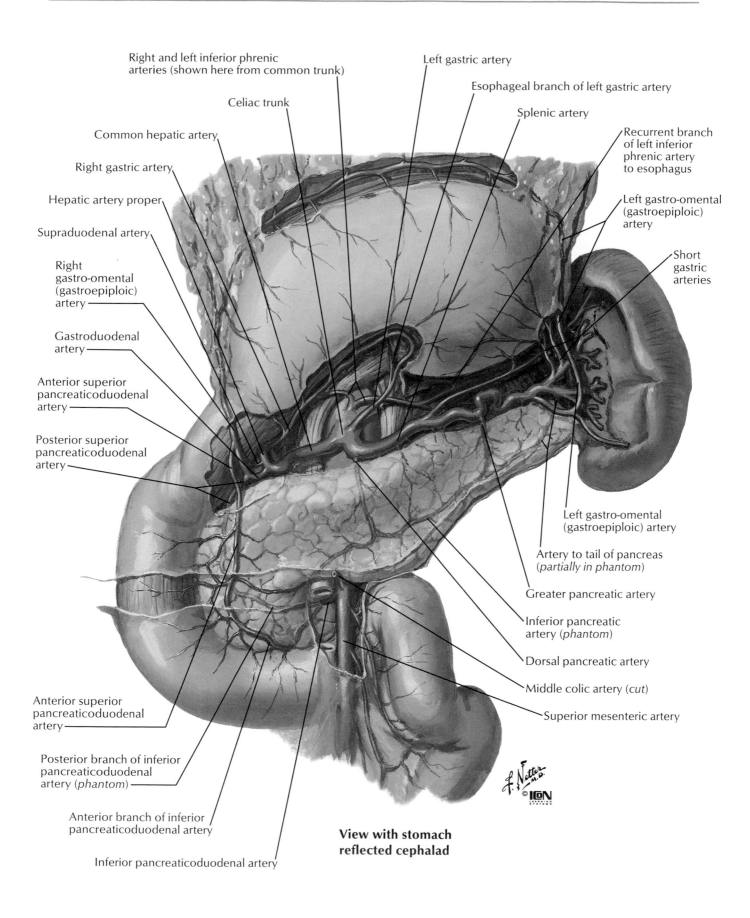

Right and left inferior phrenic arteries (shown here from common trunk)

Celiac trunk

Left gastric artery

Esophageal branch of left gastric artery

Splenic artery

Common hepatic artery

Right gastric artery

Hepatic artery proper

Supraduodenal artery

Recurrent branch of left inferior phrenic artery to esophagus

Left gastro-omental (gastroepiploic) artery

Right gastro-omental (gastroepiploic) artery

Short gastric arteries

Gastroduodenal artery

Anterior superior pancreaticoduodenal artery

Posterior superior pancreaticoduodenal artery

Left gastro-omental (gastroepiploic) artery

Artery to tail of pancreas (*partially in phantom*)

Greater pancreatic artery

Inferior pancreatic artery (*phantom*)

Dorsal pancreatic artery

Middle colic artery (*cut*)

Superior mesenteric artery

Anterior superior pancreaticoduodenal artery

Posterior branch of inferior pancreaticoduodenal artery (*phantom*)

Anterior branch of inferior pancreaticoduodenal artery

Inferior pancreaticoduodenal artery

View with stomach reflected cephalad

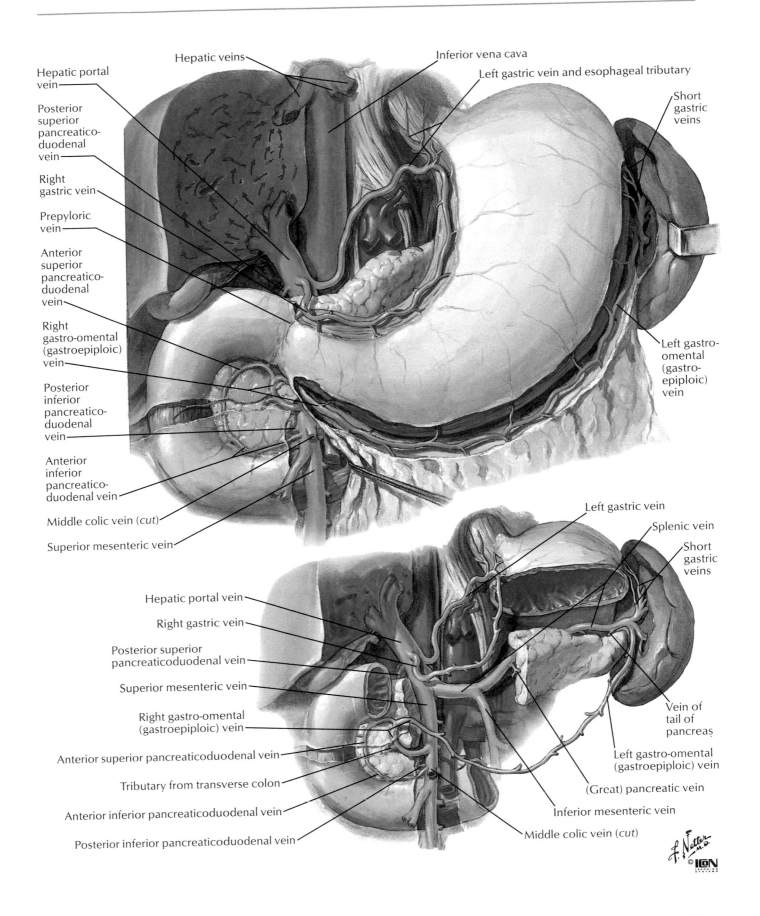

Hepatic veins

Inferior vena cava

Left gastric vein and esophageal tributary

Hepatic portal vein

Short gastric veins

Posterior superior pancreatico-duodenal vein

Right gastric vein

Prepyloric vein

Anterior superior pancreatico-duodenal vein

Right gastro-omental (gastroepiploic) vein

Posterior inferior pancreatico-duodenal vein

Anterior inferior pancreatico-duodenal vein

Middle colic vein (cut)

Superior mesenteric vein

Left gastro-omental (gastro-epiploic) vein

Hepatic portal vein

Right gastric vein

Posterior superior pancreaticoduodenal vein

Superior mesenteric vein

Right gastro-omental (gastroepiploic) vein

Anterior superior pancreaticoduodenal vein

Tributary from transverse colon

Anterior inferior pancreaticoduodenal vein

Posterior inferior pancreaticoduodenal vein

Left gastric vein

Splenic vein

Short gastric veins

Vein of tail of pancreas

Left gastro-omental (gastroepiploic) vein

(Great) pancreatic vein

Inferior mesenteric vein

Middle colic vein (cut)

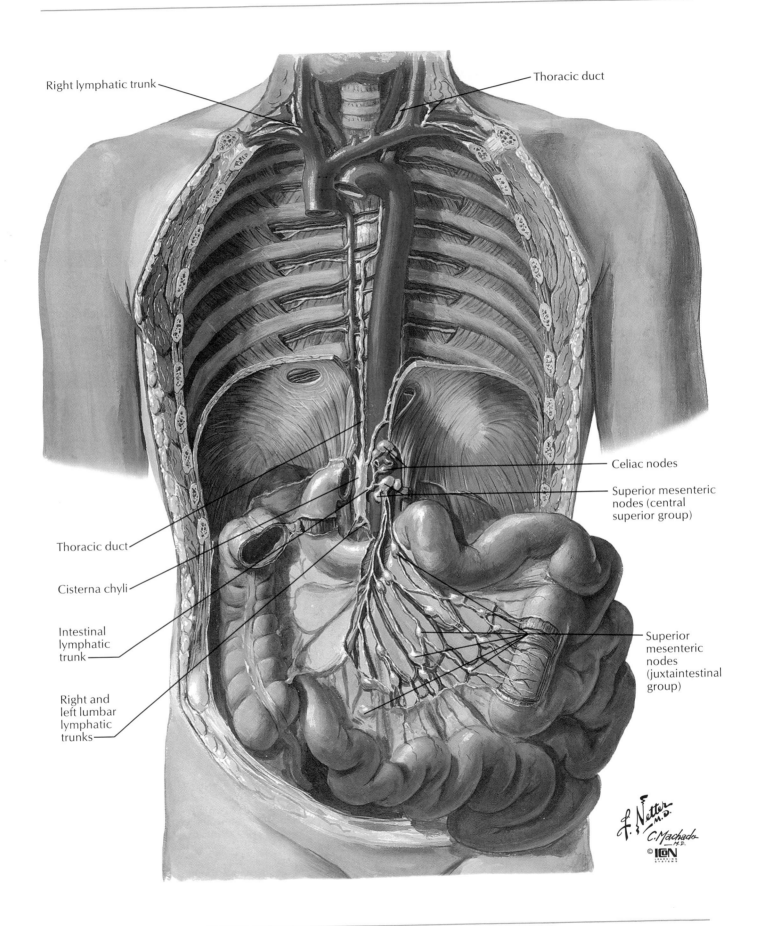

Right lymphatic trunk

Thoracic duct

Celiac nodes

Superior mesenteric nodes (central superior group)

Thoracic duct

Cisterna chyli

Intestinal lymphatic trunk

Superior mesenteric nodes (juxtaintestinal group)

Right and left lumbar lymphatic trunks

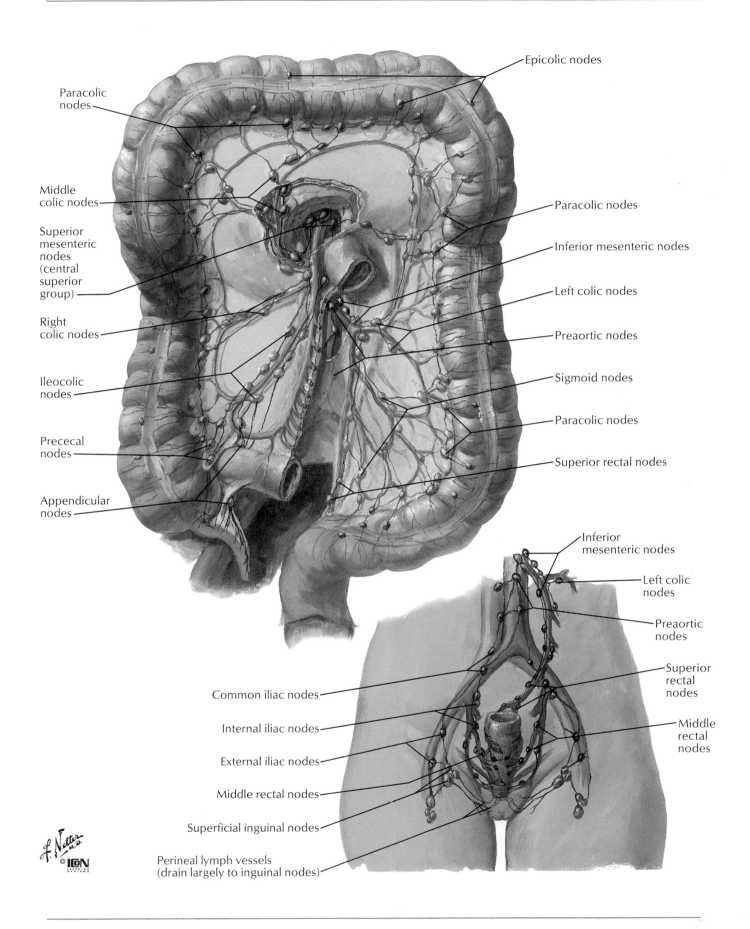

Epicolic nodes

Paracolic nodes

Middle colic nodes

Superior mesenteric nodes (central superior group)

Right colic nodes

Ileocolic nodes

Prececal nodes

Appendicular nodes

Paracolic nodes

Inferior mesenteric nodes

Left colic nodes

Preaortic nodes

Sigmoid nodes

Paracolic nodes

Superior rectal nodes

Inferior mesenteric nodes

Left colic nodes

Preaortic nodes

Superior rectal nodes

Middle rectal nodes

Common iliac nodes

Internal iliac nodes

External iliac nodes

Middle rectal nodes

Superficial inguinal nodes

Perineal lymph vessels (drain largely to inguinal nodes)

ANESTHESIA

Neck

00320 Anesthesia for all procedures on esophagus, thyroid, larynx, trachea and lymphatic system of neck; not otherwise specified, age 1 year or older

Intrathoracic

00541 Anesthesia for thoracotomy procedures involving lungs, pleura, diaphragm, and mediastinum (including surgical thoracoscopy); utilizing one lung ventilation

Upper Abdomen

00790 Anesthesia for intraperitoneal procedures in upper abdomen including laparoscopy; not otherwise specified

Lower Abdomen

00800 Anesthesia for procedures on lower anterior abdominal wall; not otherwise specified

00840 Anesthesia for intraperitoneal procedures in lower abdomen including laparoscopy; not otherwise specified

00860 Anesthesia for extraperitoneal procedures in lower abdomen, including urinary tract; not otherwise specified

SURGERY

Hemic and Lymphatic Systems

Lymph Nodes and Lymphatic Channels
Incision

38300 Drainage of lymph node abscess or lymphadenitis; simple

38305 extensive

38308 Lymphangiotomy or other operations on lymphatic channels

38380 Suture and/or ligation of thoracic duct; cervical approach

38381 thoracic approach

38382 abdominal approach

Limited Lymphadenectomy for Staging

38564 Limited lymphadenectomy for staging (separate procedure); retroperitoneal (aortic and/or splenic)

Laparoscopy

38570 Laparoscopy, surgical; with retroperitoneal lymph node sampling (biopsy), single or multiple

Radical Lymphadenectomy (Radical Resection of Lymph Nodes)

38747 Abdominal lymphadenectomy, regional, including celiac, gastric, portal, peripancreatic, with or without para-aortic and vena caval nodes (List separately in addition to code for primary procedure)

Introduction

38790 Injection procedure; lymphangiography

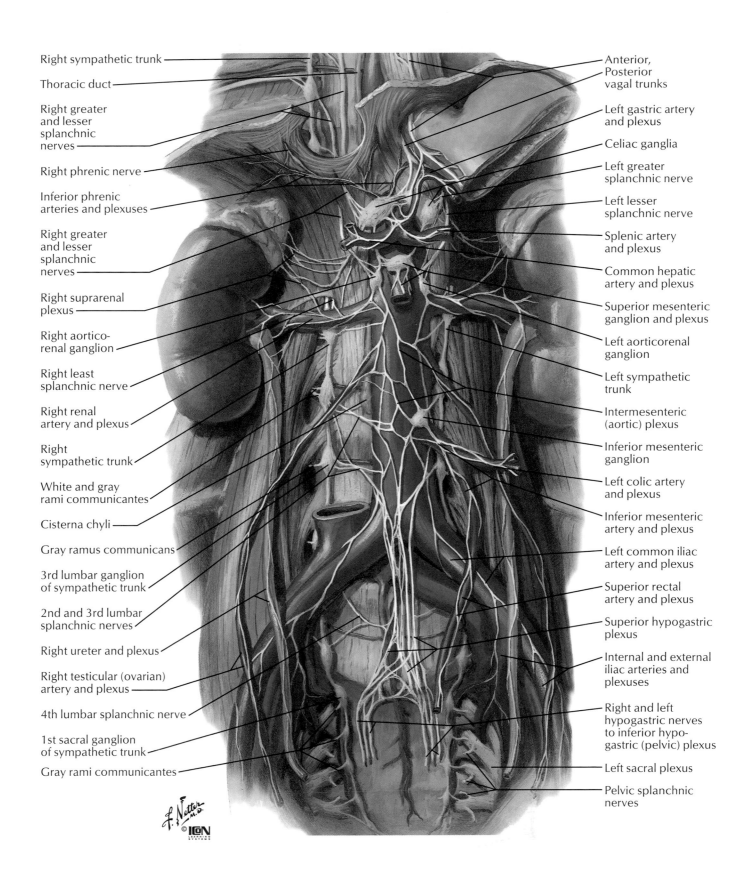

Right sympathetic trunk

Thoracic duct

Right greater and lesser splanchnic nerves

Right phrenic nerve

Inferior phrenic arteries and plexuses

Right greater and lesser splanchnic nerves

Right suprarenal plexus

Right aortico-renal ganglion

Right least splanchnic nerve

Right renal artery and plexus

Right sympathetic trunk

White and gray rami communicantes

Cisterna chyli

Gray ramus communicans

3rd lumbar ganglion of sympathetic trunk

2nd and 3rd lumbar splanchnic nerves

Right ureter and plexus

Right testicular (ovarian) artery and plexus

4th lumbar splanchnic nerve

1st sacral ganglion of sympathetic trunk

Gray rami communicantes

Anterior, Posterior vagal trunks

Left gastric artery and plexus

Celiac ganglia

Left greater splanchnic nerve

Left lesser splanchnic nerve

Splenic artery and plexus

Common hepatic artery and plexus

Superior mesenteric ganglion and plexus

Left aorticorenal ganglion

Left sympathetic trunk

Intermesenteric (aortic) plexus

Inferior mesenteric ganglion

Left colic artery and plexus

Inferior mesenteric artery and plexus

Left common iliac artery and plexus

Superior rectal artery and plexus

Superior hypogastric plexus

Internal and external iliac arteries and plexuses

Right and left hypogastric nerves to inferior hypo-gastric (pelvic) plexus

Left sacral plexus

Pelvic splanchnic nerves

ANESTHESIA

Upper Abdomen

00790   Anesthesia for intraperitoneal procedures in upper abdomen including laparoscopy; not otherwise specified

Lower Abdomen

00840   Anesthesia for intraperitoneal procedures in lower abdomen including laparoscopy; not otherwise specified

00860   Anesthesia for extraperitoneal procedures in lower abdomen, including urinary tract; not otherwise specified

Other Procedures

01991   Anesthesia for diagnostic or therapeutic nerve blocks and injections (when block or injection is performed by a different provider); other than the prone position

01992   prone position

SURGERY

Nervous System

Extracranial Nerves, Peripheral Nerves, and Autonomic Nervous System
Introduction/Injection of Anesthetic Agent (Nerve Block), Diagnostic or Therapeutic

Somatic Nerves

64408   Injection, anesthetic agent; vagus nerve

64425   ilioinguinal, iliohypogastric nerves

Sympathetic Nerves

64517   Injection, anesthetic agent; superior hypogastric plexus

64530   celiac plexus, with or without radiologic monitoring

Destruction by Neurolytic Agent (eg, Chemical, Thermal, Electrical or Radiofrequency)

Sympathetic Nerves

64680   Destruction by neurolytic agent, with or without radiologic monitoring; celiac plexus

64681   superior hypogastric plexus

Transection or Avulsion

64760   Transection or avulsion of; vagus nerve (vagotomy), abdominal

Excision

Somatic Nerves

64784   Excision of neuroma; major peripheral nerve, except sciatic

64790   Excision of neurofibroma or neurolemmoma; major peripheral nerve

64792   Excision of neurofibroma or neurolemmoma; extensive (including malignant type)

64795   Biopsy of nerve

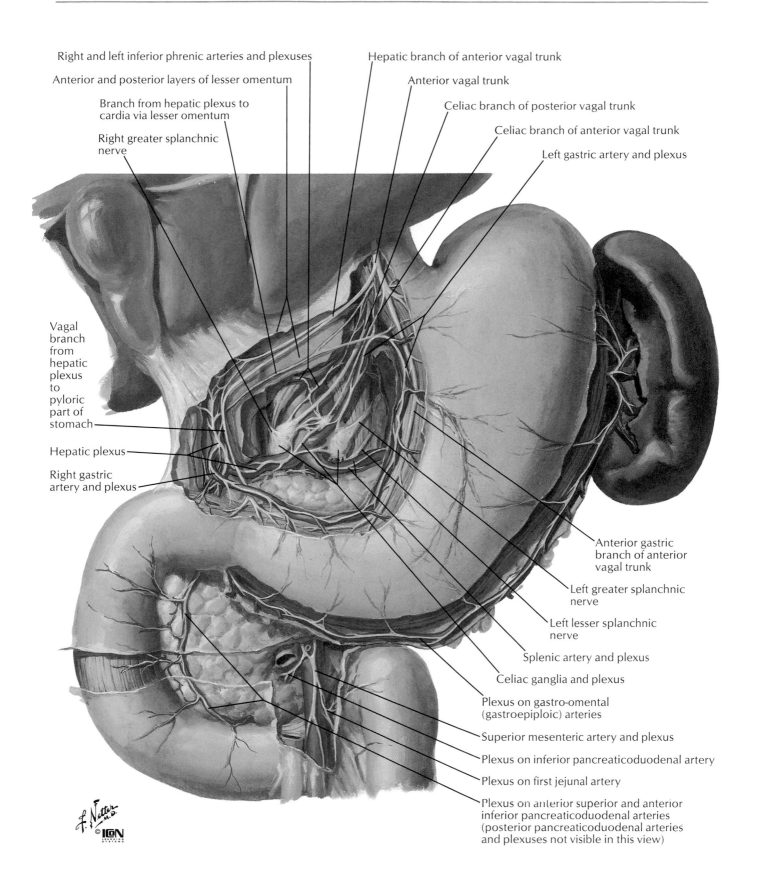

Right and left inferior phrenic arteries and plexuses

Anterior and posterior layers of lesser omentum

Branch from hepatic plexus to cardia via lesser omentum

Right greater splanchnic nerve

Hepatic branch of anterior vagal trunk

Anterior vagal trunk

Celiac branch of posterior vagal trunk

Celiac branch of anterior vagal trunk

Left gastric artery and plexus

Vagal branch from hepatic plexus to pyloric part of stomach

Hepatic plexus

Right gastric artery and plexus

Anterior gastric branch of anterior vagal trunk

Left greater splanchnic nerve

Left lesser splanchnic nerve

Splenic artery and plexus

Celiac ganglia and plexus

Plexus on gastro-omental (gastroepiploic) arteries

Superior mesenteric artery and plexus

Plexus on inferior pancreaticoduodenal artery

Plexus on first jejunal artery

Plexus on anterior superior and anterior inferior pancreaticoduodenal arteries (posterior pancreaticoduodenal arteries and plexuses not visible in this view)

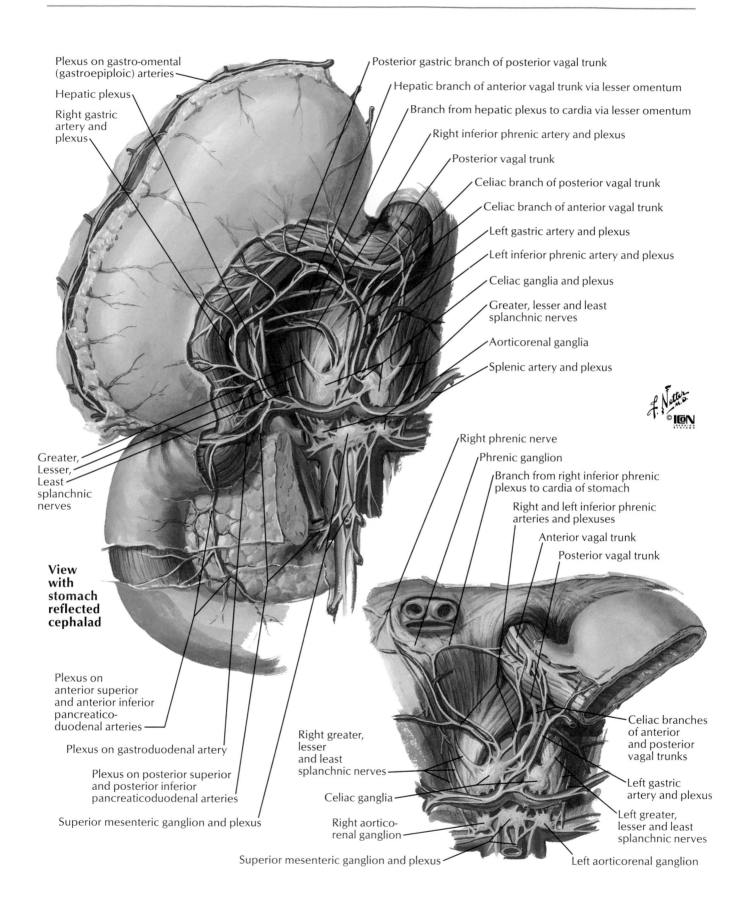

Plexus on gastro-omental (gastroepiploic) arteries

Hepatic plexus

Right gastric artery and plexus

Greater, Lesser, Least splanchnic nerves

View with stomach reflected cephalad

Plexus on anterior superior and anterior inferior pancreatico-duodenal arteries

Plexus on gastroduodenal artery

Plexus on posterior superior and posterior inferior pancreaticoduodenal arteries

Superior mesenteric ganglion and plexus

Posterior gastric branch of posterior vagal trunk

Hepatic branch of anterior vagal trunk via lesser omentum

Branch from hepatic plexus to cardia via lesser omentum

Right inferior phrenic artery and plexus

Posterior vagal trunk

Celiac branch of posterior vagal trunk

Celiac branch of anterior vagal trunk

Left gastric artery and plexus

Left inferior phrenic artery and plexus

Celiac ganglia and plexus

Greater, lesser and least splanchnic nerves

Aorticorenal ganglia

Splenic artery and plexus

Right phrenic nerve

Phrenic ganglion

Branch from right inferior phrenic plexus to cardia of stomach

Right and left inferior phrenic arteries and plexuses

Anterior vagal trunk

Posterior vagal trunk

Right greater, lesser and least splanchnic nerves

Celiac ganglia

Right aortico-renal ganglion

Superior mesenteric ganglion and plexus

Celiac branches of anterior and posterior vagal trunks

Left gastric artery and plexus

Left greater, lesser and least splanchnic nerves

Left aorticorenal ganglion

ANESTHESIA

Neck

00300   Anesthesia for all procedures on the integumentary system, muscles and nerves of head, neck, and posterior trunk, not otherwise specified

Intrathoracic

00541   Anesthesia for thoracotomy procedures involving lungs, pleura, diaphragm, and mediastinum (including surgical thoracoscopy); utilizing one lung ventilation

Upper Abdomen

00790   Anesthesia for intraperitoneal procedures in upper abdomen including laparoscopy; not otherwise specified

Other Procedures

01991   Anesthesia for diagnostic or therapeutic nerve blocks and injections (when block or injection is performed by a different provider); other than the prone position
01992   prone position

SURGERY

Digestive System

Stomach
Laparoscopy

43651   Laparoscopy, surgical; transection of vagus nerves, truncal
43652   transection of vagus nerves, selective or highly selective

Nervous System

Extracranial Nerves, Peripheral Nerves, and Autonomic Nervous System
Introduction/Inection of Anestheic Agent (Nerve Block), Diagnostic or Therapeutic

Somatic Nerves
64408   Injection, anesthetic agent; vagus nerve
Sympathetic Nerves
64530   Injection, anesthetic agent; celiac plexus, with or without radiologic monitoring

Destruction by Neurolytic Agent (eg, Chemical, Thermal, Electrical or Radiofrequency)

Sympathetic Nerves
64680   Destruction by neurolytic agent, with or without radiologic monitoring; celiac plexus

Transection or Avulsion

64746   Transection or avulsion of; phrenic nerve
64752   vagus nerve (vagotomy), transthoracic
64755   vagus nerves limited to proximal stomach (selective proximal vagotomy, proximal gastric vagotomy, parietal cell vagotomy, supra- or highly selective vagotomy)
64760   vagus nerve (vagotomy), abdominal

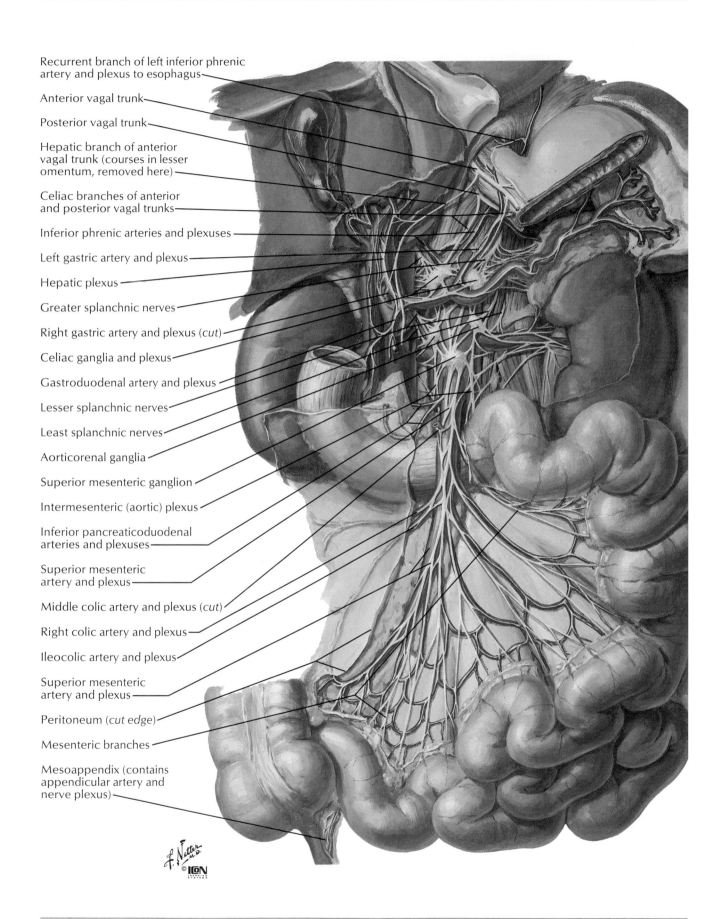

Recurrent branch of left inferior phrenic artery and plexus to esophagus

Anterior vagal trunk

Posterior vagal trunk

Hepatic branch of anterior vagal trunk (courses in lesser omentum, removed here)

Celiac branches of anterior and posterior vagal trunks

Inferior phrenic arteries and plexuses

Left gastric artery and plexus

Hepatic plexus

Greater splanchnic nerves

Right gastric artery and plexus (cut)

Celiac ganglia and plexus

Gastroduodenal artery and plexus

Lesser splanchnic nerves

Least splanchnic nerves

Aorticorenal ganglia

Superior mesenteric ganglion

Intermesenteric (aortic) plexus

Inferior pancreaticoduodenal arteries and plexuses

Superior mesenteric artery and plexus

Middle colic artery and plexus (cut)

Right colic artery and plexus

Ileocolic artery and plexus

Superior mesenteric artery and plexus

Peritoneum (cut edge)

Mesenteric branches

Mesoappendix (contains appendicular artery and nerve plexus)

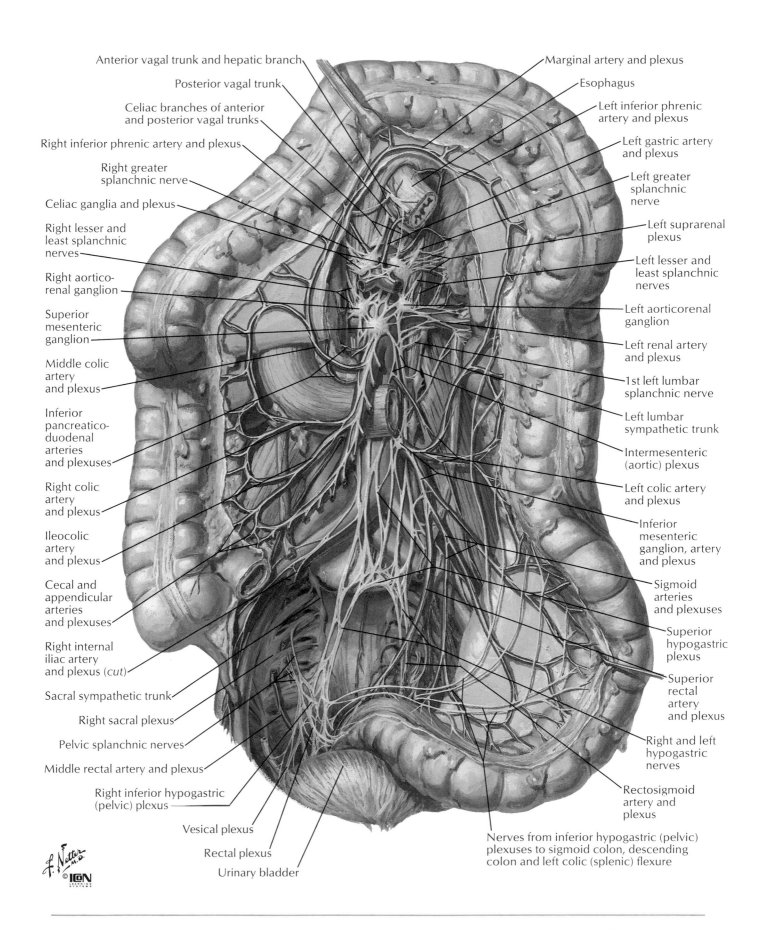

Anterior vagal trunk and hepatic branch

Posterior vagal trunk

Celiac branches of anterior and posterior vagal trunks

Right inferior phrenic artery and plexus

Right greater splanchnic nerve

Celiac ganglia and plexus

Right lesser and least splanchnic nerves

Right aortico-renal ganglion

Superior mesenteric ganglion

Middle colic artery and plexus

Inferior pancreatico-duodenal arteries and plexuses

Right colic artery and plexus

Ileocolic artery and plexus

Cecal and appendicular arteries and plexuses

Right internal iliac artery and plexus (cut)

Sacral sympathetic trunk

Right sacral plexus

Pelvic splanchnic nerves

Middle rectal artery and plexus

Right inferior hypogastric (pelvic) plexus

Vesical plexus

Rectal plexus

Urinary bladder

Marginal artery and plexus

Esophagus

Left inferior phrenic artery and plexus

Left gastric artery and plexus

Left greater splanchnic nerve

Left suprarenal plexus

Left lesser and least splanchnic nerves

Left aorticorenal ganglion

Left renal artery and plexus

1st left lumbar splanchnic nerve

Left lumbar sympathetic trunk

Intermesenteric (aortic) plexus

Left colic artery and plexus

Inferior mesenteric ganglion, artery and plexus

Sigmoid arteries and plexuses

Superior hypogastric plexus

Superior rectal artery and plexus

Right and left hypogastric nerves

Rectosigmoid artery and plexus

Nerves from inferior hypogastric (pelvic) plexuses to sigmoid colon, descending colon and left colic (splenic) flexure

Plate 124: Kidneys

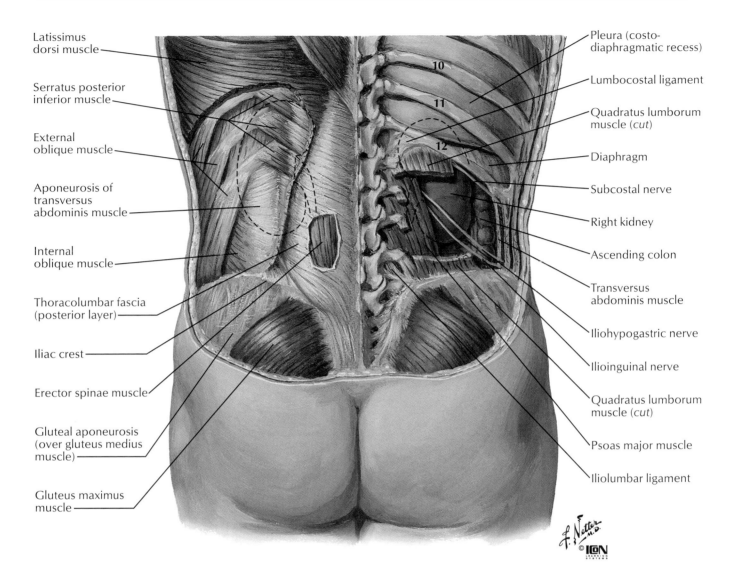

Latissimus dorsi muscle

Serratus posterior inferior muscle

External oblique muscle

Aponeurosis of transversus abdominis muscle

Internal oblique muscle

Thoracolumbar fascia (posterior layer)

Iliac crest

Erector spinae muscle

Gluteal aponeurosis (over gluteus medius muscle)

Gluteus maximus muscle

Pleura (costo-diaphragmatic recess)

Lumbocostal ligament

Quadratus lumborum muscle (cut)

Diaphragm

Subcostal nerve

Right kidney

Ascending colon

Transversus abdominis muscle

Iliohypogastric nerve

Ilioinguinal nerve

Quadratus lumborum muscle (cut)

Psoas major muscle

Iliolumbar ligament

10
11
12

F. Netter M.D.
©IGN

Nomenclature Notes

The term *suprarenal gland* is synonymous with the term *adrenal gland*.

ANESTHESIA

Lower Abdomen

00820	Anesthesia for procedures on lower posterior abdominal wall
00860	Anesthesia for extraperitoneal procedures in lower abdomen, including urinary tract; not otherwise specified
00862	renal procedures, including upper 1/3 of ureter, or donor nephrectomy
00866	adrenalectomy
00868	renal transplant (recipient)
00872	Anesthesia for lithotripsy, extracorporeal shock wave; with water bath
00873	without water bath

Perineum

00910	Anesthesia for transurethral procedures (including urethrocystoscopy); not otherwise specified

Other Procedures

01990	Physiological support for harvesting of organ(s) from brain-dead patient

SURGERY

Urinary System

Kidney
Incision

50010	Renal exploration, not necessitating other specific procedures
50020[P]	Drainage of perirenal or renal abscess; open
50021	percutaneous
50040	Nephrostomy, nephrotomy with drainage
50045	Nephrotomy, with exploration
50060[P]	Nephrolithotomy; removal of calculus

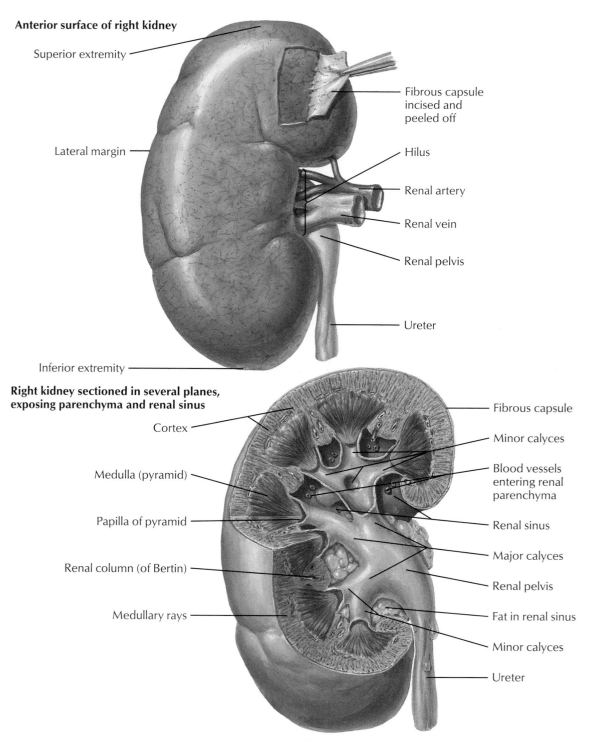

Anterior surface of right kidney

Superior extremity

Lateral margin

Inferior extremity

Fibrous capsule incised and peeled off

Hilus

Renal artery

Renal vein

Renal pelvis

Ureter

Right kidney sectioned in several planes, exposing parenchyma and renal sinus

Cortex

Medulla (pyramid)

Papilla of pyramid

Renal column (of Bertin)

Medullary rays

Fibrous capsule

Minor calyces

Blood vessels entering renal parenchyma

Renal sinus

Major calyces

Renal pelvis

Fat in renal sinus

Minor calyces

Ureter

50065	secondary surgical operation for calculus
50070	complicated by congenital kidney abnormality
50075	removal of large staghorn calculus filling renal pelvis and calyces (including anatrophic pyelolithotomy)
50080	Percutaneous nephrostolithotomy or pyelostolithotomy, with or without dilation, endoscopy, lithotripsy, stenting, or basket extraction; up to 2 cm
50081	over 2 cm

50100	Transection or repositioning of aberrant renal vessels (separate procedure)
50120	Pyelotomy; with exploration
50125	with drainage, pyelostomy
50130	with removal of calculus (pyelolithotomy, p; pelviolithotomy, including coagulum pyelolithotomy)
50135	complicated (eg, secondary operation, congenital kidney abnormality)

Excision

50200	Renal biopsy; percutaneous, by trocar or needle
50205	by surgical exposure of kidney
50220	Nephrectomy, including partial ureterectomy, any open approach including rib resection;
50225	complicated because of previous surgery on same kidney
50230	radical, with regional lymphadenectomy and/or vena caval thrombectomy
50234	Nephrectomy with total ureterectomy and bladder cuff; through same incision
50236	through separate incision
50240	Nephrectomy, partial
50280	Excision or unroofing of cyst(s) of kidney
50290	Excision of perinephric cyst

Renal Transplantation

50300	Donor nephrectomy (including cold preservation); from cadaver donor, unilateral or bilateral
50320	open, from living donor
50323	Backbench standard preparation of cadaver donor renal allograft prior to transplantation, including dissection and removal of perinephric fat, diaphragmatic and retroperitoneal attachments, excision of adrenal gland, and preparation of ureter(s), renal vein(s), and renal artery(s), ligating branches, as necessary
50325	Backbench standard preparation of living donor renal allograft (open or laparoscopic) prior to transplantation, including dissection and removal of perinephric fat and preparation of ureter(s), renal vein(s), and renal artery(s), ligating branches, as necessary
50327	Backbench reconstruction of cadaver or living donor renal allograft prior to transplantation; venous anastomosis, each
50328	arterial anastomosis, each
50329	ureteral anastomosis, each
50340	Recipient nephrectomy (separate procedure)
50360	Renal allotransplantation, implantation of graft; without recipient nephrectomy
50365	with recipient nephrectomy
50370	Removal of transplanted renal allograft
50380	Renal autotransplantation, reimplantation of kidney

Introduction

50390	Aspiration and/or injection of renal cyst or pelvis by needle, percutaneous
50391	Instillation(s) of therapeutic agent into renal pelvis and/or ureter through established nephrostomy, pyelostomy or ureterostomy tube (eg, anticarcinogenic or antifungal agent)
50392P	Introduction of intracatheter or catheter into renal pelvis for drainage and/or injection, percutaneous
50393	Introduction of ureteral catheter or stent into ureter through renal pelvis for drainage and/or injection, percutaneous
50394	Injection procedure for pyelography (as nephrostogram, pyelostogram, antegrade pyeloureterograms) through nephrostomy or pyelostomy tube, or indwelling ureteral catheter
50395	Introduction of guide into renal pelvis and/or ureter with dilation to establish nephrostomy tract, percutaneous
50396	Manometric studies through nephrostomy or pyelostomy tube, or indwelling ureteral catheter
50398	Change of nephrostomy or pyelostomy tube

Repair

50400	Pyeloplasty (Foley Y-pyeloplasty), plastic operation on renal pelvis, with or without plastic operation on ureter, nephropexy, nephrostomy, pyelostomy, or ureteral splinting; simple
50405	complicated (congenital kidney abnormality, secondary pyeloplasty, solitary kidney, calycoplasty)
50500	Nephrorrhaphy, suture of kidney wound or injury
50520	Closure of nephrocutaneous or pyelocutaneous fistula
50525	Closure of nephrovisceral fistula (eg, renocolic), including visceral repair; abdominal approach
50526	thoracic approach
50540	Symphysiotomy for horseshoe kidney with or without pyeloplasty and/or other plastic procedure, unilateral or bilateral (one operation)

Laparoscopy

50541	Laparoscopy, surgical; ablation of renal cysts
50542	ablation of renal mass lesion(s)
50543	partial nephrectomy
50544	pyeloplasty
50545P	radical nephrectomy (includes removal of Gerota's fascia and surrounding fatty tissue, removal of regional lymph nodes, and adrenalectomy)
50546P	nephrectomy, including partial ureterectomy
50547	donor nephrectomy (including cold preservation), from living donor
50548	nephrectomy with total ureterectomy

Endoscopy

50551	Renal endoscopy through established nephrostomy or pyelostomy, with or without irrigation, instillation, or ureteropyelography, exclusive of radiologic service;
50553	with ureteral catheterization, with or without dilation of ureter
50555	with biopsy
50557	with fulguration and/or incision, with or without biopsy
50561	with removal of foreign body or calculus
50562	with resection of tumor
50570	Renal endoscopy through nephrotomy or pyelotomy, with or without irrigation, instillation, or ureteropyelography, exclusive of radiologic service;

50572   with ureteral catheterization, with or without dilation of ureter

50574   with biopsy

50575   with endopyelotomy (includes cystoscopy, ureteroscopy, dilation of ureter and ureteral pelvic junction, incision of ureteral pelvic junction and insertion of endopyelotomy stent)

50576   with fulguration and/or incision, with or without biopsy

50580   with removal of foreign body or calculus

Other Procedures

50590ᴾ   Lithotripsy, extracorporeal shock wave

Bladder

Transurethral Surgery

Ureter and Pelvis

52343   Cystourethroscopy; with treatment of intra-renal stricture (eg, balloon dilation, laser, electrocautery, and incision)

52346   Cystourethroscopy with ureteroscopy; with treatment of intra-renal stricture (eg, balloon dilation, laser, electrocautery, and incision)

52354   Cystourethroscopy, with ureteroscopy and/or pyeloscopy; with biopsy and/or fulguration of ureteral or renal pelvic lesion

52355   with resection of ureteral or renal pelvic tumor

Endocrine System

Parathyroid, Thymus, Adrenal Glands, Pancreas, and Carotid Body

Excision

60540   Adrenalectomy, partial or complete, or exploration of adrenal gland with or without biopsy, transabdominal, lumbar or dorsal (separate procedure);

60545   with excision of adjacent retroperitoneal tumor

60600   Excision of carotid body tumor; without excision of carotid artery

60605   with excision of carotid artery

Laparoscopy

60650   Laparoscopy, surgical, with adrenalectomy, partial or complete, or exploration of adrenal gland with or without biopsy, transabdominal, lumbar or dorsal

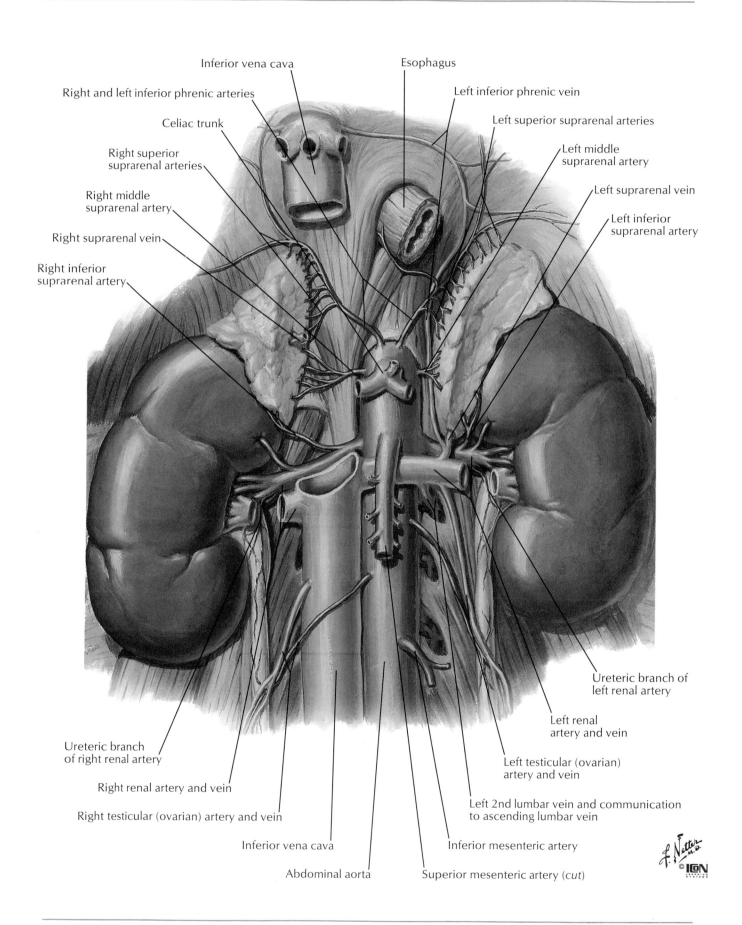

Inferior vena cava

Esophagus

Right and left inferior phrenic arteries

Left inferior phrenic vein

Celiac trunk

Left superior suprarenal arteries

Right superior suprarenal arteries

Left middle suprarenal artery

Right middle suprarenal artery

Left suprarenal vein

Right suprarenal vein

Left inferior suprarenal artery

Right inferior suprarenal artery

Ureteric branch of left renal artery

Ureteric branch of right renal artery

Left renal artery and vein

Right renal artery and vein

Left testicular (ovarian) artery and vein

Right testicular (ovarian) artery and vein

Left 2nd lumbar vein and communication to ascending lumbar vein

Inferior vena cava

Inferior mesenteric artery

Abdominal aorta

Superior mesenteric artery (cut)

ANESTHESIA

Upper Abdomen

00770   Anesthesia for all procedures on major abdominal blood vessels

Lower Abdomen

00880   Anesthesia for procedures on major lower abdominal vessels; not otherwise specified

Radiological Procedures

01916   Anesthesia for diagnostic arteriography/venography
01924   Anesthesia for therapeutic interventional radiologic procedures involving the arterial system; not otherwise specified
01926   intracranial, intracardiac, or aortic

SURGERY

Cardiovascular System

Arteries and Veins

Embolectomy/Thrombectomy

Arterial, With or Without Catheter

34151   Embolectomy or thrombectomy, with or without catheter; renal, celiac, mesentery, aortoiliac artery, by abdominal incision

Endovascular Repair of Abdominal Aortic Aneurysm

34800   Endovascular repair of infrarenal abdominal aortic aneurysm or dissection; using aorto-aortic tube prosthesis
34802[P]   using modular bifurcated prosthesis (one docking limb)
34803   using modular bifurcated prosthesis (two docking limbs)
34804   using unibody bifurcated prosthesis
34805   using aorto-uniiliac or aorto-unifemoral prosthesis
34825   Placement of proximal or distal extension prosthesis for endovascular repair of infrarenal abdominal aortic or iliac aneurysm, false aneurysm, or dissection; initial vessel
34826   each additional vessel (List separately in addition to code for primary procedure)
34830   Open repair of infrarenal aortic aneurysm or dissection, plus repair of associated arterial trauma, following unsuccessful endovascular repair; tube prosthesis
34831   aorto-bi-iliac prosthesis
34832   aorto-bifemoral prosthesis

Direct Repair of Aneurysm or Excision (Partial or Total) and Graft Insertion for Aneurysm, Psedoaneurysm, Ruptured Aneurysm, and Associated Occlusive Disease

35091   Direct repair of aneurysm, pseudoaneurysm, or excision (partial or total) and graft insertion, with or without patch graft; for aneurysm, pseudoaneurysm, and associated occlusive disease, abdominal aorta involving visceral vessels (mesenteric, celiac, renal)

35092   for ruptured aneurysm, abdominal aorta involving visceral vessels (mesenteric, celiac, renal)
35121   for aneurysm, pseudoaneurysm, and associated occlusive disease, hepatic, celiac, renal, or mesenteric artery
35122   for ruptured aneurysm, hepatic, celiac, renal, or mesenteric artery

Repair Arteriovenous Fistula

35182   Repair, congenital arteriovenous fistula; thorax and abdomen
35189   Repair, acquired or traumatic arteriovenous fistula; thorax and abdomen

Repair Blood Vessel Other Than for Fistula, With or Without Patch Angioplasty

35221   Repair blood vessel, direct; intra-abdominal
35281   Repair blood vessel with graft other than vein; intra-abdominal

Thromboendarterectomy

35341   Thromboendarterectomy, with or without patch graft; mesenteric, celiac, or renal

Transluminal Angioplasty

Open

35450   Transluminal balloon angioplasty, open; renal or other visceral artery

Transluminal Atherectomy

Open

35480   Transluminal peripheral atherectomy, open; renal or other visceral artery

Percutaneous

35490   Transluminal peripheral atherectomy, percutaneous; renal or other visceral artery

Bypass graft

Vein

35531   Bypass graft, with vein; aortoceliac or aortomesenteric
35536   splenorenal
35560   aortorenal

Other Than Vein

35631   Bypass graft, with other than vein; aortoceliac, aortomesenteric, aortorenal
35636   splenorenal (splenic to renal arterial anastomosis)

Arterial Transposition

35697   Reimplantation, visceral artery to infrarenal aortic prosthesis, each artery (List separately in addition to code for primary procedure)

Exploration/Revision

35761   Exploration (not followed by surgical repair), with or without lysis of artery; other vessels
35840   Exploration for postoperative hemorrhage, thrombosis or infection; abdomen
35907   Excision of infected graft; abdomen

Intravenous

36012   Selective catheter placement, venous system; second order, or more selective, branch (eg, left adrenal vein, petrosal sinus)

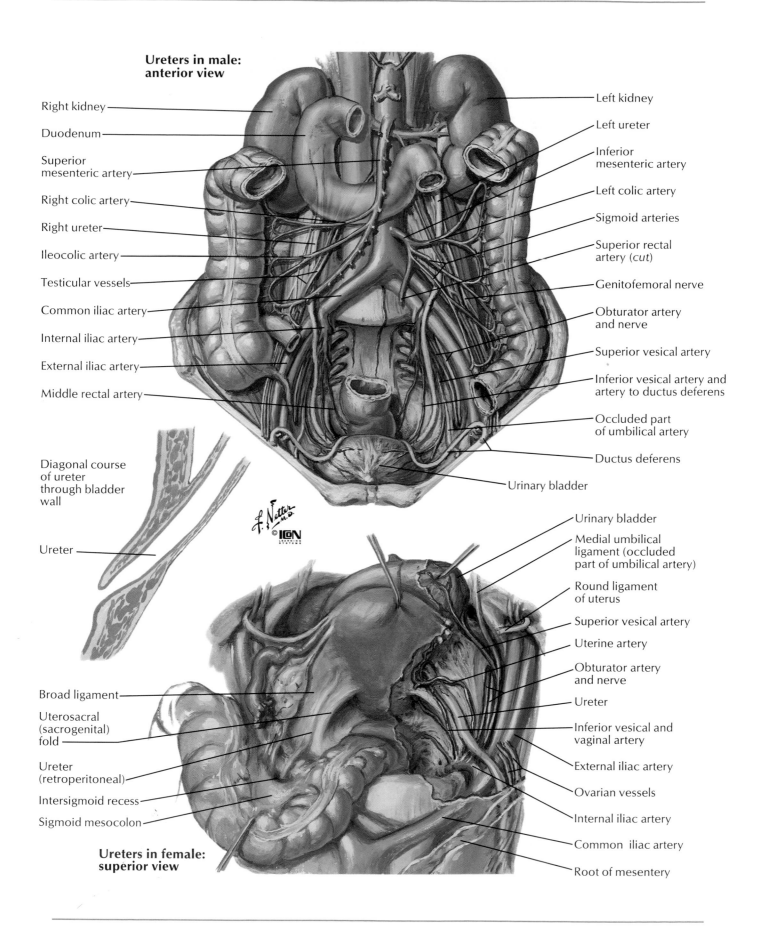

Ureters in male: anterior view

Right kidney

Duodenum

Superior mesenteric artery

Right colic artery

Right ureter

Ileocolic artery

Testicular vessels

Common iliac artery

Internal iliac artery

External iliac artery

Middle rectal artery

Left kidney

Left ureter

Inferior mesenteric artery

Left colic artery

Sigmoid arteries

Superior rectal artery (*cut*)

Genitofemoral nerve

Obturator artery and nerve

Superior vesical artery

Inferior vesical artery and artery to ductus deferens

Occluded part of umbilical artery

Ductus deferens

Urinary bladder

Diagonal course of ureter through bladder wall

Ureter

Urinary bladder

Medial umbilical ligament (occluded part of umbilical artery)

Round ligament of uterus

Superior vesical artery

Uterine artery

Obturator artery and nerve

Ureter

Inferior vesical and vaginal artery

External iliac artery

Ovarian vessels

Internal iliac artery

Common iliac artery

Root of mesentery

Broad ligament

Uterosacral (sacrogenital) fold

Ureter (retroperitoneal)

Intersigmoid recess

Sigmoid mesocolon

Ureters in female: superior view

ANESTHESIA

Lower Abdomen

00800 Anesthesia for procedures on lower anterior abdominal wall; not otherwise specified

00820 Anesthesia for procedures on lower posterior abdominal wall

00860 Anesthesia for extraperitoneal procedures in lower abdomen, including urinary tract; not otherwise specified

00862 renal procedures, including upper 1/3 of ureter, or donor nephrectomy

SURGERY

Urinary System

Kidney
Excision

50220 Nephrectomy, including partial ureterectomy, any open approach including rib resection;

50225 complicated because of previous surgery on same kidney

50230 radical, with regional lymphadenectomy and/or vena caval thrombectomy

50234 Nephrectomy with total ureterectomy and bladder cuff; through same incision

50236 through separate incision

Introduction

50391 Instillation(s) of therapeutic agent into renal pelvis and/or ureter through established nephrostomy, pyelostomy or ureterostomy tube (eg, anticarcinogenic or antifungal agent)

50393 Introduction of ureteral catheter or stent into ureter through renal pelvis for drainage and/or injection, percutaneous

50394 Injection procedure for pyelography (as nephrostogram, pyelostogram, antegrade pyeloureterograms) through nephrostomy or pyelostomy tube, or indwelling ureteral catheter

50395 Introduction of guide into renal pelvis and/or ureter with dilation to establish nephrostomy tract, percutaneous

Repair

50400 Pyeloplasty (Foley Y-pyeloplasty), plastic operation on renal pelvis, with or without plastic operation on ureter, nephropexy, nephrostomy, pyelostomy, or ureteral splinting; simple

50405 complicated (congenital kidney abnormality, secondary pyeloplasty, solitary kidney, calycoplasty)

Laparoscopy

50546[P] Laparoscopy, surgical; nephrectomy, including partial ureterectomy

50548 nephrectomy with total ureterectomy

Endoscopy

50551 Renal endoscopy through established nephrostomy or pyelostomy, with or without irrigation, instillation, or ureteropyelography, exclusive of radiologic service;

50553 with ureteral catheterization, with or without dilation of ureter

50555 with biopsy

50557 with fulguration and/or incision, with or without biopsy

50561 with removal of foreign body or calculus

50562 with resection of tumor

50570 Renal endoscopy through nephrotomy or pyelotomy, with or without irrigation, instillation, or ureteropyelography, exclusive of radiologic service;

50572 with ureteral catheterization, with or without dilation of ureter

50574 with biopsy

50575 with endopyelotomy (includes cystoscopy, ureteroscopy, dilation of ureter and ureteral pelvic junction, incision of ureteral pelvic junction and insertion of endopyelotomy stent)

50576 with fulguration and/or incision, with or without biopsy

50580 with removal of foreign body or calculus

Ureter
Incision

50600 Ureterotomy with exploration or drainage (separate procedure)

50605[P] Ureterotomy for insertion of indwelling stent, all types

50610 Ureterolithotomy; upper one-third of ureter

50620 middle one-third of ureter

50630 lower one-third of ureter

Excision

50650 Ureterectomy, with bladder cuff (separate procedure)

50660 Ureterectomy, total, ectopic ureter, combination abdominal, vaginal and/or perineal approach

Introduction

50684 Injection procedure for ureterography or ureteropyelography through ureterostomy or indwelling ureteral catheter

50686 Manometric studies through ureterostomy or indwelling ureteral catheter

50688 Change of ureterostomy tube

50690 Injection procedure for visualization of ileal conduit and/or ureteropyelography, exclusive of radiologic service

Repair

50700 Ureteroplasty, plastic operation on ureter (eg, stricture)

50715 Ureterolysis, with or without repositioning of ureter for retroperitoneal fibrosis

50722 Ureterolysis for ovarian vein syndrome

50725 Ureterolysis for retrocaval ureter, with reanastomosis of upper urinary tract or vena cava

50727 Revision of urinary-cutaneous anastomosis (any type urostomy);

(Repair continued on next page)

(Repair continued from previous page)

50728 with repair of fascial defect and hernia

50740 Ureteropyelostomy, anastomosis of ureter and renal pelvis

50750 Ureterocalycostomy, anastomosis of ureter to renal calyx

50760 Ureteroureterostomy

50770 Transureteroureterostomy, anastomosis of ureter to contralateral ureter

50780 Ureteroneocystostomy; anastomosis of single ureter to bladder

50782 anastomosis of duplicated ureter to bladder

50783 with extensive ureteral tailoring

50785 with vesico-psoas hitch or bladder flap

50800 Ureteroenterostomy, direct anastomosis of ureter to intestine

50810 Ureterosigmoidostomy, with creation of sigmoid bladder and establishment of abdominal or perineal colostomy, including intestine anastomosis

50815 Ureterocolon conduit, including intestine anastomosis

50820ᴾ Ureteroileal conduit (ileal bladder), including intestine anastomosis (Bricker operation)

50825 Continent diversion, including intestine anastomosis using any segment of small and/or large intestine (Kock pouch or Camey enterocystoplasty)

50830 Urinary undiversion (eg, taking down of ureteroileal conduit, ureterosigmoidostomy or ureteroenterostomy with ureteroureterostomy or ureteroneocystostomy)

50840 Replacement of all or part of ureter by intestine segment, including intestine anastomosis

50860 Ureterostomy, transplantation of ureter to skin

50900 Ureterorrhaphy, suture of ureter (separate procedure)

50920 Closure of ureterocutaneous fistula

50930 Closure of ureterovisceral fistula (including visceral repair)

50940 Deligation of ureter

Laparoscopy

50945 Laparoscopy, surgical; ureterolithotomy

50947 ureteroneocystostomy with cystoscopy and ureteral stent placement

50948 ureteroneocystostomy without cystoscopy and ureteral stent placement

Endoscopy

50951 Ureteral endoscopy through established ureterostomy, with or without irrigation, instillation, or ureteropyelography, exclusive of radiologic service;

50953 with ureteral catheterization, with or without dilation of ureter

50955 with biopsy

50957 with fulguration and/or incision, with or without biopsy

50961 with removal of foreign body or calculus

50970 Ureteral endoscopy through ureterotomy, with or without irrigation, instillation, or ureteropyelography, exclusive of radiologic service;

50972 with ureteral catheterization, with or without dilation of ureter

50974 with biopsy

50976 with fulguration and/or incision, with or without biopsy

50980 with removal of foreign body or calculus

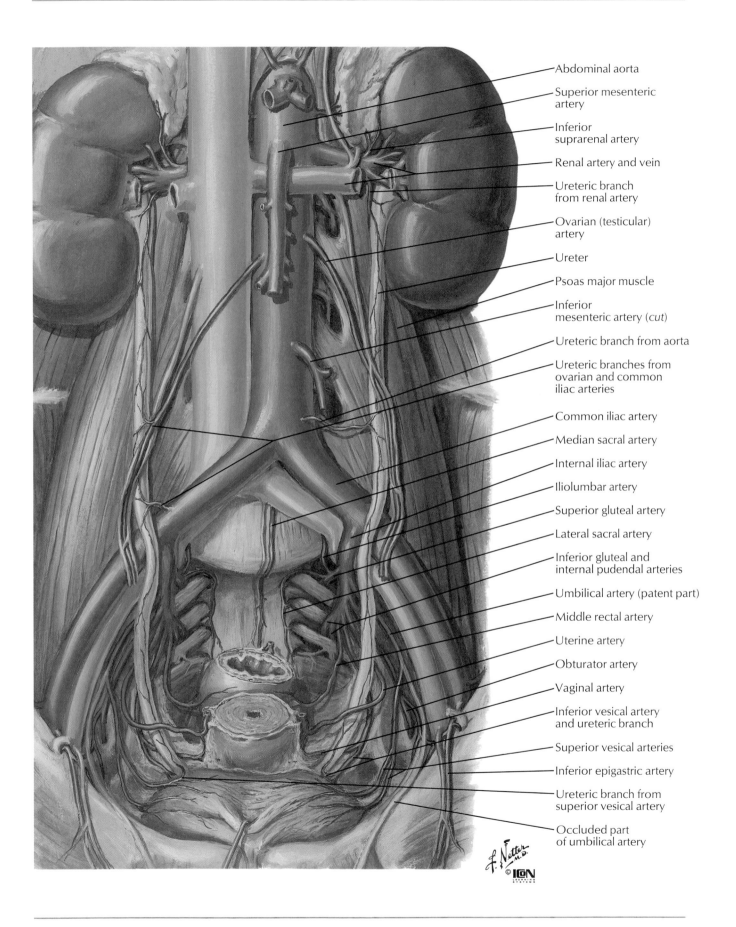

Abdominal aorta

Superior mesenteric artery

Inferior suprarenal artery

Renal artery and vein

Ureteric branch from renal artery

Ovarian (testicular) artery

Ureter

Psoas major muscle

Inferior mesenteric artery (cut)

Ureteric branch from aorta

Ureteric branches from ovarian and common iliac arteries

Common iliac artery

Median sacral artery

Internal iliac artery

Iliolumbar artery

Superior gluteal artery

Lateral sacral artery

Inferior gluteal and internal pudendal arteries

Umbilical artery (patent part)

Middle rectal artery

Uterine artery

Obturator artery

Vaginal artery

Inferior vesical artery and ureteric branch

Superior vesical arteries

Inferior epigastric artery

Ureteric branch from superior vesical artery

Occluded part of umbilical artery

ANESTHESIA

Upper Abdomen

00770 Anesthesia for all procedures on major abdominal blood vessels

Lower Abdomen

00880 Anesthesia for procedures on major lower abdominal vessels; not otherwise specified

Radiological Procedures

01924 Anesthesia for therapeutic interventional radiologic procedures involving the arterial system; not otherwise specified

01926 intracranial, intracardiac, or aortic

SURGERY

Cardiovascular System

Arteries and Veins

Embolectomy/Thrombectomy

Arterial, With or Without Catheter

34151 Embolectomy or thrombectomy, with or without catheter; renal, celiac, mesentery, aortoiliac artery, by abdominal incision

Endovascular Repair of Abdominal Aortic Aneurysm

34800 Endovascular repair of infrarenal abdominal aortic aneurysm or dissection; using aorto-aortic tube prosthesis

34802ᴾ using modular bifurcated prosthesis (one docking limb)

34803 using modular bifurcated prosthesis (two docking limbs)

34804 using unibody bifurcated prosthesis

34805 using aorto-uniiliac or aorto-unifemoral prosthesis

34808 Endovascular placement of iliac artery occlusion device (List separately in addition to code for primary procedure)

34820 Open iliac artery exposure for delivery of endovascular prosthesis or iliac occlusion during endovascular therapy, by abdominal or retroperitoneal incision, unilateral

34825 Placement of proximal or distal extension prosthesis for endovascular repair of infrarenal abdominal aortic or iliac aneurysm, false aneurysm, or dissection; initial vessel

34826 each additional vessel (List separately in addition to code for primary procedure)

34830 Open repair of infrarenal aortic aneurysm or dissection, plus repair of associated arterial trauma, following unsuccessful endovascular repair; tube prosthesis

34831 aorto-bi-iliac prosthesis

34832 aorto-bifemoral prosthesis

34833 Open iliac artery exposure with creation of conduit for delivery of infrarenal aortic or iliac endovascular prosthesis, by abdominal or retroperitoneal incision, unilateral

Endovascular Repair of Iliac Aneurysm

34900 Endovascular graft placement for repair of iliac artery (eg, aneurysm, pseudoaneurysm, arteriovenous malformation, trauma)

Direct Repair of Aneurysm or Excision (Partial or Total) and Graft Insertion for Aneurysm, Pseudoaneurysm, Ruptured Aneurysm and Associated Occlusive Disease

35081 Direct repair of aneurysm, pseudoaneurysm, or excision (partial or total) and graft insertion, with or without patch graft; for aneurysm, pseudoaneurysm, and associated occlusive disease, abdominal aorta

35082 for ruptured aneurysm, abdominal aorta

35091 for aneurysm, pseudoaneurysm, and associated occlusive disease, abdominal aorta involving visceral vessels (mesenteric, celiac, renal)

35092 for ruptured aneurysm, abdominal aorta involving visceral vessels (mesenteric, celiac, renal)

35102 for aneurysm, pseudoaneurysm, and associated occlusive disease, abdominal aorta involving iliac vessels (common, hypogastric, external)

35103 for ruptured aneurysm, abdominal aorta involving iliac vessels (common, hypogastric, external)

35121 for aneurysm, pseudoaneurysm, and associated occlusive disease, hepatic, celiac, renal, or mesenteric artery

35122 for ruptured aneurysm, hepatic, celiac, renal, or mesenteric artery

35131 for aneurysm, pseudoaneurysm, and associated occlusive disease, iliac artery (common, hypogastric, external)

35132 for ruptured aneurysm, iliac artery (common, hypogastric, external)

Repair Arteriovenous Fistula

35182 Repair, congenital arteriovenous fistula; thorax and abdomen

35189 Repair, acquired or traumatic arteriovenous fistula; thorax and abdomen

Repair Blood Vessel Other Than for Fistula, With or Without Patch Angioplasty

35221 Repair blood vessel, direct; intra-abdominal

35251 Repair blood vessel with vein graft; intra-abdominal

35281 Repair blood vessel with graft other than vein; intra-abdominal

Thromboendarterectomy

35331 Thromboendarterectomy, with or without patch graft; abdominal aorta

35341	mesenteric, celiac, or renal
35351	iliac
35361	combined aortoiliac

Transluminal Angioplasty

Open

35450	Transluminal balloon angioplasty, open; renal or other visceral artery
35452	aortic
35454	iliac

Percutaneous

35472	Transluminal balloon angioplasty, percutaneous; aortic
35473[P]	Transluminal balloon angioplasty, percutaneous; iliac

Transluminal Atherectomy

Open

35480	Transluminal peripheral atherectomy, open; renal or other visceral artery
35481	aortic
35482	iliac

Percutaneous

35490	Transluminal peripheral atherectomy, percutaneous; renal or other visceral artery
35491	aortic
35492	iliac

Bypass Graft

Vein

35500	Harvest of upper extremity vein, one segment, for lower extremity or coronary
35531	Bypass graft, with vein; aortoceliac or aortomesenteric
35541	aortoiliac or bi-iliac
35560	aortorenal
35563	ilioiliac

Other Than Vein

35631	Bypass graft, with other than vein; aortoceliac, aortomesenteric, aortorenal
35641	aortoiliac or bi-iliac
35663	ilioiliac

Exploration/Revision

35840	Exploration for postoperative hemorrhage, thrombosis or infection; abdomen
35907	Excision of infected graft; abdomen

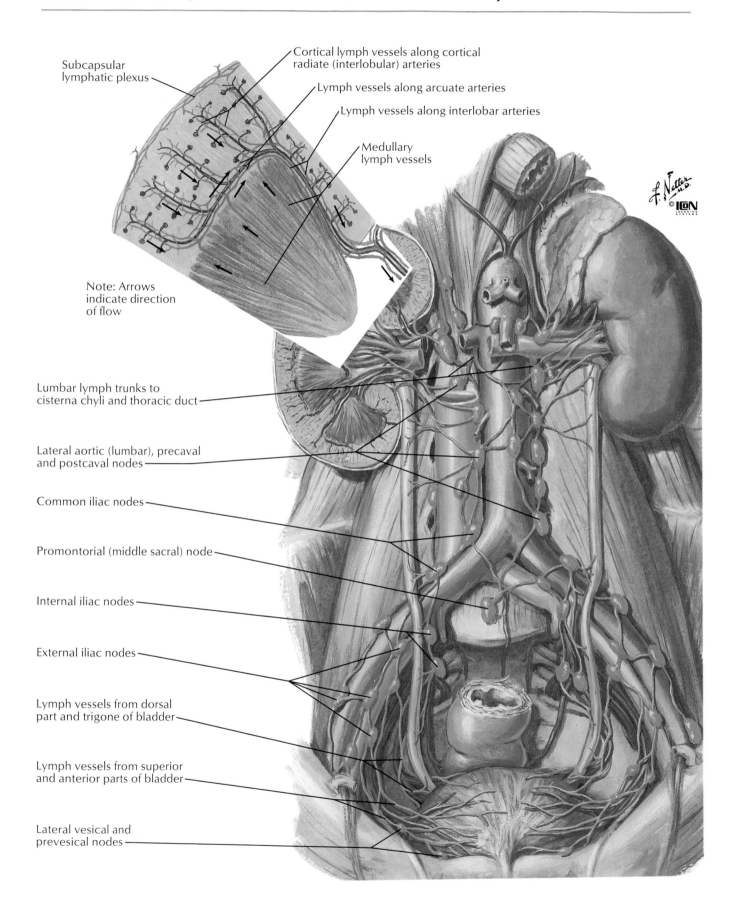

Subcapsular lymphatic plexus

Cortical lymph vessels along cortical radiate (interlobular) arteries

Lymph vessels along arcuate arteries

Lymph vessels along interlobar arteries

Medullary lymph vessels

Note: Arrows indicate direction of flow

Lumbar lymph trunks to cisterna chyli and thoracic duct

Lateral aortic (lumbar), precaval and postcaval nodes

Common iliac nodes

Promontorial (middle sacral) node

Internal iliac nodes

External iliac nodes

Lymph vessels from dorsal part and trigone of bladder

Lymph vessels from superior and anterior parts of bladder

Lateral vesical and prevesical nodes

ANESTHESIA

Lower Abdomen

00800 Anesthesia for procedures on lower anterior abdominal wall; not otherwise specified

00860 Anesthesia for extraperitoneal procedures in lower abdomen, including urinary tract; not otherwise specified

SURGERY

Hemic and Lymphatic Systems

Lymph Nodes and Lymphatic Channels
Incision

38300 Drainage of lymph node abscess or lymphadenitis; simple

38305   extensive

38308 Lymphangiotomy or other operations on lymphatic channels

Limited Lymphadenectomy for Staging

38562 Limited lymphadenectomy for staging (separate procedure); pelvic and para-aortic

38564   retroperitoneal (aortic and/or splenic)

Laparoscopy

38570 Laparoscopy, surgical; with retroperitoneal lymph node sampling (biopsy), single or multiple

Radical Lymphadenectomy(Radical Resection of Lymph Nodes)

38747 Abdominal lymphadenectomy, regional, including celiac, gastric, portal, peripancreatic, with or without para-aortic and vena caval nodes (List separately in addition to code for primary procedure)

38780 Retroperitoneal transabdominal lymphadenectomy, extensive, including pelvic, aortic, and renal nodes (separate procedure)

Introduction

38790 Injection procedure; lymphangiography

38792   for identification of sentinel node

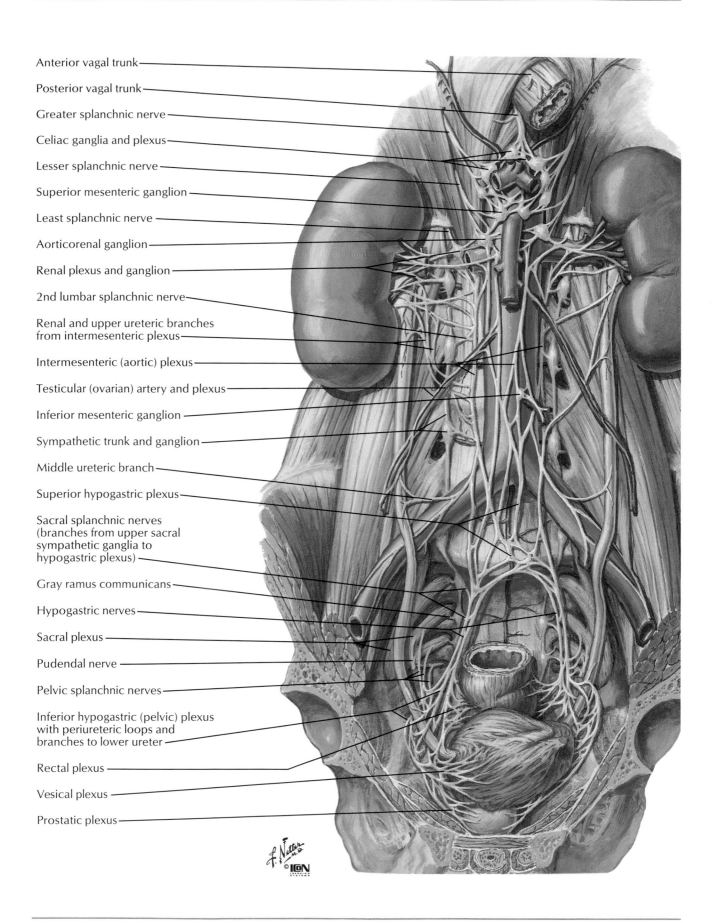

Anterior vagal trunk

Posterior vagal trunk

Greater splanchnic nerve

Celiac ganglia and plexus

Lesser splanchnic nerve

Superior mesenteric ganglion

Least splanchnic nerve

Aorticorenal ganglion

Renal plexus and ganglion

2nd lumbar splanchnic nerve

Renal and upper ureteric branches from intermesenteric plexus

Intermesenteric (aortic) plexus

Testicular (ovarian) artery and plexus

Inferior mesenteric ganglion

Sympathetic trunk and ganglion

Middle ureteric branch

Superior hypogastric plexus

Sacral splanchnic nerves (branches from upper sacral sympathetic ganglia to hypogastric plexus)

Gray ramus communicans

Hypogastric nerves

Sacral plexus

Pudendal nerve

Pelvic splanchnic nerves

Inferior hypogastric (pelvic) plexus with periureteric loops and branches to lower ureter

Rectal plexus

Vesical plexus

Prostatic plexus

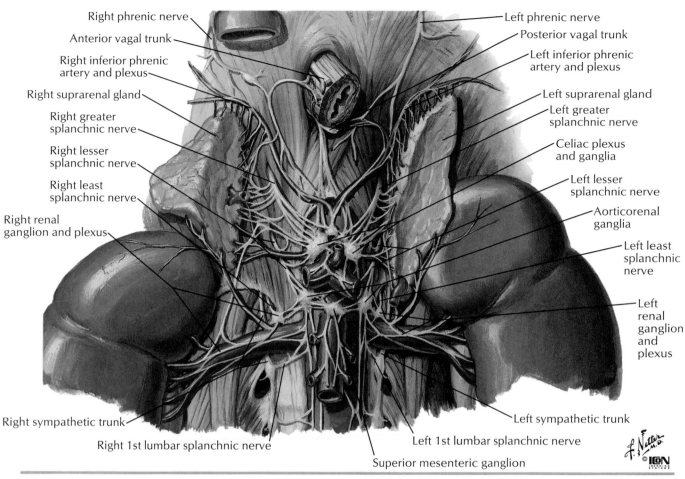

Right phrenic nerve
Anterior vagal trunk
Right inferior phrenic artery and plexus
Right suprarenal gland
Right greater splanchnic nerve
Right lesser splanchnic nerve
Right least splanchnic nerve
Right renal ganglion and plexus
Right sympathetic trunk
Right 1st lumbar splanchnic nerve

Left phrenic nerve
Posterior vagal trunk
Left inferior phrenic artery and plexus
Left suprarenal gland
Left greater splanchnic nerve
Celiac plexus and ganglia
Left lesser splanchnic nerve
Aorticorenal ganglia
Left least splanchnic nerve
Left renal ganglion and plexus
Left sympathetic trunk
Left 1st lumbar splanchnic nerve
Superior mesenteric ganglion

ANESTHESIA

Upper Abdomen

00790   Anesthesia for intraperitoneal procedures in upper abdomen including laparoscopy; not otherwise specified

Lower Abdomen

00860   Anesthesia for extraperitoneal procedures in lower abdomen, including urinary tract; not otherwise specified

Pelvis (Except Hip)

01180   Anesthesia for obturator neurectomy; extrapelvic

Other Procedures

01991   Anesthesia for diagnostic or therapeutic nerve blocks and injections (when block or injection is performed by a different provider); other than the prone position

01992   prone position

SURGERY

Digestive System

Stomach
Laparoscopy

43651   Laparoscopy, surgical; transection of vagus nerves, truncal

43652   transection of vagus nerves, selective or highly selective

Nervous System

Extracranial Nerves, Peripheral Nerves, and Autonomic Nervous System
Introduction/Injection of Anesthetic Agent (Nerve Block), Diagnostic or Therapeautic

Somatic Nerves
64408   Injection, anesthetic agent; vagus nerve
64430   pudendal nerve
64450   other peripheral nerve or branch

Destruction by Neurolytic Agent (eg, Chemical, Thermal, Electrical or Radiofrequency)

Somatic Nerves
64630   Destruction by neurolytic agent; pudendal nerve
64640   other peripheral nerve or branch

Sympathetic Nerves
64681   Destruction by neurolytic agent, with or without radiologic monitoring; superior hypogastric plexus

Transection or Avulsion

64760   Transection or avulsion of; vagus nerve (vagotomy), abdominal
64761   pudendal nerve

A

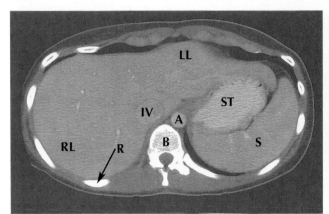

B

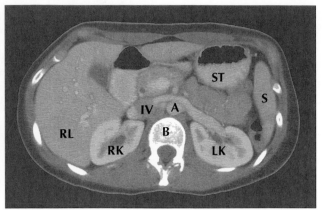

C

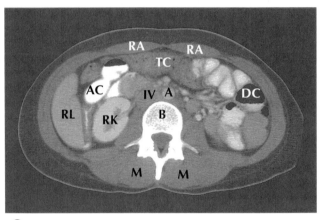

D

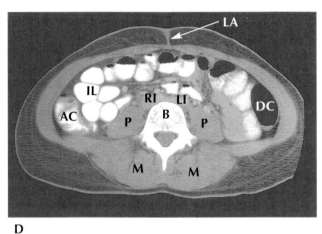

A	Aorta	**M**	Deep back muscles
AC	Ascending colon	**P**	Psoas muscle
B	Body of vertebra	**R**	Rib
DC	Descending colon	**RA**	Rectus abdominis muscle
IL	Ileum	**RI**	Right common iliac artery
IV	Inferior vena cava	**RL**	Right lobe of liver
LA	Linea alba	**S**	Spleen
LI	Left common iliac artery	**ST**	Stomach
LK	Left kidney	**TC**	Transverse colon
LL	Left lobe of liver		

RADIOLOGY

Diagnostic Radiology (Diagnostic Imaging)

Abdomen

74150	Computed tomography, abdomen; without contrast material
74160	with contrast material(s)
74170	without contrast material, followed by contrast material(s) and further sections
74175	Computed tomographic angiography, abdomen, without contrast material(s), followed by contrast material(s) and further sections, including image post-processing

Chapter 5
Pelvis and Perineum

The underlying structure of the pelvis is the bony pelvis. This structure consists of the innominate bones (or os coxae) and the sacrum. These bones make up the pelvic girdle, which is a circular bony base that forms the support for the trunk.

The pelvic cavity is the lower part of the abdominopelvic cavity. Portions of the digestive system, specifically the sigmoid colon and the rectum/anus, are found in the pelvic cavity. The illustrations of the sigmoid colon are included in Chapter 3, Abdomen, because it is continuous with the portion of the colon that lies in the abdominal cavity. Approximately the last 8 inches of the colon is called the *rectum*. The final inch of the rectum is called the *anus* or *anal canal*. The rectum stores solid waste until its elimination from the body.

The urinary bladder and urethra are also found in the pelvic cavity. The bladder is situated behind the symphasis pubis, where the two innominate bones join anteriorly. It is a retroperitoneal organ, lying behind the parietal peritoneum. The ureters themselves are located in the abdominal cavity and are illustrated in Chapter 3. The junction of the ureter and the bladder is found at the posterior part of the roughly triangular shaped floor of the bladder (trigone). The bladder is the urine reservoir of the body. The urethra serves as the conduit for excreting urine from the body. In the male, it also is the end portion of the reproductive tract, serving as a passage for excreting semen from the body. The urethera leads from the floor of the bladder to the body's exterior. The structure of the urethra is different in the male and female. In the female, it is posterior to the vagina. In the male, the urethra passes through the prostate gland and then through the penis.

The female reproductive organs—the ovaries, fallopian tubes, uterus, and vagina—are located in the pelvic cavity. The ovaries are found on either side of the uterus, below and behind the fallopian tubes. The ovaries form eggs for reproductive purposes and also secrete estrogens and progesterones as part of the endocrine system. The fallopian tubes (or oviducts) serve as ducts for the ovaries although they are not directly attached to the ovaries. The fallopian tubes are attached to the uterus at the uppermost out angles. Each of the tubes expands at the distal end to form the infundibulum. The margin of the infundibulum are fringe-like structures called fimbriae. The uterus consists of the body of the uterus and the cervix. The fundus of the uterus is the most superior portion that is a rounded prominence above where the fallopian tubes enter the uterus. The vagina is located between the rectum and the urethra and bladder. The vagina serves as the lower portion of the birth canal, as a conduit for uterine secretions and menstrual flow, and as the receptacle for the semen from the male. The female perineum is the area between the anus and the vulva.

Two of the male reproductive organs—the seminal vessels and the prostate—lie in the pelvic cavity.

The prostate gland is located below the bladder. The urethra passes through the center of the prostate. The prostate secretes the majority of the seminal fluid.

External to the pelvic cavity itself are the male reproductive organs of the penis and testes. The testes are small glands that are contained in a skin covered pouch-like structure called the *scrotum*. The testes have two main functions: sperm production and the secretion of hormones, notably, testosterone. The ducts of the testes are called the *epididymis*. The vas deferens (or seminal duct) is an extension of the epididymis that passes through the inguinal canal into the abdominal cavity, extending down the posterior surface of the bladder, where it joins the seminal vesicle duct to form the ejaculatory duct.

The penis is composed of three cylindrical erectile (cavernous) tissue masses. The *coropora cavernosa* refers to the two larger uppermost cylinders and the lower smaller cylinder is the urethra. The perineum in the male is the area between the anus and the scrotum.

Common procedures performed in the pelvic region include, but are not limited to, the following:

- Biopsy
- Proctosigmoidoscopy
- Hemorrhoidectomy
- Anoscopy
- Cystectomy
- Cystourethroscopy
- Transurethral surgery
- Male-only procedures
  —Prostatectomy
  —Destruction of prostate tissue
- Female-only procedures
  —Vaginectomy
  —Colporrhaphy
  —Fistula repair
  —Cervical cautery or conization
  —Endometrial biopsy
  —Dilation and curretage
  —Myomectomy
  —Laparoscopy
  —Transection of fallopian tubes
  —Salpingectomy

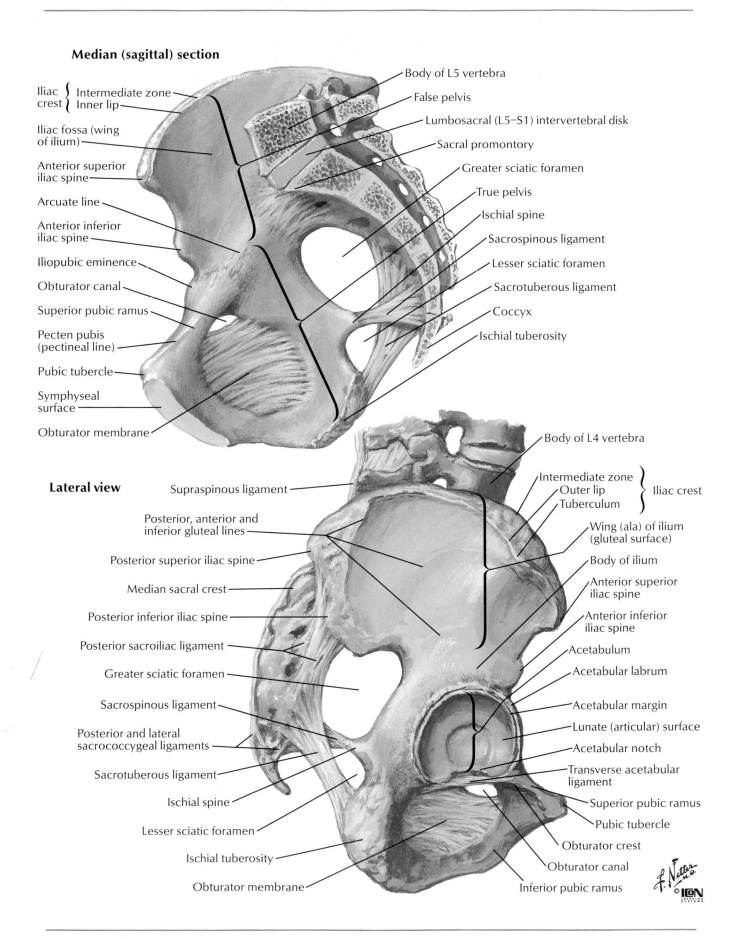

Median (sagittal) section

Iliac crest { Intermediate zone — Inner lip

Iliac fossa (wing of ilium)

Anterior superior iliac spine

Arcuate line

Anterior inferior iliac spine

Iliopubic eminence

Obturator canal

Superior pubic ramus

Pecten pubis (pectineal line)

Pubic tubercle

Symphyseal surface

Obturator membrane

Body of L5 vertebra

False pelvis

Lumbosacral (L5–S1) intervertebral disk

Sacral promontory

Greater sciatic foramen

True pelvis

Ischial spine

Sacrospinous ligament

Lesser sciatic foramen

Sacrotuberous ligament

Coccyx

Ischial tuberosity

Lateral view

Supraspinous ligament

Posterior, anterior and inferior gluteal lines

Posterior superior iliac spine

Median sacral crest

Posterior inferior iliac spine

Posterior sacroiliac ligament

Greater sciatic foramen

Sacrospinous ligament

Posterior and lateral sacrococcygeal ligaments

Sacrotuberous ligament

Ischial spine

Lesser sciatic foramen

Ischial tuberosity

Obturator membrane

Body of L4 vertebra

Intermediate zone
Outer lip
Tuberculum } Iliac crest

Wing (ala) of ilium (gluteal surface)

Body of ilium

Anterior superior iliac spine

Anterior inferior iliac spine

Acetabulum

Acetabular labrum

Acetabular margin

Lunate (articular) surface

Acetabular notch

Transverse acetabular ligament

Superior pubic ramus

Pubic tubercle

Obturator crest

Obturator canal

Inferior pubic ramus

— Nomenclature Notes —

The *innominate bone* is known as the *hip bone* and is composed of the ilium, ischium, and pubis.

ANESTHESIA

Pelvis (Except Hip)

01112	Anesthesia for bone marrow aspiration and/or biopsy, anterior or posterior iliac crest
01120	Anesthesia for procedures on bony pelvis
01140	Anesthesia for interpelviabdominal (hindquarter) amputation
01160	Anesthesia for closed procedures involving symphysis pubis or sacroiliac joint
01170	Anesthesia for open procedures involving symphysis pubis or sacroiliac joint
01173	Anesthesia for open repair of fracture disruption of pelvis or column fracture involving acetabulum

Upper Leg (Except Knee)

01200	Anesthesia for all closed procedures involving hip joint
01202	Anesthesia for arthroscopic procedures of hip joint
01210	Anesthesia for open procedures involving hip joint; not otherwise specified
01212	Anesthesia for open procedures involving hip joint; hip disarticulation
01214	Anesthesia for open procedures involving hip joint; total hip arthroplasty
01250	Anesthesia for all procedures on nerves, muscles, tendons, fascia, and bursae of upper leg

SURGERY

Musculoskeletal System

Pelvis and Hip Joint

Incision

26990	Incision and drainage, pelvis or hip joint area; deep abscess or hematoma
26991	infected bursa
26992	Incision, bone cortex, pelvis and/or hip joint (eg, osteomyelitis or bone abscess)
27000	Tenotomy, adductor of hip, percutaneous (separate procedure)
27030	Arthrotomy, hip, with drainage (eg, infection)
27033	Arthrotomy, hip, including exploration or removal of loose or foreign body
27036	Capsulectomy or capsulotomy, hip, with or without excision of heterotopic bone, with release of hip flexor muscles (ie, gluteus medius, gluteus minimus, tensor fascia latae, rectus femoris, sartorius, iliopsoas)

Excision

27050	Arthrotomy, with biopsy; sacroiliac joint
27052	hip joint
27054	Arthrotomy with synovectomy, hip joint
27060	Excision; ischial bursa
27062	trochanteric bursa or calcification
27065	Excision of bone cyst or benign tumor; superficial (wing of ilium, symphysis pubis, or greater trochanter of femur) with or without autograft
27066	deep, with or without autograft
27067	with autograft requiring separate incision
27070	Partial excision (craterization, saucerization) (eg, osteomyelitis or bone abscess); superficial (eg, wing of ilium, symphysis pubis, or greater trochanter of femur)
27071	deep (subfascial or intramuscular)
27075	Radical resection of tumor or infection; wing of ilium, one pubic or ischial ramus or symphysis pubis
27076	ilium, including acetabulum, both pubic rami, or ischium and acetabulum
27077	innominate bone, total
27078	ischial tuberosity and greater trochanter of femur
27079	ischial tuberosity and greater trochanter of femur, with skin flaps
27080	Coccygectomy, primary

Introduction or Removal

27090	Removal of hip prosthesis; (separate procedure)
27091	complicated, including total hip prosthesis, methylmethacrylate with or without insertion of spacer
27093	Injection procedure for hip arthrography; without anesthesia
27095	with anesthesia
27096	Injection procedure for sacroiliac joint, arthrography and/or anesthetic/steroid

Repair, Revision, and/or Reconstruction

27120	Acetabuloplasty; (eg, Whitman, Colonna, Haygroves, or cup type)
27122	resection, femoral head (eg, Girdlestone procedure)
27125[P]	Hemiarthroplasty, hip, partial (eg, femoral stem prosthesis, bipolar arthroplasty)
27130[P]	Arthroplasty, acetabular and proximal femoral prosthetic replacement (total hip arthroplasty), with or without autograft or allograft
27132	Conversion of previous hip surgery to total hip arthroplasty, with or without autograft or allograft
27134	Revision of total hip arthroplasty; both components, with or without autograft or allograft
27137	acetabular component only, with or without autograft or allograft
27146	Osteotomy, iliac, acetabular or innominate bone;
27147	with open reduction of hip
27151	with femoral osteotomy
27156	with femoral osteotomy and with open reduction of hip
27158	Osteotomy, pelvis, bilateral (eg, congenital malformation)

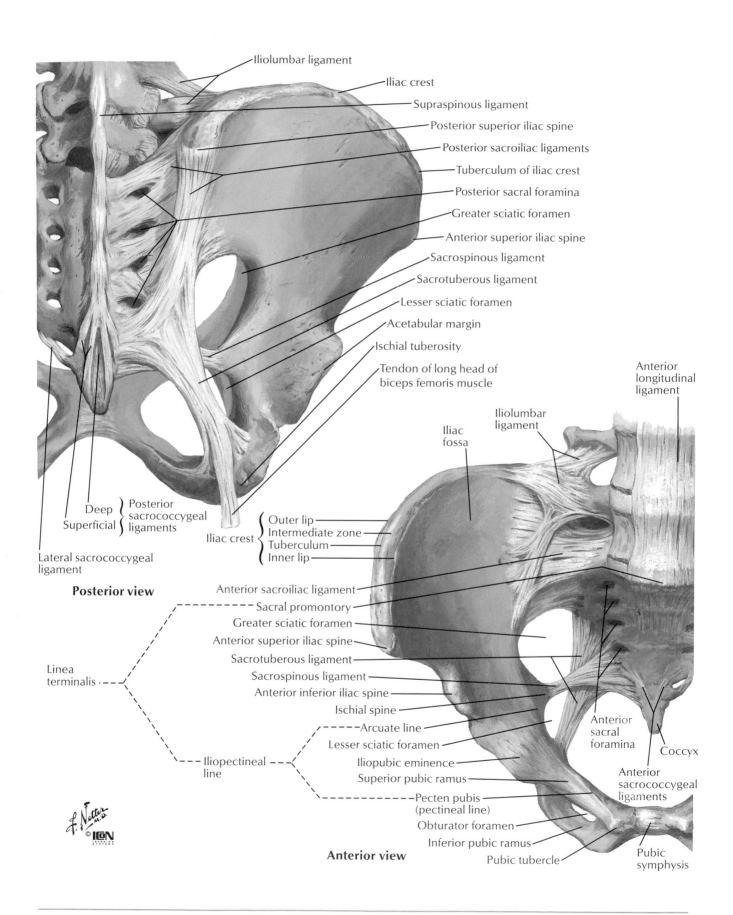

Iliolumbar ligament

Iliac crest

Supraspinous ligament

Posterior superior iliac spine

Posterior sacroiliac ligaments

Tuberculum of iliac crest

Posterior sacral foramina

Greater sciatic foramen

Anterior superior iliac spine

Sacrospinous ligament

Sacrotuberous ligament

Lesser sciatic foramen

Acetabular margin

Ischial tuberosity

Tendon of long head of biceps femoris muscle

Deep } Posterior
Superficial } sacrococcygeal ligaments

Lateral sacrococcygeal ligament

Posterior view

Iliac fossa

Iliolumbar ligament

Anterior longitudinal ligament

Iliac crest {
Outer lip
Intermediate zone
Tuberculum
Inner lip

Anterior sacroiliac ligament

Sacral promontory

Greater sciatic foramen

Anterior superior iliac spine

Sacrotuberous ligament

Sacrospinous ligament

Anterior inferior iliac spine

Ischial spine

Linea terminalis

Arcuate line

Lesser sciatic foramen

Iliopectineal line

Iliopubic eminence

Superior pubic ramus

Pecten pubis (pectineal line)

Obturator foramen

Inferior pubic ramus

Pubic tubercle

Anterior sacral foramina

Coccyx

Anterior sacrococcygeal ligaments

Pubic symphysis

Anterior view

Fracture and/or Dislocation

27193 Closed treatment of pelvic ring fracture, dislocation, diastasis or subluxation; without manipulation

27194 with manipulation, requiring more than local anesthesia

27200 Closed treatment of coccygeal fracture

27202 Open treatment of coccygeal fracture

27215 Open treatment of iliac spine(s), tuberosity avulsion, or iliac wing fracture(s) (eg, pelvic fracture(s) which do not disrupt the pelvic ring), with internal fixation

27216 Percutaneous skeletal fixation of posterior pelvic ring fracture and/or dislocation (includes ilium, sacroiliac joint and/or sacrum)

27217 Open treatment of anterior ring fracture and/or dislocation with internal fixation (includes pubic symphysis and/or rami)

27218 Open treatment of posterior ring fracture and/or dislocation with internal fixation (includes ilium, sacroiliac joint and/or sacrum)

27220 Closed treatment of acetabulum (hip socket) fracture(s); without manipulation

27222 with manipulation, with or without skeletal traction

27226 Open treatment of posterior or anterior acetabular wall fracture, with internal fixation

27227 Open treatment of acetabular fracture(s) involving anterior or posterior (one) column, or a fracture running transversely across the acetabulum, with internal fixation

27228 Open treatment of acetabular fracture(s) involving anterior and posterior (two) columns, includes T-fracture and both column fracture with complete articular detachment, or single column or transverse fracture with associated acetabular wall fracture, with internal fixation

27250 Closed treatment of hip dislocation, traumatic; without anesthesia

27252 requiring anesthesia

27253 Open treatment of hip dislocation, traumatic, without internal fixation

27254 Open treatment of hip dislocation, traumatic, with acetabular wall and femoral head fracture, with or without internal or external fixation

27256 Treatment of spontaneous hip dislocation (developmental, including congenital or pathological), by abduction, splint or traction; without anesthesia, without manipulation

27257 with manipulation, requiring anesthesia

27258 Open treatment of spontaneous hip dislocation (developmental, including congenital or pathological), replacement of femoral head in acetabulum (including tenotomy, etc);

27259 with femoral shaft shortening

27265 without anesthesia

27266 requiring regional or general anesthesia

Manipulation

27275 Manipulation, hip joint, requiring general anesthesia

Arthrodesis

27280 Arthrodesis, sacroiliac joint (including obtaining graft)

27282 Arthrodesis, symphysis pubis (including obtaining graft)

27284 Arthrodesis, hip joint (including obtaining graft);

27286 with subtrochanteric osteotomy

Amputation

27290 Interpelviabdominal amputation (hindquarter amputation)

27295 Disarticulation of hip

Endoscopy/Arthroscopy

29860 Arthroscopy, hip, diagnostic with or without synovial biopsy (separate procedure)

29861 Arthroscopy, hip, surgical; with removal of loose body or foreign body

29862 with debridement/shaving of articular cartilage (chondroplasty), abrasion arthroplasty, and/or resection of labrum

29863 with synovectomy

Hemic and Lymphatic Systems

General

Bone Marrow or Stem Cell Services/Procedures

38220 Bone marrow; aspiration only

38221 biopsy, needle or trocar

Female: midsagittal section

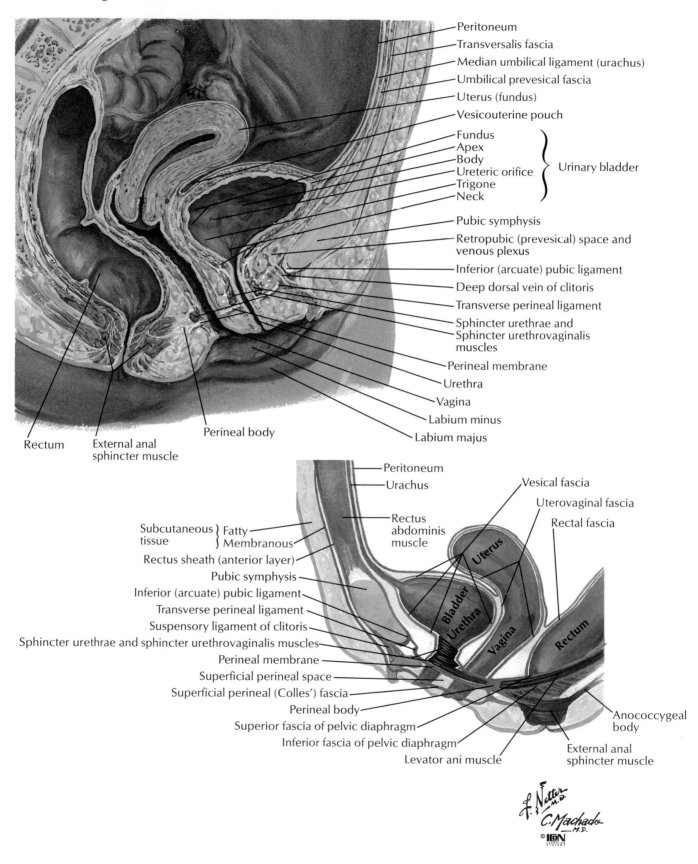

Peritoneum

Transversalis fascia

Median umbilical ligament (urachus)

Umbilical prevesical fascia

Uterus (fundus)

Vesicouterine pouch

Fundus
Apex
Body
Ureteric orifice
Trigone
Neck
} Urinary bladder

Pubic symphysis

Retropubic (prevesical) space and venous plexus

Inferior (arcuate) pubic ligament

Deep dorsal vein of clitoris

Transverse perineal ligament

Sphincter urethrae and Sphincter urethrovaginalis muscles

Perineal membrane

Urethra

Vagina

Labium minus

Labium majus

Perineal body

Rectum

External anal sphincter muscle

Peritoneum

Urachus

Vesical fascia

Uterovaginal fascia

Rectal fascia

Subcutaneous tissue } Fatty
Membranous }

Rectus abdominis muscle

Rectus sheath (anterior layer)

Pubic symphysis

Inferior (arcuate) pubic ligament

Transverse perineal ligament

Suspensory ligament of clitoris

Sphincter urethrae and sphincter urethrovaginalis muscles

Perineal membrane

Superficial perineal space

Superficial perineal (Colles') fascia

Perineal body

Superior fascia of pelvic diaphragm

Inferior fascia of pelvic diaphragm

Levator ani muscle

Uterus

Bladder

Urethra

Vagina

Rectum

Anococcygeal body

External anal sphincter muscle

ANESTHESIA

Lower Abdomen

00800 Anesthesia for procedures on lower anterior abdominal wall; not otherwise specified

00840 Anesthesia for intraperitoneal procedures in lower abdomen including laparoscopy; not otherwise specified

00848 pelvic exenteration

00860 Anesthesia for extraperitoneal procedures in lower abdomen, including urinary tract; not otherwise specified

00864 total cystectomy

00870 cystolithotomy

Perineum

00910 Anesthesia for transurethral procedures (including urethrocystoscopy); not otherwise specified

00912 transurethral resection of bladder tumor(s)

00914 transurethral resection of prostate

00916 post-transurethral resection bleeding

00918 with fragmentation, manipulation and/or removal of ureteral calculus

00920 Anesthesia for procedures on male genitalia (including open urethral procedures); not otherwise specified

00940 Anesthesia for vaginal procedures (including biopsy of labia, vagina, cervix or endometrium); not otherwise specified

00942 colpotomy, vaginectomy, colporrhaphy, and open urethral procedures

SURGERY

Digestive System

Intestines (Except Rectum)
Repair

44660 Closure of enterovesical fistula; without intestinal or bladder resection

44661 with intestine and/or bladder resection

Urinary System

Bladder
Incision

51000 Aspiration of bladder by needle

51005 Aspiration of bladder; by trocar or intracatheter

51010 with insertion of suprapubic catheter

51020 Cystotomy or cystostomy; with fulguration and/or insertion of radioactive material

51030 with cryosurgical destruction of intravesical lesion

51040 Cystostomy, cystotomy with drainage

51045 Cystotomy, with insertion of ureteral catheter or stent (separate procedure)

51050 Cystolithotomy, cystotomy with removal of calculus, without vesical neck resection

51065 Cystotomy, with calculus basket extraction and/or ultrasonic or electrohydraulic fragmentation of ureteral calculus

51080 Drainage of perivesical or prevesical space abscess

Excision

51500 Excision of urachal cyst or sinus, with or without umbilical hernia repair

51520 Cystotomy; for simple excision of vesical neck (separate procedure)

51525 for excision of bladder diverticulum, single or multiple (separate procedure)

51530 for excision of bladder tumor

51535 Cystotomy for excision, incision, or repair of ureterocele

51550 Cystectomy, partial; simple

51555 complicated (eg, postradiation, previous surgery, difficult location)

51565 Cystectomy, partial, with reimplantation of ureter(s) into bladder (ureteroneocystostomy)

51570 Cystectomy, complete; (separate procedure)

51575 with bilateral pelvic lymphadenectomy, including external iliac, hypogastric, and obturator nodes

51580 Cystectomy, complete, with ureterosigmoidostomy or ureterocutaneous transplantations;

51585 with bilateral pelvic lymphadenectomy, including external iliac, hypogastric, and obturator nodes

51590 Cystectomy, complete, with ureteroileal conduit or sigmoid bladder, including intestine anastomosis;

51595 with bilateral pelvic lymphadenectomy, including external iliac, hypogastric, and obturator nodes

51596 Cystectomy, complete, with continent diversion, any open technique, using any segment of small and/or large intestine to construct neobladder

51597 Pelvic exenteration, complete, for vesical, prostatic or urethral malignancy, with removal of bladder and ureteral transplantations, with or without hysterectomy and/or abdominoperineal resection of rectum and colon and colostomy, or any combination thereof

Introduction

51600 Injection procedure for cystography or voiding urethrocystography

51605 Injection procedure and placement of chain for contrast and/or chain urethrocystography

51610 Injection procedure for retrograde urethrocystography

51700 Bladder irrigation, simple, lavage and/or instillation

51701 Insertion of non-indwelling bladder catheter (eg, straight catheterization for residual urine)

51702 Insertion of temporary indwelling bladder catheter; simple (eg, Foley)

51703 complicated (eg, altered anatomy, fractured catheter/balloon)

51705 Change of cystostomy tube; simple

51710 complicated

(Introduction continued on page 279)

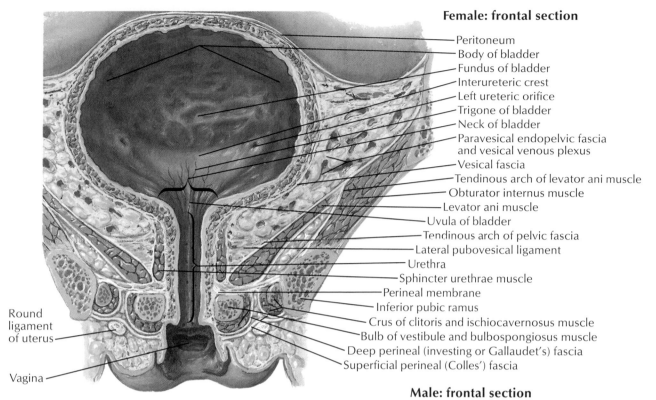

Female: frontal section

Peritoneum
Body of bladder
Fundus of bladder
Interureteric crest
Left ureteric orifice
Trigone of bladder
Neck of bladder
Paravesical endopelvic fascia and vesical venous plexus
Vesical fascia
Tendinous arch of levator ani muscle
Obturator internus muscle
Levator ani muscle
Uvula of bladder
Tendinous arch of pelvic fascia
Lateral pubovesical ligament
Urethra
Sphincter urethrae muscle
Perineal membrane
Inferior pubic ramus
Crus of clitoris and ischiocavernosus muscle
Bulb of vestibule and bulbospongiosus muscle
Deep perineal (investing or Gallaudet's) fascia
Superficial perineal (Colles') fascia

Round ligament of uterus

Vagina

Male: frontal section

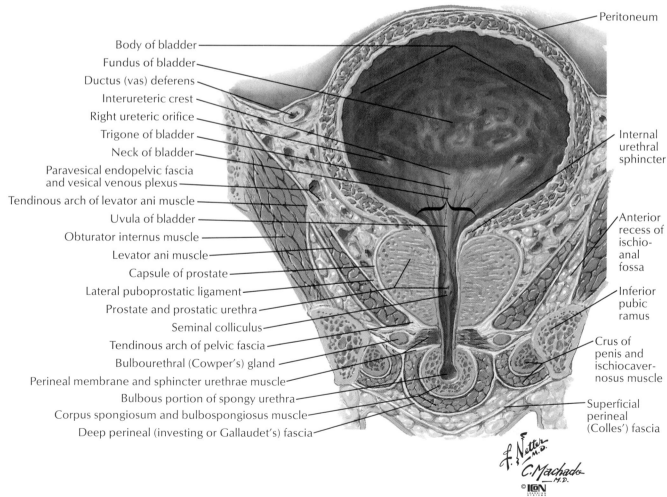

Peritoneum

Body of bladder
Fundus of bladder
Ductus (vas) deferens
Interureteric crest
Right ureteric orifice
Trigone of bladder
Neck of bladder
Paravesical endopelvic fascia and vesical venous plexus
Tendinous arch of levator ani muscle
Uvula of bladder
Obturator internus muscle
Levator ani muscle
Capsule of prostate
Lateral puboprostatic ligament
Prostate and prostatic urethra
Seminal colliculus
Tendinous arch of pelvic fascia
Bulbourethral (Cowper's) gland
Perineal membrane and sphincter urethrae muscle
Bulbous portion of spongy urethra
Corpus spongiosum and bulbospongiosus muscle
Deep perineal (investing or Gallaudet's) fascia

Internal urethral sphincter

Anterior recess of ischio-anal fossa

Inferior pubic ramus

Crus of penis and ischiocavernosus muscle

Superficial perineal (Colles') fascia

(Introduction continued from page 277)

51715 Endoscopic injection of implant material into the submucosal tissues of the urethra and/or bladder neck

51720 Bladder instillation of anticarcinogenic agent (including detention time)

Urodynamics

51784 Electromyography studies (EMG) of anal or urethral sphincter, other than needle, any technique

51785 Needle electromyography studies (EMG) of anal or urethral sphincter, any technique

Repair

51800 Cystoplasty or cystourethroplasty, plastic operation on bladder and/or vesical neck (anterior Y-plasty, vesical fundus resection), any procedure, with or without wedge resection of posterior vesical neck

51820 Cystourethroplasty with unilateral or bilateral ureteroneocystostomy

51840 Anterior vesicourethropexy, or urethropexy (eg, Marshall-Marchetti-Krantz, Burch); simple

51841 complicated (eg, secondary repair)

51845 Abdomino-vaginal vesical neck suspension, with or without endoscopic control (eg, Stamey, Raz, modified Pereyra)

51860 Cystorrhaphy, suture of bladder wound, injury or rupture; simple

51865 complicated

51880 Closure of cystostomy (separate procedure)

51900 Closure of vesicovaginal fistula, abdominal approach

51920 Closure of vesicouterine fistula;

51925 with hysterectomy

51940 Closure, exstrophy of bladder

51960 Enterocystoplasty, including intestinal anastomosis

51980 Cutaneous vesicostomy

Laparoscopy

51990[P] Laparoscopy, surgical; urethral suspension for stress incontinence

51992 sling operation for stress incontinence (eg, fascia or synthetic)

Endoscopy—Cystoscopy, Urethroscopy, Cystourethroscopy

52000 Cystourethroscopy (separate procedure)

52001 Cystourethroscopy with irrigation and evacuation of multiple obstructing clots

52005[P] Cystourethroscopy, with ureteral catheterization, with or without irrigation, instillation, or ureteropyelography, exclusive of radiologic service;

52007 with brush biopsy of ureter and/or renal pelvis

52010 Cystourethroscopy, with ejaculatory duct catheterization, with or without irrigation, instillation, or duct radiography, exclusive of radiologic service

Transuretheral Surgery

Urethra and Bladder

52204 Cystourethroscopy, with biopsy

52214 Cystourethroscopy, with fulguration (including cryosurgery or laser surgery) of trigone, bladder neck, prostatic fossa, urethra, or periurethral glands

52224 Cystourethroscopy, with fulguration (including cryosurgery or laser surgery) or treatment of MINOR (less than 0.5 cm) lesion(s) with or without biopsy

52234 Cystourethroscopy, with fulguration (including cryosurgery or laser surgery) and/or resection of; SMALL bladder tumor(s) (0.5 up to 2.0 cm)

52235 MEDIUM bladder tumor(s) (2.0 to 5.0 cm)

52240 LARGE bladder tumor(s)

52250 Cystourethroscopy with insertion of radioactive substance, with or without biopsy or fulguration

52260 Cystourethroscopy, with dilation of bladder for interstitial cystitis; general or conduction (spinal) anesthesia

52265 local anesthesia

52270 Cystourethroscopy, with internal urethrotomy; female

52275 male

52276 Cystourethroscopy with direct vision internal urethrotomy

52277 Cystourethroscopy, with resection of external sphincter (sphincterotomy)

52281 Cystourethroscopy, with calibration and/or dilation of urethral stricture or stenosis, with or without meatotomy, with or without injection procedure for cystography, male or female

52282 Cystourethroscopy, with insertion of urethral stent

52283 Cystourethroscopy, with steroid injection into stricture

52285 Cystourethroscopy for treatment of the female urethral syndrome with any or all of the following: urethral meatotomy, urethral dilation, internal urethrotomy, lysis of urethrovaginal septal fibrosis, lateral incisions of the bladder neck, and fulguration of polyp(s) of urethra, bladder neck, and/or trigone

52290 Cystourethroscopy; with ureteral meatotomy, unilateral or bilateral

52300 with resection or fulguration of orthotopic ureterocele(s), unilateral or bilateral

52301 with resection or fulguration of ectopic ureterocele(s), unilateral or bilateral

52305 with incision or resection of orifice of bladder diverticulum, single or multiple

52310 Cystourethroscopy, with removal of foreign body, calculus, or ureteral stent from urethra or bladder (separate procedure); simple

52315 complicated

52317 Litholapaxy: crushing or fragmentation of calculus by any means in bladder and removal of fragments; simple or small (less than 2.5 cm)

52318 complicated or large (over 2.5 cm)

Ureter and Pelvis

52320 Cystourethroscopy (including ureteral catheterization); with removal of ureteral calculus

52325 with fragmentation of ureteral calculus (eg, ultrasonic or electro-hydraulic technique)

52327 with subureteric injection of implant material

52330 with manipulation, without removal of ureteral calculus

52332 Cystourethroscopy, with insertion of indwelling ureteral stent (eg, Gibbons or double-J type)

52334 Cystourethroscopy with insertion of ureteral guide wire through kidney to establish a percutaneous nephrostomy, retrograde

52341 Cystourethroscopy; with treatment of ureteral stricture (eg, balloon dilation, laser, electrocautery, and incision)

52342 with treatment of ureteropelvic junction stricture (eg, balloon dilation, laser, electrocautery, and incision)

52343 with treatment of intra-renal stricture (eg, balloon dilation, laser, electrocautery, and incision)

52344 Cystourethroscopy with ureteroscopy; with treatment of ureteral stricture (eg, balloon dilation, laser, electrocautery, and incision)

52345 with treatment of ureteropelvic junction stricture (eg, balloon dilation, laser, electrocautery, and incision)

52346 with treatment of intra-renal stricture (eg, balloon dilation, laser, electrocautery, and incision)

52351 Cystourethroscopy, with ureteroscopy and/or pyeloscopy; diagnostic

52352 with removal or manipulation of calculus (ureteral catheterization is included)

52353 with lithotripsy (ureteral catheterization is included)

52354 with biopsy and/or fulguration of ureteral or renal pelvic lesion

52355 with resection of ureteral or renal pelvic tumor

Vesical Neck and Prostate

52400 Cystourethroscopy with incision, fulguration, or resection of congenital posterior urethral valves, or congenital obstructive hypertrophic mucosal folds

52402 Cystourethroscopy with transurethral resection or incision of ejaculatory ducts

52450 Transurethral incision of prostate

52500 Transurethral resection of bladder neck (separate procedure)

52510 Transurethral balloon dilation of the prostatic urethra

52601[P] Transurethral electrosurgical resection of prostate, including control of postoperative bleeding, complete (vasectomy, meatotomy, cystourethroscopy, urethral calibration and/or dilation, and internal urethrotomy are included)

52606 Transurethral fulguration for postoperative bleeding occurring after the usual follow-up time

52612 Transurethral resection of prostate; first stage of two-stage resection (partial resection)

52614 second stage of two-stage resection (resection completed)

52620 Transurethral resection; of residual obstructive tissue after 90 days postoperative

52630 of regrowth of obstructive tissue longer than one year postoperative

52640 of postoperative bladder neck contracture

52647 Non-contact laser coagulation of prostate, including control of postoperative bleeding, complete (vasectomy, meatotomy, cystourethroscopy, urethral calibration and/or dilation, and internal urethrotomy are included)

52648[P] Contact laser vaporization with or without transurethral resection of prostate, including control of postoperative bleeding, complete (vasectomy, meatotomy, cystourethroscopy, urethral calibration and/or dilation, and internal urethrotomy are included)

52700 Transurethral drainage of prostatic abscess

Urethra

Incision

53000 Urethrotomy or urethrostomy, external (separate procedure); pendulous urethra

53010 perineal urethra, external

53040 Drainage of deep periurethral abscess

Excision

53210 Urethrectomy, total, including cystostomy; female

53215 male

53220 Excision or fulguration of carcinoma of urethra

53230 Excision of urethral diverticulum (separate procedure); female

53235 male

53240 Marsupialization of urethral diverticulum, male or female

53250 Excision of bulbourethral gland (Cowper's gland)

53260 Excision or fulguration; urethral polyp(s), distal urethra

53265 urethral caruncle

53275 urethral prolapse

Repair

53400 Urethroplasty; first stage, for fistula, diverticulum, or stricture (eg, Johannsen type)

53405 second stage (formation of urethra), including urinary diversion

53410 Urethroplasty, one-stage reconstruction of male anterior urethra

53415 Urethroplasty, transpubic or perineal, one stage, for reconstruction or repair of prostatic or membranous urethra

53420 Urethroplasty, two-stage reconstruction or repair of prostatic or membranous urethra; first stage

53425 second stage

53430 Urethroplasty, reconstruction of female urethra

53431 Urethroplasty with tubularization of posterior urethra and/or lower bladder for incontinence (eg, Tenago, Leadbetter procedure)

Female Genital System

Vagina

Repair

57220 Plastic operation on urethral sphincter, vaginal approach (eg, Kelly urethral plication)

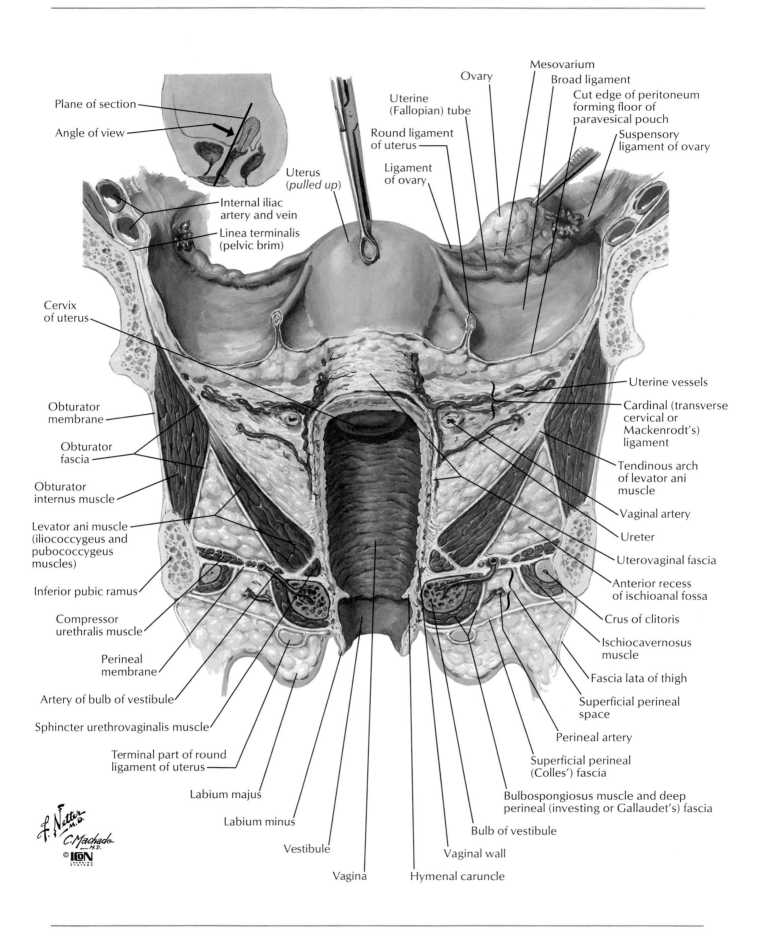

Plane of section

Angle of view

Ovary

Mesovarium

Broad ligament

Uterine (Fallopian) tube

Cut edge of peritoneum forming floor of paravesical pouch

Round ligament of uterus

Suspensory ligament of ovary

Ligament of ovary

Uterus (*pulled up*)

Internal iliac artery and vein

Linea terminalis (pelvic brim)

Cervix of uterus

Obturator membrane

Obturator fascia

Obturator internus muscle

Levator ani muscle (iliococcygeus and pubococcygeus muscles)

Inferior pubic ramus

Compressor urethralis muscle

Perineal membrane

Artery of bulb of vestibule

Sphincter urethrovaginalis muscle

Terminal part of round ligament of uterus

Labium majus

Labium minus

Vestibule

Vagina

Hymenal caruncle

Uterine vessels

Cardinal (transverse cervical or Mackenrodt's) ligament

Tendinous arch of levator ani muscle

Vaginal artery

Ureter

Uterovaginal fascia

Anterior recess of ischioanal fossa

Crus of clitoris

Ischiocavernosus muscle

Fascia lata of thigh

Superficial perineal space

Perineal artery

Superficial perineal (Colles') fascia

Bulbospongiosus muscle and deep perineal (investing or Gallaudet's) fascia

Bulb of vestibule

Vaginal wall

ANESTHESIA

Lower Abdomen

00840	Anesthesia for intraperitoneal procedures in lower abdomen including laparoscopy; not otherwise specified
00846	radical hysterectomy
00860	Anesthesia for extraperitoneal procedures in lower abdomen, including urinary tract; not otherwise specified

Perineum

00902	Anesthesia for; anorectal procedure
00904	radical perineal procedure
00940	Anesthesia for vaginal procedures (including biopsy of labia, vagina, cervix or endometrium); not otherwise specified
00942	colpotomy, vaginectomy, colporrhaphy, and open urethral procedures
00944	vaginal hysterectomy
00948	cervical cerclage
00952	hysteroscopy and/or hysterosalpingography

SURGERY

Female Genital System

Vagina
Incision

57000	Colpotomy; with exploration
57010	with drainage of pelvic abscess
57020	Colpocentesis (separate procedure)
57022	Incision and drainage of vaginal hematoma; obstetrical/postpartum
57023	non-obstetrical (eg, post-trauma, spontaneous bleeding)

Destruction

57061	Destruction of vaginal lesion(s); simple (eg, laser surgery, electrosurgery, cryosurgery, chemosurgery)
57065	extensive (eg, laser surgery, electrosurgery, cryosurgery, chemosurgery)

Excision

57100	Biopsy of vaginal mucosa; simple (separate procedure)
57105	extensive, requiring suture (including cysts)
57106[P]	Vaginectomy, partial removal of vaginal wall;
57107	with removal of paravaginal tissue (radical vaginectomy)
57109	with removal of paravaginal tissue (radical vaginectomy) with bilateral total pelvic lymphadenectomy and para-aortic lymph node sampling (biopsy)
57110	Vaginectomy, complete removal of vaginal wall;
57111[P]	with removal of paravaginal tissue (radical vaginectomy)
57112	with removal of paravaginal tissue (radical vaginectomy) with bilateral total pelvic lymphadenectomy and para-aortic lymph node sampling (biopsy)

57120	Colpocleisis (Le Fort type)
57130	Excision of vaginal septum
57135	Excision of vaginal cyst or tumor

Introduction

57150	Irrigation of vagina and/or application of medicament for treatment of bacterial, parasitic, or fungoid disease
57155	Insertion of uterine tandems and/or vaginal ovoids for clinical brachytherapy
57160	Fitting and insertion of pessary or other intravaginal support device
57170	Diaphragm or cervical cap fitting with instructions
57180	Introduction of any hemostatic agent or pack for spontaneous or traumatic nonobstetrical vaginal hemorrhage (separate procedure)

Repair

57200	Colporrhaphy, suture of injury of vagina (nonobstetrical)
57210	Colpoperineorrhaphy, suture of injury of vagina and/or perineum (nonobstetrical)
57230	Plastic repair of urethrocele
57240	Anterior colporrhaphy, repair of cystocele with or without repair of urethrocele
57250	Posterior colporrhaphy, repair of rectocele with or without perineorrhaphy
57260	Combined anteroposterior colporrhaphy;
57265	with enterocele repair
57267	Insertion of mesh or other prosthesis for repair of pelvic floor defect, each site (anterior, posterior compartment), vaginal approach (List separately in addition to code for primary procedure)
57268	Repair of enterocele, vaginal approach (separate procedure)
57270	Repair of enterocele, abdominal approach (separate procedure)
57280	Colpopexy, abdominal approach
57282	Colpopexy, vaginal; extra-peritoneal approach (sacrospinous, iliococcygeus)
57283	intra-peritoneal approach (uterosacral, levator myorrhaphy)
57284	Paravaginal defect repair (including repair of cystocele, stress urinary incontinence, and/or incomplete vaginal prolapse)
57287	Removal or revision of sling for stress incontinence (eg, fascia or synthetic)
57288	Sling operation for stress incontinence (eg, fascia or synthetic)
57289	Pereyra procedure, including anterior colporrhaphy
57291	Construction of artificial vagina; without graft
57292	with graft
57300	Closure of rectovaginal fistula; vaginal or transanal approach
57305	abdominal approach
57307	abdominal approach, with concomitant colostomy
57308	transperineal approach, with perineal body reconstruction, with or without levator plication

57310   Closure of urethrovaginal fistula;
57311   with bulbocavernosus transplant
57320   Closure of vesicovaginal fistula; vaginal approach
57330   transvesical and vaginal approach
57335   Vaginoplasty for intersex state

Manipulation

57400   Dilation of vagina under anesthesia
57410   Pelvic examination under anesthesia
57415   Removal of impacted vaginal foreign body (separate procedure) under anesthesia

Endoscopy

57420   Colposcopy of the entire vagina, with cervix if present;
57421   with biopsy(s)
57425   Laparoscopy, surgical, colpopexy (suspension of vaginal apex)

Cervix Uteri
Endoscopy

57452   Colposcopy of the cervix including upper/adjacent vagina;
57454   with biopsy(s) of the cervix and endocervical curettage
57455   with biopsy(s) of the cervix
57456   with endocervical curettage
57460   with loop electrode biopsy(s) of the cervix
57461   with loop electrode conization of the cervix

Excision

57500   Biopsy, single or multiple, or local excision of lesion, with or without fulguration (separate procedure)
57505   Endocervical curettage (not done as part of a dilation and curettage)
57510   Cautery of cervix; electro or thermal
57511   cryocautery, initial or repeat
57513   laser ablation
57520   Conization of cervix, with or without fulguration, with or without dilation and curettage, with or without repair; cold knife or laser
57522   loop electrode excision
57530   Trachelectomy (cervicectomy), amputation of cervix (separate procedure)
57531   Radical trachelectomy, with bilateral total pelvic lymphadenectomy and para-aortic lymph node sampling biopsy, with or without removal of tube(s), with or without removal of ovary(s)
57540   Excision of cervical stump, abdominal approach;
57545   with pelvic floor repair
57550   Excision of cervical stump, vaginal approach;
57555   with anterior and/or posterior repair
57556   with repair of enterocele

Repair

57700   Cerclage of uterine cervix, nonobstetrical
57720   Trachelorrhaphy, plastic repair of uterine cervix, vaginal approach

Manipulation

57800   Dilation of cervical canal, instrumental (separate procedure)

57820   Dilation and curettage of cervical stump

Corpus Uteri
Excision

58100   Endometrial sampling (biopsy) with or without endocervical sampling (biopsy), without cervical dilation, any method (separate procedure)
58120   Dilation and curettage, diagnostic and/or therapeutic (nonobstetrical)
58140   Myomectomy, excision of fibroid tumor(s) of uterus, 1 to 4 intramural myoma(s) with total weight of 250 grams or less and/or removal of surface myomas; abdominal approach
58145   vaginal approach
58146   Myomectomy, excision of fibroid tumor(s) of uterus, 5 or more intramural myomas and/or intramural myomas with total weight greater than 250 grams, abdominal approach
58150   Total abdominal hysterectomy (corpus and cervix), with or without removal of tube(s), with or without removal of ovary(s);
58152   with colpo-urethrocystopexy (eg, Marshall-Marchetti-Krantz, Burch)
58180   Supracervical abdominal hysterectomy (subtotal hysterectomy), with or without removal of tube(s), with or without removal of ovary(s)
58200   Total abdominal hysterectomy, including partial vaginectomy, with para-aortic and pelvic lymph node sampling, with or without removal of tube(s), with or without removal of ovary(s)
58210   Radical abdominal hysterectomy, with bilateral total pelvic lymphadenectomy and para-aortic lymph node sampling (biopsy), with or without removal of tube(s), with or without removal of ovary(s)
58240   Pelvic exenteration for gynecologic malignancy, with total abdominal hysterectomy or cervicectomy, with or without removal of tube(s), with or without removal of ovary(s), with removal of bladder and ureteral transplantations, and/or abdominoperineal resection of rectum and colon and colostomy, or any combination thereof
58260   Vaginal hysterectomy, for uterus 250 grams or less;
58262   with removal of tube(s), and/or ovary(s)
58263   with removal of tube(s), and/or ovary(s), with repair of enterocele
58267   with colpo-urethrocystopexy (Marshall-Marchetti-Krantz type, Pereyra type) with or without endoscopic control
58270   with repair of enterocele
58275   Vaginal hysterectomy, with total or partial vaginectomy;
58280   with repair of enterocele
58285   Vaginal hysterectomy, radical (Schauta type operation)
58290   Vaginal hysterectomy, for uterus greater than 250 grams;

(Excision continued on next page)

Plate 133: Uterus, Vagina, and Supporting Structures

(Excision continued from previous page)

58291	with removal of tube(s) and/or ovary(s)
58292	with removal of tube(s) and/or ovary(s), with repair of enterocele
58293	with colpo-urethrocystopexy (Marshall-Marchetti-Krantz type, Pereyra type) with or without endoscopic control
58294	with repair of enterocele

Introduction

58300	Insertion of intrauterine device (IUD)
58301	Removal of intrauterine device (IUD)
58321	Artificial insemination; intra-cervical
58322	intra-uterine
58323	Sperm washing for artificial insemination
58340	Catheterization and introduction of saline or contrast material for saline infusion sonohysterography (SIS) or hysterosalpingography
58345	Transcervical introduction of fallopian tube catheter for diagnosis and/or re-establishing patency (any method), with or without hysterosalpingography
58346	Insertion of Heyman capsules for clinical brachytherapy
58350	Chromotubation of oviduct, including materials
58353	Endometrial ablation, thermal, without hysteroscopic guidance
58356	Endometrial cryoablation with ultrasonic guidance, including endometrial curettage, when performed

Repair

58400	Uterine suspension, with or without shortening of round ligaments, with or without shortening of sacrouterine ligaments; (separate procedure)
58410	with presacral sympathectomy
58520	Hysterorrhaphy, repair of ruptured uterus (nonobstetrical)
58540	Hysteroplasty, repair of uterine anomaly (Strassman type)

Laparoscopy/Hysteroscopy

58545	Laparoscopy, surgical, myomectomy, excision; 1 to 4 intramural myomas with total weight of 250 grams or less and/or removal of surface myomas
58546	5 or more intramural myomas and/or intramural myomas with total weight greater than 250 grams
58550	Laparoscopy surgical, with vaginal hysterectomy, for uterus 250 grams or less;
58552	with removal of tube(s) and/or ovary(s)
58553	Laparoscopy, surgical, with vaginal hysterectomy, for uterus greater than 250 grams;
58554	with removal of tube(s) and/or ovary(s)
58555	Hysteroscopy, diagnostic (separate procedure)
58558	Hysteroscopy, surgical; with sampling (biopsy) of endometrium and/or polypectomy, with or without D & C
58559	with lysis of intrauterine adhesions (any method)
58560	with division or resection of intrauterine septum (any method)
58561	with removal of leiomyomata
58562	with removal of impacted foreign body
58563	with endometrial ablation (eg, endometrial resection, electrosurgical ablation, thermoablation)
58565	with bilateral fallopian tube cannulation to induce occlusion by placement of permanent implants

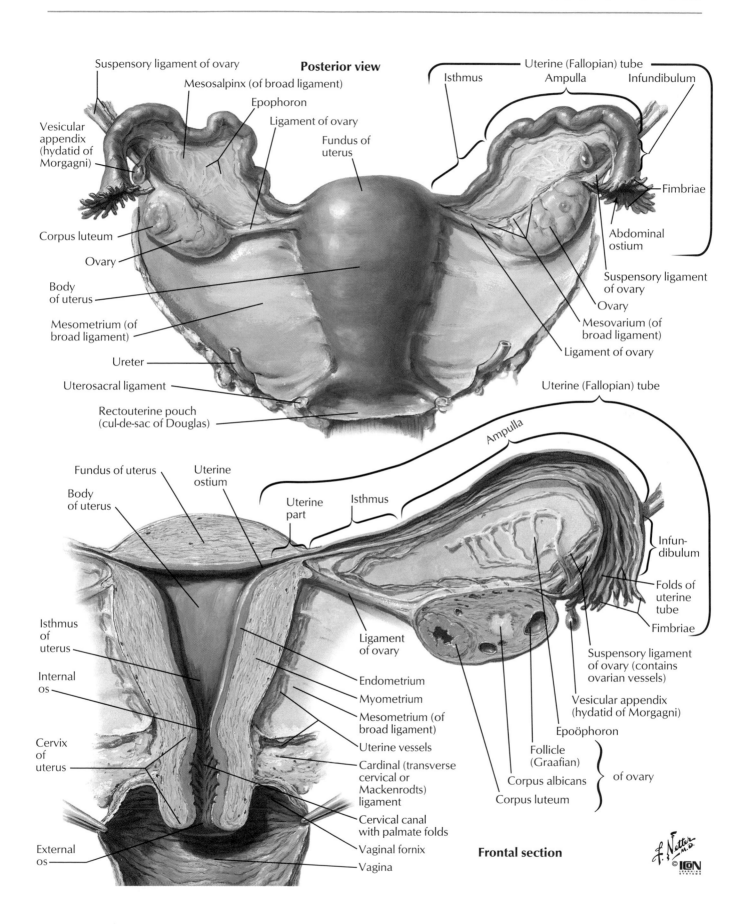

Posterior view

Suspensory ligament of ovary

Mesosalpinx (of broad ligament)

Epophoron

Ligament of ovary

Fundus of uterus

Vesicular appendix (hydatid of Morgagni)

Corpus luteum

Ovary

Body of uterus

Mesometrium (of broad ligament)

Ureter

Uterosacral ligament

Rectouterine pouch (cul-de-sac of Douglas)

Uterine (Fallopian) tube

Isthmus

Ampulla

Infundibulum

Fimbriae

Abdominal ostium

Suspensory ligament of ovary

Ovary

Mesovarium (of broad ligament)

Ligament of ovary

Uterine (Fallopian) tube

Ampulla

Fundus of uterus

Uterine ostium

Body of uterus

Uterine part

Isthmus

Infundibulum

Folds of uterine tube

Fimbriae

Suspensory ligament of ovary (contains ovarian vessels)

Vesicular appendix (hydatid of Morgagni)

Epoöphoron

Isthmus of uterus

Internal os

Cervix of uterus

External os

Ligament of ovary

Endometrium

Myometrium

Mesometrium (of broad ligament)

Uterine vessels

Cardinal (transverse cervical or Mackenrodts) ligament

Cervical canal with palmate folds

Vaginal fornix

Vagina

Follicle (Graafian)

Corpus albicans

Corpus luteum

of ovary

Frontal section

ANESTHESIA

Lower Abdomen

00840	Anesthesia for intraperitoneal procedures in lower abdomen including laparoscopy; not otherwise specified
00846	radical hysterectomy
00851	tubal ligation/transection

Perineum

00940	Anesthesia for vaginal procedures (including biopsy of labia, vagina, cervix or endometrium); not otherwise specified
00942	colpotomy, vaginectomy, colporrhaphy, and open urethral procedures
00944	vaginal hysterectomy
00948	cervical cerclage
00952	hysteroscopy and/or hysterosalpingography

SURGERY

Female Genital System

Vagina
Endoscopy

57420	Colposcopy of the entire vagina, with cervix if present;
57421	with biopsy(s)

Cervix Uteri
Endoscopy

57452	Colposcopy of the cervix including upper/adjacent vagina;
57454	with biopsy(s) of the cervix and endocervical curettage
57455	with biopsy(s) of the cervix
57456	with endocervical curettage
57460	with loop electrode biopsy(s) of the cervix
57461	with loop electrode conization of the cervix

Excision

57500	Biopsy, single or multiple, or local excision of lesion, with or without fulguration (separate procedure)
57505	Endocervical curettage (not done as part of a dilation and curettage)
57510	Cautery of cervix; electro or thermal
57511	cryocautery, initial or repeat
57513	laser ablation
57520	Conization of cervix, with or without fulguration, with or without dilation and curettage, with or without repair; cold knife or laser
57522	loop electrode excision
57530	Trachelectomy (cervicectomy), amputation of cervix (separate procedure)
57531	Radical trachelectomy, with bilateral total pelvic lymphadenectomy and para-aortic lymph node sampling biopsy, with or without removal of tube(s), with or without removal of ovary(s)
57540	Excision of cervical stump, abdominal approach;
57545	with pelvic floor repair

57550	Excision of cervical stump, vaginal approach;
57555	with anterior and/or posterior repair
57556	with repair of enterocele

Repair

57700	Cerclage of uterine cervix, nonobstetrical
57720	Trachelorrhaphy, plastic repair of uterine cervix, vaginal approach

Manipulation

57800	Dilation of cervical canal, instrumental (separate procedure)
57820	Dilation and curettage of cervical stump

Corpus Uteri
Excision

58100	Endometrial sampling (biopsy) with or without endocervical sampling (biopsy), without cervical dilation, any method (separate procedure)
58120	Dilation and curettage, diagnostic and/or therapeutic (nonobstetrical)
58140	Myomectomy, excision of fibroid tumor(s) of uterus, 1 to 4 intramural myoma(s) with total weight of 250 grams or less and/or removal of surface myomas; abdominal approach
58145	vaginal approach
58146	Myomectomy, excision of fibroid tumor(s) of uterus, 5 or more intramural myomas and/or intramural myomas with total weight greater than 250 grams, abdominal approach
58150	Total abdominal hysterectomy (corpus and cervix), with or without removal of tube(s), with or without removal of ovary(s);
58152	with colpo-urethrocystopexy (eg, Marshall-Marchetti-Krantz, Burch)
58180	Supracervical abdominal hysterectomy (subtotal hysterectomy), with or without removal of tube(s), with or without removal of ovary(s)
58200	Total abdominal hysterectomy, including partial vaginectomy, with para-aortic and pelvic lymph node sampling, with or without removal of tube(s), with or without removal of ovary(s)
58210	Radical abdominal hysterectomy, with bilateral total pelvic lymphadenectomy and para-aortic lymph node sampling (biopsy), with or without removal of tube(s), with or without removal of ovary(s)
58260	Vaginal hysterectomy, for uterus 250 grams or less;
58262	with removal of tube(s), and/or ovary(s)
58263	with removal of tube(s), and/or ovary(s), with repair of enterocele
58267	with colpo-urethrocystopexy (Marshall-Marchetti-Krantz type, Pereyra type) with or without endoscopic control
58270	with repair of enterocele
58275	Vaginal hysterectomy, with total or partial vaginectomy;
58280	with repair of enterocele
58285	Vaginal hysterectomy, radical (Schauta type operation)

58290   Vaginal hysterectomy, for uterus greater than 250 grams;

58291   with removal of tube(s) and/or ovary(s)

58292   with removal of tube(s) and/or ovary(s), with repair of enterocele

58293   with colpo-urethrocystopexy (Marshall-Marchetti-Krantz type, Pereyra type) with or without endoscopic control

58294   with repair of enterocele

Introduction

58340   Catheterization and introduction of saline or contrast material for saline infusion sonohysterography (SIS) or hysterosalpingography

58345   Transcervical introduction of fallopian tube catheter for diagnosis and/or re-establishing patency (any method), with or without hysterosalpingography

58346   Insertion of Heyman capsules for clinical brachytherapy

58350   Chromotubation of oviduct, including materials

58353   Endometrial ablation, thermal, without hysteroscopic guidance

58356   Endometrial cryoablation with ultrasonic guidance, including endometrial curettage, when performed

Repair

58520   Hysterorrhaphy, repair of ruptured uterus (nonobstetrical)

58540   Hysteroplasty, repair of uterine anomaly (Strassman type)

Laparoscopy/Hysteroscopy

58545   Laparoscopy, surgical, myomectomy, excision; 1 to 4 intramural myomas with total weight of 250 grams or less and/or removal of surface myomas

58546   5 or more intramural myomas and/or intramural myomas with total weight greater than 250 grams

58550   Laparoscopy surgical, with vaginal hysterectomy, for uterus 250 grams or less;

58552   with removal of tube(s) and/or ovary(s)

58553   Laparoscopy, surgical, with vaginal hysterectomy, for uterus greater than 250 grams;

58554   with removal of tube(s) and/or ovary(s)

58555   Hysteroscopy, diagnostic (separate procedure)

58558   Hysteroscopy, surgical; with sampling (biopsy) of endometrium and/or polypectomy, with or without D & C

58559   with lysis of intrauterine adhesions (any method)

58560   with division or resection of intrauterine septum (any method)

58561   with removal of leiomyomata

58562   with removal of impacted foreign body

58563   with endometrial ablation (eg, endometrial resection, electrosurgical ablation, thermoablation)

58565   with bilateral fallopian tube cannulation to induce occlusion by placement of permanent implants

Oviduct/Ovary

Incision

58600   Ligation or transection of fallopian tube(s), abdominal or vaginal approach, unilateral or bilateral

58605   Ligation or transection of fallopian tube(s), abdominal or vaginal approach, postpartum, unilateral or bilateral, during same hospitalization (separate procedure)

58611   Ligation or transection of fallopian tube(s) when done at the time of cesarean delivery or intra-abdominal surgery (not a separate procedure) (List separately in addition to code for primary procedure)

58615   Occlusion of fallopian tube(s) by device (eg, band, clip, Falope ring) vaginal or suprapubic approach

Laparoscopy

58660   Laparoscopy, surgical; with lysis of adhesions (salpingolysis, ovariolysis) (separate procedure)

58661   with removal of adnexal structures (partial or total oophorectomy and/or salpingectomy)

58662   with fulguration or excision of lesions of the ovary, pelvic viscera, or peritoneal surface by any method

58670   with fulguration of oviducts (with or without transection)

58671   with occlusion of oviducts by device (eg, band, clip, or Falope ring)

58672   with fimbrioplasty

58673   with salpingostomy (salpingoneostomy)

Excision

58700   Salpingectomy, complete or partial, unilateral or bilateral (separate procedure)

58720   Salpingo-oophorectomy, complete or partial, unilateral or bilateral (separate procedure)

Repair

58740   Lysis of adhesions (salpingolysis, ovariolysis)

58750   Tubotubal anastomosis

58752   Tubouterine implantation

58760   Fimbrioplasty

58770   Salpingostomy (salpingoneostomy)

Ovary

Incision

58800   Drainage of ovarian cyst(s), unilateral or bilateral, (separate procedure); vaginal approach

58805   abdominal approach

58820   Drainage of ovarian abscess; vaginal approach, open

58822   abdominal approach

58823   Drainage of pelvic abscess, transvaginal or transrectal approach, percutaneous (eg, ovarian, pericolic)

58825   Transposition, ovary(s)

Excision

58900	Biopsy of ovary, unilateral or bilateral (separate procedure)
58920	Wedge resection or bisection of ovary, unilateral or bilateral
58925	Ovarian cystectomy, unilateral or bilateral
58940	Oophorectomy, partial or total, unilateral or bilateral;
58943	for ovarian, tubal or primary peritoneal malignancy, with para-aortic and pelvic lymph node biopsies, peritoneal washings, peritoneal biopsies, diaphragmatic assessments, with or without salpingectomy(s), with or without omentectomy
58950	Resection of ovarian, tubal or primary peritoneal malignancy with bilateral salpingo-oophorectomy and omentectomy;
58951	with total abdominal hysterectomy, pelvic and limited para-aortic lymphadenectomy
58952	Resection of ovarian, tubal or primary peritoneal malignancy with bilateral salpingo-oophorectomy and omentectomy; with radical dissection for debulking (ie, radical excision or destruction, intra-abdominal or retroperitoneal tumors)
58953	Bilateral salpingo-oophorectomy with omentectomy, total abdominal hysterectomy and radical dissection for debulking;
58954	with pelvic lymphadenectomy and limited para-aortic lymphadenectomy
58956	Bilateral salpingo-oophorectomy with total omentectomy, total abdominal hysterectomy for malignancy
58960	Laparotomy, for staging or restaging of ovarian, tubal or primary peritoneal malignancy (second look), with or without omentectomy, peritoneal washing, biopsy of abdominal and pelvic peritoneum, diaphragmatic assessment with pelvic and limited para-aortic lymphadenectomy

Maternity Care and Delivery

Excision

59100	Hysterotomy, abdominal (eg, for hydatidiform mole, abortion)
59120	Surgical treatment of ectopic pregnancy; tubal or ovarian, requiring salpingectomy and/or oophorectomy, abdominal or vaginal approach
59121	tubal or ovarian, without salpingectomy and/or oophorectomy
59130	abdominal pregnancy
59135	interstitial, uterine pregnancy requiring total hysterectomy
59136	interstitial, uterine pregnancy with partial resection of uterus
59140	cervical, with evacuation
59150ᴾ	Laparoscopic treatment of ectopic pregnancy; without salpingectomy and/or oophorectomy
59151	with salpingectomy and/or oophorectomy
59160	Curettage, postpartum

Introduction

59200	Insertion of cervical dilator (eg, laminaria, prostaglandin) (separate procedure)

Repair

59300	Episiotomy or vaginal repair, by other than attending physician
59320	Cerclage of cervix, during pregnancy; vaginal
59325	abdominal
59350	Hysterorrhaphy of ruptured uterus

Other Procedures

59871	Removal of cerclage suture under anesthesia (other than local)

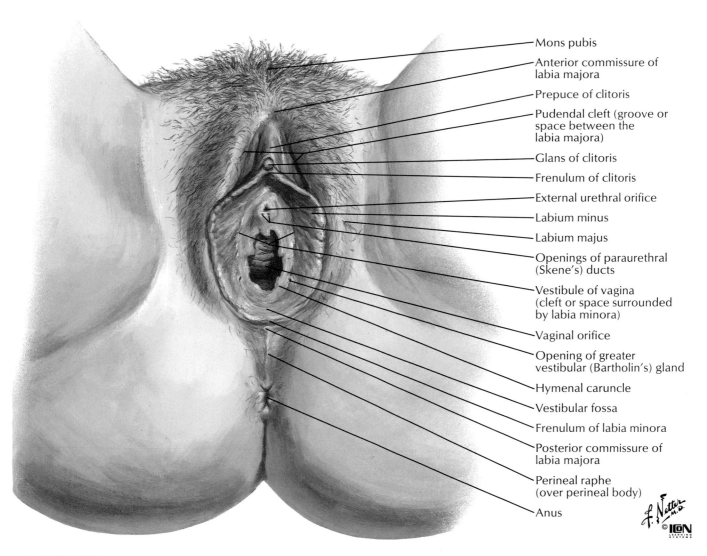

Mons pubis

Anterior commissure of labia majora

Prepuce of clitoris

Pudendal cleft (groove or space between the labia majora)

Glans of clitoris

Frenulum of clitoris

External urethral orifice

Labium minus

Labium majus

Openings of paraurethral (Skene's) ducts

Vestibule of vagina (cleft or space surrounded by labia minora)

Vaginal orifice

Opening of greater vestibular (Bartholin's) gland

Hymenal caruncle

Vestibular fossa

Frenulum of labia minora

Posterior commissure of labia majora

Perineal raphe (over perineal body)

Anus

ANESTHESIA

Thorax (Chest Wall and Shoulder Girdle)

00400   Anesthesia for procedures on the integumentary system on the extremities, anterior trunk and perineum; not otherwise specified

Perineum

00904   Anesthesia for; radical perineal procedure
00906   vulvectomy
00940   Anesthesia for vaginal procedures (including biopsy of labia, vagina, cervix or endometrium); not otherwise specified
00942   colpotomy, vaginectomy, colporrhaphy, and open urethral procedures

SURGERY

Integumentary

Skin, Subcutaneous and Accessory Structures
Excision—Benign lesions

11420   Excision, benign lesion including margins, except skin tag (unless listed elsewhere), scalp, neck, hands, feet, genitalia; excised diameter 0.5 cm or less

11421   excised diameter 0.6 to 1.0 cm
11422   excised diameter 1.1 to 2.0 cm
11423   excised diameter 2.1 to 3.0 cm
11424   excised diameter 3.1 to 4.0 cm
11426   excised diameter over 4.0 cm

Excision—Malignant Lesions

11620   Excision, malignant lesion including margins, scalp, neck, hands, feet, genitalia; excised diameter 0.5 cm or less
11621   excised diameter 0.6 to 1.0 cm
11622   excised diameter 1.1 to 2.0 cm
11623   excised diameter 2.1 to 3.0 cm
11624   excised diameter 3.1 to 4.0 cm
11626   excised diameter over 4.0 cm

Repair
Repair—Simple

12001   Simple repair of superficial wounds of scalp, neck, axillae, external genitalia, trunk and/or extremities (including hands and feet); 2.5 cm or less

(Repair continued on next page)

(Repair continued from previous page)

12002	2.6 cm to 7.5 cm
12004	7.6 cm to 12.5 cm
12005	12.6 cm to 20.0 cm
12006	20.1 cm to 30.0 cm
12007	over 30.0 cm

Repair—Intermediate

12031	Layer closure of wounds of scalp, axillae, trunk and/or extremities (excluding hands and feet); 2.5 cm or less
12032	2.6 cm to 7.5 cm
12034	7.6 cm to 12.5 cm
12035	12.6 cm to 20.0 cm
12036	20.1 cm to 30.0 cm
12037	over 30.0 cm

Repair—Complex

13131	Repair, complex, forehead, cheeks, chin, mouth, neck, axillae, genitalia, hands and/or feet; 1.1 cm to 2.5 cm
13132	2.6 cm to 7.5 cm
13133	each additional 5 cm or less (List separately in addition to code for primary procedure)

Adjacent Tissue Transfer or Rearrangement

14040	Adjacent tissue transfer or rearrangement, forehead, cheeks, chin, mouth, neck, axillae, genitalia, hands and/or feet; defect 10 sq cm or less
14041	defect 10.1 sq cm to 30.0 sq cm

Urinary System

Urethra
Incision

53060	Drainage of Skene's gland abscess or cyst

Excision

53270	Excision or fulguration; Skene's glands

Female Genital System

Vulva, Perineum and Introitus
Incision

56405	Incision and drainage of vulva or perineal abscess
56420	Incision and drainage of Bartholin's gland abscess
56440	Marsupialization of Bartholin's gland cyst
56441	Lysis of labial adhesions

Destruction

56501	Destruction of lesion(s), vulva; simple (eg, laser surgery, electrosurgery, cryosurgery, chemosurgery)
56515	extensive (eg, laser surgery, electrosurgery, cryosurgery, chemosurgery)

Excision

56605	Biopsy of vulva or perineum (separate procedure); one lesion
56606	each separate additional lesion (List separately in addition to code for primary procedure)
56620	Vulvectomy simple; partial
56625	complete
56630	Vulvectomy, radical, partial;
56631	with unilateral inguinofemoral lymphadenectomy
56632	with bilateral inguinofemoral lymphadenectomy
56633	Vulvectomy, radical, complete;
56634	with unilateral inguinofemoral lymphadenectomy
56637	with bilateral inguinofemoral lymphadenectomy
56640	Vulvectomy, radical, complete, with inguino-femoral, iliac, and pelvic lymphadenectomy
56700	Partial hymenectomy or revision of hymenal ring
56720	Hymenotomy, simple incision
56740	Excision of Bartholin's gland or cyst

Repair

56800	Plastic repair of introitus
56805	Clitoroplasty for intersex state
56810	Perineoplasty, repair of perineum, nonobstetrical (separate procedure)

Endoscopy

56820	Colposcopy of the vulva;
56821	with biopsy(s)

Vagina
Incision

57000	Colpotomy; with exploration
57010	with drainage of pelvic abscess
57020	Colpocentesis (separate procedure)
57022	Incision and drainage of vaginal hematoma; obstetrical/postpartum
57023	non-obstetrical (eg, post-trauma, spontaneous bleeding)

Destruction

57061	Destruction of vaginal lesion(s); simple (eg, laser surgery, electrosurgery, cryosurgery, chemosurgery)
57065	extensive (eg, laser surgery, electrosurgery, cryosurgery, chemosurgery)

Excision

57100	Biopsy of vaginal mucosa; simple (separate procedure)
57105	extensive, requiring suture (including cysts)

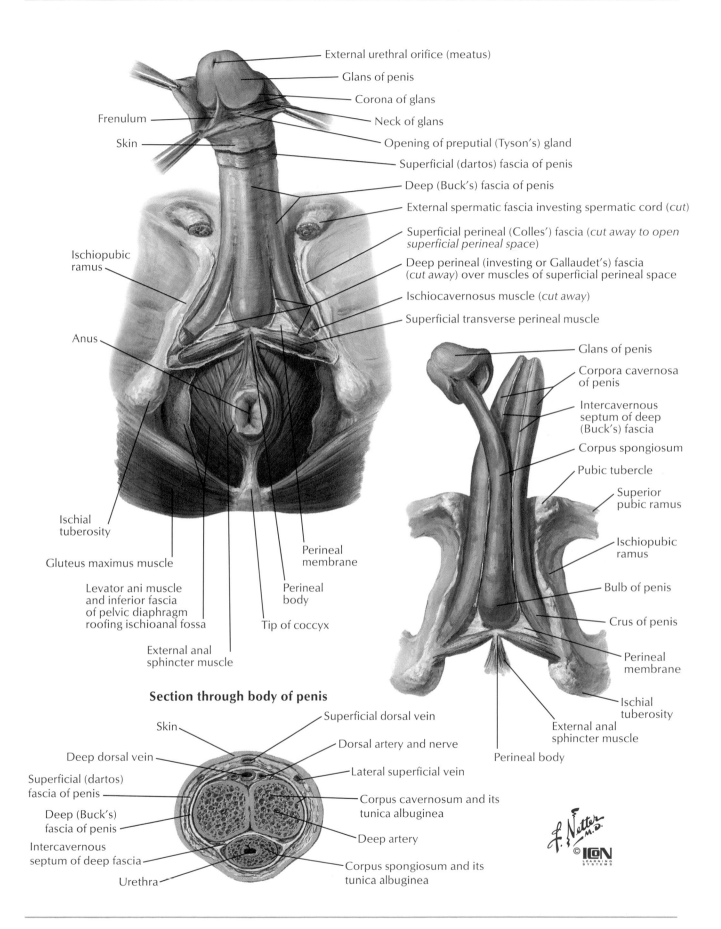

External urethral orifice (meatus)

Glans of penis

Corona of glans

Frenulum

Neck of glans

Skin

Opening of preputial (Tyson's) gland

Superficial (dartos) fascia of penis

Deep (Buck's) fascia of penis

External spermatic fascia investing spermatic cord (*cut*)

Superficial perineal (Colles') fascia (*cut away to open superficial perineal space*)

Ischiopubic ramus

Deep perineal (investing or Gallaudet's) fascia (*cut away*) over muscles of superficial perineal space

Ischiocavernosus muscle (*cut away*)

Superficial transverse perineal muscle

Anus

Glans of penis

Corpora cavernosa of penis

Intercavernous septum of deep (Buck's) fascia

Corpus spongiosum

Pubic tubercle

Superior pubic ramus

Ischiopubic ramus

Ischial tuberosity

Bulb of penis

Gluteus maximus muscle

Crus of penis

Levator ani muscle and inferior fascia of pelvic diaphragm roofing ischioanal fossa

Perineal membrane

Perineal body

Perineal membrane

Tip of coccyx

Ischial tuberosity

External anal sphincter muscle

External anal sphincter muscle

Perineal body

Section through body of penis

Skin

Superficial dorsal vein

Deep dorsal vein

Dorsal artery and nerve

Superficial (dartos) fascia of penis

Lateral superficial vein

Deep (Buck's) fascia of penis

Corpus cavernosum and its tunica albuginea

Intercavernous septum of deep fascia

Deep artery

Urethra

Corpus spongiosum and its tunica albuginea

Plate 136: Penis

ANESTHESIA

Perineum

00920	Anesthesia for procedures on male genitalia (including open urethral procedures); not otherwise specified
00932	complete amputation of penis
00934	radical amputation of penis with bilateral inguinal lymphadenectomy
00936	radical amputation of penis with bilateral inguinal and iliac lymphadenectomy
00938	insertion of penile prosthesis (perineal approach)

SURGERY

Male Genital System

Penis

Incision

54000	Slitting of prepuce, dorsal or lateral (separate procedure); newborn
54001	except newborn
54015	Incision and drainage of penis, deep

Destruction

54050	Destruction of lesion(s), penis (eg, condyloma, papilloma, molluscum contagiosum, herpetic vesicle), simple; chemical
54055	electrodesiccation
54056	cryosurgery
54057	laser surgery
54060	surgical excision
54065	Destruction of lesion(s), penis (eg, condyloma, papilloma, molluscum contagiosum, herpetic vesicle), extensive (eg, laser surgery, electrosurgery, cryosurgery, chemosurgery)

Excision

54100	Biopsy of penis; (separate procedure)
54105	deep structures
54110	Excision of penile plaque (Peyronie disease);
54111	with graft to 5 cm in length
54112	with graft greater than 5 cm in length
54115	Removal foreign body from deep penile tissue (eg, plastic implant)
54120	Amputation of penis; partial
54125	complete
54130	Amputation of penis, radical; with bilateral inguinofemoral lymphadenectomy
54135	in continuity with bilateral pelvic lymphadenectomy, including external iliac, hypogastric and obturator nodes
54150	Circumcision, using clamp or other device; newborn
54152	except newborn
54160	Circumcision, surgical excision other than clamp, device or dorsal slit; newborn
54161	except newborn
54162	Lysis or excision of penile post-circumcision adhesions
54163	Repair incomplete circumcision
54164	Frenulotomy of penis

Introduction

54200	Injection procedure for Peyronie disease;
54205	with surgical exposure of plaque
54220	Irrigation of corpora cavernosa for priapism
54230	Injection procedure for corpora cavernosography
54231	Dynamic cavernosometry, including intracavernosal injection of vasoactive drugs (eg, papaverine, phentolamine)
54235	Injection of corpora cavernosa with pharmacologic agent(s) (eg, papaverine, phentolamine)

Repair

54300	Plastic operation of penis for straightening of chordee (eg, hypospadias), with or without mobilization of urethra
54304	Plastic operation on penis for correction of chordee or for first stage hypospadias repair with or without transplantation of prepuce and/or skin flaps
54308	Urethroplasty for second stage hypospadias repair (including urinary diversion); less than 3 cm
54312	greater than 3 cm
54316	Urethroplasty for second stage hypospadias repair (including urinary diversion) with free skin graft obtained from site other than genitalia
54318	Urethroplasty for third stage hypospadias repair to release penis from scrotum (eg, third stage Cecil repair)
54322	One stage distal hypospadias repair (with or without chordee or circumcision); with simple meatal advancement (eg, Magpi, V-flap)
54324	with urethroplasty by local skin flaps (eg, flip-flap, prepucial flap)
54326	with urethroplasty by local skin flaps and mobilization of urethra
54328	with extensive dissection to correct chordee and urethroplasty with local skin flaps, skin graft patch, and/or island flap
54332	One stage proximal penile or penoscrotal hypospadias repair requiring extensive dissection to correct chordee and urethroplasty by use of skin graft tube and/or island flap
54336	One stage perineal hypospadias repair requiring extensive dissection to correct chordee and urethroplasty by use of skin graft tube and/or island flap
54340	Repair of hypospadias complications (ie, fistula, stricture, diverticula); by closure, incision, or excision, simple
54344	requiring mobilization of skin flaps and urethroplasty with flap or patch graft

54348   requiring extensive dissection and urethroplasty with flap, patch or tubed graft (includes urinary diversion)

54352   Repair of hypospadias cripple requiring extensive dissection and excision of previously constructed structures including re-release of chordee and reconstruction of urethra and penis by use of local skin as grafts and island flaps and skin brought in as flaps or grafts

54360   Plastic operation on penis to correct angulation

54380   Plastic operation on penis for epispadias distal to external sphincter;

54385   with incontinence

54390   with exstrophy of bladder

54400   Insertion of penile prosthesis; non-inflatable (semi-rigid)

54401   inflatable (self-contained)

54405   Insertion of multi-component, inflatable penile prosthesis, including placement of pump, cylinders, and reservoir

54406   Removal of all components of a multi-component, inflatable penile prosthesis without replacement of prosthesis

54408   Repair of component(s) of a multi-component, inflatable penile prosthesis

54410   Removal and replacement of all component(s) of a multi-component, inflatable penile prosthesis at the same operative session

54411   Removal and replacement of all components of a multi-component inflatable penile prosthesis through an infected field at the same operative session, including irrigation and debridement of infected tissue

54415   Removal of non-inflatable (semi-rigid) or inflatable (self-contained) penile prosthesis, without replacement of prosthesis

54416   Removal and replacement of non-inflatable (semi-rigid) or inflatable (self-contained) penile prosthesis at the same operative session

54417   Removal and replacement of non-inflatable (semi-rigid) or inflatable (self-contained) penile prosthesis through an infected field at the same operative session, including irrigation and debridement of infected tissue

54420   Corpora cavernosa-saphenous vein shunt (priapism operation), unilateral or bilateral

54430   Corpora cavernosa-corpus spongiosum shunt (priapism operation), unilateral or bilateral

54435   Corpora cavernosa-glans penis fistulization (eg, biopsy needle, Winter procedure, rongeur, or punch) for priapism

54440   Plastic operation of penis for injury

Manipulation

54450   Foreskin manipulation including lysis of preputial adhesions and stretching

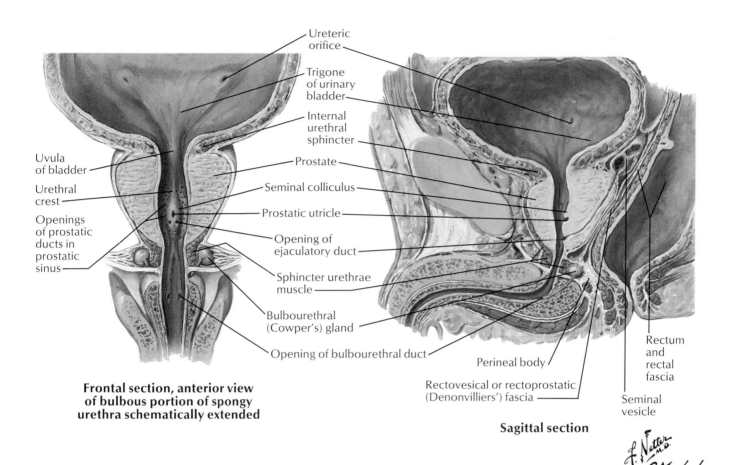

Ureteric orifice

Trigone of urinary bladder

Internal urethral sphincter

Uvula of bladder

Prostate

Urethral crest

Seminal colliculus

Openings of prostatic ducts in prostatic sinus

Prostatic utricle

Opening of ejaculatory duct

Sphincter urethrae muscle

Bulbourethral (Cowper's) gland

Opening of bulbourethral duct

Rectum and rectal fascia

Perineal body

Rectovesical or rectoprostatic (Denonvilliers') fascia

Seminal vesicle

Frontal section, anterior view of bulbous portion of spongy urethra schematically extended

Sagittal section

ANESTHESIA

Thorax (Chest Wall and Shoulder Girdle)

00400   Anesthesia for procedures on the integumentary system on the extremities, anterior trunk and perineum; not otherwise specified

Lower Abdomen

00860   Anesthesia for extraperitoneal procedures in lower abdomen, including urinary tract; not otherwise specified

00865   radical prostatectomy (suprapubic, retropubic)

Perineum

00904   Anesthesia for; radical perineal procedure
00908   perineal prostatectomy
00910   Anesthesia for transurethral procedures (including urethrocystoscopy); not otherwise specified
00912   transurethral resection of bladder tumor(s)
00914   transurethral resection of prostate
00916   post-transurethral resection bleeding
00918   with fragmentation, manipulation and/or removal of ureteral calculus
00920   Anesthesia for procedures on male genitalia (including open urethral procedures); not otherwise specified
00922   seminal vesicles

SURGERY

Urinary System

Bladder
Endoscopy—Cystoscopy, Urethroscopy, Cystourethroscopy

52010   Cystourethroscopy, with ejaculatory duct catheterization, with or without irrigation, instillation, or duct radiography, exclusive of radiologic service

Vesical Neck and Bladder

52402   Cystourethroscopy with transurethral resection or incision of ejaculatory ducts
52450   Transurethral incision of prostate
52500   Transurethral resection of bladder neck (separate procedure)
52510   Transurethral balloon dilation of the prostatic urethra
52601[P]   Transurethral electrosurgical resection of prostate, including control of postoperative bleeding, complete (vasectomy, meatotomy, cystourethroscopy, urethral calibration and/or dilation, and internal urethrotomy are included)
52606   Transurethral fulguration for postoperative bleeding occurring after the usual follow-up time

52612 Transurethral resection of prostate; first stage of two-stage resection (partial resection)

52614 second stage of two-stage resection (resection completed)

52620 Transurethral resection; of residual obstructive tissue after 90 days postoperative

52630 of regrowth of obstructive tissue longer than one year postoperative

52640 of postoperative bladder neck contracture

52647 Non-contact laser coagulation of prostate, including control of postoperative bleeding, complete (vasectomy, meatotomy, cystourethroscopy, urethral calibration and/or dilation, and internal urethrotomy are included)

52648[P] Contact laser vaporization with or without transurethral resection of prostate, including control of postoperative bleeding, complete (vasectomy, meatotomy, cystourethroscopy, urethral calibration and/or dilation, and internal urethrotomy are included)

52700 Transurethral drainage of prostatic abscess

Urethra
Excision

53250 Excision of bulbourethral gland (Cowper's gland)

Other Procedures

53850 Transurethral destruction of prostate tissue; by microwave thermotherapy

53852 by radiofrequency thermotherapy

53853 by water-induced thermotherapy

Male Genital System

Seminal Vesicles
Incision

55600 Vesiculotomy;

55605 complicated

Excision

55650 Vesiculectomy, any approach

55680 Excision of Mullerian duct cyst

Prostate
Incision

55700 Biopsy, prostate; needle or punch, single or multiple, any approach

55705 incisional, any approach

55720 Prostatotomy, external drainage of prostatic abscess, any approach; simple

55725 complicated

Excision

55801 Prostatectomy, perineal, subtotal (including control of postoperative bleeding, vasectomy, meatotomy, urethral calibration and/or dilation, and internal urethrotomy)

55810 Prostatectomy, perineal radical;

55812 with lymph node biopsy(s) (limited pelvic lymphadenectomy)

55815 with bilateral pelvic lymphadenectomy, including external iliac, hypogastric and obturator nodes

55821 Prostatectomy (including control of postoperative bleeding, vasectomy, meatotomy, urethral calibration and/or dilation, and internal urethrotomy); suprapubic, subtotal, one or two stages

55831 retropubic, subtotal

55840 Prostatectomy, retropubic radical, with or without nerve sparing;

55842 with lymph node biopsy(s) (limited pelvic lymphadenectomy)

55845 with bilateral pelvic lymphadenectomy, including external iliac, hypogastric, and obturator nodes

55859 Transperineal placement of needles or catheters into prostate for interstitial radioelement application, with or without cystoscopy

55860 Exposure of prostate, any approach, for insertion of radioactive substance;

55862 with lymph node biopsy(s) (limited pelvic lymphadenectomy)

55865 with bilateral pelvic lymphadenectomy, including external iliac, hypogastric and obturator nodes

Laparoscopy

55866 Laparoscopy, surgical prostatectomy, retropubic radical, including nerve sparing

Other Procedures

55870 Electroejaculation

55873 Cryosurgical ablation of the prostate (includes ultrasonic guidance for interstitial cryosurgical probe placement)

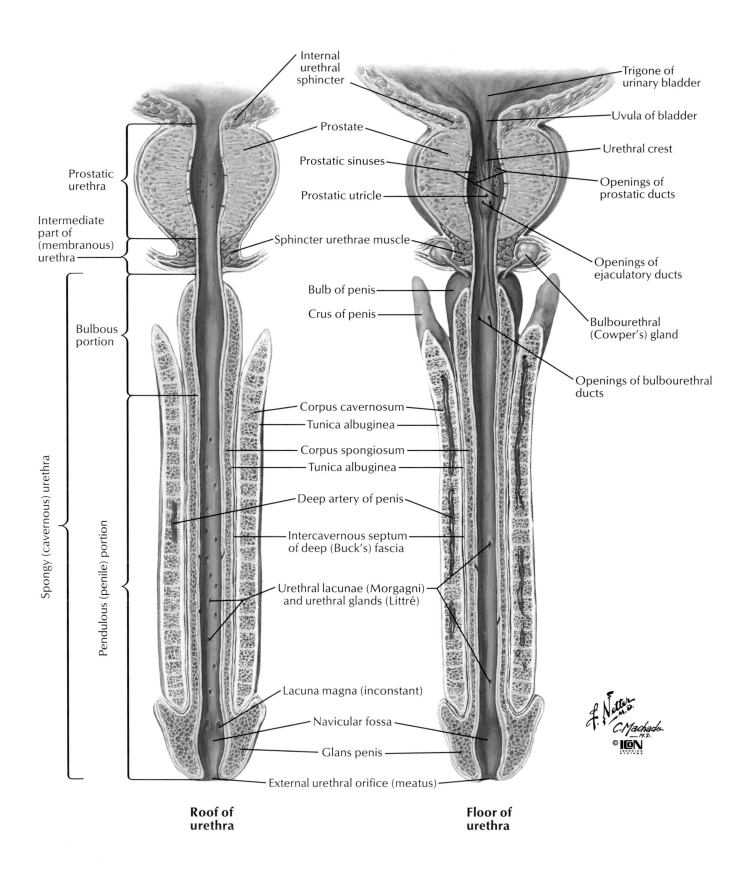

Internal urethral sphincter

Prostate

Prostatic sinuses

Prostatic utricle

Sphincter urethrae muscle

Bulb of penis

Crus of penis

Corpus cavernosum

Tunica albuginea

Corpus spongiosum

Tunica albuginea

Deep artery of penis

Intercavernous septum of deep (Buck's) fascia

Urethral lacunae (Morgagni) and urethral glands (Littré)

Lacuna magna (inconstant)

Navicular fossa

Glans penis

External urethral orifice (meatus)

Trigone of urinary bladder

Uvula of bladder

Urethral crest

Openings of prostatic ducts

Openings of ejaculatory ducts

Bulbourethral (Cowper's) gland

Openings of bulbourethral ducts

Prostatic urethra

Intermediate part of (membranous) urethra

Bulbous portion

Spongy (cavernous) urethra

Pendulous (penile) portion

Roof of urethra

Floor of urethra

ANESTHESIA

Lower Abdomen

00860 Anesthesia for extraperitoneal procedures in lower abdomen, including urinary tract; not otherwise specified

Perineum

00910 Anesthesia for transurethral procedures (including urethrocystoscopy); not otherwise specified

00920 Anesthesia for procedures on male genitalia (including open urethral procedures); not otherwise specified

SURGERY

Urinary System

Bladder
Introduction

51715 Endoscopic injection of implant material into the submucosal tissues of the urethra and/or bladder neck

Laparoscopy

51990ᴾ Laparoscopy, surgical; urethral suspension for stress incontinence

Transuretheral Surgery

Urethra and Bladder

52214 Cystourethroscopy, with fulguration (including cryosurgery or laser surgery) of trigone, bladder neck, prostatic fossa, urethra, or periurethral glands

52281 Cystourethroscopy, with calibration and/or dilation of urethral stricture or stenosis, with or without meatotomy, with or without injection procedure for cystography, male or female

52282 Cystourethroscopy, with insertion of urethral stent

52283 Cystourethroscopy, with steroid injection into stricture

Vesical Neck and Prostate

52400 Cystourethroscopy with incision, fulguration, or resection of congenital posterior urethral valves, or congenital obstructive hypertrophic mucosal folds

52510 Transurethral balloon dilation of the prostatic urethra

Urethra
Incision

53000 Urethrotomy or urethrostomy, external (separate procedure); pendulous urethra

53010 perineal urethra, external

53020 Meatotomy, cutting of meatus (separate procedure); except infant

53025 infant

53040 Drainage of deep periurethral abscess

Excision

53200 Biopsy of urethra

53215 Urethrectomy, total, including cystostomy; male

53220 Excision or fulguration of carcinoma of urethra

53235 Excision of urethral diverticulum (separate procedure); male

53240 Marsupialization of urethral diverticulum, male or female

53250 Excision of bulbourethral gland (Cowper's gland)

53260 Excision or fulguration; urethral polyp(s), distal urethra

53265 urethral caruncle

53275 urethral prolapse

Repair

53400 Urethroplasty; first stage, for fistula, diverticulum, or stricture (eg, Johannsen type)

53405 second stage (formation of urethra), including urinary diversion

53410 Urethroplasty, one-stage reconstruction of male anterior urethra

53415 Urethroplasty, transpubic or perineal, one stage, for reconstruction or repair of prostatic or membranous urethra

53420 Urethroplasty, two-stage reconstruction or repair of prostatic or membranous urethra; first stage

53425 second stage

53430 Urethroplasty, reconstruction of female urethra

53431 Urethroplasty with tubularization of posterior urethra and/or lower bladder for incontinence (eg, Tenago, Leadbetter procedure)

53445 Insertion of inflatable urethral/bladder neck sphincter, including placement of pump, reservoir, and cuff

53446 Removal of inflatable urethral/bladder neck sphincter, including pump, reservoir, and cuff

53447 Removal and replacement of inflatable urethral/bladder neck sphincter including pump, reservoir, and cuff at the same operative session

53448 Removal and replacement of inflatable urethral/bladder neck sphincter including pump, reservoir, and cuff through an infected field at the same operative session including irrigation and debridement of infected tissue

53449 Repair of inflatable urethral/bladder neck sphincter, including pump, reservoir, and cuff

53450 Urethromeatoplasty, with mucosal advancement

53460 Urethromeatoplasty, with partial excision of distal urethral segment (Richardson type procedure)

53505 Urethrorrhaphy, suture of urethral wound or injury; penile

53510 perineal

53515 prostatomembranous

53520 Closure of urethrostomy or urethrocutaneous fistula, male (separate procedure)

Manipulation

53600 Dilation of urethral stricture by passage of sound or urethral dilator, male; initial

53601 subsequent

53605 Dilation of urethral stricture or vesical neck by passage of sound or urethral dilator, male, general or conduction (spinal) anesthesia

53620 Dilation of urethral stricture by passage of filiform and follower, male; initial

53621 subsequent

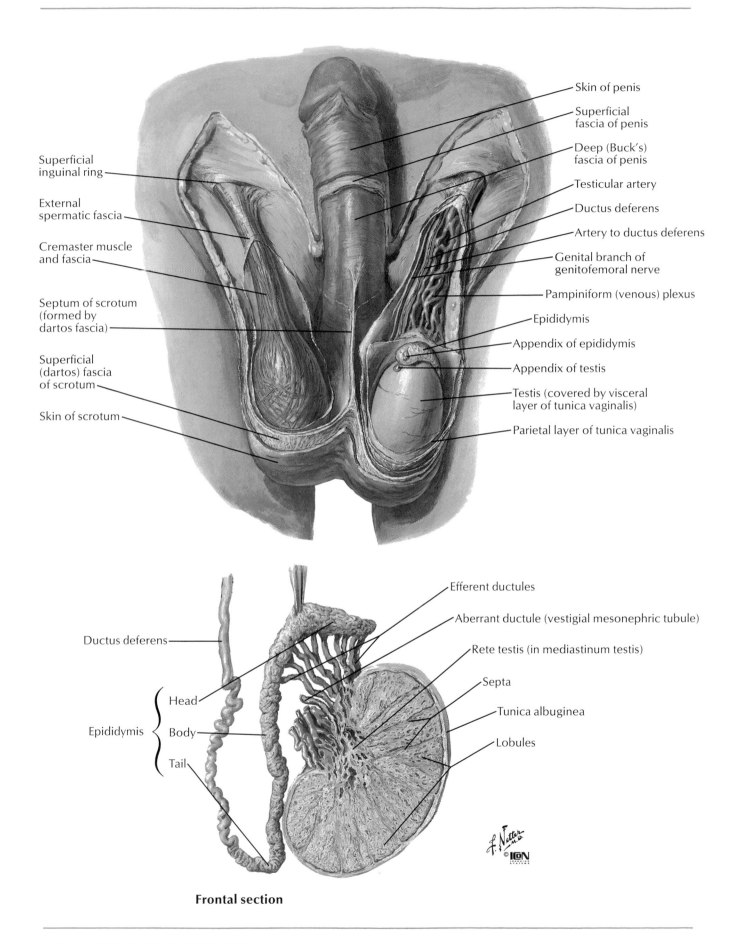

Skin of penis

Superficial fascia of penis

Deep (Buck's) fascia of penis

Testicular artery

Ductus deferens

Artery to ductus deferens

Genital branch of genitofemoral nerve

Pampiniform (venous) plexus

Epididymis

Appendix of epididymis

Appendix of testis

Testis (covered by visceral layer of tunica vaginalis)

Parietal layer of tunica vaginalis

Superficial inguinal ring

External spermatic fascia

Cremaster muscle and fascia

Septum of scrotum (formed by dartos fascia)

Superficial (dartos) fascia of scrotum

Skin of scrotum

Efferent ductules

Aberrant ductule (vestigial mesonephric tubule)

Rete testis (in mediastinum testis)

Septa

Tunica albuginea

Lobules

Ductus deferens

Epididymis

Head

Body

Tail

Frontal section

ANESTHESIA

Lower Abdomen

00840 Anesthesia for intraperitoneal procedures in lower abdomen including laparoscopy; not otherwise specified

00860 Anesthesia for extraperitoneal procedures in lower abdomen, including urinary tract; not otherwise specified

Perineum

00920 Anesthesia for procedures on male genitalia (including open urethral procedures); not otherwise specified

00921   unilateral or bilateral

00922   seminal vesicles

00924   undescended testis, unilateral or bilateral

00926   radical orchiectomy, inguinal

00928   radical orchiectomy, abdominal

00930   orchiopexy, unilateral or bilateral

SURGERY

Male Genital System

Testis
Excision

54500 Biopsy of testis, needle (separate procedure)

54505 Biopsy of testis, incisional (separate procedure)

54512 Excision of extraparenchymal lesion of testis

54520 Orchiectomy, simple (including subcapsular), with or without testicular prosthesis, scrotal or inguinal approach

54522 Orchiectomy, partial

54530 Orchiectomy, radical, for tumor; inguinal approach

54535   with abdominal exploration

54550 Exploration for undescended testis (inguinal or scrotal area)

54560 Exploration for undescended testis with abdominal exploration

Repair

54600 Reduction of torsion of testis, surgical, with or without fixation of contralateral testis

54620 Fixation of contralateral testis (separate procedure)

54640 Orchiopexy, inguinal approach, with or without hernia repair

54650 Orchiopexy, abdominal approach, for intra-abdominal testis (eg, Fowler-Stephens)

54660 Insertion of testicular prosthesis (separate procedure)

54670 Suture or repair of testicular injury

54680 Transplantation of testis(es) to thigh (because of scrotal destruction)

Laparoscopy

54690 Laparoscopy, surgical; orchiectomy

54692ᴾ   orchiopexy for intra-abdominal testis

Epididymis
Incision

54700 Incision and drainage of epididymis, testis and/or scrotal space (eg, abscess or hematoma)

Excision

54800 Biopsy of epididymis, needle

54820 Exploration of epididymis, with or without biopsy

54830 Excision of local lesion of epididymis

54840 Excision of spermatocele, with or without epididymectomy

54860 Epididymectomy; unilateral

54861   bilateral

Repair

54900 Epididymovasostomy, anastomosis of epididymis to vas deferens; unilateral

54901   bilateral

Tunica Vaginalis
Incision

55000 Puncture aspiration of hydrocele, tunica vaginalis, with or without injection of medication

Excision

55040 Excision of hydrocele; unilateral

55041   bilateral

Repair

55060 Repair of tunica vaginalis hydrocele (Bottle type)

Scrotum
Incision

55100 Drainage of scrotal wall abscess

55110 Scrotal exploration

55120 Removal of foreign body in scrotum

Excision

55150 Resection of scrotum

Repair

55175 Scrotoplasty; simple

55180   complicated

Vas Deferens
Incision

55200 Vasotomy, cannulization with or without incision of vas, unilateral or bilateral (separate procedure)

Excision

55250 Vasectomy, unilateral or bilateral (separate procedure), including postoperative semen examination(s)

Introduction

55300 Vasotomy for vasograms, seminal vesiculograms, or epididymograms, unilateral or bilateral

Repair

55400 Vasovasostomy, vasovasorrhaphy

Suture

55450 Ligation (percutaneous) of vas deferens, unilateral or bilateral (separate procedure)

Spermatic Cord
Excision

55500 Excision of hydrocele of spermatic cord, unilateral (separate procedure)

55520 Excision of lesion of spermatic cord (separate procedure)

55530 Excision of varicocele or ligation of spermatic veins for varicocele; (separate procedure)

55535   abdominal approach

55540   with hernia repair

Laparoscopy

55550 Laparoscopy, surgical, with ligation of spermatic veins for varicocele

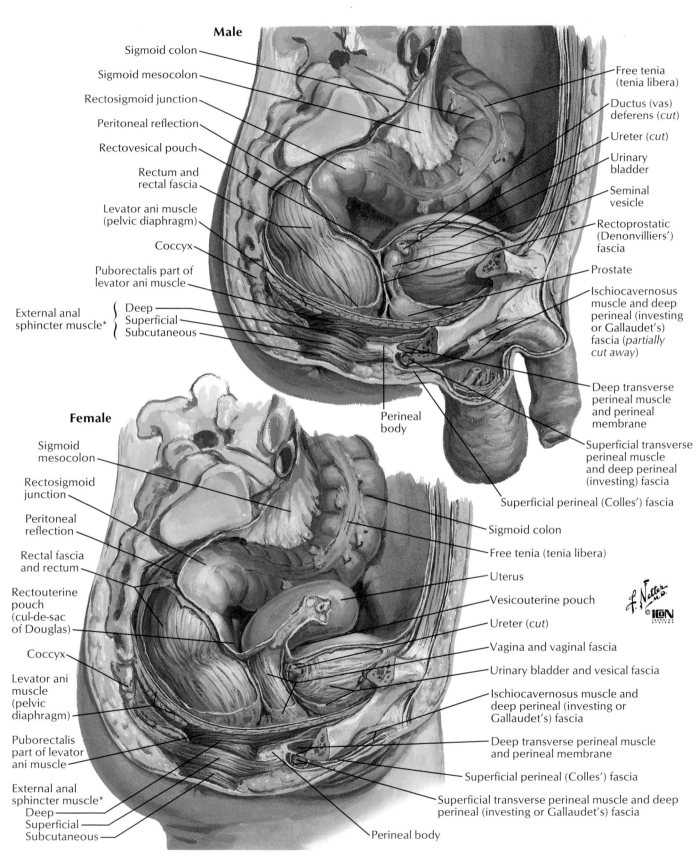

Male

Sigmoid colon

Sigmoid mesocolon

Rectosigmoid junction

Peritoneal reflection

Rectovesical pouch

Rectum and rectal fascia

Levator ani muscle (pelvic diaphragm)

Coccyx

Puborectalis part of levator ani muscle

External anal sphincter muscle* { Deep — Superficial — Subcutaneous —

Free tenia (tenia libera)

Ductus (vas) deferens (cut)

Ureter (cut)

Urinary bladder

Seminal vesicle

Rectoprostatic (Denonvilliers') fascia

Prostate

Ischiocavernosus muscle and deep perineal (investing or Gallaudet's) fascia (partially cut away)

Deep transverse perineal muscle and perineal membrane

Superficial transverse perineal muscle and deep perineal (investing) fascia

Perineal body

Superficial perineal (Colles') fascia

Female

Sigmoid mesocolon

Rectosigmoid junction

Peritoneal reflection

Rectal fascia and rectum

Rectouterine pouch (cul-de-sac of Douglas)

Coccyx

Levator ani muscle (pelvic diaphragm)

Puborectalis part of levator ani muscle

External anal sphincter muscle*
Deep
Superficial
Subcutaneous

Sigmoid colon

Free tenia (tenia libera)

Uterus

Vesicouterine pouch

Ureter (cut)

Vagina and vaginal fascia

Urinary bladder and vesical fascia

Ischiocavernosus muscle and deep perineal (investing or Gallaudet's) fascia

Deep transverse perineal muscle and perineal membrane

Superficial perineal (Colles') fascia

Superficial transverse perineal muscle and deep perineal (investing or Gallaudet's) fascia

Perineal body

*Parts variable and often indistinct

ANESTHESIA

Lower Abdomen

00840	Anesthesia for intraperitoneal procedures in lower abdomen including laparoscopy; not otherwise specified
00844	abdominoperineal resection
00848	pelvic exenteration

Perineum

00902	Anesthesia for; anorectal procedure
00904	radical perineal procedure

SURGERY

Digestive System

Rectum

Incision

45000	Transrectal drainage of pelvic abscess
45005	Incision and drainage of submucosal abscess, rectum
45020	Incision and drainage of deep supralevator, pelvirectal, or retrorectal abscess

Excision

45100	Biopsy of anorectal wall, anal approach (eg, congenital megacolon)
45108	Anorectal myomectomy
45110	Proctectomy; complete, combined abdominoperineal, with colostomy
45111	partial resection of rectum, transabdominal approach
45112	Proctectomy, combined abdominoperineal, pull-through procedure (eg, colo-anal anastomosis)
45113	Proctectomy, partial, with rectal mucosectomy, ileoanal anastomosis, creation of ileal reservoir (S or J), with or without loop ileostomy
45114	Proctectomy, partial, with anastomosis; abdominal and transsacral approach
45116	transsacral approach only (Kraske type)
45119	Proctectomy, combined abdominoperineal pull-through procedure (eg, colo-anal anastomosis), with creation of colonic reservoir (eg, J-pouch), with or without proximal diverting ostomy
45120	Proctectomy, complete (for congenital megacolon), abdominal and perineal approach; with pull-through procedure and anastomosis (eg, Swenson, Duhamel, or Soave type operation)
45121	with subtotal or total colectomy, with multiple biopsies
45123	Proctectomy, partial, without anastomosis, perineal approach
45126	Pelvic exenteration for colorectal malignancy, with proctectomy (with or without colostomy), with removal of bladder and ureteral transplantations, and/or hysterectomy, or cervicectomy, with or without removal of tube(s), with or without removal of ovary(s), or any combination thereof
45130	Excision of rectal procidentia, with anastomosis; perineal approach

45135	abdominal and perineal approach
45136	Excision of ileoanal reservoir with ileostomy
45150	Division of stricture of rectum
45160	Excision of rectal tumor by proctotomy, transsacral or transcoccygeal approach
45170	Excision of rectal tumor, transanal approach

Destruction

45190	Destruction of rectal tumor (eg, electrodessication, electrosurgery, laser ablation, laser resection, cryosurgery) transanal approach

Endoscopy

45300	Proctosigmoidoscopy, rigid; diagnostic, with or without collection of specimen(s) by brushing or washing (separate procedure)
45303	with dilation (eg, balloon, guide wire, bougie)
45305	with biopsy, single or multiple
45307	with removal of foreign body
45308	with removal of single tumor, polyp, or other lesion by hot biopsy forceps or bipolar cautery
45309	with removal of single tumor, polyp, or other lesion by snare technique
45315	with removal of multiple tumors, polyps, or other lesions by hot biopsy forceps, bipolar cautery or snare technique
45317	with control of bleeding (eg, injection, bipolar cautery, unipolar cautery, laser, heater probe, stapler, plasma coagulator)
45320	with ablation of tumor(s), polyp(s), or other lesion(s) not amenable to removal by hot biopsy forceps, bipolar cautery or snare technique (eg, laser)
45321	with decompression of volvulus
45327	with transendoscopic stent placement (includes predilation)

Repair

45500	Proctoplasty; for stenosis
45505	for prolapse of mucous membrane
45520	Perirectal injection of sclerosing solution for prolapse
45540	Proctopexy for prolapse; abdominal approach
45541	perineal approach
45550	Proctopexy combined with sigmoid resection, abdominal approach
45560	Repair of rectocele (separate procedure)
45562	Exploration, repair, and presacral drainage for rectal injury;
45563	with colostomy
45800	Closure of rectovesical fistula;
45805	with colostomy
45820	Closure of rectourethral fistula;
45825	with colostomy

Manipulation

45900	Reduction of procidentia (separate procedure) under anesthesia
45905	Dilation of anal sphincter (separate procedure) under anesthesia other than local
45910	Dilation of rectal stricture (separate procedure) under anesthesia other than local
45915	Removal of fecal impaction or foreign body (separate procedure) under anesthesia

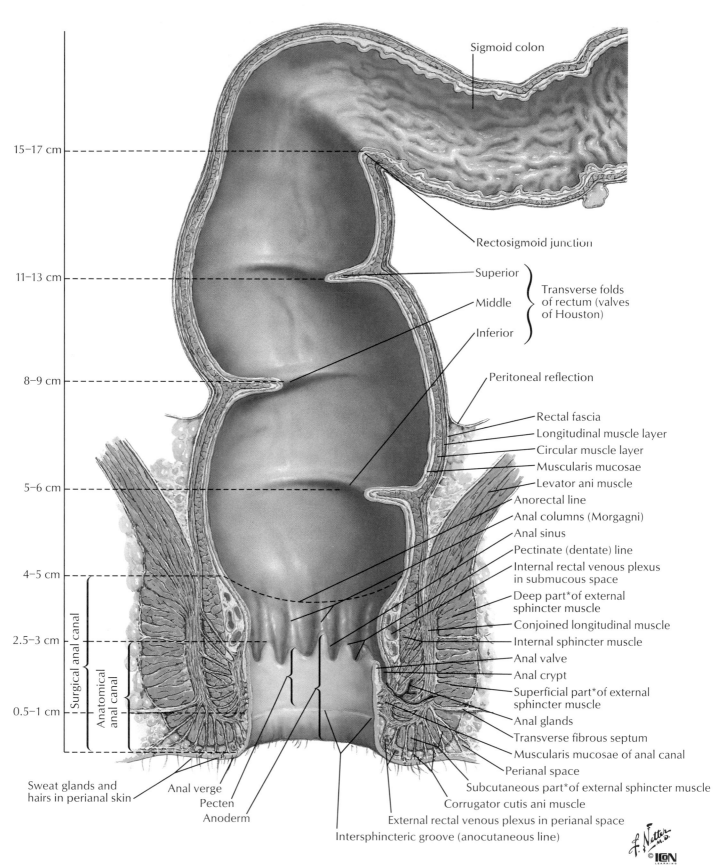

Sigmoid colon

Rectosigmoid junction

Superior

Middle

Inferior

Transverse folds of rectum (valves of Houston)

Peritoneal reflection

Rectal fascia

Longitudinal muscle layer

Circular muscle layer

Muscularis mucosae

Levator ani muscle

Anorectal line

Anal columns (Morgagni)

Anal sinus

Pectinate (dentate) line

Internal rectal venous plexus in submucous space

Deep part*of external sphincter muscle

Conjoined longitudinal muscle

Internal sphincter muscle

Anal valve

Anal crypt

Superficial part*of external sphincter muscle

Anal glands

Transverse fibrous septum

Muscularis mucosae of anal canal

Perianal space

Subcutaneous part*of external sphincter muscle

Corrugator cutis ani muscle

External rectal venous plexus in perianal space

Intersphincteric groove (anocutaneous line)

15–17 cm

11–13 cm

8–9 cm

5–6 cm

4–5 cm

2.5–3 cm

0.5–1 cm

Surgical anal canal

Anatomical anal canal

Sweat glands and hairs in perianal skin

Anal verge

Pecten

Anoderm

*Parts variable and often indistinct

ANESTHESIA

Thorax (Chest Wall and Shoulder Girdle)

00400 Anesthesia for procedures on the integumentary system on the extremities, anterior trunk and perineum; not otherwise specified

Perineum

00902 Anesthesia for; anorectal procedure
00904   radical perineal procedure

SURGERY

Digestive System

Rectum

Excision

45100 Biopsy of anorectal wall, anal approach (eg, congenital megacolon)
45108 Anorectal myomectomy

Manipulation

45905 Dilation of anal sphincter (separate procedure) under anesthesia other than local
45910 Dilation of rectal stricture (separate procedure) under anesthesia other than local
45915 Removal of fecal impaction or foreign body (separate procedure) under anesthesia

Anus

Incision

46020ᴾ Placement of seton
46030 Removal of anal seton, other marker
46040 Incision and drainage of ischiorectal and/or perirectal abscess (separate procedure)
46045 Incision and drainage of intramural, intramuscular, or submucosal abscess, transanal, under anesthesia
46050 Incision and drainage, perianal abscess, superficial
46060 Incision and drainage of ischiorectal or intramural abscess, with fistulectomy or fistulotomy, submuscular, with or without placement of seton
46070 Incision, anal septum (infant)
46080 Sphincterotomy, anal, division of sphincter (separate procedure)
46083 Incision of thrombosed hemorrhoid, external

Excision

46200 Fissurectomy, with or without sphincterotomy
46210 Cryptectomy; single
46211   multiple (separate procedure)
46220 Papillectomy or excision of single tag, anus (separate procedure)
46221 Hemorrhoidectomy, by simple ligature (eg, rubber band)
46230 Excision of external hemorrhoid tags and/or multiple papillae
46250 Hemorrhoidectomy, external, complete
46255 Hemorrhoidectomy, internal and external, simple;
46257   with fissurectomy
46258   with fistulectomy, with or without fissurectomy

46260 Hemorrhoidectomy, internal and external, complex or extensive;
46261   with fissurectomy
46262   with fistulectomy, with or without fissurectomy
46270 Surgical treatment of anal fistula (fistulectomy/ fistulotomy); subcutaneous
46275   submuscular
46280   complex or multiple, with or without placement of seton
46285   second stage
46288 Closure of anal fistula with rectal advancement flap
46320 Enucleation or excision of external thrombotic hemorrhoid

Introduction

46500 Injection of sclerosing solution, hemorrhoids

Endoscopy

46600 Anoscopy; diagnostic, with or without collection of specimen(s) by brushing or washing (separate procedure)
46604   with dilation (eg, balloon, guide wire, bougie)
46606   with biopsy, single or multiple
46608   with removal of foreign body
46610   with removal of single tumor, polyp, or other lesion by hot biopsy forceps or bipolar cautery
46611   with removal of single tumor, polyp, or other lesion by snare technique
46612   with removal of multiple tumors, polyps, or other lesions by hot biopsy forceps, bipolar cautery or snare technique
46614   with control of bleeding (eg, injection, bipolar cautery, unipolar cautery, laser, heater probe, stapler, plasma coagulator)
46615   with ablation of tumor(s), polyp(s), or other lesion(s) not amenable to removal by hot biopsy forceps, bipolar cautery or snare technique

Repair

46700 Anoplasty, plastic operation for stricture; adult
46705   infant
46706 Repair of anal fistula with fibrin glue
46715 Repair of low imperforate anus; with anoperineal fistula (cut-back procedure)
46716   with transposition of anoperineal or anovestibular fistula
46730 Repair of high imperforate anus without fistula; perineal or sacroperineal approach
46735   combined transabdominal and sacroperineal approaches
46740 Repair of high imperforate anus with rectourethral or rectovaginal fistula; perineal or sacroperineal approach
46742   combined transabdominal and sacroperineal approaches
46744 Repair of cloacal anomaly by anorectovaginoplasty and urethroplasty, sacroperineal approach

(Repair continued on next page)

(Repair continued from previous page)

46746   Repair of cloacal anomaly by anorectovaginoplasty and urethroplasty, combined abdominal and sacroperineal approach;

46748   with vaginal lengthening by intestinal graft or pedicle flaps

46750   Sphincteroplasty, anal, for incontinence or prolapse; adult

46751   child

46753   Graft (Thiersch operation) for rectal incontinence and/or prolapse

46754   Removal of Thiersch wire or suture, anal canal

46760   Sphincteroplasty, anal, for incontinence, adult; muscle transplant

46761   levator muscle imbrication (Park posterior anal repair)

46762   implantation artificial sphincter

Destruction

46900   Destruction of lesion(s), anus (eg, condyloma, papilloma, molluscum contagiosum, herpetic vesicle), simple; chemical

46910   electrodesiccation

46916   cryosurgery

46917   laser surgery

46922   surgical excision

46924   Destruction of lesion(s), anus (eg, condyloma, papilloma, molluscum contagiosum, herpetic vesicle), extensive (eg, laser surgery, electrosurgery, cryosurgery, chemosurgery)

46934   Destruction of hemorrhoids, any method; internal

46935   external

46936   internal and external

46937   Cryosurgery of rectal tumor; benign

46938   malignant

46940   Curettage or cautery of anal fissure, including dilation of anal sphincter (separate procedure); initial

46942   subsequent

Suture

46945   Ligation of internal hemorrhoids; single procedure

46946   multiple procedures

46947   Hemorrhoidopexy (eg, for prolapsing internal hemorrhoids) by stapling

Posterior view

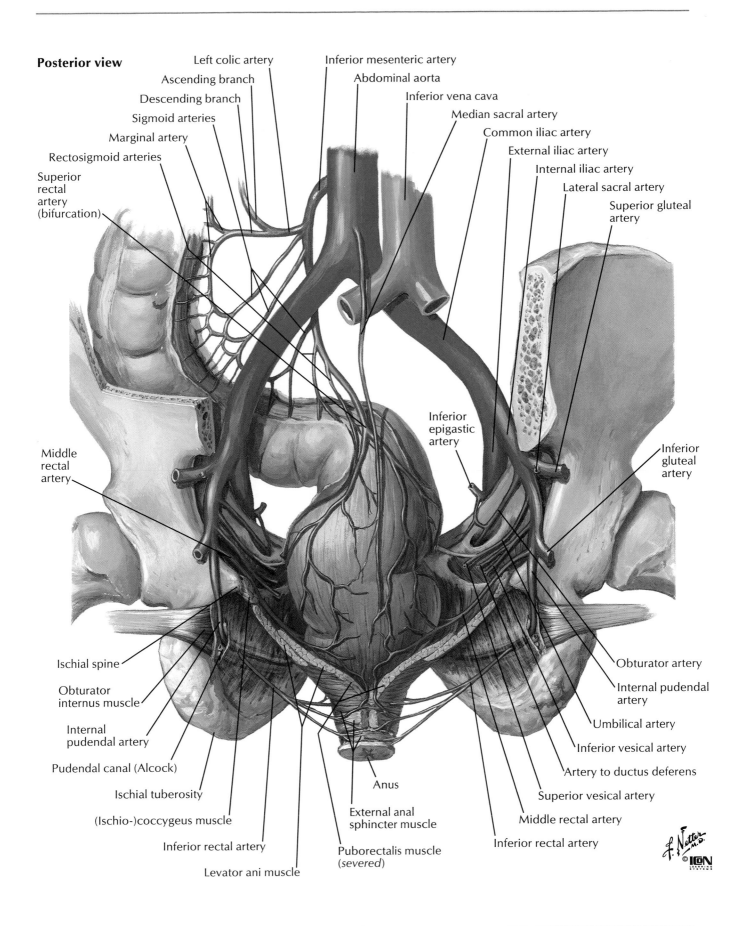

Left colic artery

Ascending branch

Descending branch

Sigmoid arteries

Marginal artery

Rectosigmoid arteries

Superior rectal artery (bifurcation)

Inferior mesenteric artery

Abdominal aorta

Inferior vena cava

Median sacral artery

Common iliac artery

External iliac artery

Internal iliac artery

Lateral sacral artery

Superior gluteal artery

Middle rectal artery

Inferior epigastic artery

Inferior gluteal artery

Ischial spine

Obturator internus muscle

Internal pudendal artery

Pudendal canal (Alcock)

Ischial tuberosity

(Ischio-)coccygeus muscle

Inferior rectal artery

Levator ani muscle

Anus

External anal sphincter muscle

Puborectalis muscle (severed)

Obturator artery

Internal pudendal artery

Umbilical artery

Inferior vesical artery

Artery to ductus deferens

Superior vesical artery

Middle rectal artery

Inferior rectal artery

ANESTHESIA

Upper Abdomen

00770 Anesthesia for all procedures on major abdominal blood vessels

Lower Abdomen

00880 Anesthesia for procedures on major lower abdominal vessels; not otherwise specified

00882 inferior vena cava ligation

Perineum

00902 Anesthesia for; anorectal procedure

Upper Leg (Except Knee)

01270 Anesthesia for procedures involving arteries of upper leg, including bypass graft; not otherwise specified

01274 femoral artery embolectomy

Radiological Procedures

01916 Anesthesia for diagnostic arteriography/venography

01924 Anesthesia for therapeutic interventional radiologic procedures involving the arterial system; not otherwise specified

01930 Anesthesia for therapeutic interventional radiologic procedures involving the venous/lymphatic system (not to include access to the central circulation); not otherwise specified

SURGERY

Cardiovascular System

Arteries and Veins
Embolectomy/Thrombectomy

Arterial, With or Without Catheter

34151 Embolectomy or thrombectomy, with or without catheter; renal, celiac, mesentery, aortoiliac artery, by abdominal incision

34201 femoropopliteal, aortoiliac artery, by leg incision

Venous, Direct or With Catheter

34401 Thrombectomy, direct or with catheter; vena cava, iliac vein, by abdominal incision

Direct Repair of Aneurysm or Excision (Partial or Total) and Graft Insertion for Aneurysm, Pseudoaneurysm, Ruptured Aneurysm, and Associated Occlusive Disease

35131 Direct repair of aneurysm, pseudoaneurysm, or excision (partial or total) and graft insertion, with or without patch graft; for aneurysm, pseudoaneurysm, and associated occlusive disease, iliac artery (common, hypogastric, external)

35132 for ruptured aneurysm, iliac artery (common, hypogastric, external)

Thromboendarterectomy

35331 Thromboendarterectomy, with or without patch graft; abdominal aorta

35351 iliac

35361 combined aortoiliac

Transluminal Angioplasty

Open

35454 Transluminal balloon angioplasty, open; iliac

35460 venous

Percutaneous

35473ᴾ Transluminal balloon angioplasty, percutaneous; iliac

35476 venous

Transluminal Atherectomy

Open

35482 Transluminal peripheral atherectomy, open; iliac

Percutaneous

35492 Transluminal peripheral atherectomy, percutaneous; iliac

Bypass Graft

Vein

35541 Bypass graft, with vein; aortoiliac or bi-iliac

35563 ilioiliac

Other Than Vein

35631 Bypass graft, with other than vein; aortoceliac, aortomesenteric, aortorenal

35641 aortoiliac or bi-iliac

35663 ilioiliac

Exploration/Revision

35761 Exploration (not followed by surgical repair), with or without lysis of artery; other vessels

35875 Thrombectomy of arterial or venous graft (other than hemodialysis graft or fistula);

35876 with revision of arterial or venous graft

Intra-Arterial—Intra-Aortic

36245 Selective catheter placement, arterial system; each first order abdominal, pelvic, or lower extremity artery branch, within a vascular family

36246 initial second order abdominal, pelvic, or lower extremity artery branch, within a vascular family

36247 initial third order or more selective abdominal, pelvic, or lower extremity artery branch, within a vascular family

36248 additional second order, third order, and beyond, abdominal, pelvic, or lower extremity artery branch, within a vascular family (List in addition to code for initial second or third order vessel as appropriate)

Ligation

37660 Ligation of common iliac vein

Digestive System

Anus
Incision

46083 Incision of thrombosed hemorrhoid, external

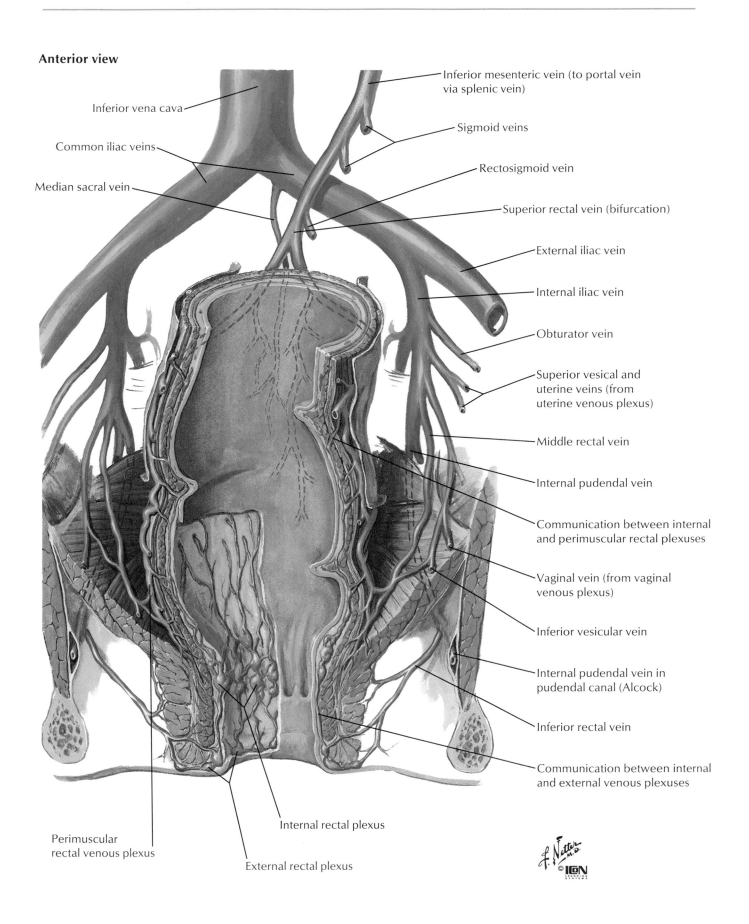

Anterior view

Inferior vena cava

Common iliac veins

Median sacral vein

Inferior mesenteric vein (to portal vein via splenic vein)

Sigmoid veins

Rectosigmoid vein

Superior rectal vein (bifurcation)

External iliac vein

Internal iliac vein

Obturator vein

Superior vesical and uterine veins (from uterine venous plexus)

Middle rectal vein

Internal pudendal vein

Communication between internal and perimuscular rectal plexuses

Vaginal vein (from vaginal venous plexus)

Inferior vesicular vein

Internal pudendal vein in pudendal canal (Alcock)

Inferior rectal vein

Communication between internal and external venous plexuses

Perimuscular rectal venous plexus

Internal rectal plexus

External rectal plexus

Plate 142: Arteries and Veins of Rectum and Anal Canal

Excision

46221   Hemorrhoidectomy, by simple ligature (eg, rubber band)

46230   Excision of external hemorrhoid tags and/or multiple papillae

46250   Hemorrhoidectomy, external, complete

46255   Hemorrhoidectomy, internal and external, simple;

46257   with fissurectomy

46258   with fistulectomy, with or without fissurectomy

46260   Hemorrhoidectomy, internal and external, complex or extensive;

46261   with fissurectomy

46262   with fistulectomy, with or without fissurectomy

46320   Enucleation or excision of external thrombotic hemorrhoid

Introduction

46500   Injection of sclerosing solution, hemorrhoids

Destruction

46924   Destruction of lesion(s), anus (eg, condyloma, papilloma, molluscum contagiosum, herpetic vesicle), extensive (eg, laser surgery, electrosurgery, cryosurgery, chemosurgery)

46934   Destruction of hemorrhoids, any method; internal

46935   external

46936   internal and external

Suture

46945   Ligation of internal hemorrhoids; single procedure

46946   multiple procedures

46947   Hemorrhoidopexy (eg, for prolapsing internal hemorrhoids) by stapling

Anterior view

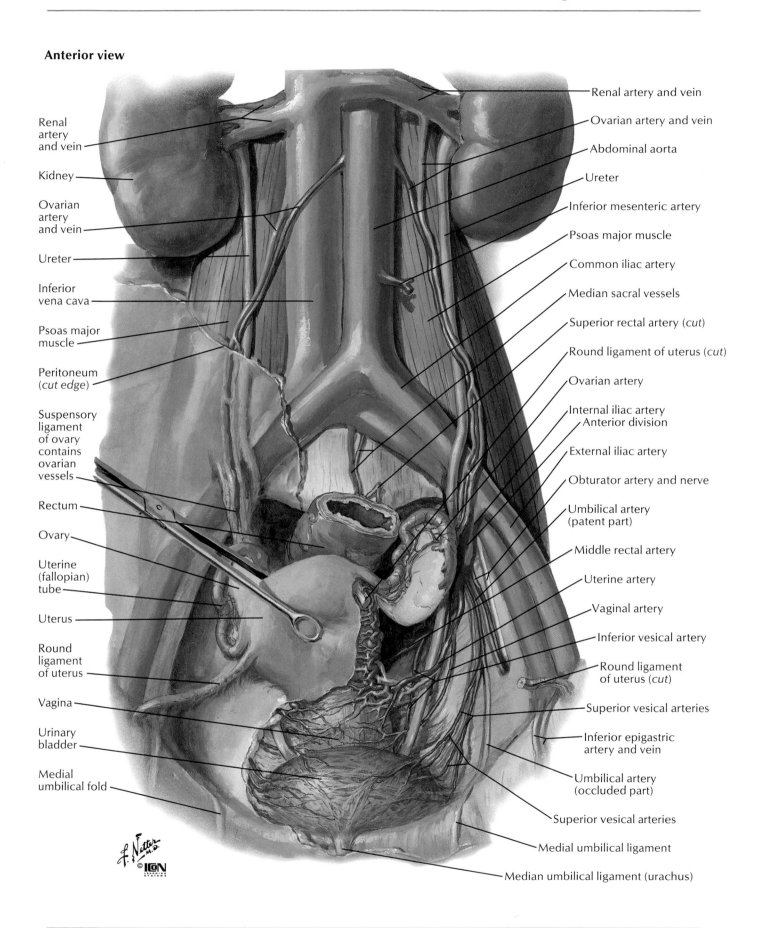

Renal artery and vein

Renal artery and vein

Ovarian artery and vein

Kidney

Abdominal aorta

Ovarian artery and vein

Ureter

Ureter

Inferior mesenteric artery

Inferior vena cava

Psoas major muscle

Psoas major muscle

Common iliac artery

Peritoneum (*cut edge*)

Median sacral vessels

Superior rectal artery (*cut*)

Suspensory ligament of ovary contains ovarian vessels

Round ligament of uterus (*cut*)

Ovarian artery

Internal iliac artery
Anterior division

Rectum

External iliac artery

Ovary

Obturator artery and nerve

Uterine (fallopian) tube

Umbilical artery (patent part)

Uterus

Middle rectal artery

Round ligament of uterus

Uterine artery

Vagina

Vaginal artery

Urinary bladder

Inferior vesical artery

Round ligament of uterus (*cut*)

Medial umbilical fold

Superior vesical arteries

Inferior epigastric artery and vein

Umbilical artery (occluded part)

Superior vesical arteries

Medial umbilical ligament

Median umbilical ligament (urachus)

ANESTHESIA

Upper Abdomen

00770 Anesthesia for all procedures on major abdominal blood vessels

Lower Abdomen

00880 Anesthesia for procedures on major lower abdominal vessels; not otherwise specified

00882 inferior vena cava ligation

Radiological Procedures

01916 Anesthesia for diagnostic arteriography/venography

01924 Anesthesia for therapeutic interventional radiologic procedures involving the arterial system; not otherwise specified

01926 intracranial, intracardiac, or aortic

01930 Anesthesia for therapeutic interventional radiologic procedures involving the venous/lymphatic system (not to include access to the central circulation); not otherwise specified

SURGERY

Cardiovascular System

Arteries and Veins
Embolectomy/Thrombectomy

Arterial, With or Without Catheter

34151 Embolectomy or thrombectomy, with or without catheter; renal, celiac, mesentery, aortoiliac artery, by abdominal incision

Venous, Direct or With Catheter

34401 Thrombectomy, direct or with catheter; vena cava, iliac vein, by abdominal incision

Venous Reconstruction

34502 Reconstruction of vena cava, any method

Endovascular Repair of Abdominal Aortic Aneurysm

34800 Endovascular repair of infrarenal abdominal aortic aneurysm or dissection; using aorto-aortic tube prosthesis

34802^P using modular bifurcated prosthesis (one docking limb)

34803 using modular bifurcated prosthesis (two docking limbs)

34804 using unibody bifurcated prosthesis

34805 using aorto-uniiliac or aorto-unifemoral prosthesis

34808 Endovascular placement of iliac artery occlusion device (List separately in addition to code for primary procedure)

34820 Open iliac artery exposure for delivery of endovascular prosthesis or iliac occlusion during endovascular therapy, by abdominal or retroperitoneal incision, unilateral

34825 Placement of proximal or distal extension prosthesis for endovascular repair of infrarenal abdominal aortic or iliac aneurysm, false aneurysm, or dissection; initial vessel

34826 each additional vessel (List separately in addition to code for primary procedure)

34833 Open iliac artery exposure with creation of conduit for delivery of infrarenal aortic or iliac endovascular prosthesis, by abdominal or retroperitoneal incision, unilateral

Endovascular Repair of Iliac Aneurysm

34900 Endovascular graft placement for repair of iliac artery (eg, aneurysm, pseudoaneurysm, arteriovenous malformation, trauma)

Direct Repair of Aneurysm or Excision (Partial or Total) and Graft Insertion for Aneurysm, Pseudoaneurysm, Ruptured Aneurysm, and Associated Occlusive Disease

35081 Direct repair of aneurysm, pseudoaneurysm, or excision (partial or total) and graft insertion, with or without patch graft; for aneurysm, pseudoaneurysm, and associated occlusive disease, abdominal aorta

35082 for ruptured aneurysm, abdominal aorta

35102 for aneurysm, pseudoaneurysm, and associated occlusive disease, abdominal aorta involving iliac vessels (common, hypogastric, external)

35103 for ruptured aneurysm, abdominal aorta involving iliac vessels (common, hypogastric, external)

35131 for aneurysm, pseudoaneurysm, and associated occlusive disease, iliac artery (common, hypogastric, external)

35132 for ruptured aneurysm, iliac artery (common, hypogastric, external)

Repair Arteriovenous Fistula

35182 Repair, congenital arteriovenous fistula; thorax and abdomen

35189 Repair, acquired or traumatic arteriovenous fistula; thorax and abdomen

Repair Blood Vessel Other Than for Fistula, With or Without Patch Angioplasty

35221 Repair blood vessel, direct; intra-abdominal

35251 Repair blood vessel with vein graft; intra-abdominal

35281 Repair blood vessel with graft other than vein; intra-abdominal

Thromboendarterectomy

35331 Thromboendarterectomy, with or without patch graft; abdominal aorta

35351 iliac

35361 combined aortoiliac

Transluminal Angioplasty

Open

35452 Transluminal balloon angioplasty, open; aortic

35454 iliac

35460 venous

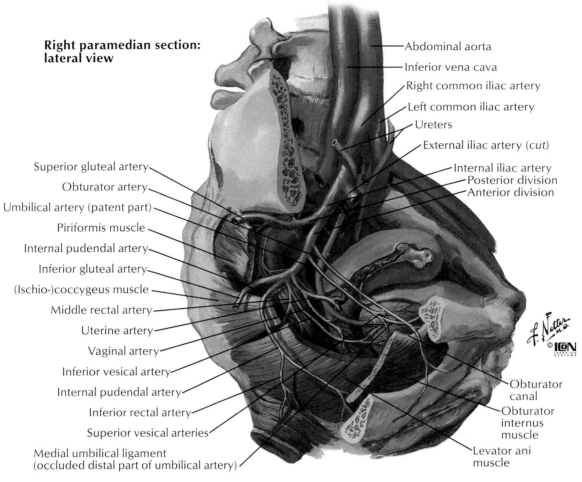

Right paramedian section: lateral view

Abdominal aorta
Inferior vena cava
Right common iliac artery
Left common iliac artery
Ureters
External iliac artery (cut)
Internal iliac artery
Posterior division
Anterior division

Superior gluteal artery
Obturator artery
Umbilical artery (patent part)
Piriformis muscle
Internal pudendal artery
Inferior gluteal artery
(Ischio-)coccygeus muscle
Middle rectal artery
Uterine artery
Vaginal artery
Inferior vesical artery
Internal pudendal artery
Inferior rectal artery
Superior vesical arteries
Medial umbilical ligament
(occluded distal part of umbilical artery)

Obturator canal
Obturator internus muscle
Levator ani muscle

Percutaneous

35472	Transluminal balloon angioplasty, percutaneous; aortic
35473[P]	iliac
35476	venous

Transluminal Atherectomy

Open

35481	Transluminal peripheral atherectomy, open; aortic
35482	iliac

Percutaneous

35491	Transluminal peripheral atherectomy, percutaneous; aortic
35492	iliac

Bypass Graft

Vein

35541	Bypass graft, with vein; aortoiliac or bi-iliac

Other Than Vein

35641	Bypass graft, with other than vein; aortoiliac or bi-iliac
35663	ilioiliac

Exploration/Revision

35761	Exploration (not followed by surgical repair), with or without lysis of artery; other vessels
35840	Exploration for postoperative hemorrhage, thrombosis or infection; abdomen

35875	Thrombectomy of arterial or venous graft (other than hemodialysis graft or fistula);
35876	with revision of arterial or venous graft
35907	Excision of infected graft; abdomen

Intravenous

36010	Introduction of catheter, superior or inferior vena cava
36011	Selective catheter placement, venous system; first order branch (eg, renal vein, jugular vein)
36012	second order, or more selective, branch (eg, left adrenal vein, petrosal sinus)

Intra-arterial—Intra-Aortic

36200	Introduction of catheter, aorta
36245	Selective catheter placement, arterial system; each first order abdominal, pelvic, or lower extremity artery branch, within a vascular family
36246	initial second order abdominal, pelvic, or lower extremity artery branch, within a vascular family
36247	initial third order or more selective abdominal, pelvic, or lower extremity artery branch, within a vascular family
36248	additional second order, third order, and beyond, abdominal, pelvic, or lower extremity artery branch, within a vascular family (List in addition to code for initial second or third order vessel as appropriate)

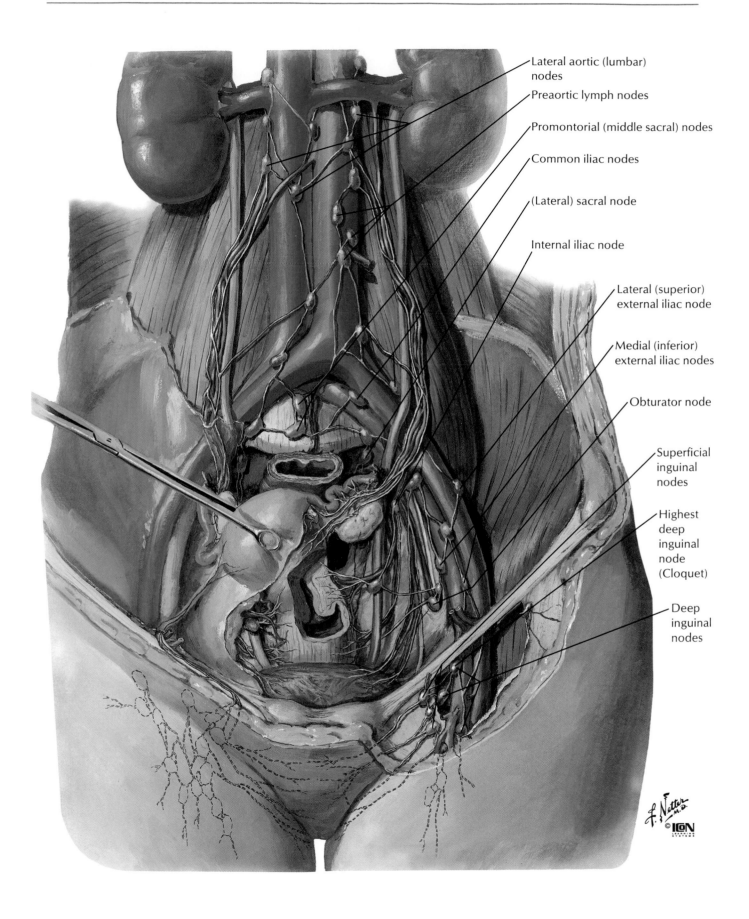

Lateral aortic (lumbar) nodes

Preaortic lymph nodes

Promontorial (middle sacral) nodes

Common iliac nodes

(Lateral) sacral node

Internal iliac node

Lateral (superior) external iliac node

Medial (inferior) external iliac nodes

Obturator node

Superficial inguinal nodes

Highest deep inguinal node (Cloquet)

Deep inguinal nodes

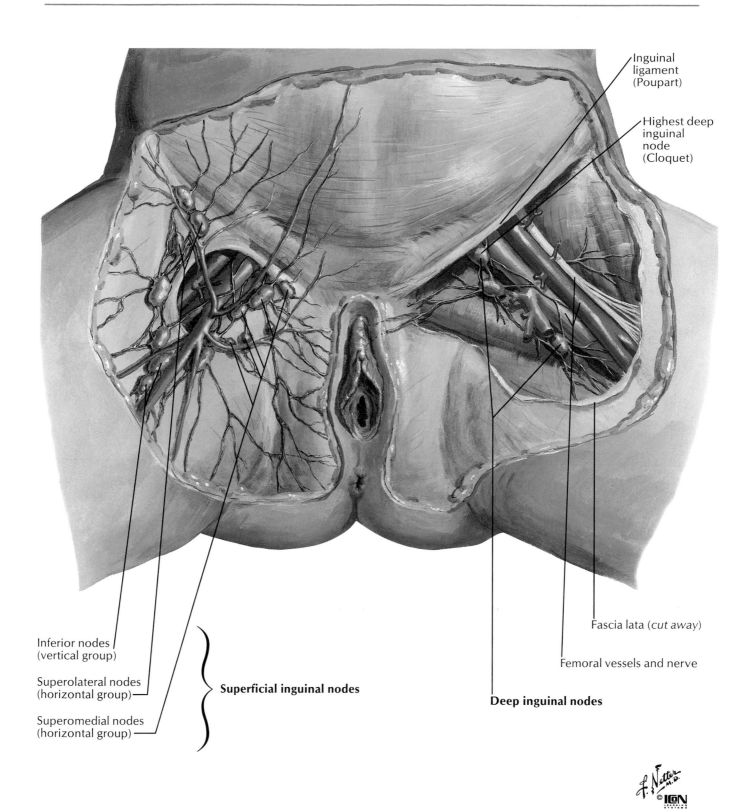

Inguinal ligament (Poupart)

Highest deep inguinal node (Cloquet)

Fascia lata (*cut away*)

Femoral vessels and nerve

Deep inguinal nodes

Inferior nodes (vertical group)

Superolateral nodes (horizontal group)

Superomedial nodes (horizontal group)

Superficial inguinal nodes

ANESTHESIA

Lower Abdomen

00800 Anesthesia for procedures on lower anterior abdominal wall; not otherwise specified

00860 Anesthesia for extraperitoneal procedures in lower abdomen, including urinary tract; not otherwise specified

Perineum

00904 Anesthesia for; radical perineal procedure

SURGERY

Hemic and Lymphatic Systems

Lymph Nodes and Lymphatic Channels
Incision

38300 Drainage of lymph node abscess or lymphadenitis; simple

38305 extensive

38308 Lymphangiotomy or other operations on lymphatic channels

Excision

38500 Biopsy or excision of lymph node(s); open, superficial

38505 by needle, superficial (eg, cervical, inguinal, axillary)

Limited Lymphadenectomy for Staging

38562 Limited lymphadenectomy for staging (separate procedure); pelvic and para-aortic

38564 retroperitoneal (aortic and/or splenic)

Laparoscopy

38570 Laparoscopy, surgical; with retroperitoneal lymph node sampling (biopsy), single or multiple

38571 with bilateral total pelvic lymphadenectomy

38572 with bilateral total pelvic lymphadenectomy and peri-aortic lymph node sampling (biopsy), single or multiple

Radical Lymphadenectomy (Radical Resection of Lymph Nodes)

38760 Inguinofemoral lymphadenectomy, superficial, including Cloquets node (separate procedure)

38765 Inguinofemoral lymphadenectomy, superficial, in continuity with pelvic lymphadenectomy, including external iliac, hypogastric, and obturator nodes (separate procedure)

38770 Pelvic lymphadenectomy, including external iliac, hypogastric, and obturator nodes (separate procedure)

38780 Retroperitoneal transabdominal lymphadenectomy, extensive, including pelvic, aortic, and renal nodes (separate procedure)

Introduction

38790 Injection procedure; lymphangiography

38792 for identification of sentinel node

Female Genital System

Vulva, Perineum and Introitus
Excision

56631 Vulvectomy, radical, partial; with unilateral inguinofemoral lymphadenectomy

56632 with bilateral inguinofemoral lymphadenectomy

56633 Vulvectomy, radical, complete;

56634 with unilateral inguinofemoral lymphadenectomy

56637 with bilateral inguinofemoral lymphadenectomy

56640 Vulvectomy, radical, complete, with inguinofemoral, iliac, and pelvic lymphadenectomy

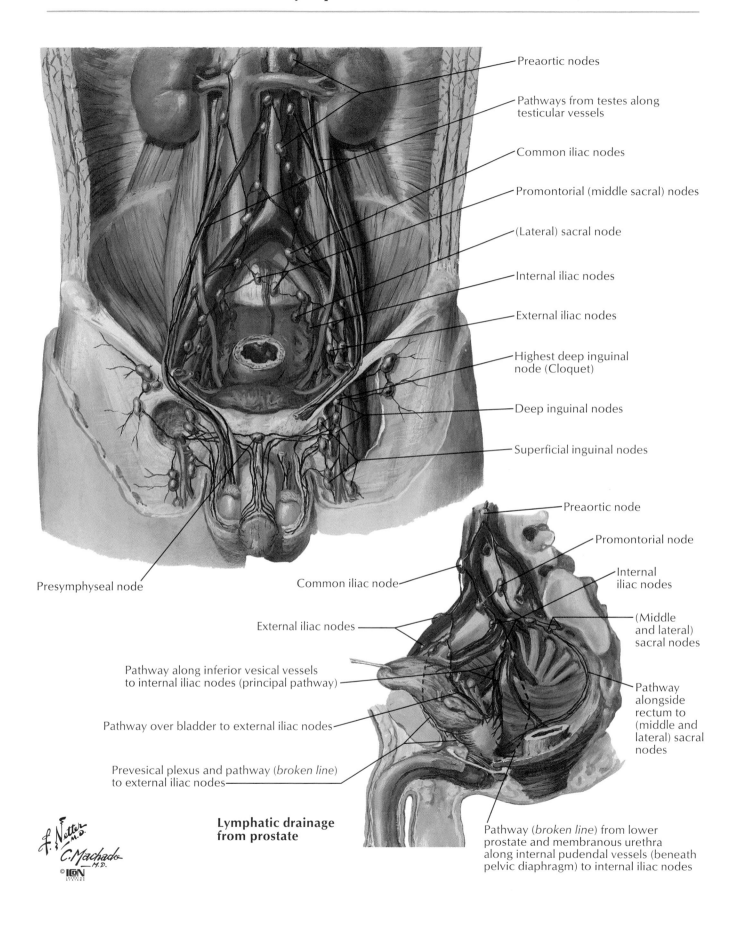

Preaortic nodes

Pathways from testes along testicular vessels

Common iliac nodes

Promontorial (middle sacral) nodes

(Lateral) sacral node

Internal iliac nodes

External iliac nodes

Highest deep inguinal node (Cloquet)

Deep inguinal nodes

Superficial inguinal nodes

Presymphyseal node

Preaortic node

Promontorial node

Internal iliac nodes

Common iliac node

(Middle and lateral) sacral nodes

External iliac nodes

Pathway along inferior vesical vessels to internal iliac nodes (principal pathway)

Pathway alongside rectum to (middle and lateral) sacral nodes

Pathway over bladder to external iliac nodes

Prevesical plexus and pathway (*broken line*) to external iliac nodes

Lymphatic drainage from prostate

Pathway (*broken line*) from lower prostate and membranous urethra along internal pudendal vessels (beneath pelvic diaphragm) to internal iliac nodes

ANESTHESIA

Lower Abdomen

00800   Anesthesia for procedures on lower anterior abdominal wall; not otherwise specified

00840   Anesthesia for intraperitoneal procedures in lower abdomen including laparoscopy; not otherwise specified

00860   Anesthesia for extraperitoneal procedures in lower abdomen, including urinary tract; not otherwise specified

Perineum

00934   Anesthesia for procedures on male genitalia (including open urethral procedures); radical amputation of penis with bilateral inguinal lymphadenectomy

SURGERY

Hemic and Lymphatic Systems

Lymph Nodes and Lymphatic Chanels
Excision

38500   Biopsy or excision of lymph node(s); open, superficial

38505   by needle, superficial (eg, cervical, inguinal, axillary)

Limited Lymphadenectomy for Staging

38562   Limited lymphadenectomy for staging (separate procedure); pelvic and para-aortic

38564   retroperitoneal (aortic and/or splenic)

Laparoscopy

38570   Laparoscopy, surgical; with retroperitoneal lymph node sampling (biopsy), single or multiple

38571   with bilateral total pelvic lymphadenectomy

38572   with bilateral total pelvic lymphadenectomy and peri-aortic lymph node sampling (biopsy), single or multiple

Radical Lymphadenectomy (Radical Resection of Lymph Nodes)

38760   Inguinofemoral lymphadenectomy, superficial, including Cloquets node (separate procedure)

38765   Inguinofemoral lymphadenectomy, superficial, in continuity with pelvic lymphadenectomy, including external iliac, hypogastric, and obturator nodes (separate procedure)

38770   Pelvic lymphadenectomy, including external iliac, hypogastric, and obturator nodes (separate procedure)

38780   Retroperitoneal transabdominal lymphadenectomy, extensive, including pelvic, aortic, and renal nodes (separate procedure)

Introduction

38790   Injection procedure; lymphangiography

38792   for identification of sentinel node

Male Genital System

Penis
Excision

54130   Amputation of penis, radical; with bilateral inguinofemoral lymphadenectomy

54135   in continuity with bilateral pelvic lymphadenectomy, including external iliac, hypogastric and obturator nodes

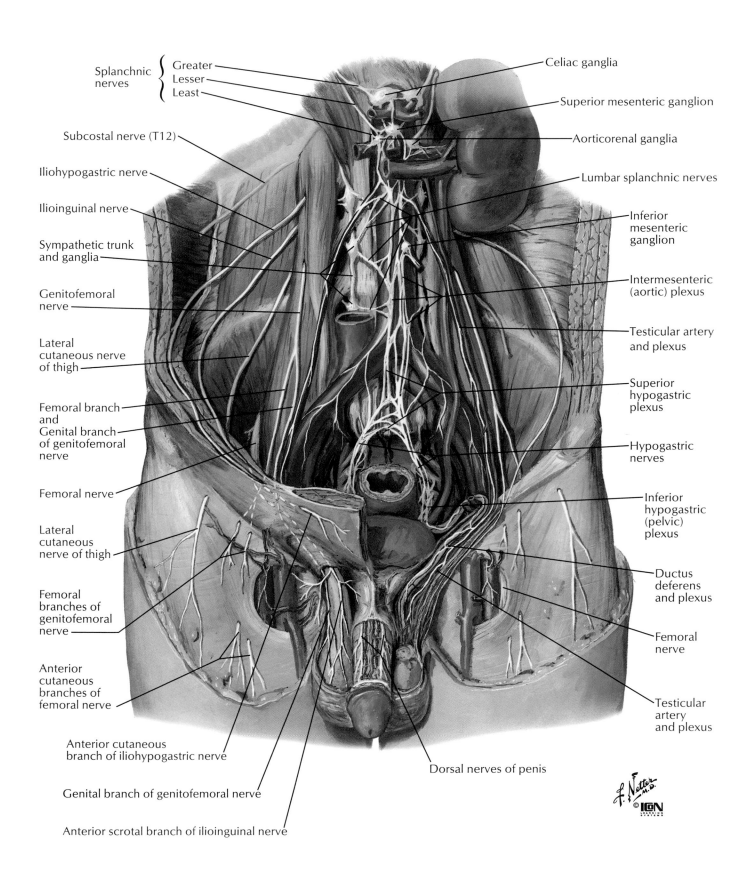

Splanchnic nerves { Greater / Lesser / Least

Celiac ganglia

Subcostal nerve (T12)

Superior mesenteric ganglion

Iliohypogastric nerve

Aorticorenal ganglia

Ilioinguinal nerve

Lumbar splanchnic nerves

Sympathetic trunk and ganglia

Inferior mesenteric ganglion

Genitofemoral nerve

Intermesenteric (aortic) plexus

Lateral cutaneous nerve of thigh

Testicular artery and plexus

Femoral branch and Genital branch of genitofemoral nerve

Superior hypogastric plexus

Femoral nerve

Hypogastric nerves

Lateral cutaneous nerve of thigh

Inferior hypogastric (pelvic) plexus

Femoral branches of genitofemoral nerve

Ductus deferens and plexus

Anterior cutaneous branches of femoral nerve

Femoral nerve

Anterior cutaneous branch of iliohypogastric nerve

Testicular artery and plexus

Genital branch of genitofemoral nerve

Dorsal nerves of penis

Anterior scrotal branch of ilioinguinal nerve

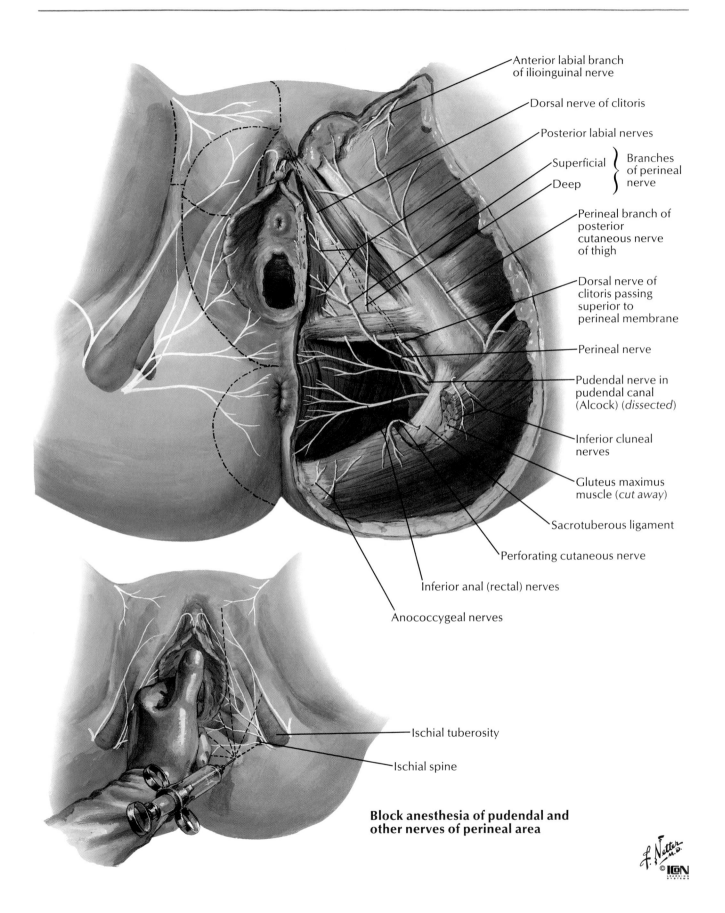

Anterior labial branch of ilioinguinal nerve

Dorsal nerve of clitoris

Posterior labial nerves

Superficial } Branches of perineal nerve

Deep

Perineal branch of posterior cutaneous nerve of thigh

Dorsal nerve of clitoris passing superior to perineal membrane

Perineal nerve

Pudendal nerve in pudendal canal (Alcock) (*dissected*)

Inferior cluneal nerves

Gluteus maximus muscle (*cut away*)

Sacrotuberous ligament

Perforating cutaneous nerve

Inferior anal (rectal) nerves

Anococcygeal nerves

Ischial tuberosity

Ischial spine

Block anesthesia of pudendal and other nerves of perineal area

ANESTHESIA

Pelvis (Except Hip)

01180   Anesthesia for obturator neurectomy; extrapelvic

Other Procedures

01991   Anesthesia for diagnostic or therapeutic nerve blocks and injections (when block or injection is performed by a different provider); other than the prone position

01992   prone position

SURGERY

Nervous System

Extracranial Nerves, Peripheral Nerves, and Autonomic Nervous System
Introduction/Injection of Anesthetic Agent (Nerve Block), Diagnostic or Therapeutic

Somatic Nerves
64425   Injection, anesthetic agent; ilioinguinal, iliohypogastric nerves

64430   pudendal nerve
64450   other peripheral nerve or branch

Destruction by Neurolytic Agent (eg, Chemical, Thermal, Electrical or Radiofrequency)

Somatic Nerves
64640   Destruction by neurolytic agent; other peripheral nerve or branch

Transection or Avulsion
64761   Transection or avulsion of; pudendal nerve

Median (A) and paramedian (B) sagittal MR images of female pelvis

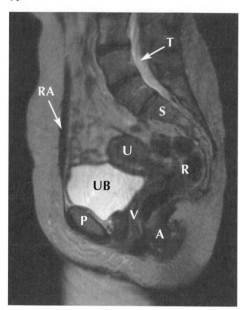

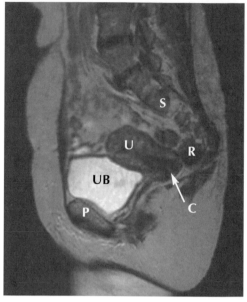

A	Anal canal	S	Sacrum
C	External os of cervix	T	Thecal sac
P	Pubic symphysis	U	Uterus
R	Rectum	UB	Urinary bladder
RA	Rectus abdominis muscle	V	Vagina

Median (C) and paramedian (D) sagittal MR images of male pelvis

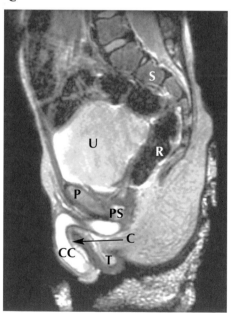

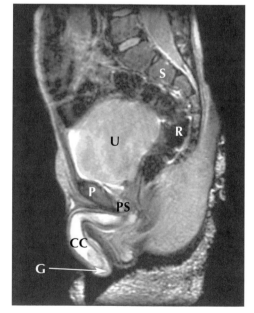

C	Corpus spongiosum	R	Rectum
CC	Corpus cavernosum	S	Sacrum
G	Glans of penis	T	Testis

ANESTHESIA

Radiological Procedures

01922　　Anesthesia for non-invasive imaging or radiation therapy

RADIOLOGY

Diagnostic Radiology (Diagnostic Imaging)

Spine and Pelvis

72195　　Magnetic resonance (eg, proton) imaging, pelvis; without contrast material(s)

72196　　　　with contrast material(s)

72197　　　　without contrast material(s), followed by contrast material(s) and further sequences

72198　　Magnetic resonance angiography, pelvis, with or without contrast material(s)

Chapter 6
Upper Limb

The upper extremity is part of the appendicular skeleton. The extremity is made up of the shoulder girdle (clavicle and scapula), the upper arm, lower arm, wrist, and hand. The shoulder is divided into three regions: the axilla, the scapular region around the shoulder blade, and the pectoral region on the front of the chest. The scapula (or shoulder blade) and clavicle form the pectoral girdle. They articulate with each other at the acromioclavicular joint, but their only articulation with the rest of the axial skeleton is where the clavicle articulates with the sternum at the sternoclavicular joint. The scapula is otherwise mobile and held in position by muscles, without any articulation with the vertebral column.

The upper arm extends between the shoulder and the elbow. The bony structure of the upper arm consists of a long bone, the humerus. The humerus articulates with the scapula and the radius and ulna. The olecranon process forms the elbow.

The forearm lies between the elbow and the wrist. The radius and ulna make up the lower arm structure with the radius situated on the thumb side and the ulna on the little finger side. These bones articulate with the humerus at the elbow joint, with each other (proximal and distal radioulnar joints), and with bones of the wrist at the radiocarpal joint. The hand consists of the wrist, the hand proper, and the digits. Eight carpal bones form the wrist. The carpal bones of the wrist are arranged in two rows of four, proximal and distal. They articulate with one another at the intercarpal joints, proximally with the radius at the radiocarpal joint (allowing pronation and supination), and distally with the metacarpals at the carpometacarpal joints. Ligaments hold the carpal bones closely together in two rows of four bones each.

Five metacarpal bones form the bony framework of the hand. These metacarpal bones articulate with the phalanges that form the fingers. Proximally, the metacarpal bases articulate with the distal row of carpal bones, and two to five articulate with each other at the intermetacarpal joints. Distally each articulates with the proximal phalanx of the corresponding digit. The digits are the thumb or pollex, the forefinger, the middle finger, the ring finger, and the little finger. Each digit has three phalanges except the thumb, which has two. The proximal phalanx articulates with the corresponding metacarpal head at the metacarpophalangeal joint. Within each digit the phalanges also articulate with each other at the proximal and distal interphalangeal joints.

The major muscles of the upper limb include the deltoid, the triceps brachii, and the biceps brachii in the upper arm; the flexor carpi radialis, flexor carpi ulnaris, flexor digitorum superficialis, flexor digitorum profundus, flexor pollicis longus, extensor carpi radialis longus, and extensor digitorum are found in the forearm. The muscles of the wrist and hand include the abductor pollicis brevis, flexor pollicis brevis, flexor digiti minimi brevis, and others that serve to provide motion to the wrist and hand.

The blood supply to the upper limb features the subclavian artery and vein, the axillary artery, the brachial artery, and radial and ulnar arteries and veins. The blood vessels of the arm are often used as an access point for transcatheter therapies or venipuncture.

The brachial plexus is a network of nerves starting from five nerve roots in the upper spine and ending in the five main nerves that control movement and sensation in the arm. It is located near where the neck joins the shoulder, behind the clavicle, between the spine and the upper arm, and distal to the axilla. The axillary and radial nerves, the ulnar nerve, the median nerve, and the musculocutaneous nerve arise from the this plexus.

Common procedures performed in this anatomic region include, but are not limited to, the following:

• Biopsy
• Arthrotomy
• Sequestrectomy
• Tenodesis
• Treatment of fractures or dislocations
• Fasciotomy
• Synovectomy
• Repair of a tendon or muscle
• Capsulorrhaphy
• Arthroplasty
• Amputation
• Nerve blocks
• Neuroplasty
• Sympathectomy
• Neurorrhaphy
• Repair of blood vessels
• Embolectomy
• Thrombectomy

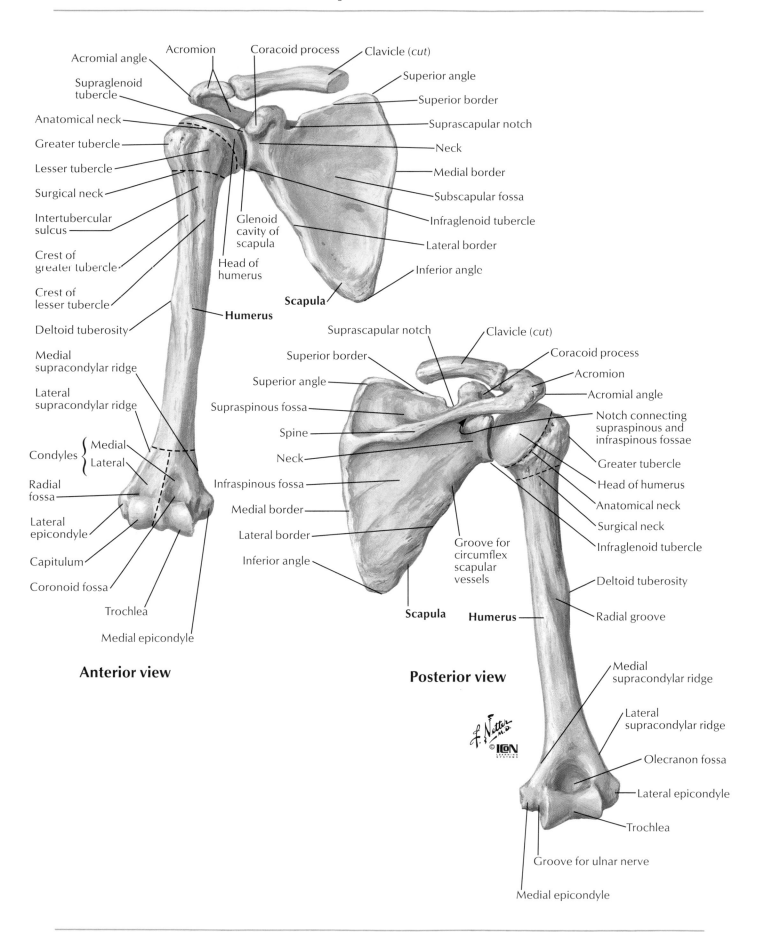

Acromion

Coracoid process

Clavicle (*cut*)

Acromial angle

Supraglenoid tubercle

Anatomical neck

Greater tubercle

Lesser tubercle

Surgical neck

Intertubercular sulcus

Crest of greater tubercle

Crest of lesser tubercle

Deltoid tuberosity

Medial supracondylar ridge

Lateral supracondylar ridge

Condyles { Medial
{ Lateral

Radial fossa

Lateral epicondyle

Capitulum

Coronoid fossa

Trochlea

Medial epicondyle

Superior angle

Superior border

Suprascapular notch

Neck

Medial border

Subscapular fossa

Infraglenoid tubercle

Lateral border

Inferior angle

Glenoid cavity of scapula

Head of humerus

Scapula

Humerus

Anterior view

Suprascapular notch

Superior border

Superior angle

Supraspinous fossa

Spine

Neck

Infraspinous fossa

Medial border

Lateral border

Inferior angle

Groove for circumflex scapular vessels

Clavicle (*cut*)

Coracoid process

Acromion

Acromial angle

Notch connecting supraspinous and infraspinous fossae

Greater tubercle

Head of humerus

Anatomical neck

Surgical neck

Infraglenoid tubercle

Deltoid tuberosity

Radial groove

Medial supracondylar ridge

Lateral supracondylar ridge

Olecranon fossa

Lateral epicondyle

Trochlea

Groove for ulnar nerve

Medial epicondyle

Scapula   **Humerus**

Posterior view

Nomenclature Notes

The *surgical neck* of the humerus is the narrow portion of the humerus that resides below the head and tuberosities.

The *anatomic neck* of the humerus is the area of transition where the rounded portion of the humeral head ends and the humeral shaft begins.

The term *greater tuberosity* is synonymous with the term *greater tubercle*.

ANESTHESIA

Thorax (Chest Wall and Shoulder Girdle)

00450	Anesthesia for procedures on clavicle and scapula; not otherwise specified
00452	radical surgery

Shoulder and Axilla

01620	Anesthesia for all closed procedures on humeral head and neck, sternoclavicular joint, acromioclavicular joint, and shoulder joint
01630	Anesthesia for open or surgical arthroscopic procedures on humeral head and neck, sternoclavicular joint, acromioclavicular joint, and shoulder joint; not otherwise specified

Upper Arm and Elbow

01730	Anesthesia for all closed procedures on humerus and elbow
01732	Anesthesia for diagnostic arthroscopic procedures of elbow joint
01740	Anesthesia for open or surgical arthroscopic procedures of the elbow; not otherwise specified
01742	osteotomy of humerus
01744	repair of nonunion or malunion of humerus
01756	radical procedures
01758	excision of cyst or tumor of humerus

SURGERY

Musculoskeletal System

General
Excision

20245	Biopsy, bone, open; deep (eg, humerus, ischium, femur)

Replantation

20802	Replantation, arm (includes surgical neck of humerus through elbow joint), complete amputation

Shoulder
Incision

23035	Incision, bone cortex (eg, osteomyelitis or bone abscess), shoulder area
23040	Arthrotomy, glenohumeral joint, including exploration, drainage, or removal of foreign body

Excision

23120	Claviculectomy; partial
23125	total
23140	Excision or curettage of bone cyst or benign tumor of clavicle or scapula;
23145	with autograft (includes obtaining graft)
23146	with allograft
23150	Excision or curettage of bone cyst or benign tumor of proximal humerus;
23155	with autograft (includes obtaining graft)
23156	with allograft
23170	Sequestrectomy (eg, for osteomyelitis or bone abscess), clavicle
23172	Sequestrectomy (eg, for osteomyelitis or bone abscess), scapula
23174	Sequestrectomy (eg, for osteomyelitis or bone abscess), humeral head to surgical neck
23180	Partial excision (craterization, saucerization, or diaphysectomy) bone (eg, osteomyelitis), clavicle
23182	Partial excision (craterization, saucerization, or diaphysectomy) bone (eg, osteomyelitis), scapula
23184	Partial excision (craterization, saucerization, or diaphysectomy) bone (eg, osteomyelitis), proximal humerus
23190	Ostectomy of scapula, partial (eg, superior medial angle)
23195	Resection, humeral head
23200	Radical resection for tumor; clavicle
23210	scapula
23220	Radical resection of bone tumor, proximal humerus;
23221	with autograft (includes obtaining graft)
23222	with prosthetic replacement

Repair, Revision, and/or Reconstruction

23480	Osteotomy, clavicle, with or without internal fixation;
23485	with bone graft for nonunion or malunion (includes obtaining graft and/or necessary fixation)
23490	Prophylactic treatment (nailing, pinning, plating or wiring) with or without methylmethacrylate; clavicle
23491	proximal humerus

Fracture and/or Dislocation

23500	Closed treatment of clavicular fracture; without manipulation
23505	with manipulation
23515	Open treatment of clavicular fracture, with or without internal or external fixation
23570	Closed treatment of scapular fracture; without manipulation
23575	with manipulation, with or without skeletal traction (with or without shoulder joint involvement)

(Fracture and/or Dislocation continued on next page)

(Fracture and/or Dislocation continued from previous page)

23585   Open treatment of scapular fracture (body, glenoid or acromion) with or without internal fixation

23600   Closed treatment of proximal humeral (surgical or anatomical neck) fracture; without manipulation

23605   with manipulation, with or without skeletal traction

23615   Open treatment of proximal humeral (surgical or anatomical neck) fracture, with or without internal or external fixation, with or without repair of tuberosity(s);

23616   with proximal humeral prosthetic replacement

23620   Closed treatment of greater humeral tuberosity fracture; without manipulation

23625   with manipulation

23630   Open treatment of greater humeral tuberosity fracture, with or without internal or external fixation

Humerus (Upper Arm) and Elbow

Incision

23935   Incision, deep, with opening of bone cortex (eg, for osteomyelitis or bone abscess), humerus or elbow

Excision

24110   Excision or curettage of bone cyst or benign tumor, humerus;

24115   with autograft (includes obtaining graft)

24116   with allograft

24140   Partial excision (craterization, saucerization, or diaphysectomy) bone (eg, osteomyelitis), humerus

24150   Radical resection for tumor, shaft or distal humerus;

24151   with autograft (includes obtaining graft)

Repair, Revision, and/or Reconstruction

24400   Osteotomy, humerus, with or without internal fixation

24410   Multiple osteotomies with realignment on intramedullary rod, humeral shaft (Sofield type procedure)

24420   Osteoplasty, humerus (eg, shortening or lengthening) (excluding 64876)

24430   Repair of nonunion or malunion, humerus; without graft (eg, compression technique)

24435   with iliac or other autograft (includes obtaining graft)

24470   Hemiepiphyseal arrest (eg, cubitus varus or valgus, distal humerus)

24498   Prophylactic treatment (nailing, pinning, plating or wiring), with or without methylmethacrylate, humeral shaft

Fracture and/or Dislocation

24500   Closed treatment of humeral shaft fracture; without manipulation

24505   with manipulation, with or without skeletal traction

24515   Open treatment of humeral shaft fracture with plate/screws, with or without cerclage

24516   Treatment of humeral shaft fracture, with insertion of intramedullary implant, with or without cerclage and/or locking screws

24530   Closed treatment of supracondylar or transcondylar humeral fracture, with or without intercondylar extension; without manipulation

24535   with manipulation, with or without skin or skeletal traction

24538   Percutaneous skeletal fixation of supracondylar or transcondylar humeral fracture, with or without intercondylar extension

24545   Open treatment of humeral supracondylar or transcondylar fracture, with or without internal or external fixation; without intercondylar extension

24546   with intercondylar extension

24560   Closed treatment of humeral epicondylar fracture, medial or lateral; without manipulation

24565   with manipulation

24566   Percutaneous skeletal fixation of humeral epicondylar fracture, medial or lateral, with manipulation

24575   Open treatment of humeral epicondylar fracture, medial or lateral, with or without internal or external fixation

24576   Closed treatment of humeral condylar fracture, medial or lateral; without manipulation

24577   with manipulation

24579   Open treatment of humeral condylar fracture, medial or lateral, with or without internal or external fixation

24582   Percutaneous skeletal fixation of humeral condylar fracture, medial or lateral, with manipulation

Amputation

24900   Amputation, arm through humerus; with primary closure

24920   open, circular (guillotine)

24925   secondary closure or scar revision

24930   re-amputation

24931   with implant

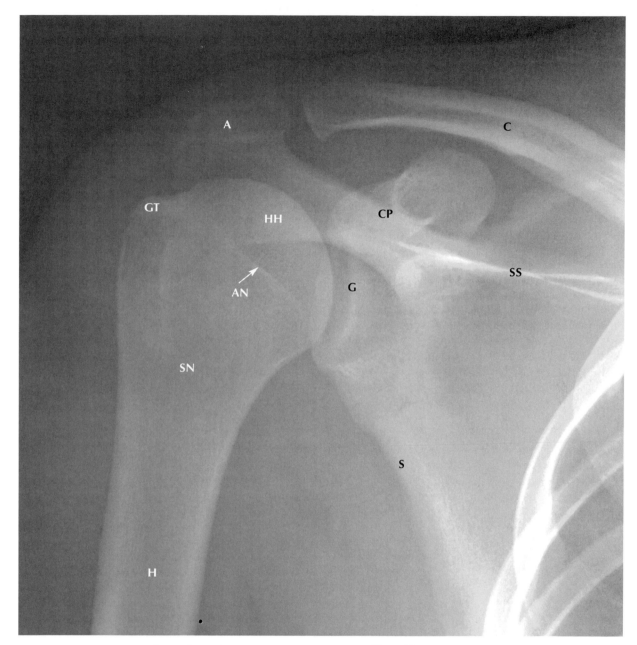

A	Acromion	**H**	Humerus
AN	Anatomical neck of humerus	**HH**	Head of humerus
C	Clavicle	**S**	Scapula (lateral border)
CP	Coracoid process	**SN**	Surgical neck of humerus
G	Glenoid cavity of scapula	**SS**	Spine of scapula
GT	Greater tubercle		

RADIOLOGY

Diagnostic Radiology (Diagnostic Imaging)

Upper Extremities

73020   Radiologic examination, shoulder; one view

Anterior view

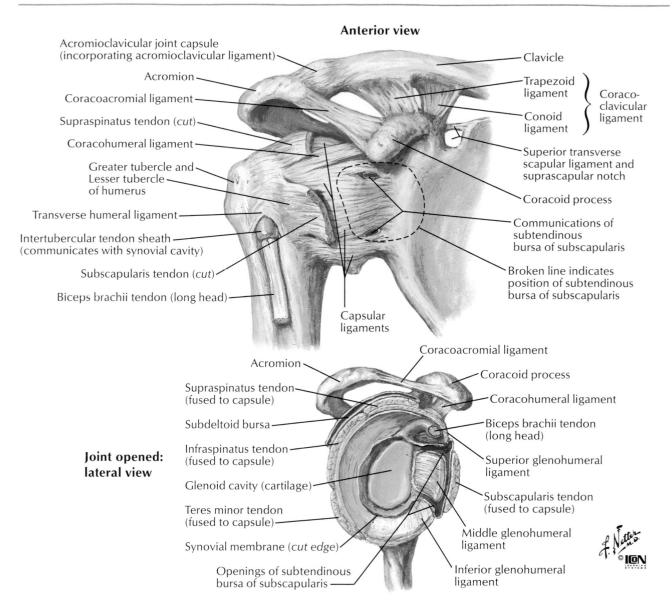

Acromioclavicular joint capsule (incorporating acromioclavicular ligament)

Acromion

Coracoacromial ligament

Supraspinatus tendon (*cut*)

Coracohumeral ligament

Greater tubercle and Lesser tubercle of humerus

Transverse humeral ligament

Intertubercular tendon sheath (communicates with synovial cavity)

Subscapularis tendon (*cut*)

Biceps brachii tendon (long head)

Clavicle

Trapezoid ligament

Conoid ligament

} Coraco-clavicular ligament

Superior transverse scapular ligament and suprascapular notch

Coracoid process

Communications of subtendinous bursa of subscapularis

Broken line indicates position of subtendinous bursa of subscapularis

Capsular ligaments

Joint opened: lateral view

Acromion

Supraspinatus tendon (fused to capsule)

Subdeltoid bursa

Infraspinatus tendon (fused to capsule)

Glenoid cavity (cartilage)

Teres minor tendon (fused to capsule)

Synovial membrane (*cut edge*)

Openings of subtendinous bursa of subscapularis

Coracoacromial ligament

Coracoid process

Coracohumeral ligament

Biceps brachii tendon (long head)

Superior glenohumeral ligament

Subscapularis tendon (fused to capsule)

Middle glenohumeral ligament

Inferior glenohumeral ligament

ANESTHESIA

Thorax (Chest Wall and Shoulder Girdle)

00450	Anesthesia for procedures on clavicle and scapula; not otherwise specified
00452	radical surgery

Shoulder and Axilla

01620	Anesthesia for all closed procedures on humeral head and neck, sternoclavicular joint, acromioclavicular joint, and shoulder joint
01622	Anesthesia for diagnostic arthroscopic procedures of shoulder joint
01630	Anesthesia for open or surgical arthroscopic procedures on humeral head and neck, sternoclavicular joint, acromioclavicular joint, and shoulder joint; not otherwise specified
01632	radical resection
01634	shoulder disarticulation
01636	interthoracoscapular (forequarter) amputation
01638	total shoulder replacement

SURGERY

Musculoskeletal System

General
Excision

20225	Biopsy, bone, trocar, or needle; deep (eg, vertebral body, femur)
20240	Biopsy, bone, open; superficial (eg, ilium, sternum, spinous process, ribs, trochanter of femur)
20245	deep (eg, humerus, ischium, femur)

Introduction or Removal

20610	Arthrocentesis, aspiration and/or injection; major joint or bursa (eg, shoulder, hip, knee joint, subacromial bursa)
20615	Aspiration and injection for treatment of bone cyst
20670	Removal of implant; superficial, (eg, buried wire, pin or rod) (separate procedure)
20680	deep (eg, buried wire, pin, screw, metal band, nail, rod or plate)

Shoulder

Incision

23040   Arthrotomy, glenohumeral joint, including exploration, drainage, or removal of foreign body

23044   Arthrotomy, acromioclavicular, sternoclavicular joint, including exploration, drainage, or removal of foreign body

Excision

23100   Arthrotomy, glenohumeral joint, including biopsy

23101   Arthrotomy, acromioclavicular joint or sternoclavicular joint, including biopsy and/or excision of torn cartilage

23105   Arthrotomy; glenohumeral joint, with synovectomy, with or without biopsy

23106   sternoclavicular joint, with synovectomy, with or without biopsy

23107   Arthrotomy, glenohumeral joint, with joint exploration, with or without removal of loose or foreign body

23120   Claviculectomy; partial

23125   total

23130   Acromioplasty or acromionectomy, partial, with or without coracoacromial ligament release

23140   Excision or curettage of bone cyst or benign tumor of clavicle or scapula;

23145   with autograft (includes obtaining graft)

23146   with allograft

23170   Sequestrectomy (eg, for osteomyelitis or bone abscess), clavicle

23180   Partial excision (craterization, saucerization, or diaphysectomy) bone (eg, osteomyelitis), clavicle

23200   Radical resection for tumor; clavicle

Introduction or Removal

23331   Removal of foreign body, shoulder; deep (eg, Neer hemiarthroplasty removal)

23332   complicated (eg, total shoulder)

Repair, Revision, and/or Reconstruction

23450   Capsulorrhaphy, anterior; Putti-Platt procedure or Magnuson type operation

23455   with labral repair (eg, Bankart procedure)

23460   Capsulorrhaphy, anterior, any type; with bone block

23462   with coracoid process transfer

23465   Capsulorrhaphy, glenohumeral joint, posterior, with or without bone block

23466   Capsulorrhaphy, glenohumeral joint, any type multi-directional instability

23470   Arthroplasty, glenohumeral joint; hemiarthroplasty

23472   total shoulder (glenoid and proximal humeral replacement (eg, total shoulder))

23480   Osteotomy, clavicle, with or without internal fixation;

23485   with bone graft for nonunion or malunion (includes obtaining graft and/or necessary fixation)

23490   Prophylactic treatment (nailing, pinning, plating or wiring) with or without methylmethacrylate; clavicle

Fracture and/or Dislocation

23500   Closed treatment of clavicular fracture; without manipulation

23505   with manipulation

23515   Open treatment of clavicular fracture, with or without internal or external fixation

23540   Closed treatment of acromioclavicular dislocation; without manipulation

23545   with manipulation

23550   Open treatment of acromioclavicular dislocation, acute or chronic;

23552   with fascial graft (includes obtaining graft)

23650   Closed treatment of shoulder dislocation, with manipulation; without anesthesia

23655   Closed treatment of shoulder dislocation, with manipulation; requiring anesthesia

23660   Open treatment of acute shoulder dislocation

23665   Closed treatment of shoulder dislocation, with fracture of greater humeral tuberosity, with manipulation

23670   Open treatment of shoulder dislocation, with fracture of greater humeral tuberosity, with or without internal or external fixation

23675   Closed treatment of shoulder dislocation, with surgical or anatomical neck fracture, with manipulation

23680   Open treatment of shoulder dislocation, with surgical or anatomical neck fracture, with or without internal or external fixation

Manipulation

23700   Manipulation under anesthesia, shoulder joint, including application of fixation apparatus (dislocation excluded)

Arthrodesis

23800   Arthrodesis, glenohumeral joint;

23802   with autogenous graft (includes obtaining graft)

Amputation

23900   Interthoracoscapular amputation (forequarter)

23920   Disarticulation of shoulder;

23921   secondary closure or scar revision

Endoscopy/Arthroscopy

29805   Arthroscopy, shoulder, diagnostic, with or without synovial biopsy (separate procedure)

29806   Arthroscopy, shoulder, surgical; capsulorrhaphy

29807   repair of SLAP lesion

29819   with removal of loose body or foreign body

29820   synovectomy, partial

29821   synovectomy, complete

29822   debridement, limited

29823   debridement, extensive

29824   distal claviculectomy including distal articular surface (Mumford procedure)

29825   with lysis and resection of adhesions, with or without manipulation

29826   decompression of subacromial space with partial acromioplasty, with or without coracoacromial release

29827   with rotator cuff repair

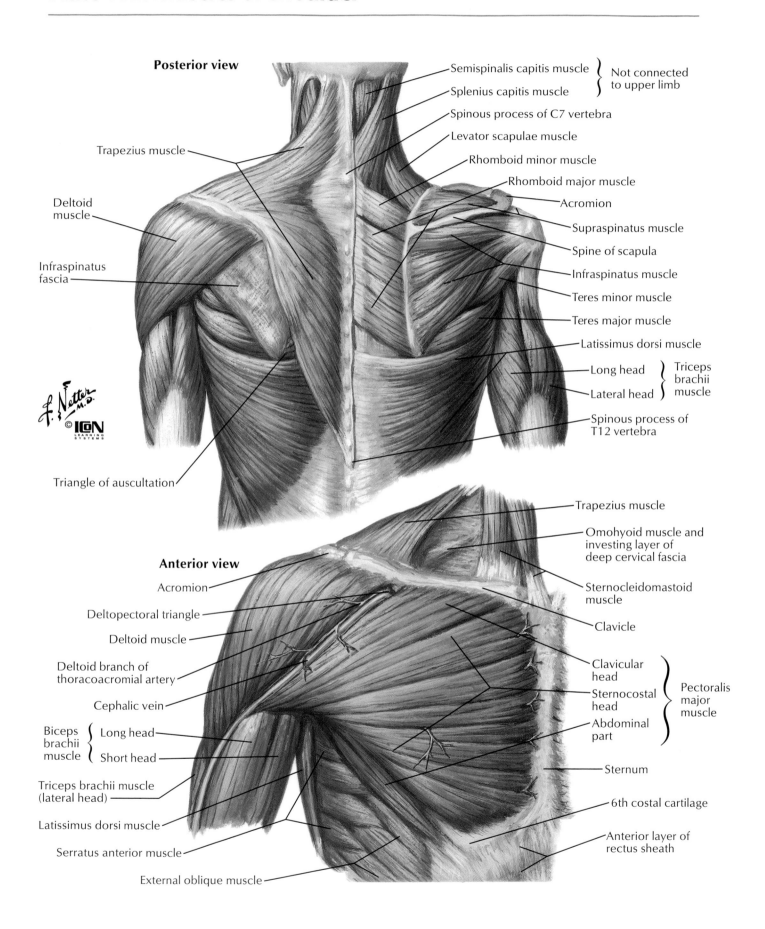

Posterior view

Semispinalis capitis muscle ⎫ Not connected
Splenius capitis muscle ⎬ to upper limb
Spinous process of C7 vertebra
Levator scapulae muscle
Trapezius muscle
Rhomboid minor muscle
Rhomboid major muscle
Acromion
Deltoid muscle
Supraspinatus muscle
Spine of scapula
Infraspinatus fascia
Infraspinatus muscle
Teres minor muscle
Teres major muscle
Latissimus dorsi muscle
Long head ⎫ Triceps
Lateral head ⎬ brachii muscle
Spinous process of T12 vertebra
Triangle of auscultation

Anterior view

Trapezius muscle
Omohyoid muscle and investing layer of deep cervical fascia
Acromion
Sternocleidomastoid muscle
Deltopectoral triangle
Deltoid muscle
Clavicle
Deltoid branch of thoracoacromial artery
Clavicular head
Cephalic vein
Sternocostal head ⎫ Pectoralis major muscle
Biceps brachii muscle ⎰ Long head
Short head
Abdominal part
Triceps brachii muscle (lateral head)
Sternum
Latissimus dorsi muscle
6th costal cartilage
Serratus anterior muscle
Anterior layer of rectus sheath
External oblique muscle

ANESTHESIA

Thorax (Chest Wall and Shoulder Girdle)

00400 Anesthesia for procedures on the integumentary system on the extremities, anterior trunk and perineum; not otherwise specified

00450 Anesthesia for procedures on clavicle and scapula; not otherwise specified

Shoulder and Axilla

01610 Anesthesia for all procedures on nerves, muscles, tendons, fascia, and bursae of shoulder and axilla

01622 Anesthesia for diagnostic arthroscopic procedures of shoulder joint

01630 Anesthesia for open or surgical arthroscopic procedures on humeral head and neck, sternoclavicular joint, acromioclavicular joint, and shoulder joint; not otherwise specified

01632 radical resection

Upper Arm and Elbow

01710 Anesthesia for procedures on nerves, muscles, tendons, fascia, and bursae of upper arm and elbow; not otherwise specified

01712 tenotomy, elbow to shoulder, open

01714 tenoplasty, elbow to shoulder

Other Procedures

01991 Anesthesia for diagnostic or therapeutic nerve blocks and injections (when block or injection is performed by a different provider); other than the prone position

SURGERY

Musculoskeletal System

General
Excision

20200 Biopsy, muscle; superficial
20205 deep
20206 Biopsy, muscle, percutaneous needle

Introduction or Removal

20520 Removal of foreign body in muscle or tendon sheath; simple
20525 deep or complicated
20526 Injection, therapeutic (eg, local anesthetic, corticosteroid), carpal tunnel

20550 Injection(s); single tendon sheath, or ligament, aponeurosis (eg, plantar "fascia")
20551 single tendon origin/insertion
20552 Injection(s); single or multiple trigger point(s), one or two muscle(s)
20553 single or multiple trigger point(s), three or more muscle(s)

Shoulder
Incision

23030 Incision and drainage, shoulder area; deep abscess or hematoma
23031 infected bursa

Excision

23065 Biopsy, soft tissue of shoulder area; superficial
23066 deep
23075 Excision, soft tissue tumor, shoulder area; subcutaneous
23076 deep, subfascial, or intramuscular
23077 Radical resection of tumor (eg, malignant neoplasm), soft tissue of shoulder area

Introduction or Removal

23330 Removal of foreign body, shoulder; subcutaneous
23331 deep (eg, Neer hemiarthroplasty removal)
23332 complicated (eg, total shoulder)

Repair, Revision, and/or Reconstruction

23395 Muscle transfer, any type, shoulder or upper arm; single
23397 multiple
23400 Scapulopexy (eg, Sprengels deformity or for paralysis)
23405 Tenotomy, shoulder area; single tendon
23406 Tenotomy, shoulder area; multiple tendons through same incision
23410 Repair of ruptured musculotendinous cuff (eg, rotator cuff) open; acute
23412 chronic
23415 Coracoacromial ligament release, with or without acromioplasty
23420 Reconstruction of complete shoulder (rotator) cuff avulsion, chronic (includes acromioplasty)
23430 Tenodesis of long tendon of biceps
23440 Resection or transplantation of long tendon of biceps

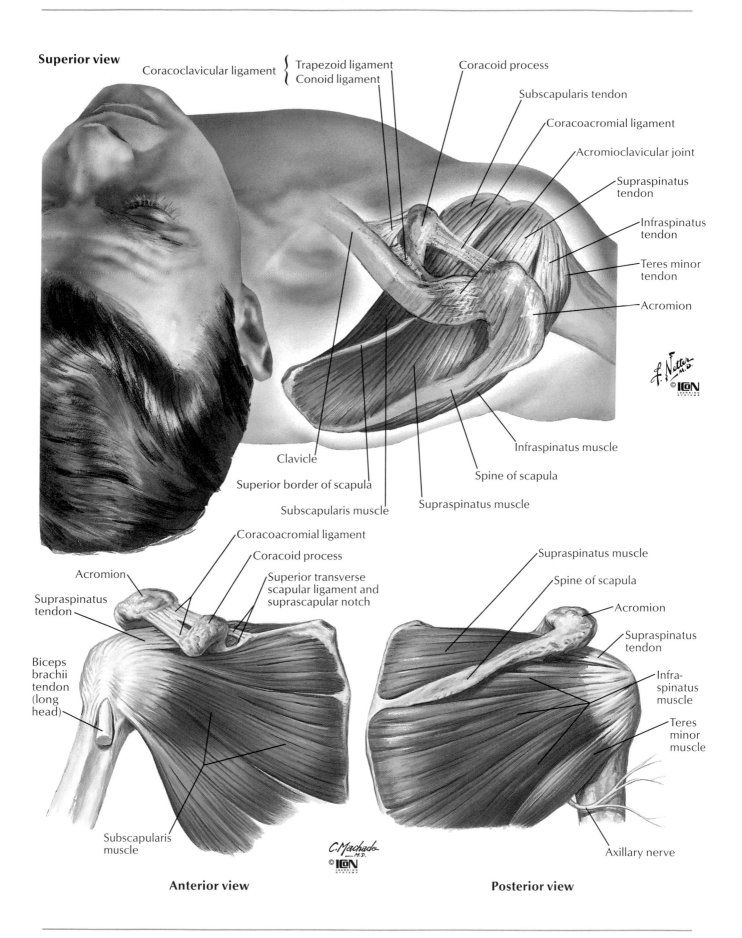

Superior view

Coracoclavicular ligament { Trapezoid ligament / Conoid ligament

Coracoid process

Subscapularis tendon

Coracoacromial ligament

Acromioclavicular joint

Supraspinatus tendon

Infraspinatus tendon

Teres minor tendon

Acromion

Infraspinatus muscle

Spine of scapula

Supraspinatus muscle

Clavicle

Superior border of scapula

Subscapularis muscle

Coracoacromial ligament

Coracoid process

Superior transverse scapular ligament and suprascapular notch

Acromion

Supraspinatus tendon

Biceps brachii tendon (long head)

Subscapularis muscle

Anterior view

Supraspinatus muscle

Spine of scapula

Acromion

Supraspinatus tendon

Infra-spinatus muscle

Teres minor muscle

Axillary nerve

Posterior view

ANESTHESIA

Shoulder and Axilla

01610   Anesthesia for all procedures on nerves, muscles, tendons, fascia, and bursae of shoulder and axilla

01630   Anesthesia for open or surgical arthroscopic procedures on humeral head and neck, sternoclavicular joint, acromioclavicular joint, and shoulder joint; not otherwise specified

SURGERY

Musculoskeletal System

Shoulder

Excision

23130   Acromioplasty or acromionectomy, partial, with or without coracoacromial ligament release

Repair, Revision, and/or Reconstruction

23405   Tenotomy, shoulder area; single tendon

23406   multiple tendons through same incision

23410   Repair of ruptured musculotendinous cuff (eg, rotator cuff) open; acute

23412   chronic

23415   Coracoacromial ligament release, with or without acromioplasty

23420   Reconstruction of complete shoulder (rotator) cuff avulsion, chronic (includes acromioplasty)

23430   Tenodesis of long tendon of biceps

23440   Resection or transplantation of long tendon of biceps

Endoscopy/Arthroscopy

29827   Arthroscopy, shoulder, surgical; with rotator cuff repair

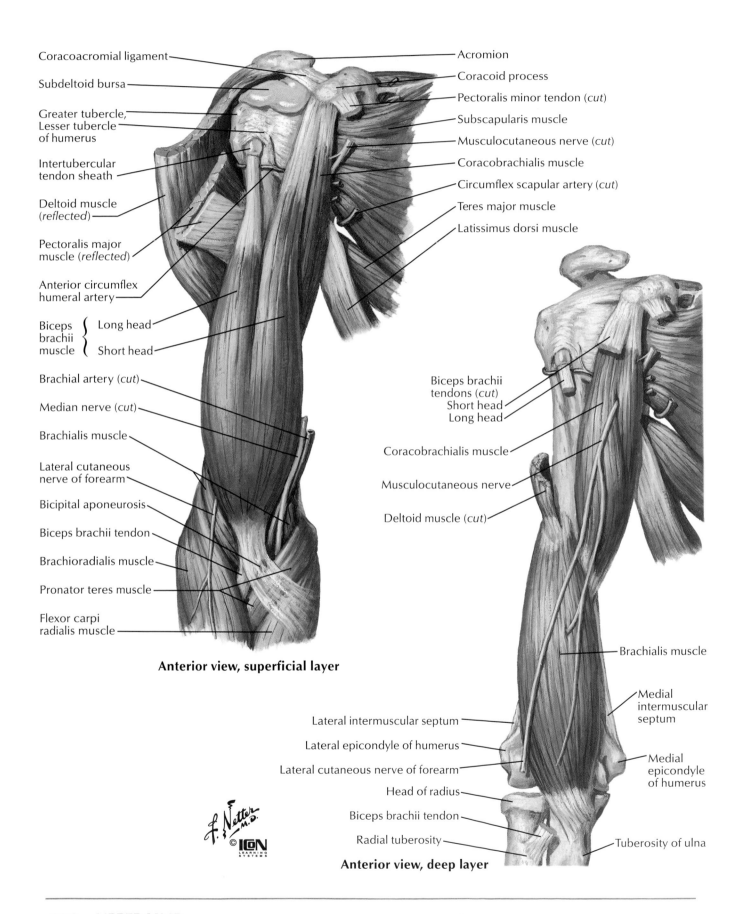

Coracoacromial ligament

Subdeltoid bursa

Greater tubercle, Lesser tubercle of humerus

Intertubercular tendon sheath

Deltoid muscle (reflected)

Pectoralis major muscle (reflected)

Anterior circumflex humeral artery

Biceps brachii muscle { Long head / Short head

Brachial artery (cut)

Median nerve (cut)

Brachialis muscle

Lateral cutaneous nerve of forearm

Bicipital aponeurosis

Biceps brachii tendon

Brachioradialis muscle

Pronator teres muscle

Flexor carpi radialis muscle

Acromion

Coracoid process

Pectoralis minor tendon (cut)

Subscapularis muscle

Musculocutaneous nerve (cut)

Coracobrachialis muscle

Circumflex scapular artery (cut)

Teres major muscle

Latissimus dorsi muscle

Biceps brachii tendons (cut) / Short head / Long head

Coracobrachialis muscle

Musculocutaneous nerve

Deltoid muscle (cut)

Brachialis muscle

Medial intermuscular septum

Medial epicondyle of humerus

Tuberosity of ulna

Lateral intermuscular septum

Lateral epicondyle of humerus

Lateral cutaneous nerve of forearm

Head of radius

Biceps brachii tendon

Radial tuberosity

Anterior view, superficial layer

Anterior view, deep layer

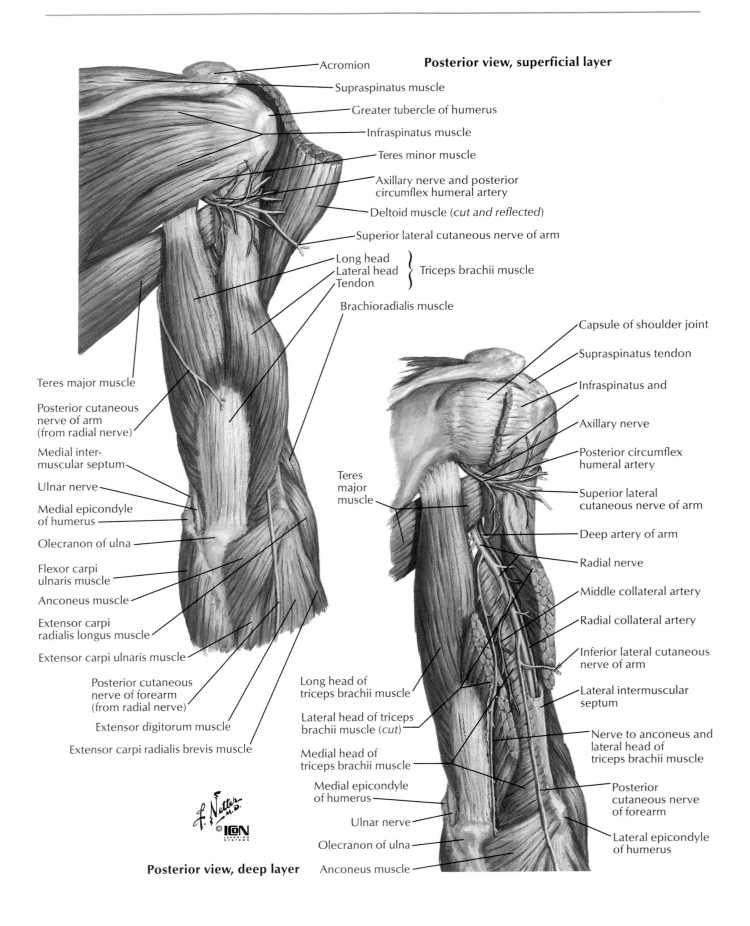

Posterior view, superficial layer

Acromion

Supraspinatus muscle

Greater tubercle of humerus

Infraspinatus muscle

Teres minor muscle

Axillary nerve and posterior circumflex humeral artery

Deltoid muscle (*cut and reflected*)

Superior lateral cutaneous nerve of arm

Long head
Lateral head } Triceps brachii muscle
Tendon

Brachioradialis muscle

Teres major muscle

Posterior cutaneous nerve of arm (from radial nerve)

Medial inter-muscular septum

Ulnar nerve

Medial epicondyle of humerus

Olecranon of ulna

Flexor carpi ulnaris muscle

Anconeus muscle

Extensor carpi radialis longus muscle

Extensor carpi ulnaris muscle

Posterior cutaneous nerve of forearm (from radial nerve)

Extensor digitorum muscle

Extensor carpi radialis brevis muscle

Posterior view, deep layer

Capsule of shoulder joint

Supraspinatus tendon

Infraspinatus and

Axillary nerve

Posterior circumflex humeral artery

Superior lateral cutaneous nerve of arm

Deep artery of arm

Radial nerve

Middle collateral artery

Radial collateral artery

Inferior lateral cutaneous nerve of arm

Lateral intermuscular septum

Nerve to anconeus and lateral head of triceps brachii muscle

Posterior cutaneous nerve of forearm

Lateral epicondyle of humerus

Teres major muscle

Long head of triceps brachii muscle

Lateral head of triceps brachii muscle (*cut*)

Medial head of triceps brachii muscle

Medial epicondyle of humerus

Ulnar nerve

Olecranon of ulna

Anconeus muscle

Plate 154: Muscles of Arm

ANESTHESIA

Thorax (Chest Wall and Shoulder Girdle)

00400 Anesthesia for procedures on the integumentary system on the extremities, anterior trunk and perineum; not otherwise specified

Upper Arm and Elbow

01710 Anesthesia for procedures on nerves, muscles, tendons, fascia, and bursae of upper arm and elbow; not otherwise specified

01712 tenotomy, elbow to shoulder, open

01714 tenoplasty, elbow to shoulder

01716 tenodesis, rupture of long tendon of biceps

01740 Anesthesia for open or surgical arthroscopic procedures of the elbow; not otherwise specified

01756 radical procedures

Other Procedures

01991 Anesthesia for diagnostic or therapeutic nerve blocks and injections (when block or injection is performed by a different provider); other than the prone position

SURGERY

Musculoskeletal System

General
Excision

20200 Biopsy, muscle; superficial

20205 deep

20206 Biopsy, muscle, percutaneous needle

Introduction or Removal

20520 Removal of foreign body in muscle or tendon sheath; simple

20525 deep or complicated

20550 Injection(s); single tendon sheath, or ligament, aponeurosis (eg, plantar "fascia")

20551 single tendon origin/insertion

20552 Injection(s); single or multiple trigger point(s), one or two muscle(s)

20553 single or multiple trigger point(s), three or more muscle(s)

Humerus (Upper Arm) and Elbow
Incision

23930 Incision and drainage, upper arm or elbow area; deep abscess or hematoma

23931 bursa

23935 Incision, deep, with opening of bone cortex (eg, for osteomyelitis or bone abscess), humerus or elbow

Excision

24065 Biopsy, soft tissue of upper arm or elbow area; superficial

24066 deep (subfascial or intramuscular)

24075 Excision, tumor, soft tissue of upper arm or elbow area; subcutaneous

24076 deep (subfascial or intramuscular)

24077 Radical resection of tumor (eg, malignant neoplasm), soft tissue of upper arm or elbow area

Introduction or Removal

24200 Removal of foreign body, upper arm or elbow area; subcutaneous

24201 deep (subfascial or intramuscular)

Repair, Revision, and/or Reconstruction

24301 Muscle or tendon transfer, any type, upper arm or elbow, single (excluding 24320-24331)

24305 Tendon lengthening, upper arm or elbow, each tendon

24310 Tenotomy, open, elbow to shoulder, each tendon

24320 Tenoplasty, with muscle transfer, with or without free graft, elbow to shoulder, single (Seddon-Brookes type procedure)

24332 Tenolysis, triceps

24340 Tenodesis of biceps tendon at elbow (separate procedure)

24341 Repair, tendon or muscle, upper arm or elbow, each tendon or muscle, primary or secondary (excludes rotator cuff)

24342 Reinsertion of ruptured biceps or triceps tendon, distal, with or without tendon graft

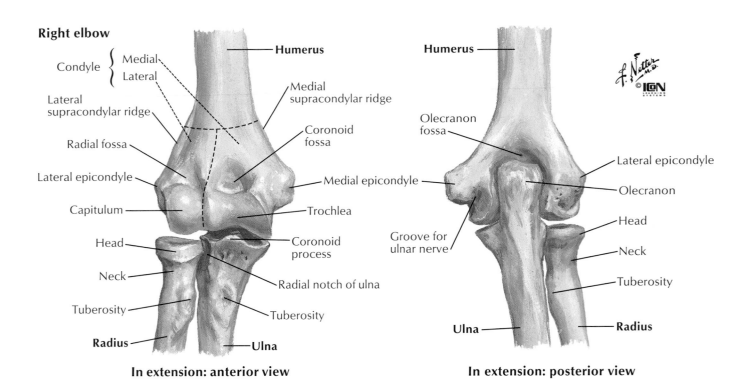

Right elbow

In extension: anterior view

In extension: posterior view

ANESTHESIA

Upper Arm and Elbow

01710	Anesthesia for procedures on nerves, muscles, tendons, fascia, and bursae of upper arm and elbow; not otherwise specified
01730	Anesthesia for all closed procedures on humerus and elbow
01732	Anesthesia for diagnostic arthroscopic procedures of elbow joint
01740	Anesthesia for open or surgical arthroscopic procedures of the elbow; not otherwise specified
01742	osteotomy of humerus
01756	radical procedures
01758	excision of cyst or tumor of humerus

SURGERY

Musculoskeletal System

General

Introduction or Removal

20605	Arthrocentesis, aspiration and/or injection; intermediate joint or bursa (eg, temporomandibular, acromioclavicular, wrist, elbow or ankle, olecranon bursa)

Humerus (Upper Arm) and Elbow

Incision

23935	Incision, deep, with opening of bone cortex (eg, for osteomyelitis or bone abscess), humerus or elbow
24000	Arthrotomy, elbow, including exploration, drainage, or removal of foreign body

24006	Arthrotomy of the elbow, with capsular excision for capsular release (separate procedure)

Excision

24100	Arthrotomy, elbow; with synovial biopsy only
24101	with joint exploration, with or without biopsy, with or without removal of loose or foreign body
24102	with synovectomy
24105	Excision, olecranon bursa
24110	Excision or curettage of bone cyst or benign tumor, humerus;
24115	with autograft (includes obtaining graft)
24116	with allograft
24120	Excision or curettage of bone cyst or benign tumor of head or neck of radius or olecranon process;
24125	with autograft (includes obtaining graft)
24126	with allograft
24130	Excision, radial head
24134	Sequestrectomy (eg, for osteomyelitis or bone abscess), shaft or distal humerus
24136	Sequestrectomy (eg, for osteomyelitis or bone abscess), radial head or neck
24138	Sequestrectomy (eg, for osteomyelitis or bone abscess), olecranon process
24140	Partial excision (craterization, saucerization, or diaphysectomy) bone (eg, osteomyelitis), humerus

(Excision continued on next page)

(Excision continued from previous page)

24145 Partial excision (craterization, saucerization, or diaphysectomy) bone (eg, osteomyelitis), radial head or neck

24147 Partial excision (craterization, saucerization, or diaphysectomy) bone (eg, osteomyelitis), olecranon process

24149 Radical resection of capsule, soft tissue, and heterotopic bone, elbow, with contracture release (separate procedure)

24150 Radical resection for tumor, shaft or distal humerus;

24151 with autograft (includes obtaining graft)

24152 Radical resection for tumor, radial head or neck;

24153 with autograft (includes obtaining graft)

24155 Resection of elbow joint (arthrectomy)

Introduction or Removal

24160 Implant removal; elbow joint
24164 radial head
24200 Removal of foreign body, upper arm or elbow area; subcutaneous
24201 deep (subfascial or intramuscular)

Repair, Revision, and/or Reconstruction

24300 Manipulation, elbow, under anesthesia
24360 Arthroplasty, elbow; with membrane (eg, fascial)
24361 with distal humeral prosthetic replacement
24362 with implant and fascia lata ligament reconstruction
24363 with distal humerus and proximal ulnar prosthetic replacement (eg, total elbow)
24365 Arthroplasty, radial head;
24366 with implant
24470 Hemiepiphyseal arrest (eg, cubitus varus or valgus, distal humerus)

Fracture and/or Dislocation

24560 Closed treatment of humeral epicondylar fracture, medial or lateral; without manipulation
24565 with manipulation
24566 Percutaneous skeletal fixation of humeral epicondylar fracture, medial or lateral, with manipulation
24575 Open treatment of humeral epicondylar fracture, medial or lateral, with or without internal or external fixation

24576 Closed treatment of humeral condylar fracture, medial or lateral; without manipulation
24577 with manipulation
24579 Open treatment of humeral condylar fracture, medial or lateral, with or without internal or external fixation
24582 Percutaneous skeletal fixation of humeral condylar fracture, medial or lateral, with manipulation
24586 Open treatment of periarticular fracture and/or dislocation of the elbow (fracture distal humerus and proximal ulna and/or proximal radius);
24587 with implant arthroplasty
24600 Treatment of closed elbow dislocation; without anesthesia
24605 requiring anesthesia
24615 Open treatment of acute or chronic elbow dislocation
24620 Closed treatment of Monteggia type of fracture dislocation at elbow (fracture proximal end of ulna with dislocation of radial head), with manipulation
24635 Open treatment of Monteggia type of fracture dislocation at elbow (fracture proximal end of ulna with dislocation of radial head), with or without internal or external fixation
24640 Closed treatment of radial head subluxation in child, nursemaid elbow, with manipulation
24650 Closed treatment of radial head or neck fracture; without manipulation
24655 with manipulation
24665 Open treatment of radial head or neck fracture, with or without internal fixation or radial head excision;
24666 with radial head prosthetic replacement
24670 Closed treatment of ulnar fracture, proximal end (olecranon process); without manipulation
24675 with manipulation
24685 Open treatment of ulnar fracture proximal end (olecranon process), with or without internal or external fixation

Arthrodesis

24800 Arthrodesis, elbow joint; local
24802 with autogenous graft (includes obtaining graft)

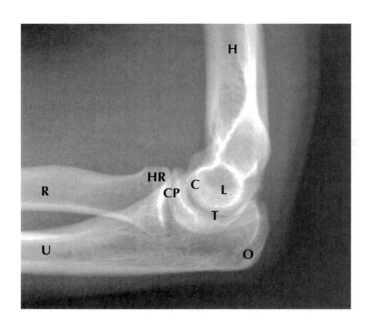

Lateral radiograph

C	Capitulum
CP	Coronoid process of ulna
H	Humerus
HR	Head of radius
L	Lateral epicondyle
O	Olecranon
R	Radius
T	Trochlear notch
U	Ulna

Anteroposterior radiograph

C	Capitulum
CP	Coronoid process of ulna
H	Humerus
HR	Head of radius
L	Lateral epicondyle
M	Medial of epicondyle
NR	Neck of radius
O	Olecranon
OF	Olecranon fossa
R	Radius
T	Trochlea of humerus
RT	Radial tuberosity
U	Ulna

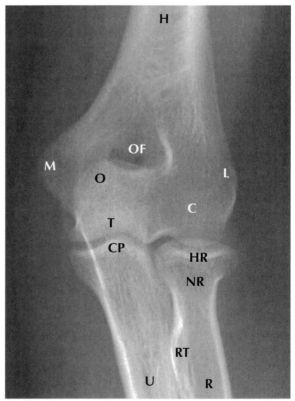

RADIOLOGY

Diagnostic Radiology (Diagnostic Imaging)

Upper Extremities

73070   Radiologic examination, elbow; two views

Plate 157: Ligaments of Elbow

Right elbow

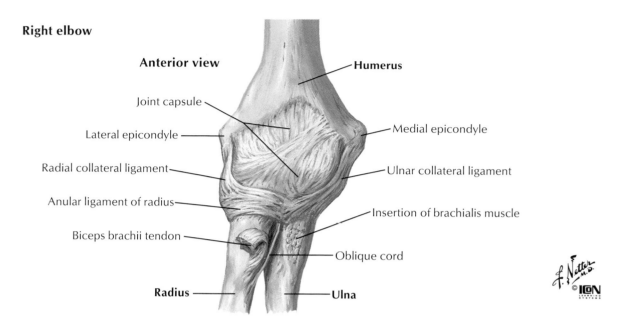

Anterior view

Joint capsule

Lateral epicondyle

Radial collateral ligament

Anular ligament of radius

Biceps brachii tendon

Radius

Humerus

Medial epicondyle

Ulnar collateral ligament

Insertion of brachialis muscle

Oblique cord

Ulna

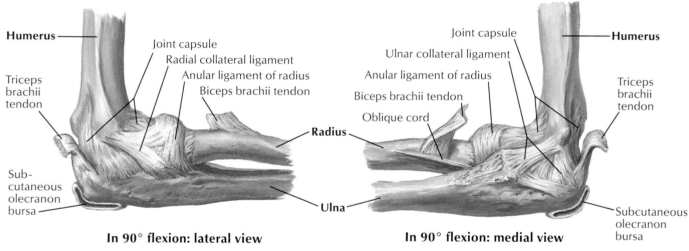

Humerus

Triceps brachii tendon

Joint capsule
Radial collateral ligament
Anular ligament of radius
Biceps brachii tendon

Sub-cutaneous olecranon bursa

In 90° flexion: lateral view

Joint capsule
Ulnar collateral ligament
Anular ligament of radius
Biceps brachii tendon
Oblique cord

Radius

Ulna

Humerus

Triceps brachii tendon

Subcutaneous olecranon bursa

In 90° flexion: medial view

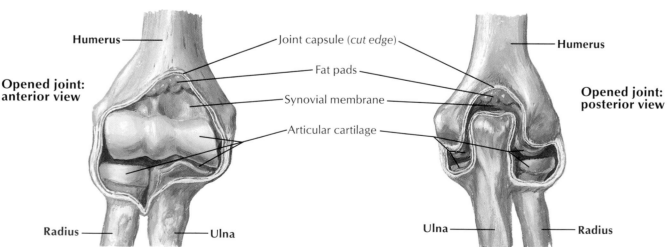

Humerus

Opened joint: anterior view

Radius

Ulna

Joint capsule (*cut edge*)

Fat pads

Synovial membrane

Articular cartilage

Humerus

Opened joint: posterior view

Ulna

Radius

ANESTHESIA

Upper Arm and Elbow

01710 Anesthesia for procedures on nerves, muscles, tendons, fascia, and bursae of upper arm and elbow; not otherwise specified

01712 tenotomy, elbow to shoulder, open

01714 tenoplasty, elbow to shoulder

01716 tenodesis, rupture of long tendon of biceps

01730 Anesthesia for all closed procedures on humerus and elbow

01732 Anesthesia for diagnostic arthroscopic procedures of elbow joint

01740 Anesthesia for open or surgical arthroscopic procedures of the elbow; not otherwise specified

SURGERY

Musculoskeletal System

Humerus (Upper Arm) and Elbow
Excision

24100 Arthrotomy, elbow; with synovial biopsy only

24101 with joint exploration, with or without biopsy, with or without removal of loose or foreign body

24102 with synovectomy

Repair, Revision, and/or Reconstruction

24301 Muscle or tendon transfer, any type, upper arm or elbow, single (excluding 24320-24331)

24305 Tendon lengthening, upper arm or elbow, each tendon

24310 Tenotomy, open, elbow to shoulder, each tendon

24320 Tenoplasty, with muscle transfer, with or without free graft, elbow to shoulder, single (Seddon-Brookes type procedure)

24330 Flexor-plasty, elbow (eg, Steindler type advancement);

24331 with extensor advancement

24332 Tenolysis, triceps

24340 Tenodesis of biceps tendon at elbow (separate procedure)

24341 Repair, tendon or muscle, upper arm or elbow, each tendon or muscle, primary or secondary (excludes rotator cuff)

24342 Reinsertion of ruptured biceps or triceps tendon, distal, with or without tendon graft

24343 Repair lateral collateral ligament, elbow, with local tissue

24344 Reconstruction lateral collateral ligament, elbow, with tendon graft (includes harvesting of graft)

24345 Repair medial collateral ligament, elbow, with local tissue

24346 Reconstruction medial collateral ligament, elbow, with tendon graft (includes harvesting of graft)

24350 Fasciotomy, lateral or medial (eg, tennis elbow or epicondylitis);

24351 with extensor origin detachment

24352 with annular ligament resection

24354 with stripping

24356 with partial ostectomy

Endoscopy/Arthroscopy

29830 Arthroscopy, elbow, diagnostic, with or without synovial biopsy (separate procedure)

29834 Arthroscopy, elbow, surgical; with removal of loose body or foreign body

29835 synovectomy, partial

29836 synovectomy, complete

29837 debridement, limited

29838 debridement, extensive

Plate 158: Bones of Forearm

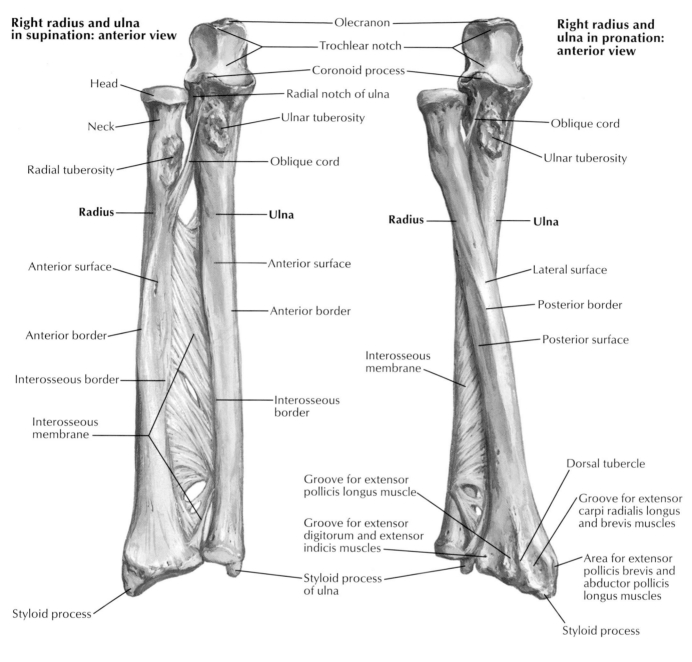

**Right radius and ulna
in supination: anterior view**

Olecranon

Trochlear notch

Coronoid process

**Right radius and
ulna in pronation:
anterior view**

Head

Neck

Radial tuberosity

Radial notch of ulna

Ulnar tuberosity

Oblique cord

Oblique cord

Ulnar tuberosity

Radius

Ulna

Radius

Ulna

Anterior surface

Anterior surface

Lateral surface

Anterior border

Posterior border

Anterior border

Posterior surface

Interosseous border

Interosseous
membrane

Interosseous
border

Interosseous
membrane

Groove for extensor
pollicis longus muscle

Dorsal tubercle

Groove for extensor
carpi radialis longus
and brevis muscles

Groove for extensor
digitorum and extensor
indicis muscles

Area for extensor
pollicis brevis and
abductor pollicis
longus muscles

Styloid process

Styloid process
of ulna

Styloid process

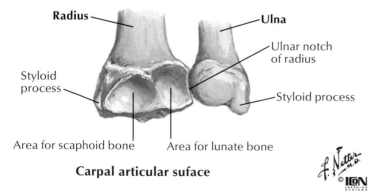

Radius

Ulna

Styloid
process

Ulnar notch
of radius

Styloid process

Area for scaphoid bone

Area for lunate bone

Carpal articular suface

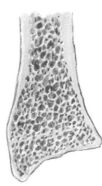

Coronal section of
radius demonstrates
how thickness of
cortical bone of
shaft diminishes
to thin layer over
cancellous bone
at di stal end

Nomenclature Notes

A *Galeazzi fracture* is a fracture of the shaft of the radius with dislocation of the distal radioulnar joint.

A *Monteggia fracture* is an angulated fracture at the junction of the proximal and middle third of ulna with anterior dislocation of the radial head.

ANESTHESIA

Upper Arm and Elbow

01730	Anesthesia for all closed procedures on humerus and elbow
01740	Anesthesia for open or surgical arthroscopic procedures of the elbow; not otherwise specified
01756	Anesthesia for open or surgical arthroscopic procedures of the elbow; radical procedures

Forearm, Wrist, and Hand

01810	Anesthesia for all procedures on nerves, muscles, tendons, fascia, and bursae of forearm, wrist, and hand
01820	Anesthesia for all closed procedures on radius, ulna, wrist, or hand bones
01830	Anesthesia for open or surgical arthroscopic/endoscopic procedures on distal radius, distal ulna, wrist, or hand joints; not otherwise specified

SURGERY

Musculoskeletal System

Humerus (Upper Arm) and Elbow
Excision

24120	Excision or curettage of bone cyst or benign tumor of head or neck of radius or olecranon process;
24125	with autograft (includes obtaining graft)
24126	with allograft
24130	Excision, radial head
24136	Sequestrectomy (eg, for osteomyelitis or bone abscess), radial head or neck
24138	Sequestrectomy (eg, for osteomyelitis or bone abscess), olecranon process
24145	Partial excision (craterization, saucerization, or diaphysectomy) bone (eg, osteomyelitis), radial head or neck
24152	Radical resection for tumor, radial head or neck;
24153	with autograft (includes obtaining graft)

Repair, Revision, and/or Reconstruction

24365	Arthroplasty, radial head;
24366	with implant

Fracture and/or Dislocation

24620	Closed treatment of Monteggia type of fracture dislocation at elbow (fracture proximal end of ulna with dislocation of radial head), with manipulation
24635	Open treatment of Monteggia type of fracture dislocation at elbow (fracture proximal end of ulna with dislocation of radial head), with or without internal or external fixation
24640	Closed treatment of radial head subluxation in child, nursemaid elbow, with manipulation
24650	Closed treatment of radial head or neck fracture; without manipulation
24655	with manipulation
24665	Open treatment of radial head or neck fracture, with or without internal fixation or radial head excision;
24666	with radial head prosthetic replacement
24670	Closed treatment of ulnar fracture, proximal end (olecranon process); without manipulation
24675	with manipulation
24685	Open treatment of ulnar fracture proximal end (olecranon process), with or without internal or external fixation

Arthrodesis

24800	Arthrodesis, elbow joint; local
24802	Arthrodesis, elbow joint; with autogenous graft (includes obtaining graft)

Forearm and Wrist
Incision

25035	Incision, deep, bone cortex, forearm and/or wrist (eg, osteomyelitis or bone abscess)
25040	Arthrotomy, radiocarpal or midcarpal joint, with exploration, drainage, or removal of foreign body

Excision

25107	Arthrotomy, distal radioulnar joint including repair of triangular cartilage, complex
25110	Excision, lesion of tendon sheath, forearm and/or wrist
25120	Excision or curettage of bone cyst or benign tumor of radius or ulna (excluding head or neck of radius and olecranon process);
25125	with autograft (includes obtaining graft)
25126	with allograft
25130	Excision or curettage of bone cyst or benign tumor of carpal bones;
25135	with autograft (includes obtaining graft)
25136	with allograft
25145	Sequestrectomy (eg, for osteomyelitis or bone abscess), forearm and/or wrist
25150	Partial excision (craterization, saucerization, or diaphysectomy) of bone (eg, for osteomyelitis); ulna
25151	radius
25170	Radical resection for tumor, radius or ulna

Repair, Revision, and/or Reconstruction

25337	Reconstruction for stabilization of unstable distal ulna or distal radioulnar joint, secondary by soft tissue stabilization (eg, tendon transfer, tendon graft or weave, or tenodesis) with or without open reduction of distal radioulnar joint

(Repair, Revision, and/or Reconstruction continued on next page)

Plate 158: Bones of Forearm

(Repair, Revision, and/or Reconstruction continued from previous page)

25350   Osteotomy, radius; distal third
25355   middle or proximal third
25360   Osteotomy; ulna
25365   radius AND ulna
25370   Multiple osteotomies, with realignment on intramedullary rod (Sofield type procedure); radius OR ulna
25375   radius AND ulna
25390   Osteoplasty, radius OR ulna; shortening
25391   lengthening with autograft
25392   Osteoplasty, radius AND ulna; shortening (excluding 64876)
25393   lengthening with autograft
25394   Osteoplasty, carpal bone, shortening
25400   Repair of nonunion or malunion, radius OR ulna; without graft (eg, compression technique)
25405   with autograft (includes obtaining graft)
25415   Repair of nonunion or malunion, radius AND ulna; without graft (eg, compression technique)
25420   with autograft (includes obtaining graft)
25425   Repair of defect with autograft; radius OR ulna
25426   radius AND ulna
25430   Insertion of vascular pedicle into carpal bone (eg, Hori procedure)
25431   Repair of nonunion of carpal bone (excluding carpal scaphoid (navicular)) (includes obtaining graft and necessary fixation), each bone
25440   Repair of nonunion, scaphoid carpal (navicular) bone, with or without radial styloidectomy (includes obtaining graft and necessary fixation)
25441   Arthroplasty with prosthetic replacement; distal radius
25442   distal ulna
25443   scaphoid carpal (navicular)
25444   lunate
25445   trapezium
25446   distal radius and partial or entire carpus (total wrist)
25447   Arthroplasty, interposition, intercarpal or carpometacarpal joints
25449   Revision of arthroplasty, including removal of implant, wrist joint
25450   Epiphyseal arrest by epiphysiodesis or stapling; distal radius OR ulna
25455   distal radius AND ulna
25490   Prophylactic treatment (nailing, pinning, plating or wiring) with or without methylmethacrylate; radius
25491   ulna
25492   radius AND ulna

Fracture and/or Dislocation

25500   Closed treatment of radial shaft fracture; without manipulation
25505   with manipulation
25515   Open treatment of radial shaft fracture, with or without internal or external fixation
25520   Closed treatment of radial shaft fracture and closed treatment of dislocation of distal radioulnar joint (Galeazzi fracture/dislocation)
25525   Open treatment of radial shaft fracture, with internal and/ or external fixation and closed treatment of dislocation of distal radioulnar joint (Galeazzi fracture/dislocation), with or without percutaneous skeletal fixation
25526   Open treatment of radial shaft fracture, with internal and/or external fixation and open treatment, with or without internal or external fixation of distal radioulnar joint (Galeazzi fracture/dislocation), includes repair of triangular fibrocartilage complex
25530   Closed treatment of ulnar shaft fracture; without manipulation
25535   with manipulation
25545   Open treatment of ulnar shaft fracture, with or without internal or external fixation
25560   Closed treatment of radial and ulnar shaft fractures; without manipulation
25565   with manipulation
25574   Open treatment of radial AND ulnar shaft fractures, with internal or external fixation; of radius OR ulna
25575   of radius AND ulna
25600   Closed treatment of distal radial fracture (eg, Colles or Smith type) or epiphyseal separation, with or without fracture of ulnar styloid; without manipulation
25605   with manipulation
25611   Percutaneous skeletal fixation of distal radial fracture (eg, Colles or Smith type) or epiphyseal separation, with or without fracture of ulnar styloid, requiring manipulation, with or without external fixation
25620   Open treatment of distal radial fracture (eg, Colles or Smith type) or epiphyseal separation, with or without fracture of ulnar styloid, with or without internal or external fixation
25650   Closed treatment of ulnar styloid fracture
25651   Percutaneous skeletal fixation of ulnar styloid fracture
25652   Open treatment of ulnar styloid fracture

Arthrodesis

25800   Arthrodesis, wrist; complete, without bone graft (includes radiocarpal and/or intercarpal and/or carpometacarpal joints)
25805   with sliding graft
25810   with iliac or other autograft (includes obtaining graft)
25820   Arthrodesis, wrist; limited, without bone graft (eg, intercarpal or radiocarpal)
25825   with autograft (includes obtaining graft)
25830   Arthrodesis, distal radioulnar joint with segmental resection of ulna, with or without bone graft (eg, Sauve-Kapandji procedure)

Amputation

25900   Amputation, forearm, through radius and ulna;
25905   open, circular (guillotine)
25907   secondary closure or scar revision
25909   re-amputation

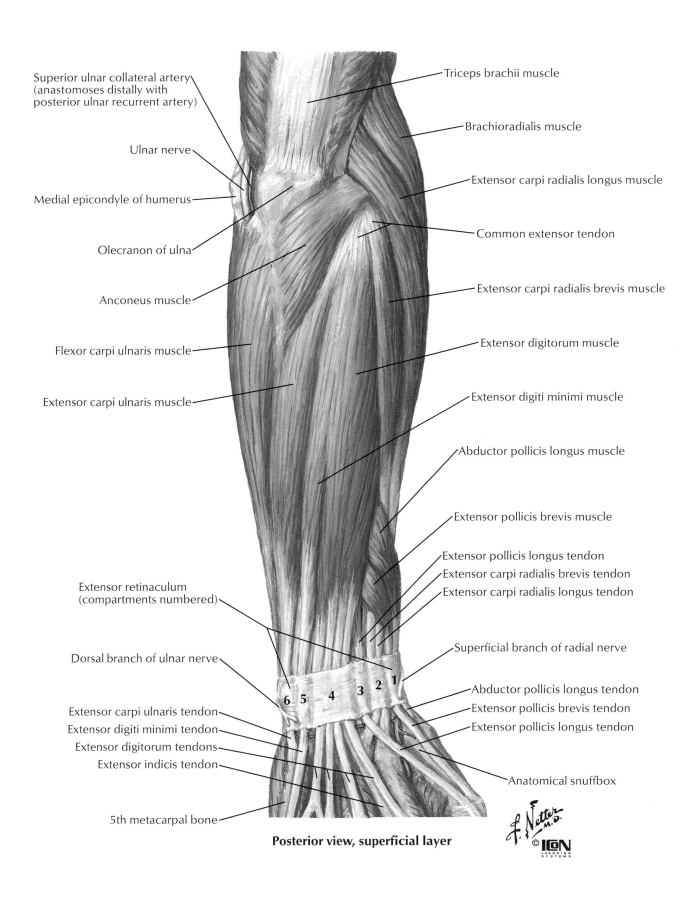

Superior ulnar collateral artery (anastomoses distally with posterior ulnar recurrent artery)

Ulnar nerve

Medial epicondyle of humerus

Olecranon of ulna

Anconeus muscle

Flexor carpi ulnaris muscle

Extensor carpi ulnaris muscle

Triceps brachii muscle

Brachioradialis muscle

Extensor carpi radialis longus muscle

Common extensor tendon

Extensor carpi radialis brevis muscle

Extensor digitorum muscle

Extensor digiti minimi muscle

Abductor pollicis longus muscle

Extensor pollicis brevis muscle

Extensor pollicis longus tendon
Extensor carpi radialis brevis tendon
Extensor carpi radialis longus tendon

Extensor retinaculum (compartments numbered)

Dorsal branch of ulnar nerve

Extensor carpi ulnaris tendon
Extensor digiti minimi tendon
Extensor digitorum tendons
Extensor indicis tendon

5th metacarpal bone

Superficial branch of radial nerve

6 5 4 3 2 1

Abductor pollicis longus tendon
Extensor pollicis brevis tendon
Extensor pollicis longus tendon

Anatomical snuffbox

Posterior view, superficial layer

Plate 159: Muscles of Forearm

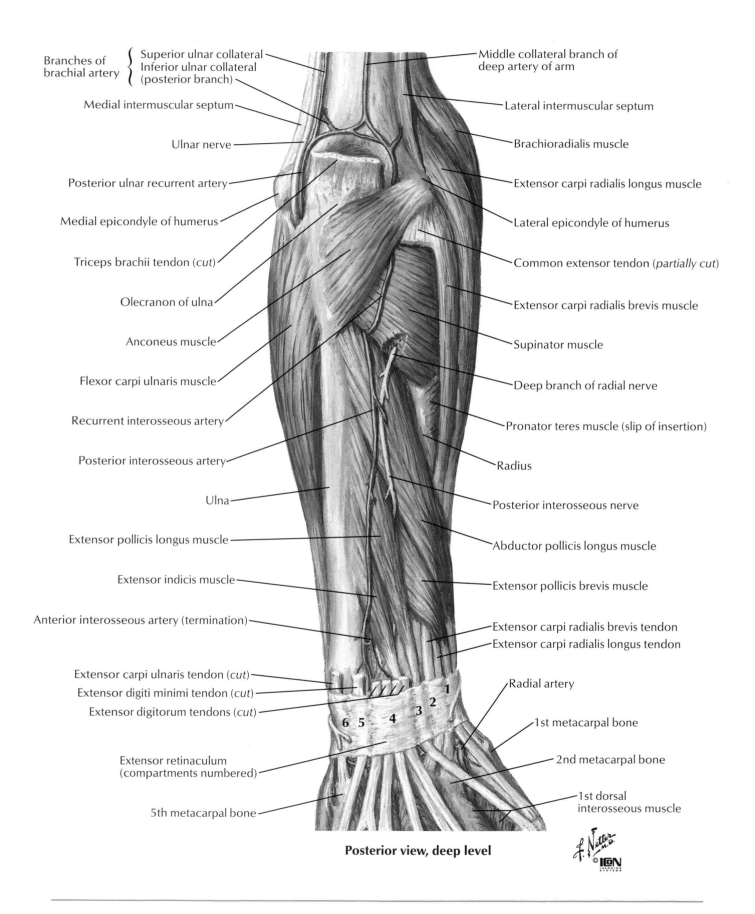

Branches of brachial artery { Superior ulnar collateral
Inferior ulnar collateral (posterior branch)

Medial intermuscular septum

Ulnar nerve

Posterior ulnar recurrent artery

Medial epicondyle of humerus

Triceps brachii tendon (cut)

Olecranon of ulna

Anconeus muscle

Flexor carpi ulnaris muscle

Recurrent interosseous artery

Posterior interosseous artery

Ulna

Extensor pollicis longus muscle

Extensor indicis muscle

Anterior interosseous artery (termination)

Extensor carpi ulnaris tendon (cut)
Extensor digiti minimi tendon (cut)
Extensor digitorum tendons (cut)

Extensor retinaculum (compartments numbered)

5th metacarpal bone

Middle collateral branch of deep artery of arm

Lateral intermuscular septum

Brachioradialis muscle

Extensor carpi radialis longus muscle

Lateral epicondyle of humerus

Common extensor tendon (partially cut)

Extensor carpi radialis brevis muscle

Supinator muscle

Deep branch of radial nerve

Pronator teres muscle (slip of insertion)

Radius

Posterior interosseous nerve

Abductor pollicis longus muscle

Extensor pollicis brevis muscle

Extensor carpi radialis brevis tendon
Extensor carpi radialis longus tendon

Radial artery

1st metacarpal bone

2nd metacarpal bone

1st dorsal interosseous muscle

Posterior view, deep level

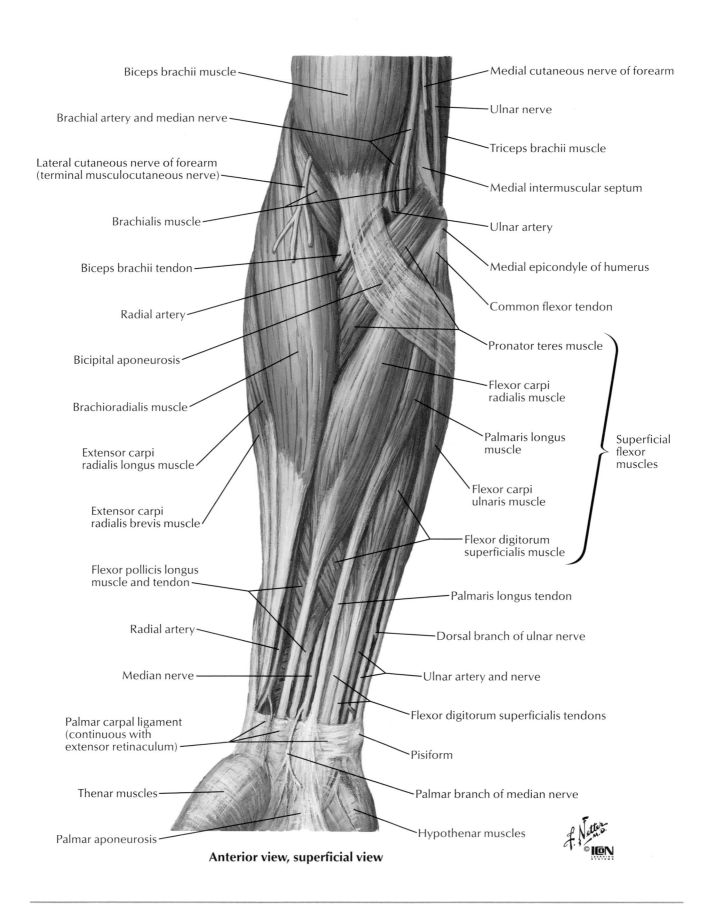

Biceps brachii muscle

Brachial artery and median nerve

Lateral cutaneous nerve of forearm
(terminal musculocutaneous nerve)

Brachialis muscle

Biceps brachii tendon

Radial artery

Bicipital aponeurosis

Brachioradialis muscle

Extensor carpi
radialis longus muscle

Extensor carpi
radialis brevis muscle

Flexor pollicis longus
muscle and tendon

Radial artery

Median nerve

Palmar carpal ligament
(continuous with
extensor retinaculum)

Thenar muscles

Palmar aponeurosis

Medial cutaneous nerve of forearm

Ulnar nerve

Triceps brachii muscle

Medial intermuscular septum

Ulnar artery

Medial epicondyle of humerus

Common flexor tendon

Pronator teres muscle

Flexor carpi
radialis muscle

Palmaris longus
muscle

Flexor carpi
ulnaris muscle

Flexor digitorum
superficialis muscle

Superficial
flexor
muscles

Palmaris longus tendon

Dorsal branch of ulnar nerve

Ulnar artery and nerve

Flexor digitorum superficialis tendons

Pisiform

Palmar branch of median nerve

Hypothenar muscles

Anterior view, superficial view

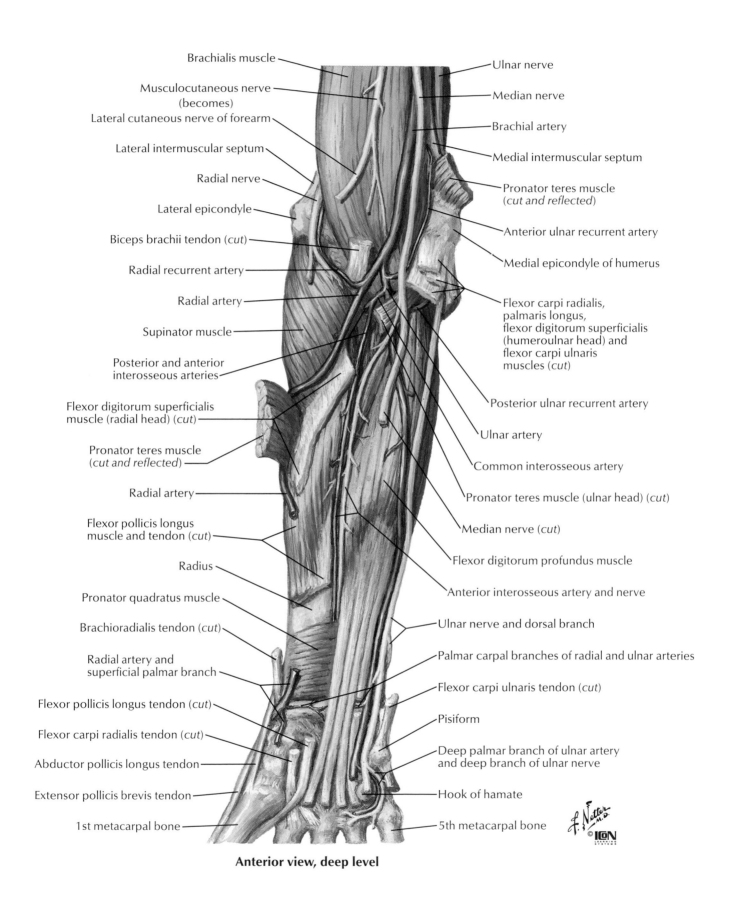

Brachialis muscle

Musculocutaneous nerve (becomes)

Lateral cutaneous nerve of forearm

Lateral intermuscular septum

Radial nerve

Lateral epicondyle

Biceps brachii tendon (cut)

Radial recurrent artery

Radial artery

Supinator muscle

Posterior and anterior interosseous arteries

Flexor digitorum superficialis muscle (radial head) (cut)

Pronator teres muscle (cut and reflected)

Radial artery

Flexor pollicis longus muscle and tendon (cut)

Radius

Pronator quadratus muscle

Brachioradialis tendon (cut)

Radial artery and superficial palmar branch

Flexor pollicis longus tendon (cut)

Flexor carpi radialis tendon (cut)

Abductor pollicis longus tendon

Extensor pollicis brevis tendon

1st metacarpal bone

Ulnar nerve

Median nerve

Brachial artery

Medial intermuscular septum

Pronator teres muscle (cut and reflected)

Anterior ulnar recurrent artery

Medial epicondyle of humerus

Flexor carpi radialis, palmaris longus, flexor digitorum superficialis (humeroulnar head) and flexor carpi ulnaris muscles (cut)

Posterior ulnar recurrent artery

Ulnar artery

Common interosseous artery

Pronator teres muscle (ulnar head) (cut)

Median nerve (cut)

Flexor digitorum profundus muscle

Anterior interosseous artery and nerve

Ulnar nerve and dorsal branch

Palmar carpal branches of radial and ulnar arteries

Flexor carpi ulnaris tendon (cut)

Pisiform

Deep palmar branch of ulnar artery and deep branch of ulnar nerve

Hook of hamate

5th metacarpal bone

Anterior view, deep level

ANESTHESIA

Thorax (Chest Wall and Shoulder Girdle)

00400 Anesthesia for procedures on the integumentary system on the extremities, anterior trunk and perineum; not otherwise specified

Upper Arm and Elbow

01710 Anesthesia for procedures on nerves, muscles, tendons, fascia, and bursae of upper arm and elbow; not otherwise specified

01756 Anesthesia for open or surgical arthroscopic procedures of the elbow; radical procedures

Forearm, Wrist, and Hand

01810 Anesthesia for all procedures on nerves, muscles, tendons, fascia, and bursae of forearm, wrist, and hand

01830 Anesthesia for open or surgical arthroscopic/endoscopic procedures on distal radius, distal ulna, wrist, or hand joints; not otherwise specified

SURGERY

Musculoskeletal System

General
Excision

20200 Biopsy, muscle; superficial
20205   deep
20206 Biopsy, muscle, percutaneous needle

Introduction or Removal

20520 Removal of foreign body in muscle or tendon sheath; simple
20525   deep or complicated

Humerus (Upper Arm) and Elbow
Excision

24065 Biopsy, soft tissue of upper arm or elbow area; superficial
24066   deep (subfascial or intramuscular)
24075 Excision, tumor, soft tissue of upper arm or elbow area; subcutaneous
24076   deep (subfascial or intramuscular)
24077 Radical resection of tumor (eg, malignant neoplasm), soft tissue of upper arm or elbow area

Introduction or Removal

24200 Removal of foreign body, upper arm or elbow area; subcutaneous
24201   deep (subfascial or intramuscular)

Repair, Revision, and/or Reconstruction

24301 Muscle or tendon transfer, any type, upper arm or elbow, single (excluding 24320-24331)
24332 Tenolysis, triceps
24340 Tenodesis of biceps tendon at elbow (separate procedure)
24341 Repair, tendon or muscle, upper arm or elbow, each tendon or muscle, primary or secondary (excludes rotator cuff)

Forearm and Wrist
Incision

25020 Decompression fasciotomy, forearm and/or wrist, flexor OR extensor compartment; without debridement of nonviable muscle and/or nerve
25023   with debridement of nonviable muscle and/or nerve
25024 Decompression fasciotomy, forearm and/or wrist, flexor AND extensor compartment; without debridement of nonviable muscle and/or nerve
25025   with debridement of nonviable muscle and/or nerve
25028 Incision and drainage, forearm and/or wrist; deep abscess or hematoma
25031 Incision and drainage, forearm and/or wrist; bursa

Excision

25065 Biopsy, soft tissue of forearm and/or wrist; superficial
25066   deep (subfascial or intramuscular)
25075 Excision, tumor, soft tissue of forearm and/or wrist area; subcutaneous
25076   deep (subfascial or intramuscular)
25077 Radical resection of tumor (eg, malignant neoplasm), soft tissue of forearm and/or wrist area

Introduction or Removal

25248 Exploration with removal of deep foreign body, forearm or wrist

Repair, Revision, and/or Reconstruction

25260 Repair, tendon or muscle, flexor, forearm and/or wrist; primary, single, each tendon or muscle
25263   secondary, single, each tendon or muscle
25265   secondary, with free graft (includes obtaining graft), each tendon or muscle
25270 Repair, tendon or muscle, extensor, forearm and/or wrist; primary, single, each tendon or muscle
25272   secondary, single, each tendon or muscle
25274   secondary, with free graft (includes obtaining graft), each tendon or muscle

Fracture and/or Dislocation

25575 Open treatment of radial AND ulnar shaft fractures, with internal or external fixation; of radius AND ulna
25600 Closed treatment of distal radial fracture (eg, Colles or Smith type) or epiphyseal separation, with or without fracture of ulnar styloid; without manipulation

Amputation

25900 Amputation, forearm, through radius and ulna;
25905   open, circular (guillotine)
25907   secondary closure or scar revision
25909   re-amputation

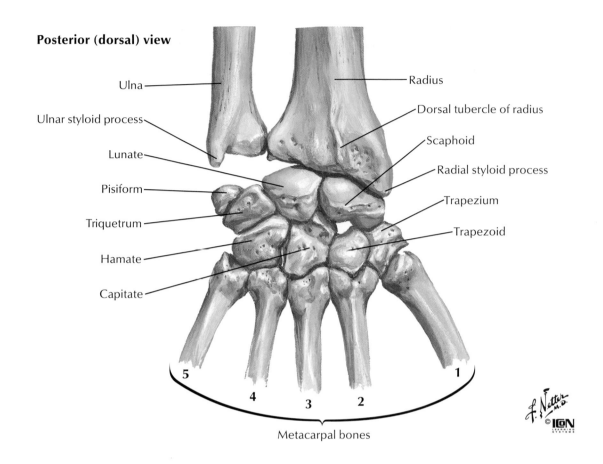

Posterior (dorsal) view

Ulna

Ulnar styloid process

Lunate

Pisiform

Triquetrum

Hamate

Capitate

Radius

Dorsal tubercle of radius

Scaphoid

Radial styloid process

Trapezium

Trapezoid

5 4 3 2 1

Metacarpal bones

ANESTHESIA

Forearm, Wrist, and Hand

01820 Anesthesia for all closed procedures on radius, ulna, wrist, or hand bones

01829 Anesthesia for diagnostic arthroscopic procedures on the wrist

01830 Anesthesia for open or surgical arthroscopic/endoscopic procedures on distal radius, distal ulna, wrist, or hand joints; not otherwise specified

01832   total wrist replacement

SURGERY

Musculoskeletal System

General
Introduction or Removal

20605 Arthrocentesis, aspiration and/or injection; intermediate joint or bursa (eg, temporomandibular, acromioclavicular, wrist, elbow or ankle, olecranon bursa)

Forearm and Wrist
Incision

25035 Incision, deep, bone cortex, forearm and/or wrist (eg, osteomyelitis or bone abscess)

25040 Arthrotomy, radiocarpal or midcarpal joint, with exploration, drainage, or removal of foreign body

Excision

25100 Arthrotomy, wrist joint; with biopsy

25101   with joint exploration, with or without biopsy, with or without removal of loose or foreign body

25105   with synovectomy

25107 Arthrotomy, distal radioulnar joint including repair of triangular cartilage, complex

25120 Excision or curettage of bone cyst or benign tumor of radius or ulna (excluding head or neck of radius and olecranon process);

25125   with autograft (includes obtaining graft)

25126   with allograft

25130 Excision or curettage of bone cyst or benign tumor of carpal bones;

25135   with autograft (includes obtaining graft)

25136   with allograft

25145 Sequestrectomy (eg, for osteomyelitis or bone abscess), forearm and/or wrist

25210 Carpectomy; one bone

25215   all bones of proximal row

25230 Radial styloidectomy (separate procedure)

25240 Excision distal ulna partial or complete (eg, Darrach type or matched resection)

Introduction or Removal

25248 Exploration with removal of deep foreign body, forearm or wrist

25250 Removal of wrist prosthesis; (separate procedure)

25251	complicated, including total wrist
25259	Manipulation, wrist, under anesthesia

Repair, Revision, and/or Reconstruction

25332	Arthroplasty, wrist, with or without interposition, with or without external or internal fixation
25335	Centralization of wrist on ulna (eg, radial club hand)
25337	Reconstruction for stabilization of unstable distal ulna or distal radioulnar joint, secondary by soft tissue stabilization (eg, tendon transfer, tendon graft or weave, or tenodesis) with or without open reduction of distal radioulnar joint
25350	Osteotomy, radius; distal third
25360	Osteotomy; ulna
25365	radius AND ulna
25370	Multiple osteotomies, with realignment on intramedullary rod (Sofield type procedure); radius OR ulna
25375	radius AND ulna
25394	Osteoplasty, carpal bone, shortening
25430	Insertion of vascular pedicle into carpal bone (eg, Hori procedure)
25431	Repair of nonunion of carpal bone (excluding carpal scaphoid (navicular)) (includes obtaining graft and necessary fixation), each bone
25440	Repair of nonunion, scaphoid carpal (navicular) bone, with or without radial styloidectomy (includes obtaining graft and necessary fixation)
25441	Arthroplasty with prosthetic replacement; distal radius
25442	distal ulna
25443	scaphoid carpal (navicular)
25444	lunate
25445	trapezium
25446	distal radius and partial or entire carpus (total wrist)
25447	Arthroplasty, interposition, intercarpal or carpometacarpal joints
25449	Revision of arthroplasty, including removal of implant, wrist joint
25450	Epiphyseal arrest by epiphysiodesis or stapling; distal radius OR ulna
25455	distal radius AND ulna

Fracture and/or Dislocation

25622	Closed treatment of carpal scaphoid (navicular) fracture; without manipulation
25624	with manipulation
25628	Open treatment of carpal scaphoid (navicular) fracture, with or without internal or external fixation
25630	Closed treatment of carpal bone fracture (excluding carpal scaphoid (navicular)); without manipulation, each bone
25635	with manipulation, each bone

25645	Open treatment of carpal bone fracture (other than carpal scaphoid (navicular)), each bone
25650	Closed treatment of ulnar styloid fracture
25651	Percutaneous skeletal fixation of ulnar styloid fracture
25652	Open treatment of ulnar styloid fracture
25660	Closed treatment of radiocarpal or intercarpal dislocation, one or more bones, with manipulation
25670	Open treatment of radiocarpal or intercarpal dislocation, one or more bones
25671	Percutaneous skeletal fixation of distal radioulnar dislocation
25675	Closed treatment of distal radioulnar dislocation with manipulation
25676	Open treatment of distal radioulnar dislocation, acute or chronic
25680	Closed treatment of trans-scaphoperilunar type of fracture dislocation, with manipulation
25685	Open treatment of trans-scaphoperilunar type of fracture dislocation
25690	Closed treatment of lunate dislocation, with manipulation
25695	Open treatment of lunate dislocation

Arthrodesis

25800	Arthrodesis, wrist; complete, without bone graft (includes radiocarpal and/or intercarpal and/or carpometacarpal joints)
25805	with sliding graft
25810	with iliac or other autograft (includes obtaining graft)
25820	Arthrodesis, wrist; limited, without bone graft (eg, intercarpal or radiocarpal)
25825	with autograft (includes obtaining graft)
25830	Arthrodesis, distal radioulnar joint with segmental resection of ulna, with or without bone graft (eg, Sauve-Kapandji procedure)

Amputation

25920	Disarticulation through wrist;
25922	secondary closure or scar revision
25924	re-amputation
25927	Transmetacarpal amputation;
25929	secondary closure or scar revision
25931	re-amputation

Endoscopy/Arthroscopy

29840	Arthroscopy, wrist, diagnostic, with or without synovial biopsy (separate procedure)
29843	Arthroscopy, wrist, surgical; for infection, lavage and drainage
29844	synovectomy, partial
29845	synovectomy, complete
29846	excision and/or repair of triangular fibrocartilage and/or joint debridement
29847	internal fixation for fracture or instability

Carpal tunnel: palmar view

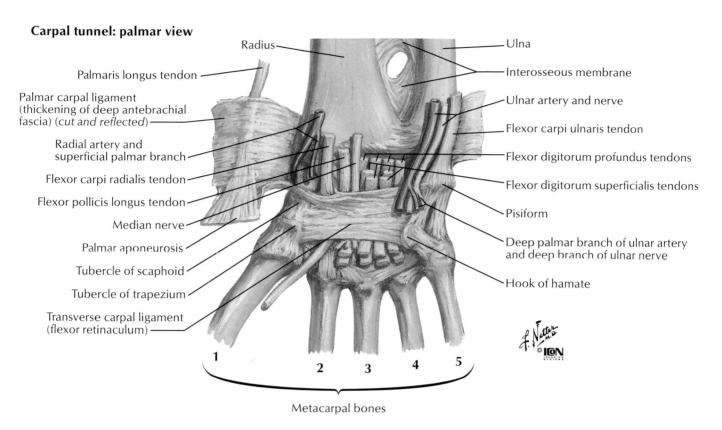

Radius — Ulna — Interosseous membrane — Palmaris longus tendon — Palmar carpal ligament (thickening of deep antebrachial fascia) (*cut and reflected*) — Radial artery and superficial palmar branch — Flexor carpi radialis tendon — Flexor pollicis longus tendon — Median nerve — Palmar aponeurosis — Tubercle of scaphoid — Tubercle of trapezium — Transverse carpal ligament (flexor retinaculum) — Ulnar artery and nerve — Flexor carpi ulnaris tendon — Flexor digitorum profundus tendons — Flexor digitorum superficialis tendons — Pisiform — Deep palmar branch of ulnar artery and deep branch of ulnar nerve — Hook of hamate

1 2 3 4 5

Metacarpal bones

ANESTHESIA

Forearm, Wrist, and Hand

01810   Anesthesia for all procedures on nerves, muscles, tendons, fascia, and bursae of forearm, wrist, and hand

Other Procedures

01991   Anesthesia for diagnostic or therapeutic nerve blocks and injections (when block or injection is performed by a different provider); other than the prone position

01992   prone position

SURGERY

Musculoskeletal System

General
Introduction or Removal

20526   Injection, therapeutic (eg, local anesthetic, corticosteroid), carpal tunnel

20550   Injection(s); single tendon sheath, or ligament, aponeurosis (eg, plantar "fascia")

Forearm and Wrist
Repair, Revision, and/or Reconstruction

25320   Capsulorrhaphy or reconstruction, wrist, open (eg, capsulodesis, ligament repair, tendon transfer or graft) (includes synovectomy, capsulotomy and open reduction) for carpal instability

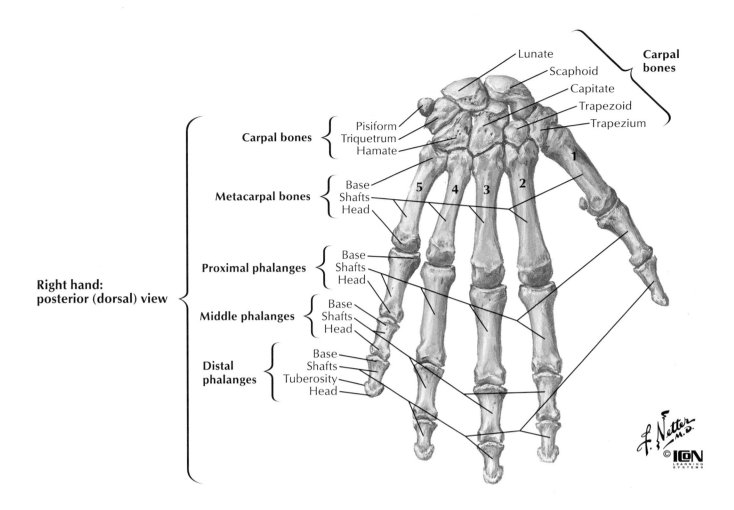

Right hand: posterior (dorsal) view

Carpal bones
- Pisiform
- Triquetrum
- Hamate
- Lunate
- Scaphoid
- Capitate
- Trapezoid
- Trapezium

Metacarpal bones
- Base
- Shafts
- Head

Proximal phalanges
- Base
- Shafts
- Head

Middle phalanges
- Base
- Shafts
- Head

Distal phalanges
- Base
- Shafts
- Tuberosity
- Head

ANESTHESIA

Forearm, Wrist, and Hand

01810	Anesthesia for all procedures on nerves, muscles, tendons, fascia, and bursae of forearm, wrist, and hand
01820	Anesthesia for all closed procedures on radius, ulna, wrist, or hand bones
01830	Anesthesia for open or surgical arthroscopic/endoscopic procedures on distal radius, distal ulna, wrist, or hand joints; not otherwise specified

SURGERY

Musculoskeletal System

Hand and Fingers
Incision

26034	Incision, bone cortex, hand or finger (eg, osteomyelitis or bone abscess)
26070	Arthrotomy, with exploration, drainage, or removal of loose or foreign body; carpometacarpal joint
26075	metacarpophalangeal joint, each
26080	interphalangeal joint, each

Excision

26100	Arthrotomy with biopsy; carpometacarpal joint, each
26105	metacarpophalangeal joint, each
26110	interphalangeal joint, each
26185	Sesamoidectomy, thumb or finger (separate procedure)
26200	Excision or curettage of bone cyst or benign tumor of metacarpal;
26205	with autograft (includes obtaining graft)
26210	Excision or curettage of bone cyst or benign tumor of proximal, middle, or distal phalanx of finger;
26215	with autograft (includes obtaining graft)
26230	Partial excision (craterization, saucerization, or diaphysectomy) bone (eg, osteomyelitis); metacarpal
26235	proximal or middle phalanx of finger
26236	distal phalanx of finger
26250	Radical resection, metacarpal (eg, tumor);
26255	with autograft (includes obtaining graft)
26260	Radical resection, proximal or middle phalanx of finger (eg, tumor);
26261	with autograft (includes obtaining graft)
26262	Radical resection, distal phalanx of finger (eg, tumor)

Plate 162: Bones of Wrist and Hand

Introduction or Removal

26320   Removal of implant from finger or hand

Repair, Revison and/or Reconstruction

26530   Arthroplasty, metacarpophalangeal joint; each joint
26531   with prosthetic implant, each joint
26535   Arthroplasty, interphalangeal joint; each joint
26536   with prosthetic implant, each joint
26546   Repair non-union, metacarpal or phalanx, (includes obtaining bone graft with or without external or internal fixation)
26548   Repair and reconstruction, finger, volar plate, interphalangeal joint
26550   Pollicization of a digit
26565   Osteotomy; metacarpal, each
26567   phalanx of finger, each
26568   Osteoplasty, lengthening, metacarpal or phalanx

Fracture and/or Dislocation

26600   Closed treatment of metacarpal fracture, single; without manipulation, each bone
26605   with manipulation, each bone
26607   Closed treatment of metacarpal fracture, with manipulation, with external fixation, each bone
26608   Percutaneous skeletal fixation of metacarpal fracture, each bone
26615   Open treatment of metacarpal fracture, single, with or without internal or external fixation, each bone
26641   Closed treatment of carpometacarpal dislocation, thumb, with manipulation
26645   Closed treatment of carpometacarpal fracture dislocation, thumb (Bennett fracture), with manipulation
26650   Percutaneous skeletal fixation of carpometacarpal fracture dislocation, thumb (Bennett fracture), with manipulation, with or without external fixation
26665   Open treatment of carpometacarpal fracture dislocation, thumb (Bennett fracture), with or without internal or external fixation
26670   Closed treatment of carpometacarpal dislocation, other than thumb, with manipulation, each joint; without anesthesia
26675   requiring anesthesia
26676   Percutaneous skeletal fixation of carpometacarpal dislocation, other than thumb, with manipulation, each joint
26685   Open treatment of carpometacarpal dislocation, other than thumb; with or without internal or external fixation, each joint
26686   complex, multiple or delayed reduction
26700   Closed treatment of metacarpophalangeal dislocation, single, with manipulation; without anesthesia
26705   requiring anesthesia
26706   Percutaneous skeletal fixation of metacarpophalangeal dislocation, single, with manipulation
26715   Open treatment of metacarpophalangeal dislocation, single, with or without internal or external fixation
26720   Closed treatment of phalangeal shaft fracture, proximal or middle phalanx, finger or thumb; without manipulation, each

26725   with manipulation, with or without skin or skeletal traction, each
26727   Percutaneous skeletal fixation of unstable phalangeal shaft fracture, proximal or middle phalanx, finger or thumb, with manipulation, each
26735   Open treatment of phalangeal shaft fracture, proximal or middle phalanx, finger or thumb, with or without internal or external fixation, each
26740   Closed treatment of articular fracture, involving metacarpophalangeal or interphalangeal joint; without manipulation, each
26742   with manipulation, each
26746   Open treatment of articular fracture, involving metacarpophalangeal or interphalangeal joint, with or without internal or external fixation, each
26750   Closed treatment of distal phalangeal fracture, finger or thumb; without manipulation, each
26755   with manipulation, each
26756   Percutaneous skeletal fixation of distal phalangeal fracture, finger or thumb, each
26765   Open treatment of distal phalangeal fracture, finger or thumb, with or without internal or external fixation, each
26770   Closed treatment of interphalangeal joint dislocation, single, with manipulation; without anesthesia
26775   requiring anesthesia
26776   Percutaneous skeletal fixation of interphalangeal joint dislocation, single, with manipulation
26785   Open treatment of interphalangeal joint dislocation, with or without internal or external fixation, single

Arthrodesis

26820   Fusion in opposition, thumb, with autogenous graft (includes obtaining graft)
26841   Arthrodesis, carpometacarpal joint, thumb, with or without internal fixation;
26842   with autograft (includes obtaining graft)
26843   Arthrodesis, carpometacarpal joint, digit, other than thumb, each;
26844   with autograft (includes obtaining graft)
26850   Arthrodesis, metacarpophalangeal joint, with or without internal fixation;
26852   with autograft (includes obtaining graft)
26860   Arthrodesis, interphalangeal joint, with or without internal fixation;
26861   each additional interphalangeal joint (List separately in addition to code for primary procedure)
26862   with autograft (includes obtaining graft)
26863   with autograft (includes obtaining graft), each additional joint (List separately in addition to code for primary procedure)

Amputation

26910   Amputation, metacarpal, with finger or thumb (ray amputation), single, with or without interosseous transfer
26951   Amputation, finger or thumb, primary or secondary, any joint or phalanx, single, including neurectomies; with direct closure
26952   with local advancement flaps (V-Y, hood)

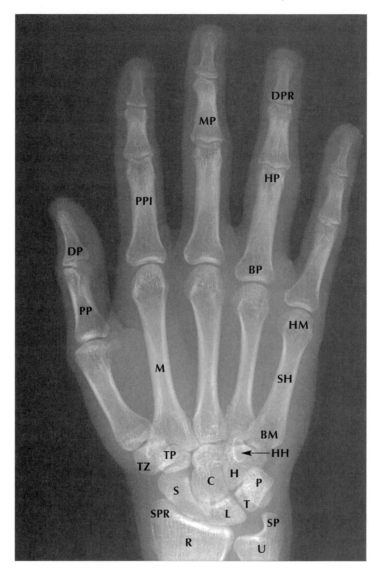

BM	Base of 5th metacarpal	**P**	Pisiform
BP	Base of 4th proximal phalanx	**PP**	Proximal phalanx of thumb
C	Capitate	**PPI**	Proximal phalanx of index finger
DP	Distal phalanx of thumb	**R**	Radius
DPR	Distal phalanx of ring finger	**S**	Scaphoid
H	Hamate	**SH**	Shaft of 5th metacarpal
HH	Hook of hamate	**SP**	Styloid process of ulna
HM	Head of 5th metacarpal	**SPR**	Styloid process of radius
HP	Head of proximal phalanx	**T**	Triquetrum
L	Lunate	**TP**	Trapezoid
M	Metacarpal of index finger	**TZ**	Trapezium
MP	Middle phalanx of middle finger	**U**	Ulna

RADIOLOGY

Diagnostic Radiology (Diagnostic Imaging)

Upper Extremities

73120   Radiologic examination, hand; two views

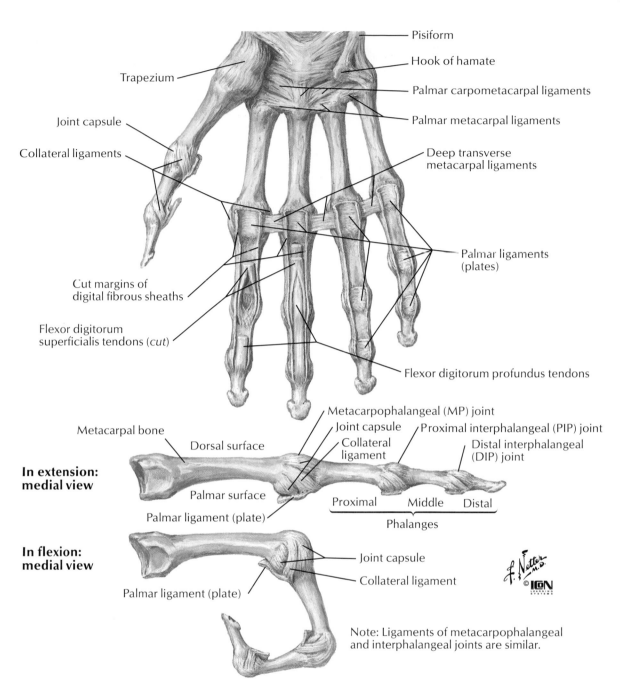

Pisiform

Hook of hamate

Trapezium

Palmar carpometacarpal ligaments

Palmar metacarpal ligaments

Joint capsule

Deep transverse metacarpal ligaments

Collateral ligaments

Palmar ligaments (plates)

Cut margins of digital fibrous sheaths

Flexor digitorum superficialis tendons (*cut*)

Flexor digitorum profundus tendons

Metacarpophalangeal (MP) joint

Joint capsule

Proximal interphalangeal (PIP) joint

Metacarpal bone

Collateral ligament

Distal interphalangeal (DIP) joint

Dorsal surface

In extension: medial view

Palmar surface

Proximal   Middle   Distal

Palmar ligament (plate)

Phalanges

In flexion: medial view

Joint capsule

Collateral ligament

Palmar ligament (plate)

Note: Ligaments of metacarpophalangeal and interphalangeal joints are similar.

ANESTHESIA

Forearm, Wrist, and Hand

01810   Anesthesia for all procedures on nerves, muscles, tendons, fascia, and bursae of forearm, wrist, and hand

SURGERY

Musculoskeletal System

Hand and Fingers
Repair, Revision, and/or Reconstruction

26540   Repair of collateral ligament, metacarpophalangeal or interphalangeal joint

26541   Reconstruction, collateral ligament, metacarpophalangeal joint, single; with tendon or fascial graft (includes obtaining graft)

26542   with local tissue (eg, adductor advancement)

26545   Reconstruction, collateral ligament, interphalangeal joint, single, including graft, each joint

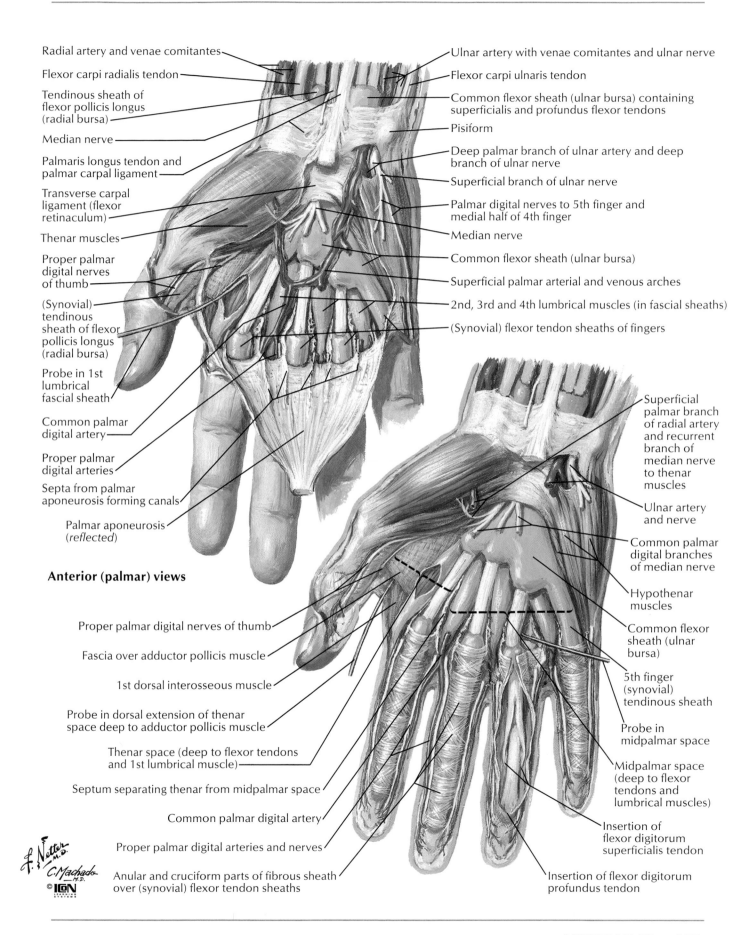

Radial artery and venae comitantes

Flexor carpi radialis tendon

Tendinous sheath of flexor pollicis longus (radial bursa)

Median nerve

Palmaris longus tendon and palmar carpal ligament

Transverse carpal ligament (flexor retinaculum)

Thenar muscles

Proper palmar digital nerves of thumb

(Synovial) tendinous sheath of flexor pollicis longus (radial bursa)

Probe in 1st lumbrical fascial sheath

Common palmar digital artery

Proper palmar digital arteries

Septa from palmar aponeurosis forming canals

Palmar aponeurosis (reflected)

Anterior (palmar) views

Ulnar artery with venae comitantes and ulnar nerve

Flexor carpi ulnaris tendon

Common flexor sheath (ulnar bursa) containing superficialis and profundus flexor tendons

Pisiform

Deep palmar branch of ulnar artery and deep branch of ulnar nerve

Superficial branch of ulnar nerve

Palmar digital nerves to 5th finger and medial half of 4th finger

Median nerve

Common flexor sheath (ulnar bursa)

Superficial palmar arterial and venous arches

2nd, 3rd and 4th lumbrical muscles (in fascial sheaths)

(Synovial) flexor tendon sheaths of fingers

Superficial palmar branch of radial artery and recurrent branch of median nerve to thenar muscles

Ulnar artery and nerve

Common palmar digital branches of median nerve

Hypothenar muscles

Common flexor sheath (ulnar bursa)

5th finger (synovial) tendinous sheath

Probe in midpalmar space

Midpalmar space (deep to flexor tendons and lumbrical muscles)

Insertion of flexor digitorum superficialis tendon

Insertion of flexor digitorum profundus tendon

Proper palmar digital nerves of thumb

Fascia over adductor pollicis muscle

1st dorsal interosseous muscle

Probe in dorsal extension of thenar space deep to adductor pollicis muscle

Thenar space (deep to flexor tendons and 1st lumbrical muscle)

Septum separating thenar from midpalmar space

Common palmar digital artery

Proper palmar digital arteries and nerves

Anular and cruciform parts of fibrous sheath over (synovial) flexor tendon sheaths

ANESTHESIA

Thorax (Chest Wall and Shoulder Girdle)

00400 Anesthesia for procedures on the integumentary system on the extremities, anterior trunk and perineum; not otherwise specified

Forearm, Wrist, and Hand

01810 Anesthesia for all procedures on nerves, muscles, tendons, fascia, and bursae of forearm, wrist, and hand

01840 Anesthesia for procedures on arteries of forearm, wrist, and hand; not otherwise specified

Other Procedures

01991 Anesthesia for diagnostic or therapeutic nerve blocks and injections (when block or injection is performed by a different provider); other than the prone position

SURGERY

Musculoskeletal System

Forearm and Wrist
Incision

25001 Incision, flexor tendon sheath, wrist (eg, flexor carpi radialis)

25020 Decompression fasciotomy, forearm and/or wrist, flexor OR extensor compartment; without debridement of nonviable muscle and/or nerve

25023   with debridement of nonviable muscle and/or nerve

25024 Decompression fasciotomy, forearm and/or wrist, flexor AND extensor compartment; without debridement of nonviable muscle and/or nerve

25025   with debridement of nonviable muscle and/or nerve

25028 Incision and drainage, forearm and/or wrist; deep abscess or hematoma

25031   bursa

Excision

25065 Biopsy, soft tissue of forearm and/or wrist; superficial

25066   deep (subfascial or intramuscular)

25075 Excision, tumor, soft tissue of forearm and/or wrist area; subcutaneous

25076   deep (subfascial or intramuscular)

25077 Radical resection of tumor (eg, malignant neoplasm), soft tissue of forearm and/or wrist area

25110 Excision, lesion of tendon sheath, forearm and/or wrist

25111 Excision of ganglion, wrist (dorsal or volar); primary

25112   recurrent

Repair, Revison, and/or Reconstruction

25260 Repair, tendon or muscle, flexor, forearm and/or wrist; primary, single, each tendon or muscle

25263   secondary, single, each tendon or muscle

25265   secondary, with free graft (includes obtaining graft), each tendon or muscle

25270 Repair, tendon or muscle, extensor, forearm and/or wrist; primary, single, each tendon or muscle

25272   secondary, single, each tendon or muscle

25274   secondary, with free graft (includes obtaining graft), each tendon or muscle

25275 Repair, tendon sheath, extensor, forearm and/or wrist, with free graft (includes obtaining graft) (eg, for extensor carpi ulnaris subluxation)

25280 Lengthening or shortening of flexor or extensor tendon, forearm and/or wrist, single, each tendon

25290 Tenotomy, open, flexor or extensor tendon, forearm and/or wrist, single, each tendon

25295 Tenolysis, flexor or extensor tendon, forearm and/or wrist, single, each tendon

25300 Tenodesis at wrist; flexors of fingers

25301   extensors of fingers

25310 Tendon transplantation or transfer, flexor or extensor, forearm and/or wrist, single; each tendon

25312   with tendon graft(s) (includes obtaining graft), each tendon

25315 Flexor origin slide (eg, for cerebral palsy, Volkmann contracture), forearm and/or wrist;

25316   with tendon(s) transfer

25320 Capsulorrhaphy or reconstruction, wrist, open (eg, capsulodesis, ligament repair, tendon transfer or graft) (includes synovectomy, capsulotomy and open reduction) for carpal instability

Amputation

25920 Disarticulation through wrist;

25922   secondary closure or scar revision

25924   re-amputation

25927 Transmetacarpal amputation;

25929   secondary closure or scar revision

25931   re-amputation

Hand and Fingers
Incision

26010 Drainage of finger abscess; simple

26011   complicated (eg, felon)

26020 Drainage of tendon sheath, digit and/or palm, each

26035 Decompression fingers and/or hand, injection injury (eg, grease gun)

26037 Decompressive fasciotomy, hand (excludes 26035)

26040 Fasciotomy, palmar (eg, Dupuytren's contracture); percutaneous

26045   open, partial

26055 Tendon sheath incision (eg, for trigger finger)

26060 Tenotomy, percutaneous, single, each digit

Excision

26115 Excision, tumor or vascular malformation, soft tissue of hand or finger; subcutaneous

26116   deep (subfascial or intramuscular)

26117 Radical resection of tumor (eg, malignant neoplasm), soft tissue of hand or finger

26121 Fasciectomy, palm only, with or without Z-plasty, other local tissue rearrangement, or skin grafting (includes obtaining graft)

26123 Fasciectomy, partial palmar with release of single digit including proximal interphalangeal joint, with or without Z-plasty, other local tissue rearrangement, or skin grafting (includes obtaining graft);

26125 each additional digit (List separately in addition to code for primary procedure)

26145 Synovectomy, tendon sheath, radical (tenosynovectomy), flexor tendon, palm and/or finger, each tendon

26160 Excision of lesion of tendon sheath or joint capsule (eg, cyst, mucous cyst, or ganglion), hand or finger

26170 Excision of tendon, palm, flexor, single (separate procedure), each

26180 Excision of tendon, finger, flexor (separate procedure), each tendon

Repair, Revision, and/or Reconstruction

26350 Repair or advancement, flexor tendon, not in zone 2 digital flexor tendon sheath (eg, no man's land); primary or secondary without free graft, each tendon

26352 secondary with free graft (includes obtaining graft), each tendon

26356 Repair or advancement, flexor tendon, in zone 2 digital flexor tendon sheath (eg, no man's land); primary, without free graft, each tendon

26357 secondary, without free graft, each tendon

26358 secondary, with free graft (includes obtaining graft), each tendon

26370 Repair or advancement of profundus tendon, with intact superficialis tendon; primary, each tendon

26372 secondary with free graft (includes obtaining graft), each tendon

26373 secondary without free graft, each tendon

26390 Excision flexor tendon, with implantation of synthetic rod for delayed tendon graft, hand or finger, each rod

26392 Removal of synthetic rod and insertion of flexor tendon graft, hand or finger (includes obtaining graft), each rod

26440 Tenolysis, flexor tendon; palm OR finger, each tendon

26442 palm AND finger, each tendon

26450 Tenotomy, flexor, palm, open, each tendon

26455 Tenotomy, flexor, finger, open, each tendon

26478 Lengthening of tendon, flexor, hand or finger, each tendon

26479 Shortening of tendon, flexor, hand or finger, each tendon

26485 Transfer or transplant of tendon, palmar; without free tendon graft, each tendon

26489 with free tendon graft (includes obtaining graft), each tendon

26490 Opponensplasty; superficialis tendon transfer type, each tendon

26492 tendon transfer with graft (includes obtaining graft), each tendon

26494 hypothenar muscle transfer

26496 Opponensplasty; other methods

26497 Transfer of tendon to restore intrinsic function; ring and small finger

26498 all four fingers

26500 Reconstruction of tendon pulley, each tendon; with local tissues (separate procedure)

26502 with tendon or fascial graft (includes obtaining graft) (separate procedure)

26504 with tendon prosthesis (separate procedure)

26508 Release of thenar muscle(s) (eg, thumb contracture)

26510 Cross intrinsic transfer, each tendon

26536 Arthroplasty, interphalangeal joint; with prosthetic implant, each joint

Amputation

26910 Amputation, metacarpal, with finger or thumb (ray amputation), single, with or without interosseous transfer

26951 Amputation, finger or thumb, primary or secondary, any joint or phalanx, single, including neurectomies; with direct closure

26952 with local advancement flaps (V-Y, hood)

Nervous System

Extracranial Nerves, Peripheral Nerves, and Autonomic Nervous System

Introduction/Injection of Anesthetic Agent (Nerve Block), Diagnostic or Therapeutic

Somatic Nerves

64450 Injection, anesthetic agent; other peripheral nerve or branch

Destruction by Neurolytic Agent (eg, Chemical, Thermal, Electrical or Radiofrequency)

Somatic Nerves

64640 Destruction by neurolytic agent; other peripheral nerve or branch

Neuroplasty (Exploration, Neurolysis or Nerve Decompression)

64702 Neuroplasty; digital, one or both, same digit

64704 nerve of hand or foot

64719 Neuroplasty and/or transposition; ulnar nerve at wrist

64721 median nerve at carpal tunnel

64722 Decompression; unspecified nerve(s) (specify)

Excision

Somatic Nerves

64776 Excision of neuroma; digital nerve, one or both, same digit

64778 digital nerve, each additional digit (List separately in addition to code for primary procedure)

64782 hand or foot, except digital nerve

64783 hand or foot, each additional nerve, except same digit (List separately in addition to code for primary procedure)

Sympathetic Nerves

64820 Sympathectomy; digital arteries, each digit
64821   radial artery
64822   ulnar artery

Neurorrhaphy

64831 Suture of digital nerve, hand or foot; one nerve
64832   each additional digital nerve (List separately in addition to code for primary procedure)
64834 Suture of one nerve, hand or foot; common sensory nerve
64835   median motor thenar
64836   ulnar motor
64837 Suture of each additional nerve, hand or foot (List separately in addition to code for primary procedure)

Neurorrhaphy With Nerve Graft

64890 Nerve graft (includes obtaining graft), single strand, hand or foot; up to 4 cm length
64891   more than 4 cm length
64895 Nerve graft (includes obtaining graft), multiple strands (cable), hand or foot; up to 4 cm length
64896   more than 4 cm length
64901 Nerve graft, each additional nerve; single strand (List separately in addition to code for primary procedure)
64902   multiple strands (cable) (List separately in addition to code for primary procedure)

Palmar view

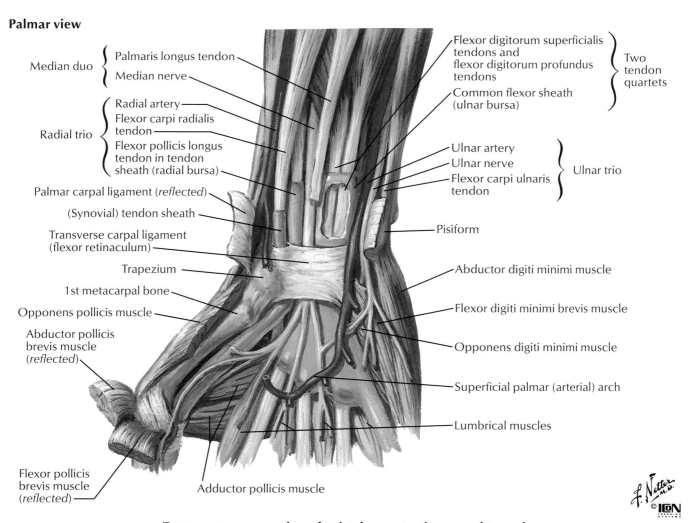

Median duo
- Palmaris longus tendon
- Median nerve

Radial trio
- Radial artery
- Flexor carpi radialis tendon
- Flexor pollicis longus tendon in tendon sheath (radial bursa)

Palmar carpal ligament (*reflected*)

(Synovial) tendon sheath

Transverse carpal ligament (flexor retinaculum)

Trapezium

1st metacarpal bone

Opponens pollicis muscle

Abductor pollicis brevis muscle (*reflected*)

Flexor pollicis brevis muscle (*reflected*)

Adductor pollicis muscle

Flexor digitorum superficialis tendons and flexor digitorum profundus tendons

Common flexor sheath (ulnar bursa)

Two tendon quartets

Ulnar artery
Ulnar nerve
Flexor carpi ulnaris tendon

Ulnar trio

Pisiform

Abductor digiti minimi muscle

Flexor digiti minimi brevis muscle

Opponens digiti minimi muscle

Superficial palmar (arterial) arch

Lumbrical muscles

Transverse cross section of wrist demonstrating carpal tunnel

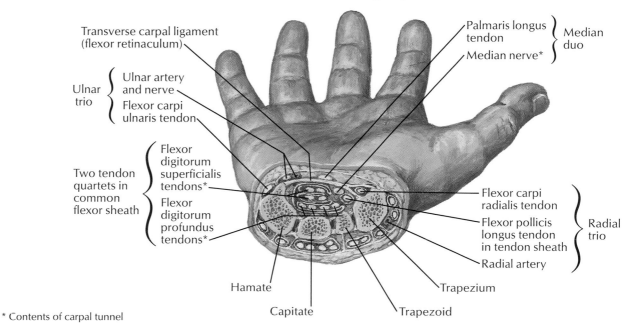

Transverse carpal ligament (flexor retinaculum)

Ulnar trio
- Ulnar artery and nerve
- Flexor carpi ulnaris tendon

Two tendon quartets in common flexor sheath
- Flexor digitorum superficialis tendons*
- Flexor digitorum profundus tendons*

Palmaris longus tendon
Median nerve*

Median duo

Flexor carpi radialis tendon
Flexor pollicis longus tendon in tendon sheath
Radial artery

Radial trio

Hamate

Capitate

Trapezoid

Trapezium

* Contents of carpal tunnel

Plate 166: Flexor Tendons

ANESTHESIA

Forearm, Wrist, and Hand

01810 Anesthesia for all procedures on nerves, muscles, tendons, fascia, and bursae of forearm, wrist, and hand

01840 Anesthesia for procedures on arteries of forearm, wrist, and hand; not otherwise specified

01842 embolectomy

SURGERY

Musculoskeletal System

General
Introduction or Removal

20526 Injection, therapeutic (eg, local anesthetic, corticosteroid), carpal tunnel

Forearm and Wrist
Incision

25001 Incision, flexor tendon sheath, wrist (eg, flexor carpi radialis)

25020 Decompression fasciotomy, forearm and/or wrist, flexor OR extensor compartment; without debridement of nonviable muscle and/or nerve

25023 with debridement of nonviable muscle and/or nerve

25024 Decompression fasciotomy, forearm and/or wrist, flexor AND extensor compartment; without debridement of nonviable muscle and/or nerve

25025 with debridement of nonviable muscle and/or nerve

Excision

25110 Excision, lesion of tendon sheath, forearm and/or wrist

Repair, Revision, and/or Reconstruction

25260 Repair, tendon or muscle, flexor, forearm and/or wrist; primary, single, each tendon or muscle

25263 secondary, single, each tendon or muscle

25265 secondary, with free graft (includes obtaining graft), each tendon or muscle

25280 Lengthening or shortening of flexor or extensor tendon, forearm and/or wrist, single, each tendon

25290 Tenotomy, open, flexor or extensor tendon, forearm and/or wrist, single, each tendon

25295 Tenolysis, flexor or extensor tendon, forearm and/or wrist, single, each tendon

25300 Tenodesis at wrist; flexors of fingers

25310 Tendon transplantation or transfer, flexor or extensor, forearm and/or wrist, single; each tendon

25312 with tendon graft(s) (includes obtaining graft), each tendon

25315 Flexor origin slide (eg, for cerebral palsy, Volkmann contracture), forearm and/or wrist;

25316 with tendon(s) transfer

25320 Capsulorrhaphy or reconstruction, wrist, open (eg, capsulodesis, ligament repair, tendon transfer or graft) (includes synovectomy, capsulotomy and open reduction) for carpal instability

Cardiovascular System

Arteries and Veins
Embolectomy/Thrombectomy
Arterial, With or Without Catheter

34111 Embolectomy or thrombectomy, with or without catheter; radial or ulnar artery, by arm incision

Direct Repair of Aneurysm, Pseudoaneurysm, or Excision (Partial or Total) and Graft Insertion for Aneurysm, Pseudoaneurysm, and Associated Occlusive Disease

35045 Direct repair of aneurysm, pseudoaneurysm, or excision (partial or total) and graft insertion, with or without patch graft; for aneurysm, pseudoaneurysm, and associated occlusive disease, radial or ulnar artery

Repair Blood Vessel Other Than for Fistula, With or Without Patch Angioplasty

35206 Repair blood vessel, direct; upper extremity
35207 hand, finger
35236 Repair blood vessel with vein graft; upper extremity
35266 Repair blood vessel with graft other than vein; upper extremity

Transluminal Angioplasty
Open
35458 Transluminal balloon angioplasty, open; brachiocephalic trunk or branches, each vessel

Percutaneous
35475 Transluminal balloon angioplasty, percutaneous; brachiocephalic trunk or branches, each vessel

Transluminal Atherectomy
Open
35484 Transluminal peripheral atherectomy, open; brachiocephalic trunk or branches, each vessel

Percutaneous
35494 Transluminal peripheral atherectomy, percutaneous; brachiocephalic trunk or branches, each vessel

Exploration/Revision

35761 Exploration (not followed by surgical repair), with or without lysis of artery; other vessels
35860 Exploration for postoperative hemorrhage, thrombosis or infection; extremity
35903 Excision of infected graft; extremity

Nervous System

Extracranial Nerves, Peripheral Nerves, and Autonomic Nervous System
Neuroplasty (Exploration, Neurolysis or Nerve Decompression)

64719 Neuroplasty and/or transposition; ulnar nerve at wrist
64721 median nerve at carpal tunnel

Excision
Sympathetic Nerves
64821 Sympathectomy; radial artery
64822 ulnar artery
64823 superficial palmar arch

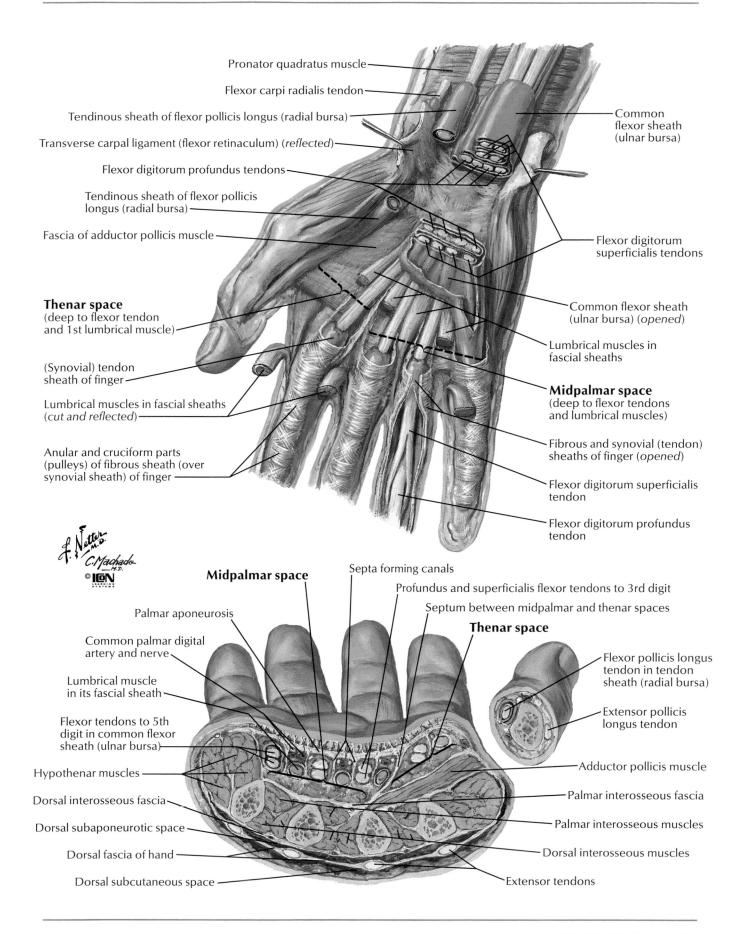

Pronator quadratus muscle

Flexor carpi radialis tendon

Tendinous sheath of flexor pollicis longus (radial bursa)

Transverse carpal ligament (flexor retinaculum) (*reflected*)

Flexor digitorum profundus tendons

Tendinous sheath of flexor pollicis longus (radial bursa)

Fascia of adductor pollicis muscle

Thenar space
(deep to flexor tendon and 1st lumbrical muscle)

(Synovial) tendon sheath of finger

Lumbrical muscles in fascial sheaths (*cut and reflected*)

Anular and cruciform parts (pulleys) of fibrous sheath (over synovial sheath) of finger

Common flexor sheath (ulnar bursa)

Flexor digitorum superficialis tendons

Common flexor sheath (ulnar bursa) (*opened*)

Lumbrical muscles in fascial sheaths

Midpalmar space
(deep to flexor tendons and lumbrical muscles)

Fibrous and synovial (tendon) sheaths of finger (*opened*)

Flexor digitorum superficialis tendon

Flexor digitorum profundus tendon

Midpalmar space

Septa forming canals

Profundus and superficialis flexor tendons to 3rd digit

Septum between midpalmar and thenar spaces

Thenar space

Palmar aponeurosis

Common palmar digital artery and nerve

Lumbrical muscle in its fascial sheath

Flexor tendons to 5th digit in common flexor sheath (ulnar bursa)

Hypothenar muscles

Dorsal interosseous fascia

Dorsal subaponeurotic space

Dorsal fascia of hand

Dorsal subcutaneous space

Flexor pollicis longus tendon in tendon sheath (radial bursa)

Extensor pollicis longus tendon

Adductor pollicis muscle

Palmar interosseous fascia

Palmar interosseous muscles

Dorsal interosseous muscles

Extensor tendons

ANESTHESIA

Forearm, Wrist, and Hand

01810   Anesthesia for all procedures on nerves, muscles, tendons, fascia, and bursae of forearm, wrist, and hand

01830   Anesthesia for open or surgical arthroscopic/endoscopic procedures on distal radius, distal ulna, wrist, or hand joints; not otherwise specified

SURGERY

Musculoskeletal System

General
Introduction or Removal

20520   Removal of foreign body in muscle or tendon sheath; simple

20525   deep or complicated

20550   Injection(s); single tendon sheath, or ligament, aponeurosis (eg, plantar "fascia")

20551   single tendon origin/insertion

Forearm and Wrist
Incision

25000   Incision, extensor tendon sheath, wrist (eg, deQuervains disease)

25001   Incision, flexor tendon sheath, wrist (eg, flexor carpi radialis)

25020   Decompression fasciotomy, forearm and/or wrist, flexor OR extensor compartment; without debridement of nonviable muscle and/or nerve

25023   with debridement of nonviable muscle and/or nerve

25024   Decompression fasciotomy, forearm and/or wrist, flexor AND extensor compartment; without debridement of nonviable muscle and/or nerve

25025   with debridement of nonviable muscle and/or nerve

Excision

25110   Excision, lesion of tendon sheath, forearm and/or wrist

25111   Excision of ganglion, wrist (dorsal or volar); primary

25112   recurrent

25115   Radical excision of bursa, synovia of wrist, or forearm tendon sheaths (eg, tenosynovitis, fungus, Tbc, or other granulomas, rheumatoid arthritis); flexors

25116   extensors, with or without transposition of dorsal retinaculum

25118   Synovectomy, extensor tendon sheath, wrist, single compartment;

25119   with resection of distal ulna

Repair, Revision, and/or Reconstruction

25275   Repair, tendon sheath, extensor, forearm and/or wrist, with free graft (includes obtaining graft) (eg, for extensor carpi ulnaris subluxation)

Hand and Fingers
Incision

26020   Drainage of tendon sheath, digit and/or palm, each

26025   Drainage of palmar bursa; single, bursa

26030   multiple bursa

Excision

26121   Fasciectomy, palm only, with or without Z-plasty, other local tissue rearrangement, or skin grafting (includes obtaining graft)

26123   Fasciectomy, partial palmar with release of single digit including proximal interphalangeal joint, with or without Z-plasty, other local tissue rearrangement, or skin grafting (includes obtaining graft);

26125   each additional digit (List separately in addition to code for primary procedure)

26145   Synovectomy, tendon sheath, radical (tenosynovectomy), flexor tendon, palm and/or finger, each tendon

26160   Excision of lesion of tendon sheath or joint capsule (eg, cyst, mucous cyst, or ganglion), hand or finger

Repair, Revision, and/or Reconstruction

26350   Repair or advancement, flexor tendon, not in zone 2 digital flexor tendon sheath (eg, no man's land); primary or secondary without free graft, each tendon

26352   secondary with free graft (includes obtaining graft), each tendon

26356   Repair or advancement, flexor tendon, in zone 2 digital flexor tendon sheath (eg, no man's land); primary, without free graft, each tendon

26357   secondary, without free graft, each tendon

26358   secondary, with free graft (includes obtaining graft), each tendon

26508   Release of thenar muscle(s) (eg, thumb contracture)

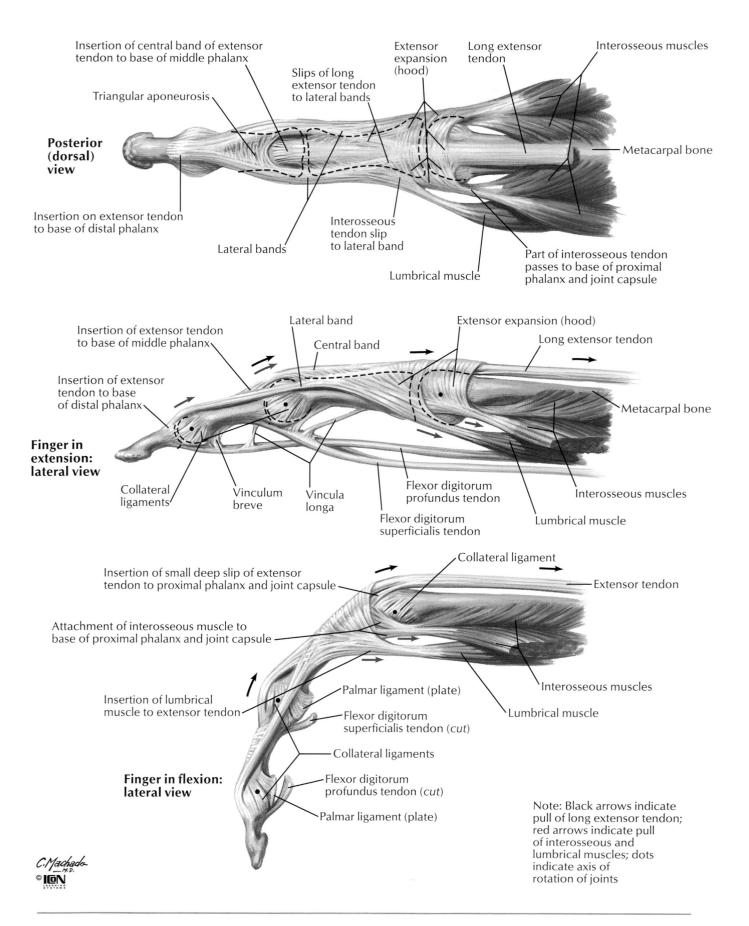

Posterior (dorsal) view

Insertion of central band of extensor tendon to base of middle phalanx

Triangular aponeurosis

Slips of long extensor tendon to lateral bands

Extensor expansion (hood)

Long extensor tendon

Interosseous muscles

Metacarpal bone

Insertion on extensor tendon to base of distal phalanx

Lateral bands

Interosseous tendon slip to lateral band

Lumbrical muscle

Part of interosseous tendon passes to base of proximal phalanx and joint capsule

Finger in extension: lateral view

Insertion of extensor tendon to base of middle phalanx

Insertion of extensor tendon to base of distal phalanx

Lateral band

Central band

Extensor expansion (hood)

Long extensor tendon

Metacarpal bone

Collateral ligaments

Vinculum breve

Vincula longa

Flexor digitorum profundus tendon

Flexor digitorum superficialis tendon

Interosseous muscles

Lumbrical muscle

Finger in flexion: lateral view

Insertion of small deep slip of extensor tendon to proximal phalanx and joint capsule

Attachment of interosseous muscle to base of proximal phalanx and joint capsule

Insertion of lumbrical muscle to extensor tendon

Collateral ligament

Extensor tendon

Palmar ligament (plate)

Flexor digitorum superficialis tendon (cut)

Collateral ligaments

Flexor digitorum profundus tendon (cut)

Palmar ligament (plate)

Interosseous muscles

Lumbrical muscle

Note: Black arrows indicate pull of long extensor tendon; red arrows indicate pull of interosseous and lumbrical muscles; dots indicate axis of rotation of joints

C. Machado M.D.
© ICON LEARNING SYSTEMS

Nomenclature Notes

A *boutonniere deformity* is a flexion of the proximal interphalangeal joint with hyperextension of the distal interphalangeal joint of the finger, caused by splitting of the extensor hood and protrusion of the head of the proximal phalanx through the resulting "buttonhole."

A *mallet finger* is an avulsion—partial or complete—of the long finger extensor tendon from the base of the distal phalanx.

The term *no man's land* refers to the area between the proximal joint crease of the finger to the distal palmar crease.

ANESTHESIA

Forearm, Wrist, and Hand

01810   Anesthesia for all procedures on nerves, muscles, tendons, fascia, and bursae of forearm, wrist, and hand

SURGERY

Musculoskeletal System

Hand and Fingers

Repair, Revision, and/or Reconstruction

26350   Repair or advancement, flexor tendon, not in zone 2 digital flexor tendon sheath (eg, no man's land); primary or secondary without free graft, each tendon

26352   secondary with free graft (includes obtaining graft), each tendon

26356   Repair or advancement, flexor tendon, in zone 2 digital flexor tendon sheath (eg, no man's land); primary, without free graft, each tendon

26357   secondary, without free graft, each tendon

26358   secondary, with free graft (includes obtaining graft), each tendon

26370   Repair or advancement of profundus tendon, with intact superficialis tendon; primary, each tendon

26372   secondary with free graft (includes obtaining graft), each tendon

26373   secondary without free graft, each tendon

26390   Excision flexor tendon, with implantation of synthetic rod for delayed tendon graft, hand or finger, each rod

26392   Removal of synthetic rod and insertion of flexor tendon graft, hand or finger (includes obtaining graft), each rod

26410   Repair, extensor tendon, hand, primary or secondary; without free graft, each tendon

26412   with free graft (includes obtaining graft), each tendon

26415   Excision of extensor tendon, with implantation of synthetic rod for delayed tendon graft, hand or finger, each rod

26416   Removal of synthetic rod and insertion of extensor tendon graft (includes obtaining graft), hand or finger, each rod

26418   Repair, extensor tendon, finger, primary or secondary; without free graft, each tendon

26420   with free graft (includes obtaining graft) each tendon

26426   Repair of extensor tendon, central slip, secondary (eg, boutonniere deformity); using local tissue(s), including lateral band(s), each finger

26428   with free graft (includes obtaining graft), each finger

26432   Closed treatment of distal extensor tendon insertion, with or without percutaneous pinning (eg, mallet finger)

26433   Repair of extensor tendon, distal insertion, primary or secondary; without graft (eg, mallet finger)

26434   with free graft (includes obtaining graft)

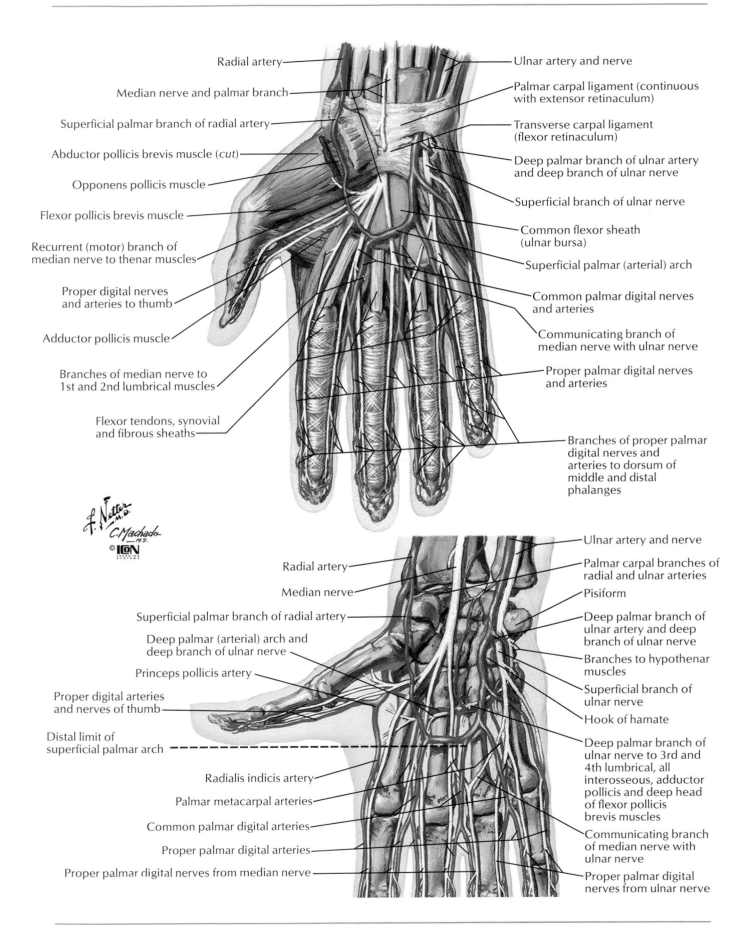

Radial artery

Median nerve and palmar branch

Superficial palmar branch of radial artery

Abductor pollicis brevis muscle (*cut*)

Opponens pollicis muscle

Flexor pollicis brevis muscle

Recurrent (motor) branch of median nerve to thenar muscles

Proper digital nerves and arteries to thumb

Adductor pollicis muscle

Branches of median nerve to 1st and 2nd lumbrical muscles

Flexor tendons, synovial and fibrous sheaths

Ulnar artery and nerve

Palmar carpal ligament (continuous with extensor retinaculum)

Transverse carpal ligament (flexor retinaculum)

Deep palmar branch of ulnar artery and deep branch of ulnar nerve

Superficial branch of ulnar nerve

Common flexor sheath (ulnar bursa)

Superficial palmar (arterial) arch

Common palmar digital nerves and arteries

Communicating branch of median nerve with ulnar nerve

Proper palmar digital nerves and arteries

Branches of proper palmar digital nerves and arteries to dorsum of middle and distal phalanges

Radial artery

Median nerve

Superficial palmar branch of radial artery

Deep palmar (arterial) arch and deep branch of ulnar nerve

Princeps pollicis artery

Proper digital arteries and nerves of thumb

Distal limit of superficial palmar arch

Radialis indicis artery

Palmar metacarpal arteries

Common palmar digital arteries

Proper palmar digital arteries

Proper palmar digital nerves from median nerve

Ulnar artery and nerve

Palmar carpal branches of radial and ulnar arteries

Pisiform

Deep palmar branch of ulnar artery and deep branch of ulnar nerve

Branches to hypothenar muscles

Superficial branch of ulnar nerve

Hook of hamate

Deep palmar branch of ulnar nerve to 3rd and 4th lumbrical, all interosseous, adductor pollicis and deep head of flexor pollicis brevis muscles

Communicating branch of median nerve with ulnar nerve

Proper palmar digital nerves from ulnar nerve

ANESTHESIA

Shoulder and Axilla

01650   Anesthesia for procedures on arteries of shoulder and axilla; not otherwise specified

Upper Arm

01770   Anesthesia for procedures on arteries of upper arm and elbow; not otherwise specified

Forearm, Wrist, and Hand

01810   Anesthesia for all procedures on nerves, muscles, tendons, fascia, and bursae of forearm, wrist, and hand

01840   Anesthesia for procedures on arteries of forearm, wrist, and hand; not otherwise specified

01842   embolectomy

Radiological Procedures

01924   Anesthesia for therapeutic interventional radiologic procedures involving the arterial system; not otherwise specified

SURGERY

Cardiovascular System

Arteries and Veins
Embolectomy/Thrombectomy

Arterial, With or Without Catheter
34111   Embolectomy or thrombectomy, with or without catheter; radial or ulnar artery, by arm incision

Direct Repair of Aneurysm, Pseudoaneurysm, or Excision (Partial or Total) and Graft Insertion for Aneurysm, Pseudoaneurysm, and Associated Occlusive Disease

35045   Direct repair of aneurysm, pseudoaneurysm, or excision (partial or total) and graft insertion, with or without patch graft; for aneurysm, pseudoaneurysm, and associated occlusive disease, radial or ulnar artery

Repair Blood Vessel Other Than for Fistula, With or Without Patch Angioplasty

35206   Repair blood vessel, direct; upper extremity
35207   hand, finger
35236   Repair blood vessel with vein graft; upper extremity
35266   Repair blood vessel with graft other than vein; upper extremity

Transluminal Angioplasty

Open
35458   Transluminal balloon angioplasty, open; brachiocephalic trunk or branches, each vessel

Percutaneous
35475   Transluminal balloon angioplasty, percutaneous; brachiocephalic trunk or branches, each vessel

Transluminal Atherectomy

Open
35484   Transluminal peripheral atherectomy, open; brachiocephalic trunk or branches, each vessel

Percutaneous
35494   Transluminal peripheral atherectomy, percutaneous; brachiocephalic trunk or branches, each vessel

Exploration/Revision

35761   Exploration (not followed by surgical repair), with or without lysis of artery; other vessels
35903   Excision of infected graft; extremity

Nervous System

Extracranial Nerves, Peripheral Nerves, Autonomic Nervous System
Neuroplasty (Exploration, Neurolysis or Nerve Decompression)

64702   Neuroplasty; digital, one or both, same digit
64704   nerve of hand or foot
64718   Neuroplasty and/or transposition; ulnar nerve at elbow
64719   ulnar nerve at wrist
64721   median nerve at carpal tunnel

Excision

Somatic Nerves
64776   Excision of neuroma; digital nerve, one or both, same digit
64778   digital nerve, each additional digit (List separately in addition to code for primary procedure)
64782   Excision of neuroma; hand or foot, except digital nerve
64783   hand or foot, each additional nerve, except same digit (List separately in addition to code for primary procedure)

Sympathetic Nerves
64820   Sympathectomy; digital arteries, each digit
64821   radial artery
64822   ulnar artery
64823   superficial palmar arch

Neurorrhaphy

64831   Suture of digital nerve, hand or foot; one nerve
64832   each additional digital nerve (List separately in addition to code for primary procedure)
64834   Suture of one nerve, hand or foot; common sensory nerve
64835   median motor thenar
64836   ulnar motor
64837   Suture of each additional nerve, hand or foot (List separately in addition to code for primary procedure)

Neurorrhaphy With Nerve Graft

64890   Nerve graft (includes obtaining graft), single strand, hand or foot; up to 4 cm length
64891   more than 4 cm length
64895   Nerve graft (includes obtaining graft), multiple strands (cable), hand or foot; up to 4 cm length
64896   more than 4 cm length

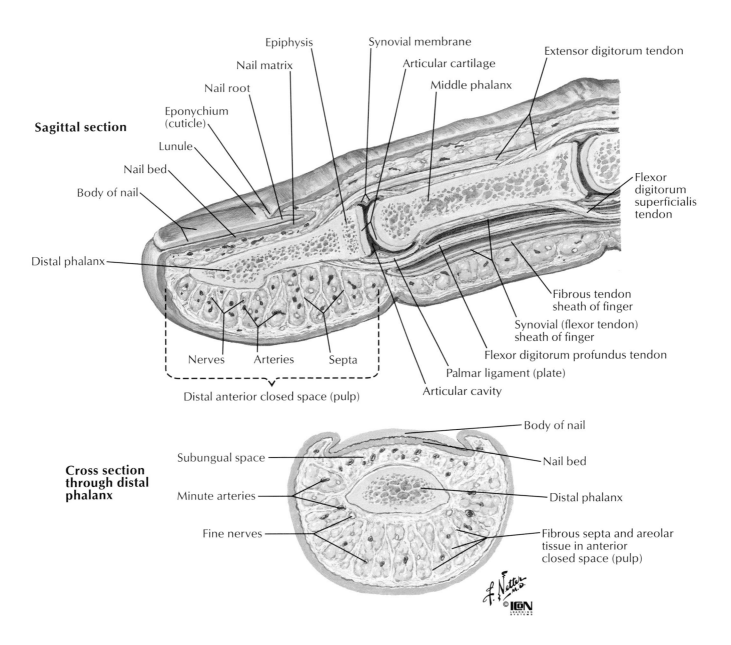

Sagittal section

Epiphysis
Nail matrix
Nail root
Eponychium (cuticle)
Lunule
Nail bed
Body of nail
Distal phalanx
Nerves   Arteries   Septa
Distal anterior closed space (pulp)

Synovial membrane
Articular cartilage
Middle phalanx
Extensor digitorum tendon
Flexor digitorum superficialis tendon
Fibrous tendon sheath of finger
Synovial (flexor tendon) sheath of finger
Flexor digitorum profundus tendon
Palmar ligament (plate)
Articular cavity

Cross section through distal phalanx

Subungual space
Minute arteries
Fine nerves

Body of nail
Nail bed
Distal phalanx
Fibrous septa and areolar tissue in anterior closed space (pulp)

ANESTHESIA

Thorax (Chest Wall and Shoulder Girdle)

00400   Anesthesia for procedures on the integumentary system on the extremities, anterior trunk and perineum; not otherwise specified

Forearm, Wrist, and Hand

01810   Anesthesia for all procedures on nerves, muscles, tendons, fascia, and bursae of forearm, wrist, and hand

01830   Anesthesia for open or surgical arthroscopic/endoscopic procedures on distal radius, distal ulna, wrist, or hand joints; not otherwise specified

Other Procedures

01991   Anesthesia for diagnostic or therapeutic nerve blocks and injections (when block or injection is performed by a different provider); other than the prone position
01992   prone position

SURGERY

Integumentary System

Nails
11719[P]   Trimming of nondystrophic nails, any number

(Nails continued on next page)

(Nails continued from previous page)

11720	Debridement of nail(s) by any method(s); one to five
11721	six or more
11730	Avulsion of nail plate, partial or complete, simple; single
11732	each additional nail plate (List separately in addition to code for primary procedure)
11740	Evacuation of subungual hematoma
11750	Excision of nail and nail matrix, partial or complete, (eg, ingrown or deformed nail) for permanent removal;
11752	with amputation of tuft of distal phalanx
11755	Biopsy of nail unit (eg, plate, bed, matrix, hyponychium, proximal and lateral nail folds) (separate procedure)
11760	Repair of nail bed
11762	Reconstruction of nail bed with graft
11765	Wedge excision of skin of nail fold (eg, for ingrown toenail)

Musculoskeletal System

General
Introduction or Removal

20600	Arthrocentesis, aspiration and/or injection; small joint or bursa (eg, fingers, toes)

Hand and Fingers
Incision

26010	Drainage of finger abscess; simple
26011	complicated (eg, felon)
26035	Decompression fingers and/or hand, injection injury (eg, grease gun)

Excision

26115	Excision, tumor or vascular malformation, soft tissue of hand or finger; subcutaneous
26116	deep (subfascial or intramuscular)
26117	Radical resection of tumor (eg, malignant neoplasm), soft tissue of hand or finger
26260	Radical resection, proximal or middle phalanx of finger (eg, tumor);
26261	with autograft (includes obtaining graft)
26262	Radical resection, distal phalanx of finger (eg, tumor)

Introduction or Removal

26320	Removal of implant from finger or hand

Repair, Revision, and/or Reconstruction

26340	Manipulation, finger joint, under anesthesia, each joint
26596	Excision of constricting ring of finger, with multiple Z-plasties

Amputation

26951	Amputation, finger or thumb, primary or secondary, any joint or phalanx, single, including neurectomies; with direct closure
26952	with local advancement flaps (V-Y, hood)

Anterior view

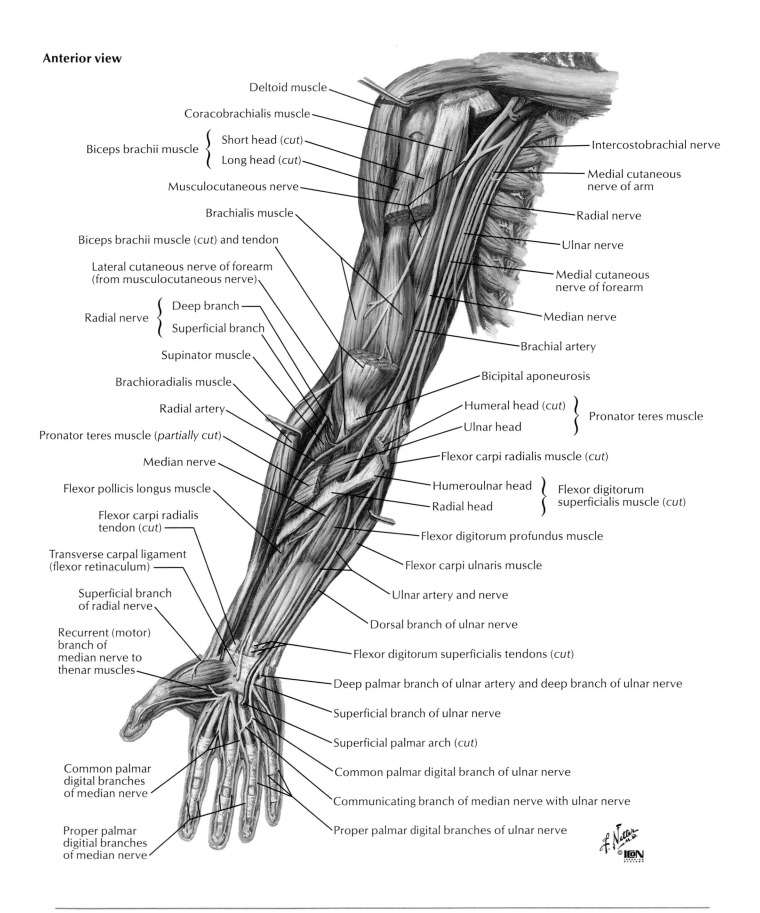

Deltoid muscle

Coracobrachialis muscle

Biceps brachii muscle { Short head (*cut*)
Long head (*cut*)

Musculocutaneous nerve

Brachialis muscle

Biceps brachii muscle (*cut*) and tendon

Lateral cutaneous nerve of forearm (from musculocutaneous nerve)

Radial nerve { Deep branch
Superficial branch

Supinator muscle

Brachioradialis muscle

Radial artery

Pronator teres muscle (*partially cut*)

Median nerve

Flexor pollicis longus muscle

Flexor carpi radialis tendon (*cut*)

Transverse carpal ligament (flexor retinaculum)

Superficial branch of radial nerve

Recurrent (motor) branch of median nerve to thenar muscles

Common palmar digital branches of median nerve

Proper palmar digitial branches of median nerve

Intercostobrachial nerve

Medial cutaneous nerve of arm

Radial nerve

Ulnar nerve

Medial cutaneous nerve of forearm

Median nerve

Brachial artery

Bicipital aponeurosis

Humeral head (*cut*) } Pronator teres muscle
Ulnar head

Flexor carpi radialis muscle (*cut*)

Humeroulnar head } Flexor digitorum superficialis muscle (*cut*)
Radial head

Flexor digitorum profundus muscle

Flexor carpi ulnaris muscle

Ulnar artery and nerve

Dorsal branch of ulnar nerve

Flexor digitorum superficialis tendons (*cut*)

Deep palmar branch of ulnar artery and deep branch of ulnar nerve

Superficial branch of ulnar nerve

Superficial palmar arch (*cut*)

Common palmar digital branch of ulnar nerve

Communicating branch of median nerve with ulnar nerve

Proper palmar digital branches of ulnar nerve

Plate 171: Arteries and Nerves of Upper Limb

ANESTHESIA

Thorax (Chest Wall and Shoulder Girdle)

00400   Anesthesia for procedures on the integumentary system on the extremities, anterior trunk and perineum; not otherwise specified

Shoulder and Axilla

01650   Anesthesia for procedures on arteries of shoulder and axilla; not otherwise specified
01652   axillary-brachial aneurysm
01654   bypass graft

Upper Arm and Elbow

01710   Anesthesia for procedures on nerves, muscles, tendons, fascia, and bursae of upper arm and elbow; not otherwise specified
01770   Anesthesia for procedures on arteries of upper arm and elbow; not otherwise specified
01772   embolectomy

Forearm, Wrist, and Hand

01810   Anesthesia for all procedures on nerves, muscles, tendons, fascia, and bursae of forearm, wrist, and hand
01840   Anesthesia for procedures on arteries of forearm, wrist, and hand; not otherwise specified
01842   embolectomy

Other Procedures

01991   Anesthesia for diagnostic or therapeutic nerve blocks and injections (when block or injection is performed by a different provider); other than the prone position

SURGERY

Cardiovascular System

Arteries and Veins
Embolectomy/Thrombectomy

Arterial, With or Without Catheter
34101   Embolectomy or thrombectomy, with or without catheter; axillary, brachial, innominate, subclavian artery, by arm incision
34111   radial or ulnar artery, by arm incision

Direct Repair of Aneurysm or Excision (Partial or Total) and Graft Insertion for Aneurysm, Pseudoaneurysm, Ruptured Aneurysm, and Associated Occlusive Disease

35011   Direct repair of aneurysm, pseudoaneurysm, or excision (partial or total) and graft insertion, with or without patch graft; for aneurysm and associated occlusive disease, axillary-brachial artery, by arm incision
35013   for ruptured aneurysm, axillary-brachial artery, by arm incision
35045   for aneurysm, pseudoaneurysm, and associated occlusive disease, radial or ulnar artery

Repair Arteriovenous Fistula

35184   Repair, congenital arteriovenous fistula; extremities
35190   Repair, acquired or traumatic arteriovenous fistula; extremities

Repair Blood Vessel Other Than for Fistual, With or Without Patch Angioplasty

35206   Repair blood vessel, direct; upper extremity
35207   hand, finger
35236   Repair blood vessel with vein graft; upper extremity
35266   Repair blood vessel with graft other than vein; upper extremity

Thromboendarterectomy

35321   Thromboendarterectomy, with or without patch graft; axillary-brachial

Transluminal Angioplasty

Open
35458   Transluminal balloon angioplasty, open; brachiocephalic trunk or branches, each vessel

Percutaneous
35475   Transluminal balloon angioplasty, percutaneous; brachiocephalic trunk or branches, each vessel

Transluminal Atherectomy

Open
35484   Transluminal peripheral atherectomy, open; brachiocephalic trunk or branches, each vessel

Percutaneous
35494   Transluminal peripheral atherectomy, percutaneous; brachiocephalic trunk or branches, each vessel

Bypass Graft

Vein
35518   Bypass graft, with vein; axillary-axillary
35522   axillary-brachial
35525   brachial-brachial

Other Than Vein
35650   Bypass graft, with other than vein; axillary-axillary

Exploration/Revision

35761   Exploration (not followed by surgical repair), with or without lysis of artery; other vessels
35860   Exploration for postoperative hemorrhage, thrombosis or infection; extremity
35875   Thrombectomy of arterial or venous graft (other than hemodialysis graft or fistula);
35876   with revision of arterial or venous graft
35879   Revision, lower extremity arterial bypass, without thrombectomy, open; with vein patch angioplasty
35903   Excision of infected graft; extremity

Nervous System

Extracranial Nerves, Peripheral Nerves, and Autonomic Nervous System
Introduction/Injection of Anesthetic Agent (Nerve Block), Diagnostic or Therapeutic

Somatic Nerves
64450   Injection, anesthetic agent; other peripheral nerve or branch

Neurostimulators (Peripheral Nerve)

64555 Percutaneous implantation of neurostimulator electrodes; peripheral nerve (excludes sacral nerve)

64560 autonomic nerve

64565 neuromuscular

64575 Incision for implantation of neurostimulator electrodes; peripheral nerve (excludes sacral nerve)

64577 autonomic nerve

64580 neuromuscular

64585 Revision or removal of peripheral neurostimulator electrodes

64590 Insertion or replacement of peripheral neurostimulator pulse generator or receiver, direct or inductive coupling

64595 Revision or removal of peripheral neurostimulator pulse generator or receiver

Destruction by Neurolytic Agent (eg, Chemical, Thermal, Electrical or Radiofrequency)

Somatic Nerves

64614 Chemodenervation of muscle(s); extremity(s) and/or trunk muscle(s) (eg, for dystonia, cerebral palsy, multiple sclerosis)

64640 Destruction by neurolytic agent; other peripheral nerve or branch

Neuroplasty (Exploration, Neurolysis or Nerve Decompression)

64702 Neuroplasty; digital, one or both, same digit

64704 nerve of hand or foot

64708 Neuroplasty, major peripheral nerve, arm or leg; other than specified

64722 Decompression; unspecified nerve(s) (specify)

Transection or Avulsion

64772 Transection or avulsion of other spinal nerve, extradural

Excision

Somatic Nerves

64774 Excision of neuroma; cutaneous nerve, surgically identifiable

64776 digital nerve, one or both, same digit

64778 digital nerve, each additional digit (List separately in addition to code for primary procedure)

64782 hand or foot, except digital nerve

64783 hand or foot, each additional nerve, except same digit (List separately in addition to code for primary procedure)

64784 major peripheral nerve, except sciatic

64788 Excision of neurofibroma or neurolemmoma; cutaneous nerve

64790 major peripheral nerve

64792 extensive (including malignant type)

64795 Biopsy of nerve

Sympathetic Nerves

64820 Sympathectomy; digital arteries, each digit

64821 radial artery

64822 ulnar artery

64823 superficial palmar arch

Neurorrhaphy

64831 Suture of digital nerve, hand or foot; one nerve

64832 each additional digital nerve (List separately in addition to code for primary procedure)

64834 Suture of one nerve, hand or foot; common sensory nerve

64835 median motor thenar

64836 ulnar motor

64837 Suture of each additional nerve, hand or foot (List separately in addition to code for primary procedure)

64840 Suture of posterior tibial nerve

64856 Suture of major peripheral nerve, arm or leg, except sciatic; including transposition

64857 without transposition

64858 Suture of sciatic nerve

64859 Suture of each additional major peripheral nerve (List separately in addition to code for primary procedure)

64861 Suture of; brachial plexus

64862 lumbar plexus

64864 Suture of facial nerve; extracranial

64865 infratemporal, with or without grafting

64866 Anastomosis; facial-spinal accessory

64868 facial-hypoglossal

64870 facial-phrenic

64872 Suture of nerve; requiring secondary or delayed suture (List separately in addition to code for primary neurorrhaphy)

64874 requiring extensive mobilization, or transposition of nerve (List separately in addition to code for nerve suture)

64876 requiring shortening of bone of extremity (List separately in addition to code for nerve suture)

Neurorrhaphy With Nerve Graft

64890 Nerve graft (includes obtaining graft), single strand, hand or foot; up to 4 cm length

64891 more than 4 cm length

64892 Nerve graft (includes obtaining graft), single strand, arm or leg; up to 4 cm length

64893 more than 4 cm length

64895 Nerve graft (includes obtaining graft), multiple strands (cable), hand or foot; up to 4 cm length

64896 more than 4 cm length

64897 Nerve graft (includes obtaining graft), multiple strands (cable), arm or leg; up to 4 cm length

64898 more than 4 cm length

64901 Nerve graft, each additional nerve; single strand (List separately in addition to code for primary procedure)

64902 multiple strands (cable) (List separately in addition to code for primary procedure)

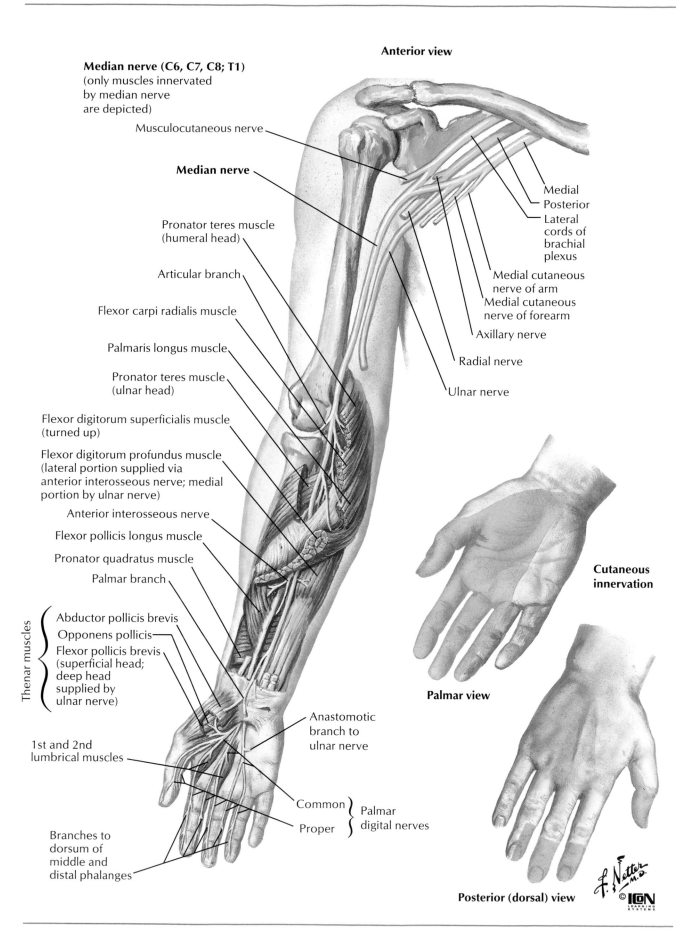

Median nerve (C6, C7, C8; T1)
(only muscles innervated
by median nerve
are depicted)

Musculocutaneous nerve

Median nerve

Pronator teres muscle
(humeral head)

Articular branch

Flexor carpi radialis muscle

Palmaris longus muscle

Pronator teres muscle
(ulnar head)

Flexor digitorum superficialis muscle
(turned up)

Flexor digitorum profundus muscle
(lateral portion supplied via
anterior interosseous nerve; medial
portion by ulnar nerve)

Anterior interosseous nerve

Flexor pollicis longus muscle

Pronator quadratus muscle

Palmar branch

Thenar muscles
{
Abductor pollicis brevis

Opponens pollicis

Flexor pollicis brevis
(superficial head;
deep head
supplied by
ulnar nerve)
}

1st and 2nd
lumbrical muscles

Branches to
dorsum of
middle and
distal phalanges

Anterior view

Medial

Posterior

Lateral
cords of
brachial
plexus

Medial cutaneous
nerve of arm

Medial cutaneous
nerve of forearm

Axillary nerve

Radial nerve

Ulnar nerve

Anastomotic
branch to
ulnar nerve

Common }
Palmar
Proper } digital nerves

**Cutaneous
innervation**

Palmar view

Posterior (dorsal) view

ANESTHESIA

Upper Arm and Elbow

01710   Anesthesia for procedures on nerves, muscles, tendons, fascia, and bursae of upper arm and elbow; not otherwise specified

Forearm, Wrist, and Hand

01810   Anesthesia for all procedures on nerves, muscles, tendons, fascia, and bursae of forearm, wrist, and hand

Other Procedures

01991   Anesthesia for diagnostic or therapeutic nerve blocks and injections (when block or injection is performed by a different provider); other than the prone position

SURGERY

Nervous System

Extracranial Nerves, Peripheral Nerves, and Autonomic Nervous System
Introduction/Injection of Anesthetic Agent (Nerve Block), Diagnostic or Therapeutic

Somatic Nerves

64415   Injection, anesthetic agent; brachial plexus, single
64416   brachial plexus, continuous infusion by catheter (including catheter placement) including daily management for anesthetic agent administration
64417   axillary nerve
64418   suprascapular nerve
64450   other peripheral nerve or branch

Neurostimulators (Peripheral Nerve)

64555   Percutaneous implantation of neurostimulator electrodes; peripheral nerve (excludes sacral nerve)
64560   autonomic nerve
64565   neuromuscular
64575   Incision for implantation of neurostimulator electrodes; peripheral nerve (excludes sacral nerve)
64577   autonomic nerve
64580   neuromuscular
64585   Revision or removal of peripheral neurostimulator electrodes
64590   Insertion or replacement of peripheral neurostimulator pulse generator or receiver, direct or inductive coupling
64595   Revision or removal of peripheral neurostimulator pulse generator or receiver

Destruction by Neurolytic Agent (eg, Chemical, Thermal, Electrical or Radiofrequency)

Somatic Nerves

64614   Chemodenervation of muscle(s); extremity(s) and/or trunk muscle(s) (eg, for dystonia, cerebral palsy, multiple sclerosis)
64640   Destruction by neurolytic agent; other peripheral nerve or branch

Neuroplasty (Exploration, Neurolysis or Nerve Decompression)

64702   Neuroplasty; digital, one or both, same digit
64704   nerve of hand or foot
64708   Neuroplasty, major peripheral nerve, arm or leg; other than specified
64713   brachial plexus
64721   Neuroplasty and/or transposition; median nerve at carpal tunnel
64722   Decompression; unspecified nerve(s) (specify)

Excision

Somatic Nerves

64774   Excision of neuroma; cutaneous nerve, surgically identifiable
64776   digital nerve, one or both, same digit
64778   digital nerve, each additional digit (List separately in addition to code for primary procedure)
64782   hand or foot, except digital nerve
64783   hand or foot, each additional nerve, except same digit (List separately in addition to code for primary procedure)
64784   major peripheral nerve, except sciatic
64788   Excision of neurofibroma or neurolemmoma; cutaneous nerve
64790   major peripheral nerve
64792   extensive (including malignant type)
64795   Biopsy of nerve

Sympathetic Nerves

64820   Sympathectomy; digital arteries, each digit
64821   radial artery
64822   ulnar artery
64823   superficial palmar arch

Neurorrhaphy

64831   Suture of digital nerve, hand or foot; one nerve
64832   each additional digital nerve (List separately in addition to code for primary procedure)
64834   Suture of one nerve, hand or foot; common sensory nerve
64835   median motor thenar
64836   ulnar motor
64837   Suture of each additional nerve, hand or foot (List separately in addition to code for primary procedure)
64856   Suture of major peripheral nerve, arm or leg, except sciatic; including transposition
64857   without transposition
64858   Suture of sciatic nerve
64859   Suture of each additional major peripheral nerve (List separately in addition to code for primary procedure)
64861   Suture of; brachial plexus
64872   Suture of nerve; requiring secondary or delayed suture (List separately in addition to code for primary neurorrhaphy)

(Neurorrhaphy continued on next page)

(Neurorrhaphy continued from previous page)

64874   requiring extensive mobilization, or transposition of nerve (List separately in addition to code for nerve suture)

64876   requiring shortening of bone of extremity (List separately in addition to code for nerve suture)

Neurorrhaphy With Nerve Graft

64890   Nerve graft (includes obtaining graft), single strand, hand or foot; up to 4 cm length

64891   more than 4 cm length

64892   Nerve graft (includes obtaining graft), single strand, arm or leg; up to 4 cm length

64893   more than 4 cm length

64895   Nerve graft (includes obtaining graft), multiple strands (cable), hand or foot; up to 4 cm length

64896   more than 4 cm length

64897   Nerve graft (includes obtaining graft), multiple strands (cable), arm or leg; up to 4 cm length

64898   more than 4 cm length

64901   Nerve graft, each additional nerve; single strand (List separately in addition to code for primary procedure)

64902   multiple strands (cable) (List separately in addition to code for primary procedure)

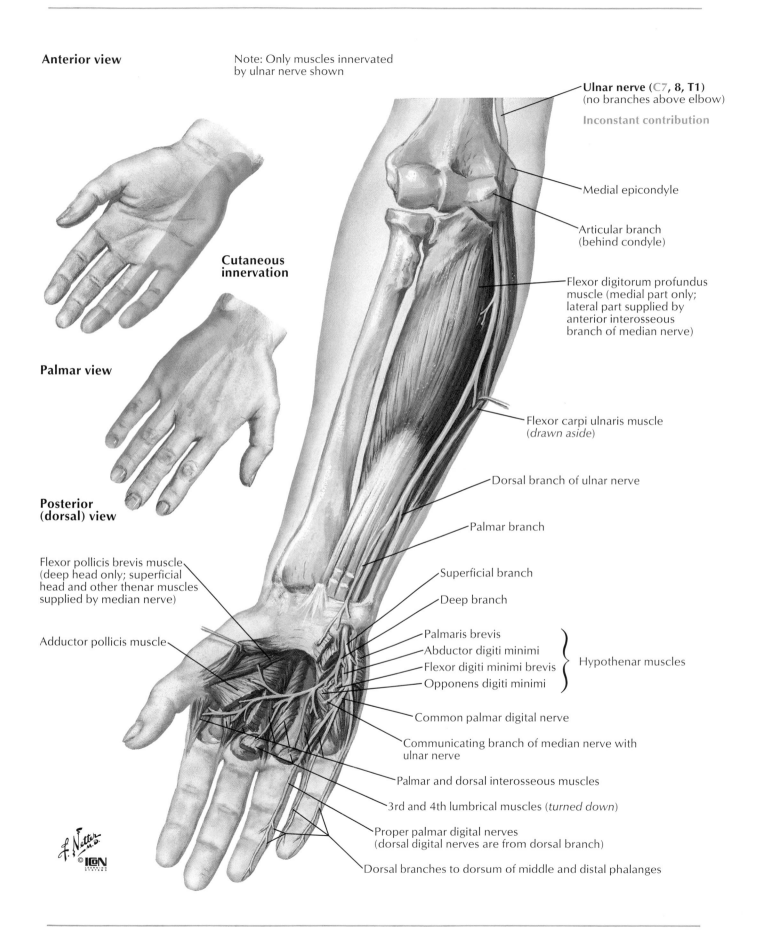

Anterior view

Note: Only muscles innervated by ulnar nerve shown

Ulnar nerve (C7, 8, T1)
(no branches above elbow)

Inconstant contribution

Medial epicondyle

Articular branch
(behind condyle)

Cutaneous innervation

Flexor digitorum profundus
muscle (medial part only;
lateral part supplied by
anterior interosseous
branch of median nerve)

Palmar view

Flexor carpi ulnaris muscle
(*drawn aside*)

Dorsal branch of ulnar nerve

Palmar branch

Posterior (dorsal) view

Flexor pollicis brevis muscle
(deep head only; superficial
head and other thenar muscles
supplied by median nerve)

Superficial branch

Deep branch

Adductor pollicis muscle

Palmaris brevis

Abductor digiti minimi

Flexor digiti minimi brevis

Opponens digiti minimi

} Hypothenar muscles

Common palmar digital nerve

Communicating branch of median nerve with
ulnar nerve

Palmar and dorsal interosseous muscles

3rd and 4th lumbrical muscles (*turned down*)

Proper palmar digital nerves
(dorsal digital nerves are from dorsal branch)

Dorsal branches to dorsum of middle and distal phalanges

Plate 173: Ulnar Nerve

ANESTHESIA

Upper Arm and Elbow

01710 Anesthesia for procedures on nerves, muscles, tendons, fascia, and bursae of upper arm and elbow; not otherwise specified

Forearm, Wrist, and Hand

01810 Anesthesia for all procedures on nerves, muscles, tendons, fascia, and bursae of forearm, wrist, and hand

Other Procedures

01991 Anesthesia for diagnostic or therapeutic nerve blocks and injections (when block or injection is performed by a different provider); other than the prone position

SURGERY

Nervous System

Extracranial Nerves, Peripheral Nerves, and Autonomic Nervous System
Introduction/Injection of Anesthetic Agent (Nerve Block), Diagnostic or Therapeutic

Somatic Nerves
64450 Injection, anesthetic agent; other peripheral nerve or branch

Neurostimulators (Peripheral Nerve)

64555 Percutaneous implantation of neurostimulator electrodes; peripheral nerve (excludes sacral nerve)
64575 Incision for implantation of neurostimulator electrodes; peripheral nerve (excludes sacral nerve)
64585 Revision or removal of peripheral neurostimulator electrodes
64590 Insertion or replacement of peripheral neurostimulator pulse generator or receiver, direct or inductive coupling
64595 Revision or removal of peripheral neurostimulator pulse generator or receiver

Destruction by Neurolytic Agent (eg, Chemical, Thermal, Electrical or Radiofrequency)

Somatic Nerves
64614 Chemodenervation of muscle(s); extremity(s) and/or trunk muscle(s) (eg, for dystonia, cerebral palsy, multiple sclerosis)
64640 Destruction by neurolytic agent; other peripheral nerve or branch

Neuroplasty (Exploration, Neurolysis or Nerve Decompression)

64702 Neuroplasty; digital, one or both, same digit
64704   nerve of hand or foot
64708 Neuroplasty, major peripheral nerve, arm or leg; other than specified
64718 Neuroplasty and/or transposition; ulnar nerve at elbow
64719   ulnar nerve at wrist
64722 Decompression; unspecified nerve(s) (specify)

Excision

Somatic Nerves
64776 Excision of neuroma; digital nerve, one or both, same digit
64778   digital nerve, each additional digit (List separately in addition to code for primary procedure)
64782   hand or foot, except digital nerve
64783   hand or foot, each additional nerve, except same digit (List separately in addition to code for primary procedure)
64784   major peripheral nerve, except sciatic
64790 Excision of neurofibroma or neurolemmoma; major peripheral nerve
64792   extensive (including malignant type)
64795 Biopsy of nerve

Neurorrhaphy

64831 Suture of digital nerve, hand or foot; one nerve
64832   each additional digital nerve (List separately in addition to code for primary procedure)
64834 Suture of one nerve, hand or foot; common sensory nerve
64835   median motor thenar
64836   ulnar motor
64837 Suture of each additional nerve, hand or foot (List separately in addition to code for primary procedure)
64856 Suture of major peripheral nerve, arm or leg, except sciatic; including transposition
64857   without transposition
64859 Suture of each additional major peripheral nerve (List separately in addition to code for primary procedure)
64872 Suture of nerve; requiring secondary or delayed suture (List separately in addition to code for primary neurorrhaphy)
64874   requiring extensive mobilization, or transposition of nerve (List separately in addition to code for nerve suture)
64876   requiring shortening of bone of extremity (List separately in addition to code for nerve suture)

Neurorrhaphy With Nerve Graft

64890 Nerve graft (includes obtaining graft), single strand, hand or foot; up to 4 cm length
64891   more than 4 cm length
64895 Nerve graft (includes obtaining graft), multiple strands (cable), hand or foot; up to 4 cm length
64896   more than 4 cm length
64901 Nerve graft, each additional nerve; single strand (List separately in addition to code for primary procedure)
64902   multiple strands (cable) (List separately in addition to code for primary procedure)

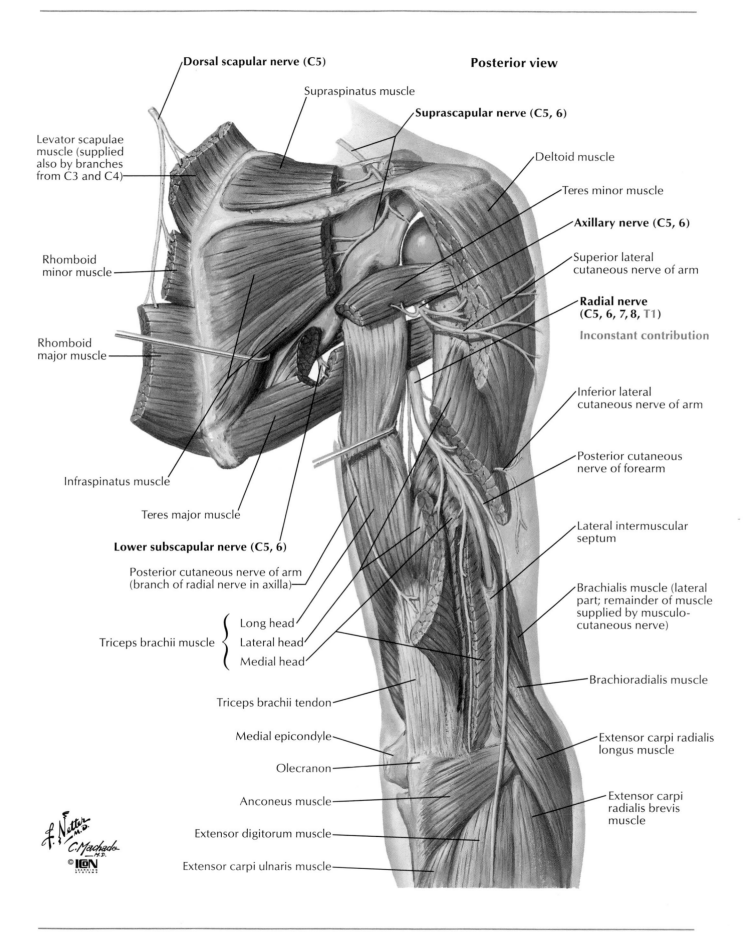

Posterior view

Dorsal scapular nerve (C5)

Supraspinatus muscle

Suprascapular nerve (C5, 6)

Levator scapulae muscle (supplied also by branches from C3 and C4)

Deltoid muscle

Teres minor muscle

Axillary nerve (C5, 6)

Superior lateral cutaneous nerve of arm

Rhomboid minor muscle

Radial nerve (C5, 6, 7, 8, T1)

Inconstant contribution

Rhomboid major muscle

Inferior lateral cutaneous nerve of arm

Posterior cutaneous nerve of forearm

Infraspinatus muscle

Teres major muscle

Lateral intermuscular septum

Lower subscapular nerve (C5, 6)

Posterior cutaneous nerve of arm (branch of radial nerve in axilla)

Brachialis muscle (lateral part; remainder of muscle supplied by musculo-cutaneous nerve)

Long head

Lateral head

Medial head

Triceps brachii muscle

Brachioradialis muscle

Triceps brachii tendon

Medial epicondyle

Extensor carpi radialis longus muscle

Olecranon

Anconeus muscle

Extensor carpi radialis brevis muscle

Extensor digitorum muscle

Extensor carpi ulnaris muscle

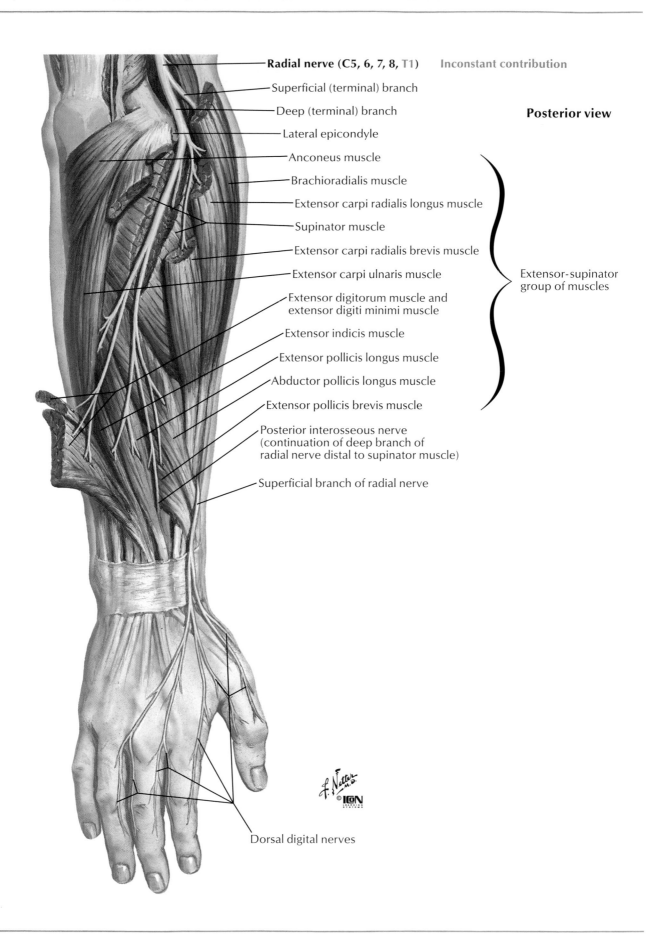

Radial nerve (C5, 6, 7, 8, T1)   Inconstant contribution

Superficial (terminal) branch

Deep (terminal) branch

Posterior view

Lateral epicondyle

Anconeus muscle

Brachioradialis muscle

Extensor carpi radialis longus muscle

Supinator muscle

Extensor carpi radialis brevis muscle

Extensor carpi ulnaris muscle

Extensor digitorum muscle and
extensor digiti minimi muscle

Extensor indicis muscle

Extensor pollicis longus muscle

Abductor pollicis longus muscle

Extensor pollicis brevis muscle

Extensor-supinator
group of muscles

Posterior interosseous nerve
(continuation of deep branch of
radial nerve distal to supinator muscle)

Superficial branch of radial nerve

Dorsal digital nerves

Plate 174: Radial Nerves in Arm and Forearm

ANESTHESIA

Upper Arm and Elbow

01710 Anesthesia for procedures on nerves, muscles, tendons, fascia, and bursae of upper arm and elbow; not otherwise specified

Forearm, Wrist, and Hand

01810 Anesthesia for all procedures on nerves, muscles, tendons, fascia, and bursae of forearm, wrist, and hand

Other Procedures

01991 Anesthesia for diagnostic or therapeutic nerve blocks and injections (when block or injection is performed by a different provider); other than the prone position

SURGERY

Nervous System

Extracranial Nerves, Peripheral Nerves, and Autonomic Nervous System

Introduction/Injection of Anesthetic Agent (Nerve Block), Diagnostic or Therapeutic

Somatic Nerves
64417 Injection, anesthetic agent; axillary nerve
64418   suprascapular nerve
64450   other peripheral nerve or branch

Neurostimulators (Peripheral Nerve)

64555 Percutaneous implantation of neurostimulator electrodes; peripheral nerve (excludes sacral nerve)
64575 Incision for implantation of neurostimulator electrodes; peripheral nerve (excludes sacral nerve)
64585 Revision or removal of peripheral neurostimulator electrodes
64590 Insertion or replacement of peripheral neurostimulator pulse generator or receiver, direct or inductive coupling
64595 Revision or removal of peripheral neurostimulator pulse generator or receiver

Destruction by Neurolytic Agent (eg, Chemical, Thermal, Electrical or Radiofrequency)

Somatic Nerves
64614 Chemodenervation of muscle(s); extremity(s) and/or trunk muscle(s) (eg, for dystonia, cerebral palsy, multiple sclerosis)
64640 Destruction by neurolytic agent; other peripheral nerve or branch

Neuroplasty (Exploration, Neurolysis or Nerve Decompression)

64702 Neuroplasty; digital, one or both, same digit
64704   nerve of hand or foot
64708 Neuroplasty, major peripheral nerve, arm or leg; other than specified
64722 Decompression; unspecified nerve(s) (specify)

Excision

Somatic Nerves
64776 Excision of neuroma; digital nerve, one or both, same digit
64778   digital nerve, each additional digit (List separately in addition to code for primary procedure)
64782   hand or foot, except digital nerve
64783   hand or foot, each additional nerve, except same digit (List separately in addition to code for primary procedure)
64784   major peripheral nerve, except sciatic
64790 Excision of neurofibroma or neurolemmoma; major peripheral nerve
64792   extensive (including malignant type)
64795 Biopsy of nerve

Neurorrhaphy

64831 Suture of digital nerve, hand or foot; one nerve
64832   each additional digital nerve (List separately in addition to code for primary procedure)
64837 Suture of each additional nerve, hand or foot (List separately in addition to code for primary procedure)
64856 Suture of major peripheral nerve, arm or leg, except sciatic; including transposition
64857   without transposition
64859 Suture of each additional major peripheral nerve (List separately in addition to code for primary procedure)
64872 Suture of nerve; requiring secondary or delayed suture (List separately in addition to code for primary neurorrhaphy)
64874   requiring extensive mobilization, or transposition of nerve (List separately in addition to code for nerve suture)
64876   requiring shortening of bone of extremity (List separately in addition to code for nerve suture)

Neurorrhaphy With Nerve Graft

64890 Nerve graft (includes obtaining graft), single strand, hand or foot; up to 4 cm length
64891   more than 4 cm length
64892 Nerve graft (includes obtaining graft), single strand, arm or leg; up to 4 cm length
64893   more than 4 cm length
64895 Nerve graft (includes obtaining graft), multiple strands (cable), hand or foot; up to 4 cm length
64896   more than 4 cm length
64897 Nerve graft (includes obtaining graft), multiple strands (cable), arm or leg; up to 4 cm length
64898   more than 4 cm length
64901 Nerve graft, each additional nerve; single strand (List separately in addition to code for primary procedure)
64902   multiple strands (cable) (List separately in addition to code for primary procedure)

Chapter 7
Lower Limb

The lower limbs or extremities are part of the appendicular skeleton and include 62 bones, beginning in the pelvis with the os coxae (or innominate bones) that are formed by the union of the ilium, ischium, and pubis.

The hip joint is a ball-and-socket joint with a deep cavity (acetabulum) into which the head of the femur fits. The joint is rarely dislocated but the neck of the femur may be fractured, particularly in the elderly. The femur, which is the longest and strongest bone in the body, comprises the bony structure of the upper leg. The patella (or kneecap) is the largest sesamoid bone in the body. (A sesamoid bone is a small, flat, round bone found in various tendons.)

The knee joint is flat, but the articular surfaces contain the medial and lateral cartilages (menisci), which are easily damaged. The joint has strong ligaments to help maintain its stability. The lower leg contains the tibia and fibula. The feet include the calcaneus (or heel bone); the talus; the cuboid, navicular, cuneiforms, metatarsals; and proximal, middle and distal phalanges. The bones and joints of the tarsus, metatarsus, and toes are made for weight bearing and walking, with the arches providing shock absorption and mobility. The arches of the foot are maintained by ligaments, long tendons, small muscles of the foot, and the plantar aponeurosis.

The muscles of the leg are arranged in compartments. In the thigh, the muscles in the anterior compartment (quadriceps) extend the knee. Muscle in the posterior compartment (hamstrings) extends the hip and flexes the knee. In the thigh, the major nerves include the femoral nerve, the obturator nerve, and the sciatic nerve.

The lower leg contains muscles in the anterior, lateral (fibular/peroneal), and posterior compartments. Major muscle groups in the lower leg include the tibialis anterior, gastrocnemius, and soleus muscles.

Major nerves in the lower leg include the tibial nerves and the common peroneal nerve. The blood supply of the lower limbs include the femoral artery and vein, the popliteal artery and vein, anterior and posterior tibial arteries, the peroneal artery, the popliteal artery, the saphenous vein, and the iliac veins.

Common procedures performed on the lower limb include, but are not limited to, the following:

- Excision of tumors and lesions
- Tendon repairs
- Arthroplasty of the knee
- Treatment of a fracture and/or dislocation
- Amputations
- Hallux valgus correction (ie, removal of a bunion, a lateral displacement of the great toe that produces deformity of the first metatarsophalangeal joint)
- Arthroscopy of the knee and ankle
- Embolectomy
- Thrombectomy
- Blood vessel repair
- Thromboendarterectomy
- Bypass grafts
- Treatment of varicose veins

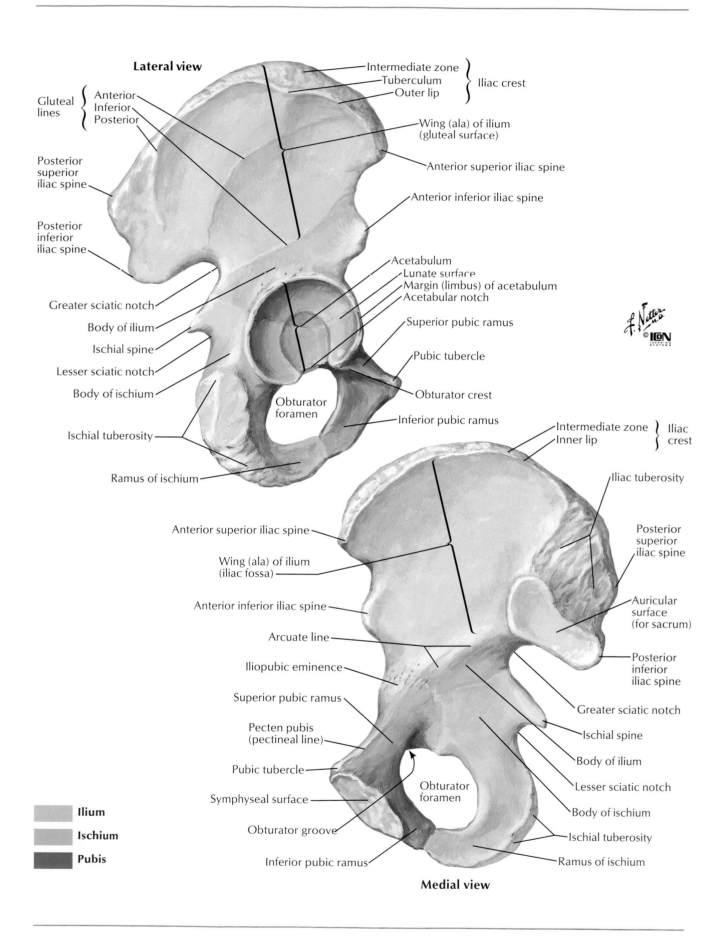

Lateral view

Gluteal lines { Anterior / Inferior / Posterior

Intermediate zone
Tuberculum } Iliac crest
Outer lip

Wing (ala) of ilium (gluteal surface)

Anterior superior iliac spine

Anterior inferior iliac spine

Posterior superior iliac spine

Posterior inferior iliac spine

Acetabulum
Lunate surface
Margin (limbus) of acetabulum
Acetabular notch

Greater sciatic notch

Body of ilium

Ischial spine

Lesser sciatic notch

Body of ischium

Superior pubic ramus

Pubic tubercle

Obturator crest

Obturator foramen

Inferior pubic ramus

Ischial tuberosity

Ramus of ischium

Anterior superior iliac spine

Wing (ala) of ilium (iliac fossa)

Anterior inferior iliac spine

Arcuate line

Iliopubic eminence

Superior pubic ramus

Pecten pubis (pectineal line)

Pubic tubercle

Symphyseal surface

Obturator groove

Inferior pubic ramus

Intermediate zone
Inner lip } Iliac crest

Iliac tuberosity

Posterior superior iliac spine

Auricular surface (for sacrum)

Posterior inferior iliac spine

Greater sciatic notch

Ischial spine

Body of ilium

Lesser sciatic notch

Body of ischium

Ischial tuberosity

Ramus of ischium

Obturator foramen

Medial view

Ilium
Ischium
Pubis

ANESTHESIA

Pelvis (Except Hip)

01160 Anesthesia for closed procedures involving symphysis pubis or sacroiliac joint

01170 Anesthesia for open procedures involving symphysis pubis or sacroiliac joint

01173 Anesthesia for open repair of fracture disruption of pelvis or column fracture involving acetabulum

Upper Leg (Except Knee)

01200 Anesthesia for all closed procedures involving hip joint

01210 Anesthesia for open procedures involving hip joint; not otherwise specified

SURGERY

Musculoskeletal System

Pelvis and Hip Joint
Incision

26992 Incision, bone cortex, pelvis and/or hip joint (eg, osteomyelitis or bone abscess)

Excision

27050 Arthrotomy, with biopsy; sacroiliac joint

27065 Excision of bone cyst or benign tumor; superficial (wing of ilium, symphysis pubis, or greater trochanter of femur) with or without autograft

27066 deep, with or without autograft

27067 with autograft requiring separate incision

Fracture and/or Dislocation

27193 Closed treatment of pelvic ring fracture, dislocation, diastasis or subluxation; without manipulation

27194 with manipulation, requiring more than local anesthesia

27215 Open treatment of iliac spine(s), tuberosity avulsion, or iliac wing fracture(s) (eg, pelvic fracture(s) which do not disrupt the pelvic ring), with internal fixation

27220 Closed treatment of acetabulum (hip socket) fracture(s); without manipulation

27222 with manipulation, with or without skeletal traction

27226 Open treatment of posterior or anterior acetabular wall fracture, with internal fixation

27227 Open treatment of acetabular fracture(s) involving anterior or posterior (one) column, or a fracture running transversely across the acetabulum, with internal fixation

27228 Open treatment of acetabular fracture(s) involving anterior and posterior (two) columns, includes T-fracture and both column fracture with complete articular detachment, or single column or transverse fracture with associated acetabular wall fracture, with internal fixation

Plate 176: Hip Joint

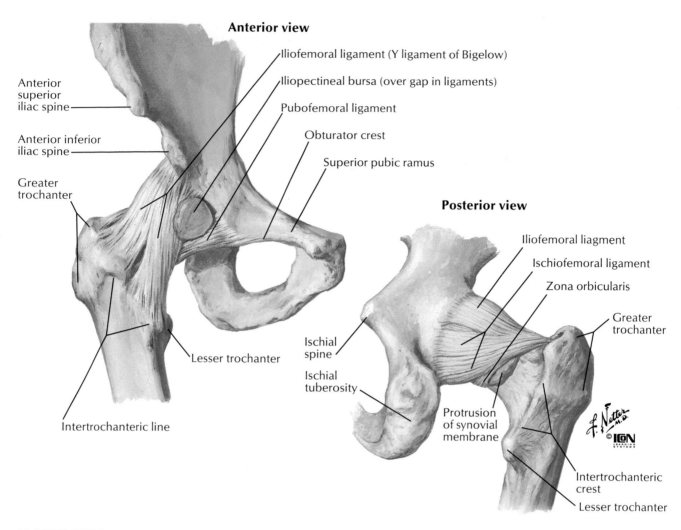

Anterior view

Iliofemoral ligament (Y ligament of Bigelow)

Iliopectineal bursa (over gap in ligaments)

Pubofemoral ligament

Obturator crest

Superior pubic ramus

Anterior superior iliac spine

Anterior inferior iliac spine

Greater trochanter

Lesser trochanter

Intertrochanteric line

Posterior view

Iliofemoral liagment

Ischiofemoral ligament

Zona orbicularis

Greater trochanter

Ischial spine

Ischial tuberosity

Protrusion of synovial membrane

Intertrochanteric crest

Lesser trochanter

ANESTHESIA

Pelvis (Except Hip)

01173	Anesthesia for open repair of fracture disruption of pelvis or column fracture involving acetabulum

Upper Leg (Except Knee)

01210	Anesthesia for open procedures involving hip joint; not otherwise specified
01212	hip disarticulation
01214	total hip arthroplasty
01215	revision of total hip arthroplasty

SURGERY

Musculoskeletal System

Pelvis and Hip Joint
Incision

27030	Arthrotomy, hip, with drainage (eg, infection)
27033	Arthrotomy, hip, including exploration or removal of loose or foreign body

Excision

27052	Arthrotomy, with biopsy; hip joint
27054	Arthrotomy with synovectomy, hip joint

Repair, Revision, and/or Reconstruction

27120	Acetabuloplasty; (eg, Whitman, Colonna, Haygroves, or cup type)
27122	resection, femoral head (eg, Girdlestone procedure)
27125[P]	Hemiarthroplasty, hip, partial (eg, femoral stem prosthesis, bipolar arthroplasty)
27130[P]	Arthroplasty, acetabular and proximal femoral prosthetic replacement (total hip arthroplasty), with or without autograft or allograft
27132	Conversion of previous hip surgery to total hip arthroplasty, with or without autograft or allograft
27134	Revision of total hip arthroplasty; both components, with or without autograft or allograft
27137	acetabular component only, with or without autograft or allograft
27138	femoral component only, with or without allograft

Fracture and/or Dislocation

27220	Closed treatment of acetabulum (hip socket) fracture(s); without manipulation
27222	with manipulation, with or without skeletal traction

27226   Open treatment of posterior or anterior acetabular wall fracture, with internal fixation

27227   Open treatment of acetabular fracture(s) involving anterior or posterior (one) column, or a fracture running transversely across the acetabulum, with internal fixation

27228   Open treatment of acetabular fracture(s) involving anterior and posterior (two) columns, includes T-fracture and both column fracture with complete articular detachment, or single column or transverse fracture with associated acetabular wall fracture, with internal fixation

Manipulation

27275   Manipulation, hip joint, requiring general anesthesia

Arthrodesis

27284   Arthrodesis, hip joint (including obtaining graft);

27286   with subtrochanteric osteotomy

Amputation

27295   Disarticulation of hip

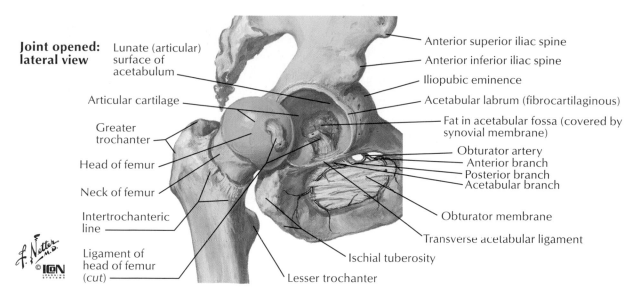

Joint opened: lateral view

Lunate (articular) surface of acetabulum

Articular cartilage

Greater trochanter

Head of femur

Neck of femur

Intertrochanteric line

Ligament of head of femur (cut)

Anterior superior iliac spine

Anterior inferior iliac spine

Iliopubic eminence

Acetabular labrum (fibrocartilaginous)

Fat in acetabular fossa (covered by synovial membrane)

Obturator artery
Anterior branch
Posterior branch
Acetabular branch

Obturator membrane

Transverse acetabular ligament

Ischial tuberosity

Lesser trochanter

ANESTHESIA

Pelvis (Except Hip)

01173 Anesthesia for open repair of fracture disruption of pelvis or column fracture involving acetabulum

Upper Leg (Except Knee)

01200 Anesthesia for all closed procedures involving hip joint
01202 Anesthesia for arthroscopic procedures of hip joint
01210 Anesthesiaesection, femoral head (eg, Girdlestone procedure)
01212   hip disarticulation
01214   total hip arthroplasty
01215   revision of total hip arthroplasty

SURGERY

Musculoskeletal System

Pelvis and Hip Joint
Incision

27030 Arthrotomy, hip, with drainage (eg, infection)
27033 Arthrotomy, hip, including exploration or removal of loose or foreign body

Excision

27052 Arthrotomy, with biopsy; hip joint
27054 Arthrotomy with synovectomy, hip joint

Repair, Revision, and/or Reconstruction

27120 Acetabuloplasty; (eg, Whitman, Colonna, Haygroves, or cup type)
27122   rhout autograft or allograft
27125 Hemiarthroplasty, hip, partial (eg, femoral stem prosthesis, bipolar arthroplasty)
27130P Arthroplasty, acetabular and proximal femoral prosthetic replacement (total hip arthroplasty), with or wit for open procedures involving hip joint; not otherwise specified
27132 Conversion of previous hip surgery to total hip arthroplasty, with or without autograft or allograft

27134 Revision of total hip arthroplasty; both components, with or without autograft or allograft
27137   acetabular component only, with or without autograft or allograft
27138   femoral component only, with or without allograft

Fracture and/or Dislocation

27220 Closed treatment of acetabulum (hip socket) fracture(s); without manipulation
27222   with manipulation, with or without skeletal traction
27226 Open treatment of posterior or anterior acetabular wall fracture, with internal fixation
27227 Open treatment of acetabular fracture(s) involving anterior or posterior (one) column, or a fracture running transversely across the acetabulum, with internal fixation
27228 Open treatment of acetabular fracture(s) involving anterior and posterior (two) columns, includes T-fracture and both column fracture with complete articular detachment, or single column or transverse fracture with associated acetabular wall fracture, with internal fixation

Manipulation

27275 Manipulation, hip joint, requiring general anesthesia

Arthrodesis

27284 Arthrodesis, hip joint (including obtaining graft);
27286   with subtrochanteric osteotomy

Amputation

27295 Disarticulation of hip

Endoscopy/Arthroscopy

29860 Arthroscopy, hip, diagnostic with or without synovial biopsy (separate procedure)
29861 Arthroscopy, hip, surgical; with removal of loose body or foreign body
29862   with chondroplasty or arthroplasty, and or resection of labrum
29863   with synovectomy

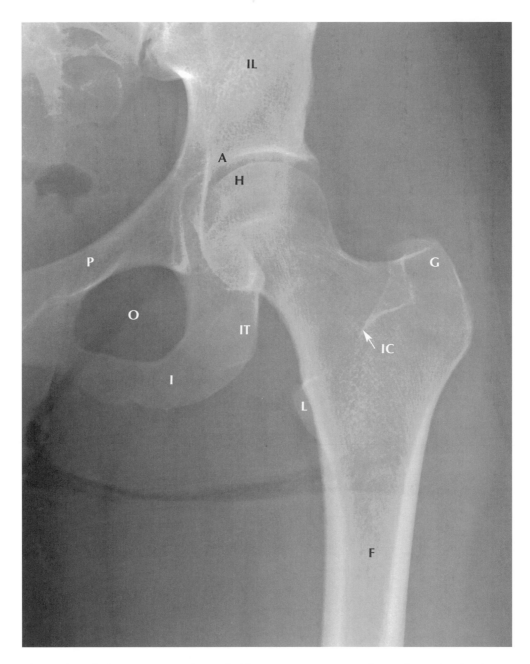

A	Acetabulum	**I**	Ischium	**L**	Lesser trochanter
F	Femur	**IC**	Intertrochanteric crest	**O**	Obturator foramen
G	Greater trochanter	**IL**	Ileum	**P**	Pubis (superior ramus)
H	Head of femur	**IT**	Ischial tuberosity		

RADIOLOGY

Diagnostic Radiology (Diagnostic Imaging)

Lower Extremities

73500   Radiologic examination, hip, unilateral; one view

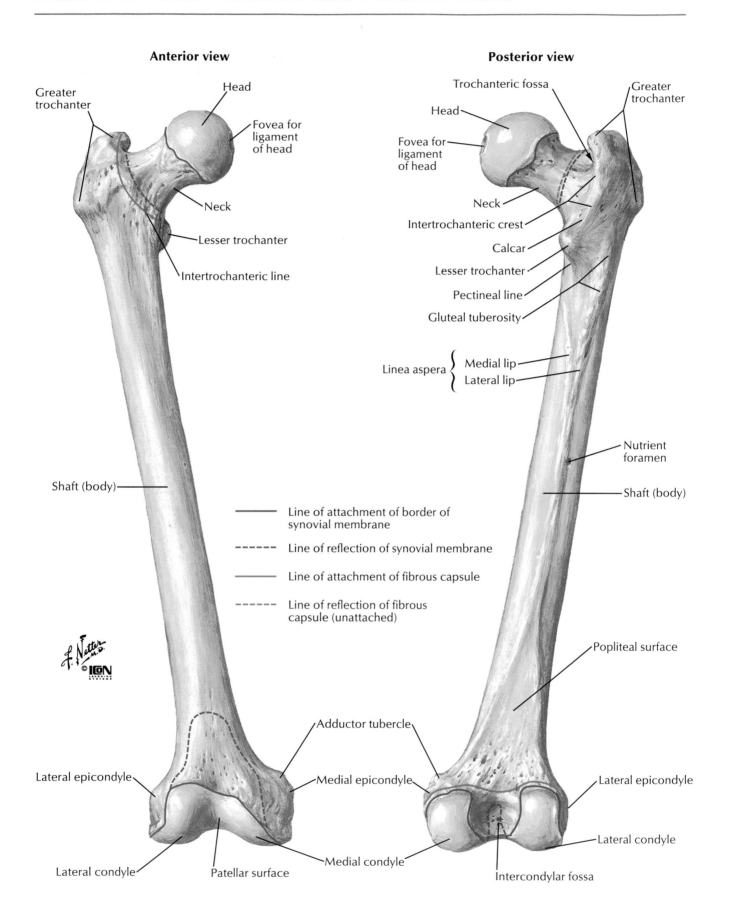

Anterior view

Greater trochanter

Head

Fovea for ligament of head

Neck

Lesser trochanter

Intertrochanteric line

Shaft (body)

Line of attachment of border of synovial membrane

Line of reflection of synovial membrane

Line of attachment of fibrous capsule

Line of reflection of fibrous capsule (unattached)

Lateral epicondyle

Adductor tubercle

Medial epicondyle

Lateral epicondyle

Lateral condyle

Patellar surface

Medial condyle

Posterior view

Trochanteric fossa

Head

Greater trochanter

Fovea for ligament of head

Neck

Intertrochanteric crest

Calcar

Lesser trochanter

Pectineal line

Gluteal tuberosity

Linea aspera { Medial lip / Lateral lip

Nutrient foramen

Shaft (body)

Popliteal surface

Lateral epicondyle

Lateral condyle

Intercondylar fossa

ANESTHESIA

Upper Leg (Except Knee)

01220 Anesthesia for all closed procedures involving upper 2/3 of femur

01230 Anesthesia for open procedures involving upper 2/3 of femur; not otherwise specified

01232   amputation

Knee and Popliteal Area

01340 Anesthesia for all closed procedures on lower 1/3 of femur

01360 Anesthesia for all open procedures on lower 1/3 of femur

SURGERY

Musculoskeletal System

Femur (Thigh Region) and Knee Joint

Incision

27303 Incision, deep, with opening of bone cortex, femur or knee (eg, osteomyelitis or bone abscess)

Excision

27355 Excision or curettage of bone cyst or benign tumor of femur;

27356   with allograft

27357   with autograft (includes obtaining graft)

27358   with internal fixation (List in addition to code for primary procedure)

Repair, Revision, and/or Reconstruction

27448 Osteotomy, femur, shaft or supracondylar; without fixation

27450   with fixation

27454 Osteotomy, multiple, with realignment on intramedullary rod, femoral shaft (eg, Sofield type procedure)

27465 Osteoplasty, femur; shortening (excluding 64876)

27466   lengthening

27468   combined, lengthening and shortening with femoral segment transfer

27470 Repair, nonunion or malunion, femur, distal to head and neck; without graft (eg, compression technique)

27472   with iliac or other autogenous bone graft (includes obtaining graft)

27475 Arrest, epiphyseal, any method (eg, epiphysiodesis); distal femur

Fracture and/or Dislocation

27500 Closed treatment of femoral shaft fracture, without manipulation

27501 Closed treatment of supracondylar or transcondylar femoral fracture with or without intercondylar extension, without manipulation

27502 Closed treatment of femoral shaft fracture, with manipulation, with or without skin or skeletal traction

27503 Closed treatment of supracondylar or transcondylar femoral fracture with or without intercondylar extension, with manipulation, with or without skin or skeletal traction

27506 Open treatment of femoral shaft fracture, with or without external fixation, with insertion of intramedullary implant, with or without cerclage and/or locking screws

27507 Open treatment of femoral shaft fracture with plate/screws, with or without cerclage

27508 Closed treatment of femoral fracture, distal end, medial or lateral condyle, without manipulation

27509 Percutaneous skeletal fixation of femoral fracture, distal end, medial or lateral condyle, or supracondylar or transcondylar, with or without intercondylar extension, or distal femoral epiphyseal separation

27510 Closed treatment of femoral fracture, distal end, medial or lateral condyle, with manipulation

27511 Open treatment of femoral supracondylar or transcondylar fracture without intercondylar extension, with or without internal or external fixation

27513 Open treatment of femoral supracondylar or transcondylar fracture with intercondylar extension, with or without internal or external fixation

27514 Open treatment of femoral fracture, distal end, medial or lateral condyle, with or without internal or external fixation

Amputation

27590 Amputation, thigh, through femur, any level;

27591   immediate fitting technique including first cast

27592   open, circular (guillotine)

27594   secondary closure or scar revision

27596   re-amputation

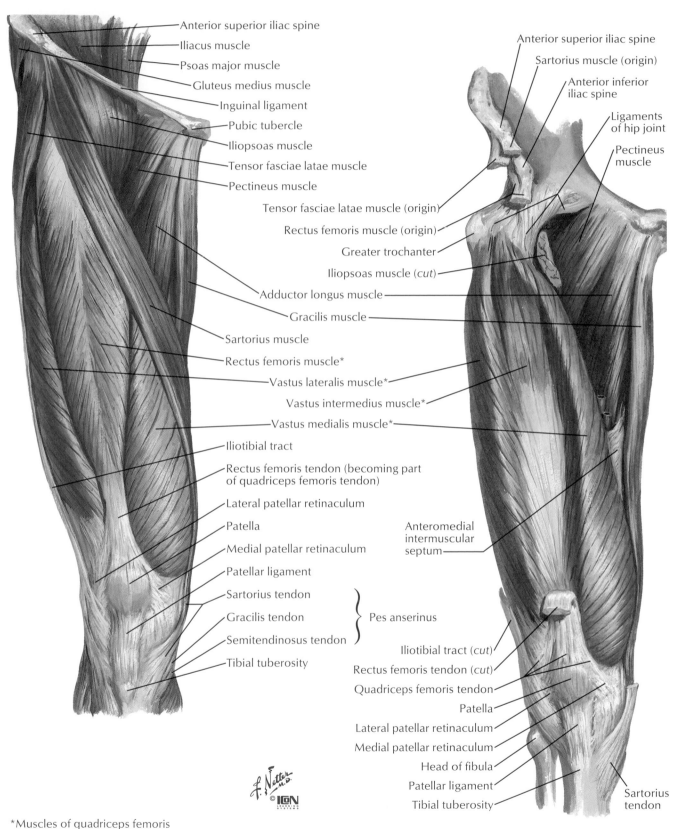

Anterior superior iliac spine
Iliacus muscle
Psoas major muscle
Gluteus medius muscle
Inguinal ligament
Pubic tubercle
Iliopsoas muscle
Tensor fasciae latae muscle
Pectineus muscle
Tensor fasciae latae muscle (origin)
Rectus femoris muscle (origin)
Adductor longus muscle
Gracilis muscle
Sartorius muscle
Rectus femoris muscle*
Vastus lateralis muscle*
Vastus intermedius muscle*
Vastus medialis muscle*
Iliotibial tract
Rectus femoris tendon (becoming part of quadriceps femoris tendon)
Lateral patellar retinaculum
Patella
Medial patellar retinaculum
Patellar ligament
Sartorius tendon
Gracilis tendon
Semitendinosus tendon
Tibial tuberosity

Anterior superior iliac spine
Sartorius muscle (origin)
Anterior inferior iliac spine
Ligaments of hip joint
Pectineus muscle
Greater trochanter
Iliopsoas muscle (*cut*)

Anteromedial intermuscular septum

Pes anserinus

Iliotibial tract (*cut*)
Rectus femoris tendon (*cut*)
Quadriceps femoris tendon
Patella
Lateral patellar retinaculum
Medial patellar retinaculum
Head of fibula
Patellar ligament
Tibial tuberosity
Sartorius tendon

*Muscles of quadriceps femoris

Anterior views

Anterior view

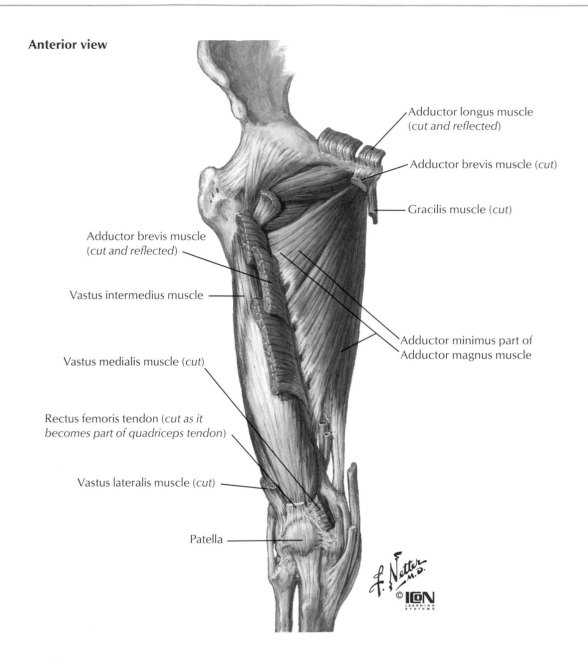

Adductor longus muscle
(*cut and reflected*)

Adductor brevis muscle (*cut*)

Gracilis muscle (*cut*)

Adductor brevis muscle
(*cut and reflected*)

Vastus intermedius muscle

Adductor minimus part of
Adductor magnus muscle

Vastus medialis muscle (*cut*)

Rectus femoris tendon (*cut as it
becomes part of quadriceps tendon*)

Vastus lateralis muscle (*cut*)

Patella

Nomenclature Notes

The term *flexor* refers to the muscle action that bends a body part, generally in a proximal direction. Flexors in the anterior thigh include the iliopsoas and rectus femoris muscles.

The term *extensor* refers to the muscle action that extends a body par. Extensors in the anterior thigh include the quadriceps femoris: rectus femoris, vastus lateralis, vastus intermedius, and vastus medialis.

The term *adductor* refers to the muscle action that draws a body part toward the medial line of the body or to a common center. Adductors in the anterior thigh include the adductor brevis, adductor longus, adductor magnus, and gracilis.

ANESTHESIA

Thorax (Chest Wall and Shoulder Girdle)

00400   Anesthesia for procedures on the integumentary system on the extremities, anterior trunk and perineum; not otherwise specified

Upper Leg (Except Knee)

01250   Anesthesia for all procedures on nerves, muscles, tendons, fascia, and bursae of upper leg

Knee and Popliteal Area

01320   Anesthesia for all procedures on nerves, muscles, tendons, fascia, and bursae of knee and/or popliteal area

SURGERY

Musculoskeletal System

Pelvis and Hip Joint
Incision

27025	Fasciotomy, hip or thigh, any type

Femur (Thigh Region) and Knee Joint
Incision

27301	Incision and drainage, deep abscess, bursa, or hematoma, thigh or knee region
27305	Fasciotomy, iliotibial (tenotomy), open
27306	Tenotomy, percutaneous, adductor or hamstring; single tendon (separate procedure)
27307	multiple tendons

Excision

27323	Biopsy, soft tissue of thigh or knee area; superficial
27324	deep (subfascial or intramuscular)
27327	Excision, tumor, thigh or knee area; subcutaneous
27328	deep, subfascial, or intramuscular
27329	Radical resection of tumor (eg, malignant neoplasm), soft tissue of thigh or knee area

Introduction or Removal

27372	Removal of foreign body, deep, thigh region or knee area

Repair, Revision, and/or Reconstruction

27380	Suture of infrapatellar tendon; primary
27381	secondary reconstruction, including fascial or tendon graft
27385	Suture of quadriceps or hamstring muscle rupture; primary
27386	secondary reconstruction, including fascial or tendon graft
27430	Quadricepsplasty (eg, Bennett or Thompson type)
27496	Decompression fasciotomy, thigh and/or knee, one compartment (flexor or extensor or adductor);
27497	with debridement of nonviable muscle and/or nerve
27498	Decompression fasciotomy, thigh and/or knee, multiple compartments;
27499	with debridement of nonviable muscle and/or nerve

Lateral view

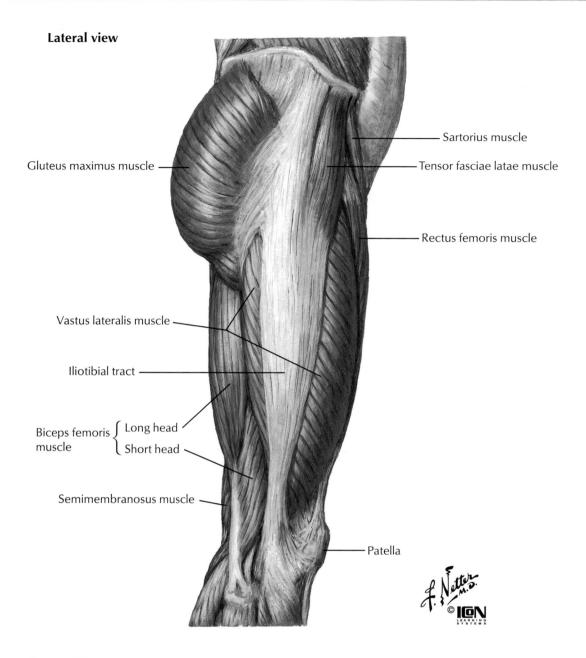

Gluteus maximus muscle

Sartorius muscle

Tensor fasciae latae muscle

Rectus femoris muscle

Vastus lateralis muscle

Iliotibial tract

Biceps femoris muscle { Long head / Short head

Semimembranosus muscle

Patella

Nomenclature Notes

The term *flexor* refers to the muscle action that bends a body part, generally in a proximal direction. Flexors in the anterior thigh include the iliopsoas and rectus femoris muscles.

The term *extensor* refers to the muscle action that extends a body par. Extensors in the anterior thigh include the quadriceps femoris: rectus femoris, vastus lateralis, vastus intermedius, and vastus medialis.

The term *adductor* refers to the muscle action that draws a body part toward the medial line of the body or to a common center. Adductors in the anterior thigh include the adductor brevis, adductor longus, adductor magnus, and gracilis.

ANESTHESIA

Thorax (Chest Wall and Shoulder Girdle)

00400   Anesthesia for procedures on the integumentary system on the extremities, anterior trunk and perineum; not otherwise specified

Upper Leg (Except Knee)

01250   Anesthesia for all procedures on nerves, muscles, tendons, fascia, and bursae of upper leg

Knee and Popliteal Area

01320   Anesthesia for all procedures on nerves, muscles, tendons, fascia, and bursae of knee and/or popliteal area

Superficial dissection

Deeper dissection

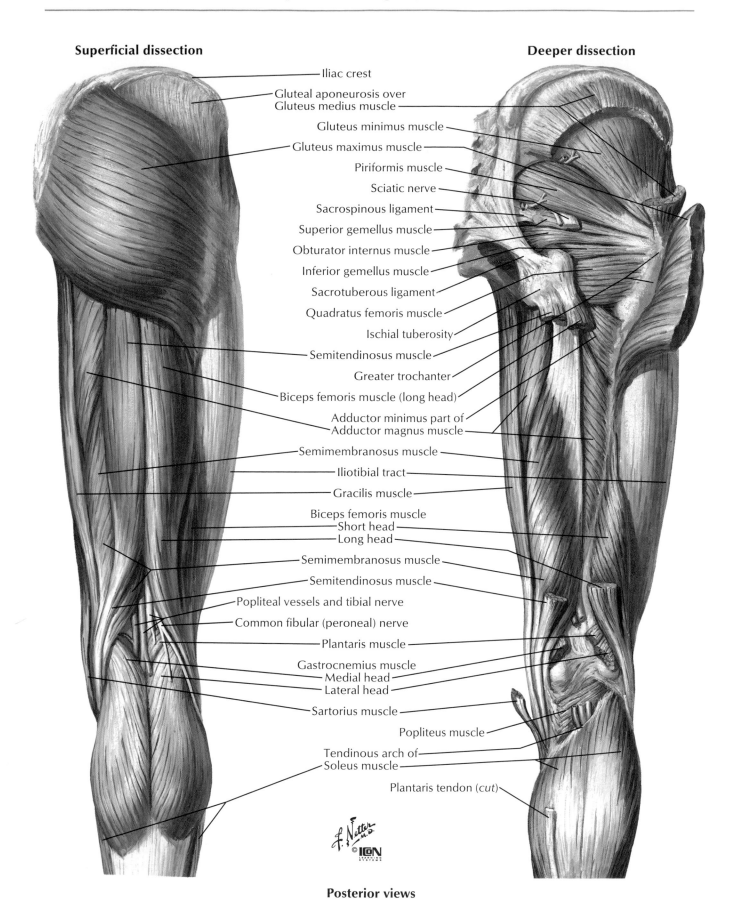

Iliac crest

Gluteal aponeurosis over
Gluteus medius muscle

Gluteus minimus muscle

Gluteus maximus muscle

Piriformis muscle

Sciatic nerve

Sacrospinous ligament

Superior gemellus muscle

Obturator internus muscle

Inferior gemellus muscle

Sacrotuberous ligament

Quadratus femoris muscle

Ischial tuberosity

Semitendinosus muscle

Greater trochanter

Biceps femoris muscle (long head)

Adductor minimus part of
Adductor magnus muscle

Semimembranosus muscle

Iliotibial tract

Gracilis muscle

Biceps femoris muscle
Short head
Long head

Semimembranosus muscle

Semitendinosus muscle

Popliteal vessels and tibial nerve

Common fibular (peroneal) nerve

Plantaris muscle

Gastrocnemius muscle
Medial head
Lateral head

Sartorius muscle

Popliteus muscle

Tendinous arch of
Soleus muscle

Plantaris tendon (*cut*)

Posterior views

SURGERY

Musculoskeletal System

Pelvis and Hip Joint
Incision

27025	Fasciotomy, hip or thigh, any type

Femur (Thigh Region) and Knee Joint
Incision

27301	Incision and drainage, deep abscess, bursa, or hematoma, thigh or knee region
27305	Fasciotomy, iliotibial (tenotomy), open
27306	Tenotomy, percutaneous, adductor or hamstring; single tendon (separate procedure)
27307	multiple tendons
27315	Neurectomy, hamstring muscle

Excision

27323	Biopsy, soft tissue of thigh or knee area; superficial
27324	deep (subfascial or intramuscular)
27327	Excision, tumor, thigh or knee area; subcutaneous
27328	deep, subfascial, or intramuscular
27329	Radical resection of tumor (eg, malignant neoplasm), soft tissue of thigh or knee area

Introduction or Removal

27372	Removal of foreign body, deep, thigh region or knee area

Repair, Revision, and/or Reconstruction

27385	Suture of quadriceps or hamstring muscle rupture; primary
27386	secondary reconstruction, including fascial or tendon graft
27390	Tenotomy, open, hamstring, knee to hip; single tendon
27391	multiple tendons, one leg
27392	multiple tendons, bilateral
27393	Lengthening of hamstring tendon; single tendon
27394	multiple tendons, one leg
27395	multiple tendons, bilateral
27396	Transplant, hamstring tendon to patella; single tendon
27397	multiple tendons
27400	Transfer, tendon or muscle, hamstrings to femur (eg, Egger's type procedure)
27496	Decompression fasciotomy, thigh and/or knee, one compartment (flexor or extensor or adductor);
27497	with debridement of nonviable muscle and/or nerve
27498	Decompression fasciotomy, thigh and/or knee, multiple compartments;
27499	with debridement of nonviable muscle and/or nerve

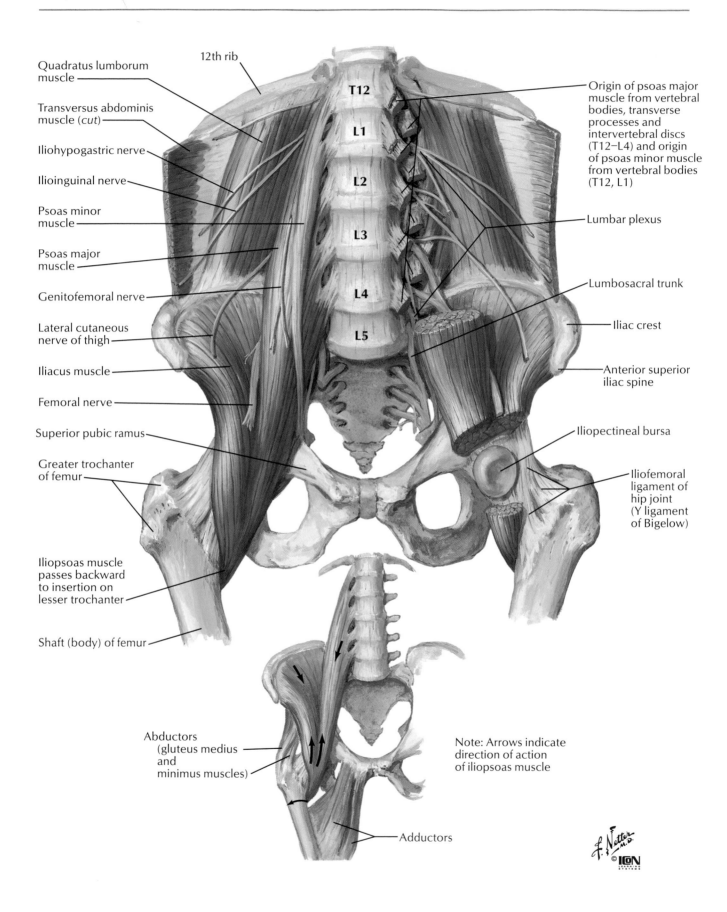

Quadratus lumborum muscle

12th rib

T12

Origin of psoas major muscle from vertebral bodies, transverse processes and intervertebral discs (T12–L4) and origin of psoas minor muscle from vertebral bodies (T12, L1)

Transversus abdominis muscle (*cut*)

Iliohypogastric nerve

Ilioinguinal nerve

L1

Psoas minor muscle

L2

Lumbar plexus

Psoas major muscle

L3

Genitofemoral nerve

L4

Lumbosacral trunk

Lateral cutaneous nerve of thigh

L5

Iliac crest

Iliacus muscle

Anterior superior iliac spine

Femoral nerve

Superior pubic ramus

Iliopectineal bursa

Greater trochanter of femur

Iliofemoral ligament of hip joint (Y ligament of Bigelow)

Iliopsoas muscle passes backward to insertion on lesser trochanter

Shaft (body) of femur

Abductors (gluteus medius and minimus muscles)

Note: Arrows indicate direction of action of iliopsoas muscle

Adductors

f. Netter
M.D.

© **ICON**
LEARNING SYSTEMS

ANESTHESIA

Thorax (Chest Wall and Shoulder Girdle)

00400   Anesthesia for procedures on the integumentary system on the extremities, anterior trunk and perineum; not otherwise specified

Pelvis (Except Hip)

01150   Anesthesia for radical procedures for tumor of pelvis, except hindquarter amputation

Upper Leg (Except Knee)

01250   Anesthesia for all procedures on nerves, muscles, tendons, fascia, and bursae of upper leg

SURGERY

Musculoskeletal System

Pelvis and Hip Joint

Incision

27001   Tenotomy, adductor of hip, open
27003   Tenotomy, adductor, subcutaneous, open, with obturator neurectomy
27006   Tenotomy, abductors and/or extensor(s) of hip, open (separate procedure)

Excision

27047   Excision, tumor, pelvis and hip area; subcutaneous tissue
27048   deep, subfascial, intramuscular
27049   Radical resection of tumor, soft tissue of pelvis and hip area (eg, malignant neoplasm)

Repair, Revision, and/or Reconstruction

27105   Transfer paraspinal muscle to hip (includes fascial or tendon extension graft)
27110   Transfer iliopsoas; to greater trochanter of femur
27111   to femoral neck

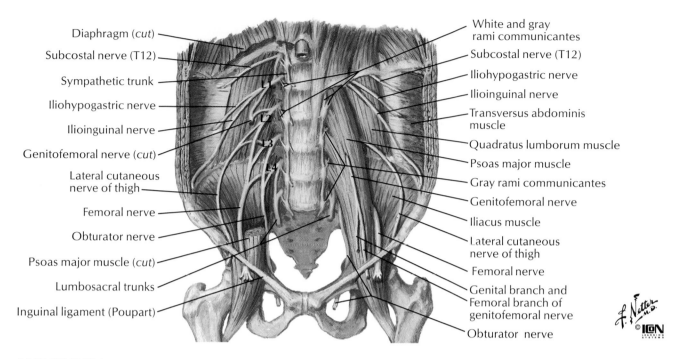

Diaphragm (*cut*)
Subcostal nerve (T12)
Sympathetic trunk
Iliohypogastric nerve
Ilioinguinal nerve
Genitofemoral nerve (*cut*)
Lateral cutaneous nerve of thigh
Femoral nerve
Obturator nerve
Psoas major muscle (*cut*)
Lumbosacral trunks
Inguinal ligament (Poupart)

White and gray rami communicantes
Subcostal nerve (T12)
Iliohypogastric nerve
Ilioinguinal nerve
Transversus abdominis muscle
Quadratus lumborum muscle
Psoas major muscle
Gray rami communicantes
Genitofemoral nerve
Iliacus muscle
Lateral cutaneous nerve of thigh
Femoral nerve
Genital branch and Femoral branch of genitofemoral nerve
Obturator nerve

ANESTHESIA

Head

00210 Anesthesia for intracranial procedures; not otherwise specified

Spine and Spinal Cord

00630 Anesthesia for procedures in lumbar region; not otherwise specified
00632 lumbar sympathectomy

Pelvis (Except Hip)

01180 Anesthesia for obturator neurectomy; extrapelvic

Upper Leg (Except Knee)

01250 Anesthesia for all procedures on nerves, muscles, tendons, fascia, and bursae of upper leg

Other Procedures

01990 Physiological support for harvesting of organ(s) from brain-dead patient
01991 Anesthesia for diagnostic or therapeutic nerve blocks and injections (when block or injection is performed by a different provider); other than the prone position
01992 prone position

SURGERY

Musculoskeletal System

Pelvis and Hip Joint
Incision

27035 Denervation, hip joint, intrapelvic or extrapelvic intra-articular branches of sciatic, femoral, or obturator nerves

Nervous System

Extracranial Nerves, Peripheral Nerves, and Autonomic Nervous System
Introduction/Injection of Anesthetic Agent (Nerve Block), Diagnostic or Therapeutic
Somatic Nerves
64425 Injection, anesthetic agent; ilioinguinal, iliohypogastric nerves
Sympathetic Nerves
64520 Injection, anesthetic agent; lumbar or thoracic (paravertebral sympathetic)

Neurostimulators (Peripheral Nerve)
64581[P] Incision for implantation of neurostimulator electrodes; sacral nerve (transforaminal placement)

Neuroplasty (Exploration, Neurolysis or Nerve Decompression)
64714 Neuroplasty, major peripheral nerve, arm or leg; lumbar plexus
64722 Decompression; unspecified nerve(s) (specify)

Transection or Avulsion
64763 Transection or avulsion of obturator nerve, extrapelvic, with or without adductor tenotomy
64766 Transection or avulsion of obturator nerve, intrapelvic, with or without adductor tenotomy

Excision
Sympathetic Nerves
64818 Sympathectomy, lumbar

Neurorrhaphy
64862 Suture of; lumbar plexus

Neurorrhaphy With Nerve Graft
64897 Nerve graft (includes obtaining graft), multiple strands (cable), arm or leg; up to 4 cm length
64898 more than 4 cm length

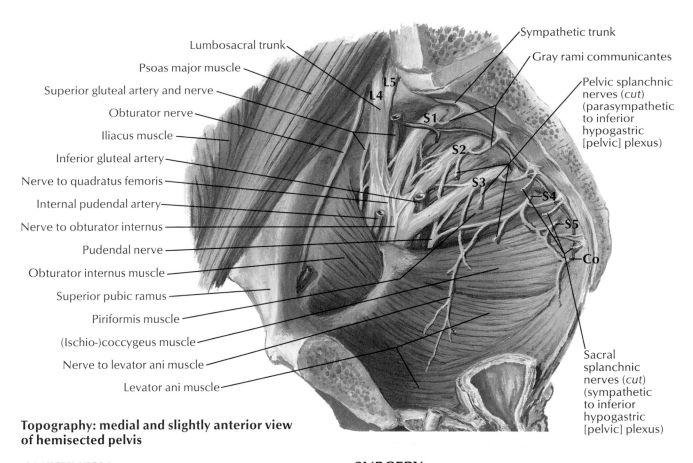

Lumbosacral trunk
Psoas major muscle
Superior gluteal artery and nerve
Obturator nerve
Iliacus muscle
Inferior gluteal artery
Nerve to quadratus femoris
Internal pudendal artery
Nerve to obturator internus
Pudendal nerve
Obturator internus muscle
Superior pubic ramus
Piriformis muscle
(Ischio-)coccygeus muscle
Nerve to levator ani muscle
Levator ani muscle

Sympathetic trunk
Gray rami communicantes
Pelvic splanchnic nerves (*cut*) (parasympathetic to inferior hypogastric [pelvic] plexus)

L5
L4
S1
S2
S3
S4
S5
Co

Sacral splanchnic nerves (*cut*) (sympathetic to inferior hypogastric [pelvic] plexus)

Topography: medial and slightly anterior view of hemisected pelvis

ANESTHESIA

Spine and Spinal Cord

00630 Anesthesia for procedures in lumbar region; not otherwise specified
00632 lumbar sympathectomy

Pelvis (Except Hip)

01180 Anesthesia for obturator neurectomy; extrapelvic
01190 intrapelvic

Upper Leg (Except Knee)

01250 Anesthesia for all procedures on nerves, muscles, tendons, fascia, and bursae of upper leg

Other Procedures

01991 Anesthesia for diagnostic or therapeutic nerve blocks and injections (when block or injection is performed by a different provider); other than the prone position
01992 prone position

SURGERY

Nervous System

Extracranial Nerves, Peripheral Nerves, and Autonomic Nervous System
Introduction/Injection of Anesthethic Agent (Nerve Block), Diagnostic or Therapeutic

Somatic Nerves
64430 Injection, anesthetic agent; pudendal nerve
64450 Injection, anesthetic agent; other peripheral nerve or branch

Destruction by Neurolytic Agent (eg, Chemical, Thermal, Electrical or Radiofrequency)

Somatic Nerves
64630 Destruction by neurolytic agent; pudendal nerve
64640 other peripheral nerve or branch

Transection or Avulsion
64761 Transection or avulsion of; pudendal nerve
64763 Transection or avulsion of obturator nerve, extrapelvic, with or without adductor tenotomy
64766 Transection or avulsion of obturator nerve, intrapelvic, with or without adductor tenotomy

Excision

Somatic Nerves
64790 Excision of neurofibroma or neurolemmoma; major peripheral nerve
64792 extensive (including malignant type)
64795 Biopsy of nerve

Superficial dissections

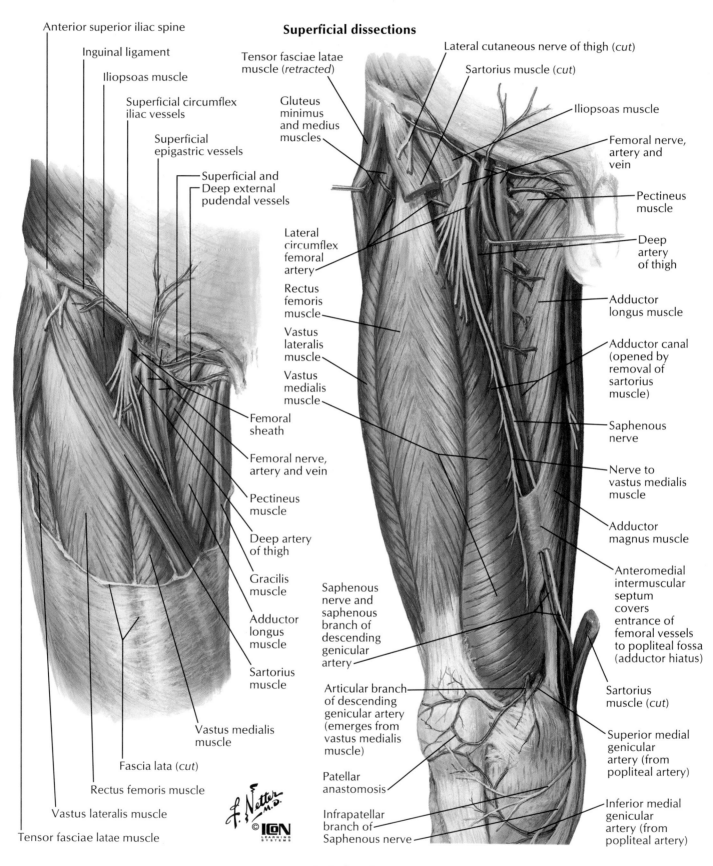

Anterior superior iliac spine

Inguinal ligament

Iliopsoas muscle

Superficial circumflex iliac vessels

Superficial epigastric vessels

Superficial and Deep external pudendal vessels

Tensor fasciae latae muscle (*retracted*)

Gluteus minimus and medius muscles

Lateral circumflex femoral artery

Rectus femoris muscle

Vastus lateralis muscle

Vastus medialis muscle

Femoral sheath

Femoral nerve, artery and vein

Pectineus muscle

Deep artery of thigh

Gracilis muscle

Adductor longus muscle

Sartorius muscle

Vastus medialis muscle

Fascia lata (*cut*)

Rectus femoris muscle

Vastus lateralis muscle

Tensor fasciae latae muscle

Lateral cutaneous nerve of thigh (*cut*)

Sartorius muscle (*cut*)

Iliopsoas muscle

Femoral nerve, artery and vein

Pectineus muscle

Deep artery of thigh

Adductor longus muscle

Adductor canal (opened by removal of sartorius muscle)

Saphenous nerve

Nerve to vastus medialis muscle

Adductor magnus muscle

Anteromedial intermuscular septum covers entrance of femoral vessels to popliteal fossa (adductor hiatus)

Sartorius muscle (*cut*)

Superior medial genicular artery (from popliteal artery)

Inferior medial genicular artery (from popliteal artery)

Saphenous nerve and saphenous branch of descending genicular artery

Articular branch of descending genicular artery (emerges from vastus medialis muscle)

Patellar anastomosis

Infrapatellar branch of Saphenous nerve

Anterior view

Deep dissection

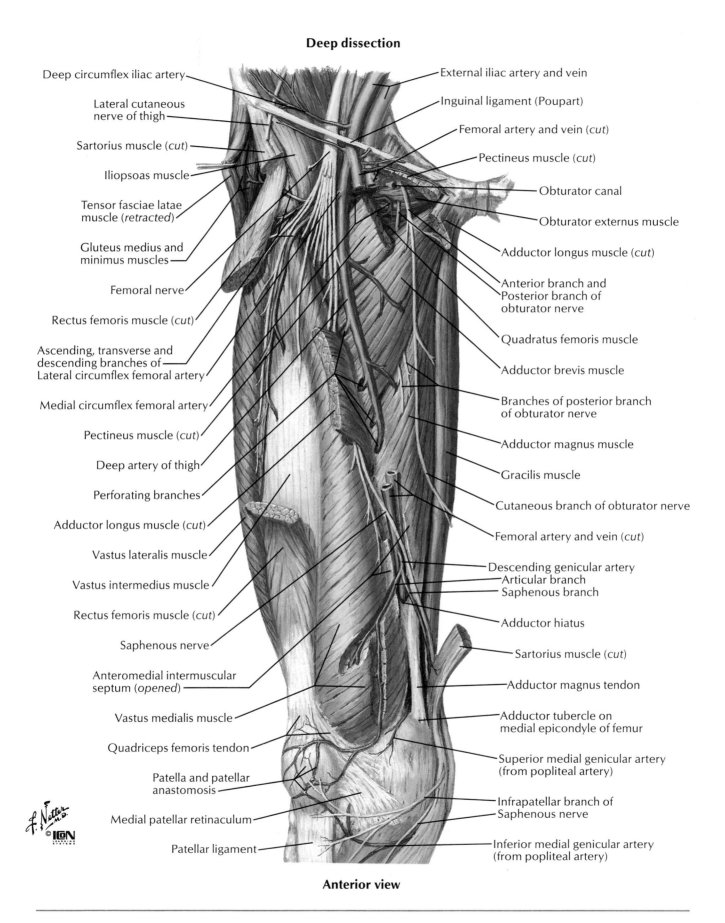

Deep circumflex iliac artery

Lateral cutaneous nerve of thigh

Sartorius muscle (*cut*)

Iliopsoas muscle

Tensor fasciae latae muscle (*retracted*)

Gluteus medius and minimus muscles

Femoral nerve

Rectus femoris muscle (*cut*)

Ascending, transverse and descending branches of Lateral circumflex femoral artery

Medial circumflex femoral artery

Pectineus muscle (*cut*)

Deep artery of thigh

Perforating branches

Adductor longus muscle (*cut*)

Vastus lateralis muscle

Vastus intermedius muscle

Rectus femoris muscle (*cut*)

Saphenous nerve

Anteromedial intermuscular septum (*opened*)

Vastus medialis muscle

Quadriceps femoris tendon

Patella and patellar anastomosis

Medial patellar retinaculum

Patellar ligament

External iliac artery and vein

Inguinal ligament (Poupart)

Femoral artery and vein (*cut*)

Pectineus muscle (*cut*)

Obturator canal

Obturator externus muscle

Adductor longus muscle (*cut*)

Anterior branch and Posterior branch of obturator nerve

Quadratus femoris muscle

Adductor brevis muscle

Branches of posterior branch of obturator nerve

Adductor magnus muscle

Gracilis muscle

Cutaneous branch of obturator nerve

Femoral artery and vein (*cut*)

Descending genicular artery
Articular branch
Saphenous branch

Adductor hiatus

Sartorius muscle (*cut*)

Adductor magnus tendon

Adductor tubercle on medial epicondyle of femur

Superior medial genicular artery (from popliteal artery)

Infrapatellar branch of Saphenous nerve

Inferior medial genicular artery (from popliteal artery)

Anterior view

Plate 185: Arteries and Nerves of Thigh

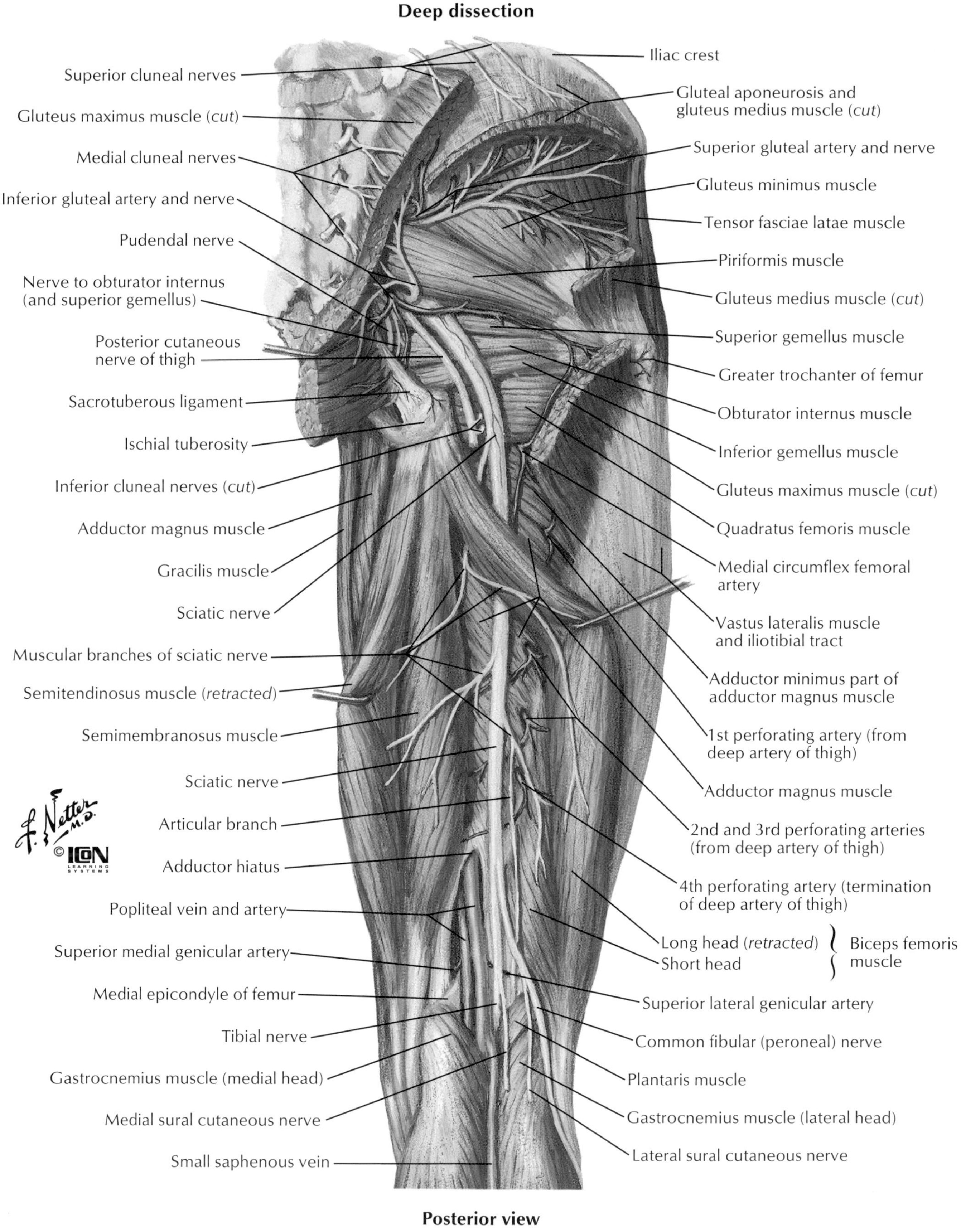

Deep dissection
Superior cluneal nerves
Gluteus maximus muscle (cut)
Medial cluneal nerves
Inferior gluteal artery and nerve
Pudendal nerve
Nerve to obturator internus (and superior gemellus)
Posterior cutaneous nerve of thigh
Sacrotuberous ligament
Ischial tuberosity
Inferior cluneal nerves (cut)
Adductor magnus muscle
Gracilis muscle
Sciatic nerve
Muscular branches of sciatic nerve
Semitendinosus muscle (retracted)
Semimembranosus muscle
Sciatic nerve
Articular branch
Adductor hiatus
Popliteal vein and artery
Superior medial genicular artery
Medial epicondyle of femur
Tibial nerve
Gastrocnemius muscle (medial head)
Medial sural cutaneous nerve
Small saphenous vein
Iliac crest
Gluteal aponeurosis and gluteus medius muscle (cut)
Superior gluteal artery and nerve
Gluteus minimus muscle
Tensor fasciae latae muscle
Piriformis muscle
Gluteus medius muscle (cut)
Superior gemellus muscle
Greater trochanter of femur
Obturator internus muscle
Inferior gemellus muscle
Gluteus maximus muscle (cut)
Quadratus femoris muscle
Medial circumflex femoral artery
Vastus lateralis muscle and iliotibial tract
Adductor minimus part of adductor magnus muscle
1st perforating artery (from deep artery of thigh)
Adductor magnus muscle
2nd and 3rd perforating arteries (from deep artery of thigh)
4th perforating artery (termination of deep artery of thigh)
Long head (retracted)
Short head
Biceps femoris muscle
Superior lateral genicular artery
Common fibular (peroneal) nerve
Plantaris muscle
Gastrocnemius muscle (lateral head)
Lateral sural cutaneous nerve
F. Netter M.D.
© ICON LEARNING SYSTEMS
Posterior view

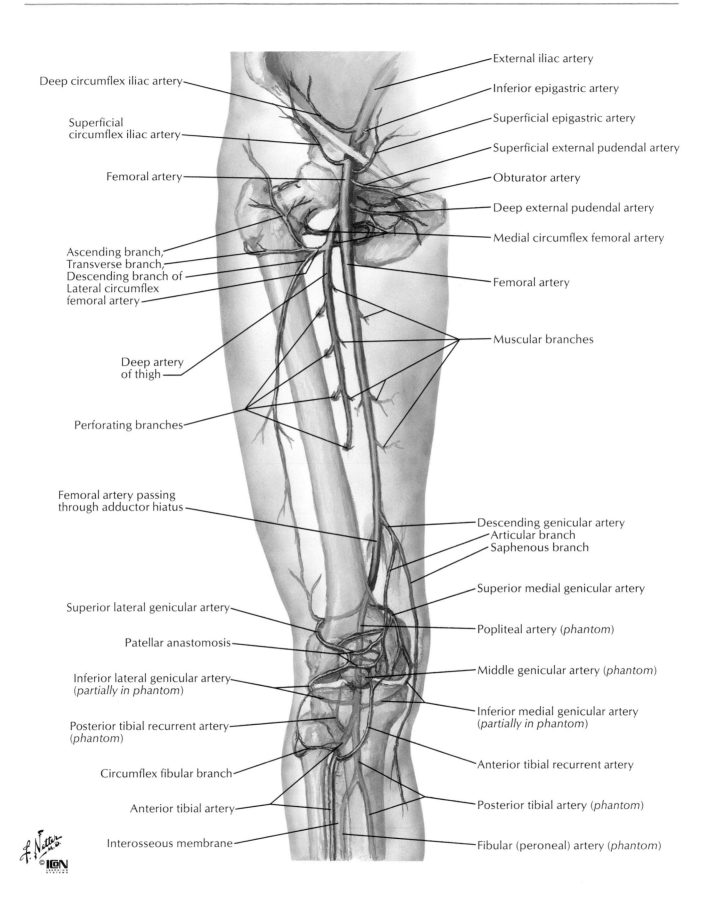

Deep circumflex iliac artery

Superficial circumflex iliac artery

Femoral artery

Ascending branch,
Transverse branch,
Descending branch of
Lateral circumflex
femoral artery

Deep artery
of thigh

Perforating branches

Femoral artery passing
through adductor hiatus

Superior lateral genicular artery

Patellar anastomosis

Inferior lateral genicular artery
(partially in phantom)

Posterior tibial recurrent artery
(phantom)

Circumflex fibular branch

Anterior tibial artery

Interosseous membrane

External iliac artery

Inferior epigastric artery

Superficial epigastric artery

Superficial external pudendal artery

Obturator artery

Deep external pudendal artery

Medial circumflex femoral artery

Femoral artery

Muscular branches

Descending genicular artery
Articular branch
Saphenous branch

Superior medial genicular artery

Popliteal artery (phantom)

Middle genicular artery (phantom)

Inferior medial genicular artery
(partially in phantom)

Anterior tibial recurrent artery

Posterior tibial artery (phantom)

Fibular (peroneal) artery (phantom)

Plate 185: Arteries and Nerves of Thigh

ANESTHESIA

Upper Abdomen

00770   Anesthesia for all procedures on major abdominal blood vessels

Lower Abdomen

00880   Anesthesia for procedures on major lower abdominal vessels; not otherwise specified

Upper Leg (Except Knee)

01270   Anesthesia for procedures involving arteries of upper leg, including bypass graft; not otherwise specified
01272   femoral artery ligation
01274   femoral artery embolectomy

Knee and Popliteal Area

01432   Anesthesia for procedures on veins, knee and popliteal area; arteriovenous fistula
01440   Anesthesia for procedures on arteries of knee and popliteal area; not otherwise specified
01442   popliteal thromboendarterectomy, with or without patch graft
01444   popliteal excision and graft or repair for occlusion or aneurysm

Lower Leg (Below Knee, Includes Ankle and Foot)

01500   Anesthesia for procedures on arteries of lower leg, including bypass graft; not otherwise specified

Shoulder and Axilla

01650   Anesthesia for procedures on arteries, shoulder and axilla; not otherwise specified

Radiological Procedures

01916   Anesthesia for diagnostic arteriography/venography
01924   Anesthesia for therapeutic interventional radiologic procedures involving the arterial system; not otherwise specified

Other Procedures

01991   Anesthesia for diagnostic or therapeutic nerve blocks and injections (when block or injection is performed by a different provider); other than the prone position

SURGERY

Cardiovasuclar System

Arteries and Veins

Direct Repair of Aneurysm or Excision (Partial or Total) and Graft Insertion for Aneurysm, Pseudoaneurysm, Ruptured Aneurysm, and Associate Occlusive Disease

35132   Direct repair of aneurysm, pseudoaneurysm, or excision (partial or total) and graft insertion, with or without patch graft; for ruptured aneurysm, iliac artery (common, hypogastric, external)

35141   for aneurysm, pseudoaneurysm, and associated occlusive disease, common femoral artery (profunda femoris, superficial femoral)
35142   for ruptured aneurysm, common femoral artery (profunda femoris, superficial femoral)
35151   for aneurysm, pseudoaneurysm, and associated occlusive disease, popliteal artery
35152   for ruptured aneurysm, popliteal artery

Repair Arteriovenous Fistula

35184   Repair, congenital arteriovenous fistula; extremities
35190   Repair, acquired or traumatic arteriovenous fistula; extremities

Repair Blood Vessel Other Than for Fistula, With or Without Patch Angioplasty

35226   Repair blood vessel, direct; lower extremity
35256   Repair blood vessel with vein graft; lower extremity
35286   Repair blood vessel with graft other than vein; lower extremity

Thromboendarterectomy

35355   Thromboendarterectomy, with or without patch graft; iliofemoral
35371[P]   common femoral
35372[P]   deep (profunda) femoral
35381   femoral and/or popliteal, and/or tibioperoneal

Transluminal Angioplasty

Open
35454   Transluminal balloon angioplasty, open; iliac
35456   femoral-popliteal
35458   brachiocephalic trunk or branches, each vessel
35459   tibioperoneal trunk and branches

Percutaneous
35470   Transluminal balloon angioplasty, percutaneous; tibioperoneal trunk or branches, each vessel
35473[P]   iliac
35474   femoral-popliteal

Transluminal Atherectomy

Open
35482   Transluminal peripheral atherectomy, open; iliac
35483   femoral-popliteal
35485   tibioperoneal trunk and branches

Percutaneous
35492   Transluminal peripheral atherectomy, percutaneous; iliac
35493   femoral-popliteal

Bypass Graft

Vein
35556   Bypass graft, with vein; femoral-popliteal
35558   femoral-femoral
35563   ilioiliac
35565   iliofemoral
35566   femoral-anterior tibial, posterior tibial, peroneal artery or other distal vessels
35571[P]   popliteal-tibial, -peroneal artery or other distal vessels

In-situ Vein

35583 In-situ vein bypass; femoral-popliteal

35585 femoral-anterior tibial, posterior tibial, or peroneal artery

35587 popliteal-tibial, peroneal

Other Than Vein

35656 Bypass graft, with other than vein; femoral-popliteal

35661 femoral-femoral

35663 ilioiliac

35665 iliofemoral

35666 femoral-anterior tibial, posterior tibial, or peroneal artery

35671 popliteal-tibial or -peroneal artery

Exploration/Revision

35721 Exploration (not followed by surgical repair), with or without lysis of artery; femoral artery

35741 popliteal artery

35860 Exploration for postoperative hemorrhage, thrombosis or infection; extremity

35879 Revision, lower extremity arterial bypass, without thrombectomy, open; with vein patch angioplasty

35881 with segmental vein interposition

35903 Excision of infected graft; extremity

Intra-Arterial—Intra-Aortic

36140 Introduction of needle or intracatheter; extremity artery

Nervous System

Extracranial Nerves, Peripheral Nerves, and Autonomic Nervous System
Introduction/Injection of Anesthetic Agent (Nerve Block), Diagnostic or Therapeutic

Somatic Nerves

64447 Injection, anesthetic agent; femoral nerve, single

64448 femoral nerve, continuous infusion by catheter (including catheter placement) including daily management for anesthetic agent administration

Excision

Somatic Nerves

64784 Excision of neuroma; major peripheral nerve, except sciatic

64790 Excision of neurofibroma or neurolemmoma; major peripheral nerve

64792 extensive (including malignant type)

64795 Biopsy of nerve

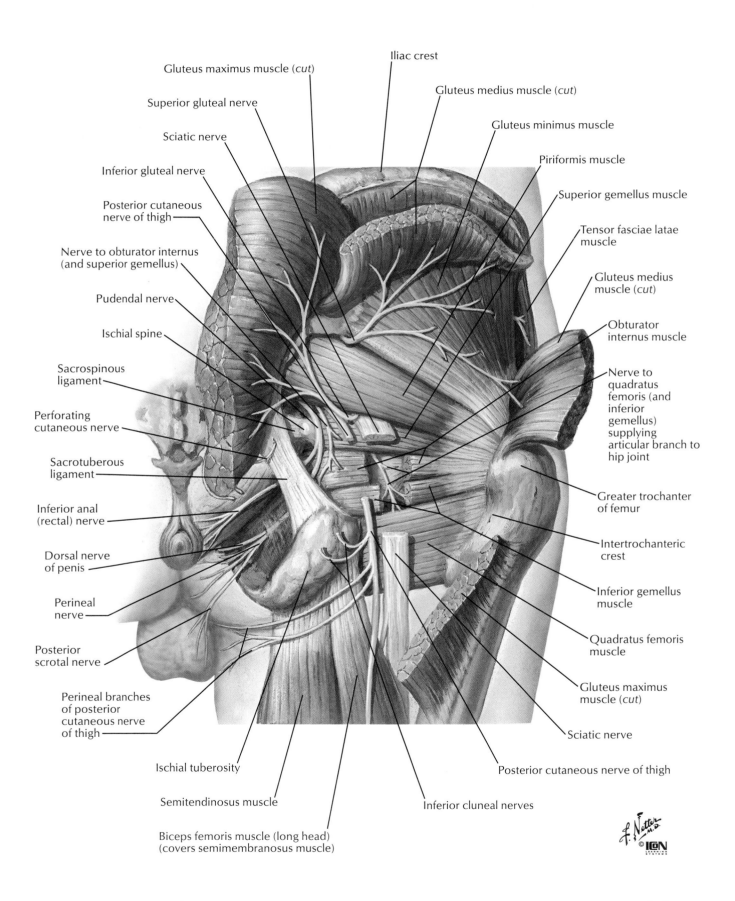

Gluteus maximus muscle (*cut*)

Superior gluteal nerve

Sciatic nerve

Inferior gluteal nerve

Posterior cutaneous nerve of thigh

Nerve to obturator internus (and superior gemellus)

Pudendal nerve

Ischial spine

Sacrospinous ligament

Perforating cutaneous nerve

Sacrotuberous ligament

Inferior anal (rectal) nerve

Dorsal nerve of penis

Perineal nerve

Posterior scrotal nerve

Perineal branches of posterior cutaneous nerve of thigh

Iliac crest

Gluteus medius muscle (*cut*)

Gluteus minimus muscle

Piriformis muscle

Superior gemellus muscle

Tensor fasciae latae muscle

Gluteus medius muscle (*cut*)

Obturator internus muscle

Nerve to quadratus femoris (and inferior gemellus) supplying articular branch to hip joint

Greater trochanter of femur

Intertrochanteric crest

Inferior gemellus muscle

Quadratus femoris muscle

Gluteus maximus muscle (*cut*)

Sciatic nerve

Posterior cutaneous nerve of thigh

Ischial tuberosity

Semitendinosus muscle

Inferior cluneal nerves

Biceps femoris muscle (long head) (covers semimembranosus muscle)

ANESTHESIA

Pelvis (Except Hip)

01180 Anesthesia for obturator neurectomy; extrapelvic

Upper Leg (Except Knee)

01250 Anesthesia for all procedures on nerves, muscles, tendons, fascia, and bursae of upper leg

Other Procedures

01991 Anesthesia for diagnostic or therapeutic nerve blocks and injections (when block or injection is performed by a different provider); other than the prone position

SURGERY

Nervous System

Extracranial Nerves, Peripheral Nerves, and Autonomic Nervous System
Introduction/Injection of Anesthetic Agent (Nerve Block), Diagnostic or Therapeutic

Somatic Nerves
64430 Injection, anesthetic agent; pudendal nerve
64445 sciatic nerve, single

64446 sciatic nerve, continuous infusion by catheter, (including catheter placement) including daily management for anesthetic agent administration
64450 other peripheral nerve or branch

Destruction by Neurolytic Agent (eg, Chemical, Thermal, Electrical or Radiofrequency)

Somatic Nerves
64630 Destruction by neurolytic agent; pudendal nerve
64640 other peripheral nerve or branch

Transection or Avulsion

64761 Transection or avulsion of; pudendal nerve

Excision

Somatic Nerves
64784 Excision of neuroma; major peripheral nerve, except sciatic
64786 sciatic nerve
64790 Excision of neurofibroma or neurolemmoma; major peripheral nerve
64792 extensive (including malignant type)
64795 Biopsy of nerve

Plate 187: Knee—Lateral and Medial Views

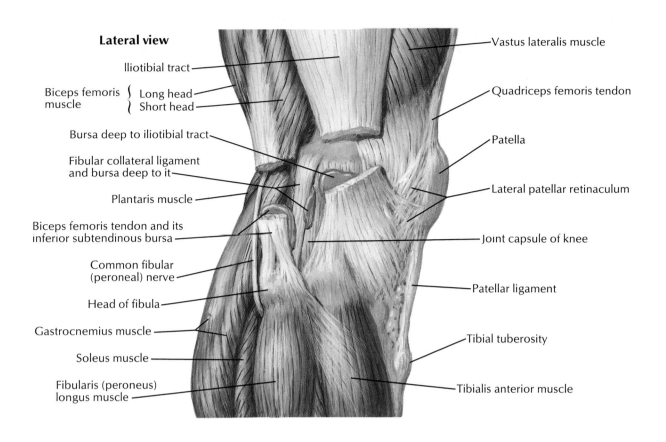

Lateral view

Iliotibial tract

Biceps femoris muscle { Long head / Short head

Bursa deep to iliotibial tract

Fibular collateral ligament and bursa deep to it

Plantaris muscle

Biceps femoris tendon and its inferior subtendinous bursa

Common fibular (peroneal) nerve

Head of fibula

Gastrocnemius muscle

Soleus muscle

Fibularis (peroneus) longus muscle

Vastus lateralis muscle

Quadriceps femoris tendon

Patella

Lateral patellar retinaculum

Joint capsule of knee

Patellar ligament

Tibial tuberosity

Tibialis anterior muscle

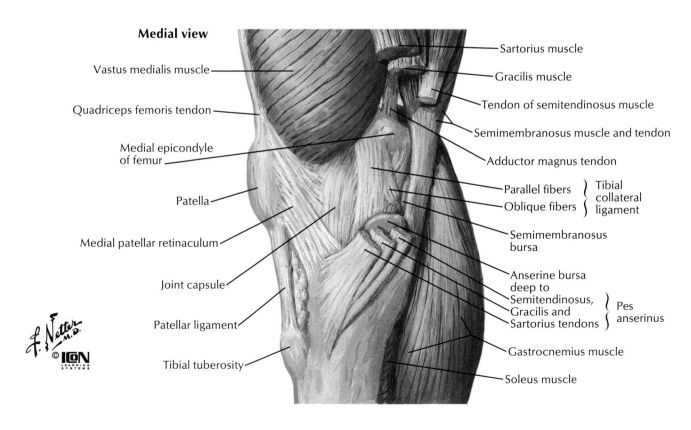

Medial view

Vastus medialis muscle

Quadriceps femoris tendon

Medial epicondyle of femur

Patella

Medial patellar retinaculum

Joint capsule

Patellar ligament

Tibial tuberosity

Sartorius muscle

Gracilis muscle

Tendon of semitendinosus muscle

Semimembranosus muscle and tendon

Adductor magnus tendon

Parallel fibers } Tibial collateral ligament
Oblique fibers }

Semimembranosus bursa

Anserine bursa deep to Semitendinosus, Gracilis and Sartorius tendons } Pes anserinus

Gastrocnemius muscle

Soleus muscle

ANESTHESIA

Thorax (Chest Wall and Shoulder Girdle)

00400 Anesthesia for procedures on the integumentary system on the extremities, anterior trunk and perineum; not otherwise specified

Upper Leg (Except Knee)

01250 Anesthesia for all procedures on nerves, muscles, tendons, fascia, and bursae of upper leg

Knee and Popliteal Area

01320 Anesthesia for all procedures on nerves, muscles, tendons, fascia, and bursae of knee and/or popliteal area

01380 Anesthesia for all closed procedures on knee joint

01390 Anesthesia for all closed procedures on upper ends of tibia, fibula, and/or patella

01392 Anesthesia for all open procedures on upper ends of tibia, fibula, and/or patella

01400 Anesthesia for open or surgical arthroscopic procedures on knee joint; not otherwise specified

01404   disarticulation at knee

SURGERY

Musculoskeletal System

Femur (Thigh Region) and Knee Joint

Incision

27301 Incision and drainage, deep abscess, bursa, or hematoma, thigh or knee region

27305 Fasciotomy, iliotibial (tenotomy), open

27320 Neurectomy, popliteal (gastrocnemius)

Excision

27323 Biopsy, soft tissue of thigh or knee area; superficial

27324   deep (subfascial or intramuscular)

27327 Excision, tumor, thigh or knee area; subcutaneous

27328   deep, subfascial, or intramuscular

27329 Radical resection of tumor (eg, malignant neoplasm), soft tissue of thigh or knee area

Introduction or Removal

27372 Removal of foreign body, deep, thigh region or knee area

Repair, Revision, and/or Reconstruction

27380 Suture of infrapatellar tendon; primary

27381   secondary reconstruction, including fascial or tendon graft

27496 Decompression fasciotomy, thigh and/or knee, one compartment (flexor or extensor or adductor);

27497   with debridement of nonviable muscle and/or nerve

27498 Decompression fasciotomy, thigh and/or knee, multiple compartments;

27499   with debridement of nonviable muscle and/or nerve

Fracture and/or Dislocation

27560 Closed treatment of patellar dislocation; without anesthesia

27562   requiring anesthesia

27566 Open treatment of patellar dislocation, with or without partial or total patellectomy

Manipulation

27570 Manipulation of knee joint under general anesthesia (includes application of traction or other fixation devices)

Arthrodesis

27580 Arthrodesis, knee, any technique

Amputation

27598 Disarticulation at knee

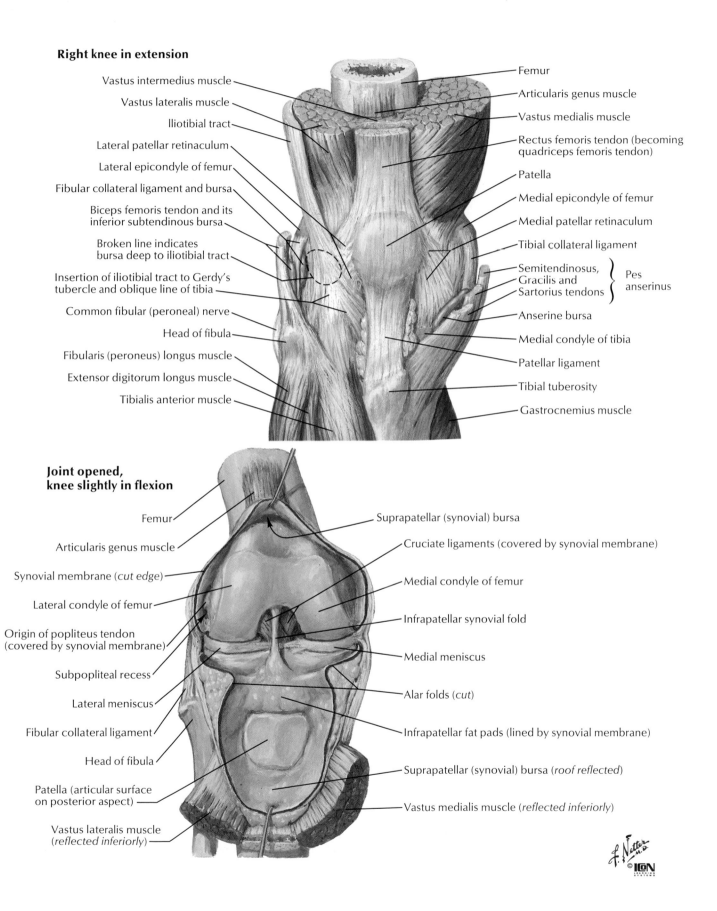

Right knee in extension

Vastus intermedius muscle

Vastus lateralis muscle

Iliotibial tract

Lateral patellar retinaculum

Lateral epicondyle of femur

Fibular collateral ligament and bursa

Biceps femoris tendon and its inferior subtendinous bursa

Broken line indicates bursa deep to iliotibial tract

Insertion of iliotibial tract to Gerdy's tubercle and oblique line of tibia

Common fibular (peroneal) nerve

Head of fibula

Fibularis (peroneus) longus muscle

Extensor digitorum longus muscle

Tibialis anterior muscle

Femur

Articularis genus muscle

Vastus medialis muscle

Rectus femoris tendon (becoming quadriceps femoris tendon)

Patella

Medial epicondyle of femur

Medial patellar retinaculum

Tibial collateral ligament

Semitendinosus, Gracilis and Sartorius tendons } Pes anserinus

Anserine bursa

Medial condyle of tibia

Patellar ligament

Tibial tuberosity

Gastrocnemius muscle

Joint opened, knee slightly in flexion

Femur

Articularis genus muscle

Synovial membrane (*cut edge*)

Lateral condyle of femur

Origin of popliteus tendon (covered by synovial membrane)

Subpopliteal recess

Lateral meniscus

Fibular collateral ligament

Head of fibula

Patella (articular surface on posterior aspect)

Vastus lateralis muscle (*reflected inferiorly*)

Suprapatellar (synovial) bursa

Cruciate ligaments (covered by synovial membrane)

Medial condyle of femur

Infrapatellar synovial fold

Medial meniscus

Alar folds (*cut*)

Infrapatellar fat pads (lined by synovial membrane)

Suprapatellar (synovial) bursa (*roof reflected*)

Vastus medialis muscle (*reflected inferiorly*)

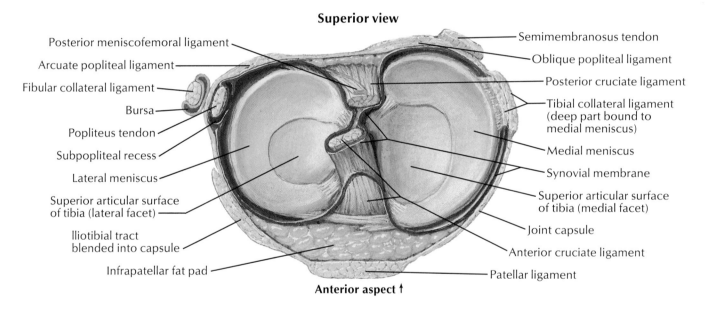

Inferior view

Iliotibial tract blended into lateral patellar retinaculum and capsule

Bursa

Subpopliteal recess

Popliteus tendon

Fibular collateral ligament

Bursa

Lateral condyle of femur

Anterior cruciate ligament

Arcuate popliteal ligament

Patellar ligament

Medial patellar retinaculum blended into joint capsule

Suprapatellar synovial bursa

Synovial membrane (*cut edge*)

Infrapatellar synovial fold

Posterior cruciate ligament

Tibial collateral ligament (superficial and deep parts)

Medial condyle of femur

Oblique popliteal ligament

Semimembranosus tendon

Posterior aspect ↑

Superior view

Posterior meniscofemoral ligament

Arcuate popliteal ligament

Fibular collateral ligament

Bursa

Popliteus tendon

Subpopliteal recess

Lateral meniscus

Superior articular surface of tibia (lateral facet)

Iliotibial tract blended into capsule

Infrapatellar fat pad

Semimembranosus tendon

Oblique popliteal ligament

Posterior cruciate ligament

Tibial collateral ligament (deep part bound to medial meniscus)

Medial meniscus

Synovial membrane

Superior articular surface of tibia (medial facet)

Joint capsule

Anterior cruciate ligament

Patellar ligament

Anterior aspect ↑

ANESTHESIA

Knee and Popliteal Area

01320	Anesthesia for all procedures on nerves, muscles, tendons, fascia, and bursae of knee and/or popliteal area
01380	Anesthesia for all closed procedures on knee joint
01382	Anesthesia for diagnostic arthroscopic procedures of knee joint
01390	Anesthesia for all closed procedures on upper ends of tibia, fibula, and/or patella
01392	Anesthesia for all open procedures on upper ends of tibia, fibula, and/or patella
01400	Anesthesia for open or surgical arthroscopic procedures on knee joint; not otherwise specified

01402	total knee arthroplasty
01404	disarticulation at knee

SURGERY

Musculoskeletal System

Femur (Thigh Region) and Knee Joint
Incision

27310	Arthrotomy, knee, with exploration, drainage, or removal of foreign body (eg, infection)

Excision

27330	Arthrotomy, knee; with synovial biopsy only
27331	including joint exploration, biopsy, or removal of loose or foreign bodies

(Excision continued on next page)

Plate 188: Knee

(Excision continued from previous page)

27332	Arthrotomy, with excision of semilunar cartilage (meniscectomy) knee; medial OR lateral
27333	medial AND lateral
27334	Arthrotomy, with synovectomy, knee; anterior OR posterior
27335	anterior AND posterior including popliteal area
27340	Excision, prepatellar bursa
27345	Excision of synovial cyst of popliteal space (eg, Baker's cyst)
27347	Excision of lesion of meniscus or capsule (eg, cyst, ganglion), knee
27350	Patellectomy or hemipatellectomy
27358	Excision or curettage of bone cyst or benign tumor of femur; with internal fixation

Introduction or Removal

27370	Injection procedure for knee arthrography
27372	Removal of foreign body, deep, thigh region or knee area

Repair, Revision, and/or Reconstruction

27380	Suture of infrapatellar tendon; primary
27381	secondary reconstruction, including fascial or tendon graft
27403	Arthrotomy with meniscus repair, knee
27405	Repair, primary, torn ligament and/or capsule, knee; collateral
27407	cruciate
27409	collateral and cruciate ligaments
27412	Autologous chondrocyte implantation, knee
27415	Osteochondral allograft, knee, open
27418	Anterior tibial tubercleplasty (eg, Maquet type procedure)
27420	Reconstruction of dislocating patella; (eg, Hauser type procedure)
27422	with extensor realignment and/or muscle advancement or release (eg, Campbell, Goldwaite type procedure)
27424	with patellectomy
27425	Lateral retinacular release, open
27427	Ligamentous reconstruction (augmentation), knee; extra-articular
27428	intra-articular (open)
27429	intra-articular (open) and extra-articular
27430	Quadricepsplasty (eg, Bennett or Thompson type)
27435	Capsulotomy, posterior capsular release, knee
27437	Arthroplasty, patella; without prosthesis
27438	with prosthesis
27440	Arthroplasty, knee, tibial plateau;
27441	with debridement and partial synovectomy
27442	Arthroplasty, femoral condyles or tibial plateau(s), knee;
27443	with debridement and partial synovectomy
27445	Arthroplasty, knee, hinge prosthesis (eg, Walldius type)
27446	Arthroplasty, knee, condyle and plateau; medial OR lateral compartment
27447	medial AND lateral compartments with or without patella resurfacing (total knee arthroplasty)

Fracture and/or Dislocation

27520	Closed treatment of patellar fracture, without manipulation
27524	Open treatment of patellar fracture, with internal fixation and/or partial or complete patellectomy and soft tissue repair
27560	Closed treatment of patellar dislocation; without anesthesia
27562	requiring anesthesia
27566	Open treatment of patellar dislocation, with or without partial or total patellectomy

Manipulation

27570	Manipulation of knee joint under general anesthesia (includes application of traction or other fixation devices)

Endoscopy/Arthroscopy

29866	Arthroscopy, knee, surgical; osteochondral autograft(s) (eg, mosaicplasty) (includes harvesting of the autograft)
29867	osteochondral allograft (eg, mosaicplasty)
29868	meniscal transplantation (includes arthrotomy for meniscal insertion), medial or lateral
29870^P	Arthroscopy, knee, diagnostic, with or without synovial biopsy (separate procedure)
29871	Arthroscopy, knee, surgical; for infection, lavage and drainage
29873	with lateral release
29874	for removal of loose body or foreign body (eg, osteochondritis dissecans fragmentation, chondral fragmentation)
29875	synovectomy, limited (eg, plica or shelf resection) (separate procedure)
29876	synovectomy, major, two or more compartments (eg, medial or lateral)
29877	debridement/shaving of articular cartilage (chondroplasty)
29879	abrasion arthroplasty (includes chondroplasty where necessary) or multiple drilling or microfracture
29880	with meniscectomy (medial AND lateral, including any meniscal shaving)
29881	with meniscectomy (medial OR lateral, including any meniscal shaving)
29882	with meniscus repair (medial OR lateral)
29883	with meniscus repair (medial AND lateral)
29884	with lysis of adhesions, with or without manipulation (separate procedure)
29885	drilling for osteochondritis dissecans with bone grafting, with or without internal fixation (including debridement of base of lesion)
29886	drilling for intact osteochondritis dissecans lesion
29887	drilling for intact osteochondritis dissecans lesion with internal fixation
29888	Arthroscopically aided anterior cruciate ligament repair/augmentation or reconstruction
29889	Arthroscopically aided posterior cruciate ligament repair/augmentation or reconstruction

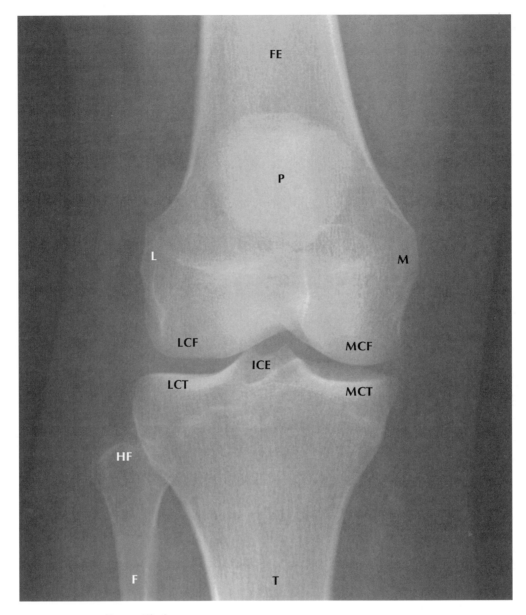

F	Fibula	LCT	Lateral condyle of tibia
FE	Femur	M	Medial epicondyle
HF	Head of fibula	MCF	Medial condyle of femur
ICE	Intercondylar eminence	MCT	Medial condyle of tibia
L	Lateral epicondyle	P	Patella
LCF	Lateral condyle of femur	T	Tibia

RADIOLOGY

Diagnostic Radiology (Diagnostic Imaging)

Lower Extremities

73560   Radiologic examination, knee; one or two views

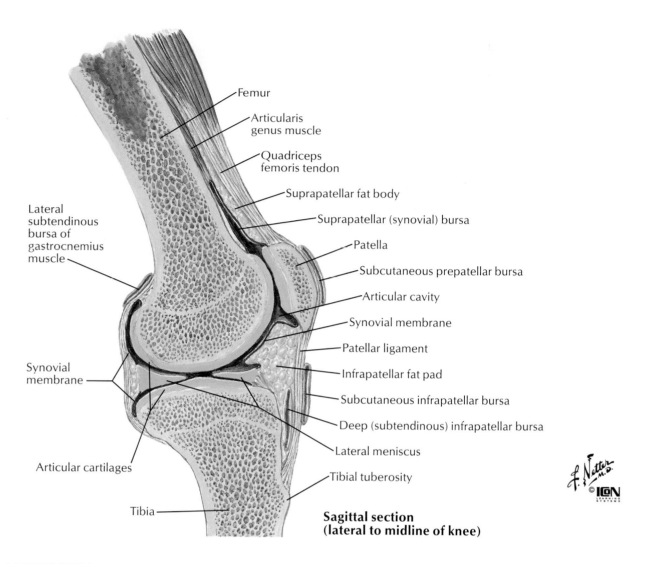

Femur

Articularis genus muscle

Quadriceps femoris tendon

Suprapatellar fat body

Suprapatellar (synovial) bursa

Patella

Subcutaneous prepatellar bursa

Articular cavity

Synovial membrane

Patellar ligament

Infrapatellar fat pad

Subcutaneous infrapatellar bursa

Deep (subtendinous) infrapatellar bursa

Lateral meniscus

Tibial tuberosity

Lateral subtendinous bursa of gastrocnemius muscle

Synovial membrane

Articular cartilages

Tibia

**Sagittal section
(lateral to midline of knee)**

ANESTHESIA

Knee and Popliteal Area

01360 Anesthesia for all open procedures on lower 1/3 of femur

01390 Anesthesia for all closed procedures on upper ends of tibia, fibula, and/or patella

01392 Anesthesia for all open procedures on upper ends of tibia, fibula, and/or patella

01400 Anesthesia for open or surgical arthroscopic procedures on knee joint; not otherwise specified

SURGERY

Musculoskeletal System

Femur (Thigh Region) and Knee Joint
Repair, Revision, and/or Reconstruction

27448 Osteotomy, femur, shaft or supracondylar; without fixation

27450   with fixation

27455 Osteotomy, proximal tibia, including fibular excision or osteotomy (includes correction of genu varus (bowleg) or genu valgus (knock-knee)); before epiphyseal closure

27457   after epiphyseal closure

27470 Repair, nonunion or malunion, femur, distal to head and neck; without graft (eg, compression technique)

27472   with iliac or other autogenous bone graft (includes obtaining graft)

27475 Arrest, epiphyseal, any method (eg, epiphysiodesis); distal femur

27477   tibia and fibula, proximal

27479   combined distal femur, proximal tibia and fibula

27485 Arrest, hemiepiphyseal, distal femur or proximal tibia or fibula (eg, genu varus or valgus)

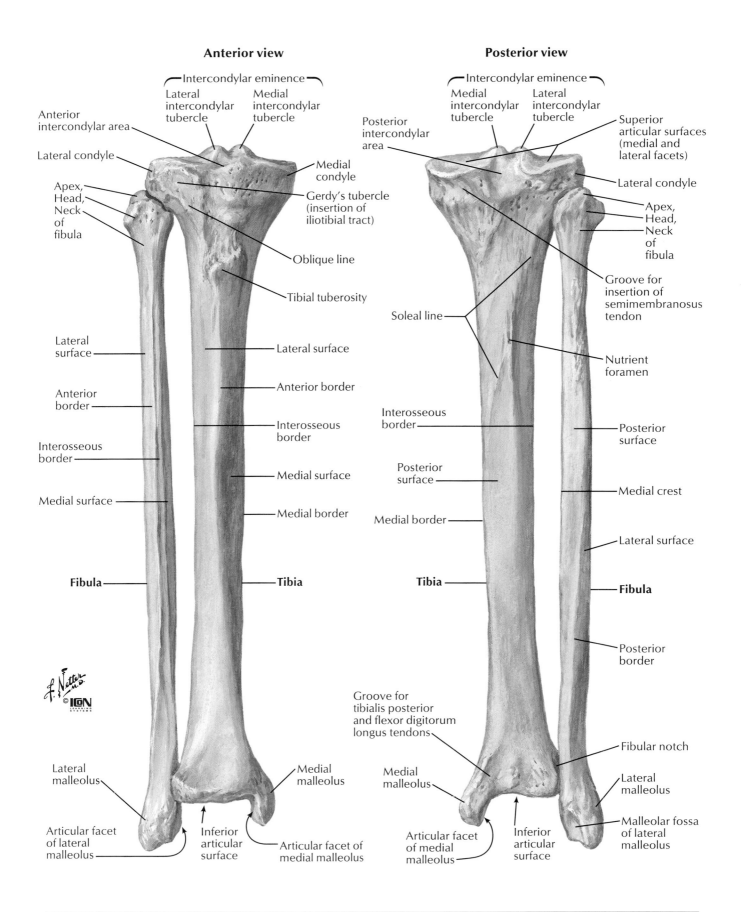

Anterior view

Intercondylar eminence

Lateral intercondylar tubercle

Medial intercondylar tubercle

Anterior intercondylar area

Lateral condyle

Apex, Head, Neck of fibula

Medial condyle

Gerdy's tubercle (insertion of iliotibial tract)

Oblique line

Tibial tuberosity

Lateral surface

Lateral surface

Anterior border

Interosseous border

Medial surface

Anterior border

Interosseous border

Medial surface

Medial border

Fibula

Tibia

Lateral malleolus

Medial malleolus

Articular facet of lateral malleolus

Inferior articular surface

Articular facet of medial malleolus

Posterior view

Intercondylar eminence

Medial intercondylar tubercle

Lateral intercondylar tubercle

Posterior intercondylar area

Superior articular surfaces (medial and lateral facets)

Lateral condyle

Apex, Head, Neck of fibula

Groove for insertion of semimembranosus tendon

Soleal line

Nutrient foramen

Interosseous border

Posterior surface

Posterior surface

Medial crest

Medial border

Lateral surface

Tibia

Fibula

Posterior border

Groove for tibialis posterior and flexor digitorum longus tendons

Medial malleolus

Fibular notch

Lateral malleolus

Articular facet of medial malleolus

Inferior articular surface

Malleolar fossa of lateral malleolus

ANESTHESIA

Knee and Popliteal Area

01360   Anesthesia for all open procedures on lower 1/3 of femur

Lower Leg (Below Knee, Includes Ankle and Foot)

01462   Anesthesia for all closed procedures on lower leg, ankle, and foot

01480   Anesthesia for open procedures on bones of lower leg, ankle, and foot; not otherwise specified

01482   radical resection (including below knee amputation)

01484   osteotomy or osteoplasty of tibia and/or fibula

SURGERY

Musculoskeletal System

Leg (Tibia and Fibula) and Ankle Joint
Excision

27635   Excision or curettage of bone cyst or benign tumor, tibia or fibula;

27637   with autograft (includes obtaining graft)

27638   with allograft

27640   Partial excision (craterization, saucerization, or diaphysectomy) bone (eg, osteomyelitis or exostosis); tibia

27641   fibula

27645   Radical resection of tumor, bone; tibia

27646   fibula

Repair, Revision, and/or Reconstruction

27705   Osteotomy; tibia

27707   fibula

27709   tibia and fibula

27712   multiple, with realignment on intramedullary rod (eg, Sofield type procedure)

27715   Osteoplasty, tibia and fibula, lengthening or shortening

27720   Repair of nonunion or malunion, tibia; without graft, (eg, compression technique)

27722   with sliding graft

27724   with iliac or other autograft (includes obtaining graft)

27725   by synostosis, with fibula, any method

27727   Repair of congenital pseudarthrosis, tibia

27730   Arrest, epiphyseal (epiphysiodesis), open; distal tibia

27732   distal fibula

27734   distal tibia and fibula

27740   Arrest, epiphyseal (epiphysiodesis), any method, combined, proximal and distal tibia and fibula;

27742   and distal femur

27745   Prophylactic treatment (nailing, pinning, plating or wiring) with or without methylmethacrylate, tibia

Fracture and/or Dislocation

27750   Closed treatment of tibial shaft fracture (with or without fibular fracture); without manipulation

27752   with manipulation, with or without skeletal traction

27756   Percutaneous skeletal fixation of tibial shaft fracture (with or without fibular fracture) (eg, pins or screws)

27758   Open treatment of tibial shaft fracture, (with or without fibular fracture) with plate/screws, with or without cerclage

27759   Treatment of tibial shaft fracture (with or without fibular fracture) by intramedullary implant, with or without interlocking screws and/or cerclage

27760   Closed treatment of medial malleolus fracture; without manipulation

27762   with manipulation, with or without skin or skeletal traction

27766   Open treatment of medial malleolus fracture, with or without internal or external fixation

27780   Closed treatment of proximal fibula or shaft fracture; without manipulation

27781   with manipulation

27784   Open treatment of proximal fibula or shaft fracture, with or without internal or external fixation

27786   Closed treatment of distal fibular fracture (lateral malleolus); without manipulation

27788   with manipulation

27792   Open treatment of distal fibular fracture (lateral malleolus), with or without internal or external fixation

27808   Closed treatment of bimalleolar ankle fracture, (including Potts); without manipulation

27810   with manipulation

27814   Open treatment of bimalleolar ankle fracture, with or without internal or external fixation

27816   Closed treatment of trimalleolar ankle fracture; without manipulation

27818   with manipulation

27822   Open treatment of trimalleolar ankle fracture, with or without internal or external fixation, medial and/or lateral malleolus; without fixation of posterior lip

27823   with fixation of posterior lip

27824   Closed treatment of fracture of weight bearing articular portion of distal tibia (eg, pilon or tibial plafond), with or without anesthesia; without manipulation

27825   with skeletal traction and/or requiring manipulation

27826   Open treatment of fracture of weight bearing articular surface/portion of distal tibia (eg, pilon or tibial plafond), with internal or external fixation; of fibula only

27827   of tibia only

27828   of both tibia and fibula

27829   Open treatment of distal tibiofibular joint (syndesmosis) disruption, with or without internal or external fixation

27830   Closed treatment of proximal tibiofibular joint dislocation; without anesthesia

27831   requiring anesthesia

27832   Open treatment of proximal tibiofibular joint dislocation, with or without internal or external fixation, or with excision of proximal fibula

Amputation

27880   Amputation, leg, through tibia and fibula;

27881   with immediate fitting technique including application of first cast

27882   open, circular (guillotine)

27884   secondary closure or scar revision

27886   re-amputation

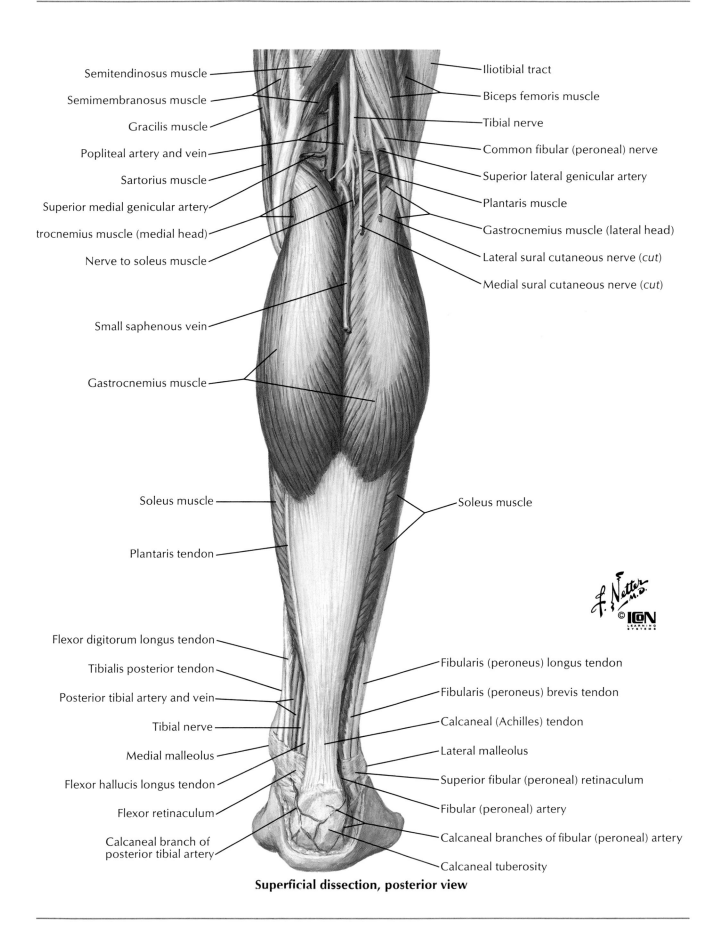

Semitendinosus muscle

Semimembranosus muscle

Gracilis muscle

Popliteal artery and vein

Sartorius muscle

Superior medial genicular artery

trocnemius muscle (medial head)

Nerve to soleus muscle

Small saphenous vein

Gastrocnemius muscle

Soleus muscle

Plantaris tendon

Flexor digitorum longus tendon

Tibialis posterior tendon

Posterior tibial artery and vein

Tibial nerve

Medial malleolus

Flexor hallucis longus tendon

Flexor retinaculum

Calcaneal branch of
posterior tibial artery

Iliotibial tract

Biceps femoris muscle

Tibial nerve

Common fibular (peroneal) nerve

Superior lateral genicular artery

Plantaris muscle

Gastrocnemius muscle (lateral head)

Lateral sural cutaneous nerve (*cut*)

Medial sural cutaneous nerve (*cut*)

Soleus muscle

Fibularis (peroneus) longus tendon

Fibularis (peroneus) brevis tendon

Calcaneal (Achilles) tendon

Lateral malleolus

Superior fibular (peroneal) retinaculum

Fibular (peroneal) artery

Calcaneal branches of fibular (peroneal) artery

Calcaneal tuberosity

Superficial dissection, posterior view

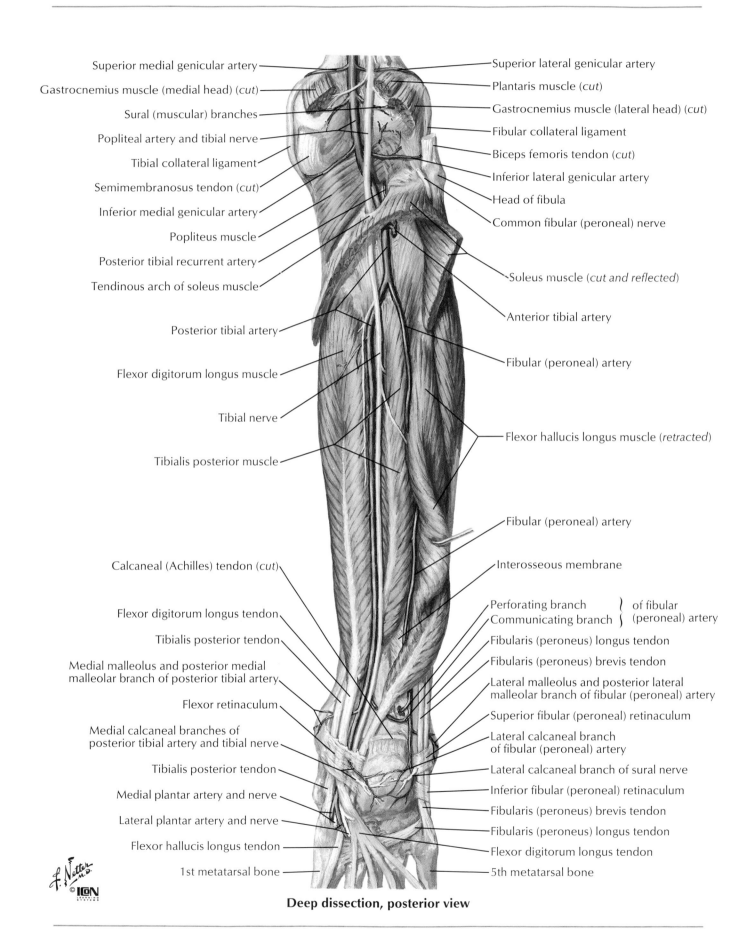

Superior medial genicular artery

Gastrocnemius muscle (medial head) (cut)

Sural (muscular) branches

Popliteal artery and tibial nerve

Tibial collateral ligament

Semimembranosus tendon (cut)

Inferior medial genicular artery

Popliteus muscle

Posterior tibial recurrent artery

Tendinous arch of soleus muscle

Posterior tibial artery

Flexor digitorum longus muscle

Tibial nerve

Tibialis posterior muscle

Calcaneal (Achilles) tendon (cut)

Flexor digitorum longus tendon

Tibialis posterior tendon

Medial malleolus and posterior medial malleolar branch of posterior tibial artery

Flexor retinaculum

Medial calcaneal branches of posterior tibial artery and tibial nerve

Tibialis posterior tendon

Medial plantar artery and nerve

Lateral plantar artery and nerve

Flexor hallucis longus tendon

1st metatarsal bone

Superior lateral genicular artery

Plantaris muscle (cut)

Gastrocnemius muscle (lateral head) (cut)

Fibular collateral ligament

Biceps femoris tendon (cut)

Inferior lateral genicular artery

Head of fibula

Common fibular (peroneal) nerve

Soleus muscle (cut and reflected)

Anterior tibial artery

Fibular (peroneal) artery

Flexor hallucis longus muscle (retracted)

Fibular (peroneal) artery

Interosseous membrane

Perforating branch } of fibular
Communicating branch } (peroneal) artery

Fibularis (peroneus) longus tendon

Fibularis (peroneus) brevis tendon

Lateral malleolus and posterior lateral malleolar branch of fibular (peroneal) artery

Superior fibular (peroneal) retinaculum

Lateral calcaneal branch of fibular (peroneal) artery

Lateral calcaneal branch of sural nerve

Inferior fibular (peroneal) retinaculum

Fibularis (peroneus) brevis tendon

Fibularis (peroneus) longus tendon

Flexor digitorum longus tendon

5th metatarsal bone

Deep dissection, posterior view

ANESTHESIA

Thorax (Chest Wall and Shoulder Girdle)

00400   Anesthesia for procedures on the integumentary system on the extremities, anterior trunk and perineum; not otherwise specified

Lower Leg (Below Knee, Includes Ankle and Foot)

01470   Anesthesia for procedures on nerves, muscles, tendons, and fascia of lower leg, ankle, and foot; not otherwise specified

01472   repair of ruptured Achilles tendon, with or without graft

01474   gastrocnemius recession (eg, Strayer procedure)

01480   Anesthesia for open procedures on bones of lower leg, ankle, and foot; not otherwise specified

SURGERY

Musculoskeletal System

Leg (Tibia and Fibula) and Ankle Joint
Incision

27600   Decompression fasciotomy, leg; anterior and/or lateral compartments only

27601   posterior compartment(s) only

27602   anterior and/or lateral, and posterior compartment(s)

27603   Incision and drainage, leg or ankle; deep abscess or hematoma

27604   infected bursa

27605   Tenotomy, percutaneous, Achilles tendon (separate procedure); local anesthesia

27606   general anesthesia

Excision

27613   Biopsy, soft tissue of leg or ankle area; superficial

27614   deep (subfascial or intramuscular)

27615   Radical resection of tumor (eg, malignant neoplasm), soft tissue of leg or ankle area

27618   Excision, tumor, leg or ankle area; subcutaneous tissue

27619   deep (subfascial or intramuscular)

27630   Excision of lesion of tendon sheath or capsule (eg, cyst or ganglion), leg and/or ankle

Repair, Revision, and/or Reconstruction

27650   Repair, primary, open or percutaneous, ruptured Achilles tendon;

27652   with graft (includes obtaining graft)

27654   Repair, secondary, Achilles tendon, with or without graft

27656   Repair, fascial defect of leg

27658   Repair, flexor tendon, leg; primary, without graft, each tendon

27659   secondary, with or without graft, each tendon

27664   Repair, extensor tendon, leg; primary, without graft, each tendon

27665   secondary, with or without graft, each tendon

27675   Repair, dislocating peroneal tendons; without fibular osteotomy

27676   with fibular osteotomy

27680   Tenolysis, flexor or extensor tendon, leg and/or ankle; single, each tendon

27681   multiple tendons (through separate incision(s))

27685   Lengthening or shortening of tendon, leg or ankle; single tendon (separate procedure)

27686   multiple tendons (through same incision), each

27687   Gastrocnemius recession (eg, Strayer procedure)

27690   Transfer or transplant of single tendon (with muscle redirection or rerouting); superficial (eg, anterior tibial extensors into midfoot)

27691   deep (eg, anterior tibial or posterior tibial through interosseous space, flexor digitorum longus, flexor hallucis longus, or peroneal tendon to midfoot or hindfoot)

27692   each additional tendon (List separately in addition to code for primary procedure)

27695   Repair, primary, disrupted ligament, ankle; collateral

27696   both collateral ligaments

27698   Repair, secondary, disrupted ligament, ankle, collateral (eg, Watson-Jones procedure)

Amputation

27880   Amputation, leg, through tibia and fibula;

27881   with immediate fitting technique including application of first cast

27882   open, circular (guillotine)

27884   secondary closure or scar revision

27886   re-amputation

27888   Amputation, ankle, through malleoli of tibia and fibula (eg, Syme, Pirogoff type procedures), with plastic closure and resection of nerves

27889   Ankle disarticulation

Other Procedures

27892   Decompression fasciotomy, leg; anterior and/or lateral compartments only, with debridement of nonviable muscle and/or nerve

27893   posterior compartment(s) only, with debridement of nonviable muscle and/or nerve

27894   anterior and/or lateral, and posterior compartment(s), with debridement of nonviable muscle and/or nerve

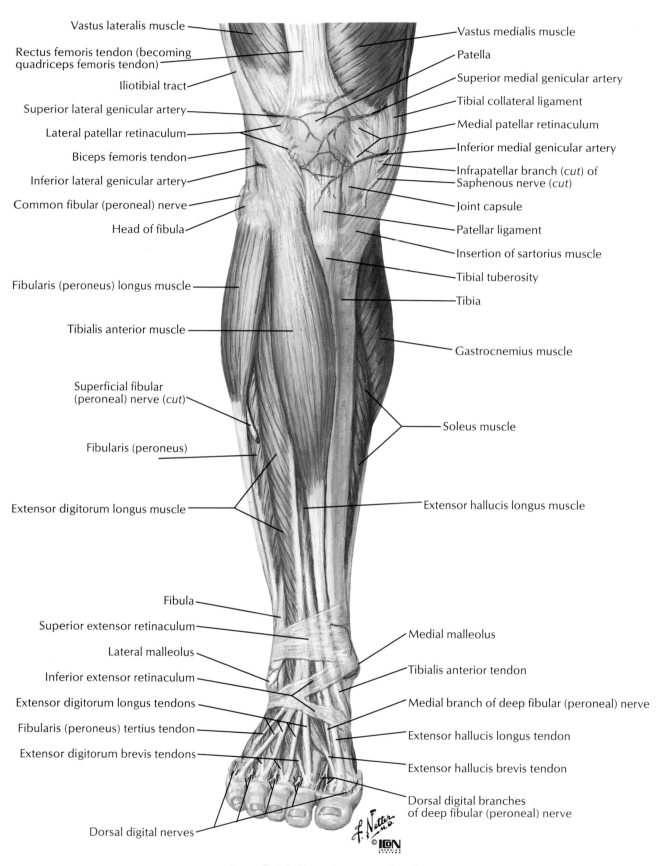

Vastus lateralis muscle

Rectus femoris tendon (becoming quadriceps femoris tendon)

Iliotibial tract

Superior lateral genicular artery

Lateral patellar retinaculum

Biceps femoris tendon

Inferior lateral genicular artery

Common fibular (peroneal) nerve

Head of fibula

Fibularis (peroneus) longus muscle

Tibialis anterior muscle

Superficial fibular (peroneal) nerve (*cut*)

Fibularis (peroneus)

Extensor digitorum longus muscle

Fibula

Superior extensor retinaculum

Lateral malleolus

Inferior extensor retinaculum

Extensor digitorum longus tendons

Fibularis (peroneus) tertius tendon

Extensor digitorum brevis tendons

Dorsal digital nerves

Vastus medialis muscle

Patella

Superior medial genicular artery

Tibial collateral ligament

Medial patellar retinaculum

Inferior medial genicular artery

Infrapatellar branch (*cut*) of Saphenous nerve (*cut*)

Joint capsule

Patellar ligament

Insertion of sartorius muscle

Tibial tuberosity

Tibia

Gastrocnemius muscle

Soleus muscle

Extensor hallucis longus muscle

Medial malleolus

Tibialis anterior tendon

Medial branch of deep fibular (peroneal) nerve

Extensor hallucis longus tendon

Extensor hallucis brevis tendon

Dorsal digital branches of deep fibular (peroneal) nerve

Superficial dissection, anterior view

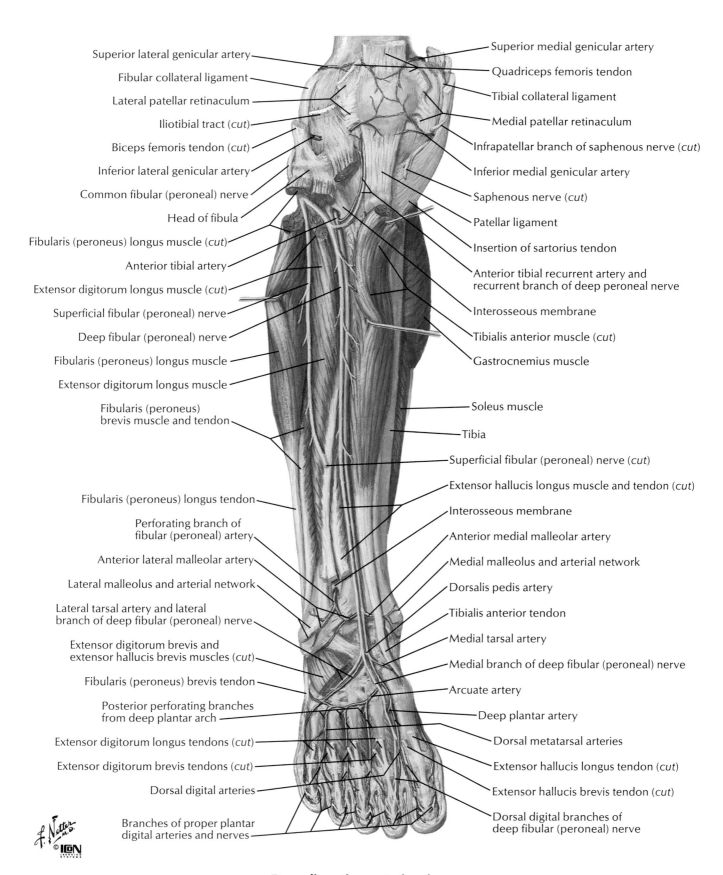

Superior lateral genicular artery

Fibular collateral ligament

Lateral patellar retinaculum

Iliotibial tract (cut)

Biceps femoris tendon (cut)

Inferior lateral genicular artery

Common fibular (peroneal) nerve

Head of fibula

Fibularis (peroneus) longus muscle (cut)

Anterior tibial artery

Extensor digitorum longus muscle (cut)

Superficial fibular (peroneal) nerve

Deep fibular (peroneal) nerve

Fibularis (peroneus) longus muscle

Extensor digitorum longus muscle

Fibularis (peroneus) brevis muscle and tendon

Fibularis (peroneus) longus tendon

Perforating branch of fibular (peroneal) artery

Anterior lateral malleolar artery

Lateral malleolus and arterial network

Lateral tarsal artery and lateral branch of deep fibular (peroneal) nerve

Extensor digitorum brevis and extensor hallucis brevis muscles (cut)

Fibularis (peroneus) brevis tendon

Posterior perforating branches from deep plantar arch

Extensor digitorum longus tendons (cut)

Extensor digitorum brevis tendons (cut)

Dorsal digital arteries

Branches of proper plantar digital arteries and nerves

Superior medial genicular artery

Quadriceps femoris tendon

Tibial collateral ligament

Medial patellar retinaculum

Infrapatellar branch of saphenous nerve (cut)

Inferior medial genicular artery

Saphenous nerve (cut)

Patellar ligament

Insertion of sartorius tendon

Anterior tibial recurrent artery and recurrent branch of deep peroneal nerve

Interosseous membrane

Tibialis anterior muscle (cut)

Gastrocnemius muscle

Soleus muscle

Tibia

Superficial fibular (peroneal) nerve (cut)

Extensor hallucis longus muscle and tendon (cut)

Interosseous membrane

Anterior medial malleolar artery

Medial malleolus and arterial network

Dorsalis pedis artery

Tibialis anterior tendon

Medial tarsal artery

Medial branch of deep fibular (peroneal) nerve

Arcuate artery

Deep plantar artery

Dorsal metatarsal arteries

Extensor hallucis longus tendon (cut)

Extensor hallucis brevis tendon (cut)

Dorsal digital branches of deep fibular (peroneal) nerve

Deep dissection, anterior view

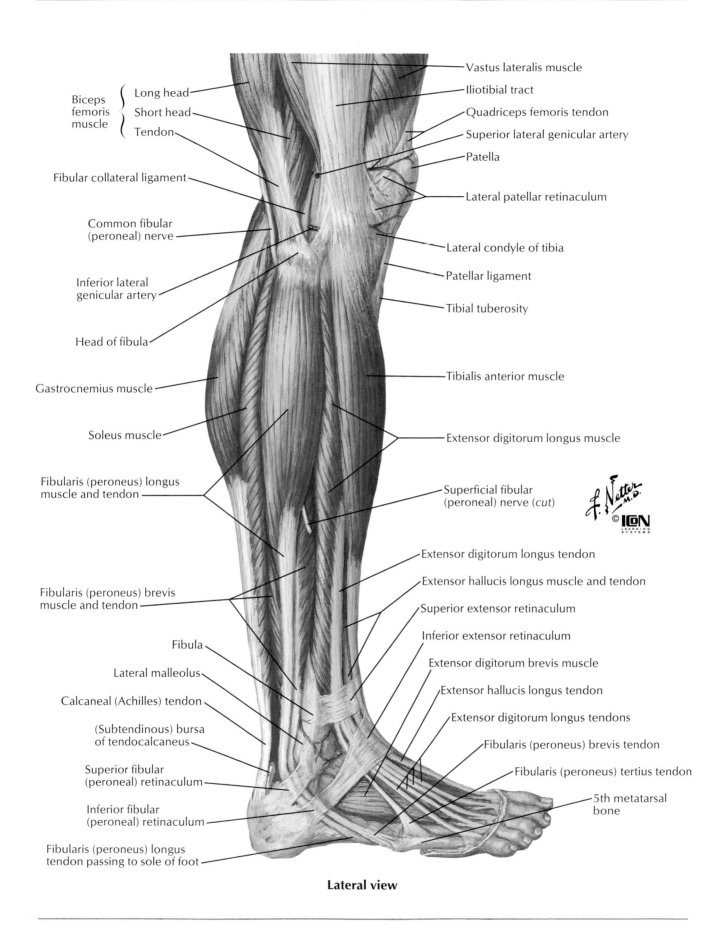

Biceps femoris muscle { Long head
Short head
Tendon

Vastus lateralis muscle

Iliotibial tract

Quadriceps femoris tendon

Superior lateral genicular artery

Patella

Fibular collateral ligament

Lateral patellar retinaculum

Common fibular (peroneal) nerve

Lateral condyle of tibia

Inferior lateral genicular artery

Patellar ligament

Tibial tuberosity

Head of fibula

Gastrocnemius muscle

Tibialis anterior muscle

Soleus muscle

Extensor digitorum longus muscle

Fibularis (peroneus) longus muscle and tendon

Superficial fibular (peroneal) nerve (*cut*)

Extensor digitorum longus tendon

Extensor hallucis longus muscle and tendon

Superior extensor retinaculum

Fibularis (peroneus) brevis muscle and tendon

Inferior extensor retinaculum

Extensor digitorum brevis muscle

Fibula

Extensor hallucis longus tendon

Lateral malleolus

Extensor digitorum longus tendons

Calcaneal (Achilles) tendon

Fibularis (peroneus) brevis tendon

(Subtendinous) bursa of tendocalcaneus

Fibularis (peroneus) tertius tendon

Superior fibular (peroneal) retinaculum

5th metatarsal bone

Inferior fibular (peroneal) retinaculum

Fibularis (peroneus) longus tendon passing to sole of foot

Lateral view

ANESTHESIA

Thorax (Chest Wall and Shoulder Girdle)

00400 Anesthesia for procedures on the integumentary system on the extremities, anterior trunk and perineum; not otherwise specified

Lower Leg (Below Knee, Includes Ankle and Foot)

01470 Anesthesia for procedures on nerves, muscles, tendons, and fascia of lower leg, ankle, and foot; not otherwise specified

01472 repair of ruptured Achilles tendon, with or without graft

01474 gastrocnemius recession (eg, Strayer procedure)

01482 Anesthesia for open procedures on bones of lower leg, ankle, and foot; radical resection (including below knee amputation)

SURGERY

Musculoskeletal System

Leg (Tibia and Fibula) and Ankle Joint

Incision

27600 Decompression fasciotomy, leg; anterior and/or lateral compartments only

27601 posterior compartment(s) only

27602 anterior and/or lateral, and posterior compartment(s)

27603 Incision and drainage, leg or ankle; deep abscess or hematoma

27604 infected bursa

27605 Tenotomy, percutaneous, Achilles tendon (separate procedure); local anesthesia

27606 general anesthesia

Excision

27613 Biopsy, soft tissue of leg or ankle area; superficial

27614 deep (subfascial or intramuscular)

27615 Radical resection of tumor (eg, malignant neoplasm), soft tissue of leg or ankle area

27618 Excision, tumor, leg or ankle area; subcutaneous tissue

27619 deep (subfascial or intramuscular)

27630 Excision of lesion of tendon sheath or capsule (eg, cyst or ganglion), leg and/or ankle

Repair, Revision, and/or Reconstruction

27650 Repair, primary, open or percutaneous, ruptured Achilles tendon;

27652 with graft (includes obtaining graft)

27654 Repair, secondary, Achilles tendon, with or without graft

27656 Repair, fascial defect of leg

27658 Repair, flexor tendon, leg; primary, without graft, each tendon

27659 secondary, with or without graft, each tendon

27664 Repair, extensor tendon, leg; primary, without graft, each tendon

27665 secondary, with or without graft, each tendon

27675 Repair, dislocating peroneal tendons; without fibular osteotomy

27676 with fibular osteotomy

27680 Tenolysis, flexor or extensor tendon, leg and/or ankle; single, each tendon

27681 multiple tendons (through separate incision(s))

27685 Lengthening or shortening of tendon, leg or ankle; single tendon (separate procedure)

27686 multiple tendons (through same incision), each

27687 Gastrocnemius recession (eg, Strayer procedure)

27690 Transfer or transplant of single tendon (with muscle redirection or rerouting); superficial (eg, anterior tibial extensors into midfoot)

27691 deep (eg, anterior tibial or posterior tibial through interosseous space, flexor digitorum longus, flexor hallucis longus, or peroneal tendon to midfoot or hindfoot)

27692 each additional tendon (List separately in addition to code for primary procedure)

27695 Repair, primary, disrupted ligament, ankle; collateral

27696 both collateral ligaments

27698 Repair, secondary, disrupted ligament, ankle, collateral (eg, Watson-Jones procedure)

Amputation

27880 Amputation, leg, through tibia and fibula;

27881 with immediate fitting technique including application of first cast

27882 open, circular (guillotine)

27884 secondary closure or scar revision

27886 re-amputation

27888 Amputation, ankle, through malleoli of tibia and fibula (eg, Syme, Pirogoff type procedures), with plastic closure and resection of nerves

27889 Ankle disarticulation

Other Procedures

27892 Decompression fasciotomy, leg; anterior and/or lateral compartments only, with debridement of nonviable muscle and/or nerve

27893 posterior compartment(s) only, with debridement of nonviable muscle and/or nerve

27894 anterior and/or lateral, and posterior compartment(s), with debridement of nonviable muscle and/or nerve

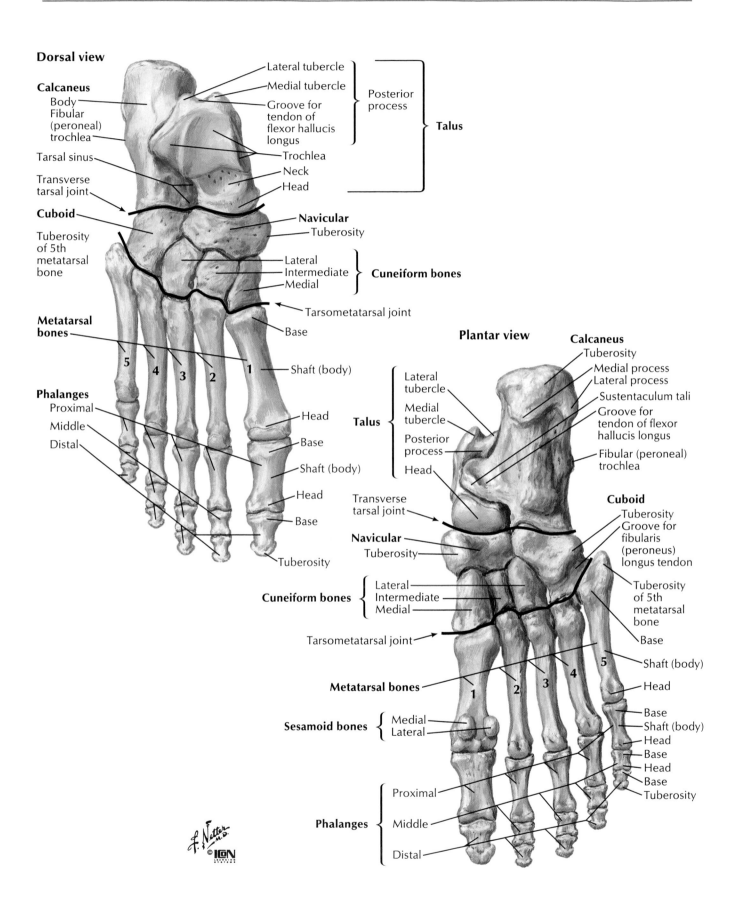

Dorsal view

Calcaneus
Body
Fibular (peroneal) trochlea
Tarsal sinus
Transverse tarsal joint
Cuboid
Tuberosity of 5th metatarsal bone

Lateral tubercle
Medial tubercle
Groove for tendon of flexor hallucis longus — Posterior process
Trochlea
Neck
Head — Talus

Navicular
Tuberosity

Lateral
Intermediate — Cuneiform bones
Medial

Tarsometatarsal joint
Base

Metatarsal bones

5 4 3 2 1

Shaft (body)

Phalanges
Proximal
Middle
Distal

Head
Base
Shaft (body)
Head
Base
Tuberosity

Plantar view

Talus
Lateral tubercle
Medial tubercle
Posterior process
Head

Transverse tarsal joint
Navicular
Tuberosity

Cuneiform bones
Lateral
Intermediate
Medial

Tarsometatarsal joint

Metatarsal bones
1 2 3 4 5

Sesamoid bones
Medial
Lateral

Phalanges
Proximal
Middle
Distal

Calcaneus
Tuberosity
Medial process
Lateral process
Sustentaculum tali
Groove for tendon of flexor hallucis longus
Fibular (peroneal) trochlea

Cuboid
Tuberosity
Groove for fibularis (peroneus) longus tendon
Tuberosity of 5th metatarsal bone
Base
Shaft (body)
Head
Base
Shaft (body)
Head
Base
Head
Base
Tuberosity

Lateral view

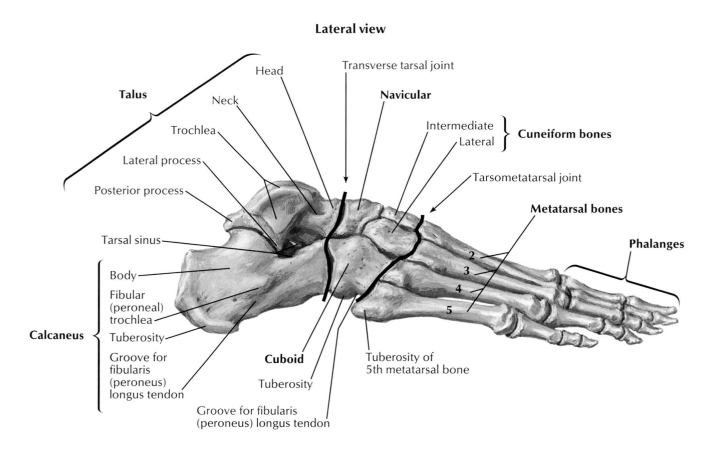

Talus

Head

Neck

Trochlea

Lateral process

Posterior process

Tarsal sinus

Calcaneus

Body

Fibular (peroneal) trochlea

Tuberosity

Groove for fibularis (peroneus) longus tendon

Transverse tarsal joint

Navicular

Intermediate

Lateral

Cuneiform bones

Tarsometatarsal joint

Metatarsal bones

2

3

4

5

Phalanges

Cuboid

Tuberosity

Groove for fibularis (peroneus) longus tendon

Tuberosity of 5th metatarsal bone

Medial view

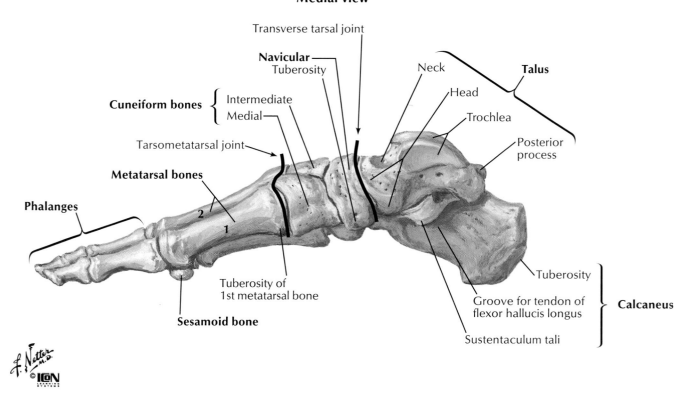

Transverse tarsal joint

Navicular

Tuberosity

Neck

Talus

Head

Trochlea

Posterior process

Cuneiform bones

Intermediate

Medial

Tarsometatarsal joint

Metatarsal bones

2

1

Phalanges

Tuberosity of 1st metatarsal bone

Sesamoid bone

Tuberosity

Groove for tendon of flexor hallucis longus

Sustentaculum tali

Calcaneus

Plate 194: Bones of Foot

ANESTHESIA

Thorax (Chest Wall and Shoulder Girdle)

00400 Anesthesia for procedures on the integumentary system on the extremities, anterior trunk and perineum; not otherwise specified

Lower Leg (Below Knee, Includes Ankle and Foot)

01462 Anesthesia for all closed procedures on lower leg, ankle, and foot

01464 Anesthesia for arthroscopic procedures of ankle and/or foot

01470 Anesthesia for procedures on nerves, muscles, tendons, and fascia of lower leg, ankle, and foot; not otherwise specified

01480 Anesthesia for open procedures on bones of lower leg, ankle, and foot; not otherwise specified

01482 radical resection (including below knee amputation)

01484 osteotomy or osteoplasty of tibia and/or fibula

SURGERY

Musculoskeletal System

Foot and Toes
Incision

28001 Incision and drainage, bursa, foot

28002 Incision and drainage below fascia, with or without tendon sheath involvement, foot; single bursal space

28003 multiple areas

28005 Incision, bone cortex (eg, osteomyelitis or bone abscess), foot

28008 Fasciotomy, foot and/or toe

28010 Tenotomy, percutaneous, toe; single tendon

28011 multiple tendons

28020 Arthrotomy, including exploration, drainage, or removal of loose or foreign body; intertarsal or tarsometatarsal joint

28022 metatarsophalangeal joint

28024 interphalangeal joint

28030 Neurectomy, intrinsic musculature of foot

28035 Release, tarsal tunnel (posterior tibial nerve decompression)

Excision

28043 Excision, tumor, foot; subcutaneous tissue

28045 deep, subfascial, intramuscular

28046 Radical resection of tumor (eg, malignant neoplasm), soft tissue of foot

28050 Arthrotomy with biopsy; intertarsal or tarsometatarsal joint

28052 metatarsophalangeal joint

28054 interphalangeal joint

28060 Fasciectomy, plantar fascia; partial (separate procedure)

28062 radical (separate procedure)

28070 Synovectomy; intertarsal or tarsometatarsal joint, each

28072 metatarsophalangeal joint, each

28080 Excision, interdigital (Morton) neuroma, single, each

28086 Synovectomy, tendon sheath, foot; flexor

28088 extensor

28090 Excision of lesion, tendon, tendon sheath, or capsule (including synovectomy) (eg, cyst or ganglion); foot

28092 toe(s), each

28100 Excision or curettage of bone cyst or benign tumor, talus or calcaneus;

28102 with iliac or other autograft (includes obtaining graft)

28103 with allograft

28104 Excision or curettage of bone cyst or benign tumor, tarsal or metatarsal, except talus or calcaneus;

28106 with iliac or other autograft (includes obtaining graft)

28107 with allograft

28108 Excision or curettage of bone cyst or benign tumor, phalanges of foot

28110 Ostectomy, partial excision, fifth metatarsal head (bunionette) (separate procedure)

28111 Ostectomy, complete excision; first metatarsal head

28112 other metatarsal head (second, third or fourth)

28113 fifth metatarsal head

28114 all metatarsal heads, with partial proximal phalangectomy, excluding first metatarsal (eg, Clayton type procedure)

28116 Ostectomy, excision of tarsal coalition

28118 Ostectomy, calcaneus;

28119 for spur, with or without plantar fascial release

28120 Partial excision (craterization, saucerization, sequestrectomy, or diaphysectomy) bone (eg, osteomyelitis or bossing); talus or calcaneus

28122 tarsal or metatarsal bone, except talus or calcaneus

28124 phalanx of toe

28126 Resection, partial or complete, phalangeal base, each toe

28130 Talectomy (astragalectomy)

28140 Metatarsectomy

28150 Phalangectomy, toe, each toe

28153 Resection, condyle(s), distal end of phalanx, each toe

28160 Hemiphalangectomy or interphalangeal joint excision, toe, proximal end of phalanx, each

28171 Radical resection of tumor, bone; tarsal (except talus or calcaneus)

28173 metatarsal

28175 phalanx of toe

Introduction or Removal

28190 Removal of foreign body, foot; subcutaneous

28192 deep

28193 complicated

Repair, Revision, and/or Reconstruction

28200   Repair, tendon, flexor, foot; primary or secondary, without free graft, each tendon

28202   secondary with free graft, each tendon (includes obtaining graft)

28208   Repair, tendon, extensor, foot; primary or secondary, each tendon

28210   secondary with free graft, each tendon (includes obtaining graft)

28220   Tenolysis, flexor, foot; single tendon

28222   multiple tendons

28225   Tenolysis, extensor, foot; single tendon

28226   multiple tendons

28230   Tenotomy, open, tendon flexor; foot, single or multiple tendon(s) (separate procedure)

28232   toe, single tendon (separate procedure)

28234   Tenotomy, open, extensor, foot or toe, each tendon

28238   Reconstruction (advancement), posterior tibial tendon with excision of accessory tarsal navicular bone (eg, Kidner type procedure)

28240   Tenotomy, lengthening, or release, abductor hallucis muscle

28250   Division of plantar fascia and muscle (eg, Steindler stripping) (separate procedure)

28260   Capsulotomy, midfoot; medial release only (separate procedure)

28261   with tendon lengthening

28262   extensive, including posterior talotibial capsulotomy and tendon(s) lengthening (eg, resistant clubfoot deformity)

28264   Capsulotomy, midtarsal (eg, Heyman type procedure)

28270   Capsulotomy; metatarsophalangeal joint, with or without tenorrhaphy, each joint (separate procedure)

28272   interphalangeal joint, each joint (separate procedure)

28280   Syndactylization, toes (eg, webbing or Kelikian type procedure)

28285   Correction, hammertoe (eg, interphalangeal fusion, partial or total phalangectomy)

28286   Correction, cock-up fifth toe, with plastic skin closure (eg, Ruiz-Mora type procedure)

28288   Ostectomy, partial, exostectomy or condylectomy, metatarsal head, each metatarsal head

28289   Hallux rigidus correction with cheilectomy, debridement and capsular release of the first metatarsophalangeal joint

28290[P]   Correction, hallux valgus (bunion), with or without sesamoidectomy; simple exostectomy (eg, Silver type procedure)

28292[P]   Keller, McBride, or Mayo type procedure

28293[P]   resection of joint with implant

28294[P]   with tendon transplants (eg, Joplin type procedure)

28296[P]   with metatarsal osteotomy (eg, Mitchell, Chevron, or concentric type procedures)

28297[P]   Lapidus type procedure

28298[P]   by phalanx osteotomy

28299[P]   by double osteotomy

28300   Osteotomy; calcaneus (eg, Dwyer or Chambers type procedure), with or without internal fixation

28302   talus

28304   Osteotomy, tarsal bones, other than calcaneus or talus;

28305   with autograft (includes obtaining graft) (eg, Fowler type)

28306   Osteotomy, with or without lengthening, shortening or angular correction, metatarsal; first metatarsal

28307   first metatarsal with autograft (other than first toe)

28308   other than first metatarsal, each

28309   multiple (eg, Swanson type cavus foot procedure)

28310   Osteotomy, shortening, angular or rotational correction; proximal phalanx, first toe (separate procedure)

28312   other phalanges, any toe

28313   Reconstruction, angular deformity of toe, soft tissue procedures only (eg, overlapping second toe, fifth toe, curly toes)

28315   Sesamoidectomy, first toe (separate procedure)

28320   Repair, nonunion or malunion; tarsal bones

28322   metatarsal, with or without bone graft (includes obtaining graft)

28340   Reconstruction, toe, macrodactyly; soft tissue resection

28341   requiring bone resection

28344   Reconstruction, toe(s); polydactyly

28345   syndactyly, with or without skin graft(s), each web

28360   Reconstruction, cleft foot

Fracture and/or Dislocation

28400   Closed treatment of calcaneal fracture; without manipulation

28405   with manipulation

28406   Percutaneous skeletal fixation of calcaneal fracture, with manipulation

28415   Open treatment of calcaneal fracture, with or without internal or external fixation;

28420   with primary iliac or other autogenous bone graft (includes obtaining graft)

28430   Closed treatment of talus fracture; without manipulation

28435   with manipulation

28436   Percutaneous skeletal fixation of talus fracture, with manipulation

28445   Open treatment of talus fracture, with or without internal or external fixation

28450   Treatment of tarsal bone fracture (except talus and calcaneus); without manipulation, each

28455   with manipulation, each

(Fracture and/or Dislocation continued on next page)

(Fracture and/or Dislocation continued from previous page)

28456 Percutaneous skeletal fixation of tarsal bone fracture (except talus and calcaneus), with manipulation, each

28465 Open treatment of tarsal bone fracture (except talus and calcaneus), with or without internal or external fixation, each

28470 Closed treatment of metatarsal fracture; without manipulation, each

28475   with manipulation, each

28476 Percutaneous skeletal fixation of metatarsal fracture, with manipulation, each

28485 Open treatment of metatarsal fracture, with or without internal or external fixation, each

28490 Closed treatment of fracture great toe, phalanx or phalanges; without manipulation

28495   with manipulation

28496 Percutaneous skeletal fixation of fracture great toe, phalanx or phalanges, with manipulation

28505 Open treatment of fracture great toe, phalanx or phalanges, with or without internal or external fixation

28510 Closed treatment of fracture, phalanx or phalanges, other than great toe; without manipulation, each

28515   with manipulation, each

28525 Open treatment of fracture, phalanx or phalanges, other than great toe, with or without internal or external fixation, each

28530 Closed treatment of sesamoid fracture

28531 Open treatment of sesamoid fracture, with or without internal fixation

28540 Closed treatment of tarsal bone dislocation, other than talotarsal; without anesthesia

28545   requiring anesthesia

28546 Percutaneous skeletal fixation of tarsal bone dislocation, other than talotarsal, with manipulation

28555 Open treatment of tarsal bone dislocation, with or without internal or external fixation

28570 Closed treatment of talotarsal joint dislocation; without anesthesia

28575   requiring anesthesia

28576 Percutaneous skeletal fixation of talotarsal joint dislocation, with manipulation

28585 Open treatment of talotarsal joint dislocation, with or without internal or external fixation

28600 Closed treatment of tarsometatarsal joint dislocation; without anesthesia

28605   requiring anesthesia

28606 Percutaneous skeletal fixation of tarsometatarsal joint dislocation, with manipulation

28615 Open treatment of tarsometatarsal joint dislocation, with or without internal or external fixation

28630 Closed treatment of metatarsophalangeal joint dislocation; without anesthesia

28635   requiring anesthesia

28636 Percutaneous skeletal fixation of metatarsophalangeal joint dislocation, with manipulation

28645 Open treatment of metatarsophalangeal joint dislocation, with or without internal or external fixation

28660 Closed treatment of interphalangeal joint dislocation; without anesthesia

28665   requiring anesthesia

28666 Percutaneous skeletal fixation of interphalangeal joint dislocation, with manipulation

28675 Open treatment of interphalangeal joint dislocation, with or without internal or external fixation

Arthrodesis

28705 Arthrodesis; pantalar

28715   triple

28725   subtalar

28730 Arthrodesis, midtarsal or tarsometatarsal, multiple or transverse;

28735   with osteotomy (eg, flatfoot correction)

28737 Arthrodesis, with tendon lengthening and advancement, midtarsal, tarsal navicular-cuneiform (eg, Miller type procedure)

28740 Arthrodesis, midtarsal or tarsometatarsal, single joint

28750 Arthrodesis, great toe; metatarsophalangeal joint

28755   interphalangeal joint

28760 Arthrodesis, with extensor hallucis longus transfer to first metatarsal neck, great toe, interphalangeal joint (eg, Jones type procedure)

Amputation

28800 Amputation, foot; midtarsal (eg, Chopart type procedure)

28805   transmetatarsal

28810 Amputation, metatarsal, with toe, single

28820 Amputation, toe; metatarsophalangeal joint

28825   interphalangeal joint

Endoscopy/Arthroscopy

29900 Arthroscopy, metacarpophalangeal joint, diagnostic, includes synovial biopsy

29901 Arthroscopy, metacarpophalangeal joint, surgical; with debridement

29902   with reduction of displaced ulnar collateral ligament (eg, Stener lesion)

Right foot

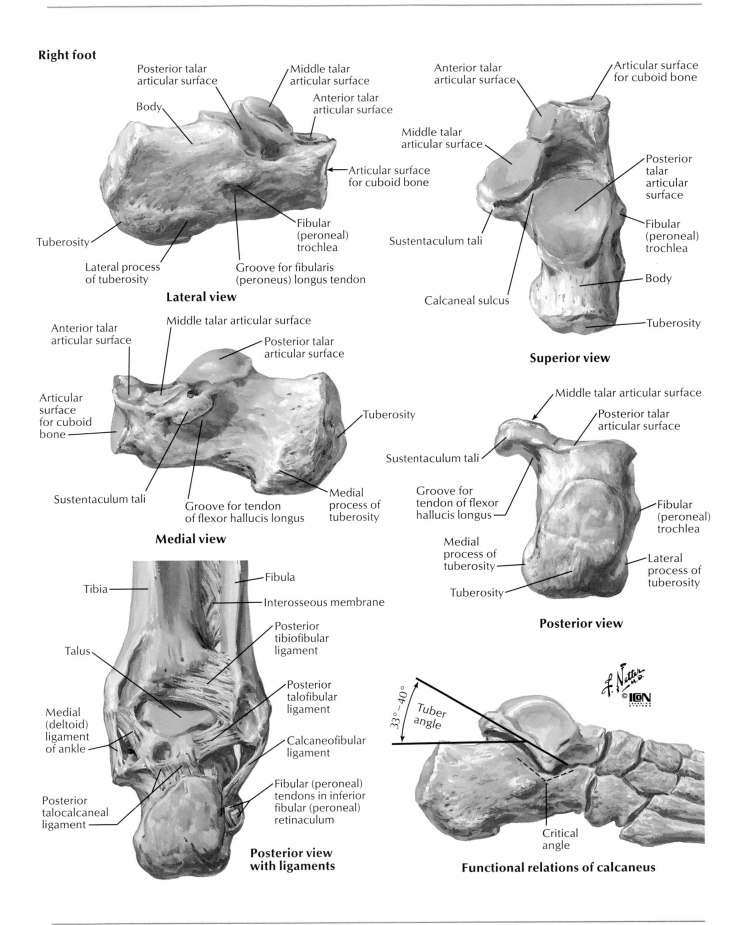

Posterior talar articular surface

Body

Middle talar articular surface

Anterior talar articular surface

Articular surface for cuboid bone

Fibular (peroneal) trochlea

Tuberosity

Lateral process of tuberosity

Groove for fibularis (peroneus) longus tendon

Lateral view

Anterior talar articular surface

Middle talar articular surface

Articular surface for cuboid bone

Sustentaculum tali

Groove for tendon of flexor hallucis longus

Posterior talar articular surface

Tuberosity

Medial process of tuberosity

Medial view

Anterior talar articular surface

Middle talar articular surface

Articular surface for cuboid bone

Sustentaculum tali

Calcaneal sulcus

Posterior talar articular surface

Fibular (peroneal) trochlea

Body

Tuberosity

Superior view

Middle talar articular surface

Posterior talar articular surface

Sustentaculum tali

Groove for tendon of flexor hallucis longus

Medial process of tuberosity

Tuberosity

Fibular (peroneal) trochlea

Lateral process of tuberosity

Posterior view

Tibia

Talus

Medial (deltoid) ligament of ankle

Posterior talocalcaneal ligament

Fibula

Interosseous membrane

Posterior tibiofibular ligament

Posterior talofibular ligament

Calcaneofibular ligament

Fibular (peroneal) tendons in inferior fibular (peroneal) retinaculum

Posterior view with ligaments

33°–40°

Tuber angle

Critical angle

Functional relations of calcaneus

ANESTHESIA

Lower Leg (Below Knee, Includes Ankle and Foot)

01462 Anesthesia for all closed procedures on lower leg, ankle, and foot

01464 Anesthesia for arthroscopic procedures of ankle and/or foot

01480 Anesthesia for open procedures on bones of lower leg, ankle, and foot; not otherwise specified

01482 Anesthesia for open procedures on bones of lower leg, ankle, and foot; radical resection (including below knee amputation)

SURGERY

Musculoskeletal System

Leg (Tibia and Fibula) and Ankle Joint
Excision

27647 Radical resection of tumor, bone; talus or calcaneus

Foot and Toes
Excision

28100 Excision or curettage of bone cyst or benign tumor, talus or calcaneus;

28102   with iliac or other autograft (includes obtaining graft)

28103   with allograft

28118 Ostectomy, calcaneus;

28119   for spur, with or without plantar fascial release

28120 Partial excision (craterization, saucerization, sequestrectomy, or diaphysectomy) bone (eg, osteomyelitis or bossing); talus or calcaneus

Repair, Revision, and/or Reconstruction

28300 Osteotomy; calcaneus (eg, Dwyer or Chambers type procedure), with or without internal fixation

Fracture and/or Dislocation

28430 Closed treatment of talus fracture; without manipulation

28435   with manipulation

28436 Percutaneous skeletal fixation of talus fracture, with manipulation

28445 Open treatment of talus fracture, with or without internal or external fixation

Arthrodesis

28705 Arthrodesis; pantalar

28715   triple

28725   subtalar

Endoscopy/Arthroscopy

29891 Arthroscopy, ankle, surgical, excision of osteochondral defect of talus and/or tibia, including drilling of the defect

29892 Arthroscopically aided repair of large osteochondritis dissecans lesion, talar dome fracture, or tibial plafond fracture, with or without internal fixation (includes arthroscopy)

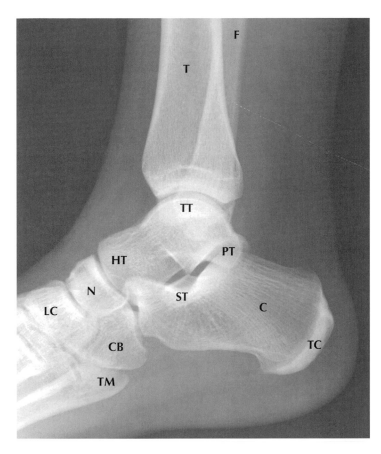

Lateral view

C   Calcaneus
CB   Cuboid
F   Fibula
HT   Head of talus
LC   Lateral cuneiform
N   Navicular
PT   Posterior process of talus
ST   Sustentaculum tali of calcaneus
T   Tibia
TC   Tuberosity of calcaneus
TM   Tuberosity of 5th metatarsal
TT   Trochlea of talus

Anterior view

F   Fibula
LM   Lateral malleolus
MM   Medial malleolus
T   Tibia
TA   Talus

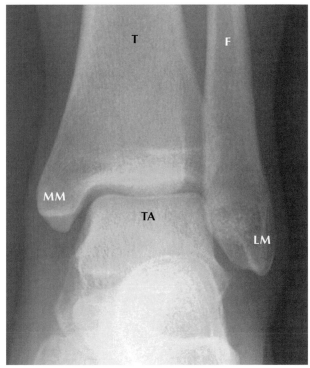

RADIOLOGY

Diagnostic Radiology (Diagnostic Imaging)

Lower Extremities

73600   Radiologic examination, ankle; two views

Right foot: lateral view

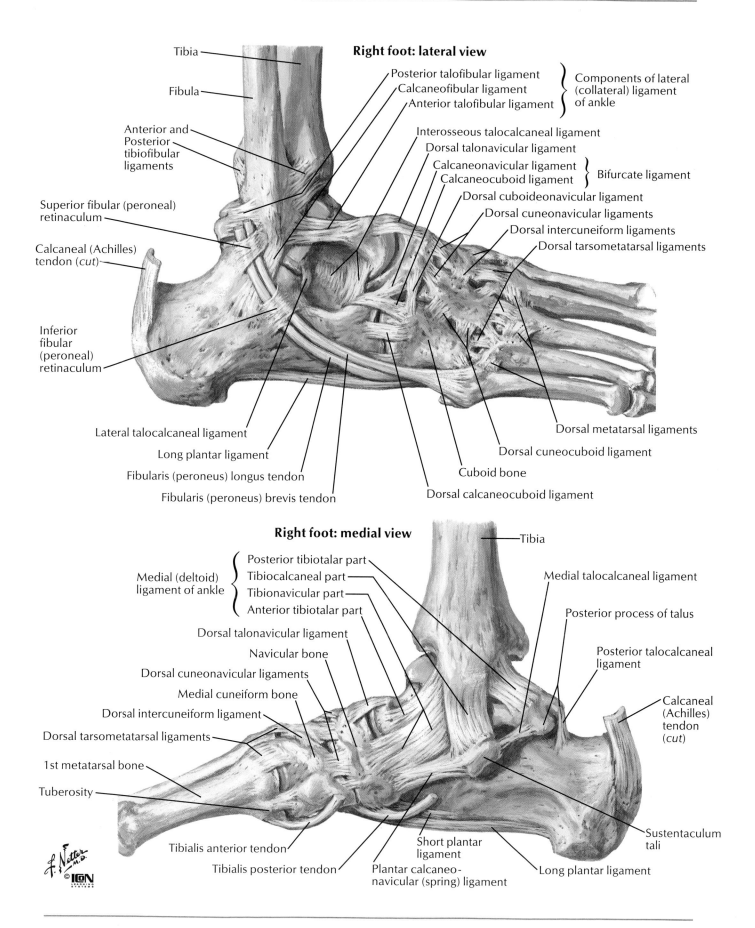

Tibia

Fibula

Anterior and Posterior tibiofibular ligaments

Superior fibular (peroneal) retinaculum

Calcaneal (Achilles) tendon (*cut*)

Inferior fibular (peroneal) retinaculum

Posterior talofibular ligament
Calcaneofibular ligament
Anterior talofibular ligament

Components of lateral (collateral) ligament of ankle

Interosseous talocalcaneal ligament
Dorsal talonavicular ligament
Calcaneonavicular ligament
Calcaneocuboid ligament

Bifurcate ligament

Dorsal cuboideonavicular ligament
Dorsal cuneonavicular ligaments
Dorsal intercuneiform ligaments
Dorsal tarsometatarsal ligaments

Lateral talocalcaneal ligament

Long plantar ligament

Fibularis (peroneus) longus tendon

Fibularis (peroneus) brevis tendon

Dorsal metatarsal ligaments

Dorsal cuneocuboid ligament

Cuboid bone

Dorsal calcaneocuboid ligament

Right foot: medial view

Medial (deltoid) ligament of ankle

Posterior tibiotalar part
Tibiocalcaneal part
Tibionavicular part
Anterior tibiotalar part

Dorsal talonavicular ligament

Navicular bone

Dorsal cuneonavicular ligaments

Medial cuneiform bone

Dorsal intercuneiform ligament

Dorsal tarsometatarsal ligaments

1st metatarsal bone

Tuberosity

Tibia

Medial talocalcaneal ligament

Posterior process of talus

Posterior talocalcaneal ligament

Calcaneal (Achilles) tendon (*cut*)

Sustentaculum tali

Tibialis anterior tendon

Tibialis posterior tendon

Short plantar ligament

Plantar calcaneo-navicular (spring) ligament

Long plantar ligament

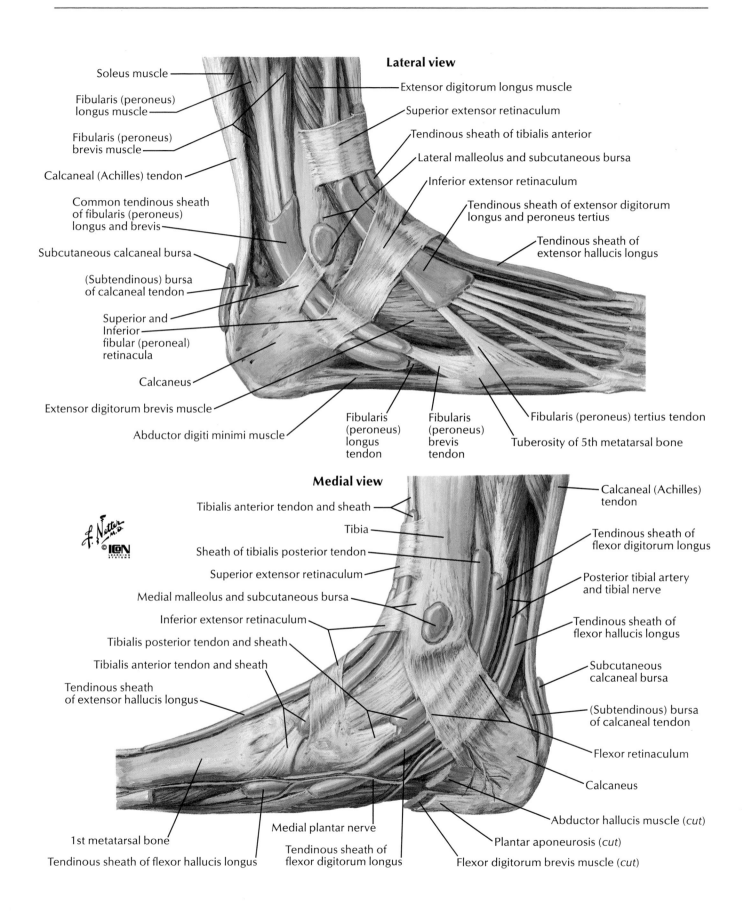

Lateral view

Soleus muscle

Fibularis (peroneus) longus muscle

Fibularis (peroneus) brevis muscle

Calcaneal (Achilles) tendon

Common tendinous sheath of fibularis (peroneus) longus and brevis

Subcutaneous calcaneal bursa

(Subtendinous) bursa of calcaneal tendon

Superior and Inferior fibular (peroneal) retinacula

Calcaneus

Extensor digitorum brevis muscle

Abductor digiti minimi muscle

Extensor digitorum longus muscle

Superior extensor retinaculum

Tendinous sheath of tibialis anterior

Lateral malleolus and subcutaneous bursa

Inferior extensor retinaculum

Tendinous sheath of extensor digitorum longus and peroneus tertius

Tendinous sheath of extensor hallucis longus

Fibularis (peroneus) longus tendon

Fibularis (peroneus) brevis tendon

Fibularis (peroneus) tertius tendon

Tuberosity of 5th metatarsal bone

Medial view

Tibialis anterior tendon and sheath

Tibia

Sheath of tibialis posterior tendon

Superior extensor retinaculum

Medial malleolus and subcutaneous bursa

Inferior extensor retinaculum

Tibialis posterior tendon and sheath

Tibialis anterior tendon and sheath

Tendinous sheath of extensor hallucis longus

1st metatarsal bone

Tendinous sheath of flexor hallucis longus

Medial plantar nerve

Tendinous sheath of flexor digitorum longus

Calcaneal (Achilles) tendon

Tendinous sheath of flexor digitorum longus

Posterior tibial artery and tibial nerve

Tendinous sheath of flexor hallucis longus

Subcutaneous calcaneal bursa

(Subtendinous) bursa of calcaneal tendon

Flexor retinaculum

Calcaneus

Abductor hallucis muscle (cut)

Plantar aponeurosis (cut)

Flexor digitorum brevis muscle (cut)

Plate 197: Ligaments, Tendons, and Sheaths of Ankle

ANESTHESIA

Lower Leg (Below Knee, Includes Ankle and Foot)

01470   Anesthesia for procedures on nerves, muscles, tendons, and fascia of lower leg, ankle, and foot; not otherwise specified

01472   repair of ruptured Achilles tendon, with or without graft

SURGERY

Musculoskeletal System

Leg (Tibia and Fibula) and Ankle Joint
Incision

27605   Tenotomy, percutaneous, Achilles tendon (separate procedure); local anesthesia

27606   general anesthesia

Excision

27630   Excision of lesion of tendon sheath or capsule (eg, cyst or ganglion), leg and/or ankle

Repair, Revision, and/or Reconstruction

27650   Repair, primary, open or percutaneous, ruptured Achilles tendon;

27652   with graft (includes obtaining graft)

27654   Repair, secondary, Achilles tendon, with or without graft

27680   Tenolysis, flexor or extensor tendon, leg and/or ankle; single, each tendon

27681   multiple tendons (through separate incision(s))

27685   Lengthening or shortening of tendon, leg or ankle; single tendon (separate procedure)

27686   multiple tendons (through same incision), each

27690   Transfer or transplant of single tendon (with muscle redirection or rerouting); superficial (eg, anterior tibial extensors into midfoot)

27691   deep (eg, anterior tibial or posterior tibial through interosseous space, flexor digitorum longus, flexor hallucis longus, or peroneal tendon to midfoot or hindfoot)

27692   each additional tendon (List separately in addition to code for primary procedure)

27695   Repair, primary, disrupted ligament, ankle; collateral

27696   both collateral ligaments

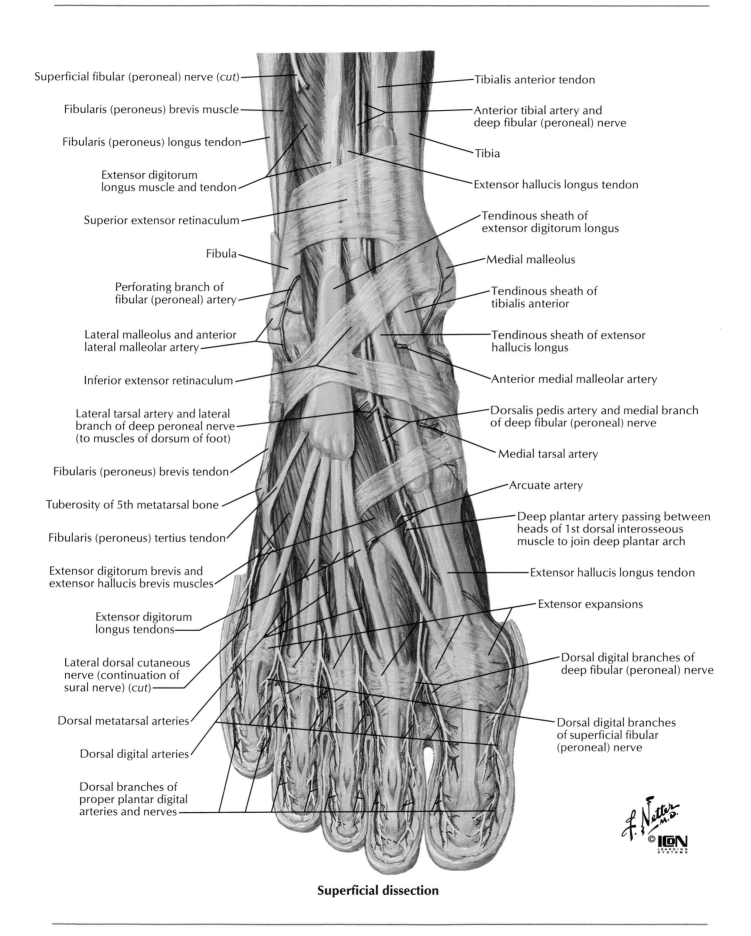

Superficial fibular (peroneal) nerve (*cut*)

Fibularis (peroneus) brevis muscle

Fibularis (peroneus) longus tendon

Extensor digitorum longus muscle and tendon

Superior extensor retinaculum

Fibula

Perforating branch of fibular (peroneal) artery

Lateral malleolus and anterior lateral malleolar artery

Inferior extensor retinaculum

Lateral tarsal artery and lateral branch of deep peroneal nerve (to muscles of dorsum of foot)

Fibularis (peroneus) brevis tendon

Tuberosity of 5th metatarsal bone

Fibularis (peroneus) tertius tendon

Extensor digitorum brevis and extensor hallucis brevis muscles

Extensor digitorum longus tendons

Lateral dorsal cutaneous nerve (continuation of sural nerve) (*cut*)

Dorsal metatarsal arteries

Dorsal digital arteries

Dorsal branches of proper plantar digital arteries and nerves

Tibialis anterior tendon

Anterior tibial artery and deep fibular (peroneal) nerve

Tibia

Extensor hallucis longus tendon

Tendinous sheath of extensor digitorum longus

Medial malleolus

Tendinous sheath of tibialis anterior

Tendinous sheath of extensor hallucis longus

Anterior medial malleolar artery

Dorsalis pedis artery and medial branch of deep fibular (peroneal) nerve

Medial tarsal artery

Arcuate artery

Deep plantar artery passing between heads of 1st dorsal interosseous muscle to join deep plantar arch

Extensor hallucis longus tendon

Extensor expansions

Dorsal digital branches of deep fibular (peroneal) nerve

Dorsal digital branches of superficial fibular (peroneal) nerve

Superficial dissection

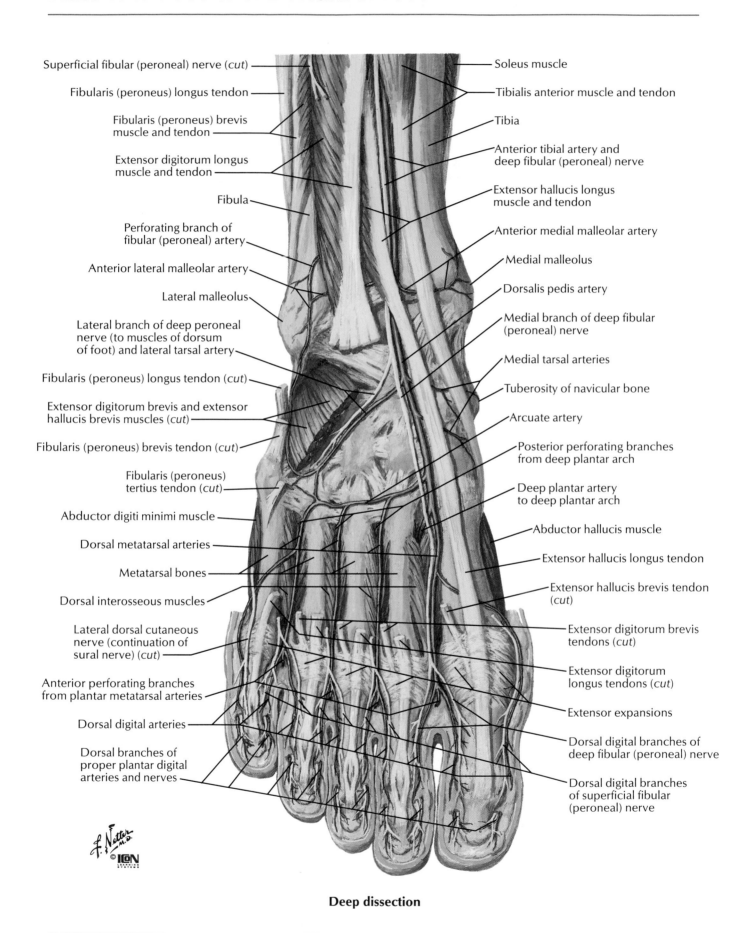

Superficial fibular (peroneal) nerve (*cut*)

Fibularis (peroneus) longus tendon

Fibularis (peroneus) brevis muscle and tendon

Extensor digitorum longus muscle and tendon

Fibula

Perforating branch of fibular (peroneal) artery

Anterior lateral malleolar artery

Lateral malleolus

Lateral branch of deep peroneal nerve (to muscles of dorsum of foot) and lateral tarsal artery

Fibularis (peroneus) longus tendon (*cut*)

Extensor digitorum brevis and extensor hallucis brevis muscles (*cut*)

Fibularis (peroneus) brevis tendon (*cut*)

Fibularis (peroneus) tertius tendon (*cut*)

Abductor digiti minimi muscle

Dorsal metatarsal arteries

Metatarsal bones

Dorsal interosseous muscles

Lateral dorsal cutaneous nerve (continuation of sural nerve) (*cut*)

Anterior perforating branches from plantar metatarsal arteries

Dorsal digital arteries

Dorsal branches of proper plantar digital arteries and nerves

Soleus muscle

Tibialis anterior muscle and tendon

Tibia

Anterior tibial artery and deep fibular (peroneal) nerve

Extensor hallucis longus muscle and tendon

Anterior medial malleolar artery

Medial malleolus

Dorsalis pedis artery

Medial branch of deep fibular (peroneal) nerve

Medial tarsal arteries

Tuberosity of navicular bone

Arcuate artery

Posterior perforating branches from deep plantar arch

Deep plantar artery to deep plantar arch

Abductor hallucis muscle

Extensor hallucis longus tendon

Extensor hallucis brevis tendon (*cut*)

Extensor digitorum brevis tendons (*cut*)

Extensor digitorum longus tendons (*cut*)

Extensor expansions

Dorsal digital branches of deep fibular (peroneal) nerve

Dorsal digital branches of superficial fibular (peroneal) nerve

Deep dissection

ANESTHESIA

Thorax (Chest Wall and Shoulder Girdle)

00400   Anesthesia for procedures on the integumentary system on the extremities, anterior trunk and perineum; not otherwise specified

Upper Leg (Except Knee)

01270   Anesthesia for procedures involving arteries of upper leg, including bypass graft; not otherwise specified

Lower Leg (Below Knee, Includes Ankle and Foot)

01470   Anesthesia for procedures on nerves, muscles, tendons, and fascia of lower leg, ankle, and foot; not otherwise specified

01480   Anesthesia for open procedures on bones of lower leg, ankle, and foot; not otherwise specified

01500   Anesthesia for procedures on arteries of lower leg, including bypass graft; not otherwise specified

Radiological Procedures

01924   Anesthesia for therapeutic interventional radiologic procedures involving the arterial system; not otherwise specified

SURGERY

Musculoskeletal System

Foot and Toes

Incision

28001	Incision and drainage, bursa, foot
28002	Incision and drainage below fascia, with or without tendon sheath involvement, foot; single bursal space
28003	multiple areas
28008	Fasciotomy, foot and/or toe
28010	Tenotomy, percutaneous, toe; single tendon
28011	multiple tendons
28030	Neurectomy, intrinsic musculature of foot

Excision

28043	Excision, tumor, foot; subcutaneous tissue
28045	deep, subfascial, intramuscular
28046	Radical resection of tumor (eg, malignant neoplasm), soft tissue of foot
28060	Fasciectomy, plantar fascia; partial (separate procedure)
28062	radical (separate procedure)
28070	Synovectomy; intertarsal or tarsometatarsal joint, each
28072	metatarsophalangeal joint, each
28080	Excision, interdigital (Morton) neuroma, single, each
28086	Synovectomy, tendon sheath, foot; flexor
28088	extensor
28090	Excision of lesion, tendon, tendon sheath, or capsule (including synovectomy) (eg, cyst or ganglion); foot
28092	toe(s), each

Introduction or Removal

28190	Removal of foreign body, foot; subcutaneous
28192	deep
28193	complicated

Repair, Revision, and/or Reconstruction

28200	Repair, tendon, flexor, foot; primary or secondary, without free graft, each tendon
28202	secondary with free graft, each tendon (includes obtaining graft)
28208	Repair, tendon, extensor, foot; primary or secondary, each tendon
28210	secondary with free graft, each tendon (includes obtaining graft)
28220	Tenolysis, flexor, foot; single tendon
28222	multiple tendons
28225	Tenolysis, extensor, foot; single tendon
28226	multiple tendons
28230	Tenotomy, open, tendon flexor; foot, single or multiple tendon(s) (separate procedure)
28232	toe, single tendon (separate procedure)
28234	Tenotomy, open, extensor, foot or toe, each tendon
28240	Tenotomy, lengthening, or release, abductor hallucis muscle
28260	Capsulotomy, midfoot; medial release only (separate procedure)
28261	with tendon lengthening
28262	extensive, including posterior talotibial capsulotomy and tendon(s) lengthening (eg, resistant clubfoot deformity)
28264	Capsulotomy, midtarsal (eg, Heyman type procedure)
28270	Capsulotomy; metatarsophalangeal joint, with or without tenorrhaphy, each joint (separate procedure)
28272	interphalangeal joint, each joint (separate procedure)

Cardiovascular System

Arteries and Veins

Repair Blood Vessel Other Than for Fistula, With or Without Patch Angioplasty

35226	Repair blood vessel, direct; lower extremity
35286	Repair blood vessel with graft other than vein; lower extremity

Transluminal Angioplasty

Open

35459	Transluminal balloon angioplasty, open; tibioperoneal trunk and branches

Transluminal Atherectomy

Open

35485	Transluminal peripheral atherectomy, open; tibioperoneal trunk and branches

Percutaneous

35495	Transluminal peripheral atherectomy, percutaneous; tibioperoneal trunk and branches

Bypass Graft

Vein
35571[P] Bypass graft, with vein; popliteal-tibial, -peroneal artery or other distal vessels

Other Than Vein
35671 Bypass graft, with other than vein; popliteal-tibial or -peroneal artery

Nervous System

Extracranial Nerves, Peripheral Nerves, and Autonomic Nervous System
Neuroplasty (Exploration, Neurolysis or Nerve Decompression)

64704 Neuroplasty; nerve of hand or foot

Excision

Somatic Nerves
64782 Excision of neuroma; hand or foot, except digital nerve
64783 hand or foot, each additional nerve, except same digit (List separately in addition to code for primary procedure

Neurorrhaphy
64831 Suture of digital nerve, hand or foot; one nerve
64832 each additional digital nerve (List separately in addition to code for primary procedure)
64834 Suture of one nerve, hand or foot; common sensory nerve
64837 Suture of each additional nerve, hand or foot (List separately in addition to code for primary procedure)

Neurorrhaphy With Nerve Graft
64890 Nerve graft (includes obtaining graft), single strand, hand or foot; up to 4 cm length
64891 more than 4 cm length
64895 Nerve graft (includes obtaining graft), multiple strands (cable), hand or foot; up to 4 cm length
64896 more than 4 cm length

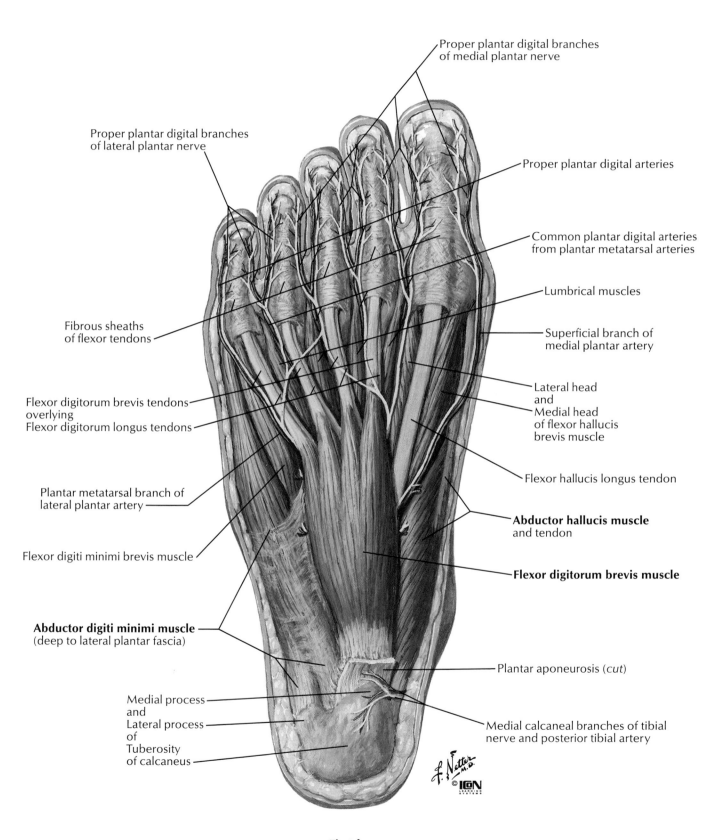

Proper plantar digital branches
of medial plantar nerve

Proper plantar digital branches
of lateral plantar nerve

Proper plantar digital arteries

Common plantar digital arteries
from plantar metatarsal arteries

Lumbrical muscles

Fibrous sheaths
of flexor tendons

Superficial branch of
medial plantar artery

Lateral head
and
Medial head
of flexor hallucis
brevis muscle

Flexor digitorum brevis tendons
overlying
Flexor digitorum longus tendons

Flexor hallucis longus tendon

Plantar metatarsal branch of
lateral plantar artery

Abductor hallucis muscle
and tendon

Flexor digitorum brevis muscle

Flexor digiti minimi brevis muscle

Abductor digiti minimi muscle
(deep to lateral plantar fascia)

Plantar aponeurosis (*cut*)

Medial process
and
Lateral process
of
Tuberosity
of calcaneus

Medial calcaneal branches of tibial
nerve and posterior tibial artery

First layer

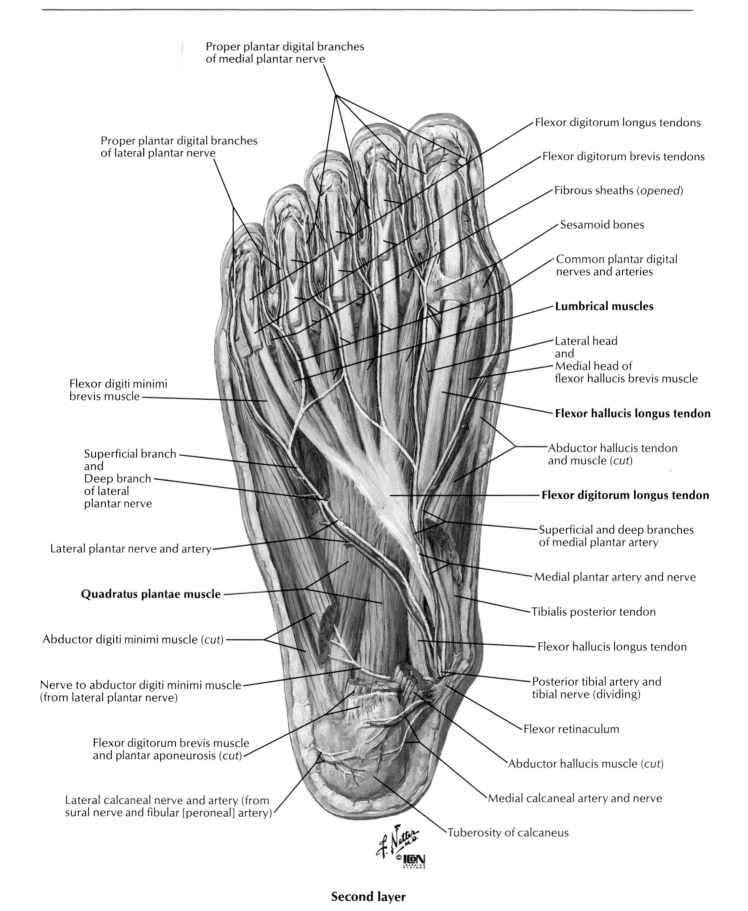

Proper plantar digital branches
of medial plantar nerve

Proper plantar digital branches
of lateral plantar nerve

Flexor digitorum longus tendons

Flexor digitorum brevis tendons

Fibrous sheaths (*opened*)

Sesamoid bones

Common plantar digital
nerves and arteries

Lumbrical muscles

Lateral head
and
Medial head of
flexor hallucis brevis muscle

Flexor hallucis longus tendon

Abductor hallucis tendon
and muscle (*cut*)

Flexor digitorum longus tendon

Superficial and deep branches
of medial plantar artery

Medial plantar artery and nerve

Tibialis posterior tendon

Flexor hallucis longus tendon

Posterior tibial artery and
tibial nerve (dividing)

Flexor retinaculum

Abductor hallucis muscle (*cut*)

Medial calcaneal artery and nerve

Tuberosity of calcaneus

Flexor digiti minimi
brevis muscle

Superficial branch
and
Deep branch
of lateral
plantar nerve

Lateral plantar nerve and artery

Quadratus plantae muscle

Abductor digiti minimi muscle (*cut*)

Nerve to abductor digiti minimi muscle
(from lateral plantar nerve)

Flexor digitorum brevis muscle
and plantar aponeurosis (*cut*)

Lateral calcaneal nerve and artery (from
sural nerve and fibular [peroneal] artery)

Second layer

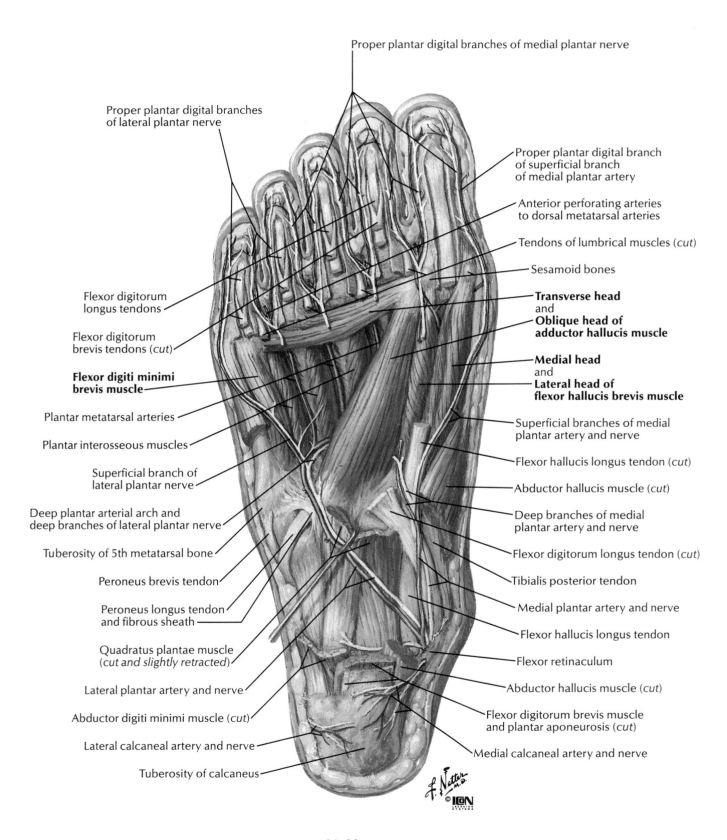

Proper plantar digital branches of medial plantar nerve

Proper plantar digital branches of lateral plantar nerve

Proper plantar digital branch of superficial branch of medial plantar artery

Anterior perforating arteries to dorsal metatarsal arteries

Tendons of lumbrical muscles (*cut*)

Sesamoid bones

Flexor digitorum longus tendons

Transverse head and **Oblique head of adductor hallucis muscle**

Flexor digitorum brevis tendons (*cut*)

Medial head and **Lateral head of flexor hallucis brevis muscle**

Flexor digiti minimi brevis muscle

Superficial branches of medial plantar artery and nerve

Plantar metatarsal arteries

Flexor hallucis longus tendon (*cut*)

Plantar interosseous muscles

Abductor hallucis muscle (*cut*)

Superficial branch of lateral plantar nerve

Deep branches of medial plantar artery and nerve

Deep plantar arterial arch and deep branches of lateral plantar nerve

Flexor digitorum longus tendon (*cut*)

Tuberosity of 5th metatarsal bone

Tibialis posterior tendon

Peroneus brevis tendon

Medial plantar artery and nerve

Peroneus longus tendon and fibrous sheath

Flexor hallucis longus tendon

Quadratus plantae muscle (*cut and slightly retracted*)

Flexor retinaculum

Lateral plantar artery and nerve

Abductor hallucis muscle (*cut*)

Abductor digiti minimi muscle (*cut*)

Flexor digitorum brevis muscle and plantar aponeurosis (*cut*)

Lateral calcaneal artery and nerve

Medial calcaneal artery and nerve

Tuberosity of calcaneus

Third layer

ANESTHESIA

Thorax (Chest Wall and Shoulder Girdle)

00400 Anesthesia for procedures on the integumentary system on the extremities, anterior trunk and perineum; not otherwise specified

Lower Leg (Below Knee, Includes Ankle and Foot)

01464 Anesthesia for all closed procedures on lower leg, ankle, and foot

01470 Anesthesia for procedures on nerves, muscles, tendons, and fascia of lower leg, ankle, and foot; not otherwise specified

01480 Anesthesia for open procedures on bones of lower leg, ankle, and foot; not otherwise specified

Other Procedures

01991 Anesthesia for diagnostic or therapeutic nerve blocks and injections (when block or injection is performed by a different provider); other than the prone position

01999 Unlisted anesthesia procedure(s)

SURGERY

Musculoskeletal System

General

Introduction or Removal

20550 Injection(s); single tendon sheath, or ligament, aponeurosis (eg, plantar "fascia")

20551 single tendon origin/insertion

Grafts (or Implants)

20924 Tendon graft, from a distance (eg, palmaris, toe extensor, plantaris)

Foot and Toes

Incision

28001 Incision and drainage, bursa, foot

28002 Incision and drainage below fascia, with or without tendon sheath involvement, foot; single bursal space

28003 multiple areas

28008 Fasciotomy, foot and/or toe

28010 Tenotomy, percutaneous, toe; single tendon

28011 multiple tendons

28030 Neurectomy, intrinsic musculature of foot

Excision

28043 Excision, tumor, foot; subcutaneous tissue

28045 deep, subfascial, intramuscular

28046 Radical resection of tumor (eg, malignant neoplasm), soft tissue of foot

28060 Fasciectomy, plantar fascia; partial (separate procedure)

28062 radical (separate procedure)

28070 Synovectomy; intertarsal or tarsometatarsal joint, each

28072 metatarsophalangeal joint, each

28080 Excision, interdigital (Morton) neuroma, single, each

28086 Synovectomy, tendon sheath, foot; flexor

28088 extensor

28090 Excision of lesion, tendon, tendon sheath, or capsule (including synovectomy) (eg, cyst or ganglion); foot

28092 toe(s), each

28119 Ostectomy, calcaneus; for spur, with or without plantar fascial release

Introduction or Removal

28190 Removal of foreign body, foot; subcutaneous

28192 deep

28193 complicated

Repair, Revision, and/or Reconstruction

28200 Repair, tendon, flexor, foot; primary or secondary, without free graft, each tendon

28202 secondary with free graft, each tendon (includes obtaining graft)

28208 Repair, tendon, extensor, foot; primary or secondary, each tendon

28210 secondary with free graft, each tendon (includes obtaining graft)

28220 Tenolysis, flexor, foot; single tendon

28222 multiple tendons

28225 Tenolysis, extensor, foot; single tendon

28226 multiple tendons

28230 Tenotomy, open, tendon flexor; foot, single or multiple tendon(s) (separate procedure)

28232 toe, single tendon (separate procedure)

28234 Tenotomy, open, extensor, foot or toe, each tendon

28240 Tenotomy, lengthening, or release, abductor hallucis muscle

28250 Division of plantar fascia and muscle (eg, Steindler stripping) (separate procedure)

Endoscopy/Arthroscopy

29893 Endoscopic plantar fasciotomy

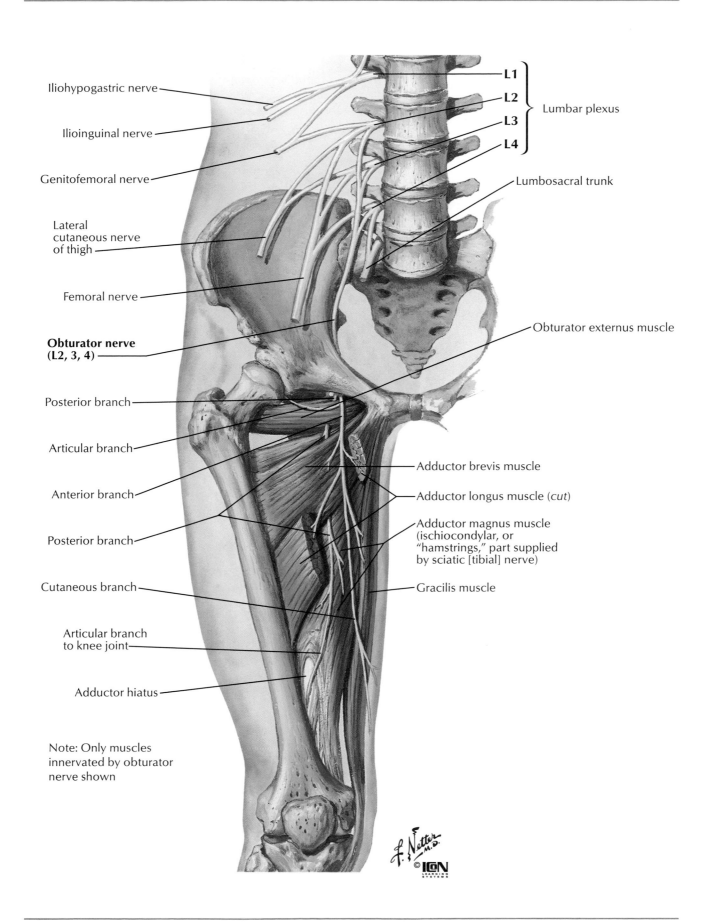

Iliohypogastric nerve

Ilioinguinal nerve

Genitofemoral nerve

Lateral cutaneous nerve of thigh

Femoral nerve

Obturator nerve (L2, 3, 4)

Posterior branch

Articular branch

Anterior branch

Posterior branch

Cutaneous branch

Articular branch to knee joint

Adductor hiatus

Note: Only muscles innervated by obturator nerve shown

L1
L2
L3
L4

Lumbar plexus

Lumbosacral trunk

Obturator externus muscle

Adductor brevis muscle

Adductor longus muscle (*cut*)

Adductor magnus muscle (ischiocondylar, or "hamstrings," part supplied by sciatic [tibial] nerve)

Gracilis muscle

Plate 200: Obturator Nerve

ANESTHESIA

Pelvis (Except Hip)

01180   Anesthesia for obturator neurectomy; extrapelvic
01190   intrapelvic

Upper Leg (Except Knee)

01210   Anesthesia for open procedures involving hip joint; not otherwise specified

SURGERY

Musculoskeletal System

Pelvis and Hip Joint
Incision

27035   Denervation, hip joint, intrapelvic or extrapelvic intra-articular branches of sciatic, femoral, or obturator nerves

Nervous System

Extracranial Nerves, Peripheral Nerves, and Autonomic Nervous System
Transection or Avulsion

64763   Transection or avulsion of obturator nerve, extrapelvic, with or without adductor tenotomy
64766   Transection or avulsion of obturator nerve, intrapelvic, with or without adductor tenotomy

---

Plate 201: Sciatic and Posterior Cutaneous Nerves of Thigh

ANESTHESIA

Thorax (Chest Wall and Shoulder Girdle)

00400   Anesthesia for procedures on the integumentary system on the extremities, anterior trunk and perineum; not otherwise specified

Upper Leg (Except Knee)

01250   Anesthesia for all procedures on nerves, muscles, tendons, fascia, and bursae of upper leg

Lower Leg (Below Knee, Includes Ankle and Foot)

01470   Anesthesia for procedures on nerves, muscles, tendons, and fascia of lower leg, ankle, and foot; not otherwise specified

Other Procedures

01990   Physiological support for harvesting of organ(s) from brain-dead patient

SURGERY

Nervous System

Extracranial Nerves, Peripheral Nerves and Autonomic Nervous System

Introduction/Injection of Anesthetic Agent (Nerve Block), Diagnostic or Therapeutic

Somatic Nerves
64445   Injection, anesthetic agent; sciatic nerve, single
64446   sciatic nerve, continuous infusion by catheter, (including catheter placement) including daily management for anesthetic agent administration

Neuroplasty (Exploration, Neurolysis or Nerve Decompression)

64712   Neuroplasty, major peripheral nerve, arm or leg; sciatic nerve

Excision

Somatic Nerves
64774   Excision of neuroma; cutaneous nerve, surgically identifiable
64784   major peripheral nerve, except sciatic
64786   sciatic nerve
64788   Excision of neurofibroma or neurolemmoma; cutaneous nerve
64795   Biopsy of nerve

Neurorrhaphy
64858   Suture of sciatic nerve

Neurorrhaphy With Nerve Graft
64892   Nerve graft (includes obtaining graft), single strand, arm or leg; up to 4 cm length
64893   more than 4 cm length
64897   Nerve graft (includes obtaining graft), multiple strands (cable), arm or leg; up to 4 cm length
64898   more than 4 cm length
64901   Nerve graft, each additional nerve; single strand (List separately in addition to code for primary procedure)
64902   multiple strands (cable) (List separately in addition to code for primary procedure)

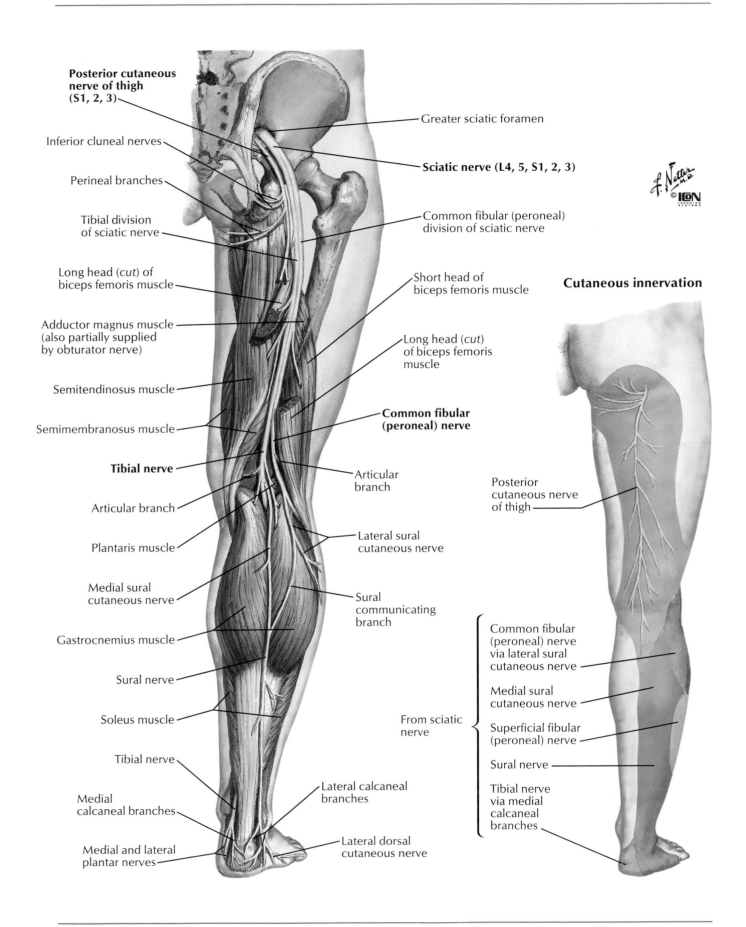

Posterior cutaneous nerve of thigh (S1, 2, 3)

Inferior cluneal nerves

Perineal branches

Tibial division of sciatic nerve

Long head (*cut*) of biceps femoris muscle

Adductor magnus muscle (also partially supplied by obturator nerve)

Semitendinosus muscle

Semimembranosus muscle

Tibial nerve

Articular branch

Plantaris muscle

Medial sural cutaneous nerve

Gastrocnemius muscle

Sural nerve

Soleus muscle

Tibial nerve

Medial calcaneal branches

Medial and lateral plantar nerves

Greater sciatic foramen

Sciatic nerve (L4, 5, S1, 2, 3)

Common fibular (peroneal) division of sciatic nerve

Short head of biceps femoris muscle

Long head (*cut*) of biceps femoris muscle

Common fibular (peroneal) nerve

Articular branch

Lateral sural cutaneous nerve

Sural communicating branch

Lateral calcaneal branches

Lateral dorsal cutaneous nerve

Cutaneous innervation

Posterior cutaneous nerve of thigh

Common fibular (peroneal) nerve via lateral sural cutaneous nerve

Medial sural cutaneous nerve

Superficial fibular (peroneal) nerve

Sural nerve

Tibial nerve via medial calcaneal branches

From sciatic nerve

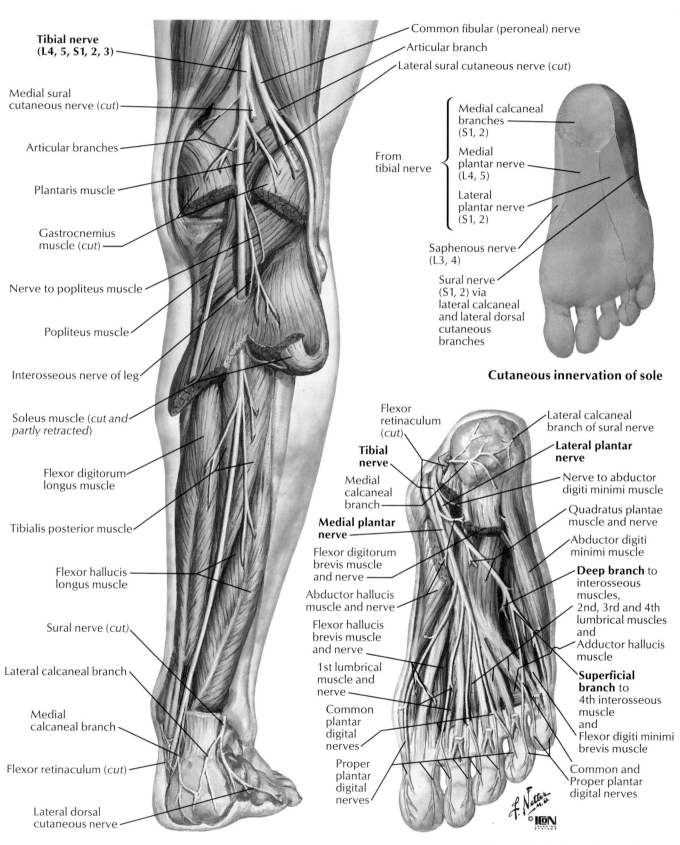

Tibial nerve
(L4, 5, S1, 2, 3)

Medial sural
cutaneous nerve (*cut*)

Articular branches

Plantaris muscle

Gastrocnemius
muscle (*cut*)

Nerve to popliteus muscle

Popliteus muscle

Interosseous nerve of leg

Soleus muscle (*cut and
partly retracted*)

Flexor digitorum
longus muscle

Tibialis posterior muscle

Flexor hallucis
longus muscle

Sural nerve (*cut*)

Lateral calcaneal branch

Medial
calcaneal branch

Flexor retinaculum (*cut*)

Lateral dorsal
cutaneous nerve

Common fibular (peroneal) nerve
Articular branch
Lateral sural cutaneous nerve (*cut*)

From
tibial nerve

Medial calcaneal
branches
(S1, 2)

Medial
plantar nerve
(L4, 5)

Lateral
plantar nerve
(S1, 2)

Saphenous nerve
(L3, 4)

Sural nerve
(S1, 2) via
lateral calcaneal
and lateral dorsal
cutaneous
branches

Cutaneous innervation of sole

Flexor
retinaculum
(*cut*)

**Tibial
nerve**

Medial
calcaneal
branch

**Medial plantar
nerve**

Flexor digitorum
brevis muscle
and nerve

Abductor hallucis
muscle and nerve

Flexor hallucis
brevis muscle
and nerve

1st lumbrical
muscle and
nerve

Common
plantar
digital
nerves

Proper
plantar
digital
nerves

Lateral calcaneal
branch of sural nerve

**Lateral plantar
nerve**

Nerve to abductor
digiti minimi muscle

Quadratus plantae
muscle and nerve

Abductor digiti
minimi muscle

Deep branch to
interosseous
muscles,
2nd, 3rd and 4th
lumbrical muscles
and
Adductor hallucis
muscle

**Superficial
branch** to
4th interosseous
muscle
and
Flexor digiti minimi
brevis muscle

Common and
Proper plantar
digital nerves

Note: Articular branches not shown

ANESTHESIA

Lower Leg (Below Knee, Includes Ankle and Foot)

01470   Anesthesia for procedures on nerves, muscles, tendons, and fascia of lower leg, ankle, and foot; not otherwise specified

Other Procedures

01991   Anesthesia for diagnostic or therapeutic nerve blocks and injections (when block or injection is performed by a different provider); other than the prone position

SURGERY

Nervous System

Extracranial Nerves, Peripheral Nerves, and Autonomic Nervous System
Introduction/Injection of Anesthetic Agent (Nerve Block), Diagnostic or Therapeutic

Somatic Nerves
64450   Injection, anesthetic agent; other peripheral nerve or branch

Destruction by Neurolytic Agent (eg, Chemical, Thermal, Electrical or Radiofrequency)

Somatic Nerves
64640   Destruction by neurolytic agent; other peripheral nerve or branch

Neuroplasty (Exploration, Neurolysis or Nerve Decompression)

64708   Neuroplasty, major peripheral nerve, arm or leg; other than specified

64722   Decompression; unspecified nerve(s) (specify)
64726   plantar digital nerve

Excision

Somatic Nerves
64774   Excision of neuroma; cutaneous nerve, surgically identifiable
64784   major peripheral nerve, except sciatic
64786   sciatic nerve
64788   Excision of neurofibroma or neurolemmoma; cutaneous nerve
64790   major peripheral nerve
64792   extensive (including malignant type)
64795   Biopsy of nerve

Neurorrhaphy

64840   Suture of posterior tibial nerve
64858   Suture of sciatic nerve

Neurorrhaphy With Nerve Graft

64892   Nerve graft (includes obtaining graft), single strand, arm or leg; up to 4 cm length
64893   more than 4 cm length
64897   Nerve graft (includes obtaining graft), multiple strands (cable), arm or leg; up to 4 cm length
64898   more than 4 cm length
64901   Nerve graft, each additional nerve; single strand (List separately in addition to code for primary procedure)
64902   multiple strands (cable) (List separately in addition to code for primary procedure)

Subject Index

Subject Index

CPT Code Index

460